The Vikings and the Victorians

INVENTING THE OLD NORTH IN NINETEENTH-CENTURY BRITAIN

The Vikings and the Victorians

INVENTING THE OLD NORTH
IN NINETEENTH-CENTURY BRITAIN

Andrew Wawn

D. S. BREWER

First published 2000
D. S. Brewer, Cambridge

ISBN 0 85991 575 1

820. 935. 203. 395
WAW

D. S. Brewer is an imprint of Boydell & Brewer Ltd
PO Box 9, Woodbridge, Suffolk IP12 3DF, UK
and of Boydell & Brewer Inc.
PO Box 41026, Rochester NY 14604–4126, USA
website: http://www.boydell.co.uk

A catalogue record for this title is available
from the British Library

Library of Congress Cataloging in Publication Data
Wawn, Andrew.
   The Vikings and the Victorians : inventing the old north in
nineteenth-century Britain / Andrew Wawn.
      p.   cm.
   Includes bibliographical references and index.
   ISBN 0–85991–575–1 (alk. paper)
   1. English literature – 19th century – History and criticism.
2. Vikings in literature.   3. Medievalism – Great Britain –
History – 19th century.   4. Old Norse literature – Appreciation
– Great Britain.   5. Great Britain – Civilization – 19th century.
6. English literature – Scandinavian influences.   7. Sagas –
Appreciation – Great Britain.   8. Europe, Northern – In literature.
9. Vikings – Historiography.   10. Vikings in art.   I. Title.
PR468.V54 W39 2000
820.9'35203395 – dc21   99–056196

This book is printed on acid-free paper

Printed in Great Britain by
St Edmundsbury Press Ltd, Bury St Edmunds, Suffolk

CONTENTS

I. HAZELLING THE GROUND

II. CREATING THE CANON

ILLUSTRATIONS

ACKNOWLEDGEMENTS

This is a book about the reception of northern antiquity in nineteenth-century Britain. Its origins are easy to identify. Like many students of medieval English literature past and present, I took a keen interest in medieval Icelandic literature, especially while writing my doctoral dissertation (on the post-medieval reception of a Chaucerian text) at the University of Birmingham during the late 1960s, encouraged in this enthusiasm by my supervisor, the late Professor Geoffrey Shepherd, and also by the late Leslie Seiffert of the German Department who voluntarily (and, these days, unthinkably) gave up his Thursday lunchtimes to lead a weekly saga-reading group of graduate students of medieval English – nowadays he would be too busy chairing a sub-committee on career development training skills. Visiting Iceland for the first time ten years later, I noticed in the Þjóðminjasafn several paintings based on sketches from the 1789 expedition to Iceland by John Thomas Stanley. The name rang a bell from my early years on Merseyside – I recalled the Stanley Hotel in Hoylake, and nearby Stanley Road, graveyard of my misdirected iron shots to the 17th green at the Royal Liverpool Golf Club for over thirty years. A visit to the Cheshire Record Office confirmed that the Hoylake Stanley was indeed the 1789 Iceland Stanley, and also the Stanley whose bookplate I discovered inside a copy of a 1786 edition of *Víga-Glúms saga* purchased in Reykjavík in 1979. Here was a subject fit for investigation – the old northern interests of a fellow Cestrian Icelandophile. It soon became clear to me that Stanley was the tip of a sizeable iceberg of late eighteenth-century British enthusiasm for the world of edda and saga, and that such enthusiasms developed vigorously in a variety of intriguing directions serving a variety of agendas during the nineteenth century. *The Vikings and the Victorians* is a study of some of those enthusiasms, directions and agendas.

Over a decade and more, in conference papers and subsequent published essays, I have sought to hazel the ground for this book by aiming sighting shots at several target topics: notably, for chapter 3, my introductory essay to a reprint of the Centenary text of Sir Walter Scott's *The Pirate* (Lerwick: Shetland Times Press, 1996); for chapter 4, a paper at a Universities of Leeds and Oslo Colloquium in 1995, eventually published as 'Samuel Laing, *Heimskringla*, and the Victorian "Berserker School" ', in Inga-Stina Ewbank (ed.) *Anglo-Scandinavian Cross-Currents* (Norwich: Norvik Press, 1999), pp. 29–59; for Chapter 5, a paper delivered at a Society for the Advancement of Scandinavian Studies in America conference, in Austin, Texas, in 1992, and published as 'The Cult of "Stalwart Frith-thjof" in Victorian Britain', in Andrew Wawn (ed.), *Northern Antiquity: The Post-Medieval Reception of Edda and Saga*. (Enfield Lock: Hisarlik Press, 1994), 211–54; for chapter 8, a paper delivered at a *Studies in Medieval-*

ix

ism conference at Bozeman, Montana in 1994, and published as 'George Stephens, Cheapinghaven and Old Northern Antiquity', *Studies in Medievalism* 7 (1995), 1–42; and, for the 'Gunnar's Howe' section of chapter 9, a lecture in the National Library of Iceland in June 1996, and published as 'William Morris and Translations of Iceland', in Shirley Chew and Alistair Stead (eds), *Translating Life: Studies in Transpositional Aesthetics* (Liverpool: Liverpool University Press, 1999), pp. 253–76. In drawing on these essays, while I have seen no reason to reword particular thoughts which I believe were well worded in the first place, all material has been fully reconsidered, reconfigured and significantly augmented. Grateful acknowledgement is offered for the permissions involved.

During the book's lengthy gestation period I was grateful for the stimulus provided by successive conference sessions on the reception of old northern texts organised by Margaret Clunies-Ross and Lars Lönnroth; and also for help in many shapes and sizes provided by Aðalgeir Kristjánsson, Gary Aho, Ben Benedikz, Jim Binns, Derek Brewer, Matthew Driscoll, Eiríkur Þormóðsson, Inga-Stina Ewbank, David Fairer, Anthony Faulkes, Finnbogi Guðmundsson, Roberta Frank, Gísli Sigurðsson, Jürg Glauser, Janet Gnosspelius, the late Grímur Helgason, Jan Ragnar Hagland, Jim Hall, Hallfreður Örn Eiríksson, Joe Harris, Fritz Heinemann, Jón Karl Helgason, Mats Malm, Gerald Morgan, Rory McTurk, Ray Page, Ólafur Pálmason, Bernard Porter, Barbara Raw, John Richowsky, Chris Sanders, Desmond Slay, Brian Smith, Sjöfn Kristjánsdóttir, Sveinn Skorri Höskuldsson, Sveinn Yngvi Egilsson, Úlfar Bragason, Kathleen Verduin, Vésteinn Ólason, John Whale, Leslie Workman, Ögmundr Helgason, Örnólfur Thorsson, and others whose names I will undoubtedly recall in embarrassment after the book has been published. I owe a particular academic debt in more than one context to the late Christine Fell. Peter Jorgensen (chapter 3), Robert Cook (chapters 6–9), and Robert Kellogg (chapter 9) were kind enough to read and comment helpfully on earlier versions of individual sections; Tom Shippey, whose own work on the reception of *Beowulf* in nineteenth-century Europe has been a constant stimulus, commented insightfully on the manuscript as a whole. I am very grateful to all these colleagues. At Boydell and Brewer Vanda Andrews, Helen Barber, Caroline Palmer and Pru Harrison have supervised the transition from script to print with efficiency, tolerance, and good humour. The errors of omission and commission which doubtless remain in the published text are entirely my responsibility.

Much of the research for and most of the writing of this book, not least this Acknowledgements section, has been done in Iceland. Several factors have made this possible and pleasurable. Firstly, awards and fellowships: a three month Snorri Sturluson fellowship in 1993 from Stofnun Sigurðar Nordals in Reykjavík; a British Academy grant in 1993; and a Leverhulme Trust Research Fellowship in 1995–6. Secondly, colleagues in the School of English at the University of Leeds have carried my end of the pedagogical and administrative log during periods of sabbatical leave. Thirdly, I have been well served by academic librarians near and far; I owe a particular debt to the staff in the

Þjóðdeild and Handritadeild at the National Library of Iceland. Fourthly, it would be hard to exaggerate the benefits to mind and spirit derived from periods of residence at the Stofnun Sigurðar Nordals, and frequent periods of study at the Stofnun Árna Magnússonar á Íslandi. This particular *farfugl* has always relished times spent perched on those scholarly branches, and greatly appreciated the warmth of the native birds' welcome. Fifthly, several Icelandic households have endured my regular visitations with at least the appearance of good humour and tolerance. A round-up of 'the usual suspects' in this context would produce the following list: Robert Cook, Guðmundur Stefánsson and Sigríður Guðmundsdóttir, Terry Gunnell and Þorbjörg Jónsdóttir, Hilmar Janússon and Ólafía Helgadóttir, Kristján Pálmar Arnarsson, and Svanbjörn Thoroddsen and Gunnhildur Sveinsdóttir – I am *very* conscious of how much I owe to these staunch and ever generous friends.

Finally, two explanatory notes. First, a word about the forms of personal and place names used in the book. Any discussion of the post-medieval reception of medieval Icelandic literature inevitably involves regular reference to both medieval Icelandic names and their Victorian transformations – to Alþingi, Freyja, Friðþjófr, Hallgerðr, Óðinn, Skarpheðinn, Valhǫll and Þórr, but also to Althingi, Frea, Frithiof, Gunnar, Hallgerd, Odin, Skarphedin, Valhalla and Thor, not to mention Althing, Freya, Fridtjof, Hallgerth, Othinn, Sarphedin, Valhöll and other variants. Some purist Victorians, proud of their hard-earned knowledge of the old language, used what they understood to be normalised Old Icelandic spellings; others used pre-normalised spellings derived from eighteenth-century editions of major texts; others were frustrated by the inability or disinclination of their publishers to cope with the Icelandic forms ð, þ, æ, ǫ and ö. Even the names of Icelandic scholars resident in Britain added to the confusion: Guðbrandur Vigfússon's name appears on title-pages as Guðbrandr, Guðbrand, Gudbrandr, or Gudbrand, while Eiríkur Magnússon's first name normally appears as Eiríkr. The broad rule of thumb adopted in this book is to use normalised Old Icelandic forms, but when discussing individual Victorian texts I use the forms favoured by each author. Such distinctions are not always easy to draw, however, and pragmatism has sometimes tempered principle. Nineteenth- and twentieth-century Icelandic names are cited in their modern forms. The principles governing the Bibliography and Index are outlined at the head of each section. Readers unfamiliar with Icelandic letters will soon become accustomed to them: ð ('eth') is a voiced consonant pronounced as the 'th' in 'this'; its unvoiced counterpart is þ ('thorn'), as with 'th' in 'thesis'; editions of medieval texts frequently employ ǫ to render the later and still current ö form.

As for my chosen title, modern academic discourse tends to avoid definite articles in titles, apparently because they signal ignorance of, or (worse still) disagreement with fixed postmodernist pieties about the impossibility and undesirability of intellectual fixity. Accordingly, I recognise that *The Vikings and the Victorians* should have been called 'Some Vikings (Not real ones, mind you, but romantic reconstructions based on philologically primitive sources) and Some (though it is hard interrogate the silence and judge how many) Victorians (with selective contextualising reference to pre- and post-Victorian events, texts and individuals within and beyond the British Isles)'. Unhappily, the book cover could not cope with this challenging alternative.

Andrew Wawn
Adel and Reykjavík
December 1999

ABBREVIATIONS

AHR	*American Historical Review*
AJ	*Alpine Journal*
AM	*Ainsworth's Magazine*
ASSL	*Archiv für das Studium der neueren Sprachen und Literaturen*
AWR	*Anglo-Welsh Review*
BAGS	*Bulletin of the American Geographical Society*
BEM	*Blackwood's Edinburgh Magazine*
BJHS	*British Journal of the History of Science*
BJRL	*Bulletin of the John Rylands Library*
BQR	*British Quarterly Review*
CCRO	Cheshire County Record Office
CM	*Cornhill Magazine*
DM	*Dublin Magazine*
DNB	*Dictionary of National Biography*
DR	*Dublin Review*
DUM	*Dublin University Magazine*
EETS	Early English Text Society
e.s.	extra series
EHR	*English Historical Review*
ER	*Edinburgh Review*
FM	*Fraser's Magazine*
FQR	*Foreign Quarterly Review*
FR	*Fortnightly Review*
GM	*Gentleman's Magazine*
HUL	Harvard University Library
ILN	*Illustrated London News*
ÍF	Íslenzk Fornrit
JEGP	*Journal of English and Germanic Philology*
JHI	*Journal of the History of Ideas*
JRL	John Rylands Library
JWCI	*Journal of the Warburg and Courtauld Institutes*
JWMS	*Journal of the William Morris Society*
LÍÁ	*Landsbókasafn Íslands: Árbók*
LM	*London Magazine*
LQR	*London Quarterly Review*
LSE	*Leeds Studies in English*
MLN	*Modern Language Notes*
MLR	*Modern Language Review*
MR	*Monthly Review*

NC	*The Nineteenth Century*
NF	*Ný Félagsrit*
n.s.	new series
PLLPS	*Proceedings of the Liverpool Literary and Philosophical Society*
PMLA	*Publications of the Modern Language Association of America*
PSAS	*Proceedings of the Society of Antiquaries of Scotland*
QR	*Quarterly Review*
RES	*Review of English Studies*
SBVS	*Saga-Book of the Viking Society*
SHR	*Scottish Historical Review*
SJL	Sidney Jones Library, University of Liverpool
SP	*Studies in Philology*
SatR	*Saturday Review*
ScotR	*Scottish Review*
SS	*Scandinavian Studies*
SSL	*Studies in Scottish Literature*
SSN	*Scandinavian Studies and Notes*
TEM	*Tait's Edinburgh Magazine*
TPS	*Transactions of the Philological Society*
TRSE	*Transactions of the Royal Society of Edinburgh*
WR	*Westminster Review*

Mig er nok,
At jeg fra Iisland og fra Norges kyst
Kan friske krandse bringe til min ven,
Og blomstre plukkede ved Engelsk haand.

(Herbert 1806, vi)

Ber ek Odins Miod
A Engla [L]iod   (Jamieson 1814, 237)
[Of Odin's mead let draught
In England now be quaff'd.]   (Green 1893, 132)

That Great-Britain belongs to the North *only*, and that she has been wrong
when in any period thinking herself belonging to the South, we can certainly state as beyond all doubt!   (Munch 1845)[1]

I say that the Church of England is wonderfully and mystically fitted for the
souls of free Norse-Saxon race; for men whose ancestors fought by the side
of Odin, over whom a descendant of Odin now rules.

(Ch. Kingsley 1851)[2]

Spirit of the Age: Why don't you try the Scandinavian Gods?
Author: The Scandy . . . how much?
Spirit of the Age: (sneeringly)
                      Oh! how new and witty!
                      The jest of ignorance indeed claims pity.

(Brooks 1851)[3]

As Iceland was Scandinavia's (especially Norway's) 2nd great colony, so was
England all Scandia's first great colony.   (Stephens 1879, 5)

I am a Barbarian, a Goth, thank God   (Hodgetts 1884, 188)

The Vikings! What a world of conjecture and romance unfolds itself before
the youthful imaginative mind at the word!   (Young 1895, 1)

Men's souls are raised by the recollection of great deeds done by their forefathers. But the study of the past has its dangers when it makes men transfer
past claims and past hatreds to the present.   (Bryce 1915, 31)

---

[1] Indrebø and Kolsrud 1924–71, I 115, PAM to George Stephens, 5.vi.1845.
[2] In Kingsley F. 1891, I 203.
[3] Brooks 1851, IV 4: work entitled 'The Exposition; A Scandinavian Sketch containing as much
irrelevant matter as possible'.

The printing of this book is made possible by a gift
to the University of Cambridge in memory of
Dorothea Coke, Skjaeret, 1951

For parents and grandparents who first took me
to Thor's Stone on Caldy Hill.

SECTION I

HAZELLING THE GROUND

CHAPTER ONE

Of Stockfish and Saga

The want of knowing the *Northern Languages*, has occasion'd an
unkind Prejudice towards them: which some have introduc'd out
of Rashness, others have taken upon Tradition.

(Elizabeth Elstob 1715, x)

We, misled by a puerile love of the Romans, revile the ruder
Goths, our fathers, as despisers of learning and the arts . . . the
Goths were the friends of every elegant art, and useful science.

(John Pinkerton 1789, I 4)

What's in a Title?

In many ways, the Victorians invented the Vikings. The word itself, in its
modern incarnation, is not recorded in the *OED* until just thirty years before the
young Princess Victoria's coronation;[1] and by 1837 only a handful of her most
scholarly subjects had begun to acquaint themselves with those Anglo-Saxon
texts in which the term had previously been recorded. Yet, within fifty years, the
word 'Viking' was to be found on dozens of title-pages – of poems, plays, pious
fables, parodies, paraphrased sagas, prize essays, published lectures, papers in
learned journals, translations, travelogues, scholarly monographs, and entries in
encyclopaedia. These were works written for all conditions of men, some conditions of women, and quite a few conditions of children. After a slow start the
floodgates opened during last two decades: amongst some three dozen titles we
find *The Viking* (1849), *The Northmen: The Sea-Kings and Vikings* (1852), *The
Vikings* (1861), *The Vikings of the Baltic* (1875), *Viking Tales of the North* (1877),
The Champion of Odin: Or Viking Life in Days of Old (1885), *The Baptism of the
Viking* (1890), *Ivar the Viking* (1893), *The Last of the Vikings* (1895), *The
Viking's Bride* (1896), *Vandrad the Viking* (1897), *King Alfred's Viking* (1898),
Kormak the Viking (1902), *The Viking's Skull* (1904), *In the Van of the Vikings*

---

[1] Earlier examples include Camden 1695, cliii: 'the Latin-writers of the history of England call
them *Wiccingi*, from their trade of piracies, *Wiccinga* (as we are assur'd by Alfric) signifying in
Saxon a *pirate*'; also Troil 1780, 66.

(1909), *Harald, First of the Vikings* (1911) and so on into the reign of George V.[2]

The ubiquity of the term 'Viking' masks a wide variety of constructions of Vikingism: the old northmen are variously buccaneering, triumphalist, defiant, confused, disillusioned, unbiddable, disciplined, elaborately pagan, austerely pious, relentlessly jolly, or self-destructively sybaritic. They are merchant adventurers, mercenary soldiers, pioneering colonists, pitiless raiders, self-sufficient farmers, cutting-edge naval technologists, primitive democrats, psychopathic berserks, ardent lovers and complicated poets. Similar variety can even be found in Victorian spellings of the word. 'Viking' had to battle with 'vikingr', 'vikinger', 'vikingir', 'wikinger', 'wiking', 'wicing', and 'wicking'.[3] Some of these variants represent hesitant transliterations of Old Icelandic *víkingr*; some were fashion statements; and others reflect old northernists' passionately held philological and political beliefs which could turn on a single phoneme. The word's etymology was much debated. For some old northernists seductive images of spray-washed 'sea-kings' led them to think in terms of 'vi-kings'; others were clear that 'it is not vi-king, but vik-ing, and is pronounced viik-ing', but less sure whether it derived 'from *víg*, battle, slaughter, or *vík* (Dan. vig) a bay of the sea'.[4] In wrestling with this problem, and more generally in their reconstructions of the Viking-age world, Victorian enthusiasts gave birth to some very strange old northern progeny. There was rarely a dull moment in the nineteenth-century marriage of Mercury and Philology.

Things were no clearer when authors or their publishers tried to settle on a stable terminology for their Viking-age reflections. 'Norse' and 'Norsemen' sufficed for many poets, novelists, and scholars – *The Norsemen in Iceland* (1858), *The Norsemen in the West* (1872), *Sagas and Songs of the Norsemen* (1894), *Myths of the Norsemen* (1908) and a dozen others.[5] For some zealots, however, 'Norsemen' signalled an unacceptable preoccupation with an exclusively Norwegian old north.[6] For Rev. Alexander Pope of Orkney, who associated Vikings with 'wickedness and daring villainy . . . murders, massacres, pyracies, invasions', this was not a problem. Alien 'Norsemen' these undesirables had always been and could remain – and the Norwegians were welcome to them. Others were less sanguine. As Victorian Britons began to uncover or redefine their affinities with the old north, and as blood-eagle carving barbarians were transformed into the progenitors of prized Victorian values, many sought to promote the idea of a

---

2   In chronological order, Zavarr 1849, White 1861, Sinding 1862, Dasent 1875, Anderson and Jón Bjarnason 1877, Hodgetts 1885, Tattersall 1890, du Chaillu 1893, Young 1895, Ferguson 1896, Clouston 1897, Whistler 1899, Hodgetts 1902, Carling 1904, Outram 1909, Young 1911.

3   See Southey 1824, 74 (vikingr); [Keightley] 1828, 238 (vikinger); Motherwell 1847, 13 (vikingir); [Busk] 1828–9, 273 (wikinger); Stephens 1857, 25 (wiking); Munch, in Farrer 1862, 25 (wicing); Gudbrand Vigfusson and Powell 1883 (wicking). More generally, see discussion in Fell 1986, 1987.

4   Charlton 1852, 188.

5   Dasent 1858, Ballantyne 1872, Major 1894, Guerber 1908.

6   Grímur Thomsen 1859.

more inclusive old northern Atlantic community represented by the term 'Northmen': as in *The Northmen* (1834), *The Northmen: The Sea-Kings and the Vikings* (1852), *The Yorl of the Northmen* (1892) *Graves of the Northmen* (1893).[7]

Another favourite term in Victorian and Edward book titles allows us to register a different controversy: *Odin, A Poem* (1817), *The Hall of Odin* (1850), *Odin's Sagas* (1882), *Champion of Odin* (1885), *Children of Odin* (1903). There was no problem with the spelling, or with issues of narrow nationalism; but disagreement raged amongst Victorian old northernists as to the identity of 'Odin'. Was he a mighty Scythian leader who had once challenged the tyranny of Rome, and who could now act as a role model for upwardly mobile Victorian young achievers? Or was he a uniquely gifted member of a primitive society invested by his awestruck fellows with supernatural authority? Or was he a prefiguration of the Christian God? Or was he part of a primeval nature myth transmitted by oral tradition? Or could his presence be found in contemporary folklore in rural Britain? As with 'Viking' and 'Norseman', the inclusion of 'Odin' in the title of a novel, essay or poem was sometimes a reflection of scrupulous scholarship, but was more often an instance of the kind of spray-on old northern atmospherics still favoured today by Scandinavian lottery operators,[8] Icelandic saga publishers,[9] French manufacturers of baby clothes,[10] American vodka distillers,[11] film producers and golf course designers.

This tension between scholarly probity and cheerful populism inevitably carried over into many other aspects of Victorian cultivation of the old north. In archaeology enthusiastic provincial antiquarians began to dig up and dust off Britain's Viking past, with interpretative creativity sometimes compensating for the modest returns on the spadework invested. Neglected cairns were opened,[12] fragmented crosses re-assembled,[13] and ancient jewellery pored over.[14] Eager eyes spotted Odinic spears and Thunoric hammers in improbable locations.[15] Runic inscriptions yielded up or had wrenched out of them long-hidden or non-existent secrets;[16] and the long-neglected Viking-age voices of local dialect and place-names were heeded again.[17] Splendid Viking banqueting halls, more Balmoral than Bergþórshvoll, emerged from the lavish fold-out diagrams of the new generation of saga translations.[18] We also meet well-kempt heroes bearing

---

[7] Sladden 1834, Sinding 1862, Strongi'th'arm [pseud.] 1892, Horsford C. 1893.

[8] The 'Vikingalottó' in Scandinavia.

[9] Viðar Hreinsson et al. 1997: subtitled 'Viking Age Classics', published by Leifur Eiríksson hf., named after the Viking-age discoverer of North America.

[10] Boyer 1994.

[11] Fell 1986, [123].

[12] Farrer 1862, Barnes 1992, 1993, 1994.

[13] Kemble 1840, Calverley 1881–2.

[14] See, for example, Wawn 1991a, 123–7.

[15] Stephens 1878.

[16] Stephens 1866–1901 and 1884.

[17] Repp 1831, Picton 1865, Ellwood 1895, Wright 1898–1905.

[18] Dasent 1861.

an uncanny resemblance to Prince Albert, and self-sacrificial heroines of Dorothea Brookean demureness.[19] Through new grammars[20] the enthusiast could
grapple with a language variously described as Icelandic, Old Icelandic, Norse,
Old Norse, Old Northern, or Scando-Anglic, and thereby enjoy privileged
access to eddas and sagas in new editions published in Denmark and Germany.
An impressive canon of English translations of many of these works emerged –
literal and paraphrastic, prose and verse, archaised and modern, reliable and
muddled, influential and neglected.[21] Viking-age society was deemed fit for
Victorian political scientists, ethnologists and comparative mythologists to
study.[22] Popular novels on Viking-age subjects were handed out as rewards for
good work at grammar school and exemplary attendance at Sunday school, and
Viking tales helped to pass the time on long Sunday afternoons at preparatory
school, and longer mid-week nights at public school.[23] Enthusiastic young converts from such early exposure grew up into the writers of, and audiences for,
more adult representations of the same Viking-age culture. The enthusiasms
aroused by such publications could be nourished by systematic contact, in
person or by post, with distinguished Icelandic philologists resident in Britain
during the latter years of Victoria's reign. Such scholars were pestered by each
of the several daily postal deliveries for information about Viking-age days of
the week, months of the year, meals of the day, laws of the land, customs of the
dead, and riders of the Valkyrie.[24] British old northern scholars were no less
painstaking than their British-based Icelandic colleagues in reaching out to a
still wider public through reviews in the periodical press[25] and lantern lectures
on the public platform.[26]

   Attempts were made to involve not just Victoria's loyal subjects, but the
monarch herself. How did the Queen react to claims that she herself was
descended from Óðinn,[27] or that the entire Hanoverian royal family was
descended from Ragnarr loðbrók, a bloodthirsty old Viking chief who met his
end in a Northumbrian snake-pit?[28] How did she view the claims of a
nineteenth-century Icelandic peasant that two of his rural friends were closely

---

19 See Dasent 1866 [iv], 104: two of C.E. St J. Mildmay's Dasent 1866 illustrations.
20 Marsh 1838, Dasent 1843, Lund 1869, Thimm 1869, Bayldon 1870, Gudbrand Vigfusson and
Powell 1879, Sweet 1886.
21 Amongst them Dasent 1842, 1861, 1866, Laing 1844, 1889, Head 1865, Morris and Eiríkr
Magnússon 1869, 1875, 1891–1905.
22 As with Cox 1872, Jón Hjaltalín 1872, Conybeare 1877, Bryce 1923.
23 Baring-Gould 1859–62, 1890, 1894.
24 See below, Chapter 12.
25 Amongst them Tremenheere 1837, Charlton 1850, [Lawrence] 1861, [Forman] 1871; see also
Tucker 1963–4.
26 Smith 1838, Browning 1876, Sephton 1887, 1894, Carlyle 1892 (1838 lectures), 1897 (1840
lectures).
27 Kingsley 1891, I 203; Blind 1899, 371.
28 Eiríkur Magnússon in Lbs. 1860 4to 17; also Morris 1910–15, VIII 238. Auðunn skǫkull was
Ragnarr's grandson; Eiríkr claims that his daughter (other sources speak of his grand-daughter)
Úlfhildr married Duke Otto of Saxland, from whom the Hanoverians were said to be descended.

related to her?[29] Had she noticed that, according to a family tree published in Charles Kingsley's *Hereward the Wake* (1866), Alexandra, Princess of Wales, who married into the British royal family in the autumn of 1863, was herself descended from King Haraldr Bluetooth?[30] What did Victoria make of the poetic eulogy written for her in Viking-age style by a latter day Icelandic skald?[31] Did she realise that her court physician Sir Henry Holland was a life-long Iceland enthusiast who had once written a field-commanding essay on the country's Viking- and saga-age history?[32] Did the Queen recall that one of her Windsor chaplains was amongst the first of the nineteenth century's many English language translators of Esaias Tegnér's hugely influential Viking-age romance *Frithiofs saga*, and that he had dedicated his translation to her in 1834?[33] Was she aware that her principal organist at St. George's Chapel had set to music the songs from Sir Walter Scott's Viking-influenced novel *The Pirate*?[34] Was the royal gaze drawn to a saga-style satire by a leading mid-century Icelandic writer in which Victoria featured (not altogether flatteringly) as a *fornaldarsaga*-style warrior queen challenging Napoleon?[35] Did Prince Arthur's report of his 1873 visit to Norway echo the sentiments of another British aristocratic onlooker at the time: 'As I sat upon the terrace . . . and watched the British squadron quit the harbour, . . . the early history of Norway came home distinctly to my memory, in which was learnt that the Vikings, Norsemen, Danes and other nations of that race, by victories at sea gave kings to neighbouring lands'?[36] Did the Queen realise the indignation of Scandinavian philologists at her German sympathies when in 1864, within months of Alexandra's marriage, Prussian troops marched into Slesvig-Holsten, for many the heartland of the Scandinavian old north?[37] And did she share her cousin Kaiser Wilhelm II's old northern enthusiasms – his 'Song to Aegir' featured at a London concert in 1896,[38] and he presented huge statues of local saga heroes to the residents of Sognefjord in Norway?[39]

In less exalted social circles, sturdy suburban houses in Middlesex were named after rime-encrusted eddic mythological halls;[40] peasant songs, proverbs and customs in Victorian Cumberland or Lincolnshire were traced back to

---

[29] Metcalfe 1861, 166.
[30] Kingsley 1866/1895, 241 (ch. 18).
[31] Harvard University Library MS Icel. 55: Jón Hjaltalín, 'Victoríukviða' (1868).
[32] See below, Chapter 2.
[33] Strong [1833].
[34] See below, p. 60.
[35] Benedikt Sveinbjarnarson Gröndal 1971, 157–78 (chs 13–14).
[36] Garvagh 1875, 198.
[37] On the philological-political outrage concerning the 1848 Prussian invasion, see Indrebø and Kolsrud 1924–71, I 360, P.A. Munch to George Stephens, 26 April 1849.
[38] Blind 1896, 96.
[39] Marschall 1991, Hougen 1996.
[40] Albany Major named his house 'Bifröst': Lbs. 2188 4to, letters to Eiríkur Magnússon.

Viking-age traditions;[41] whilst wealthy widows on the eastern sea-board of the United States commissioned designer-label stained-glass representations of the Viking-age discovery of Vínland lovingly prepared (and unscrupulously priced) by William Morris.[42] Those with no eye for a design but a good ear for a tune could sing of their old northern dreamworld. Viking themes not only found expression in lightweight Victorian parlour songs,[43] but also provided the raw material for a major cantata by late Victorian Britain's greatest native-born composer Edward Elgar.[44] They also proved seductive from an early age to colonial Australia's most famous musical son Percy Grainger ('Grettir' to his friends), whose taste for bleached hair and flagellation hint at darker currents discernible in the Victorian cult of the Viking.[45] Before the end of the century individual Viking enthusiasms within the regions and beyond the shores of Victorian Britain eventually found collective expression in national organisations such as the Viking Club in London, whose officials and offices were identifiable by painstakingly reconstructed, much derided, and soon discarded Viking-age titles: jarl, jarla-man, Viking-jarl, umboths-jarl and the rest. For all the early mockery it endured in *Punch*,[46] the society still flourishes a hundred years later. For a few select enthusiasts there were learned societies in Scandinavia to join and, in due time, to be honoured by, all committed to the study of Old Northern literature and antiquities.

It is small wonder that Victorian Britons, having joined the societies, heard the lectures, listened to the cantatas, dug up the rune-stones, deciphered the cross carvings, read the sagas, ordered the stained-glass windows, and adopted Viking-age nicknames for themselves and their houses,[47] wanted to put the authenticating seal on their enthusiasms which only travel to the saga-steads could provide. If Athens and Rome were fit destinations for the serious traveller, why not Sognefjord and Hlíðarendi? Late nineteenth-century travellers undertook pilgrimages (the word is frequently invoked)[48] to the Viking-age sites of sagas highlighted by text, tradition, and (eventually) travel agent.[49] Having learnt the language of the ancient Vikings, Victorian and Edwardian Britons could also purchase phrase-books to help them commune with the Vikings' descendants in Norway and Iceland.[50] Arriving at their chosen destination, saga

---

41 Collingwood 1902, 8; also Streatfeild 1884, Heanley 1901–3.
42 Kelvin 1984–96, II 182–3, 422–5; designs by Edward Burne-Jones.
43 The songs in Scott 1822 enjoyed a independent life: see below, Chapter 3.
44 Elgar 1896; Bennett J. [n.d]; Wawn 1998.
45 Bird 1976, 42–53.
46 Townsend 1992, 191 quotes the satirical 'Saga of the Shield-Maiden' from *Punch*, 27 January 1894. The society's 1894 inaugural session was wryly reported in *Pall Mall Gazette*, 15 January 1894, 189.
47 George Borrow signed himself 'George Olaus Borrow'. On his copiously annotated copy of Ole Worm 1636 in Norwich Guildhall Library, see Williams 1982, 23.
48 Collingwood and Jón Stefánsson 1899.
49 Advertisements in Lock 1882; also Bennett 1882.
50 [anon.] 1909.

pilgrims could row in the fjord on whose shores Friðþjófr and Ingibjǫrg courted;[51] dig for the whey-stained charred embers of 'burnt Njal';[52] and ponder the rights of man in the great natural amphitheatre of Viking-age justice and polity at Þingvellir, in a silence broken only by the running waters of the timeless Öxará, and the passing cry of whimbrel or arctic tern.[53] Enchanted by the history, humbled by the hospitality, and exasperated by feckless guides,[54] the travellers could return home to paint their pictures,[55] write their novels,[56] and add to the ever-growing list of newspaper articles and illustrated travel books about Iceland or Norway – thereby encouraging others to follow in their foam and footsteps.[57] During Queen Victoria's long reign this virtuous circle of communion with the Viking- and saga-ages was completed many times.

'Unto the Costes Colde'

It had not always been so. Though there had been travel to, and trade with, Iceland since the early thirteenth-century days when the Icelandic sagas were first being recorded on vellum, it took many centuries for Viking- and saga-age visions to earn their place in the minds of northbound travellers from Britain. The dates, order and nature of Iceland-related compounds in the *OED* reveal why intrepid individuals visited the 'costes colde': Iceland-fish (1420), Iceland-cloth (1541), Iceland-curs (1547), Iceland-spar (1771), Iceland-falcon (1771), Iceland-crystal (1805). Fishing and trade in manufactured goods give way to luxury items, raw materials for spectacle lenses, and geological research. As indicated in the *Libelle of Englysshe Polycye*, a 1430 verse treatise on the state of English commercial enterprise, it was stockfish rather than sagas which lured men into the north Atlantic. There was no reason for it to have been otherwise. By 1430 the Viking age had not yet been invented for British readers. The *Beowulf* manuscript lay gathering dust awaiting its early nineteenth-century Icelandic transcriber and editor;[58] Chaucer wrote no 'Viking's Tale'; seventeenth-century tradition held that King Arthur had once conquered both Norway and Iceland,[59] but his Orcadian knights spoke no Norn in Sir Thomas Malory's tales; and the other heroes of medieval English romance headed south and east rather than north in search of adventure – even *Havelok the Dane* offered little

[51] Characters from *Friðþjófs saga*: see below, Chapter 5.
[52] Dasent 1861.
[53] Haggard 1926, I 285.
[54] Lock 1879, 16.
[55] Haraldur Hannesson 1988. Travellers could also gaze on saga-steads at local art galleries. Adelsteen Normann's 'The Sogne Fjord' (*c*.1885), was amongst the first canvases displayed in the new (1888) Leeds City Art Gallery.
[56] Lyall 1889, Caine 1890, Downe 1902.
[57] See, for example, Dufferin 1857, Baring Gould 1863, Lock 1879, Oswald 1882; see also Aho 1993.
[58] Grímur Jónsson Thorkelin 1815; see Kiernan 1986.
[59] Arngrímur Jónsson, in Hakluyt 1599–1600, 517.

Scandinavian narrative substance, for all that early nineteenth-century old northern philologists ransacked it for Scandinavian loan-words.[60] In 1430 the earliest printed edition of any Icelandic saga, or eddic or skaldic poem, was still two centuries away. Why, in any case, would any fifteenth-century Englishman have chosen to read of Viking- or Sturlung-age strife in Norway and Iceland when, during the Wars of the Roses, there was plenty of the real thing in his own backyard and when, before the century was over, Malory would provide his own set of sagas in English about the turbulent British present, thinly disguised as the glittering Arthurian past?

The *Libelle*'s Iceland is, thus, no seductive old northern theme park:

> Of Yseland to wryte is lytill nede,
> Save of stokfische; yit for sothe in dede
> Out of Bristow and costis many one,
> Men have practised by nedle and by stone
> Thiderwardes wythine a lytel whylle,
> Wythine xij. yeres, and wythoute parille,
> Gone and comen, as men were wonte of olde
> Of Scarborowgh, unto the costes colde.
> And now so fele shippes thys yere there were
> That moche losse for unfraught they bare.
> Yselond myght not make hem to be fraught
> Unto the hawys; this moche harme they caught.[61]

The 'costis ma[n]y one' which the poet has in mind are principally east coast ports such as Yarmouth, King's Lynn and Hull which enjoyed a profitable trade with Iceland at least until the end of the sixteenth century. The silent witness of many a churchyard in such communities would have challenged the *Libelle* claim that journeying to Iceland was 'wythoute parille'. The iconography of the earliest maps confirms what an uninviting prospect Iceland could represent. In Guðbrandur Þorláksson's richly illustrated 1590 Iceland map, the southern approaches are awash with a fearsome array of predatory monsters – razortoothed catfish, ravenous sting-rays, spouting whales, winged horses, sharptoothed crocodiles, horned bisons, sinister-looking crabs, and prawns too large for any cocktail.[62] What need had Iceland of its protective land-spirits when the creatures of the deep appeared ready to consume rather than be caught by foreign fishermen? The Victorian writers who so revered the ancient Viking sea-kings might have spared a thought for the real-life mariners of late medieval and Tudor Britain who 'practised by nedle and by stone' in the bleak waters of the North Atlantic.

Other hazards were man-made: opposition from the Danish licensing

---

60 Madden 1828; see also Wawn 1991a, 118–22.
61 Warner 1926, 41, ll. 798–809.
62 See Haraldur Sigurðsson 1971–8, II 9–16; also the cover of Morris 1996.

authorities, hostility from rival Hanseatic merchants,[63] and the ever-present threat from pirates much less benevolent than Sir Walter Scott's Clement Cleveland.[64] Yet, though Thule was the 'period of cosmographie' for one Elizabethan poet,[65] level-headed Danelaw folk who went down to the sea in ships knew that trading with Iceland could be profitable.[66] English cutlery, cloths, shoes and meal were exchanged for dried fish, woollen mittens, eider duck down and tallow. Returning vessels would sometimes offer passage to Icelanders for whom, once in a while, quick wittedness, the roll of a dice, or a lucky marriage could turn rags to riches during winters spent in Yarmouth; a Sigurður Ingimundarson could be reborn as a Simon Ingham.[67]

No vessel of the Iceland fleet ever returned to Britain with its holds stacked with saga manuscripts rather than stockfish. We know of no Simon Ingham becoming Sigurður Ingimundarson, residing in a trading community such as Grindavík, and developing levels of linguistic proficiency and literary curiosity sufficient to engage with Icelandic written or oral culture.[68] We may be sure that none of the Scarborough men arraigned for illegal Iceland fishing in 1437–8[69] realised that the *Libelle* poet's 'Scarborowgh of olde' features in Snorri Sturluson's *Haralds saga Sigurðarsonar* as the assembly point for the newly-arrived Norwegian King Haraldr and his all conquering forces prior to the Battle of Stamford Bridge, and had once felt the full force of the northmen's murdering, burning and pillaging presence.[70] Britain's imaginative rediscovery of King Haraldr, his bloody progress through the north of England, and the melancholy countdown to the battle of Hastings had to wait for mid-Victorian novels by Sir Edward Bulwer-Lytton and Charles Kingsley. In late medieval and Tudor England, Æthelweardian abuse of the Vikings may have been a thing of the past, but so was any serious awareness of Britain's Viking- and saga-age links with Scandinavia.

We can identify some of these links through the eyes of a native Icelander addressing a Victorian audience. Eiríkur Magnússon, librarian, medieval scholar, and Icelander resident in Britain for fifty years from his arrival in 1862, doubtless needed little encouragement to lecture on the general theme of medieval relations between the two countries; but his talks sometimes took on an additional urgency. In 1875, acting on reports of catastrophic volcanic eruptions in his native east of Iceland,[71] Eiríkur prepared two lectures for college audi-

[63] Carus-Wilson 1967, 98–142; Björn Þorsteinsson 1970, 239–47.
[64] The eponymous hero of Scott 1822.
[65] Thomas Weelkes, in Fallowes 1967, 293, VII–VIII/1: 'period' means 'limit'.
[66] The streets of Hull were said to be paved with Icelandic stones used as ballast in returning vessels: Björn Þorsteinsson 1970, 111.
[67] Sverrir Jakobsson 1994, 39–40.
[68] Though see Wawn 1985, 115, 130.
[69] Björn Þorsteinsson 1970, 158.
[70] First available in Johnstone 1786, 200–1, with a Latin translation; Laing 1844, III 83–4.
[71] See *The Times* 1 July 1875 6c, 10 July 13c, 17 July 13f, 11 August 10c and 11a, 14 August 11c, 15 September 10b. Eiríkur had eye witness reports from family and friends.

ences in Cambridge and learned societies elsewhere in Britain. They were consciousness-raising exercises, designed to elicit support for the relief measures being coordinated by the Lord Mayor of London. 'Iceland and England 1875' was prompted by the eruption of the volcano Askja which began on Easter Monday, scarcely nine months after the much-reported millennial celebrations of Ingólfr Arnarson's pioneering voyage to Iceland. 'On early points of contact, chiefly literary, between Britain and Iceland' may have been linked to the 1882 Mansion House fund for famine victims following the desperate Icelandic winter of 1881–2.[72] Eiríkur seeks to highlight the longevity and diversity of cultural links between Britain and Iceland as a prelude to rattling the collecting box. In responding to the troubled Icelandic present, he reminds prosperous Icelandophiles in Britain about the forgotten kinship between the two peoples. For Eiríkur Magnússon, then, there was much 'nede' to 'wryte' of medieval Iceland apart from 'stockfische', and his Victorian audiences followed his words intently.

In the 'Early Points of Contact' lecture, Eiríkur claims that the 'wealthiest and most civilized' of the early settlers of Iceland came from Great Britain, and that one of them established a now famous Anglo-Icelandic literary link. Eiríkur argues that the *Beowulf* story, by this time known to Victorian scholars,[73] had been taken from Northumbria to Víðidalur in north Iceland by Auðunn skǫkull, an early settler whose maternal grandfather was the famous Viking Ragnarr loðbrók; Auðunn, in turn, was the ancestor of Grettir Ásmundarson, whose coalbiter youth, luckless life, and legendary outlawry became the stuff of *Grettis saga Ásmundarson*: 'that it [the *Beowulf* tale] was a particular favorite [sic] among the lordly descendants of Radnar [sic] . . . goes without saying'.[74] Alert Victorian readers of *The Story of Grettir the Strong* (1869), the first English translation of the saga, and the first fruits of the collaboration of Eiríkur and William Morris, might well already have spotted the similarities between Old English poem and Old Icelandic saga, notably the fights between the two heroes and their respective monsters.[75] Eiríkur also highlights the ecclesiastical links between the two lands: his earliest scholarly work in Britain had included the translation of medieval Icelandic religious prose and poetry into English,[76] and he numbered several Anglo-Catholics amongst his friends and correspondents.[77] He notes that the Anglo-Saxon language provided Icelandic with vocabulary for priestly vestments and ecclesiastical offices; and that it was from the Anglo-Saxon chronicle that the *Prose Edda* derived its habit of tracing the royal genealogies back to Óðinn, Troy and the Bible. The curiosity about England exhibited by the Benedictine monks at Þingeyrar, Iceland's oldest monastic

---

[72] Lectures in Lbs. 406 fol., 1860 4to.
[73] Via Grímur Jónsson Thorkelin 1815: see Shippey 1998, 10–24 and passim.
[74] Lbs. 406 fol. 17–18. See Magnús Fjalldal 1998.
[75] Lbs. 406 fol. 7–18.
[76] Eiríkr Magnússon 1870, 1875–83.
[77] See, below, Chapter 12; Lbs. 2189b 4to, letters from Westlake and Waterton.

establishment, is examined – notably the sagas composed about St Dunstan, King Edward the Confessor and St Thomas of Canterbury.[78] 1875 saw the publication of the first volume of Eiríkur's edition and translation of *Thómas saga Erkibiskups*,[79] and his lecture identifies the route – the Lincoln journey of Páll, nephew of Þorlákr, Bishop of Skálholt, just three years after the canonisation of St Thomas à Becket – by which such miracle stories may have reached Iceland.[80]

While some of the Anglo-Icelandic links highlighted by Eiríkur are drawn from rather deep in the river, others are underplayed. One of these deserves particular mention in view of the *Libelle* poet's reference to 'Bristowe'. Victorians on both sides of the Atlantic became familiar with the tradition[81] that it was from Bristol in the late fifteenth century that Christopher Columbus had sailed for Iceland, there to learn about and organise an expedition to explore the still more distant Vínland, discovered and abandoned by Leifr Eiríksson and his companions five centuries earlier. One Victorian Englishman, Lord Garvagh, promoted this tradition proudly: he claims that his ancestor William Canning had been allowed by the Danes (who owed him money) to continue trading with Iceland after other Bristol ships had been banned, and thus that it must have been he who carried Columbus to Iceland.[82] By this time, too, American citizens of Scandinavian descent were celebrating the idea that the earliest American settler from Europe had been Leifr Eiríksson (Norwegian/Icelandic; righteous pagan) and not Christopher Columbus (Italian; Catholic).[83] A statue to Leifr Eiríksson was unveiled in Boston in 1887,[84] not far from where the alleged site of Leifr's settlement had been located on the Charles River and within suspiciously convenient distance of Harvard University.[85] Ancient and modern, Viking and Victorian, linked arms; famous names and deeds from the past could be made to resonate powerfully in contemporary controversies about national identity, as well as in appeals for Icelandic famine relief.

'Vain Phantasies'

It is in literary London rather than commercial Bristol that the principal *Libelle* image of Iceland and its stockfish reappears in the late sixteenth century. Yet behind the bluster of Thomas Nashe's formulaic 'nothing but stock-fish, whetstones, and cods-heads' view of sixty-six degrees north,[86] there were other saltier

---

[78] Lbs. 1860 4to 32–4. See also Wawn 1991a 203–14.
[79] Eiríkr Magnússon 1875–83.
[80] Lbs. 1860 4to 34–6. For other instances of literary influence, see Taylor 1969, Jorgensen 1997, xcii–xcv.
[81] Björn Þorsteinsson 1970, 10 traces it to Finnur Magnússon.
[82] Garvagh 1875, 90–1.
[83] Brown 1887, 1890.
[84] Horsford 1888c.
[85] Horsford 1892 and Horsford C. 1893; also Fleming 1995, 1080–4.
[86] In McKerrow 1958, I 360

tales filtering down from the sub-arctic circle. Iceland had not yet become the land of the Vikings, but it was 'one of the chiefe kingdomes of the night'; it was an environmental disaster area choking on 'sulphureous stinking smoak . . . that . . . poysons the whole Countrey'; and its bottomless Lake Vether (Vättern: mysteriously relocated from Olaus Magnus's Sweden)[87] turned any passing human or animal into marble. No less fearsome was Mount Hekla, whose gaping mouth represented the earthly entrance to the hellish home of the 'perpetuis damnata'.[88] Those standing nearby could hear 'such yellings and groanes, as *Ixion*, *Titius*, *Sisiphus*, and *Tantalus*, blowing all in one trumpet of distresse, could neuer conioyned bellowe foorth'.[89] This was no land for saga heroes. That the mantle of Viking- and saga-age glory had yet to fall on the Scandinavian or Icelandic descendants of Óðinn is evident in Andrew Boorde's whimsical 1542 European travel sketches, edited for the Early English Text Society in 1870 by F.J. Furnivall, with footnotes by Guðbrandur Vigfússon, an Icelandic scholar resident in Oxford. In Boorde's portraits the Danes are good fighters who had once managed to invade England, the Norwegians are 'rewde', whilst Icelanders are simply 'beastly creatures, vnmannered and vntaughte', sometimes without even the much-derided stockfish to sustain them – 'they wyll eate talowe candells, and candells endes, and olde grece, and restye tallowe, and other fylthy thinges'.[90] Holinshed refines the topos: an Icelandic merchant's wife boards a visiting trading vessel and devours all the ship's candels as a 'iollie banket'.[91] With such privations to endure, Icelanders could hardly be begrudged the little luxuries identified by Nashe, such as frozen ale 'that they carry in their pockets lyke glue, and euer when they would drinke, they set it on the fire and melt it'.[92] This could prove efficacious to soul as well as body by functioning as a kind of sacrament on a stick. The Pope had reputedly given a dispensation to allow the Icelanders to substitute ale for wine at the Eucharist.

Cod-heads and stockfish apart, the two principal northern cultural images adopted by Nashe and his Elizabethan and Jacobean successors were 'Iselond curres' and Lapland sorcerers rather than Viking sea-kings. We may recall Shakespeare's 'prick-eared cur of Iceland', a phrase made briefly memorable as the insult directed by Ancient Pistol at Corporal Nym before they set off for Agincourt in Shakespeare's *Henry V.*[93] The suggestion of peppery aggressiveness in the image suits its immediate target well enough, yet Queen Elizabeth thought sufficiently well of her own Icelandic lap-dog to have it included in a formal portrait.[94] The fashion for returning from Iceland with 'prick-eared curs'

---

[87] Page 1963–4 231–2; Olaus Magnus 1996–8, I 62.
[88] A phrase from the 1590 Guðbrandur Þorláksson map: see above, note 62.
[89] McKerrow 1958, I 359.
[90] Boorde, in Furnivall 1870, 141.
[91] Holinshed (1587), in Seaton 1935, 14.
[92] McKerrow 1958, I 360.
[93] *Henry V* 2.i.39.
[94] Seaton 1935, 33; also Boorde, in Furnivall 1870, 32–4.

enjoyed a revival amongst Victorian Icelandophiles; though it was not until the appearance of *The Story of Burnt Njal*, George Dasent's pioneering 1861 saga translation, that readers could set the yapping reality of their prick-eared pets against the canine heroism of Sámr, the loyal Irish hound of the mighty Gunnarr of Hlíðarendi.[95] As for the Lapland sorcerers, they are first invoked by Antipholus of Syracuse, in Shakespeare's *Comedy of Errors*, to explain his bewilderment as pairs of identical twins keep stumbling upon each other on the streets of Ephesus.[96] Thereafter, Lappish sorcery enjoyed a vigorous literary life well into the eighteenth century,[97] though it was not until 1905 that the first English translation of *Vatnsdæla saga* brought the most famous of Lappish saga sorceresses to general attention.[98]

The dogs and the candle-eating, if not the sorcerers, had a basis in reality, but many of the other 'vain phantasies' and tales of 'Apparitions, Ghosts, Hobgoblins and Fairies'[99] were a source of irritation to learned Icelanders like Árngrímur Jónsson whose *Brevis commentarius de Islandia* (1593) sought to challenge 'the errors of such as haue written concerning this Island' and to confute 'the slanders, and reproches of certaine strangers, which they have vsed over-boldly against the people of *Island*'.[100] Árngrímur had no interest in tall tales about Vikings – there were more immediate misconceptions to challenge. Readers are duly assured that in Iceland whoredom *is* considered a sin (585–6), that dinner guests are *not* expected to 'wash their hands and their faces in pisse' (586), that sea-ice 'making a miserable kind of mone' off the wintry shores of the island is rarely encountered (562–3), and that any groaning sounds are those of nature, and not of lost souls heading for the mouth of Hekla (559–61, 584–5). On a more uplifting level, the Viking-age hero of *Brennu-Njáls saga* is described as a perfect Christ-like figure before popish corruption took hold of Iceland (570–1). Of the superstition that there were witches and wizards from whom favourable winds could be bought, Árngrímur is, perhaps wisely, silent. This belief proved invulnerable to hyperborean blasts of Royal Society scepticism, and survived to do service again when Sir Walter Scott was fine-tuning the presentation of his all-powerful sibyl Norna of the Fitful Head in *The Pirate*.[101] Árngrímur's overall efforts at demystification were not immediately or universally successful. It required a further heave in the mid-eighteenth century by works such as Niels Horrebow's *The Natural History of Iceland* (1758), a work admired by Dr Samuel Johnson, before much of the hocus pocus subsided.

---

[95] Dasent 1861, ch. 75.
[96] *Comedy of Errors* 4.iii.11.
[97] Farley 1906.
[98] Gudbrand Vigfusson and Powell 1905, II 290–1.
[99] Sir Thomas Craig, *Scotland's Soveraignty Asserted* (1695; written earlier), quoted in Seaton 1935, 20.
[100] Hakluyt 1599–1600, I 550.
[101] See below, Chapter 3.

A British Isle

One 'early point of contact' between England and Iceland found no place in Eiríkur Magnússon's fund-raising lectures. During the age of Boorde, Nashe and 'fables more trifling than old wives tales',[102] Britain was offered the chance to assume the governance of Iceland. The Danish king, desperate for cash, offered to cede Iceland to Henry VIII as a semi-permanent pledge against a sum of a hundred thousand florins,[103] rather as the Scottish king had previously acquired the Orkney and Shetland isles. Many Regency and Victorian old northernists, increasingly conscious of their kinship with Iceland and Scandinavia, would have jumped at the opportunity,[104] but the romance of the 'runick' old north sent no shivers up Henry's Tudor spine. He had a Reformation on his hands; Iceland was not a foreign policy priority. The proposals came to nothing, and Elizabethan and Jacobean England was left with its residual images of the far north, ancient and modern – dried fish on the table, dogs on aristocratic laps, gloomy Danish princes in the theatre,[105] and damned souls consigned to the sulphurous bowels of Hekla.

The possible annexation of Iceland reared its head again in both the eighteenth and nineteenth centuries. In the mid-1780s Denmark offered to cede Iceland to Britain, in exchange for Crab Island in the West Indies.[106] From a British point of view annexation made some sense. Iceland offered reliable supplies of sulphur for munitions, and of cod; the Faroese shipping lanes, long the haunt of pirates, could be policed more effectively; a flourishing Iceland trading fleet meant employment for British shipyards, clothing manufacturers and provision merchants, and it offered a way of keeping sailors from the British navy in training during peacetime. There was also the possibility of using Iceland as a prison colony thereby solving the age-old problem of what to do with the drunken sailor early in the morning. In addition, it was solemnly maintained that Icelandic smoked salmon could become a new staple food for the common folk of Britain – unlike white salt fish which always required a strong sauce, and was expensive in time and money for the harassed British homemaker to produce. It was further argued that Britain's diplomatic representatives in Iceland ought to be Scotsmen – the miserable climate would agree with them, and 'they are not nice as to Provisions'.[107] Both Prime Minister Pitt and his Secretary of War were sympathetic to the whole idea, but with Pitt's resignation and improving relations with Denmark, attentions were soon directed elsewhere. There were further unsuccessful attempts to revive the annexation

---

102 Hakluyt 1599–1600, I 550.
103 Björn Þorsteinsson 1957–61, 77.
104 Anna Agnarsdóttir 1979.
105 Fewer things were 'rotten in the state of Denmark' after changes to the text of *Hamlet*, prompted by James I's Danish wife, Queen Anne: Seaton 1935, 64
106 Anna Agnarsdóttir 1993.
107 My discussion in this paragraph draws on Lbs. 424 fol.

option during the Napoleonic wars; and as late as the 1860s there was talk of support for Denmark in the Slesvig-Holsten conflicts being rewarded by the gift of some Danish territory – namely Iceland.[108] Yet, all came to nothing, and old northern enthusiasts in Britain had to be content with admiring the land of myth and saga from a distance. There would be no British governor in residence. One diplomat's dreams of becoming the Earl of Iceland or Baron Mount Hekla were never realised.[109]

'Upon these shelves much Gothick Lumber climbs'[110]

While diplomats danced their wily arabesques around 'the question of Iceland', intellectual contacts between Britain and Scandinavia developed steadily. Beginning from a standing start of total ignorance, an awareness of the political and literary culture of the old north developed steadily in Britain during the seventeenth and early eighteenth centuries. The interest shown in Iceland by the newly-founded Royal Society after 1662 was one underpinning factor.[111] Secondly, the 'Gothic' old north became an important reference point in seventeenth-century political debate in Britain. The Goths were frequently cited as pioneering democrats in debates over the role of the monarchy.[112] Thirdly, the diplomatic community promoted British cultural contacts with mainland Scandinavia.[113] A fourth and major factor was the publication in Sweden and Denmark of a series of volumes which rapidly established themselves throughout Europe as canonical works of old northern scholarship. Here were the raw materials out of which, eventually, the Victorians created the Viking age – the stories, characters, deities and social contexts. These volumes enjoyed a long shelf-life in the private libraries of eighteenth- and nineteenth-century old northern enthusiasts.[114] Their contents had begun to filter through to British readers in translated summaries or popularisations by the end of the seventeenth century.[115]

Some indispensable folios of the north European renaissance – Olaus Magnus's encyclopaedic *Historia de gentibus septentrionalibus* (1555),[116] and the first edition (1514) of Saxo Grammaticus's twelfth-century *Gesta Danorum* – had

---

[108] Symington 1862, 58.
[109] Lbs. 424 fol., John Cochrane to Andrew Cochrane-Johnstone, 17 May 1797.
[110] Samuel Garth, 'The Dispensary', quoted in Quinn and Clunies Ross 1994, 207.
[111] Seaton 1935, 184ff.
[112] Kliger 1952, chs 1–2.
[113] Seaton 1935, 117, 126–8, 132–4.
[114] See, for example, [Cochrane] 1838, Bredsdorff 1965 171–4.
[115] Seaton 1935, 248–58 and passim; Fell 1992, 87–9.
[116] On Olaus's political agenda, see Foote 1996–8, I xxxvii–xxxix. The work was presented to William Cecil in 1561 to further a prospective engagement between Queen Elizabeth and King Erik XIV of Sweden.

served the old northern cause nobly for a hundred years and more.[117] They were now joined by a dozen or so major new publications:

Ole Worm, *Runer seu Danica literatura antiqvissima* (1636)
Magnús Ólafsson (ed. Ole Worm), *Specimen lexici runici* (1650)
Runólfur Jónsson, *Grammaticæ Islandicæ rudimenta* (1651)
Olaus Verelius (ed.), *Gothrici & Rolfi Westrogothiæ regum historia lingua antiqua Gothica conscripta* (1664)
Peder Resen (ed.), *Edda Islandorum* (1665)
Peder Resen (ed.), *Ethica Odini pars Eddæ Sæmundi vocata Haavamaal* (1665),
Peder Resen (ed.), *Philosophia antiqvissima Norvego-Danica dicta Woluspa* (1665)
Olaus Verelius (ed.), *Herrauds och Bosa saga* (1666)
Olaus Verelius (ed.), *Hervarar saga* (1672)
Guðmundur Andrésson, *Lexicon Islandicum* (1683)
Thomas Bartholin, *Antiqvitatum Danicarum de causis contemptæ a Danis adhuc gentilibus mortis* (1689)
Olaus Verelius (ed.), *Index lingvæ veteris Scytho-Scandicæ sive Gothicæ* (1691)
Þormóður Torfason [Torfæus], *Orcades, seu rerum Orcadensium historia* (1697)
Johan Peringskiöld (ed.), *Heimskringla, eller Snorre Sturlusone Nordländske Konunga Sagor, sive Historiæ regum septentrionalium, a Snorrone Sturlonide* 2 vols (1697).
Þormóður Torfason, *Universi septentrionis antiqvitates, seriem dynastarum et regum Daniæ, a primo eorum Sckioldo Odini filio ad Gormum grandævum Haraldi cærulidentis patrem.* (1705)

Most of these volumes drew their information and textual extracts 'ex vetustis codicibus et monumentis hactenus ineditis congesti'.[118] Resen made available newly-discovered eddic poems from the long-lost late thirteenth-century *Codex Regius*, notably *Vǫluspá* and *Hávamál*, with their evidence that old northern 'barbarians' had developed a coherent system of ethics, a mythological system, and an artful tradition of poetic composition. Verelius and Peringskiöld provide pioneering editions of, respectively, old northern *fornaldarsögur* [legendary sagas] and Snorri's *Heimskringla*; Þormóður Torfason summarises chronicle and saga material relating to the Orkneys; there are digests of runological knowledge (Worm 1636, Worm and Magnus Ólafsson 1650, Runólfur Jónsson 1651); a grammar (Runólfur Jónsson 1651); and rudimentary dictionaries (Guðmundur Andrésson 1683, Verelius 1691). In some ways the most influential of all these volumes was Bartholin's detailed treatment of what soon became a defining old northern theme – *ridens moriar*: the fearless laughter of heroes at the moment of death. Lengthy scenes from many unedited sagas are cited in Icelandic with Latin translations. In Bartholin's three lengthy sections, the heroes are followed step by step on their smiling progress from battlefield (Book 1) to grave (Book 2) to well-earned place at the feet of Óðinn in Valhǫll

---

117 Sir Walter Scott refers to Olaus Magnus: Scott 1822/1996, 347.
118 Bartholin 1689, title page. Clunies Ross 1998a 75–93 provides an authoritative examination of several of these works in relation to the preparation of [Percy] 1763.

(Book 3). Bartholin's wide-ranging and well-contextualised compendium includes illustrations of rune-stones and related antiquities, and a detailed analysis of the skald's pivotal role in old northern society. Taken together the new publications from Scandinavia provide an integrated and bracing picture of old northern life and sensibility. With Latin the international language of scholarship all these volumes found a limited but attentive readership in seventeenth- and eighteenth-century Britain; and several of them remained available in specialist bookshops well into Victorian times.[119]

Anglicisation and Dissemination

Even with Royal Society involvement, politically driven curiosity, diplomatic service networking, and new European scholarship, however, there were other needs to address before the old northern world could make a decisive breakthrough in Britain. Someone needed to produce a field-commanding work of English scholarship as an act of faith in the subject area; scholarly networks within Britain as well as overseas needed to develop further; and European old northern scholarship needed vernacular dissemination and popularisation. By the mid eighteenth century significant progress had been made on all three fronts.

Firstly, the need for a major work of English scholarship was met with a vengeance by George Hickes's *Thesaurus linguarum septentrionalium* (1703–5), a monumental project by Britain's first old northern philological giant. Under great stress as a newly-consecrated non-juring bishop after the coronation of William and Mary, Hickes worked indefatigably, supported by other British and Scandinavian scholars.[120] The place of publication was Oxford, where Christian Worm's edition of Ari Þorgilsson's *Íslendingabók* (the first Icelandic text ever printed in England) was later to appear,[121] and where scholars with old northern interests such as Thomas Marshall, rector of Lincoln College, collected Icelandic manuscripts and scholarly printed works and made contact with visiting Scandinavian scholars.[122] The *Thesaurus* was a work of extraordinary philological ambition and achievement. It offered the reader details of saga manuscripts, summaries of saga stories, a supplemented version of Runólfur Jónsson's 1651 Grammar, runic transcriptions and interpretations, and numismatic information. It promoted a strong sense of the links between 'Saxon', 'Anglo-Saxon', 'Dano-Saxon', and (even) 'Semi-Saxon' language and literature, and of the con-

---

[119] Lund 1869 [122] includes an advertisement from the bookseller Franz Thimm of Brooke Street, London; this indicates that copies of Resen's 1665 *Edda*, Guðmundur Andrésson 1683, and the three volume 1787–1828 Copenhagen *Edda* were available for sale.

[120] Harris 1992, 53–60.

[121] Worm 1716; see Harris 1992, 56.

[122] Harris 1992, 5–6. See Bodleian MSS Junius 36, 120, and Marshall 80; also Quinn and Clunies Ross 1994, 193, n. 11.

tinuities between ancient and modern literary traditions in England.[123] No wonder that Hickes's weighty volume became indispensable for anyone 'destitute of the Assistance of Books, wrote in the *Norwegian* tongues'.[124] There were plenty of scholars in this category. A Latin digest prepared by Dr William Wotton helped the *Thesaurus* to reach a wider readership. Wotton's summary was in turn translated into English by Maurice Shelton in 1735, who offers level-headed advice on a graduated programme of reading for anyone keen to engage with the '*Gothick* monuments of the Middle Ages'.[125] Having worked through the Icelandic grammar in the *Thesaurus*, students should then 'read over studiously' the entire Icelandic Bible; followed by selected reading from 'some short Histories [that is, sagas] . . . of the Northern People'. More advanced readers are then recommended to move on to Peringskiöld's *Heimskringla*, and Resen's *Edda*, 'which comprehends the whole Northern Mythology'. With all this reading dutifully undertaken, readers are assured that 'all things in the Northern Monuments will be plain and manageable' (9).

The second element needed for the awakening and coordinating of old northern interests in Britain was the emergence of a network of regionally based enthusiasts who were in contact with specialists in Oxford and in Europe. During the late seventeenth-century gestation period of the *Thesaurus*, for instance, scholars resident in the old Danelaw heartlands of Britain shared their antiquarian findings (notably runic stones and coins) with Hickes – as with Ralph Thoresby in Leeds.[126] The contacts associated with the Hickes volume prefigured the networks of old northern enthusiasts that developed on a rather grander scale in Victorian Britain.

Thirdly, British scholars familiar with the exciting publications emerging from Scandinavia began to share their often brittle knowledge with British readers[127] in works such as an English translation of the epitomised Olaus Magnus *Historia*,[128] Robert Sheringham's *De Anglorum gentis origine disceptatio* (1670; in Latin) and Aylett Sammes's more populist *Britannia antiqua illustrata; or the Antiquities of Ancient Britain derived from the Phoenicians* (1676; in English).[129] Sheringham was the first scholar to publish any Old Norse poetry in England (*Hávamál* verses derived from Worm's edition), and Sammes (not, as the *OED* records, Sir Walter Scott) first introduces the term 'berserk' into the English language.[130]

Popular poetry soon began to draw on this multilayered scholarly tradition.

---

123 Notably the alliterative tradition: Hickes 1703–5, II 195–7.

124 [Shelton] 1735, 47.

125 Ibid., 9.

126 Harris 1992, letters 196, 199 and passim. Other regional networks are revealed in Page 1995 (1965) 23–28, 127–31.

127 Fell 1996 discusses Sammes, Sheringham and, in particular, Hickes. See also Seaton 1935, Bennett 1937, 1938, 1950–1, Quinn and Clunies Ross 1994.

128 Olaus Magnus 1658, translator unknown; Latin Epitome 1558 by C. Scribonius.

129 The first Icelandic text translated into English was Arngrímur Jónsson 1609: see Purchas 1625.

130 Fell, in Faulkes and Perkins 1993, 88.

Two instances show what could happen. Weighing in at over five kilos and written in Latin, the Hickes *Thesaurus* seems an unlikely standard-bearer for a popular tradition. Yet the cult of the ubiquitous eighteenth-century poem known as 'The Waking of Angantyr' can be traced directly to its door.[131] This *Hervarar saga* poem dramatises a daughter's visit to her father's tomb to take possession of a fateful ancestral sword, and the Icelandic text in Hickes's *Thesaurus* was accompanied by an English translation – the first ever published in Britain of a complete Old Icelandic poem. This was reprinted in Dryden's *Poetical Miscellanies* (1716),[132] and in Thomas Percy's *Five Pieces of Runic Poetry* (1763).[133] Thereafter it became a kind of test piece for late eighteenth-century northern enthusiasts to paraphrase and rework; at least half a dozen versions appeared over a thirty year period from 1775,[134] as rhymesters revelled in the poem's fatalism and depiction of steely female will.

Secondly, John Campbell's impressive *A Polite Correspondence: or the Rational Amusement* (1741),[135] includes a dialogue in which Leander champions 'the study of the ancient Poets in these Northern Parts',[136] while Celadon compares the Saxon Odes favourably with their Greek equivalents (262). We find frequent respectful reference to Hickes's *Thesaurus*, 'the noblest storehouse of this kind of Learning the World has yet seen' (272). Leander claims that Viking-age religion was 'wonderfully calculated for Poetry', and offers paraphrastic samples from Saxo Grammaticus and Ole Worm. In 'An Ancient *Danish Ode*' we encounter the bracing world of the Viking sea-king, one of the most popular icons of Victorian old northernism:

> In Deeds of Arms our Heroes rise,
> Illustrious, in their Offsprings' Eyes,
>   They feared not thro' the Stormy Sea,
>   To urge their Course, – Then why should we,
>   Ingloriously such Labours flee? . . .
>
> Haste! haste! ye Heroes, haste on Board.
> Haste! haste! great *Hubba*, give the Word.
>   No more Delay, but let us fly,
>   If *Odin* please to Victory,
>   He chearful lives who does not fear to die. (293)

In the companion piece, 'Another [Ode] on *Victory*', Campbell anticipates the 'runic' style and themes of Thomas Gray by two decades. In taut half-line

---

[131] See, for example, Williams 1790; Seward 1810, III 90–103.
[132] Dryden 1716, 387f.
[133] [Percy] 1763, 13–20.
[134] Omberg 1976, 150.
[135] See McKillop 1933.
[136] [Campbell] 1741, 235.

phrases, strong end rhymes, and alliterative doublets, we meet the twin formulaic figures of Bardic singer and beast of battle (decorating a standard):

> The Combat's o'er, the Deed is done,
> The Foe is fled, the Field is won.
> Let Mirth succeed, the Day's our own.
>
> The *Raven* claps her sable Wings,
> The Bard his chosen Timbrel brings,
> With Art he plays, with Joy he sings. (294)

Such poems were vernacular doodles in the margins of scholarship, serving to create a prototypical popular iconography for the Viking age. The two 'Runic Odes' which Thomas Warton the Elder published in 1748 – via Sir William Temple out of Ole Worm – contribute to the same process:

> Yes – 'tis decreed my Sword no more
> Shall smoke and blush with hostile Gore;
> To my great Father's Feasts I go,
> Where luscious Wines for ever flow.
> Which from the hollow Sculls we drain,
> Of Kings in furious Combat slain.
>
> Death, to the Brave a blest Resort,
> Brings us to awful Odin's Court.
> Where with old Warriors mix'd we dwell,
> Recount our Wounds, our Triumphs tell;
> Me, will they own as bold a Guest,
> As e'er in Battle bar'd my Breast.[137]

We find here, firstly, the hero's eager embrace of death when fate decrees. In the accompanying poem 'on the same subject' the warrior narrator strikes a Bartholinean note: 'What's Life! – I scorn this idle Breath, / I smile in the Embrace of Death'. Secondly, in a further vernacularisation of Bartholinean learning,[138] the Warton 'runic lines' offer an image of Valhǫll [Valhalla] as the festive seat of the gods where warriors, summoned by the fatal Valkyries from their earthly battlefields, joust to the death during the day, only to be revived for the evening feasting, as all prepare for *ragnarǫk* when the frost giants will invade, and the final cosmic conflagration can no longer be prevented. Thirdly, we find an instance of the long-term consequences of a translation error from fifty years earlier: Magnús Ólafsson's Latin version of *Krákumál* in Ole Worm's *Runer seu Danica literatura antiqvissima* had mistakenly translated warriors drinking 'ór bjúgviðum hausa' [from the curved branches of skulls], that is, from drinking vessels made out of animal horns, as 'ex craniis eorum quos ceciderunt' [out of

---

[137] Warton 1748, 157–8.
[138] Bartholinus 1689, Bk2 chs viii–xiii.

the skulls of those whom they killed].[139] For all the accident of its birth (though some Victorians believed it was part of a Classicist conspiracy to denigrate the old north),[140] this macabre image was to enjoy a vigorous 200-year life of its own. By 1774 we find translator's error transformed into ethnological truth, with Thomas Warton the Younger citing late eighteenth-century Ceylonese customs as authentication of the longevity and ubiquity of the old northern practice.[141] Poets were ever eager to embellish the motif:

> Virgins of immortal line
> Present the goblet foaming o'er:
> Of heroes skulls the goblet made,
> With figur'd deaths, and snakes of gold inlaid.[142]

It was not until 1839 that English readers had the mistranslation explained to them,[143] and its eradication took even longer.

The fact that such poems and poets irritated a neo-classicist like Alexander Pope confirms the extent to which they were attracting an early eighteenth-century readership. Chaucer's *Hous of Fame* temple had no Gothic images on its supporting pillars; as recreated by Pope, however, one side of the edifice is festooned with such sanguinary elements, so that the poet can register his disapproval.[144] Inevitably, Pope has little time for the European scholars responsible for peddling such visions. For William Temple in 1690, Ole Worm 'has very much deserved from the Commonwealth of Learning';[145] in Pope's *Dunciad* he is the subject of waspish disdain:

> But who is he, in closet close y-pent,
> Of sober face, with learned dust besprent?
> Right well mine eyes arede the myster wight,
> On parchment scraps y-fed, and Wormius hight.
> To future ages may thy dulness last,
> As thou preserv'st the dulness of the past![146]

---

[139] Gordon 1957, lxix–lxx.

[140] Hodgetts 1884, 171.

[141] Warton 1774–81, I d4r, note. Warton argued that Odin's tribe emigrated 'from the confines of Persia' (1774, I d1v).

[142] Sterling 1789, 150: 'The Scalder: an Ode'.

[143] Pigott 1839, 65–6; Percy 1847, 105.

[144] *The Temple of Fame* 119–22, 125–31: Butt 1963, 177.

[145] Temple 1690, 92.

[146] *The Dunciad* iii 181–6: Butt 1963, 412–13.

Runic Pieces

It was Thomas Percy's *Five Pieces of Runic Poetry*,[147] along with his *Northern Antiquities* (1770), and the splendid 1768 Norse Odes of Thomas Gray,[148] which put the seal on the arrival of old northern literature and mythology as a recognisable influence on late eighteenth-century literary sensibility. These were the texts that rolled the pitch for the opening bowlers of Victorian old northernism, and established the canon of old northern texts that guided paraphrasers and imitators for most of the nineteenth century. The pieces were:[149]

'The Incantation of Hervor': English translation from Hickes (1703–5); Icelandic text from Verelius 1672.
'The Dying Ode of Regner Lodbrog';[150] Icelandic text from Worm 1636.
'The Ransome of Egill the Scald': Icelandic text from Worm 1636.
'The Funeral Song of Hacon':[151] Icelandic text from Peringskiöld 1697.
'The Complaint of Harold': Icelandic text from Bartholin 1689.

Five Pieces provides austere prose translations and includes Icelandic texts in an appendix intended to highlight James Macpherson's failure to do the same in his hugely successful volume of *Erse Fragments* (1760) attributed to Ossian, the ancient blind Gaelic bard.[152]

Percy's readers could learn of Hervor's unappeasable determination to avenge her murdered brothers; of Ragnarr loðbrók's Viking life; of the verbal craftiness of Egill Skallagrímsson, forced to save his neck in York not by fighting but by composing poetry;[153] of King Hákon's triumphant entry into Valhǫll;[154] and of Viking male bonding and frustrated romance in the life of King Haraldr.[155] Percy commends the 'softer passions'[156] represented by 'Harold's Complaint', and half a dozen paraphrastic versions duly appeared over the following couple of decades.[157] Other readers found the 'blood and death' more seductive, whether derived from Ragnarr's battles in Eastern Europe:

---

[147] Percy's title reflects a widespread eighteenth-century misunderstanding that there was a runic language as well as an alphabet. For an excellent account of Percy's work, see Clunies Ross 1998a, 51–104.
[148] Written 1761: Lonsdale 1969, 210–15, 220–8.
[149] See fuller discussion in Clunies Ross 1998a, 86–8.
[150] Nineteenth-century versions of the Ragnar ode include Henderson 1818, 528–35 (from Johnstone 1782), [Ferguson] 1833, [Clifford] 1865, 56–8, Headley 1875, 13–17. Hughes 1869, 74 reconstructs the night before the Battle of Ashdown – Alfred reading from the Psalms, whilst the Danes sang of 'Regner Lodbrog'.
[151] Nineteenth-century versions include Massey 1861, 13–18 ('Old King Hake').
[152] [Percy] 1763 A4v.
[153] 'Head Ransome' (*Hǫfuðlausn*) from *Egils saga Skallagrímssonar.*
[154] *Hákonarmál*: [Percy] 1763 63–70; reprinted Percy 1770, II 240–4, with omissions.
[155] [Percy] 1763, 77–9; [Percy] 1770, II 237–8.
[156] [Percy] 1763, 74.
[157] Omberg 1976, 151.

We fought with swords. I was very young, when towards the East, in the straights of Eirar, we gained rivers of blood for the ravenous wolf: ample food for the yellow-footed fowl. There the hard iron sung upon the lofty helmets. The whole ocean was one wound. The ravens waded in the blood of the slain . . .[158]

or in the heart of the Danelaw England.[159] Everywhere in the *Five Pieces* readers could relish the zest for life, the sensuous thrill of battle, and the clear-sighted way in which death is confronted with Bartholinean smiles on stiff upper lips.

The initial reception of the *Five Pieces* was by no means ecstatic, however. The whole enterprise seemed destined to be swamped by the popularity of Macpherson's Ossianic works. Scholars in England and further afield debated the authenticity of the Ossianic works – the rest of Britain and (soon afterwards) Europe simply lay back and enjoyed them.[160] Who could resist the mountain gloom, mossy streams, nodding rushes, dark waves, blasted oaks and crumbling tombs, and the assorted plaintive voices of star-crossed lovers railing against a cruel universe in which past invades present, and the barrier between life and death is momentarily lowered and then cruelly re-established? Comparison between the *Erse Fragments* and Percy's *Five Pieces* was inevitable, and generally not to the old north's advantage. The Macpherson pieces had 'the great merit of novelty'[161] whereas some sense of the old Norse spirit had already established a foothold in the public's imagination before 1763. Moreover, claims the *Monthly Review* critic, Percy had been ill-advised in his choice of pieces. Quoting 'The Incantation of Hervor' (The Waking of Angantyr) in its entirety, the reviewer remarks that he has seen better material in Bartholin.[162] Nevertheless, Percy was to be thanked for his efforts to draw attention to 'the treasures of native genius'.[163] In the *Quarterly Review* the 'Ragner Ode', an 'animated piece', is said to offer the same image of 'insane inhumanity' in war 'as is now among the savages of North-America';[164] on the other hand 'Haco' is 'a beautiful piece . . . noble . . . finely imagined' (309), and 'Harold' is deemed worthy to be quoted in its entirety (310).[165]

Three of Percy's translations received additional exposure by their inclusion (in truncated form) in his 1770 two volume translation of the Swiss antiquarian Paul-Henri Mallet's *Introduction à l'Histoire de Dannemarc, ou l'on traite de la Religion, des Loix, des Mœurs & des Usages des anciens Danois* (1755), and *Monumens de la Mythologie et de la Poésie des Celtes, et particulièrement des Anciens Scandinaves* (1756).[166] Mallet's perspective had been that of a Professor of French at

---

[158] [Percy] 1763, 27–8.

[159] Ibid., 34.

[160] Omberg 1976, 26–48; Stafford 1988.

[161] [anon.1] 1763, 281–6, at 281.

[162] Perhaps the *Darraðarljóð* from *Njáls saga*.

[163] [anon.1] 1763, 286.

[164] [anon.2] 1763, 307–10, at 308.

[165] See also Blair 1763, 11.

[166] Mallet was helped by the Icelander Jón Eiríksson: Dillmann 1996, 18, 23.

the Academy of Arts in Copenhagen, working to a commission from the Danish government. As Percy's title implies *Northern Antiquities: or, a Description of the Manners, Customs, Religion and Laws of the Ancient Danes, and other Northern Nations; Including those of our own Saxon Ancestors* was by far the fullest assemblage and discussion of old northern material yet published in English.[167] It included not only Percy's runic pieces, but also his translation of Johan Göransson's 1746 Latin version of Snorri Sturluson's *Prose Edda*.[168] Percy brought an independent mind to Mallet's huge compilation. Clearly dissatisfied with Mallet's attempts in his eddic translations to accommodate the tastes of French readers,[169] Percy includes many corrective footnotes.[170] His independence of judgement was built on wide reading, and authoritative philological guidance from his 'very learned Friend and Neighbour the Revd Mr [Edward] Lye . . . whose skill in the Northern Languages has rendered him famous all over Europe'.[171] *Northern Antiquities* has two chapters on the ancient history of Denmark; four on religion and worship; and one each on government, warfare, maritime pursuits, customs and manners, and arts and sciences. It is in these pages that the fruits of a century's European old northern learning were made available to a broader audience in Britain, in coherent and systematic form. In turn, I.A. Blackwell's revised 1847 edition of *Northern Antiquities* exposed the theories of Mallet and Percy to critical scrutiny, added four new chapters, and laid much greater emphasis than either Mallet or Percy had done on Iceland as a major player in the European old north. In this revised form *Northern Antiquties* remained a central work amongst old northern enthusiasts throughout the nineteenth century.

The unpublished Percy manuscripts from the period during which he was working on both *Five Pieces* and *Northern Antiquities* offer a revealing glimpse of the practical problems of old northern scholarship in pre-Victorian days; and also of the levels of linguistic expertise exhibited by eighteenth-century Britain's most influential scholar of the old north. Availability of books and philological competence will be recurrent themes in examining Victorian engagement with the Viking age. What sort of a standard did Thomas Percy set? Firstly, books. Surviving lists of the books which Percy owned, lent and borrowed[172] reveal problems of regular access to crucial texts by Hickes, Wotton, Bartholin, Ole Worm, Verelius, Resen, Þormóður Torfason, as he prepared Mallet's learned survey for an eighteenth-century English readership. As to the extent of Percy's competence in the old Icelandic language, his papers reveal both a dependence

---

[167] [Goldsmith] 1757, 379, 380 laments previous neglect of northern mythology, and enthuses about its 'extraordinary allegories'.

[168] [Percy] 1770, II 1–199, reprinted 1809.

[169] [Percy] 1770, II 227, note.

[170] Marked with a 'T' for 'Translator'. Percy's own efforts underwent the same treatment in [Percy] 1847.

[171] Brooks et al. 1946–77, V 3–4, TP to Evan Evans, 21 July 1761. Clunies Ross 1998b examines Lye's scholarly life; see also Clunies Ross 1998a 52–58 and passim.

[172] See, for example, Bodleian MS Percy c.9, ff. 95–98.

on published Latin translations of poems, but also some tentative efforts to acquaint himself with Icelandic.[173] Percy frequently drew on Edward Lye's more secure knowledge of Old Icelandic, Old English and runes.[174] In *Five Pieces*, for example, Percy claims to be reproducing Hickes's English translation of 'The Waking of Angantyr' 'with considerable emendations',[175] and important corrections are indeed identifiable that only Lye could have spotted for Percy.[176]

'In the manner of Mr Gray'

There is no doubting the debt that eighteenth- and nineteenth-century enthusiasts of northern antiquities owed to the painstaking scholarship of Thomas Percy and his network of philological friends. Yet, as ever, there were other ways of winning over potential old northern enthusiasts than by dogged translation. Paraphrastic and original poetry had a vital part to play in developing pre-Victorian perceptions of the Viking spirit. Thomas Percy was no poet, but one of his unpublished poetic paraphrases helps us to assess the achievement of someone who was – northern antiquity's most persuasive eighteenth-century poetic advocate, Thomas Gray.

In a May 1761 contract the publisher James Dodsley agreed to pay Thomas Percy ten pounds for the first impression of Percy's volume of translations entitled 'Five pieces of Punic [sic; corrected to Runic] Poetry'.[177] If 'Punic' was Dodsley's accident, 'Five' may have been his design, for Percy was prevented from including several additional pieces to the five actually published in 1763.[178] These five included a version of 'Darraðarljóð', the *Brennu-Njáls saga* poem which tells of the vision of a Caithness native at the moment when King Brian falls in the Battle of Clontarf.[179] The Valkyrie women weave a web of death for those due to perish in the fight; they ride over the scene of slaughter to collect fallen heroes chosen for a better life in Valhǫll, amongst them the Irish king. This was the poem which inspired Thomas Gray's influential 'The Fatal Sisters: an Ode'.[180]

The possibility of producing a poem on such a topic and with such a British Isles setting had been explored some years earlier by William Collins in his 'An Ode on the Popular Superstitions of the Highlands of Scotland, considered as

---

173 Bodleian MS Percy c.7, f. 12v.
174 See, for example, Lye's notes in Bodleian MS Percy c.7, f. 36r–39v.
175 Fell 1996, 42–3 shows that Hickes obtained a Latin or English translation of the Swedish version in Verelius 1672.
176 As Hervor leaves her father's graveside with the ancestral sword, Hickes 1703–5, II 193 reads 'So let Odin hide thee in the tombe, as thu hast Tirfing by thee'. After consultation with Lye, [Percy] 1763, 15 reads 'So let Odin preserve thee safe in the tomb, as thou hast *not* [my italics] Tirfing by thee', registering the Icelandic *eigi* in Hickes's Icelandic text.
177 Bodleian MS Eng. Lett. d.59, f. 8.
178 Itemised in Clunies Ross 1998a, 86–91.
179 *Brennu-Njáls saga*, ÍF 12, 454–8 (ch. 157).
180 Composed in 1761 and based on the Latin translation in Þormóður Torfason 1697, 36–38.

the Subject of Poetry'. The Collins poem was written at the end of 1749 but was not published until 1788, by which time its recommended themes were the height of fashion.[181] The narrator draws attention to Shakespeare's treatment of the witches in *Macbeth*. The playwright had found 'his Wayward Sisters' in native legend, 'and with their terrors dressed the magic scene' (515); and Collins urges his fellow poets to do the same (516). The appearance of the Gray and Percy versions of 'Darraðarljóð' within a few years of Collins composing these lines shows how acutely his ear had been tuned to the emerging old northern mood of the moment.

Though not published until 1768, Gray's 'The Fatal Sisters' was composed at much the same time as Percy's versions of 'Darraðarljóð', though the two men may well have worked independently.[182] It is revealing to compare briefly the responses of a conscientious scholar and a first-rank poet to their common Icelandic-Latin original, not least because Gray's poem was admired by so many in Victorian Britain. The relevant Icelandic-Latin texts appeared first in Bartholin, and were then reprinted in Torfæus's *Orcades*:[183]

Vitt er orpit	Latè diffunditur
fyrir valfalli	ante stragem futuram
rifs reidi sky	sagittarum nubes
rignir blode	depluit sangvis
nu er fyrer geirum,	jam hastis applicatur
grarr upkominn	cineracea
vefr verthiodar	tela virorum,
thær (rectius thann) er vinor fylla	qvam amicæ, texunt
raudum vepti	rubro subtegmine
randves bana	Randveri mortis
Sia er orpinn vefr	Texitur hæc tela
yta thaurmum	intestinis humanis
oc hardkliadr	staminiqve strictè alligantur
hofthum manna	capita humana
ero dreyrrekin	sunt sangvine roratæ
daurr at skoptum	hastæ pro insilibus
jarnvardr yllir	textoria instrumenta ferrea
en aurum hræladr	ac sagittæ pro radiis
skolum sla sverdum	densabimus gladiis
sigrvef thenna	hanc victoriæ telam.

The English versions of these lines produced by Gray (to the left) and (perhaps) the later of the two Percy draft versions (to the right) are as follows:

181 Lonsdale 1969, 493, 495.
182 Clunies Ross 1994, 113 and note 13.
183 Torfæus [Þórmoður Torfason] 1697, 36–7; Bartholin 1689, 617–19. For more detailed discussion see Clunies Ross 1998a, 111–18

Now the storm begins to lower,
(Haste, the loom of hell prepare,)
Iron-sleet of arrowy shower
Hurtles in the darkened air.

Glittering lances are the loom,
Where the dusky warp we strain,
Weaving many a soldier's doom,
Orkney's woe and Randver's bane.

See the grisly texture grow,
('Tis of human entrails made,)
And the weights, that play below,
Each a gasping warrior's head.

Shafts for shuttles, dipped in gore,
Shoot the trembling cords along.
Sword that once a monarch bore
Keeps the tissue close and strong![184]

Before the approaching slaughter
The cloud of arrows
Is widely scattered
The shower of blood falls
Now the ashen spear
Is knit
The web of men
Which the sisters weave
With the crimson woof
Of Randver's death

The web is woven
Of human bowels
And fast to the warp
Human heads are tied
Spears bedewed with blood
Compose the treadles
The weaving instruments are steel
And arrows are the shuttles
Let us close up with swords
The web of victory.[185]

Percy's response to his original is essentially prosaic, though written out in short lines. Had he decided to include it in *Five Pieces* the process of conversion to prose would have been easy. Gray's version confronts the reader with a wholly different level of poetic ambition. The work's haunting incantatory quality arises from paratactic syntax, phrasal and sonic parallelism, and artful variations on Miltonic diction. The neo-classical and the sublime co-exist in a creative tension. Gray's success is instructive. His late-eighteenth-century old northern imitators, no matter how sincere their flattery, tend to be long on atmosphere, but short on verbal dexterity. No matter how doggedly rhymesters followed in Gray's metrical wake,[186] autopilot deployment of grinning heroes, skull-waving drinkers, and fateful ravens wading up to their beaks through 'ensanguined' battlefields offered no guarantee of artistic success.[187] There were 'youthful Scalds' ready to 'meditate the Runic store' and 'strew their wild poetry o'er all the land',[188] but too many of them had tin ears. 'The Scalder' (1789), Joseph Sterling's homage to 'the sublime Gray',[189] is entirely characteristic of the genre:

---

184 Lonsdale 1969, 216–17.
185 Bodleian MS Percy c.7, f. 34r.
186 Having visited the Caithness saga-stead, Henry Mackenzie wrote an 'Introduction to the Fatal Sisters': Mackenzie 1808, VIII 63–5.
187 Omberg 1976 passim; also below, Chapter 2.
188 Phrases from Edward Jerningham's 'The Rise and Progress of Scandinavian Poetry': Omberg 1976, 162–7, at 166–7.
189 Sterling 1789, 146.

> Now the rage of combat burns,
> Haughty chiefs on chiefs lie slain;
>   The battle glows and sinks by turns,
> Death and carnage load the plain.
> Pale fear, grim horror stalk around;
> The blood of heroes dyes the vernant ground.[190]

Such 'disgusting and squalid subjects' became too much for some,[191] yet Gray's achievement was widely acknowledged,[192] and 'The Fatal Sisters' casts a long shadow over nineteenth-century literary old northernism. Its influence seems discernible in the supernatural machinery of a poem based on the Battle of Largs published in *The Scots Magazine* in 1803,[193] and in the northern epics of Joseph Cottle and William Herbert;[194] it enjoys further favourable exposure in one of Scott's well-upholstered appendices to *The Pirate*;[195] and it provokes the sceptical Thomas Carlyle to a perceptive passage distinguishing the world of Gray's Norse Odes from what he sees as the real spirit of Norse mythology:

> Gray's fragments of Norse Lore . . . will give one no notion of it . . . It is no square-built gloomy palace of black ashlar marble, shrouded in awe and horror, as Gray gives it us: no; rough as the North rocks, as the Iceland deserts, it is; with a heartiness, homeliness, even a tint of good humour and robust mirth in the middle of these fearful things. The strong old Norse heart did not go upon theatrical sublimities; they had not time to tremble.[196]

By 1840 the Viking age was exchanging sublimity for heart-of-oak robustness. It was ready to win a readership in the public schools and antiquarian societies of middle England.

Setting the Victorian Agenda

By the end of the eighteenth century, a raft of old northern literary and philosophical issues had emerged which, subsequently reconstructed, would form an important part of the Victorian old northern agenda. Most of them represent the breakers, backwashes or side-eddies from a tidal wave of questions about regional and national identity. These topics will feature prominently in the

---

190 Ibid., 150, v.2. See also Mathias 1781.
191 Stockdale 1778, 110–11.
192 See W. Hayley, 'Essay on Epic Poetry' (1785), quoted in Wilson 1996, 63.
193 *Scots Magazine* 65 (1803), 272–4.
194 Cottle 1816, I 25–61 (Bk 2) draws heavily on [Percy] 1770, as well as on Bartholin, Olaus Magnus, and Aylett Sammes. On Herbert, see Kirby 1912 and, more illuminating, Clunies Ross 1998a, 183–97.
195 Scott 1822/1996, 345–6 (note C to chapter 2); see also Scott's *The Antiquary* (1816), ch. 30; and [Clifford] 1865, 23–4.
196 Carlyle 1897, V 34. Gray is praised in Metcalfe 1861, 39.

present study, as the subjects of individual chapters, and as unifying elements within and between chapters. Accordingly, this outline of pre-Victorian old northernism concludes by identifying briefly the principal issues:

(i)   The old north and the new philology. Percy's *Five Pieces* originated out of a larger project 'to exhibit Specimens of the Poetry of various nations in . . . Literal Translations', and to investigate whether there was a natural poetry common to all peoples.[197] Such a notion anticipates the paradigm-challenging ideas about a long-lost common Indo-European language which were developed by scholars at the beginning of what became a golden age for comparative philology in the early nineteenth century.[198] European and British scholars of Icelandic were prominent in what became a heavily politicised scholarly field.

(ii)   The multinational old north. Many eighteenth-century scholars believed in an old northern court culture common to all Scandinavia and the North Atlantic islands.[199] Major Victorian scholars sought to rediscover that culture by investigating dialects, runes and folktales. Such investigations could also be heavily politicised.

(iii)   The Saxon versus Scandinavian, Scando-Anglian versus Norman old north. Eighteenth-century scholars had debated whether, within the British Isles, the old northern language had influenced Old Welsh, Old English and Middle English poetry.[200] For some Victorians, Old English and Old Icelandic represented two sides of the same Teutonic coin; others detected in Anglo-Saxon poetry the degenerate whingeing of an Anglo-Saxon culture in need of the *felix culpa* of the Viking invasions.[201]

(iv)   The chivalric old north. Some, ever eager to escape the 'Norman yoke', claimed that European chivalric traditions derived from the old north; others traced Mediterranean and Old Norse traditions to a common Asiatic source.[202] The chivalrous hero and demure heroine in Esaias Tegnér's *Frithiofs saga*, hugely popular in Victorian Britain, were examined in the light of this debate.

(v)   The 'barbarian' old north? Seventeenth-century European scholarship had made available old northern texts whose literary artistry and ethical systems belied humanist accusations of barbarity. This tension between Viking-age and Græco-Roman cultures, between northern and southern European values, was fully explored in Victorian writings.

---

[197] Brooks 1946–77, V 98, TP to Evan Evans, 23 July 1764. Gray proposed a similar scheme: Omberg 1976, 37.

[198] Aarsleff 1983.

[199] Warton 1774–81, I e lv; Brooks 1946–77, V 61–2, TP to Evan Evans *c.* Feb. 1764.

[200] Ibid.; also V 64–5, EE to TP, 8 March 1764; [Percy] 1770, II 197–8. Links were discussed between *Brunanburh*, *Death and Life* and 'The Waking of Angantyr'. Percy translated *Brunanburh*: Bodleian MS Percy c.7, 7v–10v; see also Warton 1774–81, I xxxviii–xl.

[201] Metcalfe 1880 142–4, 145; discussed in Poole 1994 112.

[202] [Percy] 1770, I 318–19, II 234–5; Warton 1774–81, I a lv. More recent discussion includes Kliger 1952, 229–33; on Mallet and Warton, see Omberg 1976, 98–107.

(vi)   Old northern regionalism. The 'treasures of native genius'[203] within the British Isles had been investigated by provincial antiquarians since the seventeenth century. Yet, by the beginning of the nineteenth century, there were still many texts to edit, sites to excavate and oral traditions to investigate. Old northernists living in the Danelaw regions of Victorian Britain, and in the ancient Norse kingdoms of Orkney and Shetland explored and revelled in their Viking-age history.

(vii)   The party political old north. Notwithstanding Thomas Percy's claim that *Five Pieces* was not a book about politics,[204] seventeenth- and eighteenth-century scholarship had pointed the way to the politicisation of the old north.[205] Victorian old northernists, both high Tory and hard-line Whig, picked up the political baton and ran hard with it in many directions: patriarchal family structures and female suffrage; social Darwinism and social engineering; extension of the franchise and *Führerprinzip* centralism; constitutional monarchy and republicanism; Scottish nationalism and Scottish Unionism.

(viii)   The national curriculum old north. We have identified the glimmerings of eighteenth-century pedagogical interest in the old north.[206] The promotion of old northern culture in Victorian schools and universities was much debated, and vigorous attention given to the provision of appropriate texts.

(ix)   Old northern networking. The publications of George Hickes and Thomas Percy highlight the importance of collaborative work between scholars in Britain and Scandinavia. Victorian old northernists established reading groups, antiquarian societies, and correspondence networks, often involving learned Icelanders resident in Britain. British saga translators often collaborated with these specialists.

(x)   The transatlantic old north. Though Thomas Percy knew about Þorfinnr karlsefni and his Vínland companions,[207] the publication of Rafn's *Antiqvitates Americanae* (1837) stimulated serious nineteenth-century North American interest in their old northern roots.

(xi)   The poetic and prosaic old north. For Thomas Percy Old Icelandic prose tales 'are not otherwise regarded, than as they contribute to throw light on [the poems]'.[208] English readers had to wait until the end of the eighteenth century before they had access to complete texts of *Íslendingasögur* – in the facing-page Latin translations of editions prepared in Copenhagen. If the eighteenth century was the age of eddic myth, the nineteenth century developed rapidly into the age of saga.

(xii)   Old northern travel. Visiting the saga-sites of Iceland and Norway

---

203 [anon.1] 1763, 286.
204 [Percy] 1763, 45
205 Þórmoður Torfason's *Orcades* was written to reassert the Danish crown's right to the Orkney Islands: Jensen 1995, 113–14.
206 Wotton 1735.
207 Brooks et al. 1946–77, V 17, TP to Evan Evans, 15 October 1761.
208 Ibid. V 16, TP to Evan Evans, 15 October 1761.

became a major feature of Victorian Vikingism.[209] Dr Johnson contemplated a visit to Iceland – his 'Journey to the Northern Isles' is one of the great unwritten books of the eighteenth century.[210] It was Enlightenment scientists from Edinburgh who eventually led the way north, their old northern literary interests clearly discernible either in their published works or their private papers. A group of these pre-Victorian northern travellers lived long enough to cultivate their old northern interests after the young Princess Victoria succeeded to the throne in 1837. When they were born few Britons had heard of the Vikings; by the time they died the cult of the noble old northern sea-king was securely in place. This important transitional phase in the emergence of Victorian old northernism is the subject of the next chapter.

[209] Aho 1993.

[210] Hill 1934–50, I 242, III 455: Boswell believed that Johnson would have visited Iceland had not his prospective companion died.

CHAPTER TWO

Georgian Case-Studies

The shudd'ring tenant of the frigid zone,
Boldly proclaims that happiest spot his own;
Extols the treasures of his stormy seas,
And his long nights of revelry and ease.
(Sir George Mackenzie 1811, title page)

The Edinburgh School

Three of Regency Britain's most influential students of the old and modern
north lived long enough to pursue their northern enthusiasms as loyal subjects
of the young Queen Victoria, and to watch the nature of old northernism
change. Sir John Thomas Stanley (1768–1847) spent his last days copying,
annotating and brooding over the journals that his fellow travellers had written
up at the end of the Iceland expedition he had organised nearly sixty years
earlier. During that period, as we shall see, Viking-age gods figured prominently
in his thoughts. The year 1842 saw the republication, in a truncated economy
version, of *Travels in the Island of Iceland in . . . 1810* by Sir George Mackenzie
(1780–1844), thereby making his 1811–12 account of ancient and modern
Iceland available to a new generation of potential old northern enthusiasts in
Victorian Britain. Henry Holland (1788–1873), Stanley's Cestrian protégé, was
one of Mackenzie's 1810 companions; his own expedition journal had been the
narrative source for Mackenzie's *Travels*. Holland became not just any Victorian,
but physician to Queen Victoria, a promoter of the old northern and modern
Icelandic causes in high and learned society, and a tower of supportive strength
to visiting Icelanders. Holland truly spanned the generations of nineteenth-
century old northern enthusiasm. Born in the year before Stanley's expedition
headed north in 1789, Holland lived long enough to revisit Iceland in 1871, an
astonishing sixty one years after his first exposure to life at 66 degrees north. In
Reykjavík, on this second visit, he met William Morris, late Victorian Britain's
most celebrated Icelandophile. Holland's authoritative 'Dissertation' on medieval Iceland and the old north, published in Mackenzie's *Travels*, was still
winning praise half a century after its initial publication.[1]

---

[1]   Miles 1854, 225: Holland was 'one of the most learned travellers that ever visited Iceland'.

An examination of the works, both published and unpublished, to which the northern expeditions of Stanley, Mackenzie and Holland gave rise offers an important perspective on the cultivation of the old north in Regency and early-Victorian Britain; and so do the less celebrated travels of Sir Thomas Maryon Wilson, whom we find honoured in a poem written by a young Icelander in 1830.

Sir Thomas Maryon Wilson and 'The Dream'

'The Dream' is a 170-line poem written by an Icelander living in Iceland. It exists only in a single manuscript, and would have little call on our attention had the poet been an Englishman and not Lárus Sigurðsson, 'son of a peasant in the West of Iceland'.[2] It celebrates the achievements of late eighteenth- and early nineteenth-century English travellers to Iceland. One of its twin dedicatees is an Englishman, Sir Thomas Maryon Wilson, whom Lárus seems to have met in Iceland. Remarkably, the poem is written not, as panegyric precedent would have suggested,[3] in Latin or Icelandic but in English. It may well be the first poem ever composed by an Icelander in that language.

Like a medieval dream vision the poem opens with the sleepless narrator wandering over a deserted landscape – this one is 'hard by the town [Reykjavík]'.[4] He recalls the heroic days of Iceland's ninth-century settlement period and its subsequent sad decline. Lying down to rest, he falls asleep and dreams of an encounter with the pioneering settler Ingólfr Arnarson, depicted as an heroic refugee from the centralising tyranny of King Haraldr Finehair of Norway (11–12, 17–18). Ingólfr carries the beacon of republican liberty to the new land of Iceland. Lárus claims that the same ancient Scandinavian spirit has taken root in another north Atlantic island state, Great Britain. The narrator then sights 'a reverend trail of Britons' (43), including heroes slain at the Battle of Waterloo, with the Duke of Wellington at their head.[5] He then hears Ingólfr praising British travellers in Iceland:

> 'I know, my boy, that Heav'n himself esteems
> These men as masterpieces of the times
> Proud to have made such jewels for the earth,
> And the angels love the land, that gave them birth. –' (129–32).

The first 'masterpiece' was Ebenezer Henderson (1809–79), torch- and bible-bearer for the British and Foreign Bible Society,[6] who spent the Icelandic winter

---

2 Lbs. 2208 4to, title page.
3 Henderson 1819, 499–506.
4 Lbs. 2208 4to, l. 23.
5 Ibid., ll. 67–84.
6 See Henderson 1819, 1832; Henderson T. [1859]; also Felix Ólafsson 1992.

of 1814–15 gasping in awe at Geysir,[7] glaring in horror at sites of pagan sacrifice,[8] and distributing Icelandic bibles to grateful if bewildered priests and peasants all over the country. The published account of his experiences was admired by Icelanders[9] and includes a generously illustrated discussion of old Icelandic poetry, allowing readers to reacquaint themselves with Ragnarr loðbrók's death song, in James Johnstone's 1772 translation.[10] Another British hero is Sir Joseph Banks (1743–1820), South Sea companion to Captain Cook, natural scientist, and pioneering Iceland explorer in 1772, whose fascination with Iceland's Viking- and saga-age culture underpinned his support for modern Icelandic causes:[11]

> Here come[s] great Banks . . .
> 'Twas he, that heard the complaints of my isle;
> And made her peasants in abundance smile . . .
> Thank Banks – for else you would have left the light,
> And starv'd like new-born bloom in stormy night![12]

The poem concludes by saluting its English dedicatee, the considerably less distinguished Sir Thomas Maryon Wilson.[13] No published account exists of this visit,[14] but in 'The Dream', at least, Wilson takes centre stage:

> The living love him, and the dead esteem,
> Poverty blesses him in every clime;
> To aid the poor, 'tis business of his mind
> That always is to God and virtue join'd,
> Thus has the nature (to uncertain aim,)
> But good and noble grac'd with Wilson's name.[15]

With the wish that fair winds may follow Iceland's newest 'noble friend' on his homeward journey, Ingólfr's spirit disappears over Mount Esja, the English heroes head for the harbour, the narrator wakes from his dream and, perhaps not a moment too soon, the poem comes to an end.

The work's intricate trail of references and associations is worth following briefly as evidence of the kind of network of Anglo-Icelandic contacts that

---

7 Henderson 1819, 68–74.
8 Ibid., 338–9.
9 Clark 1861, 361.
10 Henderson 1819, 528–35.
11 Halldór Hermannsson 1928, Anna Agnarsdóttir 1979, 1989, 1994.
12 Lbs. 2808 4to, ll. 139, 143–4, 151–2.
13 Ibid., 153–66. Of lesser gentry Essex stock, Thomas, like his father, studied at St John's College, Cambridge (M.A. 1823), and subsequently lived a life of modest distinction: see Venn and Venn 1954, Pt 2 VI 529; *Burke's Peerage and Baronetage* 2 vols (London, 1970), II 2849.
14 Barrow 1835, xxii expresses disappointment at this. Lbs. 604 fol., the Barrow 1835 holograph, includes two letters from Stanley recalling his 1789 experiences.
15 Lbs. 2208 4to, 157–62.

developed in the pre-Victorian years, flourished during her reign, and out of which grew so much old northern enthusiasm during the high Victorian period. We may note, firstly, that the single surviving manuscript of 'The Dream' once belonged to the poet Matthías Jochumsson (1835–1920), a visitor to Britain in the Unitarian cause, a generous host to and conscientious correspondent with many Victorian Icelandophiles,[16] and an Anglophile who translated into Icelandic English plays as dissimilar as Shakespeare's *Hamlet* and Beatrice Barmby's *Gísli Súrsson*.[17] Secondly, the poem highlights the interlocking nature of old northern interests in the nineteenth century. Travel, trade and translation were often an interconnected cultural sequence rather than a happy alliterative chance. The poem has two dedicatees – Sigurður Sívertsen, 'the first promoter of my little progress in the English language', and Wilson himself. For Sigurður Sívertsen (b. 1787) to be cited as Lárus's teacher of English would have surprised none of the British travellers who visited his home in Hafnarfjörður in July 1809 and May 1810: his linguistic prowess was frequently commented upon.[18] By accident of war, his father Bjarni (1763–1833) was an accomplished English speaker: during 1807–8 his vessels had been impounded in Britain during the Napoleonic war trade embargo against Denmark, and were only released after the intervention of Sir Joseph Banks at the highest governmental levels.[19] The ill winds of war, disrupted trade and involuntary exile thus blew the Sívertsen family and, eventually, Lárus Sigurðsson some linguistic good. It enabled his admiration for British Icelandophiles to be voiced in English and attributed to Iceland's most celebrated Viking-age settler.

Thirdly, why should Wilson – or Banks – or Holland and Mackenzie – have thought to visit Iceland in the first place, thus earning Sigurður's poetic approval? We noted in the first chapter the reasons why from the fourteenth century onwards Britons headed north on a regular basis. During the nineteenth century, while the fishing and trading continued, new interests developed. People travelled to Iceland to investigate the commercial harvesting of seaweed,[20] to study the geology of a *terra* that was never *firma*,[21] to undertake medical fieldwork,[22] to climb mountains,[23] to mine sulphur for gunpowder,[24]

---

[16] On Matthías Jochumsson's links with the manuscript, see Páll Eggert Ólason 1918–37, III 288; see also below, p. 367.

[17] Barmby 1900, 1902; Steingrímur Matthíasson 1935.

[18] Wawn 1987, 114–15; see also Henderson 1819, 47, Hooker 1813, II 233, and Symington 1862, 52–3.

[19] Anna Agnarsdóttir 1989, 47–56.

[20] Edinburgh University Library, La. III. 379/757–81, John Thomas Stanley to Grímur Jónsson Thorkelin, 28 May 1790.

[21] Notably Mackenzie 1812 and Holland: see Wawn 1987.

[22] The incidence of elephantiasis intrigued Holland (Mackenzie 1812, 400–2) as a doctor, and Henderson (1819, 234–5) as a theologian.

[23] Watts 1874, 1876.

[24] Ponzi 1995, 130–41.

to watch birds,[25] to buy wool,[26] to inspect the hot springs of Haukadalur,[27] and eventually to wander in awe through the saga-steads of Laxárdalur and Rangár-vellir.[28] There is no knowing which, if any, of these motives took Sir Thomas Maryon Wilson to Iceland. There were scholars in Cambridge during Wilson's student days who could have awakened his interest in the ancient and modern north. John Heath of King's College is a notable example.[29] He had a fine Scan-dinavian library and was well connected in Copenhagen antiquarian and philol-ogical circles. Wilson could also have read the accounts of earlier Iceland expeditions by von Troil, Hooker, Mackenzie and Henderson,[30] that found their way into the private libraries of educated gentlemen,[31] and onto the shelves of local library societies.

Wilson and his contemporaries were born too late to believe in old wives' tales about Hekla and hell, but too early to be touched by the romantic mist that enveloped Icelandic sagas and their heroes later in the nineteenth century. They observed modern Iceland with a forensic eye, and regarded the Viking age as simply 'a period when robberies and violence, by sea and land, were consid-ered as valour'.[32] 'Pyrates', the term that often translated Old Icelandic 'víkingr mikill',[33] are little commented upon. The Icelandic saga-steads were uncharted territory though Henderson's attention flickers at the runic slab at Borg which told of Kjartan Ólafsson, 'assassinated' in Svínadalr.[34] Henderson also quotes Walter Scott's explanation of the name Berserkjahraun on the Snæfellsnes penin-sula,[35] and is prompted by nearby Helgafell to reflect on the fate of Arnkell in *Eyrbyggja saga*, 'a model of civil virtues', and on the 'cruel and intriguing dispo-sition' of his persecutor 'Snorro the Pontiff'.[36] Perhaps Gunnarr's Hlíðarendi at harvest time represents the acid test. As we shall see,[37] for William Morris and other Victorian lovers of *Njáls saga*, it was a place of pilgrimage; yet in the early nineteenth century it excites no comment from Stanley, as he rides past on his way to Hekla; for Mackenzie, it is simply 'the abode of Sysselman Thoranson',[38] and for Henry Holland the new-mown fields are of interest only for the evi-

---

25 Newton in Baring-Gould 1863, 399–421.
26 Sim 1886.
27 Sumarliði Ísleifsson 1996, passim.
28 Collingwood and Jón Stefánsson 1899, Morris 1910–15, viii.
29 Bredsdorff, in Bayerschmidt and Friis 1965, 170–201.
30 There was little organised Iceland travel between the Henderson (1814–15) and Barrow (1834) expeditions, apart from Wilson (*c*. 1830), and George Atkinson (1833): on the latter, see Seaton 1989.
31 As with Sir Walter Scott: [Cochrane] 1838, Lieder 1920.
32 Troil 1780, 67; Holland in Mackenzie 1811, 16.
33 [Nicoll] 1840, 91
34 Henderson 1819, 386
35 Ibid., 330–33.
36 Ibid., 340. The reference is to Snorri goði.
37 See below, Chapters 6 and 9.
38 Mackenzie 1812, 487.

dence they reveal of hay-bale stacking techniques.[39] For this pre-Victorian travellers the bloody harvests on the battle-fields of Percy's *Five Pieces* remained more intriguing.

It was, however, in Icelandic annal and chronicle rather than edda and saga that Georgian old northernists would have encountered Ingólfr Arnarson, the ghostly presence in 'The Dream'. Ingólfr himself might have been struck by those aspects of his life and family background in which eighteenth- and nineteenth-century British travellers showed no interest. *Landnámabók* and the likely contents of a lost saga[40] suggest that his great-grandfather Hrómundr Gripsson had been a flamboyant Viking, and that his grandfather, also a violent man, had been an exile from Norway. Ingólfr himself had been a member of a successful Viking crew. He sacrificed to the pagan gods, headed for Iceland in response to a prophecy, and allowed his place of settlement (Reykjavík) to be determined by where his sacred high-seat pillars, brought from Norway, floated ashore after being thrown overboard – Thomas Percy's 'threw a wooden door into the sea' does scant justice to the fateful solemnity of the moment![41] Such exoticisms were not quite what Enlightenment-age natural and political scientists were looking for as they assembled their information-packed Iceland journals. Accordingly, they create an alternative Ingólfr: an aristocrat,[42] a principled opponent of Haraldr Finehair's despotism, and a prudent coloniser whose 'mature and well-concerted scheme' had led to the successful settlement of Iceland.[43] Only the pious Henderson scowls at Ingólfr's addiction to the 'idolatrous and superstitious customs of the age'.[44] Moreover, place names such as Ingólfshöfði, Ingólfsfell and Ingólfshaugur[45] appeared to confirm that the great coloniser was a figure of fact rather than fantasy. If Lárus Sigurðsson's poem affords Ingólfr the opportunity to thank Britain for all its post-medieval concern for his downtrodden countrymen, by the end of the nineteenth century plenty of British old northernists recognised how much they and their ancestors owed to Ingólfr and Iceland. He was accorded an honoured place in many of the works – from primary text translations to prize poems[46] – in which Victorians celebrated the land of his birth, the island that he helped to settle, and the Viking-age culture to which he contributed so significantly.

A last thought on 'The Dream'. Sir Thomas Maryon Wilson may have lived

---

[39] Wawn 1987, 261–2.

[40] Jesch, in Pulsiano 1993, 305.

[41] Percy 1859, 188, sternly corrected by Blackwell's footnote.

[42] Hooker 1813, I xii: 'of noble birth and great opulence'.

[43] Troil 1780, 64–5; Mackenzie 1811, 6–7. In 1818 Thomas Reynolds is more censorious: 'Ingulph' is 'a nobleman . . . [who] having committed an atrocious murder, fled from Justice with his retainers to Iceland': BL Add. MS 31048, f. 147.

[44] Henderson 1819, 9–10. [Nicoll] 1840, 94–7 has a fuller account, associating the spirit of Ingólfr with that expressed in Marvell's 'The Emigrants'.

[45] Hooker 1813, I xiv.

[46] Ellwood 1898, Gudbrand Vigfusson and Powell 1905 (completed 1889); Rowntree 1875, ll. 46–51.

long enough to watch a succession of major publications awakening Victorian interest in different areas of the old north: old Norway needed the early English translations of Esaias Tegnér's version of the saga of Frithiof;[47] old Sweden needed George Stephens's monumental survey of old northern rune-stones;[48] Scandinavia in general needed Samuel Laing's 1844 translation of *Heimskringla*;[49] Iceland needed George Dasent's *The Story of Burnt Njal* (1861);[50] the Faroe Islands needed C.C. Rafn's 1832 edition and translation of *Færeyinga saga*;[51] Orkney and Shetland needed Sir Walter Scott's *The Pirate*(1822); the Danelaw regions of England needed Charles Kingsley's *Hereward the Wake* (1866); and if the Isle of Man did not need Hall Caine's *The Bondman: A New Saga* (1890), it got it. We might add that Vínland was reborn with the help of Rafn's lavish *Antiqvitates Americanæ*, a volume for only the sturdiest coffee table.[52]

All these works helped to develop the Victorian perception that whilst a visit to the edda-steads of Ásgarðr and Valhǫll might require Óðinn's eight-legged steed, anyone with a sturdy Icelandic pony, sensible shoes and a stout spirit could walk around the saga-steads of Skagafjörður, Suðurey, Stiklarstaðir – or even Stamford Bridge. Inevitably, some visitors were little more than day-trippers to old northern theme parks, interested only in the water chutes (in this case Geysir), but others sought first-hand contact with what they believed was their Viking-age heritage. It was those old northern values, after all, that, in the eyes of many Victorians, underpinned the best of Britain at home and abroad – imperial power, mercantile prosperity, technological progress, social stability and justice.[53] What was more natural than to have books and travel help trace the roots of that prowess back to its Norwegian homelands,[54] or to the north Atlantic island where the legacy could still be heard in its linguistically purest form?

We do not know whether the Victorian Wilson came to share these enthusiasms. We can, however, be sure that the pre-Victorian Wilson celebrated in Lárus Sigurðsson's 1830 poem would have been baffled by such notions. His visit to Iceland marks an earlier stage in the development of British consciousness of its old northern past.

---

47 See below, Chapter 5.
48 Stephens 1866–1901 and 1884.
49 Laing 1844 and 1889. See below, Chapter 4.
50 Dasent 1861.
51 See also Metcalfe 1869, Bossche 1989.
52 Rafn 1837.
53 Laing 1844, I; Dasent 1858.
54 See Schiötz 1970–86.

John Thomas Stanley and the Eddic Gods

At first sight John Thomas Stanley seems an improbable figure to become involved with Viking lore and legend. His only two publications about the north were exclusively scientific. He went to Iceland in 1789 primarily to investigate the spectacular ebullitions of Geysir. Returning to Edinburgh with water and mineral samples, he reported his conclusions to the Edinburgh Royal Society.[55] Yet, four years earlier, the same society's Transactions published William Collins's 'An Ode on the Popular Superstitions of the Highlands of Scotland', a poem that, as we have noted, encouraged the investigation of very different mysteries.[56] In 1788, Stanley, a student at Edinburgh University, was already planning an expedition to Iceland, and may well have known Collins's 'Highland Ode'.

This duality of sense and sensibility is discernible in the response of Stanley and his party to Geysir. Here was a natural phenomenon sufficiently remarkable to furnish the English language with a rare post-medieval Icelandic loan word.[57] It fascinated European scientists at a time when Yellowstone Park's 'Old Faithful' was still the undiscovered preserve of native Americans, and when the hot springs in New Zealand were half a world away. Erasmus Darwin was just one of many in awe:

> High in the frozen North where HECLA glows,
> And melts in torrents his coeval snows; . . .
> Where, at his base intomb'd, with bellowing sound
> Fell GIESAR roar'd, and struggling shook the ground;
> Pour'd from red nostrils, with her scalding breath,
> A boiling deluge o'er the blasted heath;
> And, wide in air, in misty volumes hurl'd
> Contagious atoms o'er the alarmed world.[58]

Stanley's 'sense' produced the official published record of his Geysir investigations in the form of scientific papers; the semi-official pictorial record hints at the element of 'sensibility' helping to drive the enterprise.[59] Stanley's 1789 expedition was clearly no 'Pilgrimage to the Saga-Steads of Iceland', the title of W.G. Collingwood's artistic odyssey a hundred years later. We never see Stanley or his companions crouching in awe over Snorri's abandoned booth at the ancient parliament site at Þingvellir, or contemplating judgement circles on Kjalarnes, or digging at Bergþórshvoll for some charred relic of noble Njáll and his

---

[55] Papers read in November 1791 and April 1792: Stanley 1794. See also Black 1794.
[56] See above, pp. 27–8.
[57] The first OED reference (the Annual Register) is 1763.
[58] Darwin 1791 [fourth edition, 1799], I 147–8, quoted Hooker 1813, I 147–8.
[59] Steindór Steindórsson 1979: original sketches by Edward Dayes and Nicholas Pocock. See also John Baine's sketches in Lbs. 890 fol.

family. Instead, we find the young baronet resplendent in frock coat, fine boots and a top hat worthy of a Buckingham Palace garden party. His companions fill the middle distance, some armed with trowel and hammer, collecting botanical and geological samples for analysis; others with theodolites trained on the slopes of Hekla or Snæfellsjökull. Poets might tremble at such landscapes,[60] but the British natural scientist was made of sterner stuff. Thus, while local family groups lay aside their primitive tools of toil and gaze up in silent respect at the expedition leader, he controls and commands, monarch of all he surveys. These are scenes of summer. The snow-covered mountains and glacial expanses are objects of forensic investigation rather than sites of adventure or sources of mystery. Though a brisk wind from the south fills the sails of the voyagers' vessel as it nears the Vestmannaeyjar, lending their arrival a sense of enterprise and energy, no impertinent breeze subsequently disturbs enlightened scientific man in his fieldwork. In the paintings of Strokkur and Geysir 'sensibility' is given its head within familiar *Sturm und Drang* conventions – water colour gives way to oil, skies darken, steam belches, and water cascades. Yet amidst the drama we notice the unruffled Stanley standing at a safe distance, pointing confidently and explaining knowledgeably.[61] Another painting from the expedition tells a different tale, however. Wilder in conception and rougher in execution than the other works, it records a volcanic eruption. It was not a painting of record, for there had been no such eruption during the summer of 1789. The artist was Stanley himself,[62] and the canvas suggests a fascination with fiery spectacle. The spirit of John Thomas Stanley seems momentarily alive to the 'passionately unsettled'[63] qualities of Icelandic nature.

The expedition journals kept by Stanley's companions for the most part confirm the business-like impression of the non-Geysir pictures. Incurious about edda or saga, whether in script or print, they are primarily works of earnest scientific observation and measurement, a painstaking record of meteorology, topography, agricultural science, domestic economy, mineralogy and ethnography. With Edinburgh a buzzing centre of geological debate, a successful visit to Iceland could confer instant celebrity on those returning with rock samples from that unique natural laboratory. However, Stanley's private manuscripts confirm what his Hekla canvas hints at. Behind the public face of the scientist there lurked a private sensibility open to other and older northern voices. Moreover, Stanley remained open to such voices long after the demise of Gram and Hecla, the family's imported 'prick-eared Iceland curs'. The formative elements of that sensibility are worth mentioning: sentimental travel, German Gothicism, knowledge of Icelandic history and literature, familiarity with

---

60 See Drummond 1817, 98–100: the region of death (Hel) described in terms of an Icelandic volcano.
61 Steindór Steindórsson 1979, pictures between at 32–3.
62 Ponzi 1987, 91.
63 Stafford 1984, 341.

popular old northern poetry in Britain, a fondness for Ossian, and a north Midlands old northern network.

First, sentimental travel. Dr Charles Scott was a student friend whose over-anxious mother had prevented him from participating in the 1789 Iceland expedition.[64] Stanley was thus compelled in correspondence to serve as his friend's eyes and ears. This was no mean task, for at the very thought of Iceland, Scott's febrile imagination goes into overdrive:

> Whenever I look over a Map mine Eye untutored seeks for Iceland . . . There I seek the creeks & bays, the Cliffs and Promonteries of the forbidding Coasts, behold your landing on your beach or climbing the Summit of terrific Hecla. Every breeze from the North reminds me of my friend & every Storm alarms me for his Safety. The name of Friendship sanctifies the Pleasures of Imagination & heightens them with every benevolent affection. In the dreams of Fancy Seas & Mountains shrink before me & space has no Existence.[65]

Scott hopes that his words will stiffen the resolve of his friend in all predicaments:

> In the midst of barren Mountains, threatening Precipices & foaming Torrents let the memory of these Tidings blend one Ray of mildest hue among the dark clouds that sit upon the Mountains Top . . . tell me of your dangers that I may rejoice in your Escape but let no science take up that room in your Letter which I wish devoted to the Emanations of the heart.

Stanley's reply certainly fulfils this latter request. We hear nothing of the cool voice of Edinburgh natural science, and see nothing of the urbane self-assurance of the expedition leader depicted by Dayes and Pocock. The comfortable images of armchair primitivism he had set out with after turning the pages of Cowper, Goldsmith, James Thomson,[66] and Rousseau[67] had been brutally exposed. Stanley had gone to examine the north, and the north had examined him: 'Oh! Scot, I would persuade myself and those I wish to love me, that like a true Philosopher I could live in a humble Retreat, contented & pleas'd, with being at a distance from the World I despise. but it is not true.'[68] He responds with self-lacerating honesty:

> have I been to Iceland for the noble purpose of acquiring knowledge by contemplating in that remote Region the wonders of nature? have I been to occupy a Mind sick with itself and divert it from sensations too painfull for it to suffer? . . . I

---

64 CCRO MS DSA 7/3, CS to his mother, [n.d.] May 1789.
65 Ibid., CS to JTS, [n.d.].
66 Favourite poets of Stanley: see CCRO MS DSA 123/1.
67 JRL MS 722 includes Rousseau material copied by Stanley.
68 CCRO MS DSA 7/1, JTS to CS, 4 October 1789.

was induc'd more likely, oh! certainly in part, by Ambition, by the desire of acquiring a little of that Toy Reputation. call it vanity. half my Motives were no other.

Restored to country house comfort and metropolitan bustle in Britain, the
mood of prostrate self-examination soon passed as distance lent renewed
enchantment to Iceland. Nevertheless Stanley had learnt that there was a limit
to how much modern Icelandic reality the pre-Victorian sentimental traveller's
spirit could handle.

Secondly, Stanley encountered the Gothic spirit in Germany during his
teenage years. In 1781 he had studied at the Collegium Carolinum in Brunswick,[69] where he lost no time in tuning his responses to the local scenery and
legends.[70] The taste for German literature developed during this period led
Stanley subsequently to translate several German plays and poems.[71] In his
1796 version of G.A. Bürger's ballad 'Leonora', we read of an innocent heroine
swept away by a mysterious dark rider, with only a bare skull for a head; she
saves herself from entombment in a newly-prepared grave by ringing a churchyard bell as she races past, thereby causing her abductor to flee.

Thirdly, if the choice of the two 1796 'Leonora' title-page quotations is any
guide, Stanley not only relished Edward Young's *Night Thoughts*, a poem
known throughout Europe for its charnel house morbidity and spectral presences,[72] but also at least one old northern eddic poem, *Hárbarðsljóð*. At the end
of a lengthy flyting match between Þórr and Óðinn, in which the latter always
finds the last and best retort, his slower-witted adversary is finally dismissed
with a magisterial 'Farþv nv þars þic hafi allan gramir' [Be off to where the
demons may have you].[73] Stanley must have found the line for his 1796 title
page in the 1787 first volume of *Edda Sæmundar hinns Fróda*,[74] for many years
the definitive edition of the eddic poems for readers on both sides of the North
Sea. Published in Copenhagen, the volume took its place in the pioneering
series of old Icelandic text editions prepared under the aegis of the Arnamagnæan commission, each with a facing-page Latin translation, and most with
generous annotation and commentary. Starting with an edition of *Gunnlaugs
saga* in 1775, this set of handsomely produced volumes won for old Icelandic
literature, much of it previously unknown, a European-wide readership and
respect. Ole Worm, Þórmoður Torfason and Bartholin had served their readers
for over a century, and continued to be used well into the nineteenth century;

---

[69] Augusta, King George III's sister, married the Duke of Brunswick. Stanley's travelling tutor was
James Six, a Cambridge scholar who had befriended the family: see Wawn 1983.

[70] JRL MS 722, 18–19.

[71] His translations of Goethe's *Egmont* and *Nathan the Wise* remain unpublished: CCRO MS DSA
5/8.

[72] Jón Þorláksson's translation was popular in Iceland: Metcalfe 1861, 387.

[73] Luxdorph et al. 1787, 116. A footnote cites a plausible alternative reading 'allir', agreeing with
'gramir'.

[74] Volumes 2–3 were published in 1818, 1828. The initial editorial team included B.F. Luxdorph,
P.F. Suhm, Birgir Thorlacius and Gustav Baden.

but the Arnamagnæan series represented a major advance in scholarly provision with single volume editions not only of *Íslendingasögur* such as *Gunnlaugs saga* (1775), *Víga-Glúms saga* (1786), *Eyrbyggja saga* (1787), *Njáls saga* (1809), *Laxdæla saga* (1826), and *Kormáks saga* (1832) but also works of history (*Kristni saga* 1773, *Hungrvaka* 1778), science (*Rímbegla* 1780) and law (*Grágás* 1829). Stanley almost secured the services of Grímur Jónsson Thorkelin as his guide in Iceland in 1789[75] – the latter's 1815 edition of *Beowulf* was another publication in the Copenhagen series. Though the volumes were expensive,[76] and never easy to obtain in Britain, they found a place in some library society collections – we know that both Wordsworth and Coleridge frequently borrowed the Bristol Library Society copy of the *Edda* (1787);[77] Stanley may well have owned a copy of the same edition, as he did of the 1786 *Víga-Glúms saga* edition.[78]

We find Stanley using the Copenhagen *Edda* again fifty years after selecting his quotation for the 'Leonora' title page. A single folio leaf, written in the frail hand of his datable mid 1840s papers, contains quotations from two eddic poems, accompanied by interlinear translations, mythological information drawn from the 1787 edition, and Stanley's own etymological speculations.[79] Some lines are from *Vafþrúðnismál*, a flyting match between the ultimately victorious Óðinn and a knowledgeable giant Vafþrúðnir, in which mythological lore is imparted, including, in the Stanley extract, the giant's account of Niflhel, the deepest region to which the dead must journey. The other lines are from *Baldrs draumar*, or 'The Descent of Odin' as it was known in Thomas Gray's 1768 poem based on a Latin translation.[80] Óðinn, having journeyed on his horse Sleipnir to the gate of Hel, learns from a prophetess of the fearful fate awaiting the god Baldr, and of the ensuing *ragnarǫk*. The passage speaks of the old northern mythological region of death, whence no traveller save Óðinn returns – a subject well orchestrated to win the attention of an octogenerian Victorian Icelandophile in the final days of his own long life.

Fourthly, a 1792 manuscript notebook offers evidence of the kinds of popular old northern literature in English with which this Edinburgh-educated, Iceland-visiting, edda-reading, saga edition-owning baronet may have been familiar. In the months after the sudden death of his Irish fiancée, Stanley compiled a collection of elegiac verses.[81] He transcribes 'Elegy: To Spring' by Michael Bruce (1746–67) into his 1792 notebook from a 1782 edition of the poems. Elsewhere in the same edition we find Bruce's two 'Danish Odes',

---

[75] Edinburgh University Library, La. III. 379/757–81.

[76] Harvey Wood 1972, II 468.

[77] See Wawn 1987, 13–17, based on Bristol City Library MSS B 7473–6. The British Museum acquired Icelandic books and manuscripts belonging to Sir Joseph Banks: Lbs. 3504 8vo. On Coleridge and the *Edda*, see Demarest 1975.

[78] The present writer owns this copy. Stanley brought back from Iceland a Bible, Ari Þorgilsson's *Libellus Islandorum*, a law code, and a text of *Ólafs saga helga*: Lbs. 3888 4to 260.

[79] A loose leaf in a 1792 notebook in CCRO MS DSA 5/6.

[80] 'Vegtamsquiþa' in the 1787 Copenhagen edition.

[81] CCRO MS DSA 5/6.

which prove to be virtually the same poems as those cited by Leander in Campbell's 1741 *A Polite Correspondence*, quoted in Chapter One.[82] Another poet with old northern sympathies represented in the notebook is James Beattie (1735–1805). Not only did Beattie read over Gray's two Norse odes before their publication in 1768,[83] but it was in his philosophical poem *The Minstrel: or the Progress of Genius* (1770) that the two clearly discernible impulses behind Stanley's Icelandic interests – scientific sense and Gothic sensibility – are debated. The notebook also features an elegy by William Mason, yet another poet interested in the old north, and the biographer of Thomas Gray, with whom he discussed the old northern writings of Temple and Mallet.[84] In Mason's 1766 play *Argentile and Curan*, its Danish princely hero entertains two English courtiers with a verse version of the same 'Harold' poem that had featured as one of Percy's *Five Pieces*.[85] All these poets enjoyed a secondary life in Victorian Britain as collected editions of their works attracted new readers to their formulaic constructions of Viking-age gods and heroes.

Fifthly, to Stanley's familiarity with old northern poetic enthusiasts such as Bruce, Beattie and Mason should be added his knowledge of the Ossianic corpus. The 1792 notebook contains elegiac lines from *Carric-Thura* (1765), one of the sparest and best structured of the Ossianic pieces.[86] One Scottish enthusiast had a vast hall built whose ceiling, like some Highland Sistine Chapel, was decorated with twelve Ossianic scenes, dominated by the climactic moment in *Carric-Thura* (1765) when Fingal confronts the spirit of Loda (Macpherson's Óðinn).[87] *Carric-Thura* must have been Stanley's first encounter with the fierce Odinic spirit of Loda; how appropriate, therefore, that he should experience an Odinic epiphany of his own en route to Iceland in 1789. Annotating the Orkney section of his Iceland journals years later Stanley recalls wandering round the ancient stone circles at Stenness, pondering their origins,[88] and recalling excitedly that one particular circle (at Stenness) had been the setting for the famous Ossianic confrontation between Fingal and Loda. Stanley copies out the whole scene:[89] it is, he says, 'the most striking and beautiful episode in the whole of Ossian's poems'.[90] Frothal, a Viking chief besieges Carricthura, the Orcadian king's palace. Fingal, King of West Scotland, arrives to support the king. On the night before the battle, Fingal's young warriors feast and then sleep. The fires fade, the moon casts an eerie light, and suddenly, a terrifying air-

---

[82] See above pp. 21–2.
[83] Toynbee and Whibley 1935, iii 982–4.
[84] Ibid., ii 551–3.
[85] Mason 1811, II 235; see also I 196–8.
[86] Macpherson 1765, I 269–90. See CCRO MS DSA 5/6 7–8, 11–13, 17–18 for the Ossianic extracts. More generally, see Stafford 1988.
[87] Okun 1967; Booth 1969. On the use of Viking subjects in nineteenth-century interior decoration, see Wilson 1996 185, 1997 57.
[88] Lbs. 3886 4to, 40–50, 283–307.
[89] Ibid., 302–4.
[90] Ibid., f. 48.

borne spirit appears, with eyes flaming and nostrils flaring, and shaking a spear. It is Loda, father of the Viking Frothal. He takes up position in the stone circle; there follows an exchange of chill unpleasantries with Fingal who runs his sword through Loda, reducing the shrieking spirit to a puff of acrid smoke. Viking power in the Orkneys is destroyed. In the sad circumstances attending the compilation of the 1792 notebook, the sufferings of the young lovers in *Carric-Thura* provided verses of elegiac solace for the bereaved Stanley.

Lastly, old northern networking. While still in Edinburgh Stanley was a member of the Oyster Club, a group of young academics who met regularly to dine and discuss cultural and scientific questions. Such clubs were the stuff of intellectual life in the Athens of the North. It was at meetings of two similar associations that the young Walter Scott gave evidence of his own runic and eddic interests (or at least his capacity to paraphrase Percy's Mallet)[91] by delivering papers on 'The Manners and Customs of the Northern nations' and 'The Origins of the Scandinavian Mythology'.[92] There were family friends with whom such interests could be discussed after Stanley returned to England. Amongst the poetry of Anna Seward, 'The Swan of Lichfield', that Walter Scott edited in 1810, we find 'Herva, at the Tomb of Argantyr. A Runic Dialogue',[93] Seward's version of the still unavoidable 'Waking of Angantyr'.[94] Her friend William Bagshaw Stevens, headmaster of Repton School, recalled hearing her recite her 'long *Paraphrastic* Translation of Hervor at the Tomb of Angantyr from Hickes's *Thesaurus* which I had translated before her at the age of 17'.[95] It was through such networks of like-minded enthusiasts that the old north found a toe-hold in pre-Victorian middle England.

Stanley's old northernism was securely rooted and sustained him to the end of his life. In the 1840s Stanley could be found annotating copies of journals from the 1789 expedition, with the old north as a persistent reference point. He and his companions had been wrong to demand 'respect as . . . superiors' from folk in rural Iceland all those years ago – 'many of them were the descendants of the Earls and Barons, the Jarls & Herskers of the Norwegians of the 9th Century & constituted in fact the real Gentry of Iceland'.[96] They had misread late eighteenth-century Icelandic society by forgetting Viking-age history. Perhaps in his later years Stanley found time to read his copy of *Víga-Glúms saga* and follow the fortunes of its eponymous hero, grandson of just such a 'hersker' (OI *hersir*, 'nobleman'). His admiration for the Vikings is given an anti-Irish

---

[91] [Percy] 1770 includes a chapter on 'Customs and Manners of the Ancient Northern Nations', and four chapters of material for the 'Scandinavian Mythology' paper.

[92] See Lockhart 1838, I 91, 105, 118–19.

[93] Seward 1810, III 90–103; written *c*.1788–9, first published 1796, along with Hickes' translation. See also III 29–33, 'Harold's Complaint: A Scandinavian Ode', based on Percy's 'Complaint of Harold'.

[94] Other versions include Mathias 1781, Williams 1790, Polwhele 1792: discussed Farley 1903, 50–2.

[95] Galbraith 1965, 67–8; also 1971, 93–7.

[96] Lbs. 3888 4to, 354; West 1970–6, I 201.

spin: 'they were bold adventurers historians Poets – fame was their main object – they were the Scandinavians Conquerors of England Normandy and Sicily and the discovers of America – it is to be lamented that they had not conqurd Ireland and peopled [it] with Norwegians Danes or Anglo Saxons'.[97] Stanley ponders the clash between paganism and Christianity at the end of the first millennium.[98] In his summary of the main events, as set out in the 1773 edition of *Kristni saga*,[99] we find old Icelandic literature, modern travel and philological curiosity intersecting, as they were to do for other old northernists throughout the remainder of the nineteenth century. Stanley recalls the story of Stefnir Þorgilsson, sent by King Ólafr Tryggvason to Christianise Iceland in 996. Received icily by the heathens, he responded by destroying their temples. Bad weather forced him to shelter off Kjalarnes, which provoked heathen mockery in a poem, quoted by Stanley in Icelandic, alongside his own translation:

Vindr sleit band a landi	[JTS: the Winds freed from their Chains on land
Geysar a med isi	gushed forth with Ice
Allrickr freyr slikom	like the all powerful Goddess Freya][100]

The young Stanley had journeyed to Geysir in order to observe, measure and paint a phenomenon of nature; fifty years later, memories of that visit prompt an elderly Victorian gentleman to annotate his journals and, in translating, to stumble across the etymology of Geysir, in the course of a fine saga scene in which the collision between the forces of Viking-age and Christian Iceland is dramatised in terms of family strife, divine intervention and the weather.

Sir George Mackenzie and Helga

Early nineteenth-century Britain saw the publication of a number of small books for young readers about life in the European old and modern north, in particular Iceland. Behind all of them was the promise that 'you can learn more about the Icelanders when you are old enough to read larger books'.[101] These volumes made few concessions to the youthful imagination; they offered imperial gallons of Gradgrindian fact rather than heady flights of fancy. Thus, in *Domestic Scenes in Greenland and Iceland* by 'The Author of Everyday Wonders', we find a stodgy digest of Ari Þorgilsson's *Íslendingabók* account of Flóki and his predecessors as discoverers of Iceland, and a pot-pourri of information about native diet, dress and hot springs. There are stern, no-nonsense judg-

---

97   Lbs. 3888 4to, 290.
98   *Hungurvaka* passages about the Skálholt bishopric summarised in Lbs. 3888 4to, 346ff.
99   Suhm et al. 1773. Lbs. 3888 4to, 366ff.
100 Lbs. 3888 4to, 374. The Icelandic is correctly copied from Suhm et al. 1773, 38.
101 [anon.] 1850, 122.

ments: Naddod was a 'wicked pirate', Harold Finehair was 'a cruel king', and Ingólfr Arnarson believed 'silly falsehoods . . . and superstitions'.[102]

Of all these books, the series designed for the tiniest of pockets was Maria Hack's *Winter Evenings; or, Tales of Travellers* (1819), in which on successive evenings a mother answers questions from her two children about the social geography of nations around the world. On the tenth evening Iceland takes centre stage – its mountains, geysers and churches.[103] The title-page quotation offers the cosiest of night-time images: 'The village-matron, round the blazing hearth / Suspends the infant audience with her tales.' The Preface, however, makes clear that by 'tales' the reader is not to understand 'stories of giants and castles'[104] which 'weaken mental powers . . . exhaust the sensibility', and, worst of all, 'produce . . . listless indifference to the realities of life'. The children are exposed instead to tales of Icelandic courage, patience, fortitude, generosity, benevolence and 'reliance on the Supreme Disposer of events'. The source of the mother's information is Sir George Mackenzie's *Travels in the Island of Iceland in the Summer of the Year 1810*.[105] Maria Hack's Lucy has other worries than Icelanders being 'grave and serious':

Lucy: Though Iceland is a dismal country to live in, it abounds in curiosities. I am sorry the inhabitants live in such dirty houses. Mamma, did Mackenzie think them a disagreeable people?

Mother: While his little earthen hut is almost buried by the snows of winter, the father of an Icelandic family, by the light of an oil lamp, reads his children the lessons of knowledge and virtue.[106]

Victorian family values are thus projected onto Icelandic society, with Sir George Mackenzie as the trusted source of information. The idea of the patriarch reading by lamplight to the hushed household was to find archetypal expression in a celebrated 1860 painting by the Dane August Schiøtt, in which the 'lessons of knowledge and virtue' seem to derive from a book of sagas.[107] Mackenzie's *Travels* was also the source for the thumbnail sketches and judgements in *Near Home; or, The Countries of Europe Described* (1860):[108] Icelanders are slow and dull but honest and true; they spend too little time keeping themselves sweet and clean; and their sagas are stories 'of old times, and storms, and shipwrecks, and of fierce bears and fiercer men'.[109]

Mackenzie's own flirtation with the ancient and modern north was brief but

---

[102] Ibid., 123.
[103] Hack 1819, II 173–226.
[104] Ibid., I iii.
[105] Just as [anon.] 1825, 41–3 draws on Troil 1780, 27.
[106] Hack 1819, II 224–5.
[107] Ponzi 1986, 91.
[108] Quotations from the 1878 edition; there were five editions between 1860–1902.
[109] [Mortimer] 1878, 324.

hectic. His party spent three months in Iceland in 1810 where, like Stanley before them, they paid much attention to science and little to saga. Neverthless, during the printing of the revised 1812 edition of *Travels*,[110] Mackenzie wrote and staged *Helga*, a play (very) loosely based on Henry Holland's précis of the Old Icelandic *Gunnlaugs saga ormstungu*, included in the 1811 first edition.[111] In Holland's hands the saga becomes a sentimental melodrama; the illustrator of the 1775 Copenhagen edition clearly had the same idea. Gunnlaug is born into a family of wealth and power, but his 'turbulent and unyielding' temperament brings him into conflict with his father Illugi. He takes refuge in the house of Illugi's friend Thorstein, whose daughter Helga soon catches his eye: 'while his mind was instructed by the father, his heart was subdued by the gentleness and elegance of the daughter'.[112] With 'restless impetuosity' maturing into the 'refinement and delicacy of the youthful lover', Gunnlaug is betrothed to Helga, with Thorstein's promise that she would become his wife on his return, which must be within three years. Gunnlaug wins fame as an itinerant poet. In Sweden he befriends Rafn, a fellow skald, but the self-preoccupied Gunnlaug soon squabbles with his colleague over the relative merits of their verses. Rafn returns to Iceland and is granted the 'unwilling hand of Helga, whose heart meanwhile remained with her former lover', who had failed to return by the stipulated date. Arriving home on the day of the wedding, the 'unfortunate' Gunnlaug:

> shewed himself on a sudden among the assembled guests, eminent above all from the beauty of his person and the richness of his apparel. The eyes of the lovers hung upon each other in mute and melancholy sorrow; and the bitterest pangs went to the heart of the gentle Helga. The nuptial feast was gloomy and without joy.

Deadly enmity flares between the two rivals, with Gunnlaug humiliated and Rafn refused 'all conjugal endearments'. At the summer assembly they duel indecisively, before heading for Norway to fight to the death. With his leg severed, Rafn resolves to fight on if the trusting Gunnlaug will bring him water to slake his thirst (Fig. 1):

> Rafn, seizing the critical moment, when the water was presented to him, strikes with his sword the bare head of Gunnlaug, crying out at the same time, 'that he cannot endure that his rival should enjoy the embraces of the beautiful Helga'.[113]

Gunnlaug slays 'his perfidious opponent', before dying of his own wounds. Helga, meanwhile, succumbs to 'misery and gloom', and 'sinks an early victim to the grave, bending her last looks upon a robe she had received from Gunn-

---

110 The first edition cost £2 12s 6d and sold out in six months.
111 For an earlier précis, see Herbert 1806, 63–70.
112 Mackenzie 1812, 31.
113 Ibid., 32.

Fig. 1. Gunnlaugr and Hrafn duel to the death. Artist Georg Haas.
Sagan af Gunnlaugi ok Skalld-Rafni.

laug; and dwelling with her last thoughts upon the memory of her unhappy lover'.

W.P. Ker, his Victorian teeth cut on a more vigorous strain of Viking bravado, and meaning it as a criticism, called the saga's story 'shallow and sentimental'.[114] The early nineteenth century would have taken this judgement as a compliment. Sentiment is certainly well to the fore in Sir George Mackenzie's transformation of the story, which enjoyed the shortest run imaginable at the Theatre Royal Edinburgh. Geological controversy ensured that the play, already holed beneath its artistic water line before the curtain rose, was greeted with derision by a hostile audience.[115] At the height of its Victorian popularity, Old Icelandic literature invariably had a variety of political and intellectual breezes fluttering its flags. The fate of Sir George Mackenzie's *Helga*[116] shows what could happen earlier in the century when a breeze suddenly became a gale.

The text of the play was never published,[117] but Sir Walter Scott's specially commissioned Prologue and Epilogue both appeared in *The Scots Magazine*. Sir Walter, already a committed old northernist, does his best to create an appropriately exotic atmosphere:

[114] Ker 1896, 281.
[115] Grierson 1932–7, III 101, WS to Joanna Baillie, 4 April 1812.
[116] The full title is: 'Helga, or The Rival Minstrels, A Tragedy. Founded on an Icelandic Saga, or History'.
[117] The manuscript in now in the Henry E. Huntington Library, San Marino, California: MS Larpent 1751.

Brought from that isle where flames volcanic light
The half year's darkness of the polar night,
Where boiling streams from earth's dark caverns driven
With sleet and snow-drift mix in middle heaven
The icy Glacier and the gulph of fire;
Yet in that clime though elemental strife
Wrecks each fair trace of vegetative life,
Mid Iceland's waste of ashes and of snows,
Even there of old the Light of song arose
From her dark bosom the historic lay.
O'er Ancient Europe pourd the mental day;
In Royal halls their harps her minstrels strung
And courts and camps were silent when they sung.
Not now we aim to match their loftier strain
Or bid the runic rhyme revive again;
Enough if simply, yet to nature true,
Our wandering bard his sketch dramatic drew,
To show how sternly rival Minstrels strove
Stung by the jealousy of fame and love.[118]

Any dramatic promise held out by these lines soon disappears. Haco (Holland's Rafn) and Edgar (Gunnlaug) contend for poetic honours in front of the Swedish king. With Edgar deemed victorious, friendship sours. Haco, an old northern Iago 'determinèd to prove a villain', returns to Iceland to woo Helga:

Let pampered youths
Ride softly, softly talk, & whisper love –
That's not the way to win! Let smooth tongued
Swains go wail & weep for Mistresses unkind,
Or seek a coward death to ease their pain: –
I am of other mould, & if the truth
Were fairly told, the women do not like
Such fawning things. I'm never in a mood
For wasting breath in sighs; nor are my knees
Just made for bending – yet I'll kneel & sigh
To Helga – [aside] but not for love, no! no! no![119]

Haco's knees may not have been made for bending, but those of Emla, Sir George's own invention as the angelic Helga's faithful companion, certainly were. Familiar only with a life of pastoral tranquillity, Emla suddenly finds tragedy lurking on her rural Icelandic doorstep. She pleads in vain for Helga's father to intervene, but the combatants are determined to duel to the death, eventually leaving the stage clear for Helga's final scene of Ophelian derangement.

118 [Scott] 1812, 134–5: some punctuation added.
119 Henry E. Huntington Library, Calif., MS Larpent 1751, 2.iii.24–34.

Mackenzie's gallant attempt to popularise an Icelandic saga by transferring it to the stage proved a failure. It excited 'considerable clamour' during the final two acts, due to 'passages which were thought exceptionable'.[120] There is certainly no shortage of these, but it was geological controversy rather than dramatic hamfistedness which wrecked the evening. The problem can be traced to Mackenzie's fiery contributions to the geological debate in Edinburgh concerning the conditions under which the earth's surface was first formed. Was it the result of aqueous precipitation, as the so-called Neptunists (or Wernerians) believed, or, as the Vulcanists (or Huttonians) argued, had consolidation taken place at great heat and under great pressure beneath the ocean bed?[121] Mackenzie and his fellow explorers had investigated the Icelandic evidence. Henry Holland's Iceland journal takes a moderate Vulcanist position, but moderation was not a prominent feature of Sir George's tendentious draft chapter on mineralogy for the first edition of *Travels in the Island of Iceland in . . . 1810.* Holland, sensing trouble, dissociated himself from all theoretical statements in the published account.[122] The Wernerians were indeed offended by Sir George's chapter as published, and packed the Theatre Royal to exact revenge on the helpless play and its hapless creator.

As with Stanley, the whole episode illustrates the interlocking nature of intellectual interests amongst old northern enthusiasts on the eve of Victoria's accession. An Icelandic family saga is chosen for dramatic representation by an Iceland explorer and geologist, supported by the man who within ten years was to make his name as author of nineteenth-century Britain's first and finest old northern novel. They select a short rather than a long saga; a tale of love rather than bravado, whose protagonists are poets rather than pirates; the saga has a pronounced international dimension as the poets move effortlessly through the courts of Europe (and Britain) dazzling their royal hosts with their skaldic skills; and its resolution turns on chivalric duelling (however treacherously conducted) rather than ambush or incineration. We may note, too, the philological shallowness of Mackenzie's response to the saga. He knew no Old Icelandic, and makes no attempt to archaise or northernise the way his characters speak. Stanley was frustrated at being unable to lay hands on an Icelandic dictionary before setting sail for Iceland in 1789.[123] Sir George, one suspects, would have taken a good novel instead. Mackenzie's old north speaks only in the accents of early nineteenth-century Edinburgh.

---

[120] [Scott] 1812, 153–4.
[121] Broader contexts discussed in Rudwick 1962–3, Chitnis 1970.
[122] Lbs. 4295 4to, HH to Dr Peter Holland, 2 August 1811.
[123] Edinburgh University MS La. III. 379/757–81, JTS to Grímur Jónsson Thorkelin, 10 and 25 May 1789.

Sir Henry Holland and his 'Dissertation'

In August 1871 an improbable and unhappy meeting took place in Reykjavík between two of Victorian Britain's most fêted Icelandophiles, Sir Henry Holland and William Morris. Morris was making his first visit to Iceland; and Sir (as he was by this time) Henry Holland his second, after a gap of sixty-one years. A newly-graduated physician in 1810, Holland had subsequently attended six British prime ministers, an American president, Prince Louis Napoleon, King Leopold of Belgium, Talleyrand, Wordsworth, Sir Walter Scott, as well as Prince Albert and Queen Victoria. Yet Morris could hardly have been less in awe:

> To Mrs Maria's house again, where was dinner, and the courtly old carle, Sir Henry Holland, whose age (eighty-four) I thought was the most interesting thing about him. I was rather low, after all, and cowed by the company, and a sense of stiffness after our joyous rough life just ended.[124]

Morris's evident lack of interest in 'the courtly old carle' signals the differences that developed between two generations of northern enthusiasts in nineteenth-century Britain. Morris had come to Iceland to visit the saga-steads associated with the texts that he and Eiríkur Magnússon had been reading, translating and publishing. He knew enough Icelandic to be bad tempered in the language. Moreover, by this time the land itself had come to symbolise elements which mattered most to Morris in his life – the romance of isolation and desolation, the struggle between fate and free-will, and the ability of the human spirit to 'make and endure'.[125] He will have searched in vain for a reciprocal visionary gleam in Holland's octogenarian gaze. Holland was not deaf to Icelandic literary culture, but had learnt to view it as an Enlightenment intellectual. His account of Grettisbæli, a conically-shaped hill in the west of Iceland, is terse and sceptical:

> This hill is celebrated as having been in days of yore, the retreat of an Icelandic warrior, known in the songs; who took refuge here from his enemies; & assisted by one friend in the valley below, contrived to maintain himself in this situation for two and a half years – *Valeat quantum valere possit.*[126]

'Let it pass for what it is worth': for William Morris it was worth a great deal. With Eiríkur he translated *Grettis saga Ásmundarsonar,* and made the 'doomed tough'[127] the subject of a fine pair of sonnets marked by the poet's distinctive melancholy lyricism.[128]

---

124 Morris 1910–15, VIII 178.
125 Ibid., IX 126; more generally, see below, Chapter 9.
126 Wawn 1987, 174.
127 Auden and MacNeice 1937, 127.
128 Morris and Eiríkr Magnússon 1869, Preface; Morris 1910–15, VII xix.

Holland's 'Preliminary Dissertation on the History and Literature of Iceland', that prefaces all three editions of Mackenzie's *Travels* is an authoritative synthesis of knowledge about old northern literary culture and its post-medieval development. Holland not only knew his way around standard works by Saxo Grammaticus, Árngrímur Jónsson, Ole Worm, Resen, Björn of Skarðsá, Þormoður Torfason, Bartholin, Mallet and Percy, but was familiar with more recent works such as Hans Egede's *A Description of Greenland* (1745), Hálfdan Einarsson's *Sciagraphia historiæ literariæ Islandicæ* (1777), the early volumes of Jakob Langebek's *Scriptores rerum Danicarum medii ævi* (1772–1834), Finnur Jónsson's *Historia ecclesiastica Islandiæ* (1772–78), and the 1787 Copenhagen *Edda*. Amongst the Icelandic sagas to which he refers are *Eyrbyggja saga*, *Vatnsdæla saga*, *Ljósvetninga saga*, *Hervarar saga*, *Ragnars saga*, and *Kristni saga*; and he even owned a copy of *Víga-Glúms saga*.[129]

Holland is interested more in broad historical processes than colourful details of saga incident. He identifies three stages of Icelandic cultural development: the post-settlement golden age up to the middle of the thirteenth century; the dispiriting decline until the Reformation; and the subsequent revival of learning leading up to the late eighteenth-century publication in Copenhagen of major medieval Icelandic texts. The Viking age is viewed in characteristically Whiggish terms. Eminent Norwegians, rejecting the 'despotic sway' of monarchy at home, had settled a desolate land and made it fertile. They brought with them their annals, mythology, legends – and language. All this lore and learning was then written down in appropriately Wordsworthian circumstances:

> The summer's sun saw them indeed laboriously occupied in seeking their provision from a stormy ocean and a barren soil; but the long seclusion of the winter gave them the leisure, as well as the desire, to cultivate talents, which were at once so fruitful in occupation and delight. During the darkness of their year, and beneath the rude covering of wood and turf, they recited to their assembled families the deeds and descent of their forefathers; from whom they had received that inheritance of liberty, which they now dwelt among deserts to preserve.[130]

This is 'Time and Vellum' theory, nineteenth-century style.[131] A 'regular form of government' had reduced the incidence of violence within the community. If this meant that there was less bloodstained incident to excite the complex language of poetry, the resultant increase in peace and quiet was conducive to the cultivation of historical prose. Moreover, democratic government, with the premium it placed on persuasive oral expression and quickness of wit, represented just the stimulus to mental exertion that literary activity required, as did

---

129 The same 1786 Copenhagen edition which Stanley owned: see above, note 79. In 1811 Holland met its editor, Guðmundur Pétursson (1748–1811), who was stranded in Leith: NLS Acc. 7515, HH to Dr Peter Holland, 24 March 1811.
130 Mackenzie 1812, 18.
131 See Sigurður Nordal 1952.

an international court culture that provided a market for Icelandic Viking-age cultural wares – 'a species of commerce, in which the fruit of their mental endowments was exchanged for those foreign luxuries or comforts, which nature had denied to them from their own soil'.[132] How Adam Smith would have approved.

Holland dutifully reports on the condition of Viking-age poetry – its lack of refinement 'either of imagery and feeling' (21) can be attributed to a natural environment where 'the softer features of nature are but rarely seen'. Poetry had been a craft requiring instruction, and Holland draws attention not just to the narratives of the *Prose Edda*, but also to the skaldic practices detailed in *Skáldska-parmál* and *Háttatal*. The alliterative complexities and metaphorical ingenuities are described, but deemed too difficult for nineteenth-century readers to appreciate. Holland claims that higher honour was accorded to the writer of 'histories' – whether 'genuine', 'fictitious' or 'those of a mixed character' (29). He shows little interest in 'fabulous' tales, but acknowledges that the redeeming high seriousness of allegory can lurk beneath surface fantasy. The term 'saga' is reserved for 'mixed character' historical narratives, 'a much more . . . valuable class of compositions', that provide invaluable information about the history and customs of Iceland and other northern nations. Thus the *Eyrbyggja saga* rivalry in witchcraft between Geirríðr and Katla is cited solely in order to discuss the format of Geirríðr's trial in front of twelve men (15n) – an early form of trial by jury, whose likely northern origin was widely cited by Victorian scholars, poets and politicians.[133] Similarly, the memorable *Vatnsdæla saga* scene describing the fishing dispute between the sons of Ingimundr and the wretched Hrolleifr catches Holland's eye only because of the light it throws on the division of labour among all classes of Icelandic settlers.[134] The memorial feast for Hǫskuldr Dala-Kollsson in *Laxdæla saga* interests Holland because it illustrates 'internal supplies and means of subsistence' in rural Iceland.[135]

This buoyant picture of a golden-age domestic literary culture, and a globe-trotting skaldic elite, gives way to an account of late medieval decline and fall, with 'sedition, rapine and bloodshed' fuelled by aristocratic ambition and Norwegian royal interference. For as long as 'definite objects of ambition' existed for all members of the community, and provided that those gifted with 'vigour, activity and talent' (50) could exert political influence, then high levels of creative social energy could be maintained. After the transference of sovereignty to Norway in 1262–4, the 'apathy and indolence' of a dependency culture held sway (51). Moreover, as other European nations began to free themselves from the bondage of dark-age superstition (as Holland saw it), their native litera-

---

132 Mackenzie 1812, 19.
133 Encouraged by Scott's 'Abstract' in [Jamieson, R.] 1814.
134 Mackenzie 1812, 39; Baring-Gould 1863, 138–47 was the first Victorian writer to sense the scene's narrative richness.
135 Mackenzie 1812, 38.

tures, previously suppressed or ignored, began to revive, and the prestige previously enjoyed by itinerant Icelandic skalds declined accordingly. These poets travelled less, and Icelandic culture grew even more self-preoccupied. Holland casts a disapproving Unitarian eye on the influence of the Roman Catholic church in medieval Iceland. Priests danced more to the tune of Rome, or at least Nidaros, and less to the rhythms of native life and culture. Saga writing 'degenerated into a mere collection of ecclesiastical fables' (56); poetry became obsessed with saints and martyrs; and energies previously channelled into cultivation of the secular law were redirected to 'the rites and usage of the Catholic church'. Iceland had needed a good Reformation, and Holland describes its progress with evident relish. With the restoration of the public education system and the welcome arrival of the printing press, cultural life in Iceland was reborn. The golden age could never be restored, but the worst excesses of decline were reversed. Holland's vision of Icelandic cultural history could be challenged at any number of points; but in 1810 the surprise was not that his judgements were sometimes questionable but that he attempted them at all.

The turn-of-the-century origins of Henry Holland's involvement with the ancient north are as illuminating as those of John Thomas Stanley, his mentor. The two families were neighbours and shared the same friends, Anna Seward amongst them. Holland's early education pointed him in the right direction. From the age of sixteen Holland attended the Bristol school run by Rev. J.P. Estlin, a former pupil of Warrington's dissenting academy, who was strongly committed to humane learning in his own school. Holland's identifiable circle of country friends – Coleridge, Southey, Joseph Priestley, the Cottle and Bright families – confirms that the young Cestrian did not lack for intellectual stimulus during his Bristol years. The borrowing records of the Bristol Library Society during the first decade of the century[136] reveal an interest in old northern matters amongst the Estlin circle. Library holdings included the 1787 *Edda*, Percy's Mallet, and works by James Johnstone and the local old northern hero Amos Cottle.[137] Wordsworth and Coleridge were regular borrowers of these volumes. The popularity of Mackenzie's *Travels* is striking. From February 1812 it was borrowed twenty-eight times over a two-year period, doubtless because of local interest in both Holland and his 1810 expedition companion Richard Bright.

Again, as with John Thomas Stanley, Henry Holland remained in touch with the old and modern north for the rest of his life. A supporter of Eiríkur Magnússon after his arrival in England in 1862, Holland helped to round up influential support for the Icelandic scholar's application for a Cambridge University Library post in 1871.[138] This single act helped to ensure that tuition in

---

[136] Bristol City Library MSS B 7480–5.
[137] Works included Johnstone 1782b and Cottle 1797.
[138] See also below, p. 365.

Icelandic was available from this learned Icelander over a period of forty years to pupils near and far.[139]

Afterword

By following the old northern links and enthusiasms of four Regency Britons, this chapter has sought to contextualise 'the state of the subject' on the eve of and during the early years of Queen Victoria's reign. For most people it was an old north played very much on period instruments – the works of Hickes and Percy still guided popular taste, whilst seventeenth-century continental scholarship had eventually been supplemented by the Copenhagen saga series. It was a formulaic old north, with a relatively fixed set of heroic and mythological motifs endlessly shuffled and reassembled. It was a philologically ill-informed old north that operated most securely at a scholarly level in Latin. It had already demonstrated its potential for being a politicised old north – in the selection of texts for publication, in the presentation of Óðinn the freedom fighter, in the idea of Norwegian Vikings as virtuous colonisers. It was a tenacious old north – youthful enthusiasms never quite lost their hold on our group of travellers. It was an old north whose networks of enthusiasts were becoming increasingly cohesive both within the British Isles and into Scandinavia. It was an old north still largely populated by 'pyrates' rather than 'vikings'. Not least, it was a geographically vague old north as yet little concerned with real or imagined sagastead locations, whether in mainland Scandinavia, in Iceland or even in Britain. It is true that by 1820 many readers were familiar with Ragnarr loðbrók harrying and dying in Northumbria, and of Loda haunting the stone circles of Orkney. The more dedicated enthusiast could learn of King Hákon's campaigns in Scotland and the Isle of Man,[140] and of Kjartan Ólafsson's Irish ancestry.[141] Yet there was something missing in these Viking-age localisations. To engage the imaginations of nineteenth-century readers, individual British locations needed their old northern history dramatising and three-dimensionalising and, if necessary, inventing.

Scotland offered a glimpse of what was possible in the period 1820–22, with a royal visit in the offing. The Celtic Society of Edinburgh was founded in 1820 – its members dined in kilts and bonnets. An enterprising Bannockburn firm produced a pattern book of differentiated tartans for each clan, certificated by the Highland Society of London, and assisted by two brothers, who were English. When the king arrived, every pipe skirled, every calf was cross gartered, and the silver toggles on every sporran sparkled. The master of ceremonies and driving force behind the whole operation was Sir Walter Scott.[142] By day he

---

[139] Guðbrandur Vigfússon also held Holland in high regard: Lbs. 342c fol., GV to Bjarni Þorsteinsson, 6 March 1865.

[140] Johnstone 1784.

[141] Grímur Jónsson Thorkelin 1788.

[142] Trevor-Roper, in Hobsbawm and Ranger 1983, 26–33.

toiled at the 'tartaning' of Scotland; but by night he mused on the residual Viking spirit of the Orkneys and Shetlands. There were colourful traditions to invent and investigate; Scott was the man to do it; and his novel *The Pirate* became one of the definitive texts of the construction of the old north in nineteenth-century Britain. It is the subject of the next chapter.

CHAPTER THREE

Protectors of Northern Arts

For thither came, in times afar,
Stern Lochlin's sons of roving war,
The Norsemen, train'd to spoil and blood,
Skill'd to prepare the raven's food;
Kings of the main their leaders brave,
Their barks the dragons of the wave.

(Sir Walter Scott 1805)[1]

Huzza! my brave comrades, give way for the Haaf
We shall sooner come back to the dance and the laugh;
For life without mirth is a lamp without oil;
Then mirth and long life to the bold Magnus Troil.

(Sir George Elvey c. 1890)[2]

New friendship

In the spring of 1826 a native Icelandic philologist arrived in Edinburgh to take up his duties as Assistant Keeper of Books in the Advocates' Library in Edinburgh. His name was Þorleifur Repp, and amongst his luggage were two presentation copies of the newest saga edition in the saga text series produced by the Arnamagnæan Commission in Copenhagen. As with all the previous volumes the *Laxdæla saga* edition included a Latin translation, on this occasion the work of Repp himself. One copy was duly presented to the Advocates' Library, and the other to one of the library's most venerable members, Sir Walter Scott.[3] *Laxdæla* duly found its way into Scott's library at Abbotsford,[4] confirming that on at least one occasion 'the author of Waverley' met one of his greatest Ice-

---

1 From *The Lay of the Last Minstrel*; Scott 1904, 44.
2 From 'The Zetland Fisherman', by Sir George Elvey, Queen Victoria's organist at St George's Chapel, Windsor; the work, based on verses in *The Pirate*, was performed in front of the Queen: *Shetland Times*, 2 February 1902. I am grateful to Brian Smith, Shetland Archivist, for drawing my attention to this and other references: see below, notes 75, 82.
3 Þjóðsskjalasafn Íslands, Einkaskjöl E 182, Grímur Thorkelin to Þorleifur Repp, 31 May 1827.
4 [Cochrane] 1838, 99.

landic admirers. The work and influence of these two tribunes of the old north represent contrasting but complementary aspects of old northern enthusiasms in Scotland on the eve of Victoria's reign. In *The Pirate*, the novel that Scott wrote and Repp revered, nineteenth-century Britain's curiosity about the old north produced its first work of major and lasting influence.

In the novel Scott took the two centuries of old northern scholarship that had been 'gathered into the barns of the learned',[5] and found a way of animating it within a British context. English and Latin translations of selected British Isles-related saga scenes first became available during the 1780s. Grímur Thorkelín had published English translations of the Irish scenes from *Laxdæla saga* and the Northumbrian scenes from *Ragnars saga*;[6] and he was almost certainly the 'worthy and ingenious native of Iceland'[7] who had helped James Johnstone, British Embassy Chaplain in Copenhagen, to produce several octavo volumes of British scenes from sagas, each with an Icelandic text, and (by the standards of the time) a literal English translation intended to show 'the affinity of the English language with the most pure and original dialect of the Teutonic'.[8] The first of these volumes even provided pronunciation hints for those wishing to develop their knowledge of 'Islandic'. Johnstone had also produced a quarto volume, dedicated to the Foreign Secretary,[9] containing extracts from eight sagas or related historical works, all illuminating 'the descents made by the northern nations upon the British isles'.[10] These volumes, published in Copenhagen, achieved some currency in Britain and also found a place in Scott's capacious library.[11]

It was, however, to the well-thumbed pages of Torfaeus, Bartholin and Olaus Magnus that Scott was to turn for old northern literary materials when he decided to create a novel out of his mind's-eye recollections of Orkney and Shetland which he had visited briefly in 1814.[12] In *The Pirate* he created a late seventeenth-century fictional world in which the islands' Viking past still resonated powerfully amongst the locals. Several of Scott's characters became the imaginary companions of successive generations of Victorian readers as *The Pirate* became the first and remained the favourite old northern novel written in English during the nineteenth century. It offered British readers their first opportunity to engage with the world of Viking-age sea-kings in any sort of three-dimensional and extended literary form. It was also the first time that such Viking images were exposed to sustained critical scrutiny.

There was no greater early nineteenth-century devotee of the novels of 'Sir

---

5   [Jamieson R.] 1814, 237.
6   Grímur Thorkelin 1788.
7   Johnstone 1780 [ii]; see also Johnstone 1782a, 111 and Cowan 1972, 116.
8   Johnstone 1780 [ii].
9   The Marquis of Carmarthen. Johnstone 1782a was dedicated to Archibald Macdonald, MP for 'Newcastle under Line [sic]', whose medieval ancestors allegedly had links with the Hebrides.
10 Johnstone 1782a, vii
11 [Cochrane 1838], 64.
12 Scott 1982.

Valter Skott' than Þorleifur Repp, and he made no secret as to which was his favourite by referring to Scott not as 'The Author of *Waverley*', but as 'The Author of *The Pirate*'.[13] Repp was a shrewd judge of Scott's methods and achievement:

> he would seldom think of introducing Scandinavian letters in their primitive state without those ornamental additions which his powerful imagination so readily suggested or those decorations his art alone could arrange with so much taste and discretion – being born a protector of northern arts and letters he would not play the part of a mere usher.[14]

Much the same thing could be said about Repp himself. His own involvement with the old north was just as passionate and a good deal better informed than Scott's, and had a significant influence within and beyond educated society in Edinburgh. As a innovative and enterprising lecturer and teacher, as a collector and curator of Icelandic manuscripts, and as a pioneering runologist, Repp won a loyal following amongst early nineteenth-century Edinburgh intellectuals, though his superiors in the Advocates' Library were soon biting the carpet as they discovered that their new appointee was as difficult to have dealings with as the feistiest saga hero. He attached great importance to improving British access to old Icelandic texts and traditions. James Johnstone had sensed this need in the 1780s, but philology made great strides over the following four decades thanks to the work of Sir William Jones, Jakob and Wilhelm Grimm, and Rasmus Rask; and Repp sought to exploit those advances pedagogically.

New Philology

A new philology emerged in the early decades of the nineteenth century which drew attention to previously unrecognised patterns and systems behind the buzz and flux of world languages.[15] Interpretation of the new evidence raised fundamental cultural and political questions. Firstly, the authority and prestige previously ascribed to Greek and Latin – parent figures watching over unruly younger European languages – was challenged by the discovery of Sanskrit, a language older than either Greek or Latin. Under the revised developmental model proposed by the new philologists, Latin and Greek took their place alongside rather than towering over other tongues, all siblings of a lost Indo-European parent language, whose oldest surviving incarnation was Sanskrit. By challenging the existing Graeco-Roman linguistic (and cultural) hegemony, the new philology encouraged the investigation and celebration of other literatures and cultures previously deemed barbaric by classically trained chroniclers and

---

13 In Repp's review of Schöning 1777–1826, in Lbs. ÍB 90c fol. On Repp's philological career in Scotland, see Wawn 1991a.
14 Lbs. ÍB 90c fol.
15 Aarsleff 1983, 115–211; Lönnroth 1988, Lundgreen-Nielsen 1994, Dubozy 1998, Wolf 1998.

scholars – Viking-age literature and culture, for example. Old habits of deference were to die hard (if at all – especially in England), but new philologists claimed that there was now no reason for Anglo-Saxon or Old Icelandic literature, or for dialectal forms derived from these sources, to feel inferior in the presence of Graeco-Roman texts or vocabulary. Each language and literature, ancient and modern, could now find a new and respected place within a revised cultural world order; each was worthy of investigation and codification.

Yet, along with a revised cultural world order, there were implications for the political order of Europe and Scandinavia. Rasmus Rask, Scandinavia's leading early nineteenth-century philologist, and as patriotic as the next Dane, objected strongly to the inclusion of Scandinavian languages among J.C. Adelung's list of 'germanische Sprachen'.[16] Rask identified grammatical features of Scandinavian languages – suffixed definite articles, middle voice verbs, and infinitives ending in a vowel – which had no parallels in Germanic languages. Rask prefered the generic term 'gotisk'. Finding compromise impossible, the brothers Grimm settled on 'deutsch', a term if anything more offensive to the Scandinavians than 'germanisch'. A rising tide of German nationalism, all the stronger because there was no German nation, only a language-defined 'Volk', nourished this debate. Both sides were aware of the implications. If modern Scandinavia languages were fundamentally 'germanisch' or 'deutsch', then what about old northern literature and mythology? And, come to that, what about the Scandinavian countries themselves, particularly those areas such as Danish Slesvig-Holsten which bordered Prussia; ought they not to be more formally incorporated into a greater Germany? And what about Britain? As we shall see, the Hanoverian royal family and its supporters were very comfortable with celebrating Britain's 'Anglo-Saxon' (Grimm's preferred term) pre-Conquest heritage; but there were others, not least those living in old Danelaw areas, who abhorred the Germanisation by stealth of English culture, and sought rather to trace Victorian imperial and industrial power to the long-lasting effects of Scando-Anglian blood coursing through British veins, thanks to the Viking invasions.

Þorleifur Repp not only found an aesthetic beauty in the new philology,[17] but was anxious to exploit its pedagogical possibilities. If his students could understand the newly-codified phonological and morphological rules, they would cope more securely with the apparently random eccentricities of individual languages. In Repp's unpublished papers we find him labouring mightily to explain the medieval language of his native land by developing a systematic programme of grammatical and textual study – he was certainly the first British-based scholar in the nineteenth century to engage seriously with fundamental pedagogical problems in an Old Icelandic context. Yet Repp also understood better than most the links between philology and politics. He was a friend of the fiery anti-German old northernist George Stephens, and a passionate sup-

[16] Nielsen 1990, 25.
[17] See his tribute to Rask in Lbs. ÍB 89a fol., an outline for a proposed 'Philological Course'; also Axelsen 1996.

porter of the Slesvig-Holsten (not Schleswig Holstein – to use the German spelling was to accept the verdict of the 1864 war) cause.[18]

In the wave of creative scholarly energy (a good deal of it heavily politicised) unleashed by the new philology, many new publications appeared. New grammars,[19] folktale collections,[20] and editions of major individual texts such as the prose and poetic eddas appeared.[21] Translations, syntheses, journal articles and lectures ensured that continental scholarly insights were widely disseminated in Britain.[22] The importance of myths and oral narrative tradition was recognised, and (following the example of the Grimms) tales and traditions were systematically collected. The heroic age of philology had arrived, and there was no turning the clock back, even if some antiquarians continued to prefer the sundial. As we shall see in our examination of the work of Samuel Laing, George Dasent and George Stephens (Chapters 4, 6, 8), and of the British reception of *Frithiofs saga* (Chapter 5), the political implications of the new philology run like a steel thread through much Victorian old northernism.

Colin Kidd[23] has identified a new philological context within which the old northern writings of Scott and Repp can be read. He argues that the cultivation of Anglo-Saxon and Old Norse antiquity in enlightenment Scotland served to delay the development of a firmly focused Scottish nationalism. Many intellectuals, influenced by philologists as well as historians, came to believe that Scotland's principal cultural identity lay in its Caledonian lowland links with some broader international Teutonic racial community, whether defined as Scandinavian or Anglo-Saxon. This belief led often to the sentimentalisation or denigration of Gaelic culture. Certainly Scott's novelistic fascination with the old north and with the Scottish highlands yielded ultimately to his unionist beliefs. Repp is much less easily classified: an enthusiastic reader of German philology and theology, an Icelandic Anglophile supporting Slesvig-Holsten, a believer in unique philological links between Iceland and Scotland, and, for ten years, a Gaelic-reading Edinburgh resident, with a leading Gaelic lexicographer as a close family friend.[24]

The complementary roles of Sir Walter Scott and Þorleifur Repp as nineteenth-century protectors and ushers of the old north are the focus of this chapter. Scott died in 1832, and Repp returned permanently to Copenhagen in the year of Victoria's accession. Scott's old northern legacy was *Harold the Dauntless*, a spirited narrative poem set in Viking times; an insightful précis of *Eyrbyggja saga*;[25] essays on demonology and witchcraft which draw on Scandi-

---

18 See below, Chapter 8.
19 Rask 1811, Grimm 1819–37.
20 Grimm 1812–15, Arwidsson 1834–42.
21 Grimm 1815, Rask 1818c, 1818d.
22 Arsleff 1983, Wiley 1990.
23 Kidd 1995.
24 On all these aspects, see Wawn 1991.
25 [Jamieson R.] 1814 475–513. Originally intending to produce a précis of *Hervarar saga*, he

navian sources;[26] and two novels with a significant Scandinavian colouring to them: *The Pirate* and *Count Robert of Paris*, the latter a tale of life in the Varangian guard in Constantinople. Repp, through his journalism and other published papers,[27] through his *Laxdæla* translation[28] and one other book-length study,[29] and through his teaching, encouraged the old northern spirit to reach out from Edinburgh to antiquarians in middle England and (even) to politicians in Whitehall. He also shared Scott's fascination with ancient Orkney and Shetland, and would have relished the enthusiastic (though, alas, wholly ill-informed) involvement of his long-time Edinburgh friend Ralph Carr in interpreting the Maeshowe runes in Orkney after their discovery in 1861.[30]

Competition amongst Pirates

Turning the pages of *The Pirate*, Repp must have appreciated at once that he was being exposed to a different old north from that of eighteenth-century scholarly and popular tradition. Though, in his construction of post-medieval Orkney and Shetland, Scott draws on mythological images and disembodied presences with which readers of Percy and Gray had been familiar for half a century, the novel is also packed with artefacts, songs, folk-customs, Viking-age saints, dialectal voices, place-names, and identifiable locations in the northern islands. This three-dimensional quality had not been a feature of previous old northern works in English.

The Pirate certainly needed all the imaginative energy that Scott could summon up for it. Any novel bearing such a title faced stiff competition in the 1820's. There were dozens of swashbuckling heroes, skulls, crossbones, parrots and peg-legs vying for the reader's or theatre-goer's attention. If Scott's *The Pirate* was not to walk the critical plank in a crowded market place, its piracy needed a fresh spin. Scott had developed some of the elements he was looking for – a big theme and an old northern lore context – in *Harold the Dauntless* (1817).[31] This lengthy narrative poem tells of a battle of wills between the venerable Norse King Witikind, a Christian convert, and Harold, his hot-headed pagan son. Distraught at his father's conversion and betrayal of Viking ideals, Harold leaves home. On his travels he seeks to marry the princess Metelill who is already betrothed to an English lord; the girl's father is appalled by the bar-

found the popularity of 'The Waking of Angantyr' daunting, and chose *Eyrbyggja saga* instead: Harvey Wood 1972, II 487–8, note 7. See also D'Arcy and Wolf 1987, a strangely unsympathetic account.

26 Scott 1830.
27 As in Repp 1831 [1853 (for 1845–9)]; Repp and Jón Sigurðsson 1854.
28 Repp 1826.
29 Repp 1832. Wiley 1981, 268 cites J.M. Kemble's belief that Repp and C.C. Rafn had taken over Cleasby's papers, with a view to completing the Dictionary.
30 Carr 1868, Barnes 1993.
31 Scott 1904, 517–52.

barity of this unwelcome new suitor. Harold also encounters the ghost of his father, tormented by his son's pagan ways. Chancing upon the princess's wedding procession, Harold kills her father and only the intervention of Harold's loyal servant saves the bridegroom. In a further nightmarish vision, Harold then sees the region of death where preparations for his arrival are well in hand. He finally confronts and destroys the Odinic spirit ruling over the region. His servant proves to be a disguised and desirable Danish maiden whom Harold marries on the day of his own conversion to Christianity. Witikind may now rest in peace.

With its narrative exoticism, diversity of mood, and metrical versatility the poem exhibits some of the qualities which were to win Victorian popularity for both Tegnér's *Frithiofs saga* and Longfellow's 'Saga of King Olaf'. More immediately, several features of 'Harold' anticipate important elements in *The Pirate*: the inset songs; the supernatural scenes (visits to sacrificial shrines, fateful visions, talking trees, bizarre transformations); the variety of character and type-scenes with wild-eyed sibyls, repressive father figures, loyal retainers, quests and feasts. Thematically, there are clashes between romantic individualism and patriarchal authority (both secular and sacred), and between indigenous and invasive cultural values; and, not least, we find a rite of passage pattern as an adolescent overcomes his infatuation with destructive Viking values. The hero's stumbling progress towards maturity in Christian marriage is the controlling idea of the poem.

In Outline

When Scott came to put novelistic flesh on the bare bones of his Orcadian pirate legend, it was these elements from *Harold the Dauntless* – several of them also featuring in his 1813 précis of *Eyrbyggja saga* – which he sought to redeploy.[32] They helped him to construct the narrative platform on which he could dramatise the life and times of John Gow (or Goffe), a notorious early eighteenth-century pirate in north Atlantic waters. In that recreative process Scott rejects South Seas piratical settings in favour of bleak northern localism; he makes use of his accumulated store of island lore and legend; he finds ways of debating cultural tensions on several levels; and, not least, he enjoys crumbling through his fingers all the specialised vocabulary of island life: the avers, bee-skeps, caterans, drammocks, freits, guisards, hasps, jougs, lums, maskingfats, nowts, overlays, partans, rottons, skudlers, thiggers, voes, wadmaal and yaggers. In Scott's hands these elements added up to a good deal more than just another formulaic pirate yarn.

The novel's shape resembles that of a medieval bridal-quest romance such as *Sir Degaré*, a fourteenth-century English tale with which Scott seems to have

---

32 Signed October 1813: [Jamieson R.] 1814, 513. The elements include the yuletide feast, supernatural incidents, berserker values, due process of law, a pagan temple, and stone circles.

been familiar.[33] The young hero Mordaunt Mertoun needs first to find out who his parents are – and who they are not – before marrying one of the two daughters of the worthy Orcadian udaller Magnus Troil. He chooses Brenda, the fair-haired daughter of sense, rather than Minna, the raven-haired child of sensibility, the 'beautiful enthusiast' whose heart is set on marrying a latter-day Viking sea-king. Throughout the novel we follow the efforts of the mysterious matriarch Norna of the Fitful Head, well meaning but muddled soothsayer to the gullible, to contrive a marriage between Minna and Mordaunt, in the mistaken belief that the latter is her son by a brief and ill-starred union with Basil Mertoun. By the end of the novel Norna learns that her real son by Basil Mertoun is Clement Cleveland,[34] the charismatic pirate captain, rescued from drowning by Mordaunt, and before long his rival for Minna's affections; it is this liaison which she has sought to overturn at every stage. *The Pirate* is a romance, and its young folk need to mature and make their own decisions, with the consent of parents who themselves have lessons to learn: Magnus Troil, for example, needs to reconcile himself to having an Anglo-Spanish rather than a Shetland-Scandinavian son-in-law.

There was plenty for any thoughtful nineteenth-century reader to ponder in the novel: the clash between patriarchal benevolence (Magnus Troil) and individualistic capitalism (Triptolemus Yellowley, the meddling agrarian 'improver' from England); the exploration of gender roles and sibling rivalries (Brenda versus Minna; Clement versus Mordaunt); the universalising force of the text's interlaced historical layerings (prehistoric monuments, Viking-age sea-kings, saga-age saints, seventeenth-century poets, eighteenth-century brigands, and, ultimately, nineteenth-century ploughs); notions of nation and nationhood (Orkney vs Shetland; Orkney and Shetland vs Scotland; Orkney, Shetland and Scotland vs England); the interface between cultural margins and centres of authority (the North Atlantic islands vs mainland Britain; pirate ships vs the British navy; witchcraft and the supernatural vs scientific rationalism); atmospheric Gothicism (Norna of the Fitful Head and her Dunrossness retreat; the eery Stones of Stenness; the shadowy aisles of the St Magnus Cathedral at Kirkwall; the 'dreadful' storms and 'hideous combustions of the elements'); and dialectal and idiolectal variety (from Bryce Snailsfoot to Barbara Yellowley; from Captain Goffe to Lady Glowrowrum).

---

[33] Mitchell 1987, 3, 12, 25.

[34] Believing Norna to be dead, Basil left Orkney with their son Clement. Basil later married a Spanish woman, with whom he had another son, Mordaunt. After killing his wife, Basil moved on, and left Mordaunt at an English school in Port Royal. In due time Basil and Clement became corsairs, and were eventually left for dead by their respective rebellious crews. Basil resumes contact with Mordaunt, and the two make for the Shetlands.

Dressing the Set

The novel's densely woven old northern texture is high amongst the qualities which won for *The Pirate* a dedicated Victorian readership. The first three chapters reveal some of the elements involved. The first page confronts the reader with Jarlshof, now the joyless retreat of the desiccated Basil Mertoun but once the busy home of some 'Norwegian chief' or 'ancient earl of the Orkneys'.[35] We learn about udal tenure in Old Norwegian law, as enjoyed by Magnus Troil the local patriarch, and note how it contrasts with the feudal tenure later introduced from alien Scotland. The Troil family tenure is traced back to the days of Turf-Einar which, as readers of Torfæus's *Orcades* or Jónas Jónsson's 1780 edition of *Orkneyinga saga* would know, meant very early indeed;[36] Magnus himself is often referred to as a descendant of the early Norse earls. The northern laws of conviviality, also 'ancient', are the yardstick against which household hospitality is measured. Shetland women are immediately characterised as 'fair-haired and blue-eyed daughters of Thule', even though their most passionate old northern soul, Minna the daughter of Magnus Troil, has jet black hair. The old northern names of the Shetlandic locals (Magnus Troil, Sweyn Erickson) tell their own tale. We hear frequently of the local saints – Ronald (Jarl Rǫgnvaldr kali), Olaf (Ólafr Haraldsson, King of Norway) and Magnus the martyr (Jarl Magnús Erlendsson). We also meet Basil Mertoun's son Mordaunt who learned old northern ballads from Swertha, the aged Jarlshof housekeeper; her repertoire had also included 'dismal tales concerning the Trows or Drows (the dwarfs of the Scalds)',[37] creatures with which 'superstitious eld' had peopled every cavern and valley in Shetland. Scott's appendix informs his readers that the Drows are the successors of the diminutive old northern *dvergar*, most powerful at midnight, famed as artificers in metal.[38] Any keen late Victorian reader moved to check *dvergar* in the Cleasby-Gudbrand Vigfusson *Icelandic-English Dictionary* (1874) would immediately find there a reference to the Dwarfie Stone in Scott's *Pirate* – the novel was more than once cited in this great work of reference.[39]

It is in the first three chapters, too, that we meet the 'berserkars'. The *OED* cites Scott's novel as the first instance of the term's use, though it was employed several times by old northern scholars during the previous decade, and evidence of familiarity with the phenomenon dates back to the 1770s. In his 1811 Pre-

35 Scott 1822/1996, 8 (ch. 1).
36 Þormóður Torfason 1697, 18; Jónas Jónsson 1780, 2 and Sig. Bbbb2v. Einarr, son of Norwegian jarl Rǫgnvaldr, cleared the Orkneys of Danish Vikings, and was the first man to use turf (peat) as fuel. King Haraldr Fine-hair imposed a fine on the islands, which Einarr paid on condition that the udallers would grant him freehold of their lands.
37 Scott 1822/1996, 15–16 (ch. 2).
38 Ibid., 349 (note H to ch. 10).
39 Guðbrandur contrasts the Icelandic folk belief in the good luck attending the rescue of a drowning man, with Mordaunt's rescue of Cleveland in *The Pirate*: annotation to Jón Árnason 1862–4 (GV copy in Turville-Petre room, English Faculty Library, Oxford University).

liminary Dissertation, Henry Holland uses the terms 'berserkir' and 'berserkine' interchangeably, and, drawing on Jón Eiríksson's Latin treatise published as part of the 1773 Copenhagen edition of *Kristni saga*,[40] describes the wild men of battle thus:

> The Berserkir were wrestlers or warriors by profession, who were believed by magical means to have hardened their bodies, so that they could not be injured by fire or sword. These men, roused at times by their incantations into a sort of phrenzy, committed every species of brutal violence; rushed naked into battle, and overpowered and slew all who ventured to approach them; till, deserted by the paroxysm, their supernatural strength left them, and they immediately sunk into a state of extreme debility and wretchedness.[41]

Though Holland claims that belief in the 'Berserkine' disappeared along with other forms of magic and divination, his scientist's mind comes up with a plausible pyschological explanation for the behaviour long before the advent of group-bonding sessions by modern sportsmen and business executives. Sir Walter Scott's 1813 *Eyrbyggja saga* abstract reveals his own interest in the phenomenon:

> [there were] remarkable champions, called Berserkir, men, who, by moral or physical excitation of some kind or other, were wont to work themselves into a state of frenzy, during which they achieved deeds passing human strength, and rushed, without sense of danger, or feeling of pain, upon every species of danger that could be opposed to them; . . . these champions . . . unless . . . seized with their fits of fury, were not altogether discourteous or evil-disposed. But as any contradiction was apt to excite their stormy passions, their company could not be called very safe or commodious.[42]

Here the berserkers seem to have risen in status. They are now 'remarkable champions', a term used elsewhere by Scott as a synonym for his Viking seakings. Their frenzied feats seem more a source of wonder than rebuke; their naked brutalism has been replaced by the idea that, in between fits, they were capable of behaving normally.

In *The Pirate* we learn that the wild men were part of Mordaunt Merton's imaginative inheritance. The term is used three times in the second chapter alone: as a child he enjoyed berserker tales even more than 'the classic fables of antiquity'. We see him signalling the intensity of his father's legendary temper in berserkine terms (Scott adds a rationalising footnote about the possible psycho-

---

[40] Hannes Finnson 1773, 142–63.
[41] Mackenzie 1812, 40, 449–50.
[42] [Jamieson R.] 1814, 489. Henderson 1819 cites the same description; and Percy 1859, 517–40 reprints the Scott précis including the berserker material, with editorial annotation by Blackwell.

logical or chemical origins of the condition); and in the intensity of Swertha's credulity we can identify the ultimate source of Mordaunt's fascination:

> ay, ay . . . the Berserkars were champions who lived before the blessed days of St Olàve and who used to run like madmen on swords, and spears, and harpoons, and muskets, and snap them all to pieces, as a finner would go through a herring-net, and then, when the fury went off, they were as weak and unstable as water.
>
> (16; ch. 2)

It is in the novel's first three chapters, too, that we learn of the racial and cultural links uniting the indigenous population, such as the common celebration of '*Ioul*, the highest festival of the Goths' (22; ch. 2). We also note the power of oral tradition amongst the fishermen in preserving 'the old Norwegian sagas' (18; ch. 2) and, most striking of all, for the first time in the nineteenth-century literature of the old north, we find a sustained romantic identification between ancient saga and modern saga-stead. Of Mordaunt it is said that:

> Often the scenes around him were assigned as the localities of wild poems, which, half recited, half chanted, by voices as hoarse, if not so loud, as the waves over which they floated, pointed out the very bay on which they sailed as the scene of a bloody sea fight; the scarce-seen heap of stones that bristled over the projecting cape, as the dun, or castle, of some potent earl or noted pirate; the distant and solitary grey stone on the lonely moor, as marking the grave of a hero; the wild cavern, up which the sea rolled in heavy, broad and unbroken billows, as the dwelling of some noted sorceress. (Ibid.)

Scott's most opulent Johnsonian manner underlines what was to become a major Victorian preoccupation. Moreover, at the end of the sentence the reader is directed to an intriguing tale that Scott heard during his 1814 visit. The story goes that when Gray's 'Fatal Sisters' poem first reached Orkney, some elderly folk needed to hear only a few verses before announcing confidently that 'they knew the song well in the Norse language . . . they called it the Magicians, or the Enchantress'. Scott is speaking no more than the truth when he adds that 'it would have been singular news to the elegant translator . . . to have learned that the Norse original was still preserved by tradition in . . . those remote isles at the beginning of the eighteenth century' (345–6; Note C).

Filigree and Motifs

Inevitably this density of old northern colouring in the novel is not sustained once Minna's disillusionment with Clement Cleveland, her Norse sea-king reincarnate, and Cleveland's impatience with his admirer's naive credulity have both been established, and once old northern dreams have yielded to harsh modern scrutiny. Up to that point, however, there is plenty of filigree detail, as well as more ambitious scenes based on old northern models. Amongst the smallest-scale detail we may include the resemblance between Magnus Troil's handwriting and runic script; the threat posed to native weights and measures by those from the mainland; the use of Hjaltland as the more correct old northern name for the Shetland islands; and the numerous incidental references to pagan deities as well as local Christian saints – Odin rubs shoulders with St Olav, Thor's hammer shares the limelight with the bones and beaker of St Magnus.[43] As with the Thomas Gray references,[44] we find another of Scott's scholarly sources reappearing within the fictional framework. Magnus Troil reads (or, more accurately, is reduced to looking at the woodcuts in) Norna's copy of the Latin text of Olaus Magnus's *Historia de gentibus septentrionalibus*,[45] the same work which Scott cites in his note on King Erik of Sweden when explaining Basil Mertoun's belief in Norna of the Fitful Head's ability to sell favourable winds to anxious mariners, a gift she shared with the Swedish monarch.[46]

Creative philology could also provide authenticating detail. Minna Troil makes clear her identification with the tempestuous spirits, both male and female, of the Viking age. Neither Sir George Mackenzie's demure Helga, or (as we shall see) Tegnér's dutiful Ingeborg would have measured up to her exacting standards:

> I am a daughter of the old dames of Norway, who could send their lovers to battle with a smile, and slay them with their own hands, if they returned with dishonour. My lover must scorn the mockeries by which our degraded race strive for distinction, or must practise them only in sport, and in earnest of nobler dangers. No whale-striking, bird-nesting favourite for me; my lover must be a Sea-king, or what else modern times may give that draws near to that lofty character.
>
> (170; ch. 20)

The sea-kings are the 'flaxen-haired Kempions of the North' (46; ch. 5), with Scott underlining cultural links not with the Old French *champion* but rather with the Old Icelandic *kempa*, whose deeds are the stuff of E.J. Björner's *Nordiska kämpa dater* (1737), with its legendary tales of the Vǫlsungs, Ragnarr, Hrólfr kraki and Friðþjófr – as ever, there was a copy at Abbotsford.[47] Scott aligns 'sea-king' with 'Kiempe, or a Vi-king',[48] thereby making his own early contribution to nineteenth-century confusion on the etymology of the word. Did it derive from *wig-cyng*, 'war-king', or *wic-ing*, 'a *Pirate* that runneth from creeke to creeke'?[49] Sharon Turner hedges his bets – his Vikings were 'kings of the bays';[50] as does George Stephens – '*Vik-ingr*, Bay-Boy or War-Boy'.[51] Later

[43] Scott 1822/1996, 136 (ch. 16), 241 (ch. 29), 244 (ch. 30) and passim.
[44] See for, example, ibid. 172 (ch. 21).
[45] Ibid., 237 (ch. 29); see Foote 1996–8.
[46] Scott 1822/1996, 347–8, note E, p. 60; also Seaton 1935, 308–9; Scott 1982, 74–5.
[47] Cochrane 1838, 99.
[48] Scott 1822/1996, 170 (ch. 20).
[49] Fell 1987, 116; citation from 1610.
[50] Turner 1823, I 440 [4th ed.].
[51] Stephens 1839, 300.

in the century Guðbrandur Vigfússon and York Powell favour 'men of *the* bay [Skagerrak]' for their 'wickings'.[52] Stephens distinguishes between sea-kings and Vikings in a way that Minna Troil would have appreciated. A sea-king was:

> a Chief, generally of royal birth, who had no kingdom to inherit at home, and therefore sought one on the waters. Higher in title than the vikings, they were also commonly at the head of much more powerful fleets. Every Sea-King was a viking, but the reverse was only occasionally the case.[53]

Sharon Turner also touches on the theme of inherited wealth: old sea-kings would bury their treasures rather than pass them on to the next generation, 'that their offspring might be driven by necessity to engage in the conflicts, and to participate the glory of maritime piracy . . . that affluence only was esteemed which danger had endeared'.[54] Consideration of the modern implications of such inheritance customs featured prominently in Victorian discussion of the old north.

The ubiquitous presence of Norna of the Fitful Head in *The Pirate* is a further reminder of Scott's fondness for old northern neologism and nomenclature. Her role in the story is bound up with her name, 'which signifies one of those fatal sisters who weave the web of human fate' (47; ch. 5); and her eventual ineffectiveness serves only to confirm the folly of projecting old northern dreams onto post-medieval realities. In the early part of the novel Norna clashes with Triptolemus Yellowley, the comic 'Clod-compeller' (149; ch. 18), the intrusive mainland technocrat on an island of Viking memories. If the men of Thule no longer aspire to be champions, the spae-wife will show that 'the women have not forgotten the arts that lifted them of yore into queens and prophetesses' (46; ch. 5). Her appearance is that of some prototypical Nordic Lady of Shalotte: the wadmal upper garment, 'then much used in the Zetland Islands, as also in Iceland and Norway' (47; ch. 5), the silver girdle stamped with planetary signs, and the runic staff with calendar markings clearly visible. Norna is responsible for the first of the dozen old northern songs in the novel that subsequently enjoyed an independent life in Victorian editions of Scott's poetry. She pays for reluctantly offered hospitality with a gold coin bearing 'the rude and half-defaced effigies of some ancient northern king' (53; ch. 6). George Hickes had drawn the attention of British scholars to the historical interest of such coins; Scott removes them from the museum and momentarily restores their value as living currency. Norna's credentials as a latter-day Valkyrie are defined in terms recalling Thomas Gray: '[Norna looked at Mordaunt] with such sad and severe eyes, as those with which the Fatal Virgins, who, according to northern mythology, were called the *Valkyriur,* or "Choosers of the Slain,"

---

[52] Gudbrand Vigfusson and Powell 1883, I lxiii–iv.
[53] Stephens 1839, 288.
[54] Turner 1823, I 439

were supposed to regard the young champions whom they selected to share the banquet of Odin' (84; ch. 10).

Other authenticating detail in the novel derives from the description of real or imagined local customs, over which a light old northern wash has been sprayed. Shetland festivities mimic those of Valhǫll. The guests at Magnus Troil's great feast follow Odinic banqueting practice, while the individual responsible for preparing the libations earns the nickname Eric Punch-maker, in the same way, the reader is assured, as 'Rollo the Walker' [Gǫngu Hrólfr] earned his nickname in Viking times. The drinkers included a group of old men with 'shaggy hair and beards . . . cultivated after the ancient Norwegian fashion' (121; ch. 14). The entertainment is chiefly in the hands of a minstrel called Claude Halcro, who claims direct descent from 'Hacon Goldemund' (105; ch. 12), allegedly King Harald Fairhair's principal skald during his time in Orkney – there was never a skald of that name but who amongst Troil's guests or Scott's readers would notice? Halcro also claimed to have been a close colleague of John Dryden, a detail probably attributable to Scott's wish to squeeze one last drop from the scholarly sponge, having previously edited Dryden's poetry and written about his life.[55]

The songs of Halcro the skald (such as 'The Song of Harold Harfager') con-tribute to the debate about the old northern heroic life which is conducted in a variety of forms throughout the novel. There were those in Halcro's audience who had seen service not in the crowded coffee houses of London, but on bloody seventeenth-century British battlefields – ' "I know what war is," said an old man' (124; ch. 15). Untouched by such scepticism, Halcro's dreams of Viking conquest match those of Minna, and his exasperation at modern-day degeneracy is as strong as Norna's: 'now the descendants of Sea-Kings, and Champions and Berserkars, are become as incapable of using their swords, as if they were so many women' (123; ch. 15).

We can also discern in the novel the first significant glimmerings of Victorian fascination with the great Viking longships. Up to Scott's time the old north had been presented in largely landlocked terms. With the exception of James Johnstone's *Norwegian Account of Haco's Expedition against Scotland; A.D. 1263*, eighteenth-century texts and popular traditions featured a good deal of land-based conflict and indoor feasting (on earth or in Valhǫll). Johnstone knew about 'sea-kings',[56] and William Motherwell reflected on the different life await-ing Egill Skallagrímsson's new bride – the 'land-maiden' will become 'Queen of the sea', 'the bark of a sea king' will be her palace, with 'mad waves and winds' for her true subjects.[57] It was, however, Scott who lent lasting glamour to the

---

[55] Scott 1808.

[56] Johnstone 1782b, 111.

[57] 'The Wooing Song of Jarl Egill Skallagrim' in Motherwell 1832, 22–29. In the poem the hero loves his sword like a sibling, and learns his fate from the weird sisters after a visit to the under-world.

nomadic life of the sea-borne Viking. Claude Halcro's old northern dreams were nourished by the spray of the sea and not by the stench of stockfish:

> Ah . . . I would it were possible to see our barks, once the water-dragons of the world, swimming with the black raven standard waving at the topmast, and their decks glimmering with arms, instead of being heaped up with stockfish – winning with our fearless hands what the niggard soil denies – paying back all old scorn and modern injury – reaping where we never sowed, and felling what we never planted – living and laughing through the world, and smiling when we were summoned to quit it. (124; ch. 15)

Halcro and Minna Troil may be excused their fantasies when, within eighteen months of the publication of *The Pirate*, a scholar like Sharon Turner saw fit to devote the purplest passages of his lengthy study of the Anglo-Saxons to the same sea-born 'petty Neptunes':

> The sea-kings of the North were a race of beings whom Europe beheld with horror. Without a yard of territorial property, without any towns or visible nation, with no wealth but their ships, no force but their crews, no hope but from their swords, the sea-kings swarmed on the boisterous ocean, and plundered in every district they could approach. Never to sleep under a smoky roof, nor to indulge in the cheerful cup over a hearth, were the boasts of these watery sovereigns.[58]

Famous Viking sea-voyages such as that of Friðþjófr, the son of Þorsteinn Víkingsson,[59] sustained the idea which, by Carlyle's time, had acquired a rich complexity. The Norse sea-king represents a noble emanation of some divine Odinic energy; his sturdy simplicity contrasts favourably with the lofty dilettantism of the Greeks; and his spirit lives on in the world's greatest navy and nation:

> In the old Sea-Kings too, what an indomitable rugged energy! Silent, with closed lips, as I fancy them, unconscious that they were specially brave; defying the wild ocean with its monsters, and all men and things; – progenitors of our own Blakes and Nelsons! No Homer sang these Norse Sea-kings; but Agamemnon's was a small audacity, and of small fruit in the world, to some of them; – to . . . Hrolf, or Rollo Duke of Normandy, the wild Sea-King, has a share in governing England at this hour.[60]

It was no wonder that Clement Cleveland was anxious to end his days in receipt of the sovereign's commission. Dragon-headed barques can be found on book covers for the rest of the century. Readers of the story of King Ólafr Tryggvason, whether in Samuel Laing's translation of the medieval saga, or

---

58 Turner 1823, I 435 [4th ed.]
59 See below, Chapter 5.
60 Carlyle 1897, V 32.

Longfellow's poetic paraphrase,[61] could follow the construction of one such mighty vessel. The discovery of the Gokstad ship in 1880 confirmed excitingly all the literary representations.[62] It may be no surprise that these ships continue to feature on the spines of a prestigious series of saga editions in Iceland a century and more later;[63] but how many owners of Rover cars in Britain and Europe have noticed the Viking ship logo on the front of their cars? The origins of the company belong to the early years of the present century, when post-Victorian fascination with the Viking age still had quite a few gallons left in its tank.

Questions of Language

In *The Pirate* one of the many tensions between old Shetland and the alien culture of the south is Magnus Troil's impatience with Triptolemus's fondness for citing Greek proverbs: 'no one shall speak any other language here, save honest Norse, jolly Dutch, or Danske, or broad Scots, at the least of it' (136; ch. 16). The philological background to this momentary indignation is dense and exerts an important influence on the cultivation of old northern antiquity throughout the nineteenth century. In 1808 John Jamieson's *An Etymological Dictionary of the Scottish Language* was published, whose origins can be traced to Grímur Thorkelin's visit to Scotland in the late 1780s.[64] Prior to meeting Thorkelin at this time, Jamieson

> had held the common opinion, that the Scottish is not a language, and nothing more than a corrupt dialect of the English, or at least of the Anglo-Saxon. It was the learned Danish Professor that first undeceived him . . . and proved . . . that there are many words in our national tongue which had never passed through the channel of the Anglo-Saxon, nor been spoken in England. Before leaving . . . Thor[k]elin requested the Doctor to note down for him all the singular words used in that part of the country [Angus and Sutherland], no matter how vulgar he might himself consider them, and to give the received meaning of each.

Roused by Jamieson's claim that such forms were 'merely corruptions of English', Thorkelin replied indignantly

> If that *fantast*, [Dr Samuel] Johnson, had said so, I would have forgiven *him*, because of his ignorance or prejudice; but I cannot make the same excuse for you . . . I have spent four months in Angus and Sutherland, and I have met with between three and four hundred words purely Gothic, that were never used in Anglo-Saxon. You will admit that I am pretty well acquainted with Gothic. I am a

---

61 See below, Chapter 4.
62 Nicolaysen 1882.
63 Íslenzk fornrit.
64 Benedikz 1970.

Goth; a native of Iceland . . . All or most of these words which I have noted down, are familiar to me in my native island .[65]

The Scots language was, thus, to be viewed as a separate tongue that had 'never passed through the channel of the Anglo-Saxon', and whose origins lay in the Pictish language. Pictish, in turn, was to be understood as a Scandinavian dialect introduced to Scotland in the most exotic of circumstances. Scythian migrants had made their way into Europe, where they became known to the Romans as Piki, Peohtas, Pehts, Pihts, or other related forms – derivations from the past participle of Latin *pingo*, 'to paint', and referring to the habit of warriors painting their bodies in order to appear more warlike. Climatic variation produced consonantal changes. John Pinkerton, a philological berserker if ever there was one, describes the process:

> This seems a remarkable instance of the effect of climate upon language; for P and W are the most open of the labial letters; and V is the most shut. The former requires an open mouth; the latter may be pronounced with the mouth almost closed, which rendered it an acceptable substitute in the cold clime of Scandinavia, where the people delighted, as they still delight, in gutturals and dentals. The climate rendered their organs rigid and contracted; and the cold made them keep their mouths as shut as possible.[66]

In this way Pihts and Peohtas became first Peukini and Piki, and finally Vik(t)s, and the first modern speculative etymology for 'Viking' was born. Moving from Scandinavia to Scotland, the Scythian wanderers were confronted by a milder climate in which their organs grew less rigid and their labials reopened, allowing the frozen Vik(t)s to thaw out into Picts. This is philological Teutonism with a vengeance, with the old northern and modern nationalist wish fathering the linguistic thought.

Read against this background, Magnus Troil's brief outburst against Triptolemus makes some sense. Magnus is tolerant towards the Scots language, with its putative Scandinavian associations, but hostile towards Graeco-Roman culture which he, like John Jamieson initially, associated with Johnsonian England, and hence with alien feudal and commercial attitudes. Yet, as we have noted, by the end of the novel Magnus has to learn to accommodate not only 'broad Scottishness' but also the idea of an Anglo-Spanish son-in-law. The novel reasserts the cross-cultural benefits of union with England. The distance that Minna, too, has to travel in her rite of passage can be measured by her views on political union in the first half of the novel. She believes that Shetland had been united with the wrong land and longs for a return 'to the protection of Denmark, our parent country' (149; ch. 18). She is exasperated by the Orcadian fondness for inter-

---

65 Jamieson 1885, xv. See also Troil 1780, viii.
66 Pinkerton 1789, I 354.

marrying with 'invaders' from Scotland and England, that has deadened their spirits to 'the throb of heroic Norse blood'. Learning the error of her ways proves an uncomfortable experience.

Saga Structures

Scott's confidence in making creative use of his old northern reading can be sensed not just by small-scale scenic colouring, but by the way in which several scenes in *The Pirate* echo (in substance or spirit) old Icelandic sagas known to the novelist. In the first we discover that saga- and edda-stead visiting is not confined to Mordaunt Mertoun. Norna of the Fitful Head can be found explaining to Brenda and Minna how her father's influence lies behind her fondness for the jagged rocks and wild mountains of Shetland rather than the softer outlines of Orkney:

> I learned to visit each lonely barrow – each lofty cairn – to tell its appropriate tale, and to soothe with rhymes in his praise the spirit of the stern warrior who dwelt within. I knew where the sacrifices were made of yore to Thor and to Odin – on what stones the blood of the victims flowed – where stood the dark-browed priest – where the crested chiefs, who consulted the will of the idol – where the more distant crowd of inferior worshippers, who looked on in awe or in terror.
>
> (159; ch. 19)

One particular 'lonely barrow' had excited the young Norna's imagination more than any other – the Dwarfie Stone. James Wright, John Thomas Stanley's 1789 Iceland expedition colleague, describes it as follows:

> we went . . . to see what the inhabitants call the dwarf stone – situated in a Hollow, surrounded on every Hand except to the sea by large heath covered Mountains . . . the most remarkable circumstance with respect to this Stone, is, its being hollowed out into a kind of habitation, consisting of a Bed-place, which is supplied with a stone Pillow, & an Anti-Chamber . . . it has an opening in the Top 3 ft. in diameter, which was certainly intended for the Chimney; this I found an easier place of entrance than the Door of this Lapideous Castle . . . & before it lay, a Stone, by which the inhabitant prevented the access of impertinent intruders; but what would take Ten puny Modern Mortals nowadays to move. It is compos'd of Sand-Stone.[67]

The scientist's measuring stick yields to the sibyl's transforming imagination in Norna's lengthy account of the same spot:

> I was chiefly fond to linger about the Dwarfie Stone, as it is called, a relic of antiquity, which strangers look on with curiosity, and the natives with awe . . . The

---

[67] West 1970–76, I 19–20.

doorway is now open to the weather; but beside it lies a large stone, which, adapted to grooves, still visible in the entrance, once had served to open and to close this extraordinary dwelling, which Trolld, a dwarf famous in the northern Sagas, is said to have framed for his own favourite residence. The lonely shepherd avoids the place, for at sunrise, high noon, or sunset, the misshapen form of the necromantic owner may sometimes be seen sitting by the Dwarfie Stone. I feared not the apparition, for, Minna, my heart was as bold, and my hand was as innocent as yours. In my childish courage, I was even but too presumptuous, and the thirst after things unattainable led me, like our primitive mother, to desire increase of knowledge, even by prohibited means. I longed to possess the power of the Voluspæ and divining women of our ancient race; to wield, like them, command over the elements; and to summon the ghosts of deceased heroes from their caverns, that they might recite their daring deeds, and impart to me their hidden treasures . . . My vain and youthful bosom burned to investigate these and an hundred other mysteries, which the Sagas that I perused, or learned from Erland, rather indicated than explained; and in my daring mood, I called on the Lord of the Dwarfie Stone to aid me in attaining knowledge inaccessible to mere mortals.

(159–60; ch. 19)[68]

All the atmospheric detail is in place: the stones unhewed by earthly hand; the dwarfish inhabitant; the awe of the lonely shepherd; Norna's longing for ancestral powers of divination; and the 'burning' desire for 'inaccessible' knowledge. Yet such images prove to be only the beginning of Norna's Dwarfie Stone experiences. We learn how, seated one day on the stone, she found herself mocking the absence of the presiding deities – 'What are ye now but empty names, / Powerful Trolld, sagacious Haims' (161; ch. 19). Crashing thunder and torrential rain force her to shelter within the stone's inner recesses, where she ponders once more its eerie origins – was it the work of Trolld, the dwarf; or the tomb of a Scandinavian chief; or the last resting-place of some long forgotten anchorite; or even the random construct of a 'wandering mechanic'? Her musings are suddenly interrupted by the gruesome Trolld, speaking 'such language as was spoken in these islands ere Olave planted the cross on the ruins of heathenism' (162; ch. 19). His riddling rhymes offer the promise of awesome powers to control wind and tide, but at a terrible price: she must kill her father – 'reave thy life's giver / Of the gift which he gave'. The dwarf disappears in a cloud of sulphurous smoke recalling the destruction of Loda in *Carric-Thura*. Disturbed by the apparition and at first assigning it to the effects of isolation and over-absorption in runic studies, Norna sought out the company of friends such as Magnus Troil, with whom she fell passionately in love. In the act of eloping with Magnus she closes the door to her father's room, only to learn later of his asphyxiation by a 'suffocating vapour', perhaps from a fire – there is no suggestion of supernatural intervention. This key scene in the novel derives its force

---

68 Scott's first-hand recollections of the stone are reserved for an appendix: Scott 1822/1996 353–4, note L.

from Scott's projection of a folkloristic type-scene with old northern colouring onto a remote island location teeming with antiquarian associations.

Icelandic saga chapter and verse can certainly be found for the fortune-telling scene at Magnus Troil's home. A domestic entertainment is hijacked by Norna, who uses it to promote her dreams of a marriage between Mordaunt and Minna, at a time when her scheming seems threatened by Minna's infatuation with Cleveland the pirate captain. Scott offers two sources for the events depicted. Within the chapter readers are referred (not implausibly) to Thomas Gray's 'other' Norse Ode, 'The Descent of Odin', in which the god journeys deep into Niflheimr to learn from a sibyl the ghastly truths about Baldr's fate and Ásgarðr's future. Scott's end-note, however, confirms that the scene derives from an *Eiríks saga rauða* passage as recorded in Bartholin.[69] With its sources identified, the scene proceeds colourfully. In Magnus Troil's homestead, the assembled revellers, tense with anticipation, find Norna abruptly replacing the local sibyl. She will answer her audience's questions as posed by the inescapable Claude Halcro – how will the fishing go, will Halcro's own rhymes enjoy lasting fame, whose is the pirate ship at Kirkwall and, more problematic, will Brenda and Minna find happiness in love? It is after her slippery answer to this last enquiry that Norna is interrupted by Magnus Troil, and the scene ends.

It comes as no surprise to find Scott adding a dab of philological colour at the point when Norna is ordered to 'come forth of the tent, thou old galdragon' (180; ch. 21). Scott's coinage derives from *galdra-kinn*, (literally) 'spells-cheek'; it was but a short stumble first to **gal-drakinn*, and then to 'galdragon'. Scott first encountered the Icelandic form as Þorgríma the sorceress's nickname in *Eyrbyggja saga* while preparing his 1813 précis, published in Robert Jamieson's *Illustrations of Northern Antiquities*.[70] This volume's principal aim was to highlight Dano-Scottish links, notably in traditional balladry. The atmosphere of linguistic exploration engendered by the theories of John Pinkerton, Grímur Thorkelin, and John and Robert Jamieson may have encouraged Scott's coinages.

In a third *Pirate* scene shaped by old northern narrative we find Norna in a remote churchyard taking a piece of metal from the coffin of a Norse ancestor of Magnus Troil. From it, after much fire kindling and spell chanting, she produces a heart-shaped ingot as a restorative charm for the love-lorn Minna. This may be an echo of the *Hervarar saga* 'Waking of Angantyr' scene in which Hervor retrieves an ancestral sword from her father's grave. Scott grafts the 'grave visit' motif onto a Shetland folk tradition about spells used to cure 'the fatal disorder called the loss of a heart' (236; ch. 28). Scott certainly knew the Icelandic saga from the 1672 Verelius edition. Indeed, it had been his intention to prepare a précis as his contribution to Jamieson's *Illustrations*, but so frequently and ham-

---

[69] Scott 1822/1996, 354–6, note N reveals that Scott did not just own Bartholin 1689 but made good use of it.
[70] [Jamieson R.] 1814, 502.

fistedly had Angantyr been woken by paraphrasers since the 1760s that Scott wisely transferred his loyalties to *Eyrbyggja saga*.[71]

Reception

Analysis of the filigree detail, the philology, the folkloristic motifs and the larger narrative structures confirms that Scott worked hard to lend substance to his Orcadian and Shetlandian old northernism, and to weave it into the thematic heart of the novel. Such a novel, the first extended imaginative treatment of any aspect of the old north in the English language, had the potential to influence generations of nineteenth-century readers and writers – but did anyone in Victorian Britain or elsewhere in the English-reading world actually read it? In fact, from its first publication in December 1821, it remained available for the rest of the century, either as an individual work or in successive Victorian and Edwardian repackagings of the 'Waverley novels'.[72] *The Pirate* was also imitated, illustrated, epitomised, excerpted for children, set to music, dramatised on the London stage (within three weeks of publication),[73] and translated for readers in Europe; its many songs took their place amongst the light musical fare of fashionable soirées, and its characters were referred to in Victorian travel books about Iceland with a familiarity nowadays reserved for television soap-opera favourites. Indeed the hazy distinction between historical fact and popular fiction finally dissolved in an 1887 *New York Herald* article, subsequently republished in a Shetland newspaper, in which readers are informed that the former Miss Rae, a young Orcadian woman whose father had escorted Scott around the island sites in 1814,[74] and on whom the character of Brenda in the novel was supposedly based, is still alive and well and living as an elderly widow in Hamilton, Ontario. Indeed she had been sprightly enough to be able to pick up her well-thumbed copy of the novel, and read out to the duly deferential journalist 'the description of the two lovely daughters of "Magnus Troll" '.[75]

That artists revelled in the novel's atmosphere is confirmed by illustrated nineteenth-century editions of *The Pirate*.[76] Indeed, in George Eliot's *The Mill on the Floss* (1860), Maggie Tulliver's suitor Philip Wakem arrives one day with a volume of *The Pirate* in his hand. Maggie may have found it hard to finish the novel because of too close an identification with the fate of Minna, but the artis-

---

[71] Harvey Wood 1972, II 467–8; Cowan 1972, 121. Herbert 1815 tells of Angantyr and his sword Tirfing.

[72] The Library of Congress catalogue lists well over sixty entries (many of them American) for the novel up to 1925, and none after that date.

[73] White 1927, 162–5. See, for instance, Dibdin 1822.

[74] See Scott 1982, 70–2.

[75] [Unsigned] 'One of Scott's Characters still living: An Interview with "Brenda" ', Shetland Archive ref. D.I./135, p. 273.

[76] Illustrations could also take more elliptical form; Brown 1994 offers an 1844 set of character sketches and portraits, including (pp. 90–1) 'Minna' and 'Brenda', daughters of an Alderman Tod.

tic Philip was 'studying a scene for a picture'.[77] Several of the pictures which recur in late nineteenth-century editions derive from a set of five engravings published for members of the Royal Association for the Promotion of the Fine Arts in Scotland in 1871.[78] We observe first the sturdy domesticity of Magnus Troil in his living room along with his daughters Brenda (devoted sense) and Minna (disruptive sensibility). The former sits next to her father holding a sheet of music (cultivation of appropriately womanly arts and virtues), whilst her sister's far-away look hints at less demure visions of Viking rovers on the high seas. Another engraving depicts the foamy wildness of the storm and shipwreck from which Clement Cleveland is rescued. The artist then turns to the altercation between Cleveland and the pedlar Bryce Snailsfoot, the latter all rhymes, ribbons and repartee. We are shown the scene aboard the pirate ship in which the temporarily captive Minna receives a pistol for self-defence from the cultivated brigand Bunce – Minna's unwavering resolution contrasts with Brenda's terror-struck prostration. Lastly, and every artist's favourite subject, there is the Gothic frenzy of Norna of the Fitful Head, windswept, wild-eyed, the weirdest of sisters.

If pencil and brush played their part in popularising *The Pirate*, so, too, did music and song, and from a very early date. The novel's shifting moods find expression in several of the short lyric pieces: the Viking spirit distilled in Claude Halcro's 'Song of Harold Harfager' (122–3; ch. 15); the counterpoint between Norna and her transfixed audience in the fortune-telling scene (174–80; ch. 21); Norna's own haunting 'Song of the Reim-Kennar' delivered, as always, in her 'slow, sad, almost . . . unearthly accent' (51; ch. 6); Bryce Snailsfoot's artful rhymes of self-promotion (263; ch. 32); Cleveland's surprisingly tender love lyrics (196; ch. 22); and several boisterous pirate songs such as the 'Robin Rover' fragment (268; ch. 32), singled out for praise by the *Quarterly Review* critic.[79] These songs enjoyed a long independent life, not only in editions of Scott's verse but as individual items for private performance.[80]

Along with the pictures and the songs, Orcadian and Shetlandic actualities figured prominently in Victorian responses to *The Pirate*. As with Bernard Shaw, sitting in Thurso waiting for the boat to Kirkwall and '*re*-reading [my emphasis]'[81] *The Pirate*, it was a case of read the novel and then visit the scenes. *The Pirate* became a familiar work for the nineteenth-century Orkney and Shetland traveller in search of 'the genius of the place', and its characters became reference points for humour.[82] In his *Travels, Trips and Trots* (1903) Major General

---

[77] Eliot 1960, 405–6 (V iii).
[78] [anon.] 1871.
[79] See [anon.] 1821–2, 454–74, at 474. For early reviews see Corson 1943, 245–7.
[80] Lockhart 1838, IV 171, note; also Scott 1822/1996, 196 (ch. 22).
[81] Tompkins 1960, 86.
[82] The subtitle of [anon. 1831] reads: 'An "Excellent Lettel" Harmless Quiz upon the Funny Shetlanders; and Sketches of "Things in General," from their Bogs and Pig-Styes, to their Geese and Claude Halcro; Being a Companion to The "Pirate," without Sir Walter Scott's Leave'. The eccen-

Blacksley, late Colonel of 'The Buffs', is thrilled at being able to visit the site of the Dwarfie Stone, observe the spot where Cleveland's ship foundered, and meet Norna-style crones in Stromness selling winds of 3 knots strength for a mere two shillings.[83] Iceland travellers stopping off in Orkney and Shetland were often familiar with the novel.[84] W.G. Collingwood, writing to his 10-year-old daughter, compares the local housing in Orkney and Shetland with that described in *The Pirate*.[85] Thirty years earlier Frederick Metcalfe, most fervent of Victorian old northernists, notes that Shetlanders refuse to eat whale meat, even when they are starving: 'If Claude Halcro were still in the flesh, and had grown wiser with age, he would doubtless say with Glorious John [Dryden], "Take the good the Gods provide thee, and don't starve in the midst of plenty." '[86] So, too, when imagining the scene at the medieval Alþingi in Iceland, Metcalfe speaks of pedlars making their profitable way from booth to tent, 'the Bryce Snailfoots of those times, with silver ornaments, and cloths fine and coarse'.[87] For Metcalfe, visiting the sites of saga-age antiquity in Iceland by ship or in Shetland by novel was more than an act of whimsical antiquarianism; it was a means of renewing contact with the spiritual roots of his nation, 'that Scandinavian breed, to which, and not to the Saxon, England owes her pluck, her dash, and her freedom.'[88]

C.G.W. Lock's 1879 Iceland travel book reveals an even stronger engagement with the novel. Circumstances had prevented him from visiting Lerwick on his way north, and he does not bother to hide his disappointment that his *Pirate*-derived vision of Shetland was not to be enriched by first hand exploration:

> It was here especially that the old Norse sea-kings halted on their western voyages in search of a new home. Here many remained, and built dwellings and gave pure old Norse names to every salient feature of the landscape, names on which a thousand years have had so little corruptible effect that in Iceland alone can we find their rivals for unsullied purity. What feelings would not have been created by visiting the scenes where the inimitable Sir Walter Scott laid his story of 'The Pirate'; how vivid the realizations of the life and surroundings of the old Udaller at Burgh Westra (Icelandic, *Vestri-borg*, Western burg), and of the eccentric tenant of Jarl-

---

trics claim to have found several Magnus Troil types, as well as 'the real original of Claude Halcro': [anon.], 1831 16. A marginal note in the Shetland Archive Library copy reads: 'Dr A——E—dm—s—', an allusion to Edmonston 1809, one of the works plundered by Scott while writing the novel.

83 Blaksley 1903, 178, 185, 190.

84 En route to Iceland in 1833 George Atkinson met a Faroe islander who had learnt English 'solely' in order to read Sir Walter Scott. Atkinson's journal has several *Pirate* references: Seaton 1989, 70–71.

85 Collingwood transcripts, WGC to Mrs Collingwood, 8 June 1897.

86 Metcalfe 1861, 37.

87 Ibid., 70. In Dasent 1875, I 37–41 the name of the messenger Gangrel Speedifoot probably derives from Scott's Bryce Snailfoot.

88 Metcalfe 1861, 70.

shof (Icelandic, *Járlshof*, Earl's Court). Even the names of the persons occurring in the tale are Norse; Swertha would be called *Svarta* (Black) in Icelandic, a reminder that nicknames are no modern growth; while Sweyn Erickson (Icelandic, *Sveinn* [*Eiríksson*]) is a name common in Iceland to this hour.[89]

Many *Pirate* enthusiasts followed in Lock's wake.

Þorleifur Repp: Bearing Óðinn's Mead

Þorleifur Repp's admiration for 'Sir Valter Skott' certainly earns him an honoured place in the reception history of *The Pirate*:

> the object of this eminent genius was, of course . . . to use them [Icelandic sagas] for his own purpose, because it was on the foundation of this knowledge the learned Gent. formed and created that whole imaginary world which his readers admire . . . those very descriptions of the celebrated genius could not fail to excite in many the wish for a more intimate acquaintance with these very originals, which partly gave rise to so eminent productions, and that they would be glad to see the peculiar expressions of thought and character in the autographs of an age which so highly recommends itself by sublime sentiments, energy of thought and expression and in some points even by refined taste and learning.[90]

We know that there were Edinburgh intellectuals eager to achieve 'a more intimate acquaintance with these very originals', and Þorleifur Repp devoted himself to helping them during his ten turbulent years in Edinburgh. He brought not just presentation copies of *Laxdæla saga* to the Scottish capital but a missionary zeal to promote his own idealised vision of the old north. After humiliating dismissal from his post at the Advocates' Library compelled him to return to Copenhagen in 1837,[91] he remained eager to assert the cultural links between Britain and Iceland – through translating, editing, reviewing, and lexicography. He even acquired an English son-in-law. Readers of Percy's *Five Pieces* or of the 1809 Copenhagen edition of *Egils saga* would be familiar with Egill's 'Head-Ransome' poem,[92] in which Egill claims to be bringing the mead of Óðinn to England. This phrase appears, perhaps at Scott's suggestion,[93] as a signature verse on the title-page of Robert Jamieson's 'Popular Heroic and Romantic Ballads' section[94] of the *Illustrations of Northern Antiquities* volume which contained Scott's *Eyrbyggja* précis; and it could well have been used as the mission statement for Þorleifur Repp's decade of service in Britain. Though there were harassed officials in the Advocates Library who would happily have

---

[89] Lock 1879, 74–5.
[90] Lbs. MS ÍB 90c fol.
[91] Wawn 1991a, 56–85.
[92] Grímur Thorkelin 1809a, 427–56.
[93] Scott owned a copy of the saga: [Cochrane] 1838, 99.
[94] Jamieson 1814, 237.

rendered Repp headless, there were many others in and beyond the library who enthusiastically imbibed the Odinic mead which Repp dispensed in such generous measure through his teaching and journalism in Edinburgh. The testimonials he was able to secure after his dismissal from the library tell their own tale: 'profound knowledge of philological principles', 'almost inexhaustible fund of general knowledge . . . a most benevolent readiness to make others participant in it', 'the excellence of [his] method of teaching', 'a sort of living polyglot', 'at this moment no man in Britain equals Mr Repp in the extent of his philological acquirements'.[95] Repp understood his role clearly enough:

> It is to be lamented, that through ignorance of the ancient Norse language, and the consequent inaccessibleness of true records, and the confinement of modern historians to the very partial chronicles of timid monks, as their only source of information for the middle ages, history has been so thoroughly falsified, that it will now require the labour of learned and enlightened men for some centuries to come . . . to reconquer for the Scandinavians that lofty place which they ought to occupy in the annals of the world. There is no remedy . . . but an attentive study of the Icelandic, and a thorough perusal of ancient Northern literature, the vast extent of which is even unknown among the leading nations of modern Europe.[96]

He lost no time in providing practical assistance for those wishing to make such an 'attentive study' and 'thorough perusal'. He offered individual and group instruction in all the Scandinavian languages – £4 paid for twenty classes, each of which were well supported by carefully prepared pedagogical materials – conversation exercises, vocabulary sheets, and lectures on broader issues of the (then) new philology to equip pupils with a firm basis of understanding from which to grasp the particular eccentricities of individual languages. Repp wanted his keenest students to be independent readers of old northern texts; hence his decision to translate into English (with extensive alteration and modification) Rasmus Rask's ground-breaking 1811 Old Icelandic grammar.[97] Unhappily the translation was never published, and British enthusiasts had to wait for George Dasent's 1843 translation of the same work.[98] Repp also lectured on a wide range of old northern topics, producing entertaining prose paraphrases and recastings of eddic and saga texts – the pagan temple scene from *Eyrbyggja saga*, and sections from *Gylfaginning* and *Magnús saga* represented just the sort of supplementary materials that any reader of *The Pirate* might have welcomed the chance to study. His imaginative (if self-preoccupied)[99] expansion of material from *Færeyinga saga* may have been trig-

[95] Repp 1834: phrases from the testimonials of, respectively, William Skene, Louis Duriez, W.J. Campbell, James Browne, Sir William Hamilton.
[96] Repp 1832, 163.
[97] Lbs. ÍB 90a, translation of Rask 1811; on Repp and Rask, see Wawn 1991a, 188–90 and 247 (notes 407–8); also Axelsen 1996.
[98] Dasent 1843, translation of Rask 1818c.
[99] Wawn 1990b.

gered by Scott's Miklagard scenes in *Count Robert of Paris* (1831); it certainly follows Scott's fondness for lavish descriptions, colloquial dialogue and anti-quarian explanation. In its choice of an actual saga text as the base narrative, it anticipates mid-century writers such as George Dasent and Robert Leighton.[100] Repp also lectured on more specialised topics such as the Ruthwell runes. He and Finnur Magnússon made the first serious (albeit spectacularly incorrect)[101] attempt to decipher and interpret the Dumfries monument to whose markings George Hickes had drawn attention at the end of the seventeenth century. These fumbling efforts served not only to prompt an irate J.M. Kemble into publish-ing his own more accurate readings,[102] but also anticipated the work of George Stephens in cataloguing the runic monuments of the old north.

In all essentials Repp subscribed to the linguistic theories developed by Pink-erton and Jamieson. His vision of Scotland early in the first millennium was of a land peopled by Scandinavian Picts whose language was eventually to survive best in Old Icelandic. No Scottish tradition was immune to Repp's Icelandicis-ing tendencies. The improbable conclusion to his paper on the etymology of 'hogmanay' is that the phrase 'hogmanay, trollalay' derives from Icelandic *haug-menn á / tröll á læ* [the good mountain spirits for ever: the wicked trolls into the sea].[103] In Scott's *The Antiquary*, written shortly before *The Pirate*, the pro-Scandinavian Jonathan Oldbuck argues with his fiery young Celticist nephew about the relative merits of their respective enthusiasms:

> 'I don't pretend to much skill, uncle; but it's not very reasonable to be angry with me for admiring the antiquities of my own country more than those of the Harolds, Harfagers, and Hacos you are so fond of.'
> 'Why these, sir – these mighty and unconquered Goths – *were* your ancestors! The bare-breeched Celts whom they subdued and suffered only to exist like a fearful people in the crevices of rocks, were but their Manciples and serfs.'[104]

Oldbuck would have relished the idea of a Scandinavian hogmanay, yet his one track cultural mind would eventually have irritated Repp, who had a reading knowledge of some two dozen languages,[105] including Gaelic.

If Repp's pedagogical and journalistic efforts encouraged some of his Scot-tish readers and audiences to trace the roots of their culture back to the old north, his only book-length study in English extended that service to the whole British nation. Through an intermediary the Home Secretary commissioned Repp to compile *A Historical Treatise on Trial by Jury, Wager of Law, and Other Co-Ordinate Forensic Institutions formerly in Use in Scandinavia and Iceland* (1832). Drawing on a prodigious range of primary reading in Icelandic and

---

100 Dasent 1875, Leighton 1895; see below, Chapter 11.
101 Wawn 1991a, 122–33.
102 Kemble 1840.
103 Wawn 1991a, 105–17.
104 Scott 1816, Chapter 30 (1910 edition, p. 339).
105 Wawn 1991a, 45–55.

Latin, Repp makes a plausible case for the Scandinavian origin of the British jury system and many Victorian writers followed his lead. In a note to his *Eyrbyggja* abstract Scott mentions the twelve men assembled for Geirríða's trial;[106] Repp's 1832 treatment of the same incident is much more detailed. The jury system was 'the first fruits of liberty and its last survivor';[107] and its gradual erosion on the Scandinavian mainland led to the decline of democracy itself. Reform of nineteenth-century Scandinavian law and politics should follow modern English models, with juries as the cornerstone of judicial practice. Such views earned Repp the nickname 'the Anglo Man' amongst his Copenhagen colleagues,[108] yet his *Jury* book is also notable for its heroic presentation of his homeland and of the old north. First we hear Repp on Old Icelandic:

> a very intricate system of inflections – a great care and ingenuity displayed in the framing and beautifying of every word – the nicest harmony, proportion, symmetry, between all the elements of which a word is composed – a scrupulous avoidance of all harsh sounds, yet no prevalence of any particular letter permitted, which might create monotony or disharmony – these are the external and truly Indian characteristics of Odin's language. The style is incomparably simple and concise.[109]

In Repp's vision of philological imperialism, romance languages adopted 'a Gothic system of inflections, and Gothic laws of construction' (160), and the poetry of the romance nations is commended for being 'Gothic in form, matter, and spirit'. The extent of this Gothic cultural domination can only be appreciated by 'those who know the original, – the parent tongue of the Gothic nations, – the Icelandic'.

Turning to Iceland, Repp creates his own settlement myth: an 'aristocratic republic' (151), built around the 'flower of Norwegian aristocracy' (156) who, every bit King Haraldr's equal in 'power, dignity, and descent', had refused to bow the knee. For such 'progeny of the Gods' (154) submission would have been 'a kind of impiety – a debasement of their divine nature'. The settlers were the 'most vigorous' of the group, 'with whom it was a paramount consideration to perpetuate this ancient race and their history'. Accordingly, Icelandic culture was 'richer and more cultivated than that of any other nations during the middle ages' (156). They were more innovative law-makers, more intrepid navigators, and better historians. Repp's Home Office patron is assured – and perhaps required little convincing – that nineteenth-century colonists from the south of Europe cannot hold a candle to the energy, enterprise and glamour of their

---

106 [Jamieson R.] 1814, 484: the ceremony of compurgation formed 'the remote origin of the trial by jury'; see also Mackenzie 1812, 15, note.
107 Repp 1832, 104.
108 Lbs. Repp. Acc. 6/7/1989 fol., ÞR to Ralph Carr, 13 April 1837.
109 Repp 1832, 68–9.

medieval Icelandic forerunners. The secret of medieval Iceland's amazing literary achievement lies not in dark nights and calf skins, but rather in heroic ambition, spiritual energy and the conscious willing of ends and means.

In so many ways Repp anticipates the triumphalist constructions of the Viking-age old north in later nineteenth-century Britain and the United States: the competition between north and south; the aristocratic origins; the energy and enterprise of successful colonists; and the Scandinavian origins of an honourable judicial system. Repp's work also signals the emblematic importance of Viking and saga-age Orkney and Shetland. Firstly, after his return to Copenhagen, he helped Robert Jamieson to edit and publish (in Copenhagen) a volume of late medieval texts and translations of documents relating to land ownership on the Orkneys and Shetlands.[110] Anyone familiar with *The Pirate* could read between the lines of these intriguing documents and make contact with Magnus Troil's fellow islanders. Secondly, in 1834 whilst still in Scotland, and again in 1846 after his return to Denmark, Repp offered to revise Jónas Jónsson's errorstrewn 1780 Copenhagen edition of *Orkneyinga saga* for the Bannatyne Club in Edinburgh: 'it would be highly gratifying to me to see an Icelandic saga published in Scotland: and I am sure that most of my fellow countrymen here [Copenhagen] think as I in this respect and that they . . . would like a British edition much better than a Danish'.[111] The Bannatyne Club's response was cool, however, and later work by George Stephens and P.A. Munch on a new edition also came to nothing.[112] It was not until Gilbert Goudie and Jón A. Hjaltalín's 1873 translation that full justice was done to the principal Icelandic saga relating to the British Isles; and it was not until 1894, after acrimonious collaboration between Guðbrandur Vigfússon and Sir George Dasent, that a new edition (with translation) of *Orkneyinga saga* saw the light of day.

'Magnus Troil'

Repp had sought to illuminate the historical records of Orkney and Shetland, from oldest saga to modest inventory. In *The Pirate* Scott had bathed the same communities in a romantic fictional glow. It may be appropriate to conclude this chapter with a reference to one more devoted reader of *The Pirate*. During the 1846 General Election campaign in Orkney three pamphlets were published – all of them under the pseudonym Magnus Troil.[113] Their author was campaigning for the revival and conservation of udaller values in his native Orkney. His name was Samuel Laing, author of the pioneering and hugely influential 1844 English translation of Snorri Sturluson's *Heimskringla*. If it was Scott who

---

[110] Lbs. ÍB 90a fol., [Jamieson, trans. Repp] 1840.
[111] Lbs. ÍB 89c fol.
[112] See below, p. 241.
[113] See Sutherland Graeme 1953, 64–104, at 82–3.

first gave novelistic substance to the romance of the Viking-age legacy, it was Laing who gave the Vikings their first thoroughgoing politicisation in Britain. Laing's trenchant introductory dissertation to his three volume 'The Chronicles of the Norse kings' became a classic work of early Victorian Vikingism. This dissertation and its author are the subject of the next chapter.

SECTION II

CREATING THE CANON

CHAPTER FOUR

Dead Kings of Norroway

It is astonishing how little we in this Country know of Iceland,
scarce even is it known that the Icelanders were at one time the
Historians of the North, and the name of Snorri Sturluson has . . .
little celebrity.   (John Thomas Stanley 1791)[1]

> 'There is,' said he, 'a wondrous book
> Of Legends in the old Norse tongue,
> Of the dead kings of Norroway, –
> Legends that once were told or sung
> In many a smoky fireside nook
> Of Iceland, in the ancient day,
> By wandering Saga-man or Scald;
> Heimskringla is the volume called;
> And he who looks may find therein
> The story that I now begin.'
>   (H.M. Longfellow 1863)[2]

The pink and plume and pride of Old Norse literature.
               (Frederick Metcalfe 1880 294, on *Heimskringla*)

I live for half a dollar a day . . . This corner of the world is as good
as any other.   (Samuel Laing 1835, on life in Norway)[3]

The Berserker School

'This work', replied my uncle getting excited, 'is the *Heimskringla* of Snorre Turle-
son, the famous twelfth-century Icelandic author. It is the chronicle of the Norwegian princes who ruled over Iceland.'

'Really,' I exclaimed as well as I could. 'It's presumably a German translation?'

'What!' the professor replied animatedly. 'A translation! What would I be doing
with your translation? Who's bothered about your translation? This is the original

---

[1]   Edinburgh University Library, La. III. 379/757–81, John Thomas Stanley to Grímur Thorkelin,
1 February 1791.
[2]   From, 'The Saga of King Olaf': Longfellow 1904, 364.
[3]   From Laing's unpublished autobiographical memoir: typescript on deposit in the Orkney
Archive, p. 91.

91

work, in Icelandic: that magnificent language, both simple and rich, containing the most diverse grammatical combinations as well as numerous variations in the words.'[4]

It was a mysterious runic paper falling from his copy of Snorri Sturluson's *Heimskringla* that triggered the epic journey to the centre of the earth undertaken by Professor Lidenbrock, the prickly Hamburg academic in Jules Verne's 1864 novel. Many of Verne's readers in Victorian England came to share the professor's enthusiasm for Snorri Sturluson's thirteenth-century Icelandic chronicle of the medieval Scandinavian kings, but few could rival his mastery of the 'magnificent language' of the original. Rather like Lidenbrock's young nephew, most Victorian enthusiasts of northern antiquity certainly needed to 'bother about a translation' if they were ever to access Snorri's masterwork. Small wonder that the publication in 1844 of the first English translation of *Heimskringla* was widely welcomed in the periodical press. The three handsome volumes included a lengthy Preliminary Dissertation[5] and were the work of Samuel Laing (1780–1868), an Orcadian landowner, herring and kelp entrepreneur, political theorist and philologist.[6] Reissued in 1889, Snorri's old northern tales of dynastic growth and decay, individual loyalty and treachery, pagan defiance and Christian conquest stirred the imaginations of many nineteenth-century readers, and in its various subsequent incarnations – not least its decades of service as an Everyman's Library volume – Laing's translation has remained as Snorri's principal English voice through much of the twentieth century.[7] Along with Bishop Tegnér's *Frithiofs saga* and George Dasent's *The Story of Burnt Njal*, Laing's *Heimskringla* quickly established itself as one of a handful of canonical texts of Victorian old northernism. The present chapter examines the influence of both the translation and its accompanying Preliminary Dissertation. Laing was a founding father of what became known as the 'berserker school'[8] of old northernists, all of whose members had exhibited the necessary 'extravagant and uncritical' levels of Scandinavian enthusiasm. He was the man of Orkney who inherited Minna Troil's mantle. Powerful political and personal agendas drove what Laing wrote, causing matters of fact to dissolve into matters of fiercely expressed opinion.

---

4 Verne 1992, 8.
5 Laing 1844.
6 A native of Kirkwall, Laing studied in Edinburgh and (for two years) in Kiel. After service in the Peninsula wars, he became a mine manager in south Scotland. Returning to Orkney in 1818, he succeeded to his family's debt-encumbered estate. After his continental travels, he spent the remainder of his life in Edinburgh. On his life see Laing, 'Memoir' (see above, note 3); Anderson in Laing 1889, I xiv–xvii; [R]igg 1892; Porter 1998.
7 Laing 1889, rev. 1961. This revision incorporates Peter Foote's introduction, textual appendices and indexes.
8 [anon.] 1878, 498–500, at 498: review of Conybeare 1877.

Consulting the Runes

That the Scandinavian old north was taken seriously in Victorian Britain was due in no small measure to Laing's Dissertation and translation. The devotion which the old north could command is hinted at by the specially designed front cover of the 1889 second edition of Laing's translation, edited by Rasmus Anderson.[9] The reader is confronted with a half-page design in inlaid gold leaf on a dark blue background (Fig. 2). It is a pitch-black arctic night; the northern lights swirl in the heavens; the light from a scatter of twinkling stars picks out, on an unusually calm North Atlantic ocean, either an undersized Viking long-ship, or two oversized Viking passengers. The left-hand figure is identified as 'Snorre', hunched, hooded, hatted; he has his back to the barque's wild-eyed dragon-head, and is solemnly taking down dictation on his portable writing board. A drinking horn at his feet offers the prospect of bodily sustenance whilst the learned Icelander's spirit is nourished by the political and historical truths of which he was to be custodian. His companion is the personified figure of 'Saga', in appearance more Grecian than Gothic, as if a still unravished bride had stepped straight off the side of her Keatsian urn. She is flimsily clad for an open boat and yet her body language suggests that she is the more relaxed and authoritative of the two figures. The brightest star twinkles directly over Saga's head; her hair flows freely in the wind; and her right hand and foot appear to invade what we are now obliged to call Snorri's personal space. At one level Saga clearly represents 'history' or 'historical tradition', as conscientious Victorian readers could confirm after 1874 by checking the appropriate entry in Guðbrandur Vigfússon's *Icelandic-English Dictionary*.[10] The figure seems also to represent some powerful and possibly sacred force of nature. This is oral tradition in Victorian terms, with Saga responsible for transmitting ancestral truths which had 'floated down on the memory'.[11] As a suitable Victorian caption for this picture, we need look no further than Guðbrandur Vigfússon's 'Prolegomena' to his 1878 edition of *Sturlunga saga*, where he reflects at length on that fateful old northern moment when 'The Age of Growth of the Saga meets the Age of Writing'.[12]

In fact we do not need Guðbrandur's phrase because a number of runic markings at the base of the design serve as a title. The markings prove to be genuine long branch runes which may be read as *urþar: orþi: cueþr: elki: maþr*, or, in regularised form, 'urðarorði kveðr helgimaðr' [perhaps, 'In fateful word(s) speaks a holy man'].[13] This seems a reasonable description of Snorri's role in

9   Laing 1889. Anderson, a Norwegian-American, served for four years as a diplomat in Copenhagen. On his controversial philological career, see Hustvedt 1966.
10 Cleasby and Gudbrand Vigfusson 1874, 508–9.
11 Laing 1844, I 29.
12 Gudbrand Vigfusson 1878, xxvii.
13 I am grateful to Professor R.I. Page for his guidance in interpreting the runes.

Fig. 2. Cover design for Samuel Laing (trans.), *The Heimskringla,*
or The Sagas of the Norse Kings.

Heimskringla as he gives permanent expression to oral tradition's carefully
hoarded historical truths. Evident care has been taken in the creation of a
runologically plausible inscription. Few late nineteenth-century readers, even
berserker school adherents, would have appreciated this attention to scholarly
detail; the runes must have seemed, in the words of Professor Lidenbrock's
sceptical nephew, 'an invention by scholars to mystify the poor rest-of-the-
world'.[14] Many readers would have settled for more populist dust-jacket iconography with a hard-hearted, horned-helmeted Viking glaring at them through
rime-covered whiskers, his hand clutching a hollowed-out enemy's skull full of
ale.[15] But to Rasmus Anderson and his London publisher, the design and the
inscription were worth taking trouble over. They represented an act of scholarly
piety towards the translator, the sagas and the five hundred special subscribers.
This capacity for taking philological pains characterised many later Victorian
responses to the old north, and much of that scholarly energy can be traced back
to the influence of Laing's pioneering translation.

[14] Verne 1992, 8.
[15] The 1889 design recalls the *fjallkona* frontispiece to Powell and Eiríkr Magnússon 1866; see also
Þórunn Valdimarsdóttir 1990.

From Chronicle to Saga

Comparison of the title-pages of the two editions of Laing's translation signals one difference that forty-five years could make in the development of Victorian old northernism. The 1844 *Chronicles of the Norse Kings* became the 1889 *Sagas of the Norse Kings*. The term 'saga' took some time to develop its own prestige. Laing's best chance of winning a sympathetic audience for Snorri was to present him as a medieval chronicler, a sub-arctic Froissart, or Joinville or Villehardouin (or Homer, Herodotus, Pepys, Macaulay, Clarendon, Carlyle, Captain Marryat or James Fenimore Cooper),[16] or as a secular Icelandic equivalent to the Anglo-Saxon 'monkish' chroniclers for whom Laing reserved a special loathing.[17] He pitches his claims high: 'it may be doubted if, ever since the middle ages, any, excepting Shakspeare and Sir Walter Scott in their historical representations, have surpassed Snorro Sturleson'.[18]

None of the claims made for Snorri could be substantiated unless his works became readily available in English. As we have seen, Latin scholarship (and translations) had served scholars and laymen well over two centuries, and Laing's Dissertation reveals his own indebtedness to them.[19] Yet by the 1840s there were impatient stirrings amongst a new generation of old northernists, who either wanted better English-language dictionaries and grammars to enable them to read eddas and sagas in Icelandic[20] or who were looking for saga translations. For both groups the cupboard of scholarly provision was still bare. English versions of Rasmus Rask's 1811 grammar book did not become available until the early 1840s.[21] Dasent's translation of *Njáls saga* was only in its embryonic stages, and did not appear until 1861.[22] Thus, when Laing's *Chronicles* appeared in 1844, only one English translation of an Icelandic saga was available in print – George Stephens's 1839 version of *Friðþjófs saga*.[23] It is no wonder, therefore, that Carlyle devoured Laing's three volumes enthusiastically when they first appeared, and he was still dining off their contents in his valedictory *Lives of the Norse Kings* (1875).[24]

Laing's *Chronicles* created new possibilities as well as satisfying existing demands. In 1844 readers had one saga translation and one grammar easily

[16] Laing 1844, I 3; Johnstone 1844, 281; Dufferin 1857 (tenth edition 1895), 31–2.
[17] Laing is better than Joinville, Froissart and other medieval chroniclers: Johnstone 1844, 281.
[18] Laing 1844, III 393.
[19] Ibid., I 26, 65. He cites Ole Worm, Verelius, Bartholin and Þórmóður Torfason.
[20] On the Carlyles and Iceland, including their impatience with available grammars and dictionaries, see Gades et al. 1970–1990, XVI 124, 142–4, 149, 169, 217, 233.
[21] Marsh 1838; Dasent 1843. Marsh was an American scholar who had begun work on his grammar years earlier; see Beck 1972, 9–26.
[22] Dasent 1861 and 1866; also Head 1865.
[23] See below, Chapter 5. Stephens 1839 includes his translation of Tegnér's *Frithiofs saga*.
[24] Cowan 1979.

available in English;[25] there was no Icelandic-English dictionary,[26] no postal tuition available from British-based Icelanders,[27] only a couple of old northern novels of any substance,[28] and even Percy's *Northern Antiquities* was awaiting its 1847 facelift. That the situation had improved so dramatically on all these fronts by 1889 was due in part to the influence of the *Chronicles of the Norse Kings* – both the individual saga translations and Samuel Laing's provocative introductory essay. Rasmus Anderson's 1889 revised edition served to administer a timely booster dose.[29]

Laing made available in English Snorri's panoramic view of the old northern kings and their peoples, as narrated over seventeen sagas. Each work helped to trace the long ancestral line from the mighty Asiatic warrior Óðinn[30] in *Ynglinga saga* to King Magnús Erlingsson at the end of the twelfth century. The sagas represented a dramatic record of internal struggle and external conquest amongst north Atlantic communities, with frequent reference to parts of the British Isles – from Caithness to Cleveland, from London to Lough Larne, and from the Isle of Man to the Menai Straits. We see skirmishes in Scarborough and full-scale battle at Stamford Bridge. We sense the great tides of events affecting the fate of nations, but also attend to small-scale emblematic incidents. On the Scandinavian mainland families rise and fall, monarchs are made and broken, Things gather and disperse. The solidity of great halls, fine ships, and famous swords lies alongside the mysteries of sorcery, sacrifice and strange dreams. Sturdy bonder shares the stage with savage berserk. There is verse as well as prose. Thomas Percy had been discouraged from including several *Heimskringla* verses in his *Five Pieces*;[31] now all the verses are made available in their full prose contexts.[32]

There is only one substantial omission from Laing's translation, no doubt on the grounds of good taste. In a chapter of *Magnússona saga* (Laing's *The Saga of Sigurd the Crusader*), the exemplary King Sigurðr Jórsalafari who had dined with Byzantine emperors, pilgrimaged to the Holy Land, and been entrusted with a splinter from the holy cross, cuts a very different dash. Increasingly the victim of 'fits of insanity, and wonderful whims' (III 188), we find him sitting in his hall at Yule-tide, requesting that a plate of meat and a woman be set before him. Removing her veil the king remarks that the woman's ugly face is only just tolerable; similar remarks follow the exposure of her hands and feet.

---

[25] Marsh 1838 was never readily available in Britain.

[26] The principal help available was Björn Halldórsson 1814.

[27] Eiríkur Magnússon later offered such tuition: see below, Chapter 12.

[28] de la Motte Fouquet 1815, 1845; Scott 1822. I have not examined Petterson 1826.

[29] The actual revisions were more limited than the editor claims: Laing 1889, I xi–xiv. Anderson tidied, trimmed and signposted – and introduced new errors. On his motives for undertaking the revision, see Hustvedt 1966, 190, 332–5.

[30] Throughout this chapter when reference is made to Laing's translations, names will be spelled as in his versions.

[31] See above, p. 27, note 178.

[32] Laing 1844, I 207–9 indicates that his son helped translate the verses.

The sight of her bloated and discoloured legs, however, proves too much. William Morris and Eiríkur Magnússon, whose 1895 translation includes the chapter unblinkingly, continue as follows: ' "Fie on thy leg! it is both blue and thick, and a mere whore must thou be." And he bade them take her out, "for I will not have her." '[33] Such 'coarse and indecent' matter finds no place in Laing's old north (III 191).

Bonder values

Laing spent three years in Norway from 1834.[34] From his base on the northern shores of Trondheimsfjord he developed a good working knowledge of the modern spoken and written languages. He first discovered one of the *Heimskringla* sagas in a version borrowed from a 'bonder', to use the naturalised (by Laing) form of a common Scandinavian word – he could find no satisfactory modern English alternative that embraced the interlocking concepts of peasant, yeoman, landholder, proprietor, and statesman (I 100).[35] Laing's discovery may have been a copy of Peter Claussen's Norwegian text of *Óláfs saga helga*, that enjoyed the status of 'a house-book among the Norwegian bonders' alongside copies of the Bible, Psalter, and King Christian IV's law code (I 201). In 1837 Laing published his *Journal of a Residence in Norway during the Years 1834, 1835, and 1836 made with a View to Enquire into the Moral and Political Economy of that Country, and the Condition of its Inhabitants*,[36] a wide-ranging and authoritative work which served as a trial run for his *Heimskringla* Preliminary Dissertation. The hero worship discernible in Laing's *Journal* is not directed at Carlyle's all-powerful Odinic figures, but rather at Norwegian bonders, 'fine athletic men . . . the kernel of the nation' (258), who unlike their brothers in Denmark, Sweden and Russia had never 'crouched beneath the cudgel of the feudal baron bailiff'. They exhibit instinctively 'the feelings and proper pride of an independent man possessed of property, and knowing nothing above him but the law' (152). Primogeniture played no part in Norwegian land tenure, much to Laing's approval. He looks favourably on the equal division of inheritances; any system producing forty self-reliant bonders of equal standing was preferable to a system built around one powerful landlord and thirty-nine dependent tenants. Small freehold parcels of land created a self-sufficiency of spirit, and also expectations of high living standards which, in turn, acted as a useful restraint on population growth.

---

[33] Morris and Eiríkr Magnússon 1891–1905, V (*Heimskringla* III) 295.
[34] Laing's frustratingly brief account of this period appears in his unpublished journal: see above, note 3, pp. 90–3.
[35] Anderson (Laing 1889, I 125n) silently emends Laing's 'bonder(s)', reluctantly adopted in 1844, in favour of 'bonde(s)'.
[36] Laing 1836; all references here derive from the 1854 edition.

These same attitudes inform Laing's *Heimskringla* Dissertation, in which modern bonder virtues are represented as domestications of ancient Viking-age values. Not for nothing are the 1844 volumes entitled 'The Sea-Kings of Norway' on the spine. In the Dissertation the spirit of the romantic antiquary wrestles with the voice of the political polemicist. The essay's one hundred and eighty-seven pages promote an interlinked set of important ideas which are worth identifying.

Firstly, Laing is intrigued by the nature of that raw Viking spirit that drove a numerically insignificant group of individuals to undertake 'incredible enterprises and exertions' which exercised such a disproportionately great influence on lands near and far. He was aware that no Icelandic Viking is named in the sagas (I 58), and always looked to the Vikings' early roots in Norway rather than to their later days as gentleman farmers in Iceland. Norwegian Vikings revealed 'the human mind in a state of barbarous energy and action, and with the vitality of freedom', which invariably overcame 'the human mind in a state of slavish torpidity and superstitious lethargy' (I 15). The purest expression of that energy was to be found in the lives of the elite sea-kings: as George Stephens had already noted,[37] 'every sea-king was a viking, but every viking was not a sea-king' (I 45n).

Secondly, Laing celebrates the geological anti-feudalism of the Vikings' Norwegian homelands. Norway was a land of granite. Local lords with feudal ambitions could build their castles in the air but (unlike their Norman brothers) never on the ground (I 120–1). Royal residences were made of wood. When journeying around the country, royalty lodged in farmhouses or on-board ship; accordingly, ruler and ruled remained in close contact. Laing praises the life of the independent-minded udaller[38] whose land was inalienable by sale, gift to the church, or forfeiture. Property ownership gives people something to fight for – hence the feeble resistance of Anglo-Saxon serfs to Viking attacks.

Thirdly, Laing admired constitutional monarchy and participatory democracy. The basis of Viking-age royal legitimacy was the authority freely granted by popular assent at the local Thing (I 103): small wonder that he had no time for the Holyrood 'puppet show' of George IV.[39] Laing relished the arts of eloquence encouraged by democratic debate. The same vigorous oral culture had helped to create a literature animated with common feeling, and had fused a scattered population into a single nation. No wonder that the old northmen could overwhelm communities untouched by any such popular spirit. There were modern literary implications, too. Laing argued that, unlike nineteenth-century Germany, speech and writing shared a common idiom in Viking-influenced Britain. Few phrases from Lessing or Schiller fell from the lips of the supine German peasantry whereas, Laing claimed, many expressions from Shakespeare, Pope, Burns, Swift, Defoe, Cobbett and others enriched the

---

[37] Stephens 1839, 288.
[38] On the prestige of bonder culture, see Greenway 1977, 82–98.
[39] Laing 1854, 152.

common talk of rural England: this had resulted in 'the diffusion of one mind, one spirit, one mode of thinking and doing, through the whole social body . . . by a common language and literature . . . giving one shape and tone to the mind of all' (I 36). By his translations Laing sought to re-establish unity of mental 'shape and tone' between his fellow-countrymen and their old northern ancestors. Translation was, thus, not so much an antiquarian diversion but more a political and moral imperative.

Fourthly, Laing was relentlessly hostile to Catholicism, voicing his trenchant thoughts in a tone which seemed 'extremely objectionable' to old northern scholars in Dublin.[40] Laing argued that Anglo-Saxon lethargy grew out of monasticism whose traditions of lettered learning had created an excessively powerful political elite. The Vikings had been the saviours of the English nation, and only the monkish bias of monastic chroniclers had hidden this fact from later centuries. No barbarians could have created sagas comparable with Graeco-Roman chronicles and there was nothing primitive about old northern naval technology – 'ferocity, ignorance, and courage, will not bring men across the ocean' (I 131) without the supportive skills of ore smelting, rope making, sail-cloth weaving, provision preserving, water-cask coopering and the like. Such useful arts were superior to the drudgery of south European serfs as they quarried stone for the master-builders and sculptors of European Christendom. Christianity is also blamed for eroding the message-bearing and record-preserving roles of the old northern skald.[41] Within continental feudal societies, in particular, skalds degenerated into wandering troubadours (I 51); Widsith withered into Claud Halcro.

Fifthly, Laing was relentlessly hostile to all things German, notwithstanding an apparently agreeable 2-year-period spent in Kiel studying German language and literature around the turn of the century. He believed that far too much emphasis had been placed on searching for the roots of pre-Conquest England in Tacitus's *Germania*.[42] The Germans had always been (and remained)[43] a servile people with no tradition of democracy. The modern Danes (moderately) and Swedes (sternly) are criticised for following German ways (I 36–7).[44] The roots of nineteenth-century Britain's imperial power and social cohesion were to be traced to Norway alone, home of representative legislature, articulate public opinion, trial by jury, security of property, freedom of mind and person, and indomitable energy and courage (I 7).

Lastly, Laing enrols North America within an old northern framework. He

---

[40] [McMahon] 1848, 319.

[41] Their poetry ensured 'the accurate relation of facts, word for word, without the possibility of alteration, to all posterity'. It was a defence against royal encroachments on landholdings: Laing 1889, I 242.

[42] Laing 1844, I 8. On the political cultivation of Tacitus in seventeenth- and eighteenth-century Britain, see Kliger 1952.

[43] Laing 1842, 91 and passim.

[44] Ideas developed more fully in Laing 1839, 1842, 1852.

claims that Iceland and New England were the only colonies ever founded upon principle (I 57), and as such merited the attention of modern political scientists. There was good reason for Americans to journey to Norway to re-discover their own Viking roots, just as gentlemen salmon fishermen from Britain could visit the estates once tilled by their old northern ancestors (I 109–10). Laing devotes a substantial section of his Dissertation to the possible North American sites for Vínland (I 141–87). It was, therefore, appropriate that an American-Scandinavian scholar should supervise the 1889 revised edition of the *Heimskringla* translation, and that the venture should be financed in part by two hundred subscribers from North America.

Voicing the Old North

It was one thing for Laing to tilt at the windmills of scholarly orthodoxy in his Introduction; translating seventeen sagas represented a very different challenge. Within the emerging philological politics of Victorian Britain, the language and style of Laing's *Heimskringla* translation were as important as the ideas embodied in the sagas and analysed in the Preliminary Dissertation. For Laing, as for George Stephens, the time had come for translations into English. As we noted in Chapter 3, the pervasive influence and prestige of Latin and Greek, the 'twin linguistic tyrants',[45] had been challenged by the new philology.[46] For all his debt to seventeenth- and eighteenth-century European Latin scholarship, Laing associated Latin with the despotism and eventual decadence of Rome, and also with the intellectual one-sidedness of the medieval church. English, now the boisterous sibling rather than a dutiful son of the Graeco-Roman and Scandinavian languages, had earned the right to voice old northern texts.

The linguistic situation remained a minefield, however, and Laing's translation triggered a number of explosions.[47] In Chapter 3, we noted the role of Grímur Thorkelin in encouraging John Jamieson to undertake his Scots language dictionary. The underlying theory – Scots was a proud sibling of Icelandic rather than a degenerate waif of English – was not designed to appeal to the Unionist Tories of Edinburgh, as unsympathetic reviews of the 1828 revised form of Jamieson's *Dictionary* confirmed.[48] *The Pirate*, like *Waverley* before it, dramatises the destabilising consequences of romantic separatism. The similarly iconoclastic spirit of Laing's Dissertation was commented upon by a sceptical reviewer in the *Edinburgh Review*.[49] Though Laing never supported the crude anti-Celtic berserkerism of Pinkerton, he occasionally ended up tarred with the same brush.

---

45 Before the Grimms, 'Latin and Greek lorded it over the other languages of the earth . . . twin tyrants . . . with a pedant's rod': Dasent 1903, xviii.
46 Aarsleff 1983, 115–210.
47 Wawn 1991a, 109–15.
48 [Neaves] 1842, 61–73.
49 [Neaves] 1845, 276–318.

Laing knew little or no Old Icelandic (I iv), and (unlike later Victorian trans-lators)[50] had no modern Icelandic collaborator, but he was able to consult avail-able translations into other languages: Peringskiöld (1697: Latin and Swedish), Schöning (1777–1826: Latin and Danish) and Jakob Aall (1838–9: Norwe-gian).[51] He relied principally on Aall's version, and aimed to produce 'a plain faithful translation . . . suited to the plain English reader' (I 202). Two examples can help us to assess his success in prose and verse. Firstly, in Ólafs saga Tryggva-sonar, Rauðr the stubborn pagan endures a gruesome death at the hands of the missionary king:

Konungr vard þá reidr, oc sagdi, at Raudr skylldi hafa hinn versta dauda. Þá let konungr taca hann ok binda opinn á Slá eina, let setia kefli á millom tanna hánom oc lúka sva upp munninn: þá let konungr taca lýng-orm einn, oc bera at munni hánom . . . röcdiz þá ormrinn í munn Raudi, oc sídan í hálsinn, oc skar út um sídona; let Raudr þar líf sitt. (Schöning)[52]

Nu blev Kongen vred, og sagde at Raud skulde faae den værste Død. Derpaa lod Kongen ham binde paa en Bjælke med Unsigtet i Beiret, lod sætte en rund Pind mellem hans Tænder og lukke hans Mund op. Derefter lod Kongen tage en Lyngorm og stikke i Munden paa ham . . . Nu krøb Ormen ind i Munden paa Raud, derpaa gjennem Halsen og skar sig ud af Siden. Der lod Raud sit Liv.

(Aall)[53]

Then the king was wroth, and said Raud should die the worst of deaths. And the king ordered him to be bound to a beam of wood, with his face uppermost, and a round pin of wood to be set between his teeth to force his mouth open. Then the king ordered an adder to be stuck into the mouth of him . . . So the serpent crept into the mouth of Raud and down his throat, and gnawed its way out of his side; and thus Raud perished. (Laing I 448)

The clearest evidence of Laing's reliance on Aall is the phrase 'with his face uppermost' which appears in the Norwegian ('med Unsigtet i Beiret') but not in Schöning's Icelandic text or translations. Laing generally keeps close to his translated source in word order and vocabulary ('a round pin', 'crept' – perhaps the biblical 'serpent' seemed more portentous than 'worm'). Laing does enough to indicate the close kinship between a modern Scandinavian language and nineteenth-century English, and thus offer to linguistic underpinning to the central political thrust of his Dissertation. He could, indeed, have gone further without stumbling into creaking archaism: the compound verbal pair 'lod . . . tage . . . stikke' [caused to be . . . taken . . . stuck], and the conjunctions 'derpaa

---

[50] George E.J. Powell and Eiríkur Magnússon, William Morris and Eiríkur Magnússon, Thomas Ellwood and Eiríkur Magnússon, Gilbert Goudie and Jón Hjaltalín, George Dasent and Guðbran-dur Vigfússon.
[51] Peringskiöld 1697; Schöning et al. 1777–83; Aall 1838–39.
[52] Schöning 1777, I 284.
[53] Aall 1838, 162 (ch. 87).

... derefter' [thereupon, thereafter] could have been adopted virtually without alteration. The overall simplicity achieved stands up well against later Victorian versions of the same passage, translated from the Icelandic text. First William Morris and Eiríkur Magnússon:

> The king waxed wroth, and said that Raud should have the worst of deaths. So he let take him and bind him face up to a beam, and let set a gag between his teeth to open the mouth of him; then let the king take a ling-worm and set it to his mouth ... so ... the worm crawled into the mouth of Raud, and then into his throat, and dug out a hole in the side of him, and there came Raud to his ending.[54]

This version gives off mixed signals. The fearlessly transliterated Icelandic *láta* plus infinitive idiom sits alongside the Malorian 'waxed wroth'; in 'dug a hole' (as with Laing's 'gnawed') the translators ignore the possibility of 'shear' for OI *skera*. John Sephton's more sedate 1895 translation has its local successes (notably the alliterative triplet of 'bound . . . back . . . beam', and the neat final sentence), but as we follow the snake through the gastro-intestinal tract, the route seems laborious and our guide somewhat sqeamish:

> Whereupon the King became angry, and said that Raud should die the worst of deaths. He had him bound with his back against a beam, and a gag was placed between his teeth to keep his mouth open. A viper was then put to his mouth ... it was driven into Raud's mouth, whence it passed from his breast to his heart, and forced its way through his left side. Thus Raud lost his life.[55]

As a sample verse, we may take the poignant lines in which the poet Eyvindr Skáldaspillir laments the condition of Norway as ruled over by the sons of King Eiríkr blóðøx after the death of King Hákon:

> Snýr á Svǫlnis vóru.
> Svá hǫfum inn sem Finnar
> birkihund of bundit
> brums at miðju sumri.[56]

[It snows on Óðinn's wife = earth; so (we) have indoors, like the Finns, cattle who eat the spring buds tied up in mid summer].

> 'Tis midsummer, yet deep snows rest
> On Odin's mother's frozen breast:
> Like Laplanders, our cattle-kind
> In stall or stable we must bind. (Laing)[57]

---

[54] Morris and Eiríkr Magnússon 1891–1905, III 332–3.
[55] Sephton 1895, 330.
[56] *Haralds saga gráfeldar*, ch. 16, in Bjarni Aðalbjarnarson 1941–51, I 221.
[57] Laing 1844, I 365.

> On Swolnir's dame it snoweth,
> And so have we as Finn-folk
> To bind the hind of birch-buds
> In byre amidst of summer. (Morris and Eiríkr Magnússon)[58]

Laing's octosyllabic rhyming lines create sufficient space for the inclusion of an additional adjective ('deep'), new imagery ('frozen breast'), an alliterative doublet ('stall or stable') and the clarification of kennings ('Odin's spouse', 'cattle-kind'). The Morris version, carrying more philological firepower, seems tauter with its retention of kennings and alliteration, its internal rhyme, its avoidance of elaborately premodified noun phrases, its greater compound noun creativity, and its resistance to abstraction. It also corrects Laing's mistaken interpretation of the difficult 'Svǫlnis vǫ́ru': 'mother' becomes 'dame'. Yet in its own honest lyricism, Laing's version lends strong support to his Dissertation claims regarding the civilised values of the Viking age, which embraced literary creativity as well as governmental structures and naval technology.

Initial responses

Laing's efforts as polemicist and translator earned him generally favourable early reviews. *Tait's Edinburgh Magazine* published a poem 'suggested by the perusal of an article on the Heimskringla in the May number of *Tait's Magazine*'.[59] The opening lines address Snorri's work directly and in some awe. The Viking-age signature motifs are well to the fore – the sea, berserks, freedom:

> Oh! wild and Runic legendry,
>   Thou breath'st a living fire,
> As storm-winds to wild melody
>   Had woke the minstrel's lyre.
> A sound, as if deep ocean's waves
>   With midnight's breezes sung,
> This chant'st thou o'er the heroes' graves
>   Whose knells the Past hath rung.
>
> We read of fell Berserker rage,
>   And feel our fibres glow
> With sympathetic ire to wage
>   Like conflict with the foe.
> We long to roam the stormy main,
>   Wild Norseman-King, with thee,

---

[58] Morris and Eiríkr Magnússon 1891–1905, III 218 ('The Story of Harald Greycloak', ch. 17).
[59] [Johnstone] 1844, 381. The poem is signed 'A.G.', perhaps identifiable as Anna Gurney of Norwich (1796–1857): the poem refers to 'the chivalric De Gournay race'. Anna Gurney shared with her brother Hudson an interest in Old English and Scandinavian antiquities: see *DNB*. Hudson's handsomely bound copy of Rafn 1837 is in Stofnun Árna Magnússonar á Íslandi.

> And, scorning every dastard-chain,
>> To live for ever free. (1–16)

The excitement of battle can temporarily conceal its cruel consequences:

> Oh! in thy tales, thou War-Age grim,
>> Such spells of magic lie,
> As nerve to strength each manly limb,
>> And fire each youthful eye;
> And gazing on the glorious strife,
>> That hour we all forget,
> Which came, with death and anguish rife,
>> When battle's sun had set. (25–32)

Yet the blood-soaked realities soon reassert themselves as attention is directed to those victims for whom no modern Valholl can offer revival and rest:

> Then weakness gasped its all away
>> And youth its freshness lost,
> And fierce despair, 'neath starlight's ray,
>> Its arms to heaven uptost;
> And beauty in its anguish wild
>> Above the dying bent,
> And fiends in fearful gladness smiled,
>> And horrible content. (33–40)

A rerun of Minna Troil's collision with reality seems imminent. The siren voices of the sea-kings are rejected, and Christian compassion overwhelms a darker loðbrókian longing to 'fight with swords':

> Oh! think we but on scenes like these
>> A change comes o'er the soul;
> We hate these monarchs of the seas,
>> And long for battle's goal:
> To meet them in their tyrant ire,
>> And guarding the oppress'd,
> To cope their eager fire with fire,
>> And breast oppose to breast.
>
> Yes, 'twas a passing thought alone
>> Could make us wish as they
> To triumph in each victim's moan,
>> And weaker brethren slay.
> Thanks be to heav'n! the Christian Faith
>> A nobler goal hath given:
> The lightning blast may rend and scathe,
>> But incense soars to heaven. (41–56)

However, the poem ends more robustly than either *Harold the Dauntless* or *The Pirate*. The spirit of the Norse kings is enrolled as an instrument of foreign policy. For long-boat heroics, read gun-boat diplomacy. Old northern sea-faring courage could yet serve Britain well in future confrontations with the forces of European tyranny. Slow to rouse, the British lion can still roar in an old northern accent when compelled to:

> So may our thoughts, and words, and deeds,
>   To that blest clime aspire;
> And shrink we like to bending reeds,
>   From hate, and rage, and ire!
> Yet should the oppressor dare to blast
>   The weak with tyrant powers,
> Then rush we to the strife at last,
>   Then Norsemen's strength be ours! (57–64)[60]

This is very much the voice of Scott's Magnus Troil who, unimpressed by Claude Halcro's tavern-bar militarism, nevertheless recognises that peace should not be bought at any price:

> we are a peaceful people, – peaceful, that is, as long as any one should be peaceful, and that is till someone has the impudence to wrong us, or our neighbours; and then, perhaps, they may not find our northern blood much cooler in our veins than was that of the old Scandinavians that gave us our names and lineage.[61]

In the *Tait's Magazine* review article[62] which inspired the poem Christian Isobel Johnstone writes positively about both Snorri and Laing. The three volumes offer something for all intelligent readers – historian, antiquarian, poet and dramatist, the 'ordinary reader in search of entertainment', not to mention the new wave of Carlylean hero-worshippers. *Heimskringla* would interest those wishing to understand the elements which have 'made . . . England the freest among the European nations'.[63] We might add – the reviewer does not – that those concerned with the major issues of the hungry 1840s (Corn Law abolition, European revolution, Chartist insurrection, and the publication of the *Communist Manifesto*) could find relevant (if stern) prescriptions in Laing's account of old Norwegian polity. Snorri's work certainly exhibits the high seriousness demanded by *Tait's Magazine* of a modern novelist:

> Instead of tales of knightly love and glory, of chivalrous loyalty, of the ambition of

---

[60] Sentiments echoed in Gerald Massey's 'The Norseman' (1861): 'the noble northman stood with Robin Hood' after freedom had died under the 'cruel heart and bloody hand' of William the Conqueror, and will not be slow to answer a future call: 'Still in our race the Norse king reigns; / His best blood beats along our veins; / . . . Is danger stirring? From its sleep / Our War-dog wakes his watch to keep'.

[61] Scott 1822/1996, 125 (ch. 15).

[62] [Johnstone] 1844, 281–93, 369–81.

[63] Ibid., 281.

ancient courts, and the bygone superstitions of a half-savage state, we must have, in a new novelist, the graver themes . . . which the present condition of society suggests. We have had enough of ambitious intrigues; why not now take the magnificent subject, the birth of political principle, whose advent has been heralded for so long? Where are nobler heroes to be found than those who sustain society in the struggle; and what catastrophe so grand as the downfall of bad institutions, and the issues of a process of renovation.[64]

Heimskringla has its share of 'ambitious intrigues' and 'bygone superstitions', but when read in conjunction with the Preliminary Dissertation, it becomes a work about 'the birth of political principle' in Britain. Laing had searched for the origins of the British national character and social institutions and found them in the timeless fjords of Norway. Not for Laing the depoliticised values of Rasmus Rask as cited in another 1844 publication:

I study Icelandic, not with the object of acquiring from it political or military knowledge, or any such thing, but . . . in order to learn to think like a man, to cast out that spirit of meanness and thraldom . . . to strengthen my mind and soul that I may face dangers fearlessly, and my soul choose rather to quit than to deviate from or abjure what she has got a full and firm conviction of being right and true.[65]

Laing also wanted to 'think like a man', but a political man in Victorian Britain.

The Laing Legacy

Samuel Laing enjoyed the reputation of being Britain's foremost philosophical travel writer before the publication of his *Heimskringla* translation. His Norwegian travelogue was widely reviewed in the periodical press, and his ideas found expression in a variety of literary formats. In the *Dublin University Magazine*, William West is convinced by Laing's account of Britain's Norwegian inheritance. He acknowledges that the language of old Norway represents 'a most useful and attractive subject of investigation',[66] and reflects that the self-sufficient Norwegian bonder had much to teach the Irish peasant who marries too early, lives in a hovel, eats only potatoes, and dresses in 'a tattered great coat of raiment'.[67] Reviewing a clutch of Laing's earliest travel writings, Patrick McMahon accepts the importance of distinguishing between the individual societies of 'Scandinavia': Norway had flourished since winning independence in 1814 from a Denmark choked by a top-heavy bureaucracy; and Sweden, aspiring to be 'the France of the North', had too many people living in too

---

[64] Quoted in Boucher 1983, 78.
[65] Kavanagh 1844, I 46.
[66] West 1837, 443–52, at 443.
[67] Ibid., 450.

many private castles, and too few folk engaged in manufacturing industry.[68] McMahon is struck by how much even the physical appearance of Norwegian politicians had impressed Laing, with the austere-looking Storting building full of plainly dressed folk with the shrewd aspect of respectable farmers (285).

Even bad publicity served, at least, to draw attention to Laing's publications, especially the *Heimskringla* translation.[69] Charles Neaves found Laing's relentless anti-Germanism wearisome.[70] At a time when the discoveries of comparative mythologists and grammarians ought to be creating a renewed sense of brotherhood between Indo-European peoples, why was Laing so combative? By all means praise Viking- and saga-age culture – though if it was as wonderful as Laing asserts, why did Icelandic literature wither on the vine after 1400 – but not by misleading denigration of Teutonic achievements. Neaves detects an excess of undigested Jamieson linguistic theory; he derides the suggested connection between geology and feudalism; and he defends primogeniture – Laing's hostility represented the height of political incorrectness amongst Edinburgh followers of the liberal economist J.R. McCulloch.[71] What incentive was there for entrepreneurs to build up large family estates, only for their children to be forced by inheritance law to divide it into equal small portions? The poor would never be made rich by making the rich poor.

Laing's views remained in the public eye throughout Victoria's reign. Reviews of the 1844 translation were still appearing as late as 1871;[72] he reiterated his position in articles in the periodical press,[73] and in travelogues such as his 1852 analysis of the social and political conditions of Denmark, including the duchies of Slesvik and Holsten. This latter region had been a military battleground between Germany and Denmark in 1848, and was to be so again in 1864. Philological and cultural battles were fought over the same territory with almost equal intensity. If the settlers of England after AD 449 came from this region, did they bring Scandinavian or Germanic values with them? Laing argued that the social attitudes and structures of the two duchies resembled Denmark and England far more than a bureaucratic Germany untouched by the political freedoms which go hand in hand with successful wealth-creating economies.[74]

Laing's translation also benefited from well-timed accidents of publication. *The Chronicles of the Norse Kings* appeared shortly after the appearance of *Strife and Peace*, a newly-translated story by Frederika Bremer (in Mary Howitt's

---

[68] [McMahon] 1843, 283.

[69] Laing 1839 was reviewed sympathetically but critically in Stephens 1840a.

[70] [Neaves] 1845. See also [Neaves] 1842, reviewing a revised edition of Jamieson 1808. Jamieson's ignorance of German philological scholarship is criticised.

[71] Discussed in Wawn 1991a, 197–8.

[72] [Forman] 1871, 35–65.

[73] As in Laing 1848.

[74] Laing 1852, 120–22.

phrase) 'the Miss Austen of Sweden'.[75] Snorri's *Heimskringla* features prominently in *Strife and Peace*, and the *Tait's Edinburgh Magazine* reviewer urges readers to study Laing's translation before turning to the Bremer tale. Set mostly in Norway, *Strife and Peace* turns on the relationship between the Swedish widow Susannah and Harold Bergman, Norwegian steward to the reclusive Fru Astrid, who believed that her only son by a former profligate husband had been murdered. While Fru Astrid broods, Harold entertains Susannah and his sister Alette with stories from Jakob Aall's *Heimskringla* translation. They debate the possible Viking origins of recently discovered stone carvings at Taunton River in Massachusetts,[76] and whether Columbus learned about Vínland during his short stay in Iceland. Harold commends the familiar old northern values of laughing in the face of death (with Ragnarr loðbrók, as ever, cited as evidence); Susannah enjoys Snorri's tales of strong-minded queens such as Gunnhildr and Gyða; while Alette points to all the revenge, cruelty and oppression, claiming that sagas offer little to modern readers faced with the real-life challenges of old age and sickness. The tale ends happily with the discovery that Harold is really Astrid's long-lost son, and thus of sufficiently good stock to marry Susannah. With its inset story summaries from *Heimskringla*, its North American dimension, and its debate as to the qualities which old northern saga offers the Victorian reader, *Strife and Peace* represented an ideal trailer for Laing's full length translation.

The Trickle-Down Effect

There is an abundance of other Victorian literary evidence of the trickle-down effect of Laing's old northern ideas. Firstly, Laing looms large in William and Mary Howitt's *Literature and Romance of North Europe* (1852), an influential digest of extant northern edda and saga. This was a popular work on both sides of the Atlantic,[77] with the Howitts bathing old northern literature in a glow of imperialist triumphalism. Britain is unquestionably the foremost nation on earth. British fleets patrol the seven seas, British traders are the merchant-princes of the world, British political power is civilising millions all over the globe, and the English language marches triumphantly behind the flag. British military and financial might had subdued the greatest conqueror (Napoleon) the world had ever seen.[78] As in war and commerce, so in culture. Britain could boast of many more great authors present and past than the Germans (who, readers are informed, have only Goethe), Italy (Dante), and Greece (Homer); and, with every day that dawned, British science drives back the frontiers of

---

75 [Russell] 1844, 356.
76 The so-called Dighton Writing Rock, discussed (sceptically) in Laing 1844, I 174–80; see Bergesen 1997, 81–2.
77 Longfellow was much influenced by the Howitts: see Hilen 1947, 43.
78 Howitt 1852, 2.

darkness and ignorance on every front. Such triumphs would have been inconceivable for a people of slavish Anglo-Saxon descent (5). Lengthy sections of Laing's *Heimskringla* Dissertation are quoted approvingly in support of the proposition that though Britain had long ago absorbed and smoothed over the rough edges of its Viking inheritance, the people retain 'the old Norse fire in their veins' (9).

Secondly, amongst Laing's more avid readers in the United States was the fiery Marie Brown whose opposition to slavery is so worded as to make the cure sound almost as bad as the disease. In *The Icelandic Discovery of America, or Honour to whom Honour is Due* (1887), first published in London, the author makes Laing's anti-Romanist strictures seem ecumenical in their mildness. Brown views the proposed 1892 celebrations for the four hundredth anniversary of Christopher Columbus's arrival as a sinister Catholic conspiracy. Catholicism is the 'fowlest tyranny the world has ever seen', a monstrous snake ever eager to 'coil and crush'; Laing, 'to whom the world is deeply indebted for enlightenment', is repeatedly cited in support of such views.[79]

Thirdly, Laing can be found providing the ideological fuel for Victorian old northern novels. These will be discussed in greater detail in Chapter 11, but three brief examples here serve to establish the general point. In *Hereward the Wake* (1866) Charles Kingsley on several occasions directs his readers' attention to 'the words of a cunninger saga-man than this chronicler, even in those of the Icelandic Homer, Snorro Sturleson',[80] available in Laing's version. In Edward Bulwer-Lytton's *Harold: The Last of the Saxon Kings* (1848), much of the narrative material concerning the assault on Scarborough and York, the 'seven feet of English ground' offer from King Harald Godwinsson to King Harald Sigurdson, and the subsequent battle at Stamford Bridge, is drawn directly from Laing's 'Saga of Harald Hardrada':

> Then he brought up at Skardaborg, and fought with the people of the place. He went up a hill which is there, and made a great pile upon it, which he set on fire; and when the pile was in clear flame, his men took large forks and pitched the burning wood down into the town, so that one house caught fire after the other, and the town surrendered. (Laing III 83)

> With booty and plunder they sailed on to Scarborough, but there the townsfolk were brave, and the walls were strong. The Norsemen ascended a hill above the town, lit a huge pile of wood, and tossed the burning piles down on the roofs. House after house caught the flame, and through the glare and the crash rushed the men of Hardrada. Great was the slaughter, and ample the plunder; and the town, awed and depeopled, submitted to flame and to sword. (Lytton)[81]

---

[79] Brown 1887, 11, 16–18, 20–1, 37–9, 49, 55, 71, 73 and passim.
[80] Kingsley 1866/1895, 203 (ch. 15); see also 38 (ch. 1), 217–18 (ch. 17), 526 (ch. 41).
[81] Bulwer-Lytton 1848; cited from Ward Lock third edition [c.1900], 480–81 (II 11).

R.M. Ballantyne's *Erling the Bold* (1869), a schoolboy tale of the old north, finds the young hero's defiance of King Harald Finehair defined in recognisably Laingean terms – the centralising tyranny, the absence of consultative assemblies, the assaults on odal property. Erling's independent spirit is symbolised in his sword making, with the anvil an emblem of useful crafts in Viking-age Norway.[82] At Thing meetings Erling rails against non-constitutional monarchy. Young Victorian readers must learn to respect their political inheritance:

> we have good reason to regard their [the Norsemen's] memory with respect and gratitude, despite their faults and sins, for much of what is good and true in our laws and social customs, much of what is manly and vigorous in the British Constitution, and much of our intense love of freedom and fair-play, is due to the pith, pluck, enterprise, and sense of justice that dwelt in the breasts of the rugged old sea-king of Norway . . . Yes, there is perhaps more of Norse blood in your veins than you wot of, reader, whether you be English or Scotch (305–6).

Fourthly, in his pallid collection of portraits of the *Early Kings of Norway*,[83] Thomas Carlyle draws heavily on Laing's translation in assessing the contributions made by each monarch or ruling jarl towards the creation of 'articulate Cosmos' out of 'human Chaos' in medieval Scandinavia.[84] The *Early Kings* is a product of Carlyle's declining years; the brush-strokes are as broad as a barndoor, and the great sage's narrative attention span had grown very short. Yet when a strong-minded king is found creating order, making unrefusable offers, and taking no prisoners, Carlyle responds alertly, secure in the knowledge that the safety net of Laing's narrative offers contextualising information. No early king was more admired by Carlyle than King Ólafr Tryggvason, a 'hero-soul', a 'shining figure', the 'wildly beautifulest man, in body and in soul, that one has ever heard of in the North'.[85] Like all Carlyle's heroes, Ólafr was goal-oriented to the highest degree. Anarchy was ever the enemy, and during Ólafr's reign it wore the face of the wilful unbeliever. Such godlessness is presented either through high-priestly zealots such as Hákon jarl, a kind of Puseyite pagan,[86] or through the insouciance of bone-headed bonders. Carlyle purrs approvingly as stubborn opponents are briskly dealt with: eloquent Thing speakers are rendered dumb, temples flattened, and banquet guests threatened with sacrifice to their beloved pagan gods. As for the threats of surly malcontents, 'Tryggveson, I fancy, did not much regard all that; a man of joyful, cheery temper, habitually contemptuous of danger'.[87] It is ironic that these *Heimskringla* translations, the work of nineteenth-century Britain's greatest disciple of bonder values, should

---

82 Ballantyne 1869, 16–17.
83 Carlyle 1875a and b; also Cowan 1979.
84 Carlyle 1899, 308
85 Ibid., 233, 247. Quoted Bennett [n.d. *c*.1900?], Preface.
86 Carlyle will have recalled the elaborate pagan rites practised by Hákon jarl's father and grandfather, as recorded in Laing's translation in *Hákonar saga góða*.
87 Ibid., 237

have become part of Carlyle's advocacy of 'Human order, Regulation, and real Government',[88] in which universal suffrage and 'self government (which means no government, or anarchy)' should play no part.

It was under Carlyle's influence that Ralph Waldo Emerson's preliminary reading for his British tour of 1848–9 included Laing's Dissertation, for many of the 'English traits' about which he writes with such benevolence are traced back to the Scandinavian invasion and settlement period. Britain had been the receptacle 'into which all the mettle of that strenuous population [of Danes and Northmen] was poured',[89] and Snorri's work, the 'Iliad and Odyssey of English history' (552), had recorded the process. Emerson finds the 'traits of Odin' (555) widely disseminated: in the toughness which admires 'a fair stand-up fight' and endures the spartan life of public schools (556, 635), in maritime prowess, in stout and powerful physiques, in the fondness for 'strong, plain speech' (647), and in the 'taste for toil' which has made Britons the wealth creators of Europe. The descendants of Óðinn's smiths are Caxton, Drake, Newton, and (later) Watt, Brindley and Wedgwood who 'dwell in the troll-mounts of Britain and turn the sweat of their face to power and renown' (563). No latter day Normans, for all their aristocratic hauteur, can match this shrewd application of hard-headed science: 'What signifies a pedigree of a hundred links, against a cotton-spinner with steam in his mill; or against a company of broad-shouldered Liverpool merchants, for whom Stephenson and Brunel are contriving locomotives and a tubular bridge'.

A Concert Interlude

Laing's influence can be viewed from an additional and unusual perspective.[90] His ideas may have been recycled regularly, but only one of his saga translations achieved independent popularity and this was due to the intervention of Henry Wadsworth Longfellow, the New England poet who did for Laing what Laing had done for Snorri. Longfellow's poetic version of one saga was itself recycled in simplified form for schoolchildren; and it eventually provided a little-known provincial composer with the raw material from which he produced an old northern cantata – the first ever in Britain, and the first of a series of major choral and symphonic works that made him one of Britain's best-loved composers. Rarely, even in Victorian Britain, can a single medieval text have generated such a varied reception sequence: saga, translation, verse paraphrase, popular retellings, school text edition, libretto, published cantata, performance, publication of individual cantata items arranged for voice and solo instrument, performance of these items well into the present century, and (very recently) digital

---

88 Carlyle 1899, 308.
89 Atkinson 1950, 554.
90 See Wawn 1998.

recording and centenary revival. Some stages of this remarkable sequence merit brief comment.

In *Tales of a Wayside Inn* (1863–73), Henry Wadsworth Longfellow's act of poetic homage to Geoffrey Chaucer, one of the storytellers is a 'fair-haired, blue-eyed'[91] Norwegian musician. The longest and best of his three Scandinavian tales is 'The Saga of King Olaf' (1863) which, drawing extensively on Laing's 'King Olaf Tryggvesson's saga', presents a montage of scenes from the missionary king's life. With his Stradivarius violin, 'in Cremona's workshop's made', the musician conjures up vivid old northern images:

> The rumour of the forest trees,
> The plunge of the implacable seas,
> The tumult of the wind at night,
> Voices of eld, like trumpets blowing,
> Old ballads, and wild melodies
> Through mist and darkness pouring forth,
> Like Elivagar's river flowing
> Out of the glaciers of the North.[92]

Ann Greening, a Victorian farm-worker's daughter from Gloucestershire in England, devoured this and many other Longfellow poems, sharing her enthusiasm with her children. Years later, her son Edward, while still earning a modest living as a violin teacher in Worcester, wrote *Scenes from the Saga of King Olaf* (1896), a ninety-minute choral work based on Longfellow's poem about the Norwegian missionary king.[93] Its impact was remarkable. An unassuming composer of modest background, from unfashionable middle England and brought up in the marginalised Catholic faith of his mother, became an (almost) overnight celebrity. Britain, for so long 'a land without music', had discovered a native-born composer whose music was respected and performed in the Germany of Brahms and Wagner.[94] The composer took his pre-Conquest sounding surname from his father – William *ælfgar* (OE: 'elf-spear'), or *álfgeirr* (OI)[95] or, in its Victorian incarnation, Elgar.[96]

For all that a *Heimskringla*-derived libretto was the most likely musical response to the Victorian cult of the old north, it carried no guarantee of musical success – witness the cautionary tale of George Silke-Willoughby, a Danelaw native claiming Viking descent, who sent Guðbrandur Vigfússon a sample of 'The Norsemen to the Sea', his own dire libretto on Viking themes. Did the great Icelandic philologist know of any Scandinavian composer who

---

[91] Longfellow 1904, 347; perhaps the Norwegian violinist Ole Bull.

[92] Ibid.

[93] Handley 1987/1994.

[94] My discussion draws on Moore 1984, 1987, Anderson 1990, 1993.

[95] Reaney 1991, 6.

[96] First performed at the Victoria Hall, Hanley, which also hosted a centenary performance in 1996.

could set it to music, 'someone who has lived among the Fjords and to whom the Sea is something like what it was to our Northern Forefathers and Palna-toke, and the Jomsburg vikings and King Hakon and countless others'?

> The Viking path to fame and right
> We cleave thy crests mid laughter light
> Whilst Thunder's crashes worlds affright
> And lightening flashes day from night
> > Dark foaming Sea.
>
> In years long past when time was young
> Through Odin's halls the Fate-word rung
> From Vala lips that Norse should be
> Lords of Earth and Kings of thee,
> > Fierce surging Sea.[97]

It is hard to believe that even Edvard Grieg[98] or Carl Nielsen – or Elgar himself – could have made a musical silk purse out of this poetic sow's ear.

By 1896 there were many ways in which members of Elgarian orchestras, choruses and audiences could have come across *Óláfs saga Tryggvasonar* before hearing the music. Both Guðbrandur Vigfússon and Frederick York Powell's *Icelandic Prose Reader* (1879), and Henry Sweet's 1886 *Icelandic Primer* included extracts from the saga.[99] There were also less scholarly volumes for Elgar enthusiasts to consult. Two instances can serve for many. *Torquil, or the Days of Olaf Tryggvason* is a long and bizarre narrative poem, published in Edinburgh in 1870.[100] Laing provides the narrative context, and Longfellow the immediate poetic impetus, but the presiding spirit is that of Sir Walter Scott. Torquil, a Norseman living on one of the northern isles of Scotland, loves the saintly Maida. His pagan mother, disapproving of her son's contacts with Christianity, arranges with the aid of her niece and a pagan priest to have Maida sacrificed to appease the angry gods. Olaf Tryggvason, newly arrived in the islands, recruits Torquil, who stands loyally with the king in his final battle. Maida appears in a vision and urges Torquil to avenge her suffering by helping to convert Norway. *Torquil* wanders far from Laing's translation and Longfellow's poem – but without them it would never have been attempted.

In Robert Leighton's novel *Olaf the Glorious* (1895), Olaf was an exemplary Laingean hero. His kingship enjoyed popular legitimacy, after he had overcome many childhood challenges like some Nordic David Copperfield – the murder of his grandfather and father, escape from the predatory Queen Gunnhild, and a life of slavery in Estonia. The book's schoolboy readership would see that

---

[97] Bodleian MS Eng. misc. d.131, 24 November 1888, f. 539.
[98] Grieg had a perfect alibi: he was orchestrating music for an Olav Tryggvason opera. See 'Scenes from Olav Trygvason' (Op. 50; 1888), in Steen-Nøkleberg 1995.
[99] Gudbrand Vigfusson and Powell 1879, 152–73; Sweet 1886, 60–69.
[100] I have been unable to identify the author.

success could be achieved by the sweat of an individual's own brow. Leighton's Olaf was an *arriviste* hero, and so potentially were many of his young Victorian admirers. We follow the young man's training for life, first, amongst the slaves, the old Baltic equivalent of Victorian public school fagging. Olaf learns useful skills of hand and mind – rune carving, saga telling, harp playing, wood carving, bow bending, arrow shafting – along with the ways of old northern religion. The passing of the baton from generation to generation is signalled by an elaborate ship-burial scene as his foster-father is honoured, and by an equally elaborate ship construction scene as Long Serpent is prepared for the young leader. Thus equipped, Olaf travels widely, a generous friend and relentless foe.

Victorian reconstructions of Laing's 'King Olaf Tryggvesson's saga' were sufficiently numerous and diverse for members of Elgar's choirs and orchestras to have encountered the old northern hero before they turned to the score of the cantata. If Longfellow's poetry (along with Wagner's operas) had introduced Elgar to the old north, Longfellow's own initiation involved early familiarity with Thomas Gray's Norse odes and Scott's *The Pirate*,[101] a visit to Scandinavia in 1834, exposure to Tegnér's *Frithiofs saga*,[102] and (eventually) to Laing's *Heimskringla*.[103] He made several false starts in creating an old northern poem of his own, finding it difficult to surrender fully to the old northern pagan spirit.[104] Reading Laing's translation of *Óláfs saga Tryggvasonar* convinced Longfellow that it would be possible to compose a poetic sequence based on the missionary king's life, using Tegnér's *Frithiof* as a model. Inevitably much of Snorri's long saga finds no place in Longfellow's poem. Only twenty-seven of the 123 saga chapters feature in the poem, several of these only fleetingly. It is the climactic confrontation between Christianity and paganism in Norway following Óláfr's return from his Estonian, Jómsborgian and Orcadian *Wanderjahre* that lies at the heart of the poem.

Longfellow's realignments of Laing's text focus on Olaf's attempts to convert Norway, on his ill-starred attempts to find a loyal wife, and on his heroic death in a great sea battle. Less than half of Longfellow's twenty-two sections find a place in Elgar's work, supplemented by additional material provided by the composer's Malvern friend H.A. Acworth. The cut up and pasted sections of Elgar's dismembered edition of Longfellow are still extant. Acworth's overall libretto recasts Longfellow's interlaced narrative into three discrete blocks: conversion; Olaf's women; death of the king. For Snorri, and hence for Laing and even Longfellow, the spiritual, the emotional, and the military could interlock tragically – Sigrid's paganism earned her the exasperated slap on the cheek, which triggered her revenge and Olaf's death. For Acworth, the structure required narrative simplification and moral clarification. Norway needed

---

101 Hilen 1947, 1–2.
102 Ibid., 23–30, 47–8.
103 Ibid., 97–9.
104 'Ymer. a Poem on the Giants of the Northern Mythology', 'The Fishing of Thor', and a projected poem on Hákon jarl: Hilen 1947, 94, 104.

converting and pagan villains needed eliminating before Olaf could look for the wife who would eventually bring about his downfall.

As for Elgar's musical response to the 'King Olaf' story, we may say that if Longfellow's temperament and ideology were essentially Tegnérian, Elgar approached his assignment with his ears full of Wagner and Brahms, and with his spirit tempered by the many trials faced by a provincial lower-middle class Catholic seeking musical fame in the metropolitan, upper-middle class, Anglican musical establishment. The crusading Olaf conquered the land of his birth with his Catholic faith and scholars have suggested that Elgar saw himself – or can be seen – as a kind of Victorian crusader, if not for his Catholicism directly, then at least for his music. He, too, won over his fellow countrymen after a struggle.[105]

An authentic Elgarian atmosphere is established from the opening bars. The score's prefatory note explains that 'the performers should be looked upon as a gathering of skalds (bards); all, in turn, take part in the narration of the Saga and occasionally, at the more dramatic points, personify for the moment some important character'.[106] Elgar sets his bardic gathering in the misty key of G minor, with contrasting falling and rising figures signalling the work's fundamental conflict between 'gauntlet [Thor] and gospel [Olaf]'.[107] Elgar's fascination with Wagnerian motif construction is discernible from the outset with signature figures for Thor and his hammer, for the northern lights, for Olaf's armour and heroic presence, and for the sea over which he sails 'northward into Drontheim fiord'. The conflicts of religious faith and musical expression established in the first ten minutes are more than sufficient to fuel the remainder of this fascinating if uneven work.

The influence of Laing and Longfellow carried over from the concert hall into the classroom. Beatrice Clay, a former Cambridge pupil of Eiríkur Magnússon, prepared selections from Longfellow's poem for use as a school textbook.[108] In protecting impressionable young minds from too robust an exposure to old northern violence and impiety, only thirteen of Longfellow's sections are excerpted. We may thus imagine evenings when Victorian and Edwardian parents worked at Elgar's *Scenes from the Saga of King Olaf* at the local choral society, while their children toiled at home studying Beatrice Clay's textbook. At every stage of this process the ultimate credit belongs to Samuel Laing.

---

[105] Moore 1984, 183–4.
[106] Elgar 1896, [xii].
[107] Sveinbjörn Sveinbjörnsson's settings of Longfellow's 'The Challenge of Thor' and John Reid's 'The Viking's Grave' were published in London *c.* 1908.
[108] Clay [n.d.].

Envoi

It was in such ways that the ancient and modern Norwegian idealism of Samuel Laing and his translation found expression at all levels of Victorian literary life – from tract to travel book, novel to narrative poem, moral tale to musical reenactment. But there is a final perspective, very different and very private, which helps to account for the public agenda of Laing's Preliminary Dissertation. After all, why was an Orcadian radical wandering through Europe writing philosophical travel books and translating sagas? If Samuel Laing was so committed to the participatory democracy of the old Norwegian Thing, why was he not representing the old Viking isles of Orkney in the modern Westminster parliament?

Thereby hangs a tale. Laing had, in fact, attempted to win a parliamentary seat before leaving Orkney in 1834. The failure of a kelp marketing venture was one reason for his departure, the marriage of his daughter and her move to Edinburgh was certainly another,[109] but electoral disappointment also played its part. Over the winter of 1832–3, Samuel Laing stood unsuccessfully as a parliamentary candidate in the Orkney and Shetland Isles constituency. The election had been a shambles. A violent storm delayed the arrival of the poll books from the Shetland islands where Laing's opponent, George Traill, enjoyed majority support. Without these Shetland returns Laing enjoyed a clear lead and, according to electoral law, should have been declared the winner at the appointed time. But due process was not followed. The Lord Advocate of Scotland intervened on behalf of his friend Traill, instructing the local Sheriff substitute in Kirkwall to adjourn the poll until the storm-tossed Shetlands boat found its way to Kirkwall with the missing votes. When these eventually arrived, Laing's Orkney majority was wiped out at a stroke. Days later George Traill was duly named as member of parliament for the Orkneys and Shetlands. Laing did not take his disappointment lying down. His indignant *Address to the Electors of Scotland* (1833) criticises sharply what Laing saw as the Lord Advocate's improper interference in the democratic process.[110]

It is an ill Orcadian west wind which blows no-one any good, however. Exasperating as this experience must have been for Laing, it was one factor (along with family debt, and his children leaving home) that encouraged him to undertake his Norwegian travels, and which helped to establish the frame of mind in which he viewed that country's present state and early history. Energised by political frustration, Laing sought a better way for the modern north to live, work, and organise themselves. He found many of the answers in the fjords of Norway and in the pages of Snorri; and many Victorian berserkers followed his lead.[111]

---

109 Memoir by his daughter: Laing 1889, I xv–xvi.
110 Laing 1833; see also Sutherland Graeme 1953, 64–104, at 76–79, 82–91.
111 Laing's nephew shared his Scandinavian enthusiasms: Laing, R.M. 1841 and 1842.

CHAPTER FIVE

Frithiof of Sognefjord

It is silly for people to accuse the author [Esaias Tegnér] of sentimentality (that is, of being too sensitive and gentle of spirit, when
everything ought to match the temper and manners of the Viking
age) before they know the *Edda* poems well; for it is there that
sentimentality can be found.

(Matthías Jochumsson 1866 xxiii)[1]

Hail, Aegir, Lord of the Billows,
Whom Neck and Nix obey! . . .
As Frithjof on *Ellida*
Crossed safely o'er the sea,
On this our Dragon shield us,
Thy sons who call on thee.

(Kaiser Wilhelm II 1896)[2]

Instantly [after reading Tegnér's *Frithiofs saga* for the first time] I
was lifted into huge regions of northern sky, I desired with almost
sickening intensity something never to be described (except that it
is cold, spacious, severe, pale and remote)

(C.S. Lewis 1955 23)

An Audience for Frithiof

On the evening of 19 March 1894, John Sephton, a widely respected teacher
and old northern scholar on Merseyside,[3] read portions of his new translation of
Friðþjófs saga hins frækna to seventy-nine members of the Liverpool Philosophical and Literary Society. It was amongst the society's best attended meetings of
the 1893–1894 winter season;[4] only the theories of Charles Darwin attracted a

---

[1] 'Það er varlegt að kenna höfundinum um *sentimentalitet* (þ.e., að hann sje of viðkvæmur og
mjúkur, þar sem allt á að vera samhljóða skapferli og siðum víkingaaldarinnar), fyrr enn menn
þekkja vel Eddukvæðin; þar finna menn *sentimentalitet!*'
[2] 'Song to Aegir': quoted Blind 1896, 95–6; first sung at a 1896 London concert.
[3] See *Liverpool Daily Post*, 13 March 1895, 12f.: review of Sephton 1895.
[4] 'Gypsies' (28 members present), 'Mushroom Beds of South American ants' (50), 'Recent Social-
istic and Labour Legislation in New Zealand' (59), and 'Astrophotography' (75) fared less well:
Sephton 1894, xxix–xxxi.

larger audience than the Icelandic saga – ninety-five members heard the Liverpool surgeon John Newton discuss 'Recent Discoveries as to the Origin and Early History of the Human Race'. Why, we may ask, when others had lectured on ants, astronomy and anthropology, did Sephton decide to talk about an Icelandic saga; and why of all sagas did Sephton choose *Friðþjófs saga hins frækna*, for most of the twentieth century a forgotten work? In addressing these questions, this chapter seeks to examine the remarkable Victorian popularity and emblematic old northern status of Friðþjófr, son of Þorsteinn Víkingsson and of the saga which bears his name.[5]

Decline and Fall

The story of *Friðþjófs saga hins frækna* to which Sephton's audience was exposed can be briefly summarised. The longer of the two Icelandic versions tells of the aged King Beli of Sogn in Norway, and of a worthy freeborn man named Þorsteinn Víkingsson, lifelong friends who are eventually buried in mounds on opposite sides of the fjord. Ingibjǫrg, the royal princess, and Friðþjófr Þorsteinsson are both fostered by Hildingr, a yeoman. The two youngsters fall in love, and thus incur the wrath of Ingibjǫrg's brothers Hálfdan and Helgi, who disapprove of the lower-born suitor. Threatened by King Hringr with invasion, the brothers shamelessly ask Friðþjófr for assistance which he understandably withholds. In an unsuccessful attempt to prevent the lovers from meeting, the brothers conceal Ingibjǫrg in the temple of Baldr. Learning of the lovers' secret meetings at this sacred location, the brothers dispatch Friðþjófr to the Orkneys, ostensibly to collect tribute money, but in reality so that they can have him killed by sea-witches who conjure up storms to engulf the hero. Friðþjófr and his companions survive, emboldened by a fine sequence of heroic songs, and with the aid of his magic ship Elliði. Friðþjófr is warmly received in Orkney. The udallers refuse tribute to King Helgi but offer a substantial sum for Friðþjófr's own use. On his return to Norway he confronts the brothers, striking the arrogant Helgi with the money bag. Friðþjófr sees Helgi's wife warming the statue of Baldr over the fire, and notices that she is wearing the ring that he had once presented to Ingibjǫrg. In attempting to seize the ring, Friðþjófr causes the Baldr image to fall into the fire; the temple catches fire and soon burns to the ground. Friðþjófr escapes, and sets out on a three-year Viking voyage. In disguise he visits King Hringr who had earlier married Ingibjǫrg, under the terms of a peace-treaty with the brothers. Friðþjófr rescues the king and Ingibjǫrg from broken ice on a frozen lake, and, while out hunting, he resists the temptation to kill his sleeping host. Finally unmasking his mystery guest Hringr assures Friðþjófr that he may eventually marry Ingibjǫrg, but must rule the kingdom until the king's own children come of age. With this pledge

5 Baring-Gould 1863, 439.

duly honoured, Friðþjófr returns to Sognefjord with his bride, kills Helgi, receives Hálfdan's oath of loyalty, and accepts the title of king.

Friðþjófs saga has been a largely forgotten work during the twentieth century, enjoying none of the esteem accorded to the *Íslendingasögur*. W.A. Craigie's dismissive pre-First World War judgement can stand for many: '[*Friðþjófs saga*] is attractively written, but has not the slightest historical value'.[6] There has been no full scholarly edition published in any language for over a century,[7] and no new English translation has appeared since Sephton's 1894 version. The saga has not featured prominently in recent sympathetic revaluations of *for-naldarsögur*.[8] Such neglect would have seemed incomprehensible in Victorian Britain – and in the Victorian United States, for that matter. For the saga's first English translator, George Stephens, it was 'one of the most beautiful [sagas] in the whole Cycle of Icelandic literature'.[9] For Samuel Laing, 'this beautiful story' set in Viking-age Norway was among the high points of the 'wonderfully extensive' Old Icelandic saga corpus.[10] William Morris, one of the saga's Victorian translators, regarded it as 'lovely . . . very complete and beautiful'.[11] For Captain H. Spalding, of the 104th Fusiliers, the story was of 'surpassing beauty';[12] for Olivia Stone it was 'one of the finest . . . the world possesses';[13] and for W.P. Ker, an authoritative late-Victorian voice, *Friðþjófs saga* was 'one of the best, and one of the most famous'[14] of the romantic sagas of Iceland.[15] Few Victorian readers will have been surprised that parts of the story found their way into a volume of the 'Library of the World's Best Literature' series in 1897.[16]

In nineteenth-century Britain (and indeed throughout nineteenth-century Europe)[17] the story of Friðþjófr in either its original or one of its popularised forms, was at least as well known as any other medieval Icelandic narrative, including the most popular tales from Snorri's *Heimskringla* and *Prose Edda*. It was the first complete Icelandic saga ever published in an English translation (Stephens 1839).[18] During the nineteenth century, there were three separate

6 Craigie 1913, 95.
7 See Larsson 1901, Wenz 1914.
8 Though see Kalinke 1990, 110–29; for earlier extended comment, see Boyesen 1895, 258–77, Gould 1921–3.
9 Stephens 1839, vi.
10 Laing 1844, I 17, 23.
11 Kelvin 1984–96, I 126, 132.
12 Spalding 1872, [v].
13 Stone 1882, 27.
14 Ker 1896, 277.
15 Ibid., 281.
16 Benson 1926, 150.
17 Notably in Germany; see Zernack 1997, 68–70.
18 Earlier saga extracts are in Johnstone 1782a (the end of *Hákonar saga Hákonarsonar*); Grímur Jónsson Thorkelin 1788 (*Ragnars saga* and *Laxdæla saga*); and Skene 1834 (*Laxdæla saga*). See also Scottish Record Office, MS Heddle GD 263/124, an unpublished draft of *Orkneyinga saga* sections, translated by 'W.W.'

English translations[19] of the Icelandic saga – only one (*Eiríks saga rauða*) could boast of more.[20] Public readings by both William Morris[21] and John Sephton prior to the publication of their own translations ensured that appetites were appropriately whetted. Subsequent republication and repackaging ensured that the story continued to enjoy a high profile on both sides of the Atlantic. We find a version in *Tales of Teutonic Lands* (1872);[22] Rasmus Anderson and Jón Bjarnason arranged for the 1877 republication (in Chicago) of Stephens's 1839 translation, coupled with a translation of the later and lamer *Þorsteins saga Víkingssonar*, which tells of Friðþjófr's troll-slaying father. The Anderson initiative was well received and the Chicago volume was reprinted in his home town of Madison, Wisconsin in 1889, where the local Norwegian-American community kept the sales buoyant.[23] Anderson often wrote for the Chicago journal *Skandinaven* under the pseudonym 'Frithjof'.[24]

Friðþjófs saga and its hero found its way into the public domain in other less direct ways, even in the years before the first publication of George Stephens's translation. A case in point is Ove Malling's *Store og Gode Handlinger af Danske, Norske og Holsterne* (1777), which was translated into English by Andreas Feldborg[25] and published in 1807 as *Great and Good Deeds of Danes, Norwegians and Holsteinians*. It is not clear how widespread or well-disposed a British readership this book on Danish virtues could expect in the year of the British bombardment of the Danish navy in Copenhagen in response to Danish support for Napoleon. Nevertheless those with sufficient generosity of spirit (eleventh of sixteen virtues illustrated by Malling) to wade through the tales of Scandinavian heroes, ancient and modern, would learn that what Kjartan Ólafsson was to Integrity, and Bartholin to Learning, so Friðþjófr was to Firmness, defined as that quality of steady glowing courage whose nature surpasses the fleeting flames of instinctive bravado.[26] The saga also lived a more private life in at least two British libraries, which had custody of *Friðþjófs saga* manuscripts that British travellers brought back from Iceland.[27] Sabine Baring-Gould had acquired his manuscript under the most poignant circumstances in Akureyri: 'a native reduced to great poverty' sold it tearfully to the British traveller.[28] Baring-Gould lists 'the story of stalwart Frith-thjof' among the 'Histories of

---

[19] Stephens 1839 (reprinted Anderson and Jón Bjarnason 1877, 75–111; on its cool USA east coast reception, see Hustvedt 1966, 326); Morris and Eiríkr Magnússon 1871, 1875, and Sephton 1894.
[20] Beamish 1841, de Costa 1868, Sephton 1880, Reeves 1890; see Fry 1980, 18–21.
[21] Kelvin 1984–96, I 130.
[22] Cox and Jones 1872, 210–46.
[23] Hustvedt 1966, 325.
[24] Ibid., 137–40.
[25] Nielsen 1986.
[26] Malling 1807, 119.
[27] BL Adds. 4860 and 24972; also Adv. MS 21.2.7 of (?) Jón Espólín's *Sagaan af Hálfdani gamla og sonum hans*, a work full of Friðþjófr references: Müller 1817–1820, II 672–675.
[28] BL Add. 24972; see Baring-Gould 1863, 225.

Ancient Heroes' in the Bibliography to his 1863 Iceland travel book,[29] but makes no other comment. He had eyes only for the Icelandic saga-steads of Ingimundr goði in Vatnsdalur and (above all) of Grettir the Strong; Friðþjófr never set foot in Iceland.

The Tegnér Version

Sustained Victorian interest in the story of Friðþjófr required an additional impulse, however. This came in the form of successive English translations of Bishop Esaias Tegnér's 1825 Swedish poetic paraphrase of the Icelandic saga. While Tegnér's version follows the principal contours of the saga faithfully enough, there is much amplification and revision of incident and a completely different ending in which Frithiof, the headstrong destroyer of Balder's temple, undertakes its restoration as an act of penitence. Early nineteenth-century Scandinavian cultivation of the old northern pantheon was marked by the spiritual continuities identified between paganism and Christianity. Tegnér, like P.E. Müller (author of the pioneering *Om Asalærens Ægthed*, 1812), was a bishop.[30] In his poem the temple priest looks forward to the coming of Christ, the 'new Balder',[31] and the poem ends with Frithiof and Ingeborg prostrate in front of the deity's restored image. Reinforcing these narrative realignments, Tegnér creates a distinctive lyricism and prosodic versatility which Longfellow found so appealing.

It was, truth to tell, because of Tegnér's *Frithiof* rather than the original Icelandic saga that H.L.D. Ward's 1864 British Museum catalogue of Icelandic manuscripts could speak of 'famous Frithiof'.[32] Previously 'locked up . . . in its soft yet sonorous dialect',[33] the story suddenly became widely accessible. In the period 1833–1914 at least fifteen English versions of Tegnér's poem were published,[34] along with an assortment of retellings.[35] Tegnér's popularity spread far, wide and early in Britain. Thomas Smith, in a paper on the *Vǫluspá* read before the Leicestershire Literary Society in 1838, describes the Swedish bishop as the 'greatest of living poets', and claims that Frithiof's generosity and sang-froid are characteristic of Gothic peoples.[36] In 1841 North Ludlow Beamish could think only of Tegnér's poem when introducing the Vínland sagas to readers on both

---

29 Ibid., 439.
30 N.F.S. Grundtvig was also in holy orders: see Lundgreen-Nielsen 1994, Bradley 1994.
31 Stephens 1839, 220 (Canto 24, v. 28).
32 [Ward] 1864, 129.
33 [Smyth] 1828, 137.
34 Benson 1926.
35 There were two translations of Ferdinand Schmidt's German version: Henderson 1872, Upton 1907; see also Cappel 1882, Paget 1894, Watson 1897, Ragozin 1899, Guerber 1908 (drawing on versions by Stephens, Spalding and Longfellow).
36 Smith 1838, 56.

sides of the Atlantic.[37] A decade later William and Mary Howitt praise Tegnér's 'great [and] truly noble narrative poem'.[38] For George Dasent, in an appendix to his *Burnt Njal* translation, it was an 'immortal' poem – 'the whole work is well worth consulting for the beautiful way in which the author has caught the true spirit of the early North'.[39] A.J. Symington, an Iceland traveller and poet, celebrates Tegnér's 'beautiful northern poem' with its 'fine description of the best type of the Viking and his code of honour'.[40] Guðmundur Torfason and Matthías Jochumsson were equally enthusiastic, and completed the circle of transmission by translating Tegnér's narrative paraphrase back into Icelandic. For Guðmundur the poem is a 'snylli verk' [a work of genius],[41] and Matthías, a friend of many British Icelandophiles, finds it irresistible:

> In my opinion *Frithiofs saga* is one of the finest testimonies to the poetic life and its mental vitality. When we consider the variety to be found within the poem's individual sections we can say that the saga has become a wonderful work of art, a poetic panorama with many beautiful scenes, both parallel and contrasting . . . it is true that Tegnér's symbolism is not to the taste of the Danes or Germans and may at times be clumsy or lacking in good taste, yet it can also often be divine and wholly original. So it is that Tegnér is a true genius and as Geijer says (as I recall) creates order out of confusion.[42]

In lending this wholly new glamour to a faded medieval figure, Tegnér was to Frithiof what Longfellow became for King Ólafr Tryggvason, or Tennyson for King Arthur. Henry Sweet, a sounds rather than sentiments man, would have found few Victorians to agree with him that the poem was 'rubbish'.[43] In nineteenth-century Britain Tegnér's Frithiof outshone the Icelandic Friðþjófr, though the two figures and works were cheerfully confused and conflated by Victorian readers.

It did not take long for sections of the Frithiof story to be recycled in other fictional formats. The hero's sea-voyage to Orkney was a particular favourite, with his stirring verses stiffening the crew's resolve as they face the fearsome sea-witches. In Charles Kingsley's *Hereward the Wake*, the young hero identifies three role models – 'Harold Hardraade', 'Regnar Lodbrog' and Frithiof. The

37 Beamish 1841, i, iv, xvii, xxii, 88.
38 Howitt 1852, II 369–70; see discussion and translation of two sections, 369–98.
39 Dasent 1861, II 357–8.
40 Symington 1862, 278.
41 Lbs. ÍB 10 8vo, reverse of title-page; other copies are Lbs. 480 4to and Lbs. 2399 4to.
42 Steingrímur Matthíasson 1935, 32–3: MJ to Steingrímur Thorsteinsson, 6 May 1866 [Friðþ. er að mínum dómi einhver hinn glæsilegasti vottur um skáldlegt líf og sálarfjör, og þegar margbreytni kvæðanna er dregin saman til heildar, þá er sagan orðin allstórkostlegt listaverk, skáldlegt panórama með mörgum fegurðarmyndum ýmist samstæðum eða gagnstæðum . . . Það er satt að Symbolik Tegnérs er ekki eftir kokkabók Dana og Þjóðverja og máske slæm og smekklaus á vissum stöðum, en Symbolik Tegnérs, einmitt hans Symbolik verður líka oft guðdómleg, og fullkomlega original. Því T. er sannur snillingur og gjörir, eins og (að mig minnir) Geijer segir, óreglur að reglum]
43 Wawn 1990a, 7.

Anglo-Danish Hereward soon finds himself outlawed by the Norman-loving King Edward; in exile he and his followers sail close to Orkney in his vessel Otter, where it is shadowed by a 'witch-whale', boding ill luck. They make to attack the creature 'as did Frithiof in like case', with Hereward's rousing songs inspiring his crew.[44] The moment passes, and Frithiof's influence on the novel is at an end. Kingsley makes no fuss about the allusion; it is not footnoted. By 1866 the tale of Frithiof had become part of the familiar narrative small-change of the old northern novelist. This is confirmed in Paul du Chaillu's *Ivar the Viking, A Romantic History based upon Authentic Facts of the Third and Fourth Centuries* (1893), an extraordinary patchwork quilt of a novel in which incidents from edda and saga are reworked to illustrate the American scholar's eccentric theories about patterns of incursions in post-Roman Britain. du Chaillu believed that the Viking invasions had begun some five centuries before their conventional late eighth-century dating, and that the so-called Anglo-Saxons had in fact been Scandinavians. Early in the novel we find Ivar returning to Scandinavia after a visit to Britain to inspect the region where his ancestors had raided centuries earlier. The voyage proves as turbulent as the chapter heading 'The daughters of Ran' suggests. His vessel bears the same name as Frithiof's, and Ivar cuts up gold rings, like Frithiof before him, in order to be ready with gifts for the pagan gods of the sea should the vessel founder which, boldly steered by Ivar, it does not.[45]

Victorian fascination with Friðþjófr/Frithiof extended beyond words to pictures and music. The story attracted the attention of Scandinavian artists and illustrators soon after its publication,[46] whilst in Britain the tradition of illustrated versions of the story established by George Stephens's 1839 translations was maintained for the rest of the century. The Stephens volume offers two kinds of images – unpeopled saga-steads and decontextualised antiquities. We are shown the lonely calm of Sognefjord at Balder's Strand (Balestrand), with its cairns of King Bele and Thorsten Vikingson, and at Balder's Holm (Balholm), the traditional location of the lovers' temple meeting-place, and we see Thorsten's shield-decorated hall. As antiquities there are illustrations of a drinking horn, a festive trumpet, a harp, an arm-ring of the kind that Ingeborg 'must have' used, King Hring's sledge, a Viking long-ship, a rune-stone, and the stone circle at a Thing site. These items seem like exhibits for an as yet unbuilt museum of northern antiquities. They represent an early display of what became staple items in Victorian old northern iconography.

The text itself had a strong pictorial element which helped to promote, for instance, the glamour of the dragon-headed barque, long before actual vessels came to light in Denmark (Nydam 1863)[47] and, more famously, in Norway (Gokstad 1880; Oseberg 1904):

---

44 Kingsley 1866/1895, 116–18 (ch. 6).
45 du Chaillu 1893, 108–15. See below, pp. 329–31.
46 For example, Fahlcrantz 1829.
47 Brøndsted 1969, I 472–3.

Royal the present was; for the' oak-beams, gently-inbending,
Join'd were not, as is wont in a ship, – but had grown altogether.
Dragon-shap'd it lay on the sea; full high o'er the waters
Rose its proud head, while its wide throat flam'd, with red gold thickly cover'd.
Speckled with yellow and blue was the belly; but back, towards the rudder,
Curv'd its strong-knit tail, in a ring all scaly with silver.
Black were its wings, with edgings of gold; when each one was full-stretch'd –
Flew She with th' whistling Storm for a wager; – but the' eagle came after! –
Saw'st thou the vessel, with arm'd men fill'd – thou straightaway had'st fancied
Some King's City was floating past, or some quick-swimming fortress.
Widely renown'd was this Ship, of ships most choice in the Northland![48]

Frithiof inherits Ellidi, along with the arm-ring and a trusted sword from his father Thorstein, who himself had inherited them from his own father. Each object comes with a history and represents a challenge to every new custodian. The question is never whether sword or ship are good enough for Frithiof, but whether Frithiof is good enough for them. Yet, though custody imposes responsibilities, items such as Frithiof's sword Angurvadel are also loyal companions to be confided in at moments of stress. As illustrated in Stephens's edition, or as described in the poem, the *Frithiof* antiquities confirmed that Victorian interest in the Vikingtide[49] was no regression into cultural barbarism. The artefacts were tokens of human art, craft, and social cohesion in natural settings of rare grandeur and nobility.

After the Stephens edition had established an illustrative tradition within English language publications, we find some gentle pre-Raphaelite drawings enlivening the retellings by Cappel (1882), and Guerber (1908). In Allen's 1912 school-children's version of Tegnér's poem T.H. Robinson's colour plates present the hero on a snow-coloured hillside brandishing his gleaming Excalibur-like sword; or escorting a demurely Pre-Raphaelite Ingeborg; and in the firing of Balder's temple scene the hero is shown to be the soul of stern righteousness. Such illustrations helped to promote Frithiof as a more appropriate adolescent role model (Fig. 3) than the much lionised Sigurd the Volsung.[50] Far from troubling Victorian readers, Frithiof's sexual self-restraint represented welcome support for family values.[51]

Robinson also depicts Frithiof's perilous confrontation with the sea witches, a favourite scene for artists since the 1820s:

> Look! – as isle that loose-torn drifteth –
> Stops that Whale ELLIDA'S way;
> Sea-fiends two the Monster lifteth
> High on's back, through boiling spray:

---

[48] Stephens 1839, 39 (Canto 3).
[49] A term used by Metcalfe W. 1890, 57.
[50] [Forman] 1871, 44.
[51] Jón Hjaltalín 1872, 515.

Fig. 3. Frithiof. Artist T.H. Robinson. From
G.C. Allen, *The Song of Frithiof.*

HEJD is wrapp'd in snowy cov'ring,
   Fashion'd like the white-furr'd bear, –
HAM, 'mid whistling winds grim-hov'ring,
   Storm-bird like assaults the air.[52]

For the Dane Carl Peter Lehmann, working within a year of the poem's publication, it was a *Sturm und Drang* conflict.[53] The seas surge under an inky night-time sky with light from the moon picking out the raging spray. With no Gokstad model to guide him, Lehmann's ship is a strange affair – four sails and full rigging, at least ten oarsmen (almost engulfed and facing the wrong direction), a dragon-headed prow matched by what appears to be a dragon-tailed stern. The helmsman struggles for control, a desperate figure amidships invokes the help of the gods, and the fully armed Frithiof prepares to release a javelin at the sea-witches. We see only the heads of these grotesque emanations of the sea-gods' power, with their Medusa-like hair, fangs, red face, wild eyes and what appear to be vast earrings. The title page illustration[54] to Felix Wagner's 1904 French translation of the Icelandic saga would have been accessible to those members of the Viking Club purchasing the volume following a favourable review in *Saga-Book*.[55] In it, two passing seagulls engage a rather bored dragon head in conversation as the ship founders in mountainous seas. A Gallic Frithiof wields his club like an amateur golfer, with pencil-thin waxed moustache under winged helmet. The sea-witches may have terrified the one visible oarsman yet in their loose fitting gowns and flowing coiffeurs they seem more exotic than fearsome, as if on sabbatical leave from the Folies Bergères. The Robinson illustration is different again. The skies are bright, the sea is calm, the sea-witches are out of sight, and Frithiof seems effortlessly in control of a long-ship whose dragon head alone registers fear at the peril confronting them. The crew, bareheaded gaze up at their horned-helmeted skipper in awe and confidence. It is the spirit of a successful university boat-race crew.

The Victorian cultivation of Frithiof extended to music and travel. George Stephens's translation offered enough accompanying love songs and laments to fill (if not enliven) many a Victorian musical evening, including settings by the translator himself.[56] Years later the coronation entertainment for George V at the Drury Lane Theatre in London featured a performance of the Kaiser's 'Song

---

52 Stephens 1839, 102 (Canto 10, v. 8).
53 Wilson 1997, 36, 90–91. In 1822 Lehmann produced the pre-Tegnér, prize-winning 'Ægir and Ran': Wilson 1997, 47, 95–6.
54 By Nestor Outer.
55 [Green] 1905.
56 Some ('Frithiof at Chess', Stephens 1839, 58; 'Frithiof's bliss', 60–1; 'Ingeborg's lament', 92; 'Frithiof goes into Banishment', 136; 'The Viking-Code', 146–7; 'King Ring's Death'; 182) are settings by Bernard Crusell (see Crusell 1825), occasionally slightly revised by Stephens; others are by Stephens ('Balder's Pyre', 126–7; 'Frithiof commeth to King Ring', 158–9; 'Frithiof on his father's barrow', 200); others draw on Stephens' knowledge old Swedish folk song ('Frithiof with Angantyr', 106; 'The sledge excursion', 168).

of Aegir' based on the saga.[57] As for travel, while Iceland grew in popularity as a destination for Victorian travellers,[58] Norway retained a loyal following of British summer visitors, a number of them aware of the Friðþjófr/Frithiof story, and keen to explore saga-age Sognefjord.[59] Pocket guidebooks pointed the way.[60] One seasoned Norwegian traveller, R.G. Latham, professor of English at University College, London, not only knew the Frithiof story, but translated Tegnér's poem as *Frithiof, A Norwegian Story* (1838), before publishing a travel book, *Norway and the Norwegians* (1840). British travellers visiting the Sogn district could sometimes encounter breathless local enthusiasm about the local saga:

> My next adventure was a journey from Balholm to Sogndal over the mountains, with an old fisherman as porter. On the ascent, we had a glorious view of the scene of 'The Frithjof Saga'. My companion was enchanted, and recited the whole saga most dramatically, going up hill all the time! He lost his wind, and eventually I was obliged to carry both knapsacks.[61]

By the end of the century, indeed, the knapsacks could have been carrying copies of Edna Lyall's popular novel *A Hardy Norseman*,[62] in which Frithiof, the sturdy young Norwegian hero, successfully woos the daughter of a visiting English merchant by rowing her up and down Sognefjord, reciting the events of the local saga. Blanche Morgan could not resist the tale, and neither could many readers in Victorian Britain. The novel was based on a true story with strong links to Frithiof and tourism. The real 'Blanche Morgan' married her Balestrand 'Frithiof', whose family name was Kvikne. Opened in 1877 the Kvikne's Hotel became and remains a spectacularly sited watering hole for prosperous tourists.

Two such visitors merit a mention. Kaiser Wilhelm II's private yacht regularly cruised up the fjord during the summer months, mooring by the hotel jetty. The Kaiser so admired the local saga that he presented a large statue of King Beli and an enormous one of Frithiof to be erected at Balestrand and Vangsnes respectively.[63] They were unveiled in 1913 to a cool local reception. There was environmental disquiet at the sheer bulk of the bronze Viking – the head of a full-grown man does not reach up to the hero's calf; and there were suspicions that the essentially Teutonic rather than Viking style of the hero's armour and weaponry was yet another way of restating the familiar German philological-political claim that Scandinavian culture, ancient and modern, was

---

[57] Allen 1912 Preface. Blind 1896 prints the text.
[58] See below, Chapter 10.
[59] For example Forester 1853, 395, Anderson 1853, 16, 77. See also Schiøtz 1970–86.
[60] Bennett 1882, 92.
[61] I have been unable to retrace the source of this quotation from a late nineteenth-century book about Norway.
[62] In its eleventh edition by 1893.
[63] Hougen 1996.

really German.[64] The following year Kaiser Wilhelm's annual Balestrand visit was cut short due to the deteriorating European political situation.[65]

His departure coincided with the arrival of Mrs G.W. Kitchin and her children from Durham. A peculiar old northern poignancy attaches to their visit. Rev. G.W. Kitchin, who had died only eighteen months earlier, would surely have approved of his widow's choice of holiday location. Kitchin had been an old northern enthusiast for much of his adult life. He had lent financial and spiritual support to Guðbrandur Vigfússon in Oxford,[66] and before his translation to Durham had been a frequent summer visitor to the Lake District haunts of W.G. Collingwood and Thomas Ellwood – it was in Coniston that he helped with the proof-reading of the great Cleasby-Gudbrand Vigfusson *Icelandic-English Dictionary* (1874). How appropriate that of all the many pre-war Danelaw visitors to Sognefjord, members of this family should have been the last British guests to sign the hotel register before the 1914–18 conflict began.[67] For the next four years the saga-steads of Frithiof's Balestrand were visited only in the daydreams of British old northernists.

Reading Frithiof

Victorian and Edwardian fascination with the Sognefjord hero is more easily demonstrated than explained. The cult of Frithiof certainly received no encouragement from the cult of Iceland. With its exclusively Norwegian and Orcadian settings *Friðþjófs saga hins frœkna* could never hope to win a place in the canon of *Íslendingasögur* revered by Icelanders and their British followers. Its opening chapters offer no 'escape from the Norwegian tyranny of King Haraldr' sequence, and consequently its characters, events and spirit were never invoked by nineteenth-century Icelanders in connection with their struggle for independence. In Oxford Guðbrandur Vigfússon was baffled by the saga's popularity. Asked what he thought of the 1875 Morris/Eiríkur Magnússon *Three Northern Love Stories* volume containing translations of *Friðþjófs saga*, *Víglundar saga* (heavily influenced by *Friðþjófs saga*) and *Gunnlaugs saga*, the austere lexicographer replied, 'I am sick of love stories', regarding their 'sentimental moonshine' as an unseemly aspect of Iceland's literary past.[68] Guðbrandur's dismissive judgement, very different from his belief in the saga's historicity when he visited Sognefjord in 1854,[69] may have been connected with Eiríkur Magnússon's in-

64 Engesæter [n.d.], 56–7.
65 The Høiviksalen seat, vacated by the Kaiser when news reached him of the deteriorating European situation on 25 July 1914, remains in the hotel lounge, near two large murals of Frithiof and Ingeborg.
66 See accounts in Bodleian MS Eng. Misc. c.112; also Bodleian MS Eng. Misc. d.131, GWK to GV, especially 28 January 1889.
67 Hotel Registers at Kvikne's Hotel, Balestrand: consulted August 1997.
68 Bredsdorff 1960, 305.
69 Guðbrandur Vigfússon 1855, 38–9.

volvement with the *Three Northern Love Stories* volume. By 1875 Guðbrandur and Eiríkur, towering figures in old northern studies in Victorian England, had seen earlier friendship degenerate into bitter enmity on both a personal and professional level.[70] Yet Guðbrandur was not alone in his scepticism. The Norwegian scholar P.A. Munch might have been expected to enthuse over a tale about Viking-age Norway, especially in letters to his friend George Stephens, translator of both saga and poem. Instead he expresses incredulity at Stephens's involvement: 'Can you seriously bear to read Tegnér's Frithiof, that un-northern mixture of jingling phrases and meaningless pictures . . . the whole thing reminds me of sugar cakes and marzipan artificial flowers'.[71] Munch's scholarly sense of an authentic Norwegian past led to his rejection of a modern Swedish vulgarisation.

As a co-translator of the saga, Eiríkur Magnússon (like Stephens) was inevitably more favourably inclined towards the Frithiof story. His library contained four English translations of Tegnér's poem,[72] as well as Felix Wagner's French translation of the Icelandic saga.[73] When yet another Tegnér translation was under consideration, Eiríkur was invited to write the introduction.[74] Eiríkur was also consulted by his former pupil Beatrice Clay, the Chester schoolteacher responsible for the schools edition of Longfellow's *King Olaf* poem. Following the example of Frederick Winbolt,[75] she had written a play based on the Icelandic *Friðþjófs saga*. Could Eiríkur advise her on Ingibjǫrg's costume, pagan priestly vestments, Old Icelandic forms of divination, and on her proposed alternative ending to the saga, created to 'bring the conclusion in accord with modern feeling'?[76] Winbolt's blank verse melodrama had also deviated from both saga and poem. The vengeful Helgi tricks his sister into believing that a ship burning in the distance is that of Frithiof, returning from Orkney; Ingeborg dies of a broken heart; arriving home too late to save his beloved, Frithiof contemplates suicide, but is persuaded by King Ring to live a full and active life until his reunion with Ingeborg beyond the grave.

For all his many-faceted involvement with the Icelandic saga and the Swedish poem, Eiríkur's explanation for the original saga's popularity is disappointingly simplistic. He claims that *Friðþjófs saga* was written 'for the evident purpose of

---

[70] See below, Chapter 12.

[71] 'Kan De virkelig udstaa Tegners Fridthjof, dette u-nordiske Conglomerat af klingende Tale-maader og hule Billeder . . . det Hele vækker hos mig Idee-association af Sukkerbagværk og kun-stige Marcipan-Blomster': P.A. Munch to GS, 28 April 1850, in Indrebø and Kolsrud (et al.) 1924–7, I 425.

[72] Latham 1838, Matthías Jochumsson (in Icelandic) 1864, Spalding 1872 (heavily annotated), Hamel 1874. Catalogued by Bertha Phillpotts: Lbs. 405 fol.

[73] A complimentary copy from the translator.

[74] Lbs. 2189a 4to, Robert Pritchett (on behalf of Messrs Marcus Ward) to Eiríkur Magnússon, undated.

[75] Winbolt 1902.

[76] Lbs. 2186b 4to, BC to EM, 27 September 1911. The play was never published.

. . . making the listeners merely merry'.[77] Eiríkur had no patience with fashionable solar myth readings, such as that of G.W. Cox: 'Gods and men all mourn the absence of the bright being without whom life and gladness seem alike to be lost'.[78] Frithiof was the solar hero – born to be great but for a time eclipsed by others.[79] Ingibjǫrg's marriage to Hringr, Baldr's death, and Iðunn's abduction are all assigned to Cox's infinitely flexible 'absences of the bright' category.[80] Cox, Eiríkur felt, had been wounded by the mistletoe of one-sidedness.

The issue of Friðþjófr's/Frithiof's popularity in Victorian Britain can certainly be addressed more searchingly than either Guðbrandur or Eiríkur managed to do. Firstly, the lingering popularity of Ossian was certainly a contributory factor. Like C.C. Rafn before him[81] the Reverend William Strong, first English translator of the Tegnér version, includes on his 1834 title-page a quotation from the Swedish bishop which confirms the link. Those drawn to the misty melancholy of the Ossianic corpus would also enjoy the Frithiof romance:

> If you prefer the significant and profound, what ministers to seriousness and contemplation; if you delight in the gigantic, but pale forms which float on the mist, and darkly whisper of the world of the spirits, and of the vanity of all things save true honour – then I must refer you to the hoary – to the saga-stored world of the North, where Vala chanted the key tone of creation, whilst the moon shone upon the cliffs, the brook trilled its monotonous lay, and seated on the summit of a gilded birch, the night-bird sang an elegy upon the brief summer – a dirge over expiring nature.

Ossian was referred to in the commentary notes of British translators throughout the nineteenth century.[82] There were even those who argued that, unlike Frithiof, an historical Ossian actually visited Iceland around the third century AD.[83] Secondly, the story of Friðþjófr/Frithiof could be read as a bridal-quest medieval romance. As such it was always likely to find a receptive readership amongst British antiquaries investigating their own native traditions of medieval chivalry and romance. The hero's remarkably patient wait to recover his bride was seen by some as justification for relocating the origins of medieval chivalry in the vigorous north rather than the decadent south of Europe.[84] Thirdly, the story of Friðþjófr/Frithiof earned its popularity through the memorable poetic sequence from the hero's hazardous voyage to the Orkneys.

---

77 In a draft review of Goddard 1871: Lbs. 405 fol.
78 Goddard 1871, xiv.
79 Cox and Jones 1872, 27.
80 Cox claims that Ingeborg and Frithiof resemble Penelope and Odysseus; that King Ring is like the Mountain Troll in 'The Old Dame and Her Hen' (Dasent 1859); and that Ingeborg's claustration resembles the seizure of Iðunn and her apples.
81 Rafn 1821–6, III [iv], title page to his Danish translation of *Friðþjófs saga*.
82 For example Heckethorne 1856, 176.
83 Waddell 1875, 325–38.
84 Muckleston 1862, v.

One of the earliest British reviews of Tegnér claims that 'a more animated picture of danger at sea, and heroism amidst it, was never drawn',[85] whilst to the Oxonian old northernist Frederick Metcalfe it is a scene 'so vivid and lifelike that our breath bates and our limbs move in unison as we read of hair-breadth escapes and deeds of daring'.[86] Plenty of nineteenth-century Britons saw their nation as the world's greatest sea-power and never tired of nautical adventure stories. Nor were these simply *Boys' Own* tastes. In his 1877 Oxford prize-winning essay *The Place of Iceland in the History of European Institutions*, C.A. Vansittart Conybeare claims that 'it is to the seafaring instincts of the [Norwegian Viking] race that England owes that naval supremacy which has long been her glory, and is still her strength'.[87] Such feelings were still afloat half a century later when the perilous voyage sections of the Morris/Eiríkur Magnússon *Friðþjófs saga* translation were included in a collection of *Great Sea Stories of All Nations*.[88] The moral dimension of these sea-faring instincts was brought out in Tegnér's poem. Life on-board ship under Frithiof's Viking code was no 'peg legs and pieces of eight' operation. The sea-king sleeps under the stars; never furls his sails in a storm; shuns drink and women during a voyage; seeks glory not bounty; regards his wounds as marks of honour which must remain untended for a day; is merciful to those who beg for peace; fights with a short sword; and must earn his crew's loyalty. The section of the poem outlining this code,[89] imported by Tegnér from *Hálfs saga og Hálfsrekka*,[90] became a favourite of translators such as George Borrow[91] and George Dasent who, citing it in the 'Vikings' appendix to his *Burnt Njal* translation, describes it as 'the most perfect summary of the rights and duties of the generous Viking'.[92] There is very little in this 'Vikingabalk' which was out of line with the corporate culture of a Victorian public school, regiment or gentleman's club.

A fourth contributory element to the popularity of the Frithiof story in Britain is, not unnaturally, its Orcadian episode. We have noted that the first Icelandic saga fragments ever translated into English were published principally because of their local British interest – in Orkney, Shetland, the Western Isles, Scotland and Ireland.[93] Victorian readers of *The Pirate* might well have followed the progress of Frithiof to and through Orkney with particular interest. It is indeed possible to identify one potential Orcadian-related readership more precisely. The Udal League was established in the 1880s by London-based exiles from the northern islands. The League aimed to promote a revival of the Norse

---

85 [Smyth] 1828, 137–61, at 151.
86 Metcalfe 1880, 287.
87 Conybeare 1877, 4.
88 Tomlinson 1930, 993–9.
89 Stephens 1839, 149–52 (Canto 15).
90 Rafn 1829–30, II 37. Tegnér would have known the saga from Björner 1737 (ch. 10).
91 Borrow 1923–4, VIII 109–15; translated in 1854.
92 Dasent 1861, II 358–60; see also 1875, I 227–8.
93 Johnstone 1780, 1782a, 1784, 1786; Grímur Jónsson Thorkelin 1788; Skene 1834.

characteristics of the British nation.[94] Angantyr, the Orcadian chief who dealt so nobly with Frithiof, seems an admirable embodiment of these qualities.

Fifthly, the interest which Thomas Carlyle took in *Friðþjófs saga* while working on his study of Oliver Cromwell is instructive. He drew parallels between the destruction of the Baldr temple and early seventeenth-century hostility to Archbishop Laud and his fondness for 'beauty of holiness' ecclesiastical ceremonial. Carlyle would have deplored Tegnér's final Canto in which the temple is restored.[95] So it is that one great Victorian old northernist was able to find within *Friðþjófs saga* the kind of conflicts between high and low church which feature so entertainingly in the Barsetshire novels of Anthony Trollope, himself a visitor to Iceland in the 1880s.

The Language of Old Norway

Merry evenings at home, a taste for salty sea-stories, Ossianic romanticism, Orcadian localism, high vs low church controversy: all these factors certainly helped to win an audience for the story of Friðþjófr/Frithiof in Victorian Britain. Yet there were broader intellectual currents playing around its reception, and as with Laing's *Heimskringla* one of them was language. For Laing and (to a much greater extent) George Stephens, it was important that the language of their translations was English and not Latin, the language of despotic Rome.[96] Written in an old northern vernacular, sagas ought always to be translated into a modern equivalent. Stephens's particular problem as *Friðþjófs saga*'s first translator was to find an appropriate voice for Icelandic saga in a nineteenth-century English language much of whose educated vocabulary and syntax remained resolutely Latinate. He was flying blind, with no stylistic models to work from. He did however have a distinctive philological position which, discussed in greater detail in Chapter 8, requires brief explanation before we examine a representative passage from his translation of *Friðþjófs saga*.

Stephens believed that there had once been a common old northern language which survived best not in the late, bookish forms of Old Icelandic, but in the language of old northern England – its runes, poems and dialect.[97] Much influenced by Rasmus Rask, Stephens strongly resisted claims that English was a Teutonic language, and like Samuel Laing despised 'the modern tendency to Germanicise England and the English'.[98] Thus, when considering the first appearance of the Icelandic *Friðþjófs saga* in English, we need to recognise that each linguistic old northernism has a political charge to it and should not be dis-

---

94 Lbs. 2186b 4to, Alfred Johnstone to Eiríkur Magnússon, 25 March 1887. See also Davis 1842, Thomson 1985.
95 Fielding 1984, 3–10, 35.
96 Stephens 1883, 413–14.
97 Ibid., 320–2.
98 'den modern trafik at germanisere England og Englænderne': Stephens 1890, 27.

missed automatically as old-bufferish eccentricity. The opening paragraph reads as follows in Björner's 1737 text which Stephens used:[99]

Sva byriar þessa Sogu, at *Beli* kongur styrþi *Sygna fylki* i Noreye, hann atti þriu born, *Helgi* het son hans annar, enn *Halfdan* annar, *Yngibiorg* dottir. Yngibiorg var væn at aliti enn vitur at hyggiu, hun var fremst kongs barna. Þar geck strond nockur fyrer vestann fiorþinn, þar var bær stor sa bær var kallaþur i *Ballþurs haga*, þar var *gripastaþur* ok *hof* mikit ok *skyþgarþur* mikill um, þar voru *morg goþ* þo var af *Ballþur* mest hallþit, þar var sva mikit vandlæti giort af heiþnum monnum, at þar *skyllþi aungvo granþ giora hvorki fe nie monnum, einginn viþskipti skyllþu þar karlar viþ konur eiga*. A *Syrstronþ* het þar eþ kongur reþi fyrer, enn hinu meigin fiarþarins stoþ eirn bær, ok het a *Framnesi*, þar bio sa maþur er *Þorsteirn* het ok var *Wikingsson*, bær hans stoþst a viþ kongs aþsetu. Son atti Þorsteirn er *Friþþiofur* het, hann var allra manna stærstur ok sterkastur ok vel at iþrottum buinn þegar i æsku, hann var kallaþur Friþþiofur *hinn frækni*. Har var sva vinsæll at allir baþu honum goþs . . .[100]

This is George Stephens's 1839 version of the passage:

This Saga begins as follows. – King Bele governed Sygna-fylke, in Norway; he had three children; Helge was his first son, Halfdan his second, and his third child was Ingeborg, a daughter. Ingeborg was fair to look upon, and of great understanding, and was reckoned first and best among the royal offspring. There, west of the frith, stretched the strand, and thereupon stood a considerable village called Balder's Hage, where was a Sanctuary and a great Temple, hedged round with a lofty plank-work. Here were many Gods, but Balder was the most honoured among them all; and so zealous were those heathen men, that they had forbidden any harm being done there to either man or beast, nor could a male have any converse with a woman. At Syrstrand was the dwelling of the King, but on the other side the firth was a village called Framnås, where lived that man hight Thorsten the son of Viking, and his village lay opposite the residence of the King. Thorsten's spouse bore him a son called Frithiof, who was the tallest and strongest of men, and, from his very youth, was versed in all manner of exploits; hereby got he the name Frithiof the Bold, and was so happy in his friends that all men wished him well.[101]

Stephens achieves a variety of archaistic effects: coordinate syntax, inversion ('hereby got he the name'), alliterative pointing ('stretched the strand'), phrasal contraction ('where was a sanctuary'), neologistic compounding ('plank-work'), and some old northern vocabulary ('reckoned', 'strand'). This, however, finds itself mixed in with Latinate and French usages ('governed', 'sanctuary', 'considerable village'). Overall the translation seems uncertain in its register, with saga-like plainness subverted by moments of regency verbosity ('hedged around with' for *um*, 'versed in all manner of exploits' for *vel at iþrottum buinn*). This

---

99 Stephens 1839, [2].
100 Björner 1737, 1–2 [pagination not continuous from saga to saga].
101 Stephens 1839, 3–4.

early attempt falls some way short of the idealised style which he partially practised and certainly preached fifty years later – 'that mighty and noble and
thoroly Scandinavian (*Old* Scandinavian) NORTH ENGLISH which is now
the birth-tung of England and her colonies'.[102] In 1839 he knew what his target
was but he was still trying to find the range.

Victoria's Frithiof

If there was a cultural politics to the style of Stephens's *Friðþjófs saga* translation,
similar resonances are soon identified in the story itself. The Frithiof story could
be made to sound a very Laingean text, un-Teutonic and hostile to hereditary
power, characteristics not guaranteed to commend the saga to the very Teutonic
and hereditary Queen Victoria. Laing, for instance, commends the old Norwegian notion that a royal daughter could marry a bonder: 'there was no idea of
disparagement, or inferiority, in such an alliance';[103] and, in the saga, the frank-
lin Friðþjófr duly marries the princess Ingibjǫrg/Ingeborg, whereas courtiers
had been compelled to search the royal palaces of Europe for a suitably well-
born consort for Victoria. How, then, did Queen Victoria and the household at
Windsor cope with the saga of Frithiof?

This is no idle question. After all, as we have noted, the first translation of
Tegnér's poem was dedicated to the youthful Princess Alexandrina Victoria, just
four years before her coronation. *Frithiofs saga* was, thus, not just a Victorian
story. From its earliest exposure in nineteenth-century Britain it was Victoria's
story. The translator was the Reverend William Strong, King George IV's
Chaplain in Ordinary at Windsor. Its title-page identifies the work as 'a Skandi-
navian Legend of Royal Love', while the preface assures readers that Victoria
represents 'a living impersonation of the graces and attractions, of the inflexible
rectitude and fine sensibility, of the conscious dignity and patriotic devotion, of
all the native attributes ascribed by the fiction of the poet to the Royal Maiden
of Norway'.[104] Here, then, was just the old northern tale to encourage Victorian matrons, shocked by Sarah Bernhardt's Cleopatra, to cry 'how *very* like the
home life of our own dear Queen'.[105] Tegnér's Ingeborg is beautiful but
demure; obedient to her brothers; and places duty to family and country before
personal happiness, 'the glorious conquest of the sense of female dignity and
patriotic duty, over fervent and deep-rooted affection'.[106] Passive female stoicism is made to seem an active virtue – was it admiration for these same qualities that led George Stephens to name his own daughter after Tegnér's

---

102 Stephens 1884, xv.
103 Laing 1844, I 104–105.
104 Strong 1833, Preface.
105 *Oxford Dictionary of Quotations* 1980, 5/20.
106 Strong 1833, xiii.

heroine?[107] Throughout Strong's translation the two lovers are presented far more lyrically than in the Icelandic saga, where Ingibjörg in particular seems moody and taciturn. The courage and cameraderie of Frithiof and his crew during their sea-voyage are properly celebrated but, unlike the end of the Icelandic saga where Friðþjófr has to kill Helgi before Hálfdan submits, Tegnér's hero never draws his sword. Helgi dies ignominiously, crushed by a falling idol in a Finnish pagan temple.[108] Indeed, despite the wit, nautical prowess, and poetic skills of Tegnér's hero, it is the Ingeborg/Victoria figure on whom all the hero's actions and most of the reader's thoughts are focused. Strong's edition thus serves as a decorous tribute to the future head of Britain's beloved royal family.

In 1830s Britain, however, members of the royal family were not especially beloved. By no means everyone felt obliged to imitate the royal chaplain's obsequiousness. This was, after all, the age of revolution in Europe; the age of the Chartists in Britain. There were Britons for whom the monarchy had degenerated into a circus full of (mostly Prussian) foreigners. Much of the majesty of monarchy was the creation of late nineteenth-century royal spin-doctors. David Cannadine has reminded us of the comic seediness and chaos surrounding royalty in the early nineteenth century.[109] The sour *Times* obituary for George IV pulls no punches: 'most reckless, unceasing and unbounded prodigality . . . tawdry childishness . . . indifference to the feelings of others', and, even worse, 'the late King had many generations of intimates with whom he led a course of life, the character of which rose little higher than that of animal indulgence'.[110] At the time of the young Princess of Kent's accession, the monarchy could not assume the unquestioning respect of all its subjects. There was no guarantee that the British monarchy would last the century or even the decade. Viewed in this light, it is not difficult to read a monitory element into the royal chaplain's version of Tegnér's *Frithiof*, with Ingeborg serving as a royal role model, and the story as a whole assuming the role of a contemporary Mirror for Princes(ses).

The spirituality at the heart of Bishop Tegnér's *Frithiofs saga* was also likely to commend it to Princess Victoria's chaplain. Balder is treated with more respect than in the Icelandic saga. Indeed, the love of Frithiof and Ingeborg is seen as an earthly reflection of Balder's love for his wife Nanna in old northern myth; and the poem's paganism is the natural religion of righteous heathens awaiting fulfilment in Christianity. The restoration of Balder's temple is 'a victory of the religious principle over youthful arrogance'. George Stephens was amongst those to claim that in Victorian England any 'religious principle' – even pagan-

[107] Obituaries of Stephens in *Proceedings of the Society of Antiquaries of Newcastle upon Tyne* 7 (1895), 14; ibid. 8 (1897), 17, 83.
[108] Stephens 1839, 222–3 (Canto 24, v. 30).
[109] Cannadine 1983, 118.
[110] Hibbert 1976, 782–783.

ism and even (just about) Catholicism – was preferable to materialistic nihilism.[111]

This was indeed the view of late Victorians like John Newton in his Liverpool Philosophical and Literary Society lecture as they tried to accommodate
the intellectual paradigm shift represented by Darwin's theories. The publication in an English translation of J.J.A. Worsaae's *The Primeval Antiquities of
Denmark* (1849),[112] a study of stone- and iron-age Denmark, had challenged the
idea of literal biblical time, and of original Edenic purity which had undergone
subsequent degeneration. History should be seen as progress – but what sort of
progress? Scientific rationalism had identified a random evolutionary process
governed by the laws of physics and chemistry rather than by the dispensations
of divine providence. Skulls grew larger, and brains expanded to fill the space.[113]
It was hard to depict such developments in terms of a ladder leading up towards
some single divine purpose. Evolution had more in common with a tree
without a central bough. The new philology also offered disturbing evolutionary insights.[114] Clarification of ancient linguistic relationships went hand in
hand with uncertainty as to their future development. In nineteenth-century
evolutionary or linguistic theory, what place was there for human or divine
authority? It is small wonder, then, that a royal chaplain should have seized on
Tegnér's Frithiof tale as a source of spiritual guidance; or that, as the century
progressed, other readers empathised with the poem's piety: 'its story is that of a
fine nature, driven half-unwittingly into wrong-doing; of his repentance, atonement, and final forgiveness'.[115] *Friðþjófs saga* was an old northern saga rediscovered in the wake of the new philology; yet in Bishop Tegnér's version it could be
reconciled securely with the primacy of the 'religious principle'.

Beyond Windsor

Within the walls of Windsor Castle the story of Frithiof may have promoted
duty, loyalty and righteous pagan spirituality, but outside the royal circle a range
of more robust readings emerged. Firstly, the story's treatment of the
Friðþjófr/Frithiof figure drew attention to the theme of 'manliness', a favourite
Victorian notion in connection with the old north. Charles Kingsley genderised
the pre-conquest invasions – the Anglo-Saxons represented a female impreg-
nated by the 'great male race', the Norse Vikings.[116] Tegnér's image of old
northern masculinity involved the Viking hero being physically strong and
brave; chivalrous and trustworthy; a witty and resourceful poet; respectful to his

---

111 Bodleian MS Eng. Misc. d.131, GS to Guðbrandur Vigfússon, 9 March 1887.
112 Translation of Worsaae 1843.
113 The Iceland explorers Sir George Mackenzie and Robert Chambers were interested in such theories: on Chambers see Bowler 1989, 88–9.
114 Dowling 1986, 46–103.
115 Watson 1897, 30.
116 Kingsley 1891, I 201.

father; wary of women;[117] and a cool but clubbable leader of men. This latter quality is, needless to say, celebrated in the Orkney voyage scenes, in which the storm at sea contrasts with Frithiof's sang-froid:

> 'Better felt soft kisses
> From my Bride with BALDER,
> Than, as here I stand, to
> Taste this up-thrown brine.
> Better 'twas to' encircle
> ING'BORG'S Waist so slender, –
> Than, as here, tight-clasping
> This hard Rudder-bar!'[118]

And, if, in the translated saga and poem, the hero did not speak 'with a manly mouth', in Dasent's phrase, it would only be because standard Victorian English remained irreparably tainted with the 'mincing' diphthongs of decadent, house-bound West Saxons.[119]

Outside Windsor, too, the Friðþjófr/Frithiof story was read as a challenging account of old northern democratic processes. The tale depicts the orderly trans-fer of power from older to younger generation. The two brothers offer a nega-tive model of this process. Inheriting their father's royal power by hereditary succession, they abuse it, and are unable to defend it convincingly against foreign forces. Their public authority is weak because of their personal imma-turity. The young men demand as an inherited right a deference which they have yet to earn. They huddle regressively on their dead father's mound, and are unable to raise a popular force to resist the elderly, urbane and (in his way) fatherly King Ring because their power has no popular legitimacy. They invoke the supernatural power of the witches (interpretable as displaced mother figures) to sustain their authority. Frithiof, by contrast, is not of royal stock and thus has to be granted any authority he is to exercise. When the brothers torch his home it is as if, in the underlying symbolic logic of the story, the hero is compelled to become his own man, to leave home, to place himself in jeopardy, and to wait like the most patient of Prince Charmings until his Sleeping Beauty wakes up. King Ring's children by Ingeborg will rule their kingdom, whilst Frithiof and his new wife establish a new dynasty based on popular consent. There were plenty of opportunities for Frithiof to seize power by stealth, but he shuns them. He could, for instance, have usurped the throne from Ring's chil-dren, but instead (as with Beowulf and Hygelac's heir) he guards it selflessly until they are old enough to exercise the power formally bestowed at a Thing meeting at the end of Tegnér's poem.

Such is the model of constitutional royal power on offer, certainly in Tegnér's

---

[117] Stephens 1839, 23: Canto 2, v. 28.
[118] Ibid., 99–100.
[119] Dasent 1873, I 14; see below, Chapter 6.

work: an elective monarchy serving a supportive people, exactly as commended to their respective sons by the dying King Bele and Thorstein Vikingson.[120] George Stephens's annotation to his translation makes his own views clear:

> The Kingship of the old North was originally, as it should be, – an Elective Presidency; though the history of the Scandinavian Kingdoms affords melancholy proof enough, how respect for the 'divine races' (as the families said to have been descended from Oden were called) overwhelmed the land with destructive minorities or imbecile manhood. With the 'hereditary principle,' whether monarchic or aristocratic equally cementing Dynasties formed in Kingdoms gained by the sword, came in also 'hereditary degredation.'[121]

For the fiery ex-patriot Englishman, William IV's brief reign had been the last straw, with the king dismissing the government three times in seven years, twice dissolving parliament prematurely, and interfering in the formation of coalition administrations.[122]

The emphasis in *Frithiofs saga* on the democratic legitimacy of central authority will also have played well with those sympathetic to the small shopkeeper Anglo-Saxonism which Olive Anderson[123] has identified in Victorian England. This was marked by enthusiasm and desire to reactivate in appropriate modern form the ancient folk-moot and shire-moot system. A more responsive relationship between monarch and people could be achieved through an extended parliamentary franchise and shorter parliaments. Approval of best pre-Conquest practice went with disapproval of post-Magna Carta concentration of power in a small number of influential families. Participation in government at whatever level ought to be determined by intellectual capacity rather than accidents of birth.

Darwinian Perspectives

We may recall that the two best attended 1893–4 lectures at the Literary and Philosophical Society of the British Empire's greatest commercial port of Liverpool were about *Friðþjófs saga* and Charles Darwin's theories. Darwin's description of man's ascent, from ape to conquest of savagery to global multiplication was just the image of upward social mobility to appeal to those ambitious ranks in Victorian society who could cope with the theological implications. As a recent biographer puts it, what Darwin offered to Britain's *nouveau riche* was 'a romantic pedigree, an epic genealogy. Disregarding the apes, as many did, they found the *Descent [of Man]* a tremendous family

---

120 Stephens 1839, 18–22 (Canto 2).
121 Ibid., 228; Alexander Pope, *Essay on Man* III 241–248, IV 205–216 is cited in support.
122 Gash 1965, 5. The 1848 European convulsions caused some *Frithiof* enthusiasts to shy away from radical constitutional change on old Norwegian models: Forester 1850, 457–59.
123 Anderson 1967.

saga'.[124] It is a striking image to use about a mid-century period that was able for the first time to read real Icelandic sagas in newly-available translations. John Ruskin, quoted by Carlyle at the end of *Early Kings*, posed what for all social Darwinians and many old northernists remained the crucial question for the governance of any community: ' "Who is best man? . . ." and the Fates forgive much, – forgive the wildest, fiercest, cruelest experiments – if fairly made for the determination of that'.[125] Read in this context, the story of Frithiof could be read as encoding a powerful set of *arriviste* middle-class values. The saga community of Sogn ended up with the 'best man' as leader, precisely because the succession of King Bele's sons was unsustainable. To ambitious Victorian ears the story of Frithiof must have sounded deeply reassuring: one reviewer of Stephens's *Frithiof* volume makes great play of Frithiof being a self-made man who rose entirely 'through personal ascendancy and dauntless bearing'.[126] The romance shape of the story generates successive images of authoritarian hostility (ill-natured brothers, predatory sea-witches, raging berserks) overcome by individual prowess and underlying social cohesion. By the end the fearsome margins of existence have been confronted and contained, the illegitimate centre has been overthrown, and a new order established. The long-delayed but star-crossed marriage of the hero finally takes place. It is an optimistic and humane vision reminiscent of Shakespearean romance. If the evidence of the story's widespread diffusion is any guide, Victorian readers of saga and poem responded eagerly to the mood.

The Kaiser's Song

There is no record of any Victorian parent in Britain ever having a child christened Ægir, after the old northern god of the sea. Similarly, even in Iceland, where Óðinn and Þórr (and eventually even Friðþjófur) were common first names, as late as 1920 there had only ever been one Ægir, and there is no record of any girl named Rán until 1940.[127] Yet by 1896 'not a few' loyal German parents were naming their sons after the old northern god of the sea, others were seeking a government ruling as to the legality of the name[128] and, more ominously, a German battleship of that name was launched in 1896. The reason is not difficult to identify. Kaiser Wilhelm II, with his enthusiasm for *Frithiofs saga* still at the short poem rather than giant statue stage, had composed his 'Song to Aegir', which includes and celebrates Frithiof's maritime adventures. It was translated into English by one of Oxford's leading comparative philologists Max Müller, was the subject of an article by Karl Blind published in the *Scottish*

---

[124] Desmond and Moore 1992, 580.
[125] Carlyle 1899, 309.
[126] Forman 1871, 45.
[127] Guðrún Kvaran and Sigurður Jónsson 1991, 236, 455, 603.
[128] Blind 1896, 97.

Review in 1896 and, as we noted earlier, featured in the coronation entertainment organised for King George V. Blind's etymological study allows us a final word on both the popularity and the politicisation of Frithiof the Viking hero.

Blind assures his British readers that Ægir is by no means an alien deity, for in Danelaw areas the name survives to describe the tidal wave which moves periodically up the Rivers Ouse and Trent. Carlyle had noted this in his 'Hero as Divinity' lecture in 1840:

> Sea Tempest in the Jötun *Aegir*, a very dangerous Jötun; – and now to this day, on our river Trent, as I learn, the Nottingham bargemen, when the River is in a certain flooded state (a kind of backwater, or eddying swirl it has, very dangerous to them), call it *Eager*; they cry out, 'Have a care, there is the *Eager* coming!' Curious; that word surviving, like the peak of a submerged world![129]

Thomas Wright's great *English Dialect Dictionary* (1905) offered geographical chapter and verse: *aiger* (NE Yorks), *aigre* (EYorks and SW Lincs), *æger, ager, eger, eygre* (N Lincs), *egor* (E Yorks), *eygre, hygre* (N Lincs). Little interest is shown in possible links with Old English *egor*, 'water'. Carlyle observes that the more general speech of ordinary Danelaw folk 'is still in a singular degree Icelandic . . . its Germanism has still a peculiar Norse tinge'.[130] For Carlyle, with his Prussian sympathies, the old north was essentially Teutonic, and Karl Blind, a British-based refugee from Germany, wholeheartedly agreed.[131] The Eager refers to a 'Germanic' deity integral to the 'creed of the Jutes, the Angles, the Saxons, the Frisians, and other German tribes who made Britain into England'.[132] Blind also notes that the River Eider in Schlesvig-Holstein derives from the same etymological source. The river's original form Egdora or Ægidora ('door to the sea') now seemed even more appropriate with the opening of a ship canal connecting the German ocean with the Baltic – this, claims Blind, was one of the happy fruits of the two former Danish provinces being 're-united with the Fatherland' (98).

As we have seen with Laing and will see with Stephens, not all Victorian old northernists would have joined in the celebration. Even Blind recognises that the Kaiser's intention to devote all proceeds from performances of his 'Song of Ægir' towards a memorial to Kaiser William I, under whose leadership that 'reunification' with the Fatherland had taken place, might not prove universally popular – Ægir himself 'in his hot heathen temper' might 'stir up a fresh tumult of waves' (103). Yet this awareness does not hold Blind back from a final throw of the sycophant's dice: the Kaiser's poem resembles the meeting between Ægir and Bragi (the god of poetry) in the prose eddic *Skáldskaparmál*. On such occasions in the modern British parliament, the normal cry is, 'Give him a job'.

---

[129] Carlyle 1897, V 18–19.
[130] Ibid., 19.
[131] See also Blind 1877, 1879, 1899.
[132] Blind 1896, 97.

So it is that *Frithiofs saga* having begun its Victorian life in the fiery custody of the fanatically anti-German George Stephens ends the century firmly in the sinister hands of the Kaiser and his ever-loyal supporters in Britain. The venerable runologist would have been spinning in his freshly dug grave. It is there that we must leave him until Chapter 8, whilst we turn to the third great canonical text of Victorian old northernism, George Dasent's *The Story of Burnt Njal*.

CHAPTER SIX

George Dasent and *Burnt Njal*

It was the foster-father's duty, in old times, to rear and cherish the child which he had taken from the arms of its natural parents, his superiors in rank. And so may this work [*Burnt Njal*], which the translator has taken from the house of Icelandic scholars, his masters in knowledge, and which he reared and fostered so many years under an English roof, go forth and fight the battle of life for itself, and win fresh fame for those who gave it birth. It will be reward enough for him who has first clothed it in English dress if his foster-child adds another leaf to that evergreen wreath of glory which crowns the brows of Iceland's ancient worthies.

(G.W. Dasent 1861, xx)

How strange it all seemed. The stern reality of the story; the romantic incidents connected with the place; the splendid qualities and chivalrous courage of the man. And what remained? An old-world legend and this heap of battered stones.

(S.E. Waller 1874, 115, on visiting the howe of Gunnarr of Hlíðarendi)[1]

A Wide Screen Epic

In 1861 George Dasent, Professor of English Language and Literature at King's College in London,[2] published his translation of *Brennu-Njáls saga* and by doing so initiated a remarkable new phase in the cultivation of old northern literature in Victorian Britain. Pre-publication sales of a thousand copies[3] in a depressed market following the death of Prince Albert[4] hinted at the favourable reception awaiting the translation. Dasent's *The Story of Burnt Njal* duly became the work through which many Victorian readers made their first acquaintance with the specifically Icelandic as opposed to Scandinavian old north. *Burnt Njal* would never replace Snorri's *Heimskringla* or Tegnér's *Frithiof* in Victorian affections. Yet the encyclopaedic breadth of *Heimskringla* made it a work to be

---

1 Waller 1874, 114. Waller heard an old man read the story of Gunnarr's howe at the site.
2 On Dasent, see Halldór Hermannsson 1919.
3 Lbs 367 fol., GWD to Grímur Thomsen, 21 March [?1861].
4 Ibid., GWD to Grímur Thomsen, undated.

dipped into rather than swallowed whole. Moreover, its focus was dynastic rather than domestic. Both the King Ólafr figures could serve as role models for Victorian muscular Christians, but many novel readers empathised more with the household dramas involving Gunnarr of Hlíðarendi and Njáll Þorgeirsson, Hallgerðr and Bergþóra. As for the story of Frithiof, its Viking-age vision is essentially postcard sized whereas that of *Burnt Njal* fills the widest screen. *Frithiof* has no more than a dozen significant characters; *Njála* has well over a hundred, any one of whom can impact powerfully on the fate of a whole community through a single act of courage or folly. The *Frithiof* story has a single narrative line, that of *Njála* is more like a valkyrie's web. The action of *Frithiof* is concentrated in two principal locations, neither of them delineated in much detail; the events of *Njála* take place not only in the courts and on the high seas of northern Europe, but also in vividly depicted locations on the plains of southern Iceland. Both *Frithiof* and *Njála* present an old north in which the simplicities of the freebooting Viking life are set alongside the complexities of living among family and friends, kin and community but, in Victorian terms, *Frithiof* was a short story while *Njála* was a full-length novel. *Frithiof* is primarily rite of passage romance; the story of Gunnarr and Njáll is the stuff of epic tragedy. It is a tale of law and lawlessness, Christianity and paganism, noble heroes and tempestuous heroines, sibling rivalry and motiveless malignity, the star-crossed and the doomed, creators and destroyers, innocent youth and gnarled age, of royalty and beggarfolk, lawyers and soothsayers, loyal dogs and devious friends, idle travel and gainful trade, taunt and truce, accident and contrivance, songs and spells, sin and saintliness, prevarication and resolve, and of reckless unconcern for, and burdensome knowledge of, the future. If *Frithiof* draws on the myth of Baldr, the narrative shape of *Njáls saga* follows the contours of old northern cosmology overall[5] – the regions of Fljótshlíð and Landeyjar have their local Þórr, Óðinn, Loki, and Freyja figures, and many a minor *ragnarǫk* is played out in daily life as the best seek to ward off (and the worst to advance) the day when the frost-giants of social disruption can be resisted no longer. Yet for all its mythic underlay, the saga creates its own three-dimensional secondary world in which danger can lie in the path of a reckless horse, the theft of a piece of cheese, the snapping of a shoe-thong, the gift of a silk cloak, the glint of a shield, or the proximity of a patch of chickweed. It also dramatises a human world in which goodness can lie in patient attention to detail, generous hospitality, the loyalty of friends and family, the tireless defence of honour, the determination to contain human disruption within a framework of law, and the capacity to feel intensely but to retain self-control. And even when society seems hell-bent on self-destruction, there is an even worse condition to imagine – outlawry from that society. In its depiction of a noble hero who rejects such outlawry and then laughs at the death which follows that defiance, and in its portrayal of that noble hero's noblest friend in his own last earthly moments,

---

5   Allen 1971, 130–1.

Dasent's *Burnt Njal* presented Victorian Britain with unforgettable Bartholinean images which old northern enthusiasts read and relished for the rest of the century. Chaucer's *Canterbury Tales* may have failed Matthew Arnold's 'high seriousness' test – not so *The Story of Burnt Njal*.

Stockholm Preparations

Though *Burnt Njal* was not published until 1861, George Dasent had completed much of the first draft by 1843,[6] during his five year (1840–45) tour of diplomatic duty in Stockholm. Very few other Englishmen at that time would have been able to wrestle convincingly with the saga's language. George Borrow had translated portions of the saga during the 1820s but 'no London publisher, or indeed magazine editor would look at anything from the Norse, Danish etc'.[7] Thomas Carlyle's letters from 1843 reveal his own efforts to come to grips with *Njála*. 'I am deep in Norse sagas', he reports. He had learnt to read Danish, had acquired the 1772 Copenhagen edition of the saga, and had secured access to Rasmus Rask's dictionary – 'I want only the Grammar [Dasent 1843] to begin reading'.[8] It is not clear how much fruit his efforts bore, but he would certainly have fared better with access to the two teachers who helped Dasent: Séra Ólafur Pálsson (1814–76),[9] and George Stephens, both then based in Stockholm. Dasent acknowledges Stephens's help, 'his favours . . . are so numerous that the writer despairs of being able to enumerate them'.[10] Dasent's four Stockholm translation projects – the *Prose Edda* (1842),[11] Rask's Icelandic *Grammar* (1843), *Njáls saga* (begun *c.* 1843), and *Theophilus* (1845) – confirm the diversity of his intellectual sympathies: mythology, grammar, saga, vernacular piety. The published prefaces highlight three of the key factors motivating Dasent's early old northernism: medievalism, the new philology, and interest in questions of translation.

Dasent's medievalism is defined in robust terms. During his student years in Oxford, Dasent like many of his contemporaries was touched by the teachings of Cardinal Newman.[12] The *Theophilus* project, with its tale of a man who sold his soul to the devil and was rescued by the intercession of the Virgin Mary, seems at first sight to lie within that Anglo-Catholic framework. As the Preface reveals, however, the Puseyite dream soon faded and Dasent is anxious to protect his old northern medievalism against charges of stagnant Mariolatry. He

6 Dasent 1861, I xv. Lbs. 367 fol., GWD to Grímur Thomsen, 8 March 1852, indicates that *Burnt Njal* is 'nearly ready to go to press': see Wawn 1991b, 78.
7 Borrow 1923–4, XII 250; see also 251–53.
8 Gades et al. 1970–90, XVI 149, 157, 169 and passim.
9 Snæbjörn Jónsson 1956. Séra Ólafur translated Icelandic folk tales for Symington 1862.
10 Dasent 1845, viii.
11 Dasent 1842. Dasent eventually owned a late paper manuscript of Snorri's *Edda*, the gift of Eiríkur Magnússon: King's College, London, MS Icelandic 2.
12 Dasent 1903, 8.

realises that some will find in these legends 'new proof of monkery and superstition'; others will embrace them too eagerly in their craving for some 'fresh
morning breeze of five centuries back'.[13] Dasent had little sympathy for such
lack of faith in the modern world: 'why should we not encrease our Machinery a
million-fold, and spin Cotton sufficient for the whole world, and still be free at
heart, holding our heads on high, and believing in God?' (iv). Dasent's medievalism seeks common cause with the new entrepreneurialism; his Vikings were
the heroic merchant adventurers of the old north. As for any Mariolatry in the
Theophilus legends, this belonged to the childhood of religious faith. It was now
beyond revival but ought also to be above contempt. Such tales had 'once
[been] the comfort of many an aching heart, and did good service in their day
to the cause of Truth in combating the dark powers of Hell and Death' (vi).
Images of Vikings sailing the seven seas, or of holy men ministering to the
long-forgotten faithful, belied any simple-minded notions of the 'Dark Ages'.
Those centuries had been 'filled with a proper Measure of Light, by which great
and noble deeds were done' (iii).

Dasent's eagerness to protect the medieval north from misunderstanding also
extended to its pagan traditions. His translation of 'Gylfaginning' from the *Prose
Edda*, dedicated to Thomas Carlyle, banishes to the end of the volume Snorri's
prologue, with its thirteenth-century Christian humanistic attempt to locate
Norse mythology within a recognisable biblical framework, with the origins of
Þórr and Óðinn traced back to Saturn, Lord of Crete, and thence to the sons of
Noah. Such 'false conceptions' are rejected, as is Carlylean euhemerism, according to which the gods were simply mighty heroes whose divinity was a con-
struction of their awed fellow men.[14]

Turning to philology, we find that in his Preface to the *Grammar*, Dasent
underlines the importance of the Icelandic language for British readers. Speaking in the apocalyptic tones of the Coleridgean clerisy as they strive to defend
the English language,[15] his diagnosis is bleak: the English language is degenerating fast, under the influence of 'base and barbarous' vocabulary in 'Novels,
Annuals, and a certain class of periodicals'.[16] The remedy is straightforward:
better English teaching in schools undertaken by teachers who have studied
Anglo-Saxon, Anglo-Norman, Old, Middle and New English, early German
and – granted a privileged position – Old Norse:

> putting aside the study of Old Norse for the sake of its magnificent Literature, and
> considering it merely as an accessory help for the English student, we shall find it
> of immense advantage, not only in tracing the rise of words and idioms, but still
> more in clearing up many dark points in our early History . . . I cannot imagine it

---

[13] Dasent 1845, i.
[14] See below, Chapter 7.
[15] Dowling 1986, 29–37.
[16] Dasent 1843, iv.

possible to write a satisfactory History of the Anglo Saxon Period without a thorough knowledge of the Old Norse Literature.[17]

Not only could old northern philology remind the Victorians of their nation's linguistic roots; larger issues were at stake. For the education system not to respond would signal a cultural death-wish. The danger had been well defined by Friedrich Schlegel, as translated by J.G. Lockhart, Sir Walter Scott's son-in-law:

> The care of the national language I consider as at all times a sacred trust and a most important privilege of the higher orders of society. Every man of education should make it the object of his unceasing concern, to preserve his language pure and entire, to speak it, so far as is in his power, in all its beauty and perfection . . . A nation which allows her language to go to ruin . . . testifies her willingness to cease to exist.[18]

Dasent agreed wholeheartedly. For too long, he claimed, 'the twin tyrants [Greek and Latin] ruled all the dialects of the world with a pedant's rod'.[19] The days of such tyranny were numbered, now that the new philology had legitimised the study of other previously unfashionable ancient languages, notably Old English and Old Icelandic: 'Let our philology, therefore, be rather home-born than foreign.'[20]

As for his attitude to translation, Dasent claimed to be making Rask's *Edda* available to English readers in a manner 'as faithful as possible' to the original,[21] whilst acknowledging that many passages will seem 'harsh and abrupt' to 'polished' nineteenth-century ears.[22] As an example we may follow the final part of the scene in which Þórr, travelling in the region of the frost-giants, is confronted by the sleeping Skrýmir. Þórr has already learnt the limits of his legendary powers. Now, after two ineffective blows to Skrýmir's head from his hammer, Þórr winds up for a third and, he hopes, decisive strike. Rask's 1818 Stockholm edition reads as follows:

> Þá hugsaþi Þórr þat, ef hann qvæmi svâ í fære at slá hann it þriþia havgg, at alldri skylldi hann siá sik siþan: liggr nú oc gætir, ef Skrýmir sofnaþi fast. En litlu firir dagan þá heyrir hann at Skrýmir mun sofnat hafa, stendr þá upp oc hleypr at honum, reiþir þá hamarinn af avllu afli, oc lýstr á þunnvángan þann er upp vissi; savkkr þá hamarrinn upp at skaptinu. En Skrýmir settiz upp, oc strauk of vángan oc mælti: hvârt munu foglar nokqvorir sitia í trènu yfir mèr? mic grunar er ec

17 Ibid., vii.
18 Quoted Dowling 1986, 29.
19 Dasent 1903, xviii. Barnes 1869, 101–2 talks of the 'slighting' of Germanic languages in schools and universities.
20 Dasent 1873, II 41.
21 Dasent 1842, vi.
22 Ibid., vii.

vaknaþa, at tros nokqvat af qvistunum fèlli í havfut mèr, hvârt vakir þú Þórr? Mál mun vera upp at standa oc klæþaz.[23]

Dasent's translation reads:

> Then Þórr made up his mind, if he should come to be able to strike him the third blow, that he should never see him more: he lies now and watches if Skrýmir slept fast; but a little before day then hears he that Skrýmir must have slumbered; then stands he up and runs to him, grasps the hammer with all his strength, and dashes it on the cheek that he saw upmost; then sinks the hammer up to the haft. But Skrýmir sat up and stroked his cheek and said. 'Be there any birds sitting in the tree over me? Methought as I woke some moss from the branches fell on my head: what, are you awake Þórr! It must be time to stand up and clothe one's self. . . .'[24]

This is indeed literal translation,[25] bordering at times on transliteration, in terms of vocabulary, syntax and tense variation. Dasent's chosen style suggests a relish for the linguistic and cultural links which the new philology had revealed between England and the old north. The overall radicalism of Dasent's 1842 version would have struck any Victorian reader who took the trouble to compare it with Bishop Percy's 1770 translation, included in I.A. Blackwell's revised *Northern Antiquities* in 1847:

> He however resolved that if he had an opportunity of striking a third blow, it should settle all matters between them. A little before day-break he perceived that Skrymir was again fast asleep, and again grasping his mallet, dashed it with such violence that it forced its way into the giant's cheek up to the handle. But Skrymir sat up, and stroking his cheek, said – 'Are there any birds perched on this tree? Methought when I awoke some moss from the branches fell on my head. What! Art thou awake, Thor? Methinks it is time for us to get up and dress ourselves. . . .'[26]

Percy achieves some gentle archaism ('Methought . . . methinks'); he catches the parallel between *strauk* and 'stroked'; and Dasent looks to have borrowed 'Methought as I woke some moss from the branches fell on my head' word for word. There are omissions in Percy, however: Þórr's impatient wait for Skrýmir to fall asleep, his rush towards the giant with the hammer, and Skrýmir lying with his cheek upturned. Moreover 'settle all matters between them' seems more an urbane paraphrase than a translation of 'alldri skylldi hann sia sik siþan' [never should he see him afterwards]. A new philologically alert era of old northernism would do better than this. Early Victorian English readers

---

[23] Rask 1818d, 52–3.
[24] Dasent 1842, 56.
[25] 'I first read the younger Edda without translation, and then get Dasent's to shew me whether I had missed the sense . . . it being directly and even painfully literal, and at times more difficult than the original': Bodleian MS Eng. Misc. d.131, J.A. Carlyle to Guðbrandur Vigfússon, 5 August 1866.
[26] Percy 1859, 438.

deserved a fresh translation of Snorri's *Edda*, and Dasent brought to his work a scholarly energy and focus previously unknown. The same qualities were soon put to the service of *Njáls saga*.

Dasent in the 1850s: An Old Northern Vision of Life

It is as the translator of *Burnt Njal* that Dasent won his Victorian celebrity. Work on the saga was well under way by 1843. It was subsequently delayed as Dasent took on demanding responsibilities as assistant editor of *The Times*, and became distracted by other projects (notably translating Norwegian folktales). Yet ultimately the translation was all the better for such delays, which allowed Dasent's competence and confidence as a translator to develop. The end result was a style less defensively literal than in the *Edda*.

As published in 1861 *Burnt Njal* was the third and last of a group of old northern publications that occupied Dasent in the late 1850s. The other two works were *The Norsemen in Iceland* (1858), a barnstorming tour of the old northern horizons published in the 'Oxford Essays' series;[27] and *Popular Tales from the Norse* (1859), forty-six translated stories from the first volume of Peter Chr. Asbjørnsen and Jørgen Moe's *Norske Folkeeventyr*, published in Norway in 1843. Taken together these contrasting projects represented the most comprehensive and authoritative vision of the old or traditional north that Victorian Britain had yet been offered. The prefaces are less overtly politicised than Laing's *Heimskringla* Dissertation. To an even greater extent than in George Stephens's *Frithiof* translation, due attention is paid to the material culture of the northman – accommodation, clothing, weaponry, transport. The relationship between old northern literary and British popular culture is highlighted for the first time; and the impact of the new philology on old northern studies is analysed with a fresh and well-informed eye.

The Norseman in Iceland is, in effect, a dry run for the *Burnt Njal* introductory essay. Dasent's use of the term 'Norseman' caused some irritation – as it still can today.[28] Unlike the more inclusive 'Northmen', 'Norsemen' was seen to privilege the Norwegian old north. The ground covered by Dasent's essay – the colonisation of Iceland, pagan mythology, legal institutions, kinship ties – was much the same as that dealt with in Holland's 1811 Preliminary Dissertation, but everywhere there are new insights and emphases. We may note Dasent's fascination with the different types of spear and sword[29] and the inner life with which precious weapons are endowed by names and poetic imagery. Dasent contrasts the 'heartiness, pathos and truth' of old northern spirituality with the spiritual aridity of Victorian Britain.[30] He warms to the Norseman's preference

[27] Hogg 1859 provides a more sober treatment of the same issues.
[28] Grímur Thomsen 1859, 4–16, at 4; Egerton 1848, xi–xii. For Dasent's response, see Wawn 1991b, 88; more generally, see Jónas Kristjánsson 1994.
[29] Dasent 1858, 173–4.
[30] 'Practical Atheism is reserved as the misery of a civilized age': ibid., 200.

for the freedom of the *tún* over the claustration of the town: '[he] loved better to hear the lark sing than the mouse squeak' (202). He shows a shrewd under-standing of Viking-age vengeance culture, for all that he refuses to condone it nine hundred years later in respect of British treatment of Indian mutineers (214). He respects the high premium placed on steadfast male friendship ('You made a friend and kept him; he lasted for life; he was not changed every half year, like a coat'), and also on the diverse roles of women in old northern society, whether as pioneering colonisers, itinerant sibyls (211–12), vulnerable household maidens protected by locked bed closets from 'any gay Lothario among her father's guests' (205), or the kind of venerable *Märchenfrauen* posited in Dasent's interpretation of the much debated term 'Edda' (187).[31]

But it was not just what Dasent said; it was the way he said it. Like so many nineteenth-century scholars of the old north Dasent communicates the excite-ment of the old north stylistically, through cascading metaphor, sensuous adjec-tives, doublet phrases, parallelism, alliteration, all held in place by a richly oratorical syntax. Of Viking territorial expansion he writes: 'Everywhere...in western and central Europe, where there was traffic to be driven or plunder to be got, where a keel would float or an anchor hold, where winds blew and billows rolled, these dauntless rovers showed their fair, but terrible features' (176). Of Viking-age ships as animate objects: 'The Norseman's ship was a dragon, an eagle, a snake, a horse, a stag, an elk, a reindeer, an ox . . . and as in those simple sensuous minds the belief in evil eyes was firmly set, the staring eyeballs and gaping jaws of the monster were supposed not only to terrify but to charm and bewitch the foe on whom they yawned and glared' (177). And saga-age Icelanders were 'the bravest warriors, the boldest sailors, and the most obstinate heathen; but they were the best husbands, the tenderest fathers, and the firmest friends of their day' (214). Dasent's admiration for the Viking past shines out of every paragraph he writes. His faith in the present remains clear but cautious and as for the future, much would depend on the active promotion of his pre-Darwinian version of social Darwinism. The 'ploughshare of Destiny' must not be hindered by meddlesome legislation. So well fertilized were the furrows into which the seeds of old northern freedom had fallen that they should survive all attempts to uproot them. Destiny and Dasent's Darwinism demanded that nature rather than nurture should determine a man's future. Accordingly, his 'Norsemen in Iceland' essay charts carefully the path along which an old northern baby moves: from birth, to acceptance in the household by its father, to fostering, to maturation. Society's demands are stated baldly and with approval:

No 'tenth transmitter of a foolish face' would then have been tolerated merely because one of his ancestors, generations back, had been a man of merit. Society required an earnest and pledge from the man himself that he was worth some-thing, and in this the youth found his noblest incentive to action. 'Place, king!'

31 See below, p. 209.

cries a new guest to a king of Norway. 'Place! find a place for yourself; turn out one of my Thanes if you can. If you can't, you must sit on the footstool.' (212)

Old northern society welcomed individuals sound in wind and limb, irrespective of birth, but was intolerant of incapacity and refused it legal protection. The 'great purposes of Providence' and the 'great rush of progress' had always required 'frequent and bitter sacrifices' – the alternative was social and cultural ruin.[32] Though it seems almost too neat to be true, we know that on his 1861-2 travels in Iceland the excitable and knowledgeable Dasent, a gushing spring of Icelandic antiquity, was known to his fellow travellers as Darwin. On the basis of the 1858 essay alone it is not hard to see why.[33]

The year 1859 not only saw the publication of *The Origin of Species* but also of 'Darwin' Dasent's *Popular Tales from the Norse*. For all the celebrity later enjoyed by *Burnt Njal*, Dasent's translated selection of Norwegian folktales enjoyed at least as wide a readership over as long a time. The 1859 volume sold a thousand copies in the first three months,[34] and the individual tales, variously packaged, were constantly finding new readers: from the publication of 'The Master Thief' in *Blackwood's Magazine* in 1851[35] to the appearance of 'Mother Roundabout's Daughter' in the first volume of a 1918 series improbably entitled 'Oxford Story Readers for Serbians'; from *A Selection from the Norse Tales for the Use of Children* (1861-2) to *Norse Wonder Tales* (1909), a modest children's series published in Glasgow. Yet few readers, of whatever age and condition of life, would have sensed the importance attached by Dasent to these relics of old northern legend. Apart from an odd troll or Norwegian first name, and disregarding the volume's title, the old northern origins of *Popular Tales* would have gone unnoticed had not attention been drawn to them in Dasent's wideranging introductory essay. In his 1858 essay he had noted that 'few would recognise the dreaded Norn of the Norsemen in those witches and "wise women" whose charms are still potent in many an English village'.[36] It is this same sense of abandoned or crippled myths that Dasent seeks to highlight in his 1859 Introduction.

Dasent's thesis, much influenced by the theories of Asbjørnsen and Moe, is that such popular stories are no mere pastimes of an idle hour but witnesses to a rich old northern heritage. They represent the residue of tales once known throughout pre-migration Indo-European society. The process of their transmission westwards mirrors that of the Indo-European language as revealed by the new philology. For Dasent, the western migrants were like the younger son in many a popular tale who, bursting with energy and self-belief, 'went out into the world, with nothing but his good heart and God's blessing to guide him;

---

[32] See also Browning 1876, 9.
[33] [Clifford] 1865.
[34] Cowan and Hermann Pálsson 1972, 15.
[35] Dasent 1851.
[36] Dasent 1858, 212.

and now has come to all honour and fortune, and to be king, ruling over the world'.[37] The western branch 'went out and *did*' while the easterners 'sat down . . . and *thought*' (xvii).[38] The pattern was still discernible centuries later. Dasent disapproved of the British treatment of Indian mutineers in the 1850s, but had no doubts as to which nation had earned the right to be benevolent master and which was destined to be loyal subject. A hothouse plant, however exotic its blooms, was no match for the sturdy oak, deeply rooted, tempered by sun and storm (xvii–xix). No excuse was needed, therefore, for studying the popular survivals of the myths and legends of the western post-migration branch as preserved in Norway. Dasent had never explained in his 1842 *Edda* translation why he thought Norse mythology was so valuable. By 1859, with the arguments of two Norwegian nationalist scholars ringing in his ears, he was in no doubt. Old northern myths represented in refracted form the beliefs, values and spirit of the old northern forefathers of Asbjørnsen and Moe – and of George Dasent and his fellow countrymen. Even the simple language of the Norwegian folktales was as much a virtue as the expressive straightforwardness of the sturdy bonders of the old and modern north 'who call a spade a spade, and who burn tallow, not wax' (lxxx).[39]

The lyrical final page of Dasent's Introduction reveals the depth of his attachment to the idea of Norway and old Norseman just before he transferred his loyalties to Iceland after two successive summer visits. Dasent was capable of feeling a culture as well as thinking it:

[The] constant, bright blue sky, those deeply-indented, sinuous, gleaming, friths, those headstrong rivers and headlong falls, those steep hill-sides, those long ridges of fells, those peaks and needles rising sharp above them, those hanging glaciers and wreaths of everlasting snow, those towering endless pine forests, relieved by slender stems of silver birch, those green spots in the midst of the forest, those winding dales and upland lakes, those various shapes of birds and beasts, the mighty crashing elk, the fleet reindeer, the fearless bear, the nimble lynx, the shy wolf, those eagles and swans, and seabirds, those many tones and notes of Nature's voice making distant music through the twilight summer night, those brilliant, flashing, northern lights when days grow short, those dazzling, blinding storms of autumn snow, that cheerful winter frost and cold, that joy of sledging over the smooth ice, when the sharp-shod horse careers at full speed with the light sledge, or rushes down the steep pitches over the crackling snow through the green spruce wood – all these form a Nature of their own . . . belong . . . to no other land. When in the midst of all this natural scenery, we find an honest manly race, not the race of towns and cities, but of the dales and fells, free and unsubdued, holding its own in a country where there are neither lords nor ladies, but simple men and women. Brave men and fair women, who cling to the traditions of their forefathers, and whose memory reflects as from the faithful mirror of their native steel

---

[37] Dasent 1859, xvi–xvii.
[38] Reviewers praised this distinction: [Christophers] 1859, 360–1.
[39] The distinction is between bees' wax and the more lowly (animal fat) tallow.

the whole history and progress of their race. When all these natural features, and such a manly race meet, then we have the stuff out of which these tales are made, the living rock out of which these sharp-cut national forms are hewn. (lxxxvii–viii)

We need perhaps to remind ourselves that such soaring lyricism represents as heavily politicised a vision as does the austere impenetrability of much academic discourse a century and more later.

Burnt Njal

George Dasent translated *Brennu-Njáls saga* with (for the most part)[40] great accuracy from the only edition of the Icelandic text then available, that of Ólafur Olavius (Copenhagen 1772), with readings clarified when necessary by Guðbrandur Vigfússon, then still resident in Copenhagen.[41] Dasent was no passive transmitter of earlier textual traditions. In what Robert Cook has called the 'Dasent shift',[42] he realigns a cluster of chapters in the middle of the saga in order to consolidate two separated sections dealing with the Christianising of Iceland and the murder of Njáll's foster-son Hǫskuldr Hvítanesgoði. Similar critical self-confidence is discernible throughout Dasent's introductory essay which remains, almost a century and a half later, a well-stocked introduction to the literary and material world of the Icelandic old north. Several features catch the eye. Firstly, it draws on the latest scholarship from Iceland, mainland Scandinavia and Germany. Secondly, Dasent offers a generous range of supplementary saga-derived illustration as when, discussing the exploits of Viking-age Icelanders abroad, he provides the first ever translation of *Auðunar þáttr*;[43] or when an explanation of the internal organisation of an Icelandic hall leads him to translate for the first time chapters from *Gísla saga* relating to the *dyngja*, the room in which the women weave and talk.[44] The reader senses that if only time and space permitted dozens of other sagas could have been quoted at length, each

---

[40] The saga's most recent translator (Cook in Viðar Hreinsson 1997, III 1–220) has made a detailed study of Dasent's translation. The number (some two dozen) and nature of the errors identified testify to Dasent's care and consistency of approach (personal communication, 2 September 1996). For brief discussion see Jakob F. Ásgeirsson 1998.

[41] Sources identified in Dasent 1861, I xix–xx. See also Wawn 1991b, 79. The 1844 Viðeyjarklaustur version was based on Olaus Olavius 1772. Dasent had access to the Grímur Jónsson Thorkelin 1809b Latin translation.

[42] Cook 1998. Dasent's arrangement allows the conversion account (1772 edition and 1809 translation, chs 101–105; 1844 and later editions chs 100–104) to follow the introduction of Hallr of Síða (1772 and 1809, ch. 97; 1844, ch. 96; Dasent ch. 95). The Hǫskuldr chapters (1772 and 1809 chs 98–100; 1844 chs 97–99; Dasent chs 102–4: marriage, murder, revenge on Lýtingr's brothers) are followed directly by the murder of Lýtingr himself (1772 and 1809, ch. 107; 1844 edition ch. 106; Dasent ch. 105).

[43] Dasent 1861, I clxxiii–clxxxiii.

[44] Ibid., I cviii–ix. Dasent 1866, 29ff. differs somewhat from this earlier version.

worthy of full-length translation into English.[45] Thirdly, George Dasent was the barrister son of a colonial attorney-general, and it shows in his response to *Njáls saga*. For Dasent the saga is about law and its greatest hero is Iceland's greatest lawyer. Thirty of the introductory essay's two hundred pages are devoted to the theory and practice of old Icelandic law,[46] with Dasent saluting the nobility of its aims, and despairing at its inability to protect Njáll and his family.

It is no coincidence, also, that Dasent grew up in the age of the great Victorian novelists: *Burnt Njal* appeared just four years after *Barchester Towers*, two years after *Adam Bede*, and in the same year as *Great Expectations* and *Silas Marner*. It is not difficult to read Dasent's fascination with the domestic world of Hlíðarendi and Bergþórshvoll in the light of that flourishing prose narrative tradition. Indeed Anthony Trollope, returning from Iceland in 1878, makes just this point in an article in the *Fortnightly Review*.[47] Dasent's Introduction shows that he understands the interests of a novel-reading age: what was the local geography of Hlíðarendi; what was it like to gaze back up the slope as Gunnarr had famously done;[48] how was a great chief's hall decorated (I xcviii–ci); where did people sleep; how was food prepared and at what times was it served; what were the duties of servants; what were the differences between ceremonial and everyday clothing? The Alþingi site at Þingvellir is described in detail (accompanied by two diagrams; I cxxiv and cxxx); there are sacrificial bowl by bowl accounts of pagan temples (I xxxviii–xlii); and the descriptions of the ceremonial stone circles where law courts met are realistic enough to encourage visitors to locate and explore the sites.[49] Dasent's old northern history was about dates and times as well as places. We are told, for instance, that Njal was burnt on a Monday night in August 1011, at the age of seventy, and with his sons in their forties (I xcvi–vii). The Norse fairy tales that Dasent translated may transcend every neo-classical narrative unity, but not so Icelandic sagas as read by the *Burnt Njal* translator, under the influence of mid-century Icelandic scholars eager to assert the historicity of what had become pivotal documents in their struggle for political independence.

With the chronological and architectural infrastructure of saga life so firmly in place, it is hardly surprising that Dasent responds to the saga characters as if they stalked the pages of *Middlemarch*. Kári is all dash and gallantry, Gunnarr the quintessence of 'goodness and manliness' (I clxxxvi), while Njáll becomes the resourceful country town lawyer, his spirit weighed down with foreknowledge, and content eventually to die a martyr's death. Dasent has a harder time with the wives of the two heroes. Jane Carlyle commented memorably on the tragic inability of Icelandic saga heroes to find suitable wives:

---

[45] Candidates included *Vatnsdæla saga* and *Hallfreðar saga*: [Clifford] 1865, 44, 64–70.
[46] Dasent 1861, I cxl–clxx.
[47] Trollope 1878a, 175.
[48] Dasent 1861, I lxix–lxxi. Dasent had not yet visited Iceland, and drew on Metcalfe 1861.
[49] Adolf Friðriksson and Orri Vésteinsson 1992.

> I feel there was a savagery about some of the Icelandic *Ladies* which made one shudder even to think of! One wd not like to think that the *Arch Enemy* himself would be capable of some of the deeds ascribed to these *Ladies*! No wonder that the advice is given 'Believe not a maiden's word' (nor her Mother's neither) . . . some of the men were very beautiful characters if they had been rightly mated.[50]

Bergþóra is redeemed by her famous declaration of wifely loyalty, but Dasent is icily unforgiving towards Hallgerðr – 'that noble frame, so fair and tall, and yet with so foul a heart, the abode of all great crimes, and also the lurking place of tale-bearing and thieving' (I clxxxvi). The cairn of 'this wicked woman' was still to be seen, and 'is said to be always green, summer and winter alike' (I cxx–cxxi).[51] Her villainy is of Lady Macbethean proportions and the judgement is of biblical severity. Queen Gunnhildr was 'wicked' too, but sufficiently fascinating to earn a twenty-page appendix (II 377–96). Dasent the rationalist is convinced that the only witchcraft she ever exercised was through her 'lovely face and artful mind' (II 380). Morðr, too, seems to have stepped off the stage of some Victorian melodrama – the 'greatest villain, perhaps, in all Icelandic story', 'the very counterpart of Loki', the 'Iago of this Icelandic tragedy' (I lxxxix, xciv).

A further immediately striking feature of Dasent's *Burnt Njal* Introduction is the modernity of some of its broader interpretative judgements. His account of the eventual integration of the traditions of secular orality and clerical literacy when sagas were 'reduced to writing' later in the twelfth century would ruffle few literary-critical feathers almost a century and a half later (I x–xi). The same is true of his analysis of the potentially destabilising nature of gifts as he reflects on the reluctance of freemen to accept land except by purchase (I xliv–v); and of his account of the tensions between pagan and Christian, action and restraint, revenge and forgiveness at the heart of the saga (I clxxxvii). He even proves to be a revisionist on the subject of Vikings and alcohol; despite constant references to their drinking, the sea-rovers were not drunks (I cxv–vi). Yet such interpretative modernities have to fight for their place in the sun with other more distinctly Victorian judgements. Early settlers of Iceland were marked by 'natural nobleness and manliness of character' (I xxxv), and saga 'bare-serks' can be likened to native Malayans out in the Empire – as they run amok 'the intoxicating fumes of bangh or arrack are said to be the cause of their fury' (I xxii).[52]

A key test for the Victorianism of Dasent's *Burnt Njal* might lie in the two favourite themes of Victorian novelists, love and land or, put more directly, sex and money. Of Killer Hrappr's relationship with Gunnarr's widow Hallgerðr we read reports in the saga that there was great friendship between the two and that 'hann fifldi hana' (I xxxv). For modern translators 'he seduced her' or 'he

---

[50] Bodleian MS Eng. Misc. d.131, JC to Guðbrandur Vigfússon, 5 March 1882.
[51] See also Matthías Johannessen 1958, Jón Karl Helgason 1998, 51–75.
[52] Dasent notes the theory that the word should be 'bear-serk' (1861 I xxii).

slept with her' have sufficed;[53] Dasent is content with 'he led her astray'. Hrutr's psycho-sexual problems with his wife following his dealings with Queen Gunnhildr are also treated with great circumspection. The saga is unblinking in its account of Unnr's conversation with her father. We may first follow the passage in the newest English translation:

> Mord said to his daughter: 'Now tell me everything that's happened between you two, and don't make things worse than they are.'
>
> 'So be it,' says she. 'I want a divorce from Hrutr, and I can tell you what my main grievance against him is: he is not able to have sexual intercourse in a way that gives me pleasure, though otherwise his nature is that of the manliest of men.'
>
> 'How can this be?' said Mord. 'Give me more details.'
>
> She answered: 'When he comes close to me his penis is so large that he can't have any satisfaction from me, and yet we've both tried every possible way to enjoy each other, but nothing works. By the time we part, however, he shows that he's as normal physically as other men.'[54]

In comparison Dasent's translation may seem comically evasive. Old northern bonders may have called a spade a spade, but their greatest Victorian admirer appears disinclined to call an enlarged penis anything at all:

> and then Mord said to his daughter –
>
> 'Now, tell me all that is between you two, and don't make more of the matter than it is worth.'
>
> 'So it shall be,' she answered, and sang two songs, in which she revealed the cause of their misunderstanding; and when Mord pressed her to speak out, she told him how she and Hrut could not live together, because he was spell-bound, and that she wished to leave him.[55]

The reference to 'two songs' is not to be attributed solely to prudish evasion on Dasent's part. Three such songs, all omitted in modern editions, were to be found in the 1772 text from which Dasent translated.[56] It is true that detail about the enlarged limb finds expression in one of these verses, but it does not appear in the accompanying prose which Dasent translated. Thus, Dasent's evasion is not quite as it seems from comparison with modern editions alone, but consists only in the decision to report rather than translate the (themselves elliptical) verses.

No such reticence attends Dasent's treatment of money, however. He devotes a twenty-page appendix to the topic and seems anxious that his readers should understand what everything cost in the old north – a silver ring, a ship, or a

---

53 Cook in Viðar Hreinsson 1997, III 105; Bayerschmidt and Hollander 1955, 185; Magnus Magnusson and Hermann Pálsson 1960, 193 (ch. 88); Olaus Olavius 1772, 135 (ch. 89).

54 Cook in Viðar Hreinsson 1997, III 11.

55 Dasent 1861, I 24–5.

56 Olaus Olavius 1772, 13; also in Grímur Jónsson Thorkelin 1809b, 21–4. See Einar Ólafur Sveinsson 1954, 3, 465–6.

life.[57] Dasent produced a chart to show that an old Icelandic hundred in silver (the unit of payment in fines or compensation) was equivalent to £4 10s 0d in Victorian money. Having read of the Njálssons' killing of their foster-brother Hǫskuldr Þráinsson, a reader could register the awfulness of the crime by calculating the compensation sum agreed at the Alþingi – six hundreds of silver was equivalent to £27. This was the equivalent of six weeks' wages for Eiríkur Magnússon in Cambridge University Library, or over three times the first class return fare to Iceland in 1880,[58] or nearly two-thirds of the cost of the dying Guðbrandur Vigfússon's final consultation with his physician in 1889.[59] Noting that Njáll's own blood-fine was three hundreds in silver, Dasent remarks in all solemnity, 'we think we see fresh proof that the hundred in Njal's time was £4 10s., rather than £2 10s. A man of Njal's worth was surely worth £13 10s, and £7 10s would have been too little for him.'[60] At the published price of £1 8s 0d[61] the exchange rate works out at 13 copies of Burnt Njal for one burnt Njáll. Dasent spares no effort to find the right wavelength for a nation of shopkeepers.

'Real Homeric stuff'

From its first appearance in 1861 The Story of Burnt Njal was never long out of the public eye and, if one Iceland traveller is to be believed, 'is [to be] found in the library of every educated gentleman'.[62] The publisher was certainly proud of it – 'I have always considered it one of my choicest publications';[63] and Dasent was proud of the publisher who 'had spared no expense or pains to lay Njal before the world in a beautiful or becoming shape . . . no work has seen the light of late years in this country with a better index'.[64] There were occasional dissenting voices in private – 'vulgar translation . . . in the original [the saga] is so clear . . . [I] detest the slang which Dasent introduces',[65] but published reviews, in both Iceland[66] and Britain, were generally positive: 'we have no hesitation is ascribing to Njala, regarded from an ethnographic point of view, a weight equal to that of the Iliad';[67] 'wonderfully perfect in its construction, marvellously lifelike in all its portraits . . . narrated in a style of such simple

[57] Wawn 1991b, 86–7.
[58] As advertised in Lock 1882.
[59] Invoice included in Bodleian MS Eng. Misc. c.112.
[60] Dasent 1861, II 415.
[61] Wawn 1991a, 87
[62] [Banks] 1881, 52.
[63] Cowan and Pálsson 1972, 16.
[64] Dasent 1861, xviii.
[65] Bodleian MS Eng. Misc. d.131: J.A. Carlyle to Guðbrandur Vigfússon, 25 December 1874. Disapproval of the title and anglicised names surfaces in Lbs. 1484a 4to, correspondence between Lord Dufferin and Sigurður Jónasson.
[66] Guðbrandur Vigfússon 1861: the only criticisms are of anglicised names and incorrect diagrams of Þingvellir.
[67] [Forman] 1871, 60.

beauty';[68] and descriptions done 'with the fidelity of daguerrotype'.[69] Reviewers sought to situate the saga within more familiar literary traditions – the saga man was the Icelandic Plutarch; Gunnarr's rejection of exile parallels Ulysses's rejection of Calypso's offer;[70] Flosi's dream recalled the Flodden Field vision in Scott's *Marmion*; saga speech and conversation were reminiscent of Shakespeare,[71] and the 'good taste' of the prose was worthy of Samuel Richardson.[72] Following Dasent's own example, characters were discussed as if they had either come straight out of a novel or play: Mord 'out Iago's Iago', Flosi was 'a dastard', whilst Hallgerðr is simply an 'infamous, ambitious, insatiate harlot'.[73] In the publishers' advertisements at the end of Dasent's 1866 translation of *Gísla saga Súrssonar*, the tributes continue: *Burnt Njal* 'has a merit equal in our eyes to that of the Homeric poems themselves' (*Edinburgh Review*); 'a story . . . which for simple force and truthfulness is . . . unequalled in European history and poetry, and is not unworthy of being compared . . . for the insight, which it gives into ancient society, with the Homeric poems' (*The Guardian*); 'unsurpassed by any existing monument in the narrative department of any literature, ancient or modern' (*Saturday Review*); 'there are few portions of it [*Burnt Njal*] that are not pregnant with interest and instruction for the reflective mind' (*Athenaeum*).

Admiration was not confined to literary journals. The Danish ambassador in London rewarded Dasent for his efforts by presenting him with a replica old northern horn – musical rather than drinking, we may assume from the allusion to Heimdallr, the 'watchful warden'. In view of the imminence of fresh conflict in Slesvig-Holsten, Dasent's letter of thanks sounds an ironic note which the Englishman, not blessed with the foresight of Njáll, could only have appreciated in retrospect:

> for the Horn, let me say that I think it is a true work of art . . . I am fully aware of the hidden meaning which the excellent artist who designed it has conveyed to those who look rightly at this masterpiece. When the watchful warden blows his horn, and when the wakeful cock crows, when the sturdy seaman who supports the insignia of Denmark strains his eyes on the look out, and when the crowned Lion of the North rouses himself – Then we may trust that the old Northern heart will harden itself for deeds of high emprise, and the stout arm nerve itself to smite down foe after foe.[74]

---

[68] [Lawrence] 1861, 330.

[69] Lowe 1861, 431. The reviewer, a leading parliamentarian and educational reformer, composed prefatory verses in Greek hexameters for Head 1866 [v].

[70] Lowe 1861, 432, 440.

[71] [Lawrence] 1861, 341, 346, 349.

[72] Lowe 1861, 431.

[73] [Forman] 1871, 63–4.

[74] Wawn 1991, 89; letter dated 4 February 1862.

The time for 'deeds of high emprise' was nigh but Britain seemed agog with indifference – 'how hard it is to get people here to enter into the details of the Holstein and Schlesvig quarrel'.[75] When the balloon went up late in 1863, the 'crowned Lion of the North' soon found that it had few friends in the jungle of European diplomacy.

Repackaging

Burnt Njal flourished in a variety of formats well into the twentieth century, thanks to its 1911 reincarnation as an Everyman Library text. Earlier repackagings had also reached out to a broad readership. The original two-volume edition contained the translation, a 200-page introductory essay fully justifying the book's subtitle 'Life in Iceland at the End of the Tenth Century', three appendices (about Vikings, Queen Gunnhild, and money), two maps (of Iceland, and of the main saga-steads), and four plates of an old Icelandic hall.[76] The edition's front cover featured James Drummond's heroic design (Fig. 4), created around the chief weapons mentioned in the saga – Gunnarr's bill, Skarpheðinn's axe and Kári's sword, each held in place by a Viking-age brooch of the kind 'found in a Viking's hoard in Orkney'.[77] Framing the design are two of the saga's memorable saws: 'Bare is back without brother behind'[78] and 'But a short while is hand fain of blow'.[79]

Few of these elements survived the Victorian and Edwardian process of republication and popularisation. E.V. Lucas's 1900 single volume version of the complete translation retains the cover illustration, but discards the appendices and nearly all of the introduction: for most readers 'a good story is the first consideration, and its bearing upon a nation's history a secondary one – or is not considered at all'.[80] The maps and hall designs are also omitted; in their place we find just a single picture of what by the end of the century had become the saga's most famous scene. Gunnarr of Hlíðarendi had been sentenced to a three-year period of overseas exile for his involvement in a sequence of crimes and killings. His friend Njáll had helped to secure this relatively lenient sentence and urges Gunnarr to adhere to the settlement. Gunnarr and his brother Kolskeggr prepare to leave Hlíðarendi and head for shore, ship, and safety. Dasent's translation continues:

> They ride down along Markfleet, and just then Gunnar's horse tripped and threw him off. He turned with his face up towards the Lithe and the homestead at Lithend, and said –

[75] Wawn 1991, 85, George Dasent to Grímur Thomsen, undated.
[76] The work of Sigurður Guðmundsson.
[77] Dasent 1900 [v].
[78] Dasent 1861, II 316 (ch. 151; Einar Ólafur Sveinsson 1954, 436).
[79] Ibid., I 132, II 95, 201 (ch. 42, 104, 133; Einar Ólafur Sveinsson 1954, 109, 253, 349).
[80] Dasent 1900, vii.

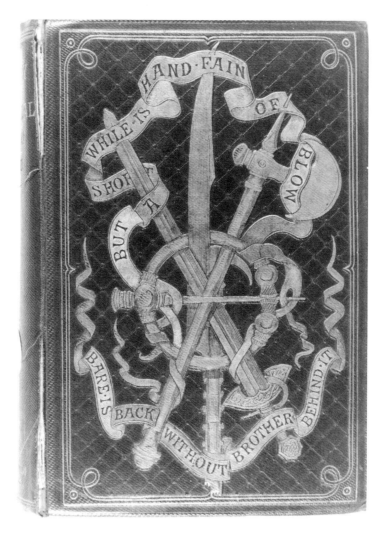

Fig. 4. The chief weapons in *Brennu-Njáls saga*: Gunnarr's
hallberd, Kári's sword and Skarpheðinn's axe. Artist James
Drummond. Cover design for George Webbe Dasent
(trans.), *The Story of Burnt Njal*.

'Fair is the Lithe; so fair that it has never seemed to me so fair; the corn fields are white to harvest, and the home mead is mown; and now I will ride back home, and not fare abroad at all.'

'Do not this joy to thy foes,' says Kolskegg, 'by breaking thy atonement, for no man could think thou wouldst do thus, and thou mayst be sure that all will happen as Njal has said.'

'I will not go away any whither,' says Gunnar, 'and so I would thou shouldest do too.'[81]

Gunnarr was Gunnarr of Hlíðarendi; in accepting exile he was surrendering a crucial part of his identity, and this on a day when his home fields had never looked lovelier. It was a narrative moment of such power and poignancy that by the end of the nineteenth century a visit to Hlíðarendi in order to gaze up that same slope had become part of any saga pilgrim's Iceland experience. Even Sir Richard Burton, most sceptical of travellers, acknowledges that 'It [Dasent's *Burnt Njal*] . . . will send many an English tourist to gaze upon the Lithe-end.'[82] Before we examine the Lucas edition picture, it is worth looking in more detail at a short section from the translation which it served to illustrate.

The 1772 Icelandic text from which Dasent was working reads:

þeir ríða fram með Markarflióti. þá drap hestr Gunnars fæti ok stokk hann af baki. honom varð litið upp til hlíðarinnar. ok bæarins at Hlíðarenda ok mællti. fogr er hlíðin sva at mer hefir hon alldri iafnfogr sýnz. bleikir akrar. en slegin tún. ok man ek ríða heim aptr. ok fara hvergi.[83]

Many individual features of Dasent's version catch the eye: the extra drama created by translating *þá* as '*just* then'; the anti-heroic nature of Gunnarr's separation from the horse, caused by mistakenly taking *hann* as the object of *stokk* rather than its subject;[84] the willed nature of 'turned with his face' as opposed to catching an accidental glimpse of the slope; the retention of Lithe and Lithend in the archaic sense of 'slope', recorded in a single mid-nineteenth-century *OED* citation (Dasent's readers may well have been puzzled by the usage);[85] the triple repetition of 'fair' and double repetition of 'so fair' will have seemed incantatory, flat-footed, or determinedly plain style according to taste; the lyric amplification 'are white *to harvest*'; the semi-archaism[86] of 'home mead' for *tún*, setting up alliteration with 'mown'; the echo of the Icelandic *fara* in the archaic 'fare'; and the gratuitous 'abroad' at the end. Taken as a whole, there is relatively little lily gilding; this is hardly the paragraph that launched a thousand tourist ships. It is

---

81 Dasent 1861, I 236–7 (ch. 74; Einar Ólafur Sveinsson 1954, 182).

82 Burton 1875, I 252.

83 Olaus Olavius 1772, 112 (ch. 76).

84 Acknowledged in Dasent 1861, II 503: 'slipped off his horse' suggested instead.

85 The *OED* refers to a place name at an ancestral English home.

86 Dasent's archaising was inconsistent: he used verbal inversion, and 'thou' with -*est* forms, but -*s* rather than -*eth* third person forms.

the scene itself rather than any verbal tricks by Dasent which drew the pilgrims to Hlíðarendi.[87]

Passages rendered purple by tradition are as hard for the illustrator as they are for the translator. Reviewing Dasent's translation in 1862 an old northern scholar asks, 'Will not Mr. Maclise, who some time since showed us so admirably the deeds of Gunnar's brethren at Hastings, trace the line a little higher up, and show us the death of Gunnar himself at Lithend'.[88] The answer, alas, was – no. The picture in E. V. Lucas's 1900 volume does little to satisfy the need or rise to the occasion. It is a parade of old northern iconographic cliché. The blond-haired, horned-helmeted, cross-gartered, breast-plated, chain-mailed, cloak-clasped, shield-bearing, bill-clutching Gunnar gazes back up the slope over the reader's shoulder, whilst the less extravagantly clad Kolskegg looks on with reins in hand, eager to be off down the path (Fig. 5).

Bare is the back without brother, the saga reminds us,[89] and bare is the book without pictures. When *Burnt Njal* next saw the light of published day in 1906 it had shed not only the hall plates and maps, but now also its cover design and the 1900 Gunnar at Lithend illustration. The Lucas volume had been prepared 'simply as a brave story for men who have been boys and for boys who are going to be men'.[90] Far greater things were planned in the 1906 Norrœna Society volume, *The Story of Burnt Njal, The Great Icelandic Tribune, Jurist and Counsellor*. The Norrœna Society was the hollow invention of Rasmus Anderson, Laing's one-time editor, and by now a venerable professor in Wisconsin.[91] Under its flag of convenience, recycled translations of texts devoted to 'The History and Romance of Northern Europe' could sail into the homes of prosperous readers in London, Copenhagen, Stockholm, Berlin and New York (the places of publication cited on the title page), where they would represent a clear cultural statement about pride in old northern origins.[92] Eight expensive volumes were duly published in a limited edition, including Oliver Elton's Saxo Grammaticus translation, Benjamin Thorpe's 1866 *Edda*, Thomas Percy's *Northern Antiquities* in the revised 1847 version, Laing's *Heimskringla*, and two volumes by George Dasent – *Popular Tales from the Norse*,[93] and *Burnt Njal*. This latter volume is an almost word-for-word reprint of the 1900 Lucas abridgement, though now illustrated with artworks of arguably greater distinction and

---

[87] See also: (i) Cox and Jones 1872, 358 (with Gunnar still on his horse): ' "How fair is Lithend in the summer sunshine! Never has it seemed to me so fair. The corn-fields are yellowing to harvest. They are carrying the hay from the home-field – how sweet it smells! I cannot leave the old place, brother; by my life I will not leave it!" ' (ii) Leith 1897 172 translates the relevant lines in Jónas Hallgrímsson's 'Gunnarshólmi': 'Ne'er saw I yet the earth's increase so fair! / The cattle spread them o'er the field to graze, / Against pale cornfields roses redden there'.
[88] King 1862, 117. The allusion is to Daniel Maclise: see also Wilson 1997, 58–9, 95.
[89] Dasent 1861, 1900 incorporate the phrase into their cover designs.
[90] Dasent 1900, vii.
[91] Hustvedt 1966, 334.
[92] Ibid., 335.
[93] Retitled as *A Collection of Popular Tales from the Norse and North German*; Dasent's eighty-page introduction is substantially reduced.

Fig. 5. Gunnar refuses to leave home. Artist George Morrow. From
E.V. Lucas's revised version of George Webbe Dasent (trans.),
The Story of Burnt Njal.

assuredly less relevance. As a frontispiece we find I.L. Lund's 'The Last Skald' in colour reproduction; the poet looks thoroughly forlorn, as well he might in view of the pointlessness of his presence in the *Burnt Njal* volume; there is C.E. Anderson's 'The Death of Earl Hacon' which does at least refer to a character from the saga, even if the form of death in the picture (arrow through breast) does not match his death in the saga (knife through throat);[94] and Lorenz Froelich's 'Blood-Badet – Blood revel' illustrates a passage (ch. 83) in which not a drop of blood is spilt.

There could hardly be a greater contrast between Anderson's lavish but inert recycling of Dasent's text, and the pocket-sized, pictureless, but pedagogically well judged *Njal and Gunnar, A Tale of Old Iceland* (1917). It was compiled by H. Malim, late Principal of the Government College in Mangalore, India. If, as the name suggests, Malim was of Anglo-Indian extraction, we may recall Dasent's 1859 remarks about the cultural and ethnographic irony which found Britain ruling the same land where, many centuries earlier, a common Indo-European culture had flourished:

> the Highlander, who drives his bayonet through the heart of a high-caste Sepoy mutineer [in the 1856 Indian Mutiny], little knows that his pale features and sandy hair, and that dusky face with its raven locks, both come from a common ancestor in Central Asia, many, many centuries ago.[95]

Dasent's colonial background will have helped him appreciate the point.[96] Returning home from the family estate in the West Indies on the death of his father in 1832, Dasent was sent to the Whiggish Westminster School. *Njal and Gunnar* could have served admirably as a reading book for later generations of the school's preparatory pupils. Its young readers in India are unlikely to have been descendants of Sepoy mutineers but rather the likes of Billy Bunter's Greyfriars friend Hurree Jamset Ram Singh. After a brief introduction,[97] fourteen specially adapted chapters treating the main events lead first to Gunnar's death, and later to the burning of Njal. A list of saga characters is provided, helpfully divided into family groupings (121), as are 'subjects for essays' (122–3) and suggestions for further reading (124).

Dasent's text undergoes sensible linguistic modification. The 'Fair is the Lithe' passage now reads:

> They got as far as Markfleet without once looking back. There Gunnar's horse tripped, and he fell to the ground with his face towards home. 'Fair is Lithend!' said he; 'so fair that it has never seemed to me so fair. The cornfields are white, and the home meadow is mown; now will I ride home and not go abroad at all.'

---

[94] Dasent 1861, II 63.

[95] Dasent 1903, xxviii.

[96] Dasent was born in 1817. His family had owned a West Indian estate since the seventeenth century, and his grandfather had been Chief Justice of St Nevis: Dasent 1903, 'Memoir', 5–7.

[97] Malim 1917, vii–xi.

'Do not give this joy to your foes,' said Kolskegg. 'No man could think that you would break the atonement. And if you do so all will happen as Njal said.'

'I will not go,' said Gunnar. (38)

There is a little extra pointing of the 'looking back' motif, which now seems more involuntary; archaic 'mead' and 'fare' become 'meadow' and 'go'; the ellipsis of 'do not this joy to thy foes' is expanded; and Kolskegg's syntactically complex sentence is broken down into its constituent elements.

The suggested essay topics highlight the lessons which *Burnt Njal* could teach the class of 1917: geography ('Describe Iceland'); narrative understanding ('Tell the story of Hallgerda's Theft', with the young essayist encouraged to 'invent details from your own imagination'); character analysis ('Compare the characters of Njal and Gunnar, Kari and Flosi'); philosophy ('Does civilisation make men less cruel?'); law and morality (How does the story confirm that 'Whom God would destroy he first drives mad?'); history, technology, and (unhappily) current affairs ('Contrast sea-fighting in the tenth and twentieth centuries'); poetic composition (Compose *Burnt Njal*-related poems in ballad form, blank verse, or the metre of Morris's *Sigurd the Volsung*); and, lastly, cartography and technical drawing ('Draw a map of Iceland, and a picture of a Viking ship'). 'A Tale of Old Iceland' it may be, but *Njal and Gunnar* was not to be taught as some childish escape from human realities, nor as a bellicose allegory of imperialism. There was knowledge to absorb and romantic images to respond to, but also sad truths and sordid treacheries to ponder.

Malim's *Njal and Gunnar* brought Dasent's *Burnt Njal* into classrooms across the empire. Albany Major and E.E. Speight had shown the way with their *Stories from the Northern Sagas* (1899), whose worthy aim was 'to get the Saga Stories into English Schools, to bring a little of the Northern atmosphere to the children'.[98] There were problems to overcome, as when John Dasent had refused permission for any of his father's translation to be reprinted, forcing the editors to produce their own version of the selected extract, 'to the detriment of our little book'.[99] Beatrice Clay also worked to promote saga literature in Edwardian schools: 'it seems to me such a pity that children should grow up knowing nothing of this wonderful literature and I am afraid they will only read it in a modern form'.[100] Her plan was to rewrite and publish a set of 'Stories from the Saga of Burnt Njal'. Eiríkur Magnússon is questioned rigorously by his former Cambridge pupil about the saga: how does the fifth court system work; why does Mǫrðr state his suit against Flosi twice; what is the nature of the insult when Skarpheðinn taunts Skapti about having put pitch on his head; what was the name of Njáll's third daughter, and much else besides.[101]

98 Lbs. 2188 4to, Albany Major to Eiríkur Magnússon, 14 July 1899.
99 Ibid., John Dasent was waiting for Dasent 1900 to appear.
100 Lbs. 2186b 4to, Beatrice Clay to Eiríkur Magnússon, 22 March 1909.
101 Her version of the Hlíðarendi lines is, 'Fair is the Lithe, so fair as never before has it seemed to these eyes of mine. The cornfields are white to harvest and the home-field is mown': Clay [?1909] 167.

Allen French's *Heroes of Iceland* (1905) is a novelistic adaptation of Dasent's *Burnt Njal* for youngish readers on both sides of the Atlantic. The adaptor's introduction anxiously makes the case for admitting *Brennu-Njáls saga* to the inner canonical circle of the world's great books. This was not easy, for old habits died hard, and the old northern long-ship still tended to be moored at a respectful distance from the great galleons of Greece and Rome. New translations of Icelandic sagas were prefaced by verses praising northern freedom written in Greek hexameters.[102] Books on Iceland were deemed suitable school and university prizes for high attainment in Greek and Latin.[103] British reviewers showered praise on *Burnt Njal* by emphasising its Homeric virtues. The battle to establish the credentials of old northern literature had to be fought anew with every generation, on every continent. Could its works offer majesty of theme, heroic characters, a sufficiently tragic plot, unity of conception and action, and poetic justice? French offers affirmative answers. The turbulent life of a vibrant society is a noble subject; the climactic burning of Njáll is of Graeco-Roman tragic intensity; Gunnarr and Njáll rival Achilles and Nestor; justice, whether poetic or otherwise, governs the outcome of the saga; and the Gunnarr and Njáll narratives are shapely and unified, or they would be by the time French has reduced Dasent's 158 chapters to his own twenty-five, omitting genealogical material, 'irrelevant' episodes, legal technicalities, minor characters, and many of the verses. He claims that the unadorned simplicity of the prose style matches the austere understatement of modern drama. As for the value of *Njáls saga* for the modern reader, French identifies three principal elements: it tells a good story; it shows 'our' ancestral kinsman the Norseman in his natural surroundings ('because he was what he was, we are today, in part, what we are');[104] and it reveals all the finest virtues of the old north – honesty, hospitality, friendship, the habit of work, love of family, respect for women, and moral and physical courage.

French is also able to situate the saga within a Darwinian vision of human evolution and a W.P. Ker framework of world epic.[105] *Burnt Njal* itself was a literary emblem of successful human evolution. Just as the world renews itself from age to age through the emergence of new races, so each new race produces at least one 'imperishable book'[106] about its heroes. *Burnt Njal* or, in French's more generalised title, *Heroes of Iceland* is the imperishable book of the northmen. In his excellent recent study of the international reception of *Njáls saga*, Jón Karl Helgason has drawn attention to the American cultural politics of

---

[102] See Head 1866, p. [v].

[103] The Seðlabanki Íslands library copy of Forbes 1860 was awarded to Robert Wilson, Kings College, London, as an 1861 prize for attainment in Greek. The present writer's copy of Cox and Jones 1872 was presented to E.C. Taylor for attainment in Classics at Leeds Grammar School in 1874.

[104] French 1905, xxi.

[105] Ker 1897.

[106] French 1905, ix.

French's work, published in Boston in 1905.[107] The period of 'old immigration' from Britain and Western Europe had passed; by 1907 81% of immigrants were from eastern and southern Europe and even further afield. In the six years immediately prior to the book's publication, annual immigration into Massachusetts had doubled, with disproportionately large numbers of Greeks and Italians. In *Heroes of Iceland* Allan French, a Bostonian of seventeenth-century English immigrant stock, celebrates the old northern values of 'our part-ancestor'[108] at the very time when the local definition of 'our ancestry' was becoming ever more problematic. He notes that southern folk 'fall far short of the heroic standard of the Teutonic races' (xxiii)[109] at a time when Boston was awash with immigrants from such lands. The forcefield around French's book celebrates 'Mayflower' values and turns its back on destabilising modernity.

In French's editorial custody the abridged story carries a dozen pages of sensible notes, a rudimentary map of south-west Iceland, a table of historical dates, and, enterprisingly, a guide to the pronunciation of names, which seems an admirable idea until we meet the statement that 'the simplest rule . . . is to treat all vowel and consonant sounds as if they were German' (xliv). This would have pleased Thomas Carlyle rather more than Samuel Laing. In E.W.D. Hamilton's four illustrations Iceland's early settlers walk around in dapper deer-stalker hats and little else (78), as when Gizur kills an implausibly aged and unfit Gunnar. Dasent's text is followed with reasonable fidelity in the saga's most famous moments, such as the 'Fair is the Lithe' passage where the only deviation is the omission of 'by breaking thy atonement, for' in Kolskegg's response to Gunnarr.

Pilgrims and Pilgrimage

Few of Allan French's Bostonian readers will have visited the saga-steads about which he wrote, but a number of Victorian Britons seized the chance when it came. With *Burnt Njal* in hand they landed in Reykjavík and trekked eastwards to Fljótshlíð. As we noted in Chapter Two, in the decades before *Burnt Njal* Icelandic saga-steads were rarely visited and never celebrated. For Henry Holland, Hlíðarendi was notable only as having been the birthplace of Mackenzie's disreputable guide Ólafur Loptsson, and the site of a memorable encounter with Sæmundur Hálfdanarson, the snuff-taking, brennivín-soaked local priest.[110] Ebenezer Henderson, for whom rapture came easily, strikes a phlegmatic tone about Hlíðarendi: 'the abode of Gunnar, who occupies so conspicuous a place in the Saga of Niál Thorgeirson'.[111] *Burnt Njal* had still not been published

---

107 Jón Karl Helgason 1999, 65–79.
108 French 1905, xxi.
109 See also French 1904, ix.
110 Wawn 1987, 267.
111 Henderson 1818, I 335.

when A.J. Symington visited Iceland in 1859 and had barely been digested by the time he wrote his 1862 travel account. He was aware that the southern plains had been 'rendered classic ground'[112] by the saga, but visited none of major *Njála* sites. Sabine Baring-Gould's 1863 travel book lists *Burnt Njal*,[113] but his priorities lay rather in tracing the more northerly steps of his own favourite saga heroes Grettir Ásmundarson and Ingimundr goði. Within a decade, however, a visit to Bergþórshvoll had become in the eyes of some a visit 'to the – can I say hallowed? – spot, where Njal delved and Bergthora span'.[114] The opening sentence of S.E. Waller's *Six Weeks in the Saddle: A Painter's Journal in Iceland* (1874) leaves the reader in no doubt what lay behind the author's Icelandic travels: 'It was "Burnt Njal" that was at the bottom of it.'[115] For a party of Liverpudlian travellers in 1880, the saga sites, and memories of the conflicts in *Burnt Njal* 'will make a traveller's "very toes tingle and his pulse beat higher . . . if he has any soul in him"'.[116] By 1882 amongst the suggested routes for summer travellers, W.G. Lock's *Guide to Iceland* offers one entitled 'Through "The Njál Country"', complete with a ten-page plot summary of the saga.[117] In 1888 H. Rider Haggard can be found writing of Þingvellir, so prominent in the saga, 'every sod, every rock, every square foot . . . is eloquent of the deeds of great men'; of Hlíðarendi, 'I am writing this on the site of Gunnar's hall, which I distinctly trace'; and of Njáll's hall, '[we] dug last night and found various relics of the burning'.[118] There is a special chapter devoted (in every sense) to the 'Country of Burnt Njal' in W.G. Collingwood's *A Pilgrimage to the Saga-Steads of Iceland*.[119] The story of Gunnarr is now deemed 'too well known' to need recounting, but Collingwood cannot resist having a go at the famous sentence: ' "Fair is the lyth," he said. "I never thought it so fair. Blake (yellow) are its acres, and green its meadows. I will ride home and never leave it." '[120] A black and white picture of 'the lyth', a pale shadow of Collingwood's fine water colour,[121] accompanies his account of the area:

In the morning we learnt once more that scenery and romance are inseparable. Gunnar's home which he so passionately loved was worthy of his affection – even from the sentimental view of the landscapist. He may not have known why he 'thought it so fair': perhaps the blake acres commended themselves to him as much for practical farming as for poetical fancy. But no modern traveller can fail to note that the one place of all the world where a man, in those distant and rude days,

112 Symington 1862, 177.
113 Baring-Gould 1863, 441.
114 Lock 1879, 61.
115 Waller 1874, 1.
116 [Banks] 1881, 4.
117 Lock 1882, 116–23 (route); 65–74 (saga summary).
118 Haggard 1926, I 285–86.
119 Collingwood and Jón Stefánsson 1899, 20–32.
120 Ibid., 28.
121 Haraldur Hannesson 1988, 279.

chose deliberately to die, rather than go out into exile from it, was so magnificently situated.

Almost 'no modern traveller', that is. An insensate member of Anthony Trollope's party of Tory tourists achieves the feat. Perhaps with Victorian corn-law debates still ringing in his ears, he cites the same scene from Dasent's translation solely in order to note that corn was once but is no longer grown in Iceland.[122]

A Poet's Response

A modern traveller particularly responsive to the beauty of Hlíðarendi was Mrs Disney Leith, who visited Iceland over three successive summers from 1894.[123] She chronicled her experiences in *Three Visits to Iceland*, a work whose lengthy sub-title draws the distinction proper for a Victorian Anglo-Catholic between a 'Pilgrimage to Skalholt' (the ancient episcopal seat in pre-Reformation times) and 'Visits to Geysir and the Njala District'. She knew her way around Dasent's translation[124] but had learnt Icelandic well enough to enable her to produce translations of modern Icelandic poems on saga subjects.[125] In this way *Burnt Njal* becomes cross-pollinated with nineteenth-century Icelandic responses to the same saga. She recalls her visit to Oddi, where 'we talked a good deal about Njála', to the 'Land-Isles of Dasent's Burnt Njal',[126] and to Bergþórshvoll, built on the site traditionally associated with Njáll's hall:

> the excavations, from which charred wood was brought to the museum some years ago, were just under our room; so, as Arni [their host] put it in his terse English, 'You are just on the place where Njál was!' A great thought for me, who have loved Njál and his Story for so many years, and now at last have travelled over the country once so familiar to his wise and kindly eyes. (143)

No less memorable was the following day's visit to 'Fleet-lithe – so dear to Gunnar's eyes that he could not tear himself away into exile'. The response is predictably awe-struck: 'Looking at it, though even on this rather dreary cloudy day, I cannot wonder at his attachment, for the district seems beautiful and fertile above most' (145). The flower-filled grasslands remind her of the same scene as depicted in Jónas Hallgrímsson's famous poem 'Gunnarshólmi'.

Mrs Leith was not the first Victorian traveller to Iceland who became familiar with Jónas's poetry. The opening lines from his equally celebrated 'Ísland',

122 [anon.], articles on Iceland in Macleod 1879, 559–65, at 564–5.
123 Other Victorian women travellers to and writers about Iceland include Oswald 1876, 1882; Harley 1889; Clerke 1891; Hall [?1900].
124 Leith 1897, 173.
125 Mrs Leith learned Icelandic by corresponding with Brynjólfur Jónsson: Lbs. 1706 4to. Brynjólfur (with Grímur Thomsen) translated several of her poems into Icelandic.
126 Leith 1897, 141.

which rejoice in Iceland's natural beauty, appear opposite the contents page of Baring-Gould's *Scenes and Sagas* volume.[127] Yet neither of Jónas's poems is an innocent idyll. 'Ísland' argues that Iceland was once a beautiful land colonised by great heroes such as Gunnarr and Njáll; centuries later it remains a beautiful land but the energy and enterprise of the heroes has fallen 'í gleymsku og dá' [into oblivion and ruin]. Dasent sensed this degeneration himself when visiting Þingvellir.[128] 'Gunnarshólmi', translated by Mrs Leith in an appendix, also deals with saga-age beauty and loss, and strikes its own note of defiance at the end. As another of Collingwood's water colours shows,[129] the location is the spit of land near the Markár River on which the hero stood before rejecting exile and riding back to Hlíðarendi. The landscape has been much eroded over a thousand years as 'the rushing Mark/o'er sandbanks roars', but, as presented in Mrs Leith's version of Jónas's poem, Gunnarr's headland remains, stubbornly resisting the geological and cultural change all around it:

> Fled are the dwarfs, the rock-troll's hammer still,
> Drear is the plain, the folk by need are bowed;
> But never sheltering warmth and grace may lack
> That grassy holm, whence Gunnar turned his back.[130]

In Jónas's imagination, the modern landscape had briefly once again played host to saga-age figures, notably Gunnarr and Kolskeggr as they head for their ship, lying at anchor in the distance:

> But Gunnar turns his face towards the land;
>   No fear the righteous hero's dismal soul dismays,
> Though fierce the threatenings of the hostile band.
>
> 'Ne'er saw I yet the earth's increase so fair!
>   The cattle spread them o'er the field to graze,
> Against pale cornfields roses redden there.
>
> Here will I spend the number of my days,
>   Yea, all that God shall send me. Fare thou well,
> Brother and friend!' Thus Gunnar's saga says.[131]

Although the note on the facing page directs readers to Dasent's *Burnt Njal*, Mrs Disney Leith herself was able to read the sagas in Icelandic. Her other translations of Icelandic literature, ancient and modern, confirm a lack of interest in grinning Vikings in their death agonies. She was drawn rather to the

---

[127] Baring-Gould 1863, [vi].
[128] [Clifford] 1865, 13.
[129] Haraldur Hannesson 1988, 280.
[130] Leith 1897, 173.
[131] Ibid., 172.

noble saints and martyrs of saga-age Catholic Iceland,[132] amongst the lower ranks of whom, we may imagine, she placed Gunnarr and Njáll.

If the evidence of Mrs Leith's nine 'Songs from the Sagas' is to be believed, even Skarpheðinn was a candidate for sanctity. In both the 'Death Song of Skarphedin' and 'The Finding of Burnt Njal',[133] the dominant figure proves to be the 'wild warrior', ugly and wilful in life, single-minded and fearless in death, an elemental life force unconquered by weapon or flame, and able in death to reach out to the Christian god to whom he had paid all too little heed in life. The cross found burned on his chest signals his welcome within the fold of Mrs Leith's repentant saga sinners. Skarpheðinn also figures indirectly in 'Kári's Revenge'. At Earl Sigurðr's Yuletide feast one of the burners, Gunnarr Lamba-son, boasts of the terrible events at Bergþórshvoll.[134] His claim that Skarpheðinn had cried in the face of death proves too much for Kári who lay in hiding outside. His entrance is swift, his vengeance fierce, and the poet's gaze is as unblinking as Skarpheðinn's in the heat of the fire:

> Not to right or left looked Kari,
>   Not a single word he spoke;
> But upon the son of Lambi
>   Straight he dealt th'unerring stroke.
>
> Stoutly on the neck he smote him
>   With his tried and trusty sword;
> And the head of that false speaker
>   Rolled upon the reeking board.[135]

Yet the two most haunting poems in the Leith *Burnt Njal* ballad cycle concern two women beyond the reach of solace or sanctity – Hallgerðr and Queen Gunnhildr. The slow unfurling of Hallgerðr's revenge for her husband's long-remembered slap is well served by the relentless pulse of the balladic metre, with the twin refrains highlighting an unfathomable paradox for ideologically unre-constructed Victorian readers – so beautiful, so destructive. The last verses are as follows:

> 'Hast thou not smitten me once?' she said
>   (Soft as silk and yellow as grain),
> 'So give I thee never a hair of my head'
>   (And arrows are falling like Odin's rain).
>
> 'Hold thou out little, hold thou out long'
>   (Soft as silk and yellow as grain),

---

[132] Gunnar Guðmundsson 1993. See, for example, Leith's 'Christmas at Skálholt A.D. 1193 (Thorlákssaga)', in Leith 1895a, 116–17.
[133] Leith 1895a, 101–2.
[134] Dasent 1861, II 325 (ch. 154; ÍF xii 442–3).
[135] Leith 1895a, 108

'I care no whit so I wreak my wrong'
(And arrows are falling like Odin's rain).

And all for the lack of two locks of her head
(Soft as silk and yellow as grain),
On the floor of his dwelling the chief lies dead,
(And arrows are falling like Odin's rain).[136]

Though wholly different in concept and execution, and not striving for acceptance as high art, this Leith poem arguably deserves a place alongside William
Morris's 'Gunnar's Howe above the House at Lithend' (see Chapter Nine) as
the two most arresting poems in English inspired by *Burnt Njal*. 'Queen Gunnhild' does not lag far behind. In stanzas of eight *fornyrðislag* length lines, the
poem reconstructs Gunnhildr's death, drawing on Dasent's appendixed
account.[137] The exiled queen, lured to Denmark by the prospect of a royal marriage, is betrayed by her companions who abandon her in a bog afterwards
known as 'Gunnhillda's Moss'. In the Leith poem the defeated queen, surveying
her final earthly domain, weeps with only the wailing wind in attendance.[138]
Dasent was intrigued by the 'wicked' queen, but Mrs Leith proves an unforgiving judge.

Dasent and Dissolution

We have seen something of the effect which *Burnt Njal* could have on its
readers. But what, finally, of its influence on Dasent's own later old northern
work and of its place within his overall scholarly career? After spending the
summers of 1861–2 travelling in Iceland, he returned home dreaming of land
purchase there,[139] and determined to pursue other old northern interests.[140] In
his essay writing he focused more on Scandinavian courts and dynasties and
other *Heimskringla*-related issues,[141] but *Burnt Njal* incidents and characters
feature significantly in his effortful three-volume paraphrastic version of *Jómsvíkinga saga*. We might say that in Dasent's later publications he was filling in the
gaps round *Burnt Njal*. How had early Icelandic society operated long before
Gunnarr and Njáll ruled the plains of Rangárvallasýsla? What sort of Viking
lives did the sons of Njáll experience before settling down at Bergþórshvoll?
And, more generally, what impact was the old north still exercising on Britain,
centuries after the visit of Njáll's son-in-law Kári Sǫlmundarson?

Dasent's *The Story of Gisli the Outlaw* (1866) addresses the first of these

---

[136] Ibid., 69
[137] Dasent 1861, II 394–5.
[138] Leith 1895a, 111–12.
[139] Sidney Jones Library MS 3.33, f. 60: Jón Sigurðsson to Guðbrandur Vigfússon, 28 November
1865.
[140] Dasent 1866, 1873, 1875, 1876, 1882; Gudbrand Vigfusson and Dasent 1887–94.
[141] Dasent 1873, I 198–309, II 154–353.

issues.[142] *Gísla saga*, in many ways comparable in quality to *Njáls saga*,[143] tells of Norwegian emigré and Icelandic settler life a generation and more before the period dramatised in *Burnt Njal*.[144] Set principally in the north-west of Iceland, an area unvisited by Dasent, the saga tells of a community forced to resolve its own conflicts without recourse to the structures of an Alþingi. The publisher was the same Edinburgh company of Edmonston and Douglas who had served *Burnt Njal* well, and many format features of the 1861 translation are repeated in 1866. On both the cover and the main title page we find a design featuring the saga's fateful weapon, this time the sword Graysteel.[145] There is a map, a chronological table, and an insightful introduction. A set of seven engravings[146] casts a veil of quiet Victorian dignity over the saga's bloody deeds. In the bearded Gisli there is more than a hint of the late Prince Consort. In 'Gisli in Sæbol', the trilby-hatted hero, dull-eyed but determined, snuffs out the lamp before moving in to murder Thorgrim (Fig. 6); while 'Gisli, Gudrida, and Auda' shows the family unit undisturbed by its troubles – Gisli, erect and wary, walks through an un-Icelandic looking forest, accompanied at a deferential distance by Auda who gazes loyally but anxiously into her husband's haunted eyes. Overall, the volume attracted much less attention than *Burnt Njal*.[147] The doomed Vestein could claim that 'now all the streams fall towards Dyrafirth'[148] but few nineteenth-century saga pilgrims found their way to the remote north-west fjords. Nevertheless, Dasent's translation was reprinted around the turn of the century,[149] spiced up with a bizarre new set of illustrations. Gisli appears in an assortment of dazzlingly coloured outfits, as if modelling the new 'Viking range' of wadmal wear.

No such illustrative levities, family dramas, or Icelandic settings feature in Dasent's three-volume work *The Vikings of the Baltic* (1875), a paraphrastic reworking of events from *Jómsvíkinga saga* deploying motifs, character types, and antiquarian learning which Dasent had absorbed during almost forty years of old northern reading. *Burnt Njal* includes overseas Viking adventures, yet its principal focus remained the workings of a fissile and complex community back in Iceland. *The Vikings of the Baltic* investigates the Viking life, the 'honourable profession . . . of sea-roving', which both Gunnarr and the sons of Njáll[150] expe-

---

142 The translation was based on the longer redaction, edited by Gísli Konráðsson in 1849.
143 'one of the finest, if not . . . the very finest' of the shorter sagas: Dasent 1866, vii.
144 Dasent 1866 [xxxvii] calculates that Gísli died aged 44 in 978.
145 Dasent accepted the *Sturlunga saga* claims that this weapon, recast as Gísli's spear, was still in use in the thirteenth century: 1866, xxxii–xxxiii. See Perkins 1989, 250–1; also Fox [1906].
146 The work of C.E. St John Mildmay.
147 Though see [Forman] 1871, a review of Stephens 1839; Laing 1844; Dasent 1861, 1866; Head 1866; Morris and Eiríkur Magnússon 1869, 1870. See also Fox [1906] and Sims 1909, published in a series called 'All Time Tales'.
148 Dasent 1866, 37.
149 Dasent [?1900].
150 The dealings of Helgi and Grímr, sons of Njáll, with Þráinn Sigfússon and Killer Hrappr (Einar Ólafur Sveinsson 1954, 208–25, chs 87–90) are recycled in the novel (Dasent 1875, II 144–79) to establish the authority of Hákon jarl before his confrontation with the Jómsborgers.

Fig. 6. Gisli kills Thorgrim. Artist C. St J. Mildmay. From George
Webbe Dasent (trans.), *The Saga of Gisli the Outlaw*.

rienced as young men – the daily tests of nerve and sinew, masculine camarade-
rie, and indifference to dynastic aggrandizement and organised commerce. The
novel's potential readership extended far beyond the world of the Victorian
schoolboy. For many a male-menopausal patriarch of middle England, burdened
by commitments to family, business, community, church and state, the idea of
the free-booting Viking life must have held its attractions. Dasent's friends certainly recognised this longing in the great translator himself:

> Of Herculean height and strength, with his long black beard descending to his
> waist, he resembled a Viking of old, and such I conceive he at times supposed
> himself to be. In fact, so deeply was he imbued with the spirit of antiquity that a
> continual antagonism between the past and the present, or rather, I should say
> between the imaginary and the real, existed in his breast. He was two gentlemen at
> once . . . In dull fact, he was an excellent citizen, a householder, paying rates and
> taxes, an affectionate husband, and the good father of a family; but in the dream,
> the fancy . . . he was a Berserker, a Norse pirate, ploughing the seas in his dragon-
> beaked barque, making his trusty falchion ring on the casques of his enemies,
> slaying, pillaging, burning, ravishing and thus gratifying a laudable taste for
> adventure. I fear he preferred the glorious dream to the sober reality. I think he
> inwardly pined at his own respectability.[151]

The Vikings of the Baltic, based on a saga cited by scholars since the days of Bartholin,[152] uses 'glorious' Viking dreams to address 'sober' Victorian anxieties
about social dissolution and degeneracy.[153]

These issues can best be approached briefly via two scenes from *Jómsvíkinga
saga*. In the first, a feast in the young Danish King Sveinn Haraldsson's court
marks his accession to power following the death of his father King Haraldr
Gormsson, shot through the eye by Pálna-Tóki, Sveinn's foster-father. A page-
boy is instructed to carry a golden arrow round the hall so that its owner could
be identified. Pálna-Tóki claims it unflinchingly, 'I parted with it by bowstring
when I shot your father.'[154] He then manages to escape, together with his loyal
companion Bjǫrn the Welshman. They head for the land of the Wends where
King Búrisleifr allows them to settle at a place called Jóm in return for help in
defending the kingdom. The two Vikings establish a fortification, and Pálna-
Tóki creates a comprehensive code of conduct for the elite Jómsborg corps:[155]
no member is to be older than fifty or younger than eighteen; membership is on
merit rather than kinship; no-one may refuse to fight anyone as strong as
himself; each must avenge the other as his own brother; no-one must feel or
give expression to fear; looted goods are to be shared equally; no-one is to stir
up dissension; no women may reside in the stronghold; absences from Jóms-

[151] [Clifford] 1865, 3–4.
[152] Bartholinus 1689, 3–4, 40–43 and passim.
[153] See Dunn 1894.
[154] 'Ek skilðumk við á bogastrengnum þá er ek skaut í gegnum feðr þinn': Blake 1962, 16.
[155] Ibid., 17–18.

borg are limited to three days; and any warrior found to have killed a relative of another troop member must submit to the judgement of Pálna-Tóki. This brisk regime resembles life on-board ship for Frithiof's crew or, in Victorian terms, life at Rugby School for Tom Brown and Frederick York Powell (later nicknamed Jórvíkur Powell),[156] saga translator and for many years the Oxford amanuensis of Guðbrandur Vigfússon. We might also note that it was another Rugbeian, Matthew Arnold (son of Dr Thomas), whose *Balder Dead*, an embryonic *Idylls of the Gods*, shares Dasent's *Vikings of the Baltic* concern with crumbling nobility and self-destructing brotherhoods.[157]

There were few signs of crumbling nobility among the Jómsvikings at the outset. They were to be an elite troop whose code would encourage Darwinian processes of natural selection to work their magic. In true Bartholinean fashion the results of this robust regime were to be measured in the way the hero faced his death. So it was at the end of the saga, in the second of our two key scenes. At the funeral feast for his own father, the new Jómsborg leader Sigvaldi pledges to drive the hated Hákon jarl out of Norway. As so often, bold evening words produce bleak morning deeds. In the climactic battle at Hjǫrungavágr many Jómsborgers are captured. Their training had failed to bring victory but would at least keep them defiant when facing execution. A different fate awaits Pálna-Tóki's grandson, Vagn, a reformed teenage coalbiter, and his crotchety foster-father Bjǫrn. They trick and kill the executioner; the surly Hákon is furious, but his more gracious son Eiríkr intervenes and invites both men to join his own warrior troop.

Two *Jómsvíkinga saga* scenes: one showing the foundation of the Jómsborg Vikings, and the other testing that Viking code under the greatest pressure. Pálna-Tóki, the founding father, was long dead, but as the spirit of *drengskapr*[158] passed down to his successors there were no signs of degeneration. Indeed it had been Vagn's success in earning membership of the Jómsborg group at the illegally early age of twelve that had been the making of this previously sullen youth. There were even fewer signs of degeneration on his mother's side of the family. Vagn's maternal grandfather Véseti had been a bold warrior, whilst uncle Búi provides his young nephew with an exemplary paradigm of Viking virtues: he is laconic, proud, strong and (often a good sign) ugly. Loyal to his leader, he fights ferociously in the final sea battle, keeping a stiff upper lip even when his lower one was hacked off: 'Kissing us will now seem less agreeable to the Danish woman in Bornholm.'[159] There is no chance to confirm this. Under renewed attack, Búi's hands are cut off at the wrists, and he escapes overboard, his bleeding stumps jammed into the handles of the chests full of gold which his

---

[156] York Powell 1896, xxxix. For the nickname see Lbs. 2185 4to, Jón Stefánsson to Eiríkur Magnússon, 24 November 1898.

[157] Discussed below, pp. 204–5.

[158] Cleasby and Gudbrand Vigfusson 1874, 105 identifies the richness of this concept: courage, high-mindedness, manliness, bluffness, fellowship.

[159] ' "Versna mun nú hinni dǫnsku þykkja at kyssa oss í Borgundarhólmi" ': Blake 1962, 37.

enterprise had won him over the years. The last we hear of Búi is of his transformation into a serpent lying in the gold hoard at the bottom of the sea,[160] a coiled and curmudgeonly distillation of uncompromising Viking rectitude.

There was no degeneracy, then, on either side of the Pálna-Tóki family line, and in his more sanguine moments Dasent sees few signs of degeneracy in Victorian Britain. The Vikings had been an elemental life force, and Dasent viewed eighteenth- and nineteenth-century British inventors and entrepreneurs in very much the same light:

> They [the Vikings] were like England in the nineteenth century: fifty years before all the rest of the world with her manufactories, and firms – and five-and-twenty years before them with her railways. They [the Vikings] were foremost in the race of civilisation and progress; well started before all the rest had thought of running. No wonder, then, that both won.[161]

And how had these Viking qualities established themselves in the blood of Englishmen? Dasent, like Laing before him, looks for the answer in the Viking raids on Pre-Conquest Britain. The dark, slavish and town-loving Celts had been overthrown by the vigorous Anglo-Saxons.[162] Subsequent Anglo-Saxon degeneracy had enabled the Vikings to overwhelm the priest-ridden King Edward the Confessor.[163] Dasent's Vikings, like Laing's, had brought to the British Isles 'an infusion of Northern blood into its sluggish veins'.[164] When, in turn, the Normans conquered England, they were merely the continental descendants of the noble Viking Gǫngu-Hrólfr,[165] their raw energy 'wonderfully bettered by their cross with the Romance stock' (I 245–6). As ever, Dasent was fascinated by the Darwinian sense that only the fittest races survive 'the everyday battle of life . . . that long unceasing struggle which race wages with race, not sword in hand alone, but by brain, will and feeling' (I 3). Saxon had beaten Celt, Viking had beaten Saxon, Norman had beaten everyone; and, by the middle of the nineteenth century, the British imperial successors of this Saxon-Viking-Norman tradition had beaten and colonised much of the world. Who could beat them?

This last question cast its shadow across Dasent's optimistic vision. Dasent was sensitive to Viking gloom as well as glory. As *Burnt Njal* and *The Origin of Species* had shown in their respective ways families, communities and races wane as well as wax – even Viking-descended races. As Dasent had seen, Þingvellir, once the centre of due legal process in *Burnt Njal*, now lay covered in moss and berries with only ravens holding court.[166] In Dasent's Darwinian vision, a system of government was like a sword, passed down from generation to gen-

160 Ibid., 43.
161 Dasent 1873, I 247.
162 Ibid., II 3. See also Curtis 1968.
163 Dasent 1873, I 198–243.
164 Dasent 1858, 166.
165 Dasent 1873, II 328.
166 [Clifford] 1865, 13.

eration. It was for each successive age to show itself worthy of the inheritance. All the more important, then, that the disappearance of true old northern government in Iceland should be balanced by its robust survival in the British Isles, whether in Westminster or the Isle of Man. Yet such survival could only be the result of 'long *unceasing* [my italics] struggle' and who was to say that the seeds of British decline were not already planted and germinating, or that the struggle was not already slackening?[167]

The assertions of Victorian manly heartiness everywhere in evidence on the surface of *The Vikings of the Baltic* could not wholly conceal the nagging rumbles of social disintegration. Dasent's lifelong fondness for old northern mythology may be linked to his sense that it 'carried about with it that melancholy presentiment of dissolution which has come to be so characteristic of modern life'.[168] Even I.A. Blackwell's generally gung-ho 1847 repackaging of Percy's *Northern Antiquities* is not immune to such concerns. At one moment it celebrates British imperial power: 'England, matchless in the mechanical arts, irresistible in arms, sweeping from the surface of the ocean the fleets of every rival nation that dares dispute her maritime supremacy'.[169] Yet, on the next page, sober contemplation sets in:

> The day . . . must necessarily arrive when the Teutonic race, after running its destined career from barbarism to civilization, from civilization to decay, will have, either to cede that heritage to a more primitive or vigorous race, or to be regenerated by that fusion of nations which a century of war and destruction has at different epochs inevitably produced. May that day be still far distant; but when German philosophy degenerates into Hellenic sophistry, and British refinement into Roman luxury, we may safely conclude that the Teutonic race has reached its point of culmination, and must necessarily fall before the race destined, by the inscrutable design of an Allwise Providence, to carry on the development of humanity on earth. (45)

Dasent identified several social and cultural signs indicating that *ragnarǫk* may be on the way. Firstly, he claims that whilst there had been more crime in Viking-age England than in Victorian times, there had been less vice;[170] secondly, the Vikings had treated their women more equally and liberally than did nineteenth-century Britain (212); and thirdly, Viking-age mythology at least showed that the Vikings had a spiritual dimension to their lives, 'which is more than all the professors of a true religion can [now] say' (213). Matthew Arnold was not alone in hearing the sounds of retreating faith on Dover Beach. An additional sign of degeneracy involved questions of families, inheritance and succession. Dasent despised the tendency of meddling modern law to interfere with the healthy processes of natural selection. Unlike Jómsborg, where 'a man

---

[167] Brantlinger 1988, 42–44 and passim identifies factors which undermined imperial confidence.
[168] Dasent 1903, lxxi.
[169] Percy 1847, 44.
[170] Dasent 1858, 204.

was of age as soon as he was fit to do man's work' (212), Victorian legislators had sought to define when a man shall 'come of age'. More importantly, inheritance law protected life's inadequates:

> We do not, now-a-days, stop to inquire if the infant be deformed or a cripple. With us an old house will stand as well upon a crooked as upon a straight support. But in Iceland, in the tenth century, as in all the branches of that great family, it was only healthy children that were allowed to live. The deformed, as a burden to themselves, their friends, and to society, were consigned to destruction by exposure to the mercy of the elements . . . In this old age of the world the law holds us in her leading-strings, as though we had fallen into second childhood . . . for incapacity that [Viking] age had no mercy.[171]

No wonder that Dasent was fascinated by celebrated weapons such as Skarp-heðinn's curved axe in *Brennu-Njáls saga*, pestering Guðbrandur Vigfússon and Grímur Thomsen for the minutest details about its shape.[172] For Dasent heroic conflict meant wielding rather than hurling weapons. A hand-held sword was an emanation of a Viking's self, the externalisation of 'personal prowess [which] had not been equalized by cunning invention',[173] and as such was an essential part of natural selection. Poets had already been attracted to the idea:

> Dull builders of houses,
> Base tillers of earth,
> Gaping, ask me what lordships
> I owned at my birth;
> But the pale fools wax mute
> When I point with my sword
> East, west, north, and south,
> Shouting, 'There am I Lord!'[174]

The only Viking laws of succession were those of the battle-field and not of parliament. In *The Vikings of the Baltic* Dasent chooses to modernise an Icelandic saga one of whose principal structural features is a set of parallel feast scenes in which a son formally takes over the responsibilities of a dead father, scenes which by definition highlight the twin possibilities of continuity or dissolution in family or kingdom. Irritation with hereditary succession sounds loud and clear:

---

171 Ibid., 211–12.
172 Wawn 1991b, 84.
173 Dasent 1858, 174.
174 Motherwell 1847, 21 (from 'The Sword Chant of Thorstein Raudi', *c*.1828). The sword assumes a sensuous quality: 'Joy Giver! I kiss thee . . . women may change, but a sword's forever' (23–4). Hodgetts 1884 devotes a lecture to swords: Norman cowardice had led to the lengthening of weapons; Frithiof is quoted – 'Short is the shaft of the hammer of Thor / Frey's sword an ell in the blade; / 'Tis long enough for the brave, but the longest in war / Is too short if the owner's afraid' (89).

An Earldom is not a title that descends from father to son. Sometimes . . . it is a good thing to keep a good title in a good stock, but if the stock be bad the title should perish; for what is worse for a land than to have over it an Earl who is neither good in arms or counsel.[175]

Even developments in philology contributed to the mid-nineteenth-century tension between triumphalism and dissolution which informs Dasent's treatment of *Jómsvíkinga saga*. As we noted in Chapter 3, the new philology had lent intellectual legitimacy to the serious study of old northern languages and literatures. It had been the intellectual mood music behind Dasent's early venture into translating Snorri's *Edda*, from which Dasent's old northern 'melancholy presentiments of dissolution' derived. At a deeper level, however, philology could create its own gloom. Firstly, some romantic philologists had believed that in the languages of individual nations could be heard the distinctive voice of 'the people', the *Volksstimme*:[176] 'language is the outward appearance of the intellect of nations: their language is their intellect and their intellect their language: we cannot sufficiently identify the two'.[177] Dasent certainly held this to be true. It lay behind his enthusiastic promotion of the virtues of learning Old English and Old Icelandic, rather than allowing readers to be satisfied with even the best English translations.[178] Dasent stressed the invigorating influence of old northern vocabulary and phonology on Saxon English. As if in some phonological and morphological re-enactment of the Viking raids, West Saxon features had been largely superseded by Northumbrian ones, with wholly beneficial results for pronunciation centuries later:

As for our pronunciation, it certainly appears to be much more Northern than Saxon. There are some young ladies indeed who talk of . . . *kjind* and *chjild*, for 'kind' and 'child'; some, too, talk of *cjare* for 'care'; and some clodpoles in the West talk of being *sceared* for being 'scared' or frightened, or of a *meare* for a 'mare'; but as a nation we speak with less mincing mouth. We speak our vowels out broadly and boldly; in speech at least, we have sent the West Saxon broken vowels to the right about, and even where we have kept them to the eye, as in *swear* . . . we have lost them to the ear, for though we write *swear*, we pronounce *sware*.[179]

Yet, even as Dasent rejoiced that 'our forefathers spoke with a manly mouth', and set to work on *The Vikings of the Baltic*, a new generation of scientific linguists would have looked askance at such notions. For them, language was simply an arbitrary system of signs pointing to signifieds, ever subject to linguistic changes wholly unrelated to any perceived characteristics of peoples or countries. The distinctively old northern timbre that Dasent had sensed in

---

[175] Dasent 1875, II 82.
[176] Dowling 1986, 15, 25–9.
[177] Quoted Dowling 1986, 35.
[178] Dasent 1843, Preface.
[179] Dasent 1873, II 13–14.

English speech, and which he had sought to register periodically in his old northern translations, would have been dismissed as mere subjective whimsy. Linguistic 'manliness' and 'mincing' were all in the mind. Dasent, once the liberated new philologist of the 1840s, was now in danger of being overtaken by the unheeded implications of theories which he long supported.

Secondly, Dasent accepted an evolutionary view of linguistic history: 'In language as in race the rule holds that the weakest must go to the wall.'[180] This explained the unstoppable mid-century march of the English language worldwide. August Schleicher makes the broader point:

> In the present period of the life of man the descendants of the Indo-Germanic family are the conquerors in the struggle for existence; they are engaged in continual extension, and have already supplanted or dethroned numerous other idioms.[181]

Yet this notion was also open to challenge by scientific philology which saw language as by definition subject to perpetual change. There never had been or would be a golden age of language. Linguistic change was a matter of quantitative investigation rather than qualitative judgement. Scientific linguists were more interested in the evolution of the latest than in the survival of the fittest. Moreover, though the new linguistics was not a profane science, there was certainly nothing godly about it. Walter Skeat may have been anxious for language to be studied 'in a spirit of reverence',[182] but for others God would have to take his place in the queue.

Dasent knew all this, and his head prompted him to write approvingly about the 'internal law[s]' of linguistic 'progression' – 'languages, so long as they are living . . ., are always in a state of change and progression';[183] but his heart remained unconvinced and, arguably, the doubts wash over into *The Vikings of the Baltic*. As Dasent first began reflecting on *Jómsvíkinga saga* in the 1860s,[184] Britannia may have ruled the waves, the Empire may have dominated half the world, English may have become a major international language, but intellectual and social factors hinted at future dislocation and dissolution. In a straight translation of the saga, the Jómsborg spirit could have radiated defiance in the face of such instabilities. But Dasent's novelistic adaptation allows other voices to be heard within the text, none of them more important than that of Bjǫrn the Welshman.

---

180 Ibid., II 4. See Beer 1989.
181 In *The Darwinian Theory and the Science of Language*, quoted by Koerner 1983, 64 from E.V.W. Dikker's 1869 translation.
182 Skeat 1879–82, xv.
183 Dasent 1873, I 333.
184 As early as 1859, Dasent (1859/1903 xxxvi–viii) discusses Pálna-Toki's link with the William Tell legend; the saga is discussed in his 1865 essay on 'England and Norway in the Eleventh Century' (Dasent 1873, I 216ff.).

Bjǫrn the Welshman

The Vikings of the Baltic has no introduction, illustrations, annotation, appendices, or any of the other scholarly apparatus of *Burnt Njal*. All such cultural information is incorporated into the main body of his novel, helping Dasent in the era of Gerard Manley Hopkins to promote his own 'inscapes' of the Viking world. He grafts on to the *Jómsvíkinga saga* root stock sections from other sagas (including Killer-Hrapp from *Burnt Njal*), and expands existing scenes in order to debate the central oppositions of Viking life – fishing against fighting, sea against city, youth against age. Above all, he develops the character of Bjǫrn (Beorn) into the central comic figure of the novel: he becomes the Claude Halcro of the Baltic. It is through the curmudgeonly Beorn that the Victorian fears of dissolution and degeneracy find expression.

In his fleeting appearances in *Jómsvíkinga saga*, Bjǫrn is the choric voice of traditional Viking values in a Jómsborg whose new leader, Sigvaldi, is showing signs of compromising its ice-clear honour code. Dasent's Beorn becomes the conscience of old Jómsborg, always ready to denounce 'niddering', that is, acting shamefully. For Sigvaldi, the Vikings' code is like a strong but flexible leather thong (I 19). For Beorn it is like a block of coal – chip a piece off and the whole slab may splinter. Soon bored by Jómsborg feasts, the Welshman craves action: 'I long for the whining of the arrow in the air and for the hurtling of spears. Sweeter far to me is the scream of the sea-mew than the bleating of sheep' (I 245). Jómsborg, for Beorn, has gone soft; there are too many on sick-parade, too much fighting with stones and spears rather than swords, too much shirt changing, too much bathing, too many Wendish priests given houseroom, too little questing for adventure, too many who regarded Jómsborg as a cosy home environment, thereby forgetting that 'a Viking has no home; like the bird in the air or the fish in the sea, his home is wherever spoil or fame are to be found' (I 155). It is, accordingly, by acts of physical daring, such as his successful fight with a full-size bear,[185] that the precocious Vagn wins Beorn's approval.

Above all, Victorian readers will have been struck by Beorn's curmudgeonly attitude towards women, in gnomic asides, and in the anxious counselling and world-weary grumbling with which he seeks to defend the ark of the Jómsborg covenant. Thus, when even his young companion Vagn shows a disturbing interest in the beautiful Ingeborg, he grumbles:

> I never could see the use of women. Why can't men be born as they were in old times, when one leg of Borr the giant rubbed itself against the other and out came a man. But ever since men have been born of women there has been naught but strife in the world. (I 248)

---

[185] He returns with the bear's snout, a motif borrowed from *Víga-Glúms saga*, which Dasent knew well, having helped with Head 1866 (see xvi).

For Beorn, widowed when young, the Jómsborg rot sets in when Sigvaldi wishes to marry:

> The castle would be filled with screaming women and squalling children. The good old Viking times are over, you know; you can't spit a baby now on a spear, or get rid of it in that way. We should all quarrel. The castle would be filled with gossip and slander. Tale-bearing would follow child-bearing. (I 14)

Similar sentiments are heard in Thorstein's *Hávamál*-like instructions to his son Frithiof.[186] This sense of the destabilising influence of women on Jómsborg *esprit de corps* mirrors Victorian censoriousness towards 'harlot' Hallgerðr, or Guðrún Ósvífrsdóttir – or Guinevere. For Beorn women will be 'the ruin of the brotherhood'. Dasent himself was alive to such old northern-Arthurian parallels, as in an essay on King Magnús the Good of Norway:

> in Sighvat Skald he had his Merlin, in Sweyn he found the traitor Mordred. Harold was his Lancelot, but the Guinevere whom the great warrior sought to win was none other than that fair land of Norway; though unlike the guilty queen she was true to her liege lord, and only gave herself up with a sigh to her wooer when death had cut asunder the tie which bound her to her first love.[187]

Dasent's *Vikings of the Baltic* is no parable of dissolution like Tennyson's *Idylls*. Like its Icelandic source it ends happily or at least justly. Yet the reader is prompted to ponder the idea of dissolution, and it is not clear that the uncertainties, fears and tensions embodied in Beorn are resolved comfortably in the novel's final pages. Matthew Arnold's 'Dover Beach' ends by pointing bleakly to the 'darkling plain' behind the 'land of dreams' which 'hath really neither joy, nor love, nor light / Nor certitude, nor peace, nor help for pain'. In Sir George Webbe Dasent's urgent championing of the dreamland of medieval Viking culture we may perhaps sense a longing for ethical certainties not always securely available in Victorian England. As the title of his translation confirms, such stabilities had not been available in *Burnt Njal*; and they prove just as elusive in *The Vikings of the Baltic*.

---

[186] Stephens 1839, 23 (v. 28).
[187] Dasent 1873, II 247.

CHAPTER SEVEN

The Eddas

But we never hear anything about Northern Mythology at school.
(Annie and Elizabeth Keary 1857, 6)[1]

Yes, people sneer at the old English chronicles now-a-days, and prefer the Edda, and all sorts of heathen stuff, to them.
(Thomas Hughes 1859 [1989], 37)[2]

He is gone like Balder to the realm of night, never to return.
(G.W. Dasent 1874 ciii, on the death of Richard Cleasby in 1847)[3]

The English reader – even the cultured reader – is the veriest igno-ramus as regards Northern Mythology.   (G.A. Hight 1912)[4]

The Percy Legacy

In February 1886 the *Pall Mall Gazette* published William Morris's list of the world's hundred greatest books. In nineteenth place Morris recommends 'some half-dozen of the best Icelandic sagas', amongst which he would probably have included *Friðþjófs saga*, which he had translated, and *Njáls saga* which he revered. In eighteenth place it is no surprise to find *Heimskringla*, which he and Eiríkur Magnússon were later to translate. Occupying fourth place we find 'The Edda', by which Morris meant primarily the mythological and heroic poems of the so-called *Sæmundar Edda* attributed by late eighteenth-century Copenhagen editors to Sæmundr Sigfússon, twelfth-century priest of Oddi in the south of Iceland. 'The Edda' takes its place among Morris's elite group of texts which were 'far more important than any literature . . . in no sense the work of individuals . . . [they] have grown up from the very hearts of the people.'[5]

---

[1] A disgruntled schoolboy speaks.
[2] An old man speaks.
[3] Cleasby and Gudbrand Vigfusson 1874, ciii. Cleasby read the poetic *Edda* four times a week in 1839 with Konráð Gíslason (lxxviii–lxxix); the inadequacy of available dictionaries led him to 'promote the preparation of a good sound Old Northern Lexicon'.
[4] Lbs. 2187b 4to, GAH to Eiríkur Magnússon 29 March 1912.
[5] Kelvin 1984–96, II 514–18. It was the *Poetic Edda* which 'fetched Morris most': Morris and Eiríkr Magnússon 1891–1905, VI xiv.

Unlike the other old northern texts selected by Morris, eddic narratives had enjoyed a vigorous pre-Victorian life. In Britain, popular poets in Britain had fed voraciously off the tales of valkyries and Valhǫll included in Thomas Percy's 1770 *Northern Antiquities*. Between 1809 and 1902 *Northern Antiquities* was reissued six times in a variety of formats. I.A. Blackwell's much revised version appeared in 1847, without Percy's five runic pieces and Johan Göransson's 1746 Latin translation of the eddic poems, but now featuring Blackwell's translation of the *Prose Edda*,[6] Scott's abstract of *Eyrbyggja saga*, and detailed editorial annotation. Blackwell was a well-informed commentator on the early nineteenth-century scholarship which the mythological poems had attracted in Denmark and Germany. Even the 1770 volume's subtitle had been recast in order to reflect the 1814 political realignments in Scandinavia. No longer is the reader offered 'an historical account of the manners, customs, religion and laws, maritime expeditions and discoveries, language and literature of the ancient Danes including those of our own Saxon ancestors', but rather of 'the ancient Scandinavians (Danes, Swedes, Norwegians and Icelanders) with incidental notices respecting our Saxon ancestors'. *Northern Antiquities* in its revised 1847 form soon became part of the influential Antiquarian Library series promoted by H.G. Bohn and reissued in 1887, 1898 and 1902.[7] It thus represented the natural starting point for any adult Victorian reader wanting to learn about Viking-age myth and religion.[8]

Just as the title page and contents of *Northern Antiquities* underwent a mid-nineteenth-century facelift, so the knowledge and expectations which readers brought to Percy's volume changed during Victoria's reign. Increasingly during the nineteenth century the eddas were read in the light of the sagas, and vice versa. Blackwell's inclusion of Scott's *Eyrbyggja saga* abstract encourages this linkage and the three canonical texts discussed above (Chapters 4–6) will have been read with greater understanding as a result. The role of Baldr worship in the story of Frithiof will have seemed more suggestive; readers of *Burnt Njal* will have better appreciated the forces confronting Þangbrandr during his missionary visit to Iceland and the achievement of Þorgeirr the pagan law-speaker in resolving peacefully the crisis of rival faiths at the Alþingi. In *Heimskringla* the defiant figures of Rauðr, Járn-Skeggi and Hákon jarl will have seemed more substantial – and perhaps more sympathetic – to readers aware of all they stood to lose as their spiritual world crumbled around them.

The tales of *Northern Antiquities* could also illuminate conversion dramas much nearer home than Þingvellir or Trondheim. An 1881–2 paper interpreting carvings on the ancient crosses at Gosforth in Cumberland includes a sonnet written by Hardwicke Drummond Rawnsley (1850–1920):[9]

6   Anderson 1880, 16 dismisses Blackwell 1847 as 'a poor imitation of Dasent'.
7   The series also included [Keightley] 1828, Thorpe 1853.
8   Victorian Old Icelandic primers included eddic extracts: for Lund 1869, 64 the *Poetic Edda* is 'one of the most incomparable works of the human race'.
9   Calverley 1881–2, 403. His other old northern poems include 'A Cumberland War Song', and

We are not wiser than the seers of old,
Our fathers – they twelve hundred years agone,
   Hewed from its silent place this prophet stone,
And bade the sacred Yggdrasil uphold
A Balder-Christ whose triumphs should be told
   In pagan picture – here the battle won
   By Horn's blast; there the Horse with Death thereon
Cast down for years whose coil is endless rolled.
Preacher of Christ, stone-lipped, and not in vain,
Preacher of Woman's love to help her Lord
   By faithful tendance, yea, though earth should quake,
   For lo! her feet upon the buried snake,
Here Mary stands beside the Christ in pain!
Then Loki's queen prevents with cup the poisons poured!

The Gosforth cross, with its Christian form and old northern mythological imagery, was examined by the indefatigable philologist George Stephens (see below, Chapter 8) visiting from Copenhagen in 1882.[10] Under his influence the carvings were seen as the work of an early missionary (or perhaps a local Danish convert) who sought to convert English pagans by including scenes from their mythology within the panelled framework of a Christian cross. As at the end of *Frithiofs saga* the new religion is presented as transcending the old one. The old northern images identified include Óðinn on horseback, Víðarr propping open the jaws of Fenrisúlfr, Þórr's fishing expedition with Hymir, and Loki's wife trying to prevent the Miðgarðsormr's poison from reaching the lips of her once treacherous and now helpless husband.[11] As Rawnsley's sonnet confirms, such iconography was open to Christian interpretation: Baldr becomes Christ crucified on the world tree Yggdrasill, and Sigyn (Mary) weeps for Loki (Christ in torment). The carvings seemed to confirm the existence of a common old northern pagan mythology preserved alike in eddic prose and verse and in early English sculpture.[12]

By the time the Gosforth paper was published even more radical claims were in the pipeline. The introductory dissertation to Guðbrandur Vigfússon and Frederick York Powell's *Corpvs Poeticvm Boreale* (1883) argued that such tales had not only flourished in the British Isles before and during the 'Wicking' period, but that the eddic poems in which they find their earliest expression were actually composed in the 'Western Isles' of Britain – the Hebrides, or the Orkney and Shetland Isles, or the Isle of Man, or Ireland. Nineteenth-century Irish scholars had speculated about the possible debt of Icelandic saga to Irish

---

'Sons of the Viking Men'. Poems prompted by old northern archaeological finds included Whittier 1843, 6–10; Longfellow 1904, 46–7.
[10] Parker 1896, 7; see Stephens 1884.
[11] See Calverley 1881–2, 403; reprinted in Parker 1896, 63–4.
[12] Kemble 1840 revealed the links between the Ruthwell cross and *The Dream of the Rood*; see also Finnur Magnússon 1836–7, Wawn 1991a, 122–33.

narrative tradition.[13] Now the two Oxford scholars offered a possible route for transmission of insular culture to Iceland: a 'Western Islander', captain of a trading vessel, spends the winter in Iceland and is invited to tell a story at some gathering: 'he recites one of the poems he has heard at entertainment in his own land',[14] that is, eddic poems recited by Viking settlers from Scandinavia. The 'western' captain's Icelandic host records the poems he hears. An alternative transmission route involved an Icelander wintering in the western isles, then returning to Iceland where he retold the poems he had heard recited on festive occasions. For some Victorian old northernists such a theory will have seemed irresistible. Was there no limit to the British Isles' Viking-age greatness? Not only had great saga heroes such as King Ólafr Tryggvason, Egill Skallagrímsson and Friðþjófr visited and left their mark, and not only had ancient myths found artistic expression in ecclesiastical sculpture, but it now appeared that the famous poems of the *Codex Regius* could be added proudly to the British literary heritage alongside *Beowulf*, Chaucer, Shakespeare and Scott.

Folklorists were uncovering additional reasons for celebrating the old northern mythological heritage of England. By the end of the nineteenth century 'Merry Olde Englande' was the subject of fevered investigation.[15] The folk customs of rural England, notably of Danelaw areas, were recorded and studied by scholars convinced that in sword-dances, May-games, mummers' plays, and seasonal feasts could be found the residue of a once vigorous Viking-age pagan faith. It is easy to forget that though E.K. Chambers' *The Medieval Stage*, with its lengthy and densely annotated section on folk drama, was still being reissued in the 1970s, it was first published in 1903 as very much a product of late Victorian folklore research. Papers at the Viking Club in London covered the same topics. A Fenland vicar shares tales of Yule logs, pre-Crimean War plough bullocks carrying horse's skulls (Óðinn the Wild Huntsman carrying Sleipnir's head), bees being first informed of the death of a household head and then fed with food from the funeral feast (compliant bees produce honey; mead requires honey; the gods drank mead in Valhǫll),[16] and lucky horseshoes which when banged to the accompaniment of the appropriate polytheistic charm ward off ague:

> Feyther, Son and Holy Ghoast,
> Naale the divil to this poast.
> Throice I smoites with Holy Crok
> With this mell Oi throice dew knock,
> One for God,

---

[13] Todd 1867, xxviii–ix.
[14] Gudbrand Vigfusson and Powell 1883, lxxiii; see also lx–lxiv, and Gudbrand Vigfusson and Powell 1886. For discussion of the theories, see [Metcalfe F.] 1884 and Metcalfe W. 1890.
[15] See Hodgetts 1884.
[16] Heanley 1901–3.

An' one for Wod
An' one for Lok.[17]

Late nineteenth-century speculations such as these fed off curiosities aroused much earlier in Victorian Britain. The first fifty years of Victoria's reign had seen an unprecedented proliferation of editions, translations, paraphrases, poetic amplifications, selections, simplifications and interpretations of eddic tales. The poems of the *Poetic Edda*, and the tales of Snorri Sturluson's *Prose Edda* became the subject for public lectures. The origins of the old northern pantheon were pondered in the light of new continental theories of mythology; and, as befits an age of Gothic architectural revival, the places and practices of Viking-age worship attracted attention – could the mysterious temples at Uppsala and Hofsstaðir hold a candle to those of Sir George Gilbert Scott?[18] Could their interior furnishings match those designed by William Morris and Edward Burne-Jones? The eddas were, thus, just as much canonical works of the Victorian old north as they had been for late eighteenth-century readers. Accordingly, Victorian books, lectures and other treatments of eddic texts are the subject of this chapter.

A section from George Dasent's 1858 'The Norsemen in Iceland' essay offers a useful textual benchmark in our discussion. He quotes a famous passage from *Vǫluspá* in which the old northern apocalypse is chillingly predicted:

> Brothers shall fight together,
> And be one the other's bane;
> Sisters' children
> Their kin shall kill.
> Hard is't with the time,
> Whoredoms many.
> An axe-age, a sword-age,
> Shields are cloven;
> A wind-age, a wolf-age,
> Ere the world stoops to doom.[19]

These lines are taken from Snorri's thirteenth-century *Prose Edda* which George Dasent had translated in 1842.[20] The passage became almost a neck-verse for Victorian old northernists responsive to its Dasentian 'presentiments of dissolution'. Various treatments of this passage can serve as reference points as we investigate the diversity of Victorian responses towards the old northern pantheon.

---

[17] Ibid., 53.

[18] Victorian readers would be familiar with Scott's description of Þórólfr Mostrarskegg's Hofs-staðir temple from Percy 1859, 518. On the cult of romantic archaeology in nineteenth-century Iceland, see Adolf Friðriksson 1994, 48–74.

[19] Dasent 1858, 197.

[20] Dasent's 'sister's [sic] children their sib shall spoil' (1842, 78) becomes 'Sisters' children / their kin shall kill' (1858, 197).

Theories of Origin and Interpretation

The Óðinn who arrived in Regency Britain was frequently understood to have been a great military leader at war with tyrannical Rome. In Robert Southey's 'The Race of Odin' (1827), for instance, an all-conquering warrior, migrating westwards from Asia, adopts the name and claims the honours due to the god Odin.[21] His northern kingdom is peopled by 'the free-born offspring of the free-born sire',[22] with Scandinavia's 'hardy soil' producing a strong and vigorous plant. It is there that 'genuine poesy' emerges, destined to stiffen the resolve of warriors (two of Percy's *Five Pieces* are echoed);[23] the emergence of the crack force of Jómsborg Vikings is celebrated; and the poem ends at the 'destin'd hour' when the Romans are defeated, slavery is abolished, ' "and lo, the world is again free!" ' (712, l. 115). In the companion piece, 'The Death of Odin', we find the great warrior in his death throes even as his troops drive on to final victory. Odin exhibits all the old northern qualities which a hundred and fifty years of learned European scholarship had clarified, and a hundred years of English verse had popularised. He embraces death eagerly, knowing that his spear will still direct his forces in his absence; his warriors know that those chosen by the valkyries will be borne by Odin himself to their last and best resting place, where foaming 'sweet-smiling' skulls full of 'hydromel' await them (712, l. 123).

No such interpretative clarity attended his entry into Edwardian Britain a hundred years later. Over the intervening period euhemerism jostled with vegetation myth, monotheism with polytheism, Graeco-Roman origins with Indo-European or Scandinavian. Some sense of the vigorous Victorian debate about the origins and significance of the old northern pantheon emerges from a brief examination of six early Victorian discussions of the *Edda*: Thomas Smith's 1838 lecture to the Leicestershire Literary Society on *Vǫluspá*;[24] Grenville Pigott's 1839 compendium of mythological lore; the first of Thomas Carlyle's 1840 London lectures 'On heroes and hero worship'; I.A. Blackwell's 1847 revision of Percy's *Northern Antiquities*; an 1852–3 review by William Roscoe of current eddic scholarship; and George Dasent's reflections on the eddas in his 1858 'The Norsemen in Iceland' paper.

Thomas Smith illustrates his *Vǫluspá* lecture from his own translation of the poem, based on the text in the 1828 third volume of the Copenhagen *Edda* edition. The keynote passage reads:

> Brother brother slays
> Rent asunder are

---

[21] See also Herbert 1806, 15–20; [Percy] 1809, I 51–62; Drummond 1817.

[22] Southey 1829, 711; reprinted in Omberg 1976, 171–6.

[23] Southey 1829, 711 ['The Ransome of Egill the Scald', ll. 73–82; 'Regner Lodbrog', 83–90].

[24] See also [Busk] 1835, 1836. Heavily influenced by Grundtvig's allegorical readings. On Grundtvig and the eddas, see Lönnroth 1988, Lundgreen-Nielsen 1994.

The bonds of kindred;
Hard will be the time!
Luxury prevails;
Axe-time, sword-time!
Shields are cleft.
Wolf-time, storm-time,
Ere the world falls!
Nor shall one man
Another spare.[25]

Smith almost certainly relied primarily on the Copenhagen Latin translation. Without Dasent's training in Icelandic, his translation does scant justice to the Icelandic text's verbal spikiness, and the evasive 'luxury prevails' enables him to dodge the bullet of 'hórdómr micill' [L adulteria freqventia].[26] Smith's philological instincts and sense of decorum were those of the late eighteenth century, but he is aware of the theories of Finnur Magnússon concerning the origins of old northern mythology.[27] Rejecting the euhemerism of Snorri Sturluson, which had underpinned Mallet's readings, Finnur's theory, romantic to the core, was that the myths reflected primitive responses, sensuous and intense, to the natural forces governing individuals' lives since the dawn of civilisation. In Smith's chosen examples Baldr represents summer light in May, and Hǫðr's deadly assault marks the onset of winter darkness. In *Þrymskviða* the giant (winter) has stolen Þórr's thunderbolt (summer storms) and demands Freyja (the moon) in exchange – a concession that would fundamentally destabilise nature. Þórr and Loki then combine to overcome the forces of winter.[28] Though respecting Finnur's 'vast learning' and 'the felicity of his conjectures',[29] Smith resists the notion that the ash tree Yggdrasill represents an imperfectly integrated alternative theory of creation to the one represented by Ymir and Auðhumla (31).[30] For Smith the tree betokens the earth in its organised state, while the Auðhumla story tells of the earlier stages of creation.

Smith identifies continuities between the Viking-age spirit and nineteenth-century industrial and scientific progress. British success is attributed not to Viking blood in Victorian veins but to the Gothic spirit in Victorian minds. The Goths' wildness of imagination transcended the bounds of the existing world; the eddas represent the mythic distillation of that impulse. Just as the soaring lines of medieval Gothic architecture could inspire the earthbound soul, so

[25] Smith 1838, 50.
[26] Luxdorph 1787–1828, III 46.
[27] Finnur Magnússon 1824–6; see also [Keightley] 1828.
[28] Smith 1838, 39–40. [Neuberg] 1854, 316, noting the post-1848 popularity of eddic myth and legend in Germany, speaks of 'potions from Mimir's well to nourish the tree of Nationality'. He notes German belief in the indigenous nature of the myths: ibid., 318.
[29] Smith 1838, 37.
[30] Finnur ([Keightley] 1828, 229n) saw the two models as anticipating nineteenth-century geological controversy between Neptunists and Vulcanists.

nineteenth-century science seeks to challenge, harness and control the forces of nature. The Goths were only barbarians in the eyes of their ultimately defeated Roman opponents (56). The moral lessons of eddic mythology, its sense of reward and punishment in the afterlife, 'are not . . . the characteristics of blind and brutal barbarism' (53). The Goths were 'of gentle and sedate disposition' except when roused to war; they were capable of generosity of spirit (Frithiof is cited, amidst glowing praise of Tegnér's poem; 56); and Valhǫll offered no welcome to murderers, perjurers or cowards. From the broadest perspective Smith claims that the study of eddic texts, and also of parallel Eastern mythological systems (Finnur Magnússon had linked Norse mythology with Buddhism and the Koran; 36–7), could contribute excitingly to clarifying the Indo-European stages of mankind's history, much as comparative philology had done.

Thomas Smith was addressing a single learned society in middle England; Grenville Pigott's *A Manual of Scandinavian Mythology, Containing a Popular Account of the Two Eddas and of the Religion of Odin* (1839) reached out to a national readership. It was essentially a work of synthesis, assembled originally without any view to publication – hence the absence of footnotes.[31] He claims no originality for the volume's format (based on E.L. Heiberg's 1827 *Die deutsche Mythologie*),[32] for its introductory discussion and appendices (based on Finnur Magnússon and Bishop P.E. Müller), or for the choice of texts (guided by Percy). There are, however, distinctive elements in the volume. Pigott may have been the first British scholar to give a detailed explanation of the seventeenth-century Latin mistranslation which had prompted the belief that Vikings and Valhǫll revellers drank wine out of the skulls of their slain foes.[33] The volume succeeds in its aim of making available in succinct form information about the Old Norse gods that was 'spread throughout many a costly volume' and 'shut up in languages not studied in England'.[34]

The euhemeristic traditions rejected by Thomas Smith and Pigott find renewed support in Thomas Carlyle's celebrated 1840 lecture 'The Hero as Divinity'. Carlyle deals not with the overall sweep of what he calls the 'Hyper-Brobdingnagian business'[35] of old northern mythology, but with the single individual responsible for its initial articulation and codification. It was Óðinn who gave written form and shape to his fellows' unvoiced perceptions about the 'beautiful, awful, unspeakable'[36] world in which they lived. Like all great heroes he produced cosmos out of chaos.[37] His was the vivid pictorial language of a

---

[31] Pigott 1839, xiii. [Keightley] 1828 (reprinted 1860) was more international in coverage, but dated in its sources.
[32] Even the idea of quoting Oehlenschläger comes from Heiberg.
[33] Pigott 1839, 65–6.
[34] Ibid., xiii.
[35] Carlyle 1897, V 20.
[36] Ibid., V 7.
[37] Carlyle 1899, V 210: such abilities, 'hugely in discredit at present', were 'not unlikely to be needed again . . . before all is done'.

soul intensely charged with primeval insight. Óðinn's ability to create a runic record of the truths he had revealed so astonished his fellows that they regarded him first as a magician and then as a incarnate divinity. As a seer, inventor and poet he was worthy of worship – a hero as divinity. Óðinn's runic wisdom, transformed by poets and scribes, reappeared centuries later in the two eddas. While Carlyle enjoyed tales such as Þórr's adventures in Útgarðr, he regarded these as products of a self-consciously playful literary age, for all their residual flecks of 'real antique Norse gold'. In the case of Þórr, the antique elements were his 'right honest strength'; as the presence of his faithful retainer Þjálfi signals, Þórr was ever the peasant's friend.[38] In Þórr's humiliation at the hands of Skrýmir Carlyle sees 'mirth resting on earnestness and sadness, as the rainbow on black tempest' (39), part of the 'sublime uncomplaining melancholy' (36) to be found in old northern, Victorian – and American backwoods – hearts. Carlyle laments that little remains of Þórr save in nursery memories of Jack the Giant Killer. As for Óðinn, whose last earthly appearance was as the 'one-eyed stranger' at a feast of the missionary King Ólafr Tryggvason in Snorri's saga (and Laing's translation and Longfellow's poem), he survives only in a handful of place names and a single day of the week. But the spirit of both figures had become part of the British character, a source of strength and stability in times of abhorred (by Carlyle) Chartist turmoil in Britain and popular insurrection in Europe.

A glance at Percy's unrevised 1770 *Northern Antiquities* confirms the extent to which Carlyle's euhemeristic approach draws on Mallet's understanding of Óðinn. Readers are told that Óðinn may have been Sigge, a Scythian rebel against Rome, charismatic leader of the Æsir people whose principal city was Ásgarðr. As chief priest Sigge adopted the name of Óðinn, the all-father god. Fleeing from Pompey's all-conquering forces Óðinn and the Æsir moved west and north and found refuge in Jutland. Leaving his son Skjǫldr behind to rule Denmark (and to found the Scylding dynasty), Óðinn then moved east to Sweden, whose leader Gylfi was so dazzled by the Scythian's military prowess that he regarded him as a god. The Swedes crowned Óðinn's son Yngvi, thus founding the Yngling dynasty. After further conquests in Norway, Óðinn returned to Sweden to die, declaring that he would rejoin the other gods at the eternal banquet in Ásgarðr. Though the secondary deities do not pass muster with the eighteenth-century rationalising mind,[39] the main precepts of the religion appeared civilised enough: 'to be brave and intrepid in war, to serve the gods, and to appease them by sacrifices, not to be unjust, to show hospitality to strangers, to keep their words inviolably, and to be faithful to the marriage bed'.[40]

Mallet-Percy euhemerism and monotheism underwent thorough revision by

38 Carlyle 1897, V 35; he here draws on Uhland 1836.
39 [Percy] 1770, I 103.
40 Ibid., 101.

I.A. Blackwell in 1847.[41] Blackwell saw primitive polytheism undergoing rapid systematisation, out of which emerged a single dominant deity. Worship and doctrine were then formalised, with the priestly elite viewing the original elemental deities as mere symbols of natural phenomena. Poets, in turn, gave expression to these esoteric understandings. Blackwell concluded that these 'higher doctrines' had little or no impact on the simple faith of the commonalty, which involved loyalty to one or two favoured gods, and a general sense that 'all who died with arms in their hands . . . would partake of the boisterous joys of Valhalla'.[42] Amongst the historical, ethnological, astronomical, physical and psychological interpretations vying for attention in the middle of the nineteenth century Blackwell remains a cautious cherry-picker. Along with euhemerism, ethnological readings of myths as allegorised tribal disputes are rejected.[43] He is more sympathetic to 'physical' and 'psychological' readings – the early codifiers were capable of giving mythic expression to the conflicting forces in their universe (light vs dark, summer vs winter, good vs evil, barbarism vs civilisation). Blackwell is wary though not dismissive of Finnur Magnússon's astronomical explanations: Finnur had noted parallels between the twelve celestial mansions described in *Grímnismál* and the twelve signs of the zodiac.[44] Thus Álfheimr (whose tutelary deity is Freyr) corresponds to Capricorn, Breiðablik (Baldr) to Gemini, and Nóatún (Njǫrðr) to Libra and so on. It seemed 'very appropriate' to have the sun god correspond to the winter solstice (which marked the annual birth of the sun); the impartiality of Baldr's son Forseti, the god of justice, is fittingly signalled by the autumn equinox (midway between summer and winter); and Baldr in Cancer marks the going down of the sun – a belief dimly discernible in the midsummer custom of lighting bale fires on the festival of the nativity of John the Baptist.[45]

In Blackwell's *Prose Edda* translation, the benchmark *Vǫluspá* lines read:

> Then shall brethren be
> Each other's bane,
> And sisters' children rend
> The ties of kin.
> Hard will be the age,
> And harlotry prevail.
> An axe-age, a sword-age,
> Shields oft cleft in twain,
> A storm-age, a wolf-age,
> Ere earth shall meet its doom.[46]

---

[41] Blackwell is less sanguine about euhemerism than Petersen 1849, 121–3.
[42] Percy 1859, 468.
[43] Ibid., 478.
[44] Luxdorph 1787–1828, III 1011; Percy 1859, 503–4.
[45] Percy 1859, 504–5.
[46] Ibid., 451–2.

This is a far cry from Percy's 1770 translation of Mallet:

> Brothers becoming murderers, shall stain themselves with brothers blood; kindred shall forget the ties of consanguinity; life shall become a burthen; adultery shall reign throughout the world. A barbarous age! an age of swords! an age of tempests! an age of wolves! The bucklers shall be broken in pieces; and these calamities shall succeed each other till the world shall fall to ruin.[47]

Blackwell favours shorter sense units, compound nouns, terser verb phrases, and a less Latinate vocabulary ('kin' for 'consanguinity'). The Old French derived 'harlotry' and 'adultery' enable him to tiptoe past the problem of 'hórdómr'.

The fifth voice in this preliminary survey of nineteenth-century British responses to the eddas is that of William Roscoe in his 1852–3 review of new translations by Karl Simrock and Benjamin Thorpe.[48] While Carlyle and Blackwell had hinted at the possibilities of reading old northern mythology as natural science, Roscoe reports its full potential as set out in Thorpe's reading of Þórr.[49] The deity himself represents electricity; his belt is a condenser; his gloves are conductors; his son Magni represents magnetism, and Þórr's journey into the realm of Útgarðaloki represents the diffusion of terrestrial magnetism in the vegetable kingdom. In the stories of the creation and subsequent theft of the poetic mead, the brewing dwarfs are putrefaction and fermentation; Gillingr, the giant who drowns when the dwarfs' boat capsizes, signifies post-fermentation dregs; his vengeful son Suttungr is spiritous drink (perhaps referring to his capacity to fly after Óðinn who had stolen the mead); and Suttungr's daughter Gunnlǫð who was left in charge of the mead is to be understood as carbonic acid. Roscoe remains quizzical, and, overall, he misses in current eddic scholarship any mention of the two great 'practical' gods of the Vikings, 'honour and self'. The old northern pantheon may have served as a useful safety net on a stormy night in an open boat, but the most fundamental Viking-age belief was self reliance.[50] Roscoe anticipates one major focus of late Victorian eddic research – ought the poems to be regarded as 'the shattered remains of ancient religious drama'?[51] Based on his study of the Baldr legend Sir James Frazer was later to suggest[52] that the poems represented performance texts for annual sacred rituals, with seasonal fires lit to commemorate the pyre in which Baldr died, in the hope of ensuring continued sunshine. Continental scholars had pondered such readings since the end of the eighteenth century,[53] but Roscoe's may be the first formulation of the claim in English: 'they [the

---

[47] [Percy] 1770, II 159–60.
[48] Roscoe 1852–3.
[49] Thorpe 1851–2, I 126–7. His work draws on Petersen 1849. On Thorpe, see Pulsiano 1998.
[50] Roscoe 1852–3, 487–9; Dasent 1875, I 278.
[51] Phillpotts 1920, 114.
[52] Frazer 1913.
[53] Discussed in Gunnell 1995, 1–7.

Vikings] were the first to discover the drama in its fullest sense. The stage they had not, but their imaginations had long been familiar with all that finds in the stage its highest development.'[54]

George Dasent, the final witness in this preliminary survey of Victorian responses to the old northern gods, was, as we have seen, mid-Victorian Britain's most accomplished old northernist, and inevitably his judgements carried a special authority. He reveals himself to be a Blackwellian revisionist though with some distinctive notes of his own. He identifies six developmental stages. The sensuous imagination of primitive man assigns names to the natural forces ruling his life.[55] The tribes abandon their mid-Asiatic homelands taking with them their common store of mythic lore, which slowly mutates in the light of local conditions. In Dasent's second stage men attempt to impose themselves on their environment. Technological progress and growing prosperity went hand in hand with a move to monotheism; the forces of nature are now seen as having been tamed by Óðinn, 'the disposer and arranger of the . . . universe'.[56] In the third stage, Óðinn's attributes were soon devolved to a dozen inferior divinities: Þórr as the summer thundercloud against the frost giants; Freyr as the god of fecundity and so on. Giants and trolls, the 'old Tories' of mythology, are distant echoes of a 'simple primitive race, whose day is past and gone',[57] driven to the woods and rocky fastnesses, their hunting fields having fallen prey to agriculture and tillage. In the fourth stage, the peaceful tribes over whom Óðinn has presided benevolently began to fight with each other, with Óðinn emerging as a battle god able to bestow luck and victory in war. The fifth stage sees the reversal of human civilisation's temporary triumph over the hostile forces of nature. As Dasent's version of our benchmark *Vǫluspá* quotation reveals, mankind would self-destruct and the axe-age, sword-age, wind-age, wolf-age would arrive. Eventually, though, a new generation of gods would herald a new age of unending prosperity. However, as Dasent reminds his readers, this period of apocalypse and rebirth never happened. In the sixth and final stage, Christianity overwhelmed paganism. Hel became a place rather than a person, and the Æsir themselves were as much a defeated and exiled group as their former gigantic enemies. For Dasent this final stage had its own sense of melancholy. His Langlandian vision sees the simple truths of early Christianity decaying under the leaden weight of papist bureaucracy, corruption and unnatural clerical celibacy.

The pagan gods, stubbornly resistant to the new faith, survived unrecognised through the Middle Ages, and on into Dasent's own Victorian age in the form of folktale, peasant custom, and rural superstition, as when Óðinn, degraded by Christianity, became the demon huntsman of popular belief.[58] He could be spotted in the clouds, and his hunting cries heard on spring and autumn eve-

---

[54] Roscoe 1852–3, 522–3.
[55] Dasent 1858, 199.
[56] Ibid., 188–9.
[57] Dasent 1859, lxxiii.
[58] Ibid., xliii; Baring-Gould 1863, 199–203.

nings as sea birds took to the air.[59] Strenuous efforts were made to enlist Shakespeare to the old northern cause, with his small Latin, less Greek, but much folklore. Herne the Hunter in *The Merry Wives of Windsor* (4 iv 28–38) becomes a displaced Óðinn figure, walking round oak trees in Windsor Forest on winter nights, wearing a set of horns, killing cattle and shaking a chain. The weird sisters in *Macbeth* are the norns of old northern myth – Urðr, 'the past', Verðandi, 'the present', and Skuld, 'the future'.[60]

At various levels of mythic displacement these were the silenced old northern voices which keen folklorists were eager to rediscover in their own culture, for all that this would fly in the face of Christian dogma, universal education and scientific rationalism. Though Dasent believed that such myths found their richest expression in Norway, his native land was not far behind. Indeed, this very thought triggers an old northern note in his vocabulary: 'in England there are old names of the land and towns, which one may skill [OI *skilja*, 'to understand'] to know that they have been given in another tongue than this'.[61] These folk narratives were collected by Thomas Keightley, Dasent, and Benjamin Thorpe.[62]

Dasent's work also stressed the need for a translation of the *Poetic Edda*; the importance of producing books of old northern lore for children; the possibility of creating a major modern epic poem about the Norse gods and old northern heroes; and the role which new understandings of the northern mythology could play in illuminating the history of Britain, and, indeed, the history of mankind. It is to these Victorian issues that the present chapter now turns.

Translating the Eddas

Only one (incomplete) translation of Snorri Sturluson's *Edda* was published in Britain during Queen Victoria's lifetime.[63] No complete English translation of the *Poetic Edda* became available before the appearance of Benjamin Thorpe's 1866 version,[64] and only one other (by Guðbrandur Vigfússon and Frederick York Powell) appeared before the end of the century.[65]

Amos Cottle's 1797 paraphrastic versions of a dozen or so eddic poems was based on the facing page Latin translations in the first volume of the Copenha-

---

[59] Dasent 1859, xlv; On Shetland, see Blind 1879, 1105ff. Discussed Mjöberg 1967, 46; Wilson 1997, 69, 97.

[60] Blind, as quoted in Anderson 1880, 253–6. See also Pigott 1839, vii; Browning 1876, 39.

[61] Dasent 1842, 111.

[62] (i) [Keightley] 1828, republished 1860 in Bohn's Antiquarian Library; eddic and saga material, pp. 60–75; Scandinavian folklore, pp. 78–155 (1860 edition) (ii) Dasent 1859 (iii) Thorpe 1851–2. Thorpe 1853 is a popular repackaging.

[63] Dasent 1842. Anderson 1880, published in Chicago, had limited exposure in Britain.

[64] Translations of individual poems appeared earlier: see, for example, Anster 1853.

[65] Eiríkur Magnússon's translation was rejected for publication: Lbs. 2188b 4to, John Murray to EM, 19 April 1871.

gen *Sæmundar Edda*; *Vǫluspá* was included in the edition's 1828 third and final volume, too late to be 'Cottled'. The 1828 text and Latin translation was used by many nineteenth-century commentators and popularisers, though due account was taken of later editions by P.A. Munch, Hermann Lüning and others.[66] In our benchmark passage, Thorpe's 1866 translation (based on Lüning's 1859 text)[67] adds, reorders and amends lines. Comparison with Thomas Smith's 1838 version reveals Thorpe's greater willingness to swim against the tide of linguistic expectation in word order and alliteration. There is no back-sliding from the 'whoredom' translation pioneered by Dasent in 1858:

Brœðr munu berjask	Brothers shall fight,
ok at bönum verðask,	and slay each other;
munu systrungar	cousins shall
sifjum spilla:	kinship violate.
grundir gialla,	The earth resounds,
gifr flíugandi,	The giantesses flee;
mun engi maðr	no man will
öðrum þyrma.	another spare.
Hart er í heimi	Hard it is in the world,
hórdómr mikill	great whoredom,
skeggöld, skálmöld,	an axe age, a sword age,
skildir 'ro klofnir,	shields shall be cloven,
vindöld, vargöld,	a wind age, a wolf age,
áðr veröld steypisk.	ere the world sinks.[68]

An air of hesitancy marks the actual publication of Thorpe's work, for all that it represents the natural follow-up to his *Northern Mythology* and draws on the latest European eddic scholarship. He allowed the second part (the heroic poems) to be published only after receiving reassuring notices about the first; and it was only on the publisher's insistence that Thorpe identified himself at the end of the second volume's preface. The translator wanted to produce 'a small work at a moderate cost', which would be 'a homely representation of the original' and fill a 'chasm in our literature':[69] his volume fulfils these objectives.

Later English translators tended to favour either prose or alliterative long lines. In their *Corpvs Poeticvm Boreale* (1883) Guðbrandur Vigfússon and York Powell (like Dasent) translated the verse from Snorri's *Edda*:[70] 'It shall go hard with the world: much of whoredom, an age of axes, an age of swords, shields shall be cloven, an age of storm, an age of wolves, ere the world falls in ruins.'[71] Olive Bray's 1908 Viking Club Translation Series version, sporting its W.G.

66 Thorpe used Lüning's edition: 1866, I vi–viii.
67 Lüning 1859, 11.
68 Thorpe 1866, I 9; Lüning 1859, 150–1.
69 Ibid., I viii, II iii.
70 Gudbrand Vigfusson and Powell 1883, I 192.
71 Ibid., I 198.

Collingwood illustrations, was based on the *Codex Regius* text, printed on the facing page:

Brothers shall fight   and be as murderers
sisters' children   shall stain their kinship.
'Tis ill with the world;   comes fearful whoredom,
a Sword age, Axe age,   – shields are cloven,
a Wind age, Wolf age,   ere the world sinks.
Never shall man then   spare another.[72]

At the end of the nineteenth century, then, as at the beginning, the most likely way for British readers to access the broad sweep of old Norse myths and legends was by reading the text and following the critical discussion of Snorri's *Prose Edda* in Blackwell's revision of Percy's *Northern Antiquities*. The Copenhagen *Poetic Edda*, with its Latin translation, also remained in use in both private homes and public libraries. Eventually, readers could read a serviceable English translation of the poems in Thorpe's pocket-sized edition, along with the same scholar's versions of Scandinavian folktales. Some of these folktales were also made available as a Christmas book for children,[73] confirming that at least one scholar understood the importance of winning the hearts and minds of new generations of potential old northern enthusiasts.

Children's Corner

The most influential attempt to introduce Viking-age mythology to young Victorian readers was Annie and Elizabeth Keary's *The Heroes of Asgard and the Giants of Jötunheim; or, The Week and its Story* (1857). The introductory section describes a family Christmas, during which the children find Aunt Helen and Uncle Alick in the library studying Percy's *Northern Antiquities*.[74] Starved of such knowledge at school,[75] the children are promised that on each of the seven days of the Christmas week, they will learn about the name of the day and at least one related old northern myth. Thus, beginning on Wodensday, the children learn first of Óðinn, and then of residual Yule-tide elements such as the Boar's Head, perhaps a distant echo of Sæhrímnir whose renewable flesh fed the revellers in Valhǫll. They learn that the English idiom 'a little bird told me' could refer to the two ravens Huginn and Muninn who kept Óðinn informed about events all over creation. Thursday prompts reflections on the links between Þórr's hammer (Fig. 7) and the engineering works at Crewe, both symbolising man's desire to subdue matter by strength and ingenuity.[76] As the discussion

---

[72] Bray 1908, 291.
[73] Thorpe 1853.
[74] Keary 1857, 5.
[75] Speight 1903 was an alternative school reader, including passages from Snorri's *Edda*.
[76] Keary 1857, 101–2.

Fig. 7. The giant Skrymir and Thor. Artist Huard. Cover design for A. and E. Keary, *The Heroes of Asgard*.

develops, and clearly under Blackwell's influence, the adults concede that 'no end' of explanations are possible for each mythic element – Þórr could be a symbol of thunder ('meagre, unsatisfactory', claims Alick), or of human toil subduing the earth (rejected by Aunt Margaret).[77] Friday produces a précis of *Skírnismál* with Gerðr (the earth) married to Freyr (the summer sun), followed by Aunt Margaret's speculation that Freyr's boar-drawn chariot may lie behind the annual Yorkshire chariot-drawing custom, about which she been told by her grandmother. Saturday's tale of the theft of Iðunn's apples is again accompanied by a moral reading (innocence restored through pain and suffering) and a nature-myth one (spring captured but eventually released by autumn). After the Sabbath has been kept decorously free from storytelling, Baldr is Monday's featured deity. For Aunt Margaret the god is a figure of innocence whose death symbolises the fall of man, with Hǫðr representing that blind force of evil which led Adam and Eve astray; young Alick prefers a 'summer stolen by winter' reading. Tuesday is devoted to the binding of Fenrir (the wolfish nature of sin); no-one seems able to explain why Loki deserved the loyal support of his wife as she sought to protect him from the dripping poison. At the end of the story sequence the children learn that their Christmas tree is a reminder of Yggdrasill, and that the post-Ragnarǫk new world confirms that while righteous pagans can approach God's truths through the revealed world, only Christ can defeat death – a fact celebrated by a Christmas carol.

Title alterations to subsequent Victorian editions of the Keary work suggest that publishers were uncertain how to pitch the volume for their young audience: *Christmas Week and Its Stories, or the Heroes of Asgard* (?1860) became *The Heroes of Asgard: Tales from Scandinavian Mythology* (1883 and 1891). These latter editions dispense with the library discussions, and include snatches of eddic verse, including our benchmark verses from *Vǫluspá*, in which there is no tasteless tangling with 'adulteria':

Then brother contended with brother, and war had no bounds. A hard age was that.

> An axe age,
> A sword age,
> Shields oft cleft in twain;
> A storm age,
> A wolf age,
> Ere the earth met its doom.[78]

The Heroes of Asgard lived on in a variety of formats well into the twentieth century. Kipling's casual reference to 'Heroes of Asgard' Thor' in the 'Weland's Smith' tale in *Puck of Pook's Hill* (1906) confirms the volume's enduring popu-

---

[77] Ibid., 104.
[78] Keary 1901, 299.

larity.[79] A repackaged children's edition in 1930 was still being reprinted by Macmillan in 1963. The 1891 edition was also the source for the 1944 Macmillan's English Literature Series volume on Norse mythology 'for the use of schools'. The wartime introduction highlights the Laingean spirit of the original preface: the myths reveal the nobility of heroic forefathers whose Viking blood still flows in modern veins (ix–x). If *The Heroes of Asgard* lost its way after 1944, it will not have been helped by a world war fought against a state whose leaders were still fantasising about rebirth after Ragnarǫk from the *Führerbunker* in 1945.[80]

The young readership for which the Keary volume was intended could also turn to Ruth Pitt's *The Tragedy of the Norse Gods* (1893), in which claims for the importance of Old Norse mythology are pitched high. These deities had 'informed, upheld and influenced' the Norseman in his 'hard and stern heroism . . . contempt for cowardice . . . reverence for home . . . steadfastness to duty, obedience, truth, and trust – virtues on which our family and national constitution are founded'.[81] The myths, to be read as 'one story' (4), are retold in prose with each chapter headed by an eddic verse, not least our *Vǫluspá* lines, with the 'whoredom' firmly in place:

> Hard is it in the world,
> Great whoredom,
> An axe age, a sword age,
> Shields shall be cloven,
> A wind age, a wolf age,
> Ere the world sinks. (177)

The chapters themselves are written in a wide-eyed lyrical style, as if a roll of William Morris's wallpaper had suddenly come to life, as in the description of Yggdrasill:

> It was springtime, and buttercups were springing in the long grass, and daffodils were nodding their yellow heads. Here and there the tender tears of the dew still lingered on the tall spikes. Apple trees, lilacs, and laburnums shed a shower of pink, blue, and yellow blossom on the scented air. The birds sent forth a full melody of song, unabashed by the presence of divinity. (64)

Stranger still is the conversation between Frea and Odin in Ásgarðr. The 'world--mother' senses the onset of evil and the matter is discussed in a tone reminiscent of anxious Victorian parents awaiting their children's important examination results:

---

[79] Kipling 1993, 14.
[80] Toland 1966, 74.
[81] Pitt 1893, 3.

'How happy the children are.'

'And why should they not be happy, dear heart?' asked Odin, who sat above her, one large hand resting on her golden hair.

'Because – because – Ah! I don't know. Because there are shadows among the trees.'

But he who loved her was not to be put off. His brow darkened as he drew her to him, and lifted up the flower-like face till he could look straight into the troubled eyes.

'What is it, Frea?'

She put her head down on his shoulder, and, to his alarm, sobbed, with deep-drawn breaths between. (25)

'A Place in Our Songs'

In the preface to his translation of Snorri's *Edda*, Rasmus Anderson longs for the day when 'some young son or daughter of Odin' would write 'a Teutonic epic' based on eddic material.[82] This would signal an end to the sad neglect of this rich cultural inheritance amongst English speaking people of old northern descent. There had been too much grovelling before the gods of 'foreign nations' (Greece and Italy). The eddas

> are the concentrated result of their [the forefathers' of Anderson and his Scandinavian-American readers] greatest intellectual and spiritual effort, and it behooves us to cherish this treasure and make it the fountain at which the whole American branch of the Ygdrasil ash may imbibe a united national sentiment. It is not enough to brush the dust off these gods and goddesses of our ancestors and put them up on pedestals as ornaments in our museums and libraries . . . The grand-son must use what he has inherited from his grandfather . . . ancestral deities want a place in our hearts and in our songs.[83]

Anderson wanted Norse epics not odes, though had he known of Sir William Drummond's bloated *Odin, A Poem; in Eight Books and Two Parts* (1817) he might have thought again.[84] Scandinavian poets had shown the way early in the century. Adam Oehlenschläger's epic-scale *Nordens guder* (1819) was translated by W.E. Frye, and much cited in Pigott's *Manual*. In Frye's version of our benchmark lines, we find a remarkable transformation of 'hordómr mikill':

> Brother shall fight with brother
> And slay each other:
> The bonds of affection and parentage
> Shall be rent asunder:
> Evil reigns in the world;

[82] Anderson 1880, 10.

[83] Ibid., 29–30.

[84] Published in a lavish folio volume; draws heavily on Mallet. Drummond 1817, xxvi states that the reception of the experimental Part 1 would determine whether Part 2 would appear; it never did.

> Libidinous excess triumphs;
> The sword, the axe
> Shall be in constant employ:
> Shields shall be cloven;
> Times of tempest, of wolfish ferocity,
> Before the world finally ends;
> No man shall spare his neighbour.[85]

It seems appropriate that a version so replete with romance vocabulary should have been published jointly in London and in Paris; its dedicatory epistle to King Christian VIII of Denmark was written in the French capital. As was to be expected in the early 1840s the introductory essay reveals the influence of Finnur Magnússon's nature myth readings – the two men had met in Copenhagen (xxiv–ix, xxxi–lxxv). The Æsir are the 'creative, embellishing and conservative powers of nature' while the giants represent the 'defacing, corrupting, destructive' powers (xii). In the more ethnographic reading also offered, the giants represent the aboriginal tribes present in Scandinavia when Óðinn and the Goths arrived from the east (xi–xiv).

If Frye's Oehlenschläger translation was not the new poem which Rasmus Anderson was looking for, Julia Clinton Jones's *Valhalla, The Myths of Norseland: A Saga, In Twelve Parts* (1878), published in San Francisco, was certainly right on target in terms of subject matter; and if the author was not quite a 'daughter of Odin', at least her grandfather had been governor of New York State. The preface strikes a truculent note: deplorable ignorance of Scandinavian mythology still prevails; modern England and the United States have their Gothic ancestors to thank for having planted the seeds of liberty, for their scorn of luxury, and for their dedication to temperance and morality – qualities which have placed England 'in the foremost rank of the nations, and which are blazoned forth on the glorious flag of her daughter, our own United States'.[86] The author believes that 'the bold Vikings . . . went deeper into the grand scheme of Creation, and recognized the power of God working in the heart of Nature, in a fuller sense than in the mere Jötun force displayed in the earthquake shock, or tempest blast' (14–15). Baldr was clearly an anticipation of Christ, Loki of Satan, and Ragnarǫk prefigured the great Christian Judgement Day. Our *Vǫluspá* lines are briefly discernible in the poem's final canto:

> More fiercely than the lurid glare
> Of conflagration, hideously
> Shone on men's faces Murder's flame!
> Brother slew brother – father child;
> Men turn to tigers, mad for gore!
> Creation raged! war followed war;

---

[85] Frye 1845, 371.
[86] Jones 1878, 11–12.

> Impiety, Injustice piled
> Huge heaps of horror to the sky. (120–1)

The Miltonic syntax and eighteenth-century poetic diction seem well past their sell-by date. The poet lacks the imaginative and stylistic firepower to reanimate her original tellingly.

Though Rasmus Anderson had been looking for a Scandinavian-American 'son or daughter of Odin' to write the great old northern epic, several Englishmen also made the attempt, with Morris's *Sigurd the Volsung* (1876) coming closest to becoming the literary masterwork that would have so benefited the old northern cause in Victorian Britain. It will be discussed in Chapter 9. William Herbert's three lengthy epics, *Helga* (1815), *Hedin* (1820) and *Attila* (1838), all enjoyed Victorian exposure in reprinted editions.[87] *Helga* (1815), in some ways the most influential, has its feet very much in the late eighteenth century. The poet adds mythological ballast to the doomed love affair of Helga and the great Viking chief Hialmar – the poem's characters and events are freely adapted from the early chapters of *Hervarar saga* and *Örvar-Odds saga*.[88] In a dream Helga consults a Hel-based Vala (a scene heavily indebted to Gray's 'beautiful . . . Descent of Odin'),[89] and Hialmar's death produces an elaborate vision of his welcome in Valhalla. Ossianic melancholy and school of night Gothicism play across the narrative, and the shaping influence of *Gunnlaugs saga ormstungu* also seems discernible. The subsequent popularity of Tegnér's tale of Frithiof and Ingeborg casts an ironic shadow over Herbert's decision to change the name of his heroine to Helga from its *Örvar-Odds saga* form Ingibjǫrg on the grounds that the latter was 'too uncouth' for English poetry.

Imitation of Herbert's 'Helga' in the pseudonymous Zavarr's *The Viking, An Epic* (1849) doubtless represents the sincerest form of flattery. The poem's combative Preface anticipates Rasmus Anderson's call to arms: 'unmerited indifference' has been shown to the mythology of 'our Norse and Saxon ancestors'; 'our greatest bards have been contented with anything but their own' and would do well to copy the *amor patriæ* of the 'ancient and foreign poets' whom they imitate.[90] Zavarr's poem is the first of a series written to illustrate the various mythological systems of the world. Its acknowledged sources include Herbert's 'Helga', Scott's *Harold the Dauntless*, Oehlenschläger, and Blackwell's revision of Percy (280).[91] The poem, stylistically by Ossian out of Milton, follows the path of the Viking Vali from paganism to Christianity, a transformation brought about by the love of the Saxon maiden Edgiva. Dream visions produce lengthy inset descriptions of Ásgarðr (74–94), but in the third and final book ('Sólarspá')

---

[87] See also Herbert 1806.
[88] Hialmar's killer is Angantyr, entombed presence in the 'Waking of Angantyr'; Herbert 1815, 254n claims to have worked without ready access to *Örvar-Odds saga*.
[89] Herbert 1815, 205, 207.
[90] All quotations from Zavarr 1849, vii–x.
[91] The volume contains 130 pages of dense annotation.

Christian love proves the stronger and Vali's loðbrókian spirit finally yields.[92] This is perhaps not surprising in view of his revelation (uncannily anticipating the theories of Sophus Bugge)[93] that before setting out for England he already read about Christianity in captured monastic manuscripts that his Viking sea-king father had brought back from earlier raids (51).

Matthew Arnold's *Balder Dead* (1860) has its roots in Milton (as a kind of 'Ásgarðr Lost') and Keats rather than eighteenth-century sublimity, and is an intriguing attempt to breathe poetic life into a favourite myth. Earlier poets had hinted at the possibilities[94] but it is Arnold's poem which places Balder centre stage and guides the reader towards a surprisingly modern conclusion. In the approved epic mode there are journeys between worlds, debates and dissent amongst the gods, and elaborate similes aplenty – none more spectacular than that describing the moment when (almost) all creation weeps, thus apparently fulfilling the conditions for Balder's release from subterranean bondage:

> North, south, east, west, they struck, and roamd the world,
> Entreating all things to weep Balder's death.
> And all that lived, and all without life, wept.
> And as in winter, when the frost breaks up,
> At winter's end, before the spring begins,
> And a warm west-wind blows, and thaw sets in –
> After an hour a dripping sound is heard
> In all the forests, and the soft-strewn snow
> Under the trees is dibbled thick with holes,
> And from the boughs the snowloads shuffle down;
> And, in fields sloping to the south, dark plots
> Of grass peep out amid surrounding snow,
> And widen, and the peasant's heart is glad –
> So through the world was heard a dripping noise
> Of all things weeping to bring Balder back.[95]

This pastoral mood is broken by the confrontation with the toothless, dry-eyed old crone Thok (Loki); her scornful repetition of the word 'weep' shoots its own mistletoe barb through the heart of the epic simile. Unfamiliar camera angles allow us to catch sight of the flinty streets, lighted windows, and gate-house of Asgard; to learn of the resentment of Hela which hardens her heart against the pleas of the grieving gods; and to follow the debate between the hot-headed Odin, whose sentence was assuredly for open war, and his far-seeing wife Frea who reminds him that Hela 'holds by right her prey'. The reader may

---

[92] His defiance upon capture is a *Krákumál* paraphrase (ibid., 23–5); his night thoughts before execution take the form of a 'Dauðadrápa', with a Bartholinean 'I will smile as I die' refrain (ibid., 132ff.).

[93] Bugge 1881–9; Stephens 1883.

[94] Call 1875, 47: 'Balder' (1849).

[95] Allott and Allott 1979, 413, ll. 304–18.

reflect on the fate of the wretched Hoder, as his grief turns the scornful heart of Hermod to pity, and may ponder the intriguing speeches of Balder with which the poem closes – the gods of Asgard may long for his return, but does Balder wish to rejoin them? The daring question produces a striking answer:

> But not to me so grievous, as, I know,
> To other Gods it were, is my enforced
> Absence from fields where I could nothing aid . . . (ll. 500–2)

Like Njáll with his family, Balder bears the burden of knowing that all but a handful of the gods are doomed. He cannot help them survive the coming conflagration and, even if such deliverance were within his power, it is not clear that such a relentlessly bloodthirsty way of life is worth saving:

> For I am long since weary of your storm
> Of carnage, and find, Hermod, in your life
> Something too much of war and broils, which make
> Life one perpetual fight, a bath of blood.
> Mine eyes are dizzy with the arrowy hail;
> Mine ears are stunnd with blows, and sick for calm. (ll. 503–8)

For Hermod Balder was 'underground, / Rusting for ever', but the fallen deity at least has the companionship of his wife Nanna, Hela's 'iron frown' has relaxed, and the companies of the dead need leadership. Balder is content to await 'the happier day' when, with the turmoil of Ragnarök at an end, he and Hoder will rejoin the 'small remnant' of surviving deities in a new world 'more fresh, more verdant than the last' (l. 529). Not for Arnold the Tegnérian certainty that a still better world with Christ the redeemer at its head was imminent, but for both poets the sense that Asgard had run its course.

Balder found still more extended and ambitious exposure in Robert Buchanan's mystical reverie, 'Balder the Beautiful: A Song of Divine Death' (1866). Readers are warned to dismiss all memories of the eddas, or treatments of the deity by Oehlenschläger, Johannes Ewald,[96] and Arnold. Though Buchanan's Balder is 'bright, beautiful and palpably divine',[97] his mother was human, and her son retains a profound sympathy for the plight of humanity enslaved by Death. Apparently rejected by his fellow gods in heaven, Balder returns to earth and sets off, like a saintly incarnation of Chaucer's *Pardoner's Tale* riotours, to catch 'this thing / Which will not let man rest' (459). Confronted with images of the bloodhound Death hunting humanity, Balder offers himself as a sacrifice:

---

[96] For an English translation of Ewald's 1773 poem, see Borrow 1889.
[97] Buchanan 1877, I 434.

> Let me die in my brethren's stead –
> Let me die; but when I am dead,
>   Call back thy Death to heaven! (471)

In a trance-like state the Norse God meets Christ who recognises the affinity between them: 'O Balder, these thy Brethren were / Surely as they were mine' (476–7). On waking Balder journeys again to Asgard, confronts a hostile Odin who associates the bright god with the eventual doom of the gods. Winter storms surround them, Ragnarök is at hand, but in the final scene, after Death has overwhelmed the gods, there are signs of spring as Christ calls on any divine souls amongst the fallen deities to return to life: 'All that is beautiful shall abide, / All that is base shall die' (492). More clearly even than in Tegnér's poem, Buchanan's Balder dissolves into the risen Christ. By the end of the century it took an enterprising poet to buck this particular trend.[98]

Baldr may have been the favourite Victorian old northern deity,[99] but it is Óðinn who produced a greater variety of responses, and from an earlier date. In William Drummond's euhemeristic *Odin, a Poem* (1819), the god is cast in his familiar eighteenth-century role of an heroic Teuton avenging his earlier humiliations in Rome. In A.T. de Vere's 'Odin the Man' (1884) we watch the deity retreating to the north after his initial defeat by the Romans, declaring 'Four centuries I need'[100] to train his people for the vengeful return journey. The anonymous Mancunian poet of the 'Odin Sagas' (1882) dwells on even earlier stages of the deity's life – Creation of the world, birth of the hero, reconciliation of the Æsir and Vanir, migration of the tribes, and deification of the leader.[101] Menella Bute Smedley's chilling 'Odin's sacrifice' (1863) finds a diseased land praying in vain to the unappeasable god until the queen, unwilling to sacrifice her son, places herself on the sacrificial stone, and the god's wrath is finally assuaged.[102] Gruesome scenes of this kind were not the way to win a poetry prize at Oxford, however. In 1850 the prescribed topic was *The Hall of Odin* and the two top prizewinners' submissions were published. In T.F.S. Rawlins's response we follow the tribes west, glimpse sacrificial scenes in the Uppsala temple but, crucially, rejoice at the defeat of Odinism by Christianity – 'Dark suspicion, and her hellish brood / Have fled'.[103] Rawlins's Vikings are still drinking from 'the reeking skulls of enemies' (3); more worryingly, the main sources cited are Pindar and Edward Gibbon! The second prize was won by William Christopher Valentine whose Valhalla feasters also fill their 'foemen's

---

98   Tattersall 1890, 1–3: a rough viking, about to be baptised, enquires about the fate of his pagan mother; told that 'quenchless fire' awaits her, he rejects baptism and storms from the church; the pagan gods respond from on high – ' "Thou hast done well!" '
99   See also Stockbridge 1894; and a trickle of post-Victorian responses, such as Lutyens [1929].
100 de Vere 1884, 204, l. 38.
101 H. L. 1882: a privately circulated volume addressed to a female readership.
102 In Smedley 1863, 296–313. 'Song of Odin', Egerton-Warburton 1887, 37–8, deploys more familiar images of the god's ferocity.
103 Rawlins [?1850] 5.

skulls' (7) with ale as the poet shuffles motifs from Percy's *Five Pieces*,[104] *North-ern Antiquities*, and Southey's Odinic poems, before announcing that life's cowards ended up in Niflheim – a fate made to sound little worse than deten-tion at Dr Arnold's Rugby School. Half a century later, however, the time for joking had passed. F.W. Bourdillon's 'False Gods' (1914)[105] characterises Odin as the false god of the same Prussian race against whom the British Empire is now at war. For forty years Britain had feared Prussia as a untrustworthy friend, but there is now no fear of Prussia the militant foe – they, like Odin's Roman foes before them, are heading for a crushing defeat.

The final Victorian poetic word properly belongs to the old north's greatest pagan leader, who stood most to lose by the fall of his favourite gods. In *Heimskringla* Snorri Sturluson celebrated the deeds of Norway's two great Christian kings, the two King Ólafr figures. It was left to nineteenth-century writers to bang the drum for the defiant pagan Hákon jarl.[106] An Icelandic grammar and reader features Snorri's description of Hákon's sacrificial practices at the shrines of Óðinn and Njǫrðr,[107] while Hákon's relationship with Þórr is recalled by the same Robert Buchanan who had serenaded Balder. This fine poem, written *c.* 1867–8, confirms that, as with Mrs Leith's *Burnt Njal* sequence, the old north is invariably well served by the brisk dignity of ballad metre:

> Hakon of Thule, ere he died
> Summoned a Priest to his bed-side.
>
> 'Ho, Priest!' with blackening brow quoth he,
> 'What comfort canst thou cast to me?'
>
> The young Priest with a timorous mouth,
> Told of the new gods of the South, –
>
> Of Mary Mother and her Child,
> And holy Saints with features mild;
>
> Of those who hate and those who love,
> Of Hell beneath and Heaven above.
>
> Then Hakon laughed full loud and shrill –
> 'Serve thy puny gods who will!'
>
> Then, roaring to his henchman red,
> 'Slit me the throat o' the Priest,' he said;

[104] Yet again *Krákumál* is most favoured: Valentine [?1850], 12.
[105] See also Wallace 1917, 1–7: Odin's faltering army is unmistakably German.
[106] Notably in Oehlenschläger's *Hakon jarl*; no Victorian English translation was published.
[107] Lund 1869, 93–6. *Saga of King Hakon the Good*, ch. 16: Laing 1889, II 19–21.

'His red heart's blood shall flow before,
As steaming sacrifice to Thor!'[108]

Swedenborgian Visions

Hákon jarl might well have reached for his own knife had he known Sir J.J. Garth Wilkinson's *The Book of Edda called Völuspá, A Study in its Scriptural and Spiritual Correspondence* (1897). Victorian Britain produced no stranger old northern publication. Wilkinson was a devoted Icelandophile who had studied the eddas with Jón A. Hjaltalín, an Edinburgh-based scholar whom Wilkinson had met in Reykjavík.[109] Wilkinson's devotion to Icelandic literature began, inevitably, with Tegnér's *Frithiofs saga*, and his *Vǫluspá* study represented its final flourish, with a full prose translation prefacing his relentless allegorical reading. The familiar benchmark lines run as follows:

> Brothers shall battle, and each become bane to each. Sisters' sons shall murder family. Hardness is in the world. Whoredom grievous. Axe of axebarbs, age of swords. Shields are cloven. Wind-age, wolf-age, ere manage crumbles. Foundations groan. Giantess a-flying. No man shall have pity for other men.[110]

Like Jón Hjaltalín and Annie Keary,[111] Wilkinson was a lifelong follower of the teachings of the Swedish scientist and mystic Emmanuel Swedenborg (1688–1772). So, come to that, were Balzac, Emerson, Strindberg, Yeats and many other eminent Victorians. Swedenborg had abandoned natural sciences and turned to visionary experience. He claimed that he could access the spirit world as easily as the natural. His central belief was that all created things 'correspond' to a spiritual reality; all created things originated in divine love and wisdom; evil came from mankind's misuse of freedom; the world needed a restoration of harmony between the material and spiritual by following Christ's example, as revealed by Swedenborg.[112] Wilkinson's book-length analysis of the *Vǫluspá* is driven by his belief that the poem's 'Vala' was an old northern predecessor of Swedenborg. The poem was an anointed source of spiritual and moral instruction, its primary narrative surrounded by a richer layer of allegory. Baldr represents the highest state of human brotherhood, in which no brother could ever 'become bane to other'. Baldr's murder is an act of violence done to that truth. Selfhood, unless governed by brotherhood, destroys all around it. Loki is the 'intellectual selfhood of the race determined to evil, and enjoying it'.[113] The

---

108 Buchanan 1901, I 247. The poem dates from 1867–8.
109 Wilkinson 1897, x. The author describes himself as 'a Lover of Iceland, her Hospitality and Genius': handwritten dedication, Landsbókasafn Íslands copy.
110 Ibid., 15.
111 [Keary] E. 1882, 134.
112 See *The Oxford Dictionary of the Church* (1974, repr. 1977), pp. 1327–8.
113 Wilkinson 1897, 58.

mistletoe on Hǫðr's spear comes from the tree of death, a 'parasitic intruder, the viscid friend, the snare of birds, the glue of thought'.[114] Fjalarr and the giants represent a 'dethroned deity' and 'enthroned science'. As for Askr and Embla, mankind's parents occupying Ásgarðr, they represent reformers such as Wyclif, Tyndale and Luther who released the word of god from its ecclesiastical entombment. For some readers, at least, it must have seemed time to seek refuge in drink.

The Irish Edda

Parading eddic myths as Reformation allegories was certainly not the way to guarantee them an enthusiastic readership in Ireland. Irritated by anti-Celtic and pro-Scandinavian propaganda,[115] weary of fulsome flattery of everything English,[116] and feeling no nostalgic warmth towards Viking destroyers of early monasteries, Irish scholars looked for ways of accommodating the myths of Þórr and Óðinn. Edward Charlton reviews the eddic-related writings of Thorpe, and of William and Mary Howitt[117] with some impatience. He claims that the attribution of nineteenth-century British imperial triumphs to Viking blood in Victorian veins is absurd. If Christianity had been so enervating for the Anglo-Saxons, why did not the northmen succumb to the same ennui after adopting the new faith? Had not cheap raw materials from the colonies contributed to nineteenth-century British commercial dominance? Was not Britain's easily defended island status an immense advantage? The church's role in preserving the eddas themselves was too easily forgotten – Sæmundr, after all, had been a cleric at Oddi.[118] Charlton may have known that Oddi's chief interest for Victorian philologists was as the place name from which the term 'Edda'[119] derived – or did the word mean (great)-grandmother;[120] or art;[121] or could it be derived from some obsolete Old Icelandic verb æða, 'to teach';[122] or from óðr; 'mind, soul';[123] or from Latin edo, 'to compose (poetry)';[124] or German erda;[125]

---

[114] Ibid., 56.

[115] Wawn 1991a, 108–15; Curtis 1968.

[116] [Crolly] 1852, 184–220.

[117] Charlton 1852b. The Howitts were scorned by the likes of George Stephens, Daniel Wilson, and P.A. Munch: Indrebø and Kolsrud 1924–71, II 84–5, 91.

[118] Also Kennedy 1872, 486.

[119] Eiríkr Magnússon 1896, 21.

[120] Pigott 1839, xlii; Kennedy 1872, 482; Lund 1869, 64; Cleasby and Gudbrand Vigfusson 1874, 114; Anderson 1880, 26; Keary 1883, 14, 16 (*Poetic Edda* – 'but, oh dear! you mumble so much and make use of such old-fashioned words we can scarcely understand you'; *Prose Edda* – 'a very queer old lady indeed').

[121] Browning 1876, 16

[122] Henderson 1819, 539.

[123] Holland ascribes this view to Árni Magnússon: Mackenzie 1812, 26n.

[124] Attributed to Magnús Ólafsson (1609) by Faulkes 1977, 37.

[125] Eiríkr Magnússon 1896, 8 reports Guðbrandur Vigfússon's theory: an Icelander, hearing a

or Sanscrit *Veda*, 'knowledge'? With this, as with many other eddic issues, Victorian scholars agreed to disagree. For Charlton the finest eddic poem was the pious 'Sólarljóð', omitted by Thorpe and Olive Bray from their edda translations (perhaps because they felt it smacked of 'popery'), though it was translated by Charles Sprague Smith, a pupil of Guðbrandur Vigfússon.[126] For Charlton the poem was 'immeasurably superior to the dark records of Thor, or Odin in Valhalla'.[127]

For Irish scholars looking for ways of Christianising old northern myth help was also at hand from an unexpected direction. The Norwegian scholar Sophus Bugge set the cat among the old northern pigeons by arguing that a fully fledged system of old northern paganism had developed in Scandinavia only after Viking raiders in Britain had returned to Norway and Denmark with manuscripts containing fragmentary pagan lore, seized from Celtic monasteries where it had been collected.[128] Bugge claimed that such old lore was a metamorphosed residue of Graeco-Roman mythic tradition, much as some scholars argued that old northern runes were of Grecian origin rather than the 'primitive underived literal characters of the Gothic race'.[129]

Bugge's theory shocked but convinced many scholars, Willard Fiske wrote in early January 1880 to the Icelandic poet Steingrímur Thorsteinsson lamenting that the eddic poems were about to be snatched from the grasp of their Icelandic 'owners' at a single scholarly stroke:

> Do you poets not hear the pipes of Pan dying mournfully away in the distance? Do you not see the light of Valhöll glimmering fainter and fainter afar off. Do you not feel the rustling garments of the old deities, as they rush past and vanish forver, like frightened ghosts, into the gloomy recesses of oblivion . . . The ancient gods are dethroned, as Saturn by his sons, and the realm of poesy shall know them no longer. Out of the Edda they march . . . For whom will you sing now? Whose deeds will you chant? When Balder is gone, who is there left to praise? . . . I can only sigh with you over the tarnished splendor of the ancient myths.[130]

How brittle the old north could prove to be; and how unshakeable the stranglehold of Graeco-Roman culture – and of Celtic Christian – culture.

George Stephens in Copenhagen was having none of it, and launched a withering attack on Bugge's theory. Firstly, at the time when the Vikings were supposed to have headed home with the pagan lore manuscripts, paganism was all

---

poem about the origin of the earth in a Germanic tongue, could have misheard the word for 'earth' as 'Edda'.

126 Smith C. 1891a; see Chapter 12.
127 Charlton 1852b, 120–1.
128 Bugge 1881–9; see also his 'English hypothesis' regarding *Grettis saga* analogues: Magnús Fjalldal 1998, 81–8.
129 [Keightley] 1832, 445.
130 Nanna Ólafsdóttir 1982, 39–41. See also Lbs. 4374 4to, Willard Fiske to Geir Zoëga, 26 January 1880.

but dead in England. Secondly, how were contacts established between the church and these manuscript-reading Vikings; chronicle evidence suggested that the two parties came into contact only in circumstances of murder and pillage:

> We are now . . . called upon to believe that at this moment of rapid heathen decay and transition, the most intelligent Scandinavian adventurers . . . after ravaging and firing churches and monasteries where almost alone skin-books were kept, and after slaughtering the monks and nuns and clergy and leading men . . . suddenly run about to read the codices they had destroyed and to hold friendly talk with the wise men they had butchered, and in this way pickt up a lot of legends and traditions and details . . . And so they went home and elaborated heathen genealogies and myths and tales for the use of a population whose masses had already *abandoned* and now openly *ridiculed* not a little of what they had inherited.[131]

Stephens was instinctively hostile; others, like W.G. Collingwood took their time. His novel *Thorstein of the Mere* (1895) was written 'to illustrate the position laid down by Professor Bugge by showing the meeting point of pagan and Christian thought'.[132] Within a year Eiríkur Magnússon[133] had convinced Collingwood of the need to give more weight to the role of pre-Christian paganism. Accordingly, Collingwood planned to revise the novel in any second edition.

Anticipating Morris

The next two chapters examine the contribution of two giant personalities to the development of Victorian old northernism: George Stephens and William Morris, the voices of Philology and Mercury respectively. We have just heard George Stephens in characteristically robust voice; the present chapter may conclude with a glimpse of William Morris's view of the *Poetic Edda*. We know what a Morris version of *Vǫluspá* might have looked like from lines quoted in his only extant Iceland-related lecture, delivered in Hammersmith in 1887.[134] His audience was told that Iceland was 'a Holy land', a 'casket' for the stories of 'the great Germanic race'; that its early residents were 'the bravest men and the best tale-tellers whom the world has ever bred'. Morris's discussion of the northern gods includes our benchmark lines, with 'whoredom' now an alliterative necessity:

[131] Stephens 1883, 304–5.
[132] Lbs. 2186b 4to, WGC to Eiríkur Magnússon, 29 July 1895. See below, pp. 337–8, for discussion of the novel.
[133] Eiríkr Magnússon 1896, 189.
[134] Kelvin 1984–96, II/2 318 refers to a lecture to the Sheffield Secular Society on 'Iceland, Its ancient literature and myths'.

Then brethren shall battle
And be bane of each other
And their sons of one sister
Their kindred shall spill.
Hard times in the world then
And mighty the whoredom:
An axe age a sword age
The shields shall be cloven
A wind age a wolf age
Before the world waneth.[135]

These lines were well known to Morris long before he took to the political plat-form. We will find them woven into the heart of his great epic *Sigurd the Volsung*, to be discussed in Chapter Nine.

[135] Le Mire 1969, 189.

SECTION THREE

PHILOLOGY AND MERCURY

CHAPTER EIGHT

The Errander of Cheapinghaven

The Philologists I am getting tired of, they are such dry sticks.
(Guðbrandur Vigfússon 1887)[1]

Wikings were the scourge of God, an intolerable plague and calamity, bloody barbarians, sparing neither age nor sex, mainsworn oath-breakers of their own holiest heathen oaths . . . living only for plunder and desolation.
(George Stephens 1883, 14/302)

Reading the Dagmar Cross

'For his stubborness [sic] he has suffered a charlatan's fate,' remarks the compiler of a sale catalogue of books from the library of George Stephens (Fig. 8), the Viking-hating titan of Victorian old northernism, 'and history has not always treated him kindly'.[2] Truth to tell, until recently history has scarcely treated him at all.[3] The sale catalogue's pen-portrait represents a rare modern glimpse of a man whose work as a scholar of northern antiquity had earned him by 1884[4] the titles Knight of the Northern Star (Sweden), Knight of St Olaf (Norway), Knight of the Dannebrog (Denmark), and led to his election as a Fellow of the Society of Antiquaries in London, and Honorary Fellow of the Royal Historical Society of London, of the Society of Antiquaries of Scotland, of the Royal Historical and Archaeological Association of Ireland, and of the 'Antiquarian Guilds' of Cumberland-Westmoreland, Newcastle-upon-Tyne, Yorkshire, Helsingør, Trondheim, Gothenburg, and Stockholm. This represents quite a haul for a 'charlatan' and his 'ludicrous'[5] scholarship. However, the contradictory verdicts sounded by the 'fair and foule trumpes' of philological

---

[1] SJL, University of Liverpool, MS 3.32, p. 97: Guðbrandur Vigfússon to Sephton, 29 March 1887.
[2] *Northern Books. Rulon-Miller Books. Catalogue 99* (St Paul, Minnesota, 1991), iv. Over 600 items listed.
[3] B[radley] 1897–8, 1060–1; Dehn-Nielsen 1933–44; Page 1973, 8–9; Stanley 1975, 83–5; Barnes 1992, 1993 350–1, 1994 passim; Kabell 1996.
[4] Listed on the title-page of Stephens 1884.
[5] Bradley, as in note 3.

215

Fig. 8. George Stephens. Artist J. Magnus Petersen. Frontispiece to
George Stephens, *The Old-Northern Runic Monuments of
England and Scandinavia*.

history can always bear re-examination. Indeed, some hundred years after Stephens's death modern academe, only too familiar with politicised literary theorists and jet-setting mandarins, may be unusually well equipped to cope with George Stephens's own brand of politicised, transnational philology. The topics which underpin the Englishman's sixty years of scholarly publications[6] now sound eerily fashionable: language and national identity, colonialism and multiculturalism, orality and literacy, linguistic 'correctness' and diversity, and interplay between the lettered and material worlds. Modern literary discussion is also much exercised by the questions of minority and marginality; the once peripheral becomes central, thereby creating a fresh set of (cheerfully neglected) margins and minorities. Such an irony would have been relished by George Stephens, a fascinatingly marginal figure – an exile by choice, a rebel by temperament, glowering across the North Sea from his book-lined Copenhagen study at the (in his view) unhappy condition of England. Modern literary theory is not, it is true, sympathetic to biography – not surprisingly, some may think, in view of recent revelatory books about revered gurus.[7] Yet out of the details of Stephens's life and times we can discern the kinds of inner tensions and contradictions which theorists might relish – the English nationalist exiled in Scandinavia, the high Anglican fascinated by old northern paganism, the British anti-royalist hired to translate a treatise in favour of an hereditary Danish monarchy.[8] Moreover, as this chapter will suggest, there is in Stephens's views on old northern language development a hint of the philological deconstructionist, if such a being can be imagined. Finally, in the breadth of Stephens's intellectual sympathies we find just that plurality, multiplicity and diversity perhaps more often preached than practised in the world of learning a century after the Englishman's death. In his published scholarship we find Stephens ranging from the third to the nineteenth century; he was as comfortable with runes on a stone or carvings on a door as with words on a page; and he was as well disposed towards popular ballads and folk tales as towards canonical masterworks. He translated Icelandic sagas whilst contributing to their reoralisation by writing saga-based parlour songs; he taught Shakespeare whilst himself writing plays on old northern subjects in Elizabethan style; and he contributed vigorously and unashamedly to popular polemics. His tireless work as a collector of runic inscriptions in Britain and Scandinavia is honoured to this day by runologists, and as an interpreter he cannot be relied upon always to be wrong. Throughout his life Stephens was, in his own coinage, a political and philological 'errander'[9] with a mission to promote his distinctive old northern vision to the widest possible audience. As passionately as Samuel Laing, and with much greater fleetness of philological foot, George Stephens set out to defy what he

---

6 Erslev 1858–68, III 268–78 lists over 300 publications by Stephens up to 1868.
7 See, for example, Lehman 1992.
8 Stephens 1853b.
9 Stephens 1883, 150.

(like Rasmus Rask before him)[10] saw as a rising tide of nineteenth-century German imperialism in old northern scholarship and modern European diplomacy. No matter what triumphs Prussia enjoyed on the battlefields of Slesvig-Holsten in 1864, George Stephens proposed to win back the old north for the Anglo-Scandinavians. Sifting through hundreds of his publications written over six decades it is hard to find more than a handful untouched by this all-consuming and passionate intellectual agenda.

So vast was Stephens's old northern scholarly output that any examination of it risks disappearing under the sheer weight of primary material. The main part of this chapter attempts to define his distinctive old northernism by allowing the light from a representative group of his publications to play across the pages of a single work – his Viking-age chamber drama *Revenge, or Woman's Love* (1857).[11] However, we can cut a preliminary swathe through the complex intellectual hinterland of Stephens the playwright and militant medievalist by examining an 1863 pamphlet,[12] in which he discusses a small enamelled cross on display in a museum in the Danish capital. The artefact was a copy of the thirteenth-century original which King Frederik VII of Denmark presented to his daughter Princess Alexandra on her departure for England in March 1863 as the soon-to-be bride of the Prince of Wales. Taken together, as we shall see, the medieval cross, the modern royal marriage, and the contemporary pamphlet represent the intersection of intellectual currents which find momentary expression in the 1863 booklet, and prolonged exemplification in the scholarly life of George Stephens.

The original ornament had been designed to celebrate the marriage of Waldemar II of Denmark to Dagmar Margareta, daughter of King Otakar I of Bohemia in 1205.[13] The new queen's warmth and generosity immediately won a loyal following in Denmark. Popular Danish ballads record her wedding day wish that all prisoners be released and financial exactions on the common people reduced (8, 10–11). It was a touchingly appropriate memento for King Frederik to the future Queen of England. If the wedding gift was a token of fatherly advice, the 1863 pamphlet had its own political message. Readers are reminded that only two other Danish queens ever matched the popularity of Dagmar. First there was Queen Thyre who built the Danne-Virke across the southern boundary of Slesvig in order to deter Saxon invaders. That renowned fortification, its 'winding line [. . .] newly-strengthened' (9) in 1848 and again in 1850, is (claims Stephens) 'still a watchword and a battle-cry', a clear reference to the (in 1863) just dormant but long-contentious issue of the sovereignty of the Slesvig-Holsten territories. The second popular queen cited was Margaret, ' "the Semiramis of the North" . . . who by the famous Calmar Union first gave shape to that deep longing for a Scandinavia, one free and great,

---

[10] Nielsen 1990; more generally, see Aarsleff 1983, 161–210.
[11] There is no record of performance in Nicoll 1946 and 1959.
[12] Stephens 1863.
[13] Ibid., 8.

which daily draws nearer to its fullest accomplishment'. Yet the italicised incantation 'Fortune's Wheel stayeth not' (10–11), twice repeated by Stephens, reminds the reader of the fragility of all human achievements. Queen Dagmar died in childbirth after only seven years of marriage and the Dagmar cross only came to light when her grave was pillaged in the eighteenth century (11). Stephens might have added that the Calmar Union itself had collapsed irreparably by 1448 and was formally abrogated in 1523; but, as we shall see, the Englishman's own political-philological agenda kept him strongly committed to the idea of a united old north of which his native England was an integral part. As for the 'free and great' Scandinavia 'daily' (9) drawing nearer, its southern boundaries secured by the Danne-Virke – what a cruel difference a year could make. In October 1864, the newly-crowned King Christian IX of Denmark ceded the Duchies of Slesvig and Holsten to the Emperor of Austria and the King of Prussia, following overwhelming Danish defeat in two short but decisive campaigns.[14] The ineffectiveness of the Danne-Virke had proved to be of Maginot line proportions. Subsequently the Treaty of Prague confirmed the transfer of sovereignty to Prussia alone, subject to a plebiscite in North Schleswig (its new spelling). This codicil was formally abrogated by the Treaty of Vienna in 1878. As for the royal House of Hanover in Britain, it is easy to imagine how the rumbling aftermath of German-Danish hostilities might have impacted on the reception of the very Danish Princess Alexandra, new bride to the considerably German Prince of Wales.

The manner of Stephens' Dagmar pamphlet is as significant as its matter. The substance of the text promotes three principal propositions: firstly, the virtue of a robust Danish nationalism directed against territorial and cultural invasion from Austria-Prussia (the English Stephens had by this time become more Danish than the Danes); secondly, a strong commitment to Slesvig-Holsten's Danish identity alongside a profound nostalgia for the lost days of a united old north; and thirdly, as we have noted, the idea that royal authority is better secured by works than words. Each of these themes is developed in the text with the aid of an interlace of literary references, all deployed in a boisterous tone that constantly tests the limits of generic decorum. Thus the 'true Gentility'[15] of Dagmar and Margaret is underscored with famous lines from Chaucer's Wife of Bath:

> Lok who that is most vertuous alway,
> Privé and pert, and most entendith ay,
> To do the gentil dedés that he can,
> Tak *him* for the grettest gentil man.
> Crist, wol he clayme *of him* our gentilesse,
> Nought of oure eldres for her olde richesse. (7)

14 Sheehan 1988, 682–3, 890–6.
15 Stephens 1863, 7.

Similarly, recalling the ghoulish circumstances under which the Dagmar Cross came to light in the eighteenth century, Stephens invokes the grave-diggers from *Hamlet*. Scholarly discourse dissolves into a dramatic cameo:

> So! Walk up, Ladies and Gentlemen! Queen DAGMAR'S Scull! A penny a peep! – And thereafter, away with it to the Bone-house: 'chapless, and knocked about the mazzard with a sexton's spade', – or to the nearest dunghill: – 'That scull had a tongue in it, and could sing once: How the knave jowls it to the ground, as if it were Cain's jaw-bone, that did the first murther!' (12)

As for Dagmar's wedding wishes, Stephens, a pioneering ballad editor himself, cites ballads from Sven Grundtvig's *Danmarks Gamle Folkeviser*.[16] George Stephens believed passionately in the value of such works as voice-prints of a precious pre-literary past, 'folk-speech' rather than 'book-tung', and thus uncontaminated by nineteenth-century linguistic standardisation. Such regulation was as unwelcome for Stephens in language and literature as in the 'melancholy alterations and "restorations" ' [17] inflicted on medieval churches during his lifetime.

Medieval antiquities, the ballad tradition, Chaucerian debate, incantations about transience, a Shakespearean-style vignette, reflections on royal legitimacy and a recent royal marriage, the Slesvig-Holsten question, and more general Dano-Prussian tensions stretching from either side of the Danne-Virke as far as the turrets of Windsor Castle: this is a fair harvest from a fourteen-page pamphlet describing a tiny medieval cross. There are, moreover, two additional factors about its author's interests discernible from the booklet. Firstly, a full-page advertisement on the rear flyleaf draws attention to Stephens's earlier publications. This selection, it turns out, is entirely representative of his teeming scholarly creativity in many fields over the six decades which followed the appearance of his first publication in 1836: attention is drawn to editions of the Old English *King Waldere's Lay* (1860),[18] and the Middle English romance *Sir Amadace* (1860),[19] Stephens's own balladic celebration of the centenary of Robbie Burns's rescue in 1759 from otherwise certain childhood death,[20] a text-book offering rudimentary study notes on six of Shakespeare's plays (1855),[21] an English translation of a Swedish treatise on the merits of pan-Scandinavianism (1858),[22] and *Revenge, or Woman's Love. A Melodrama in Five Acts* (1857), available with separate libretto.[23] 'Disappointment' awaited anyone hoping to buy Stephens's pioneering translations of the Old Icelandic and

---

[16] Ibid., 8, 10–11. Grundtvig's ballads translated in Prior 1860.
[17] Stephens 1863, 9.
[18] Stephens 1860a.
[19] Stephens 1860b.
[20] Stephens [1859a].
[21] Stephens 1855.
[22] Stephens 1858.
[23] Stephens 1859b.

modern Swedish versions of the Frithiof story – the volume was 'for the present' out of print.

The second additional feature of the Dagmar Cross discussion relates to language. Stephens cultivated a prose style reminiscent in tone and syntax of Wulfstan's fierier sermons, and with a marked preference for old northern rather than Graeco-Roman forms. The Dagmar pamphlet seems relatively restrained in comparison, yet a scatter of archaised spellings[24] and an isolated compound ('large-hearted' for 'generous')[25] hint at a dormant philological awareness, and so do two of Stephens's most personal linguistic signatures, that appear on the title page. In 'Cheapinghaven' for 'Copenhagen', Stephens asserts the cognate relationship between Old English *ceap* and *hæfen*, Old Icelandic *kaup* and *höfn*, and their Modern Danish equivalents *køb* and *havn*. He believed that he was restoring the 'old northern' (or at least Mercian, if we remember the likes of Chipping Camden) English form to its proper use. Stephens, as we shall see, believed that there had once been a common Scandinavian language and culture, and that 'old northern' English as preserved on the earliest runic inscriptions or in 'Old-English Edda Songs'[26] like *Waldere* was the truest available guide to its nature. This proposition is central to his scholarly life. It informed and energised his editorial and rune-collecting activities, and its influence is discernible throughout his Viking-age play *Revenge, or Woman's Love*.

The Genesis of an Enthusiasm

If the old north lies near the heart of George Stephens's *Revenge*, it had also cast a light across the playwright's early years on Merseyside, an area of north-western England rich in ancient Scandinavian place names and modern northern enthusiasms. Born in Liverpool in December 1813, George Stephens grew up within sight of the Horne and Stackhouse merchant ships returning from trading voyages to Iceland, and unloading their cargoes of stockfish, fox skins, woollen mittens and whale oil at Pier Head.[27] Merseyside was, we may recall from Chapter Two, a region which had fathered two of England's most important explorers of Iceland – John Thomas Stanley and Henry Holland. Stephens's formal education differed in one important respect from that of Stanley and Holland. He studied at the newly-opened University College, London rather than in Edinburgh.[28] R.G. Latham (*Frithiof* translator, Norway lover, philologist)[29] was one of its early professors, but there is little direct evidence to suggest that during his university years Stephens was much exposed to native

---

24 Stephens 1863: 'chaunt' (11), 'scull', 'murther', 'exprest' (12).
25 Ibid., 1863, 8.
26 Stephens 1860a, x.
27 Wawn 1985, 98, 130.
28 See above, Chapter 2.
29 Latham 1838, 1840, 1862.

linguistic and literary traditions.[30] In London, as in Oxford and Cambridge, the principal commitment remained that of educating English gentlemen in the spirit of Greece and Rome.

The specific link between Stephens and the Viking-age north can be traced more to family than formal education. His 'dear and distinguished' brother Joseph Rayner Stephens[31] was a fiery Lutheran who left Britain in 1826 to establish a mission in Stockholm, and returned four years later to live a life of rebellious non-conformity on the Lancashire and Cheshire borders, addressing huge gatherings before being imprisoned in 1839. It was under his influence that George moved to the Swedish capital in 1834, where he earned his living as an English teacher.[32] It was also Joseph Stephens, the 'tribune of the poor',[33] who had first 'recommended to my eager study the literature of the North in general', the first fruits of which were the 1839 Frithiof translations.[34] Both works had been 'unrolled before me by an oral translation' from Joseph, who was languishing in Chester prison when the volume was published. It proved to be George Stephens's first and, for reasons to be considered later, last major published engagement with an Old Icelandic text. Viewed with hindsight we can see that Tegnér's *Frithiof* was in line with Stephens's already well developed social, political and aesthetic instincts[35] – the philologist even named his daughter after the saga's heroine.[36] It was, as we have noted, a tale in which royal authority had to be confirmed in each generation through fresh deeds of derring-do; a tale in which the yeoman Frithiof had royal status conferred upon him by a district Thing meeting; a tale which projects an identity of spirit between Frithiof and independent-minded Orcadian jarls; and a tale in which the pagan religion of Scandinavia could be viewed as a natural and noble faith awaiting only its final fulfilment in Christianity. Moreover, by including in the 1839 volume a translation of the original Icelandic saga, Stephens was able to experiment with developing a style which drew consciously on the Old English and Old Icelandic elements in the English wordhoard. It is also clear that Stephens's feisty and richly metaphorical prose style, full of echoes of oral tradition (transferred to the printed page by parentheses, italics, capitalisation and exclamation marks), was already well established by the end of his 1839 preface, as in this not especially humble Englishman's version of a humility topos:

---

[30] Chambers 1939, 342–58 draws a dispiriting picture of philological scholarship in the college before 1850.

[31] A[lexander] G[ordon], 'Joseph Rayner Stephens', *DNB* XVIII 1065–6.

[32] See Stephens 1836, 1837.

[33] Stephens 1839, ix.

[34] Stephens's translation of the Icelandic saga was republished in Anderson and Jón Bjarnason 1877. Stephens and Anderson knew each other in Copenhagen. After the 1888 presidential elections, Anderson's diplomatic posting was terminated, in spite of lobbying by Danish supporters, including Stephens: Hustvedt 1966, 200, 210, 324.

[35] See above, Chapter 4.

[36] *Proceedings of the Society of Antiquaries of Newcastle upon Tyne* 7 (1895), 14; 8 (1897), 17, 83.

> Do not let the Master [Tegnér] suffer for the faults of the pupil [Stephens] . . . should Criticism – seated on the throne of the Thunderer, and wielding the God's own bolts – 'Hurl its indignant lightenings at our head' – and annihilate a work vainly hoping for subsistence – our consolation will be, *'non omnia possumus omnes,'* and we shall abandon the field to some more gifted champion.[37]

This is almost certainly Stephens's first published reference to his favourite old northern deity: the Englishman was in many ways an earthly emanation of the Norse god's tempestuous spirit.

The Swedish capital remained George Stephens's home, and old Swedish literature remained his principal scholarly interest in the years up to his appointment as Lektor in English at the University of Copenhagen in 1851. His pamphlet *Hurrah for Denmark* (1848) suggests that he was deftly preparing the way for his move well ahead of time. Whilst in Stockholm he edited Swedish saints' lives[38] and Arthurian legends,[39] wrote articles on Sweden and its ballad tradition for publication in Britain,[40] and translated traditional Swedish legends and fables,[41] not to mention the Stockholm port regulations, first prepared by Oscar I, King of Norway and Sweden.[42] Like other Victorian philologists, Stephens understood the cultural and linguistic importance of non belle-letristic texts.

George Stephens's move to Copenhagen marks the beginning of a period of concentrated scholarly activity for him, carried out against a background of political tension and instability. The period embraces his appointment as Professor of English at the university in 1855, the publication of a string of important works, including all those advertised in the Dagmar pamphlet, and culminating in the first volume of his magisterial *The Old-Northern Runic Monuments of Scandinavia and England* in 1866. The decade also saw the undermining of the brittle Slesvig-Holsten peace agreement from the 1852 Convention of London. It is against the background of these works and conflicts that Stephens's drama *Revenge, or a Woman's Love*, the focus of the remainder of this present chapter, needs to be read.

The Play's the Thing

On its rough-hewn surface *Revenge, or Womans Love* appears to have little connection with learned philology or contemporary diplomacy. Read in the light of Stephens's other works of the period, however, it reflects many of the English-

---

[37] Stephens 1839, x.

[38] Stephens 1847–58.

[39] Stephens and Liffman 1845–9. Stephens 1872 discusses the Valþjófsstaðir church door carvings which may derive from the same legend; see also Harris 1970.

[40] Stephens 1840a and 1840b.

[41] Tales such as 'The Monk' and 'The Boy and the Shadow,' in *The People's Magazine* 1841, 13–18, 302.

[42] Stephens 1848.

man's most passionately held philological and political beliefs about northern-ness and the old north. The play is set alternately in North Sweden and England in the mid-tenth century during the reigns of King Eric the Victorious and King Athelstan. We meet first Rowena, young wife of Edgar, Earl of Mercia, who feels neglected as her impressionable husband falls increasingly under the malign influence of his Iago-like counsellor Odo. Rowena finds solace in reading the Old English Gospels and Alfred's *Orosius*, and listening to medieval songs in the company of a faithful Nurse, a pallid reincarnation of Juliet's matronly companion. Rowena learns of the love of Elfwina, Edgar's sister, for her childhood playfellow Sibert, a stout-hearted Mercian yeoman. She also learns of Edgar's opposition, prompted by Odo, to this potential breach of courtly *degre*. Odo persuades his young master, 'Our bold beigh-giver, the BALDOR of our chieftains' (17), to undertake a pilgrimage to the holy lands, so that the treacherous counsellor can once again pay court to the vulnerable Rowena. Her celebration of stable patriarchal domesticity – 'man's heaven on earth / Is Home and Wife and bonny Bairns; weak Woman's – Man's true Heart is *her* earth-nest' (20) – is interrupted by Edgar's abrupt announcement of his Palestinian travels. Rowena attributes the whole insane idea to 'glozing monks', 'false-tongued plotting courtiers', a 'vague thirst for change or ramble', and 'arrant fancy' – 'Here, as on Calvary's Mount, may Sin be wept' (23). With Edgar's resolve unshaken, Rowena, most patient of old northern Griseldas, dutifully acquiesces:

> openly I questioned
> Thy will, first utter'd; else thy thrall I were
> Not thy life's partner; but as thus unchang'd
> Thy purpose seems, with equal zeal I hasten
> Obedience to thy wish. Her wit and wisdom
> Woman oft showeth best by – waiving them. (24)

The play's second act is set in Sweden, near whose coast Edgar's voyage of pilgrimage has been interrupted by a Viking band (25) who delivered the Mercian earl a prisoner to 'Swea's Victorious Ruler' (26). King Eric enters 'the great Idol-temple in Upsala' (34),[43] and instructs the pagan priests to mimic the rites of sacrifice as Edgar enters, so as to convince him that he is their next intended victim. Eric then names the price of life and liberty for his English captive: Rowena must be summoned and sacrificed. As the dumb-struck Edgar awaits the answer to his letter home, Stephens produces a pyrotechnic display of crypto-Shakespearean lyricism, full of newly-minted compounds, anaphoric elaboration, and (alas) syntactic congestion:

---

[43] The Uppsala site had been made famous by Adam of Bremen's description from *Gesta Hammaburgensis ecclesiæ pontificum* (Hanover, 1846), Bk 4, xxvi.

Ere thrice that wondrous world-light
Sun call'd by Men but Star by lofty Deities,
Strange lovely earth-long course at last completing,
Her car-borne disk behind yon mounds hath driven;
Ere thrice Night's King, the Moon, the shining Year-teller,
Soft source of slumber-joys and dear Dream-father,
Slow climbs the gloam-vault, countless star-bands round him,
His wain by RIME-MANE drawn, whose fierce-champt bit
O'er hill and dale and farthest furrow tosses
Those glist'ring foam-sparks here we Dew-drops clepe;
Ere thrice our Valhall's kemps in spear-lit feast-house
Nod o'er their oft-drain'd mead-horns; – answer wait I.[44]

Act Three finds Rowena reading Edgar's letter, horrified by his apparent willingness to sacrifice her. The predatory Odo insinuates himself into her favour by agreeing to help avenge her husband's spinelessness. A defiant message is duly carried to Sweden by a Viking minstrel, whilst Sibert and Elfwina meet in secret before the worthy yeoman sets off to fight for 'Athelstane and England' (51), perhaps at the Battle of Brunanburh. Like an Ossianic heroine, Elfwina is fearful but steadfast: 'tho Edgar still deny, Sibert's or Death's unspotted bride I'll die!' (53). By Act Four Edgar is reduced to a dishevelled King Lear-like figure. He lives in wretched rural exile, dreaming of home, hearth, and the Christian faith, tormented by 'self-caus'd griefs' (60), and glimpsing his wife only in visions conjured up by a cairn-dwelling witch, reminiscent of Walter Scott's Norna. King Eric, meanwhile, entertains a spirited English minstrel (identified as Oswald) in the royal hall in Uppsala. The visitor sings songs of battle, peace and freedom and, as he requests, is rewarded with the humiliated Edgar's release, much to Odo's fury back in England. Restored to his native soil, Edgar now allows Elfwina to marry Sibert, and agrees to abolish slavery (81–2). Still hopelessly susceptible to Odo's wiles, however, he is urged to punish Rowena for her earlier apparent refusal to sacrifice her own life to save her husband. In the climactic scene, set in Edgar's banqueting hall, the Mercian ruler denounces his wife, who flees in distress. With the sudden reappearance of the minstrel Oswald, Odo is exposed and flees; the minstrel then reveals *her*self to be not Oswald but rather Rowena, the loyal wife who, we now learn, had first rescued her husband by guile and now forgives him through love. Domestic hierarchy is restored:

Now my Spouse once more
Mine own sweet Lord reigns, as in days of yore.
Now, while as erst in mine Old Home I move,
Brightly shall shine my Sun – a Husband's Love! (86)

[44] Stephens 1857, 40.

The 'serpent' Odo is banished and the wife's 'charitable' revenge on her imma-
ture but ultimately worthy husband is complete.

For all its breathless and confusing denouement, there is much lively writing
in the play, and it would be ponderous to miss the element of *jeu d'esprit* which
helps to drive the whole work. Yet there is surely 'ernest' amidst the 'game'.
Revenge dramatises issues which lay at the heart of George Stephens's deeply
personal and heavily politicised old northern philology. We noted a number of
them in the Queen Dagmar fragment; in *Revenge* they take on a more refracted
form. In brief, they can be identified as: the nature of nobility, the significance
of Mercia, the role of religion, the value of popular literary tradition, runic
remains and, over-arching everything, the idea and ideal of the old north.

The Themes of Revenge

To take the seemingly simplest point first. One of the beneficial effects of
Edgar's unhappy rite of passage in Sweden is that he learns to redefine his idea
of gentility and thus to allow the Mercian yeoman Sibert to marry Elfwina,
Edgar's sister. Edgar's initial stubbornness echoes that of the brothers Halfdan
and Helgi in the early cantos of Tegnér's *Frithiofs saga*, as translated by Stephens. Their arrogant obsession with birth and status[45] exactly matches that of
Edgar at the start of Stephens's play:

> [. . .] here on earth
> Earldoms like thistles spring not, and Rock-eagles
> Seek seld their peers mong brown-heath chirrupers.
> Strong is thine arm; but Mercia's loftiest beauties
> It therefore grasps not; and thy cottage-home
> Nature's first needs may give thee, – find thee then
> Some pretty franklin-spouse, and all is well![46]

'Bold' Sibert, a lion on the battlefield and a lamb in the chamber, is a noble
'gentleman' by virtue of brave deeds of arms performed for King Athelstan with
no thought of material reward, and also because of his proven love for the fair
Elfwina. As with Dasent's Jómsborg, accidents of birth play no part in establishing his worth.

Inevitably linked to Stephens's understanding of nobility and gentility are his
ideas about royalty. Stephens pinned his colours to the mast of constitutional
monarchy early in his career. Annotating his Tegnér translation, he expresses his
approval for the old northern 'Elective Presidency' form of kingship. As the
hereditary principle developed, 'cementing Dynasties formed in Kingdoms

---

45 Stephens 1839, 54–64 (Canto 4).
46 Stephens 1857, 16.

gained by the sword', so inevitably did 'hereditary degradation'.[47] In *Revenge*, the 'ancient Monarchy of Sweden' is ruled by an hereditary king whose testing of Edgar is stern but shrewd, and who is happy to yield to the disguised Rowena's intercessions. There is no suggestion that the hereditary monarch should be deposed, but Rowena's moderating role is significant. She personifies the necessary checks and balances to which all legitimate authority, whether domestic or national, should be exposed. The Swedish kingdom is strong and well defended, and so is Athelstan's England, thanks to loyal worthies like Sibert, who joins his king in a successful offstage battle against Viking forces: strength comes from the unity of leader and led. Thus, *Revenge* is no text of revolutionary republicanism. It promotes instead the cautious democratic instincts of a lifelong Tory radical.

Though Stephens shared George Dasent's hostility to the hereditary principle, he views Vikings very differently. Dasent's Jómsborg heroes were cheery (or, at worst, roguish) sea-rovers, like a hearty college rugby team travelling to an away match. Stephens was not so sanguine. Though his play includes Gudmund, a cheerfully benign Viking, the real menace lies offstage, first in the 'damn'd Bare-serk crew / Of Wikings, bay-boys, pirates, heathen hell-hounds'[48] who waylay Edgar, and then in the shadowy figures who threaten Athelstan's England.[49] In his other writings Stephens displays no romantic admiration for what he saw as the essentially sour and destructive Viking spirit:

> the scourge of God, an intolerable plague and calamity, bloody barbarians, sparing neither age nor sex, mainsworn oath-breakers of their holiest heathen oaths . . . living only for plunder and desolation . . . the Wicking sought partly fame; but his *real* trade was beef and beer and booty, gold and gauds, silks and slaves and silver, wines and women and war-gear. These things he would get by all hazards, by foul means (fire and sword) or by fair (commerce), and foul means were the easiest and commonest.[50]

By the tenth century the heathen faith of the Vikings was dying out, transcended by 'the Spirit of Christ, the Law of Love', as predicted by the temple priest at the end of Bishop Tegnér's *Frithiof*. George Stephens seems never to have forgotten that he was a son of the manse. In his construction of the old north, Christian England represents a higher stage of spiritual development than pagan Scandinavia. Scandinavian scholars like N.F.S. Grundtvig shared his belief that northern paganism was a splinter of the true light,[51] whereas in Germany the study of eddic myth was driven by the desire to identify and celebrate the heathen roots of their culture.

[47] See Stephens 1839, 228; also Dasent 1858, 211–12.
[48] Stephens 1857, 25.
[49] Ibid., 51.
[50] Stephens 1883, 14/302.
[51] Bradley 1994, passim; Lundgreen-Nielsen 1994, 54–7.

The Mercian setting is another important politicised element in the play. Sibert sets off to fight 'gainst invaders / Of Athelstane and England', but it is to 'Mercia's realms' and its 'drooping Harvest's checquer'd shrivel'd yellow'[52] that he hopes to return, and in which he looks forward to marrying. For Stephens, both personally and culturally, Mercia represented a more sympathetic region of England than Wessex. Liverpool, his birthplace, was situated on what became Mercia's northern margins;[53] at least as important, Stephens associated Alfredian Wessex with oppressive cultural centralisation. The Old English language had, he felt, suffered at the hands of Winchester scribes, who had obliterated just that diversity of linguistic forms which, in Stephens's mind, gave life to any 'folk-tung'.[54] Multiplicity was the mark of the folk; standardisation was the sign of the scholar. Stephens sought to restore the once vigorous but now inaudible voice – or rather the voices – of the folk, through the humane practice of comparative philology. This was, he claimed, very different from nineteenth-century German scholarship whose 'iron'[55] rules silenced such voices. Stephens celebrates the 'folk-tung' of Mercia. In the Old English *Battle of Maldon*, Ælfwine, a loyal follower of Byrhtnoth, is proud of his Mercian origins ('ic wæs on Myrcon miccles cynnes';[56] [I was of noble kin in Mercia]) yet fights as part of a multi-regional troop of diverse social status. So does Sibert in the play – a stalwart Mercian fights for king and country; and he sets off for battle speaking the words of Byrhtnoth's prayer before that warrior's final encounter with the Vikings.[57] For George Stephens regional pride could embrace the broader body politic.

Sibert's Mercian origins are important for the play and so also is his yeoman status. His non-courtly origins link up with another cultural discourse much esteemed by Stephens, and highlighted in his play: folk songs, ballads, legends, proverbs, 'racy saws and idiotisms',[58] and all the other surviving emanations of a once-vigorous popular oral tradition. The 'book-dialect' in Rowena's copy of Alfred's *Orosius* represents the standardised language of an educated elite. The rawer 'folk-tung' material that found a role in the Dagmar booklet also features tellingly in *Revenge*, as the delightfully named 'Borrowed feathers' (Notes on Sources and Analogues) section confirms. The intertextual plumage is plucked from a wide range of old northern popular texts, many of them newly rediscovered, reassembled and edited in Scandinavia following the example of the Grimms in Germany. Stephens played a major role in encouraging this work

---

52 Stephens 1857, 51.
53 Wainwright 1975, 63–130 examines Danish and Norse influence in old northern Mercia.
54 On non-West-Saxon elements in West-Saxon orthography and morphology, see Campbell 1959, 9.
55 As Tennyson's sonnet 'To J[ohn] M[itchell] K[emble]' shows, some Victorians relished iron linguistic discipline: Ricks 1986, I 280; see also Simmons 1992.
56 Compare Stephens 1857, 51–2 with *Battle of Maldon*, l. 217 (Dobbie 1942, VI 13).
57 *Maldon*, ll. 173–80 correspond to Sibert's prayer beginning 'Lord of hosts [. . .]': Stephens 1857, 52.
58 Stephens 1857, 88.

before he left Sweden.[59] Thus Sibert's serenade to Elfwina, performed under her garden window,[60] derives from Arwidsson's *Svenska Fornsånger*;[61] as does the aubade[62] sung to Rowena by her maid Ethelfleda; 'the Sweet Rescue, or the Maid that was Sold Away' (29–33) sung by women at King Eric's court is recycled from Geijer and Afzelius's *Svenska Folkvisor*;[63] and Rowena in her minstrel disguise responds to an heroic ballad[64] from Gudmund the Viking with the Middle English lyric 'Summer is i'comen in' (57). When to these popular songs are added Sibert's Old English prayer (52), the English soldiers' battle song (51–2),[65] and the temple priests' chants (36–9), which were Stephens's own creations in the alliterative style of eddic verse, the overall effect is to unify, at least for the duration of the play, the old northern literary world – Old Icelandic, Old English, Middle English, and Old Swedish reunite in nineteenth-century English. Such a unity was one of George Stephens's most precious ideals. When one of King Eric's skalds dares to mock the songs of this unsung tradition:

> Pooh! Whining love-songs are all he [a fellow scald] e'er learn'd.
> Too bold, methinks, his jinglings he'd intrude
> Mong grey-beards school'd in Runes and champion-lay.[66]

he is immediately silenced by the worthy Signe, in appropriately proverbious if not actually proverbial style: 'Peace, cank'rous croaker! [. . .] By Death of BALDER! Bard gibes not his Brother'.

For Stephens this popular bardic tradition certainly extended as late as Shakespeare. The 'Afterwords' assure readers that the alliterative chants of the Uppsala temple priests match those in *Vǫluspá, Beowulf*, 'all our Old, Early and Middle-English Poets', and Shakespeare. Indeed Shakespeare's stylistic influence is glaringly apparent throughout *Revenge*, in style, structure and character stereotype, with Stephens drawing on his experience as a teacher of English language and literature having produced study guides such as *The Shakespear Story-Teller* (1855).[67] The overall pattern of intertextual reference in *Revenge* represents, in effect, George Stephens's 'Great Tradition', almost a century before the equally peppery F.R. Leavis developed his. It involves belief in a continuous process of Anglo-Scandinavian oral and literary creativity in Britain, still discernible in Shakespeare's lifetime, still alive in the nineteenth-century spoken word and, as we have seen Rasmus Anderson lamenting, still awaiting literary revival.

Stephens eagerly anticipates such a revival, though he can hardly have seen

---

[59] Stephens 1843–5; Jón Samsonarson 1991.
[60] Stephens 1857, 48–9.
[61] Arwidsson 1834–42.
[62] Stephens 1857, 12–13.
[63] Geijer and Afzelius 1880.
[64] Stephens 1857, 54–6.
[65] From *The Battle of Brunanburh*.
[66] Stephens 1857, 64.
[67] A detailed commentary on five plays.

Revenge as other than the most stumbling of initial steps. Nearly all his other publications in the 1852–66 period promote aspects of that Anglo-Scandinavian literary-linguistic continuum. Even an apparently slight piece such as *The Rescue of Robert Burns, February 1759. A Centenary Poem*[68] can be read against this background. The poem recalls how the newly-born Burns was rescued from a disintegrating house during a violent storm. Stephens dramatises the battle waged for the helpless baby between the Fairy Queen and her attendant benevolent fairies, and a dwarfish chorus supported by ill-natured witches. This popular legend, says Stephens, can perform a fruitful modern service. In the far-flung quarters of the Empire, ballads can boost the morale of intrepid colonisers by reminding them of their distant homeland as they recite the oral ballads of their youth – tales of Arthur, Alfred, Ossian, Robin Hood, Wallace, Bruce and Burns. Stephens urges that the tradition be continued: 'In Old Scotland's sounding tongue, / In Old England's sister-lay, / In Old Scandinavia. / Scotia, sing thy Ballads still!'[69] Stephens's enthusiastic advocacy of these popular lyric traditions, his sense of the Anglo-Scandinavian continuities they embody, is driven by his desire to see an extension of such continuities into philology, politics and diplomacy.

Stephens and Old Northern Religion

Paganism and Christianity could also have a popular basis, and were thus as important for Stephens as popular lyric tradition, though their operation in the play is more complex. At the end of his life Stephens writes to Guðbrandur Vigfússon heaping praise on the newly-completed Anglican Church in Copenhagen, the beauty of the liturgy, and the fine singing of the surpliced choir. George Stephens was no Obadiah Slope.[70] He sees a simple spiritual choice for Victorian Britain – 'one Catholic Church, or one infernal atheism', with Roman Catholicism dismissed as a mere 'Schism [. . .] blasphemous fetishism'.[71] Late Victorian Britain witnessed a growing interest in the Christian old north, notably amongst aristocratic devotees of the Oxford movement.[72] Stephens was still supportive of the liturgical practices of the early English Catholic church before it succumbed to 'transubstantiation and other errors and superstitious belief'.[73] In his own Stockholm and Copenhagen publications he had certainly paid his dues to the 'one Catholic church' of pre-Reformation Europe. He had

---

68 Stephens [1859a].

69 Ibid., 16.

70 Anthony Trollope's puritanical Barsetshire chaplain.

71 Bodleian MS Icelandic d. 131, GS to Guðbrandur Vigfússon, 9 March 1887. See also Kabell 1996 36–9.

72 See, for example, Eiríkr Magnússon 1870, Metcalfe 1881, Elton O. 1890, Gunnar Guðmundsson 1993. See also below, p. 366.

73 Stephens 1853a, 7: 'Transsubstantiationen og andre Kætterier og overtroiske Lærdomme'.

collected runic inscriptions from Christian graves,[74] edited saints' lives[75] as well as more austere documents bearing witness to long forgotten holy lives.[76] In *Revenge*, however, pre-Reformation Catholicism is presented ambiguously. The worthy ideal of properly organised piety is cruelly compromised by shifty spiritual shepherds. It is 'glozing' monks who help to fill Edgar's head with vainglorious thoughts of pilgrimage. These same monks plot against Rowena on her return from Sweden. Yet the play ends with the eerie calm of priests chanting Latin praise of the Virgin Mary – a dramatic convenience, no doubt, but also a celebration of the beauty of non-doctrinal holiness.

The priestly chants have to compete with more secular, if not pagan, cries of 'wassail, drinkheil' from the royal revellers. We have noted Stephens's unambiguous condemnation of Viking culture, and the eventual collapse of paganism in the face of the White Christ and his gospel of love. There was, though, a strong streak of pragmatic syncretism in the English scholar, for right up to the end of his life he retained much sympathy both for the spirituality of old northern paganism (notably its concern for the proper burial of the dead in battle),[77] and for the particular values that he identified in individual pagan deities, especially Thor. In *Revenge* the Uppsala temple priests address prayers to their respective gods, as with the artfully crafted lines addressed to the god of thunder:

> THÓR, the Tróll-smiter
> Thrúndvang rúleth,
> Hámmer húrling
> gainst hósts of fóne;
> ÉARTH'S and ÓDEN'S
> héir he bóasts him,
> Héaven's best Héro
> and Hópe of Mén![78]

That Thor could be a 'Hópe of Mén' was, for George Stephens, no idle concession to alliterative convenience. In 1878 he published a paper identifying the figure of 'Thunor the Thunderer' carved on a font at Ottrava in Skara, Västergötland, from the year 1000. The identification of Thunor (Stephens characteristically preferring the Old English form to the Old Icelandic Þórr) leads, first, to a tirade against German editors who have attempted by emendation to obliterate the old northern god from *Beowulf*,[79] and then to a celebration of a deity whose dauntless spirit was woven into the fibre of every Briton. It is the hammer-wielder of the old north, 'our great ancestral Symbol-god . . . speaking

---

[74] Stephens 1866–1901, passim.
[75] See above, note 38.
[76] Stephens 1852b.
[77] Stephens 1884, xvii–xviii.
[78] Stephens 1857, 37.
[79] Stephens 1878, 56 discusses German emendations to *Beowulf* l. 177.

alway of STRENGTH, WORK, DUTY, TRUTH; HONOR BRIGHT', who exemplifies memorably the virtues of 'Self-Sacrifice FOR THE GOOD, THE RIGHT and AGAINST THE BAD, THE WRONG' (58). Thunor still survives in properly edited texts of *Beowulf*; on funeral stones, to ensure that the dead can rest in peace; on jewels and amulets as a charm; and he can even be spotted on a holy font 'perpetually preaching that the Christian soldier should FIGHT AT LEAST AS BRAVELY against Baseness as ever did the Hammer-wielder'. Thunor served 'our Scando-Gothic forefathers' well a thousand years ago, and there was evidently a great deal of work for him still to do in a Victorian society whose declining spirituality he, like Matthew Arnold, deplored. Stephens makes the point in his most flamboyantly Wulfstanian style:

> In a time like this, of -isms endless, the one more damnable, ignoble, driveling or doltish than the other; – of foulness, fetishism, or frantic blasphemy, flaunting paper crowns overscrawled 'infallible' and 'high science'; – of 'rings' and riots, blacklegs and bribers, falseness and fraud, adulteration and adultery, capitalism and club-law, – of softness, sentiment, sophism, weakness and wilfulness, pendriving and paradox; – of morbid materialism, luxury run mad, license unbounded, a literature most leprous, – LAW the while become LAWLESSNESS, a slow and costly sham and swindle, a cobweb wide open for wasps and dragon flies and catching only silly gnats, a comedy contemptible as it is costly; – 'Punishment' now smothered in maundering 'Philanthropy', CRIME (even Rape, Murder, Burnings) REWARDED with pensions in palaces built with the sweat and tearful savings of the toilsome non-criminal million; of 'Blood-and-Iron' and Bankruptcy; – 'Examinations' and hot-house 'Education', in other words Cant and Cram and an unbearably arrogant but in real life worthless 'Little of Everything' (palsying the limbs and blearing the eyes of our daily feebler youth), these now the only Ten Commandments, the only 'Religion of the Future' of States *called* Christian. (58)

Stephens also targets scientific materialism, nihilism, Darwinism, and even 'the almighty Dollar', before thundering on to his conclusion. Scholarly investigation of the pagan gods underlines the importance of a spiritual dimension within any community. This is the lesson to be learnt from 'Our Northern fore-elders'. Stephens pleads: 'At such a moment THUNOR, our great ancestral Symbol-god, should never leave us [. . .] God help that Hearth, that Home, that Land, that Age where NO THUNOR IS' (58–9). Certainly Thunor continued to be a part of England for as long as George Stephens could wield a pen, and write works such as *Revenge*.

The Slesvig-Holsten Dimension

The spirit of Thunor was certainly not patrolling the corridors of the British Foreign Office during the Slesvig-Holsten war in 1864. The supine British failure, as Stephens regards it, to offer military or diplomatic support to the Danes struck at the heart of his sense of Anglo-Scandinavian wholeness as reflected in *Revenge*, as did the absence of Swedo-Norwegian assistance. Stephens believes that Britain had been settled in immediately post-Roman times by people from Slesvig-Holsten and Jutland, integral parts (he never ceased to believe) of his adopted homeland of Denmark. His antipathy towards German philology and philologists colours his view of the Slesvig-Holsten question. The loss of these provinces to Germany in 1864 is not just a military and diplomatic defeat for Denmark, but a humiliation for the land of his birth, whose leaders do not share his sense of cultural identification with the old north.[80]

There was certainly some British sympathy for the Danes, as Bligh Peacock, a Tyneside merchant and old northernist,[81] confirms in letters to Jón Sigurðsson, by the mid-1860s the most influential of the Copenhagen based Icelanders:[82]

[I] hope you will escape from the miseries of war with Germany, but if you are unfortunately driven to defend the rights of your country by force of arms, you may be sure that the sympathy of all Englishmen is with you, whatever may be the conduct of our government. We do not pretend to understand the merits of the question at issue between Denmark and Holstein, but we are satisfied that the Germans have no right to set a foot in Slesvig and if they do we sincerely hope they will be ignominiously expelled. (1 February 1864)[83]

Peacock reports widespread popular support for the Danish cause, and laments the ensuing settlement:

I don't know what is going to become of Denmark but I sincerely trust that the robbers will quarrel over their prey, and that Prussia and Austria may yet pay very dear for the Duchies. As for Holstein I think the inhabitants have found already that they have changed masters considerably for the worse, and they deserve what they have got. (3 March 1865)

There was even talk of France being presented with Iceland by Denmark as a reward for any support offered against Prussia.[84]

But, as Peacock and Stephens knew well, Germany had many well connected supporters in Britain, not least in royal circles. John Kemble, doyen of British Anglo-Saxonists, who had dedicated his *The Saxons in England* (1849) to Queen Victoria, wrote to Jakob Grimm at the time of the Slesvig conflict: 'I desire you may whop and wallop the Danes into shivers . . . I hold them to be a mere outpost of Russia . . . you have my good will to thrash them to their

[80] Shippey 1994a and 1998, 16–18 and passim examines the Schleswig-Holstein dimension in nineteenth-century *Beowulf* criticism. Storm (*Saga-Book* 2/2 244) cites Stephens's work in support of there having always been a racial boundary line at the one-time Danish border: no runic monuments were found south of the line.
[81] See below, pp. 349, 365, 367.
[82] Páll Eggert Ólason 1929–33.
[83] Þjóðskjalasafn Íslands, E. 10 (11), BP to JS; see also JS 143 fol., letters to JS. On Peacock's other Icelandic correspondents, see Lbs. ÍB 93–105 fol., to Jón Borgfirðingur Jónsson; Lbs. 3633 4to, to F.P. Eggerz.
[84] Symington 1862, 58.

heart's content.'[85] Many Britons, uncomfortable with extremist fervour, may have felt more at home with the weary insouciance of the old northernist Sabine Baring-Gould. He hears all about the rights and wrongs of the Slesvig crisis from a Danish merchant while visiting Hofsós in the west of Iceland in 1862, but spares his readers the details – 'I never did understand them [the causes of the conflict], and fear that I do not comprehend them a bit better now.'[86] Such heedlessness would have appalled Stephens, whose philology argued for kinship links which diplomacy and military strength consistently failed to support. Twenty-five years later, celebrating the anniversary of King Christian IX's accession to the throne, Stephens recalls the humiliations of 1864 in a 'Cantata' for the University of Copenhagen:

> Fierce howl'd the storm, with crash of horrid thunder,
> By some long fear'd, but not of them foreseen.
> Blue lightenings flam'd, earth's self gan split asunder
> And yawn'd where from of yore one soil had been
>
> Allies we call'd to aid, and still hoped fondly
> In cousins' fairness, such noble in nearest kin;
> In desert drear soon died our voice despondly,
> To our fate they left us, beggarly truce to win.[87]

For the poet, these are no ritual words of laureate distress. They are driven by the same passion for old northern Anglo-Scandinavian unity that had nourished his *Revenge* play a generation earlier.[88]

'Quaintly carv'd Rune-Stones'

Act 4 Scene 2 of *Revenge* opens with a meeting between Edgar and his wife Rowena disguised as a witch. It is evening and the stage directions prescribe 'wild northern scenery', featuring a 'sepulchral mound, on which stands a tall quaintly carv'd Rune-stone'. It would have been surprising if the play had not found room for rune-stones in some shape or form, for the recording and interpretation of runic inscriptions on grave slabs, crosses, rings, swords and other articles occupied much of George Stephens's long life. His four-volume *Old-Northern Runic Monuments* (1866–1901) represents a formidable testimony to his energy and enterprise in this then underdeveloped field of study. Over his lifetime Stephens examined plenty of real-life sepulchral mounds and quaintly carved rune-stones. At the time that he was writing *Revenge*, however, a famous Orcadian mound with its runic inscriptions was about to attract his full atten-

[85] Wiley 1981, 278, 21 April 1849.
[86] Baring-Gould 1863, 170.
[87] Stephens 1888, 1–2.
[88] On mid-nineteenth-century Pan-Scandinavianism, see Andrés Björnsson 1990.

tion for the first time. James Farrer, member of parliament for South Durham and a keen amateur archaeologist, had undertaken a preliminary examination of Maeshowe in the Orkneys in the mid-1850s. The runic carvings on the chamber walls excited great interest, both locally and in Scandinavia. The opinions of three Scandinavian-based professors were sought – P.A. Munch, C.C. Rafn, and George Stephens – and their (frequently divergent) readings published side by side in an 1862 volume which, as recently as 1993, was described as 'still the nearest thing we have to a full edition of the Mæshowe inscriptions'.[89] Some of Stephens's readings reveal more about his preconceptions than about the runes themselves. Properly understood, the inscriptions seem to represent little more than 'light hearted medieval graffiti'.[90] Yet, with the breeze of many a misreading in his sails, George Stephens is able to construct an exciting tale of Viking times: the mound represents a pre-Viking-age tumulus once used as a refuge by the sons of Ragnarr loðbrók and their English hostage after they had avenged the death of their father in Northumbria (their runic carvings were to be dated c.870–80).[91] Victorian Britain could access the 'Death Song of Ragnar Lothbrok' in a variety of forms, and it continued to serve as a favourite statement of the indomitable Viking spirit.[92] George Stephens's Maeshowe readings, taken as a set, offer an atmospheric picture of the old north – weary sea-kings seeking shelter, memorials to fallen comrades, battlefield messages sent via trusty officers, buried treasure on nearby islands, pillaging Jerusalem pilgrims,[93] and a handful of forgotten Vikings whose names and faceless presence lent substance to the world of their more celebrated contemporaries.[94]

Stephens's runic readings could, in fact, have gone further. It may be symptomatic of the Cheapinghaven scholar's relative indifference to the *Íslendingasögur* that, unlike P.A. Munch, he does not pick up an allusion to Gaukr Trandilsson (from *Njáls saga*) in Inscription 16: '– with this Axe which Goukr Traenaldson owned . . . on the south side of the country'.[95] Gaukr was killed by his fosterbrother Ásgrímr Elliða-Grímsson, a friend of both Gunnarr of Hlíðarendi and Njáll as recorded in the saga. Ásgrímr was related to Gizurr the White, leader of Gunnarr's assailants. In turn, Gizurr's great, great, great grandson was Þórhallr Ásgrímsson who brought Rǫgnvaldr jarl and his men back to Orkney from Norway after their 1153 Jerusalem faring.[96] Stephens would have had little difficulty in convincing Victorian devotees of *Burnt Njal* that the same axe that had carved Inscription 16 was once held by a man who had once shaken hands with Gunnarr and Njáll and his sons!

89 Barnes 1993, 350.
90 Ibid., 364. Barnes M. 1994 is the most recent authoritative study.
91 Farrer 1862, 35–6: Inscription 20.
92 See, for example, Henderson 1818, I 345–52, [Ferguson] 1833, [Crolly] 1852, Kennedy 1864, [Clifford] 1865, 55–9, Blayney 1882, 9–11.
93 Discussed in Barnes M. 1994, 117–18, 189.
94 Constructed out of Farrer inscriptions I, II, VII, XIV, XVI, XIX, XX, XVI.
95 In Farrer 1862, 34; saga cited as 'Burnt Njal'. Inscription discussed Barnes M. 1994, 144–58.
96 Hermann Pálsson 1970, 53.

George Stephens's experience at Maeshowe helped him to construct his own sort of 'alternate history', as this now fashionable academic discourse is called. Stephens's tireless work on his heroic *Old-Northern Runic Monuments* project reminded him daily about the evanescence of communities and of life itself. Inscriptions turn to dust, artefacts disappear, nineteenth-century road building and farming methods unearth and then destroy monuments which had survived undisturbed for centuries. Stephens cites the case of King Knut. There must once have been hundreds of memorials to this mighty monarch, yet by 1870 the whole of northern Europe could produce (at best) four – three in Sweden and one in Norway: such was the 'irrepressible annihilation by time and men of the hardest granite and the most burnisht brass', and hence the importance of pro-moting systematic 'diggings [archaeology] and speech-craft [philology] and rune-lore [runology]'[97] to help recover and preserve these lost chapters in British history. Understanding such history would help in restoring nineteenth-century identification with the old northern 'rune-wielding class whose Scando-Anglian home became the mother-hive of . . . mighty nations' (includ-ing Britain). A more active awareness of that inheritance might in turn lead to greater Victorian resolve in the face of then current Prussian or Russian milita-rism. Had King Knut lived, the Mongols would never have torn the heart out of Europe – Poland would have remained a shield in the West, Finland in the North, and the Caucasus and Crimea in the South and East (1–2). Scandinavia as mother land and England as colony would have stood united against the world. But Knut perished too early, the Mongols did their worst, the old north was and remains sundered, and Stephens's prophecy is gloomy: 'broken into provinces and exposed to piecemeal ruin, they [the Scando-Anglians] are yet of one stock and blood and speech, have risen together, and together will set and perish. Only *love* and *union* can save them' (21). England's failure to support Denmark was a 'sure harbinger' of her own fall (2). This is archaeological, phi-lological and runological politics on an apocalyptic scale. As our discussion of Stephens the speechman will show, it was not an isolated outburst.

Postmodern Speechman

This discussion of George Stephens's *Revenge* has sought to examine the issues of nobility, national self-imaging, popular lyric tradition, religion, runology and contemporary politics which help to determine its form and substance. There remains the many-stranded question of the play's use of and attitudes to lan-guage. In George Stephens's linguistic theories, we find Rasmus Rask's early nineteenth-century hostility to Prussian philological imperialism recycled and vernacularised for an English readership.[98] His originality lies largely in the high levels of indignation which he brought to the task. Firstly, he loathed the term

---

[97] Stephens 1870, 21.
[98] See above, Chapter 3.

'Anglo-Saxon', used by Jakob Grimm and his British supporters.[99] Stephens argues that the term implies legitimisation of German appropriation (or recovery, as some German scholars saw it)[100] of literary works more appropriately described as 'Old English' or, more broadly, 'Old Northern'. Thus, at the start of *Revenge*, the stage directions state that amongst the books on Rowena's table are Alfred's *Orosius* and 'the Gospels in Old-English', whilst in the textual 'Afterwords' (Notes) Stephens refers only to 'Old-English' dialect, and 'Old-Northern' poetry. The reader is referred to two recent articles in *The Gentleman's Magazine* in which Stephens defends his insistent use of 'the expression Old-English, for the oldest form of our Mother-tongue, instead of that absurd misnomer and barbarous and dangerous modernism "Anglo-Saxon" '.[101] Germanisation of the origins of the old northern 'folk-group' in England must stop. The bulk of pre-Conquest settlers, he argues, were Angles from Slesvig; the Saxons were from Holsten. The old northern cultural continuities are still discernible: 'a farm-laborer (from Jutland for instance) can after a couple of days be hob and nob with the peasantry in Northern England and Southern Scotland – the olden North-English march. [. . .] in the Old-Northern Runic age all these folkships could get on well together'.[102] For the Prussian military to capture the two regions – those 'clan-lands of our forefathers'[103] – in the battles of 1864 is bad enough; for their philologists to invade them without resistance is unthinkable. In this seemingly coordinated military and philological pincer movement[104] Stephens rejects Grimm's reclassification of the English as an essentially southern Teutonic race, separate from the Scandinavian Teutons. As we noted in Chapter 3, morphology lay at the heart of the German claims. The northern Teutonic language is seen to have three distinguishing marks:[105] infinitives ending in *-a* (Old Norse *hafa*, compared with Old English *habban*), suffixed definite articles, and a middle voice that enabled verbs to indicate reflexive, reciprocal or passive usage. No such features are to be found in German, ancient or modern, or in Old English; therefore the English language and people had and have no deep-rooted Scandinavian ties.

The indignant Stephens has an alternative theory. The oldest Scandinavian manuscript sources date from the twelfth century, and need to be checked against evidence from the old northern runic inscriptions that Stephens had been labouring mightily to collect, and which he dates from the third century

99 Wiley 1990.

100 Stanley 1975, 6–7 and passim.

101 Stephens 1857, 88.

102 Stephens 1884, 225; see also Stephens 1853a, 1. Barnes 1863, 1 senses these same linguistic continuities; his remarks about the Danes holding sway over Slesvig-Holsten, 'fatherland of the Anglo-Saxons', are ironic in view of the article's date.

103 Stephens 1884, 226.

104 Stephens often used military imagery in such contexts. Arguments against German philology were a 'wall of bayonets': Stephens 1884, xi.

105 Stephens 1852a, 472; translated into Danish in 1854 by Gísli Brynjólfsson – see Stephens 1860a, 32, note [3].

onwards.[106] These demonstrably old northern runes, claims Stephens, had none of the allegedly diagnostic morphological features identified by German philologists. Moreover, these same features are less marked in the earliest old northern literary texts recorded – eddic poems and prose homilies – than in later works such as the *Íslendingasögur* and Snorri's works. Accordingly, Stephens argues, the features represent late dialectal variations of a common old northern speech whose purest surviving representation is in old northern English. The middle voice inflections are a 'book speech' development, unknown in West Denmark and Jutland 'except by the "eddicated" ',[107] and yet Jutlanders 'speak as good Danish there as any part of the monarchy, rather better, although the capital calls it a dialect'. Stephens further suggests that in Old English there must once have been a suffixed definite article form, residual traces of which are still to be found in words like 'garden' and 'burden' (473). Stephens discusses the status of Gothic, recently 'authoritatively announced' as an essentially German language. He suggests rather that it represents the oldest south Scandinavian 'folk-belt' language covering an area including Norway, South Sweden, the greater part of Denmark, and Jutland. As such it was a major formative influence on the language of the early English settlers from these regions and it, too, lacks suffixed definite articles, and *-a* infinitives. As for 'Frisic' (Frisian; 474), it features *-a* infinitives and suffixed definite articles, yet is viewed by German philologists as an essentially German language, albeit 'weakened' by northern influence. Stephens concludes: 'In one word, the Gothic is the most south-eastern, the Old-English and the Frisic the most south-western of the northern tongues' (473). None of them is German. Old English *-n* infinitives represent the courtly affectation of a Wessex literary and political elite (474), unrepresentative of northern England (Mercia included), especially in its spoken language. Northern English forms remained much more Scandinavian in character than 'Old South-English'. He further notes that /w/, universal in England yet uncommon in Norwegian, Swedish, and Copenhagen Danish, suggests links with Jutland, where the sound is very common. It does not suggest any links with the German language, where /w/ developed into /v/. A similar shift can be seen with /th/: universal in Denmark, Iceland, Faroes and England, it becomes /z/ in German (475).

Stephens concludes that modern German linguistic theories were 'an insult to our nationality and scholarship' (475), as, for that matter, was their corresponding attempt to claim as German a mythology that is essentially northern: 'the wholesale annexation, the theft bodily, by Germany in modern times [. . .] of the whole mythic store of Scandinavia and England'.[108] A limp hand of philological friendship is briefly extended: 'We are all brethren, we are all "Indo-Europeans", members of that famous stock of free folk-tribes from Scandinavia

---

[106] Norwegian finds are dated third century; the earliest English artefacts fifth century: Stephens 1884, 53–7, 111.
[107] Stephens 1852a, 473.
[108] Stephens 1883, 18.

to the Switzer Alps.'[109] But the gesture proves to be merely a prelude to the final onslaught:

> German nationality is not ours; certainly *its* faults are not *our* faults. Their speech is not ours; their body, and mind, and soul, and tendencies are far from being ours, which are altogether cast in the Northern mould, in our opinion one much purer and more noble. . . . As a people we are an independent race, of ancient north extraction and speaking a Northern tongue . . . our nearest homeland is Denmark; our furthest kin-land is Germany. (475)

The article ends with group-bonding slogans: 'Blood is thicker than water. Let us cleave to our own. Let us not "Germanize". It will not be to our profit' (476). The defence of the realm is at stake: 'Our people and our language, our nationality, and our long line of glories are being rapidly transferred to a race with whom we have no particular connection, and whose qualities are not such as to make any amalgamation desirable [. . .]. Of all foreign yokes, those of "Romanism" and "Saxonism" are most impertinent, hurtful, unnecessary, and degrading.' A final call to verbal arms follows: 'Let us speak out. Let us do our duty by our holiest inheritance: let us guard it from the hands of the invaders!'

If objections to the term 'Anglo-Saxon' represent one form of George Stephens's defence of the 'holy inheritance', broader-based resistance involved his assault on the ungrounded fixities of nineteenth-century comparative philology. This seems an iconoclastic stance for a philologist born in the heroic age of comparative philology early in the nineteenth century.[110] We recall Þorleifur Repp, a Copenhagen contemporary of Stephens,[111] marvelling at the linguistic cosmos out of chaos created by the revelations of Rasmus Rask. Stephens remained sceptical, however. He was not against fixity as such – after all, his own views changed little over fifty years – but he hated philological fixities that threatened his dreams of old northern unity.

Stephens's dislike of the 'infallible' rules of philological theory becomes very important for him in the period immediately after Pope Pius IX's declaration of Papal Infallibility in 1870. Stephens frequently linked 'Romanism' with 'Saxonism':

> We may all commit faults. And we all know the strange facility with which modern omnipotent philologists have changed their opinions, whilst at the same time each following Pope has excommunicated his fore-ganger. Only, the mischief is, that each decree is equally infallible as long as it lasts – and it sometime may last a long while.[112]

---

[109] Stephens 1852a, 475.

[110] T.A. Shippey (*Times Literary Supplement*, 22 July 1994, 22) notes the still unresolved tension in medieval studies between 'justified scepticism and hard-won knowledge'.

[111] In 1851 Stephens succeeded Repp as lektor in English at Copenhagen University: see Jens Axelsen [Review of Wawn 1991], *Scandinavica* 32/2 1993, 253.

[112] Stephens 1883, 4.

Such decrees, whether theological or philological, serve only to silence the voice of the common man, in defence of whose rights Stephens's brother had once served time in jail. George Stephens attempts to find a way round the problem in works such as his 1879 pamphlet on the dialect of an early Swedish printed book of 1495.[113] There is much detailed commentary on the work's morphology, out of which two claims emerge. Firstly, the single language spoken (Stephens believed) throughout Scandinavia could never have been strictly standardised; and secondly, that language could not have resembled Old Icelandic as reconstructed in nineteenth-century grammars. Some mainland Scandinavian runes and dialects predate by many centuries the 'polisht . . ., uniformized . . . *Mandarin lingua franca*'[114] of 'classical' Old Icelandic. Stephens attacks the basis of these modern misconceptions: the German obsession with rules and standardisation – 'so far therefore from the watchword of Modern Philology, "Unity and Iron Laws", we must largely build on very different TRUTHS – "variety and endless Caprice", as *all Nature thro*' (214). Multiplicity, diversity, change, instability are to be the watchwords:

> *Now* we certainly *have* a 'language', – a sham and convention, a gradually growing artificial 'book-dialect' which we agree to use, and which, thanks to our tremendous Centralization and to the Press and Railways and Folk-schools and Cultus-ministers and Policemen, is rapidly killing all the old local tungs. But in *olden* times it was not so. There has indeed always been the conventional talk of the Chief or King and his Chancery, and of the Priests and the Cloister, even from Egypt and Babylon downward, largely determined by the province where the ruling power was throned. But *there was not*, and could not be, that centralized official iron uniformity in all the many folk-lands which we *now* call the Book-language. The great folk-land tungs were then living mightily, and sometimes suddenly rose up as state-dialects, when violent changes took place or the political capital or victorious clan-seat was flitted from one speech-land to another. Thus they might at any time re-appear, simply or mixt, when the official dialect was broken or interrupted.[115]

It is the true philologist ('speechman') who alone can restore contact with the plurality of ancient 'shiretalks'. Doing so requires long hours and hard work on long-neglected, non-canonical, sometimes barely legible ancient texts (4). The prize at stake is the development of what sounds like a kind of postmodernist philology:

> So far from one 'Grammar' or 'Wordbook' in one great land-group for 1000 winters, every independent document or monument from the old uncentralized times has in a certain sense and to a certain degree in every country *its own* Grammar and *its own* Wordbook, with endless transitional forms and meanings

---

[113] Stephens 1879.
[114] Stephens 1884, xv–xvi.
[115] Stephens 1879, 3.

and pronominal twists or survivals in the changing local dialects: – for no caprice is so capricious as the caprice of language, as long as it *lives*, is not bound down by central violence, or has not become a venerable mummy. (6)

An additional 'violence' done to the old northern language is the failure of the Roman alphabet to represent adequately the full range of surviving old northern sounds. Anticipating the experiments of Henry Sweet, Stephens some-times writes to his friends using a spelling system that re-establishes the distinc-tion between voiced and unvoiced consonants, notably by reactivating runic þ and ð, long displaced by Roman *th*. Thus we find Stephens writing to the Nor-wegian scholar P.A. Munch about their new edition of *Orkneyinga saga* (never completed).[116] Stephens agrees to mark significant variants in a specially pur-chased copy of the saga: 'It will be ðe best for me to buy here a copy ov ðe *Orkn. Saga*. My own iz too fine a one to be uzd for ðis purpose. Ðe expense ov ðis copy you can afterwardz refund. I await your answer.'[117]

Not to put too fine a point on it, what did Stephens stand to gain out of all this? What broader intellectual benefit does the old northern cause derive from idiosyncratic spelling systems and deconstructed morphology? The answer may lie in the creation of a scepticism-free zone inside which his own runic decipher-ings and broader dreams of old northern glory can have free rein. Stephens is able to defend his readings of runes or rhymes against criticism that they contra-dicted the grammatical orthodoxies of Old English or Old Icelandic, as these became more familiar to English readers.[118] He is thus able to restate at every opportunity his fundamental philological message: it is on the runic monu-ments of the Scando-Anglian colony of Britain that the surviving vestiges of that great Old Scandian empire are still to be found carved (or, better still, 'risted'); and old northern English is the truest guide to the original common Scandinavian tongue introduced to Britain by the colonisers. It is this belief that fuels Stephens's editorial zeal in making what he regarded as old northern English texts available to his students and the wider scholarly audience,[119] and that prompts him to attempt the difficult task (when based in Copenhagen) of preparing a dictionary of Northumbrian dialect.[120] His overall philological agenda is clear by 1840, and it never altered. The title of an 1890 pamphlet asks *Er Engelsk et Tysk Sprog?* The answer, as ever, is a scornful, 'No'.

One thing that Stephens's half a century of frenetic activity never secured him was a job back in England. He coveted the chair of Old English at Oxford, to which Joseph Bosworth was appointed.[121] Ironically, we find Stephens's letter

---

[116] Indrebø and Kolsrud 1924–71, II 121, 123, 142–44.

[117] Ibid., II 123. Hodgetts 1884, 65–6 supported such reforms.

[118] Notably in Dasent 1843, Cleasby and Gudbrand Vigfusson 1874.

[119] The work of a 'North-English Minstrel': Stephens 1860b, 5.

[120] Never published; his daughter presented the manuscript to the Society of Antiquarians of Newcastle upon Tyne in 1897: *Proceedings* 8 (1897), 83.

[121] 'Stephens vill nú gjarnan þángað, ef kostur væri i pláz Bosworths': SJL MS 3.33, p. 57, Jón Sigurðsson to Guðbrandur Vigfússon, 13 November 1865.

of congratulation to Bosworth bound into the front of a presentation copy of the Copenhagen scholar's edition of *Two Leaves of King Waldere's Lay* (1860),[122] precisely the sort of exciting publication that ought to have secured the Oxford position for himself – an edited fragment, discovered in a Copenhagen library, from a work that must once have been part of a complete early English eddic cycle. *Beowulf*, Stephens claimed, could now be regarded as 'only *one of many*' English epics, produced in the great patriotic days before 'the great Christian Corporation in England – many of them Italians or other foreigners' rejected the English language and succumbed to the lure of Latin.[123] The Copenhagen scholar sends warm good wishes, and claims that Bosworth's appointment is a timely blow struck against German philological arrogance:

> Do not grow weary. It is high time that we should be up and doing, if this whole study should not press into the hands of . . . grasping and stealing Germans, who then turn round and taunt us with our being unable to publish our own remains, and publish our finest things as pieces in 'a dialect of High-German'!

It is clear that the old northern cause is proving financially unrewarding in Copenhagen:

> As for myself, I have spent all my life and all my private fortune in a devoted and continued study of my mother-tongue, and of those languages which are nearest allied to it and from which it may best be illustrated . . . I am now advancing in years, and long – like a bird – to fly home again, and work in our own libraries. If some men good and true would follow the example of Oxford and found an O.E. Chair in Cambridge,[124] and would honour me by calling me to fill it – how great would be my delight! But I suppose that there is no chance of anything so reasonable, and that I must die in exile. I have not even oil for my lamp, ie a literary pension – (similar to that enjoyed by Kemble and Thorpe) from the Crown, to assist in keeping the wolf from the door. So I labor, as you may imagine, under great disadvantages and discouragements.

This *crie de cœur* represents a momentary, and touching, concession to frailty. Þórr's most loyal champion was soon thundering again, not to be silenced finally for another thirty years.

Efterord

For over fifty years George Stephens's fiery advocacy of his old northern dreams met with many disappointments. The threat from Prussia signalled by the mid-century bloodshed in Slesvig-Holsten was merely a prelude to far more painful

---

122 Volume in the Bodleian Library, Oxford.
123 Stephens 1860a, xi–xii.
124 Written above: 'or in King's College, London'.

conflicts which he foresaw but happily did not live long enough to witness. Unlike Edgar, Stephens never returned to England, though there was talk of possible posts in Oxford and Cambridge. His philological theories found few long-term disciples in Britain.[125] His credibility was not helped by the revelation that his reading of 'half-Scandian'[126] runes on the Brough stone in Westmoreland proved to be somewhat wide of the mark – the inscription was written in Greek hexameters![127] The English language remained stubbornly resistant to reconstructions of alphabet and vocabulary based on old northern models. English dialects were recorded assiduously[128] but the pressures towards standardisation of linguistic usage were relentless. The term 'Anglo-Saxon' proved ineradicable. Moreover, Wessex and the south of England re-established itself as the centre of political and administrative power in Victorian Britain, for all the proven wealth-creating capacities of Stephens's native Mercia. The romantic adulation of the ancient north that certainly developed in Victorian Britain never gave birth to a really outstanding English epic poem, play, novel, painting or musical work drawing on the materials which scholarship had made available. The old north remained the eager enthusiasm of the few rather than a major concern of the many.[129]

In reviewing Stephens's career it may thus seem hard to avoid the conclusion that his was a life of ultimate scholarly failure, with the political and philological waves deaf to his commands. Happy endings were possible only in fictions such as *Revenge*. Yet this would be too bleak a judgement. The corpus of runic materials that he assembled over half a lifetime provided a rich legacy for his more discriminating scholarly successors. His pioneering editorial work in Old and Middle English extended the text corpus importantly. He made a major contribution to the collection and classification of northern folk-tale and legend. His politicisation of philology and literary theory anticipates the late twentieth-century's addiction to such practices. Yet the final thought in this chapter relates rather to George Stephens and J.R.R. Tolkien. These two professors of English philology may have had little in common temperamentally or politically. It was certainly easier to fight the Germans in the columns of the *Gentleman's Magazine* than in the trenches of World War One. Yet in a play such as *Revenge*, Stephens can be seen as a very modest standard-bearer for a type of philologically-driven literary creativity that was eventually to find a world-famous champion. We recall Stephens's belief, stated at the end of the play, that 'our Princes of Song in England' would 'doubtless [. . .] vigorously restore' the once flourishing alliterative tradition of old northern oral and written tradition.

---

125 Metcalfe 1880, 260–76, 462–4 followed Stephens's writings enthusiastically.
126 Stephens 1884, 116.
127 Learning of his error, Stephens declared breezily that he 'ought to be beaten': Hodgkin 1895, 52. On the Scandinavian element in pre-Conquest stone sculpture in Northern England, see Cramp, Bailey, Lang et al. 1984–91, I–III.
128 Notably in Wright 1898–1905.
129 On the parallel case of nineteenth-century Denmark, see Lundgreen-Nielsen 1994.

If Stephens's own restorative efforts buttered few parsnips, Professor Shippey has revealed the extent to which Stephens's wishes were fulfilled in the work of his fellow Mercian professor. It may not have been in the way that Stephens would have imagined but it is hard to believe that he would have disapproved. George Stephens was no J.R.R. Tolkien, and *Revenge* is no *Lord of the Rings*. The play's readers could be numbered in tens, whereas Tolkien's novel remains one of the most widely read books in the world. Stephens saw himself in a far more politicised, public and laureate role than the Oxford professor. There is no evidence that Tolkien knew Stephens's scholarly or literary work, and, even had he done so, there was little to trigger his inspiration, apart from its fundamental proposition that lost worlds are recoverable through a grammar-laden imagination. Similar philological training afforded Stephens and Tolkien access to a similar range of materials with which to fictionalise their vision. That one should succeed commandingly whilst the efforts of another languish in obscurity is best explained not by the literary theories of claustrated academia but by the chaos theory of real human lives.

CHAPTER NINE

William Morris
and the Old Grey North

the man who loved a battle shout better than a symphony . . . the
Defender of Guinevere and of Gudrun . . . the Viking in the blue
byrnie . . . the Hector of Hammersmith and Varangian Guard of
his own Metropolitan District – William Morris

(Violet Hunt 1881)[1]

Lagði lofsæll
listamaðr
ungr ást
við Ingólfs fóstru;
drakk Són og Boðn
sjálfrar hennar
sem mjólkurbarn
af móðurbrjósti.

(Matthías Jochumsson c.1896)[2]

'In the North forever dwells my heart'

On 7 September 1871 a 'quite bewildered'[3] middle-aged Englishman stood on
the railway station in Edinburgh. He was a striking presence if hardly a commanding figure: five feet six inches tall, overweight, bull-necked, red-faced,
bearded, and with a shock of hair. He had been away from Britain for the whole
summer on what he came to regard as the most important overseas visit of his
life. Now, on his return, everything looked very strange and, as he bade farewell
to his travelling companions Eiríkur Magnússon and Jón Sigurðsson, he hardly
knew where to purchase a ticket to. William Morris had been to Iceland and

---

[1]   Quoted MacCarthy 1994, 427.
[2]   From 'Vilhjálmur Morris': Matthías Jochumsson 1956–8, I 567–8. Translation: 'while still
young the blessed artist dedicated his love to the fosterling of Ingólfr [Iceland]; he drank her mead
of poetry like a nursing child from his mother's breast'. Matthías died in 1920; in 1923 his son
arranged for the publication of the poem, and a c.1906 account of Morris's life.
[3]   Morris 1910–15, VIII 185.

been deeply affected by the experience, as the final entry in his travel journal confirms: 'Iceland is a marvellous, beautiful and solemn place . . . where I had been in fact very happy.'[4]

When he arrived home the mood was still upon him. He copied out and sent to Jón Sigurðsson, by this time back in Copenhagen, two short poems that he had written about Iceland. The idea was for Jón to have them translated into Icelandic and published in *Ný Félagsrit*, the literary journal that he helped to edit. After reading both poems, Jón wrote to Eiríkur Magnússon, indicating that he had reservations about them: the poet 'considers our mother [Iceland] to be rather grey and scrawny, drab and sad'.[5] Jón's letter concedes that there may be something melancholy about Iceland but he would like the poems to promote a more positive and heroic image.[6] He asks Steingrímur Thorsteinsson to translate 'Iceland first seen';[7] as for the other piece, 'I don't think we'll bother with it.'[8] So it was that 'Í landsýn við Ísland' appeared in *Ný Félagsrit* in 1872,[9] nearly twenty years before English readers first set eyes on the English original in Morris's 1891 collection *Poems by the Way*, where it stood alongside the rejected (and subsequently revised)[10] 'Gunnar's Howe above the House at Lithend', and other old northern inspired pieces such as the brief 'To the Muse of the North'.

It is not difficult to understand why Jón found Morris's Iceland lyrics depressing. In its twenty-one lines 'To the Muse of the North' has three references to death, and single references to 'the doom of the world', 'great sorrow' and 'grief'. 'Iceland first seen' talks of pain, grief, death, desolation, dreadful ice, and grey wastes. As for 'Gunnar's Howe' we find 'ruin', 'dead hands', 'toil' (twice), 'tomb' (three times) and four instances of 'grey'. Morris indeed had plenty to feel grey and gloomy about as he set off on his first visit to Iceland. He was under financial pressure, as previously secure income from family mining investments dwindled alarmingly. The man who in 1862 had been able to draw dividends of £913 from his mining shares was not able to draw a penny in 1871.[11] At the same time the previously buoyant church-building industry, on which the earlier success of Morris, Marshall, Faulkner and Company had been based, was in the grip of recession.[12] Visiting Iceland was a costly business,[13] and we may doubt whether, in normal circumstances, Morris would have contemplated it until the financial boat had been refloated. Yet, if Morris could

---

4 Ibid.
5 'þykkir móðir vor heldur gráleit og gelgjuleg, dauf og döpur': Finnbogi Guðmundsson 1971, 135.
6 Ibid.
7 Icelandic title 'Í landsyn við Íslands'.
8 'Eg held við reynum ekki við það': Finnbogi Guðmundsson 1971, 135.
9 *Ný Félagsrit* 29 187–9.
10 Lbs. JS 400–2 4to (IVb): holograph copies of both poems.
11 Harvey and Press 1991, 24.
12 Ibid., 62–6.
13 Baring-Gould 1863, 445–7 costs his two month stay in Iceland at £100.

scarcely afford to go to Iceland in either 1871 or 1873, emotionally he could hardly afford not to. The story of Janey Morris's long-term liaison with Dante Gabriel Rossetti has been told many times.[14] Just weeks before he left for Iceland in 1871 Morris incurred the additional expense of acquiring (in joint tenancy with Rossetti) Kelmscott Manor, a country house retreat in Oxfordshire, that offered his wife and her lover some respite from the inquisitive metropolitan gaze.

Exposure to Iceland renewed Morris's spirits, as is discernible in the two poems sent to Jón Sigurðsson. Far from being gloomy and presenting a negative image of Iceland, Morris's early Iceland lyrics may be seen as a kind of Victorian equivalent to Egill Skallagrímsson's 'Sonatorrek', an elegy composed on the death of his sons. Morris knew the saga and the incident well.[15] The Viking skald's grief is overwhelming; his daughter saves him from a suicidal fast; and his poem represents a triumph of will as Egill eventually finds the mental resolve to allow the forms of ancient Icelandic poetry to harness and give shape to intense feelings. It may be said that Morris's emotional desolation was also intense; and that the solemnity and stoicism which he came to associate with Iceland afforded him real succour. His Iceland lyrics give vivid expression to the consolatory power of the ancient and modern land through which he had travelled on horseback and in his mind. They represent tough-minded wisdom distilled from elemental experience. We read in them the fascination which the idea of Viking- and saga-age Iceland exerted on William Morris before he first travelled there; we sense the profound effect that first-hand exposure to modern Iceland had on his weary spirit; and we know that Iceland was still working its spell on him in 1891 when these private lyrics became public property in England. These were not the poems that made Morris a household name in late Victorian Britain; but they distil the qualities of the ancient and modern north which inspired him to create 'The Lovers of Gudrun' (from *The Earthly Paradise*) and *Sigurd the Volsung*, narrative poems that earned him an international reputation as Victorian Britain's most arresting poetic spokesman for the old north. Morris and his old northern writings are, accordingly, the subject of this chapter.

There are many claims which cannot be made about William Morris's relationship with Iceland, even with the generous spirit engendered by the 1996 celebrations marking the centenary of his death. As we shall see in Chapter 10, Morris was not the first traveller to produce a memorable journal of his Iceland travels. Nor was he the first Iceland traveller able to speak and understand some Icelandic (Forbes, Baring-Gould).[16] Nor was the fact that Morris visited Iceland twice anything remarkable (Dasent, Henry Holland). It is, indeed, more puzzling why Morris, in spite of many passing references in his letters to the possi-

---

[14] Most recently by MacCarthy 1994, 251–9.
[15] Kelvin 1984–96, I 100.
[16] There are journal references to Morris speaking Icelandic: Morris 1910–15, VIII 18, 26, 46, 63, 68, 96, 103.

bility, never returned to Iceland after 1873.[17] Morris was certainly not the first traveller to head for the saga-steads (Metcalfe, Baring-Gould). He was not the first Victorian to translate a full-length Icelandic saga (Stephens), nor the first to work closely with an Icelandic collaborator (Dasent worked with Grímur Thomsen and Guðbrandur Vigfússon).[18] Morris was certainly not the first Victorian to write poems on old northern subjects (Motherwell, Symington);[19] nor was he the first to lecture to provincial audiences on old northern subjects (Smith, Browning).[20] He was neither the first nor the only Victorian to have one of his Iceland-related works translated into Icelandic (Symington, Barmby).[21] Morris was not the only Victorian Icelandophile to become the subject of an Icelandic poem (George Powell, Barmby),[22] or to play an active role in journalism and politics (Lowe, Bryce, Howorth).[23] He was not even the only famous Victorian Icelandophile to die in 1896 – but there were no centenary exhibitions, conferences, or radio and television talks to celebrate the old northern achievements of George Dasent.

'Many men, many minds, the old saw saith',[24] and so it proved in centenary celebration discussion of Morris. Was he a pioneering political activist on behalf of oppressed workers who needed all the help they could find, or a champagne socialist whose copy of *Das Kapital* was bound in 'deep turquoise leather with elaborate gilt-tooled decoration of buds and spots and stars'?[25] Did he preach the anti-enterprise culture attitudes of a university-educated elite which pointed the way to Britain's subsequent industrial decline,[26] while practising brisk capitalist efficiency in his own business?[27] For some it has remained tempting to set Morris's loathing of 'ministering to the swinish luxury of the rich'[28] alongside his cultivation of the same swine as potential customers for the designer-label luxury goods that his company produced. One of his wealthiest clients (in Morris's words 'monstrously rich . . . hurrah for the social revolution')[29] was Catherine Lorillard Wolfe in Newport, Rhode Island, among the features of whose new house (named 'Vinland') were to be stained glass windows designed by Edward Burne-Jones, with Morris as literary consultant. These featured scenes

[17] Kelvin 1984–96, I 198, 14 September 1873; 203, 22 October 1873; 287 [n.d.; March 1876].
[18] Wawn 1991b. MacCarthy 1994, 290 ignores the achievement of Dasent (and Baring-Gould) in claiming that Morris was 'certainly the first Englishman in Iceland who arrived with such a knowledge of its language and literature'.
[19] Motherwell 1847, Symington 1862.
[20] Smith 1838, Browning 1876.
[21] Matthías Jochumsson 1902; Symington 1862, 279–81, 287–8.
[22] Matthías Jochumsson 1956–8, I 573–6 on Powell; and I 580 on Barmby, 'Sigrún Suðurlands'.
[23] See Lowe 1861, Bryce 1874, 1923; Howorth 1894, 1920.
[24] 'The Folk-Mote by the River', Morris 1910–15, IX 173.
[25] MacCarthy 1994, 592. Visiting Engels Morris spotted a copy of the *Poetic Edda*: MacCarthy 1994, 509.
[26] Wiener 1981.
[27] Harvey and Press 1991.
[28] MacCarthy 1994, 412.
[29] Kelvin 1984–96, II.2 182.

from the Norse discovery of America: three presiding gods (Óðinn, Þórr and Freyr); three Vínland stalwarts (Þorfinnr karlsefni, Guðríðr Þorbjarnardóttir, Leifr Eiríksson); and a Viking ship.[30]

With all scepticism registered, the claims to be made for Morris the Victorian old northernist remain substantial. He wrote by far the best Victorian poems on eddic and saga subjects. His Iceland journal, with its arresting personal subtext, offers a unique blend of complex responses to ancient saga-steads, and sharp-eyed sensitivity to the shifting moods and colours of modern Icelandic nature. By their philological alertness the saga translations of Morris and his (too easily ignored) collaborator Eiríkur Magnússon earned an honoured place in the history of attempts to tune in the English language to these elusive narratives – 'Morrisian' language, for all the disdain it could generate, attracted many imitators.[31] William Morris devoted himself to many other enthusiasms in the remaining quarter century of his life after returning from Iceland in 1873, but the old north and its modern manifestations remained major public and private reference points for him. While his friends looked to the European south for their literary inspiration, Morris's gaze, like his Viking-sized personality and simmering berserker rages,[32] remained loyal to the north:

> O, South! O, sky without a cooling cloud;
> O, sickening yellow sand without a break;
> O, palm with dust a-lying on thy leaves;
> O, scarlet flowers burning in the sun:
> I cannot love thee, South, for all thy sun,
> For all thy scarlet flowers or thy palms;
> But in the North forever dwells my heart.
> The North with all its human sympathies,
> The glorious North, where all amidst the sleet,
> Warm hearts do dwell, warm hearts sing out with joy;
> The North that ever loves the poet well.[33]

Morris's greatest Icelandic champion called him a giant, a lion-maned Welsh Volsung, the Þórr of the study from whom thundering was not unknown.[34] Fading fast in September 1896 his spirit could still be stirred when recalling Scandinavian travels earlier in the year – a visit to Sognefjord, site of the saga of Friðþjófr that he had translated twenty-five eventful years earlier.[35]

Published translations of some two dozen sagas, verse translations of Danish

---

[30] Ibid., 182, 423.

[31] Alfred Wyatt 'deems' it appropriate to write to Eiríkur Magnússon about Vínland: 'deem . . . is such a Morrisian word': Lbs. 2190 4to, AW to EM, 11 November 1908.

[32] See, for example, May Morris in Morris 1910–15, XII xiii.

[33] 'The Dedication of the Temple' (1855), quoted in Erhleman 1940, 129.

[34] Matthías Jochumsson, in Steingrímur Matthíasson 1935, 126; see also Eiríkur Magnússon 1896–7, 109.

[35] Morris and Eiríkr Magnússon 1891–1905, VI xii.

ballads,[36] sonnets on saga heroes, lyrics triggered by saga reading and saga-stead visits, translations and reanimations of eddic legends, prose romances set in misty old northern locations, lectures about old Icelandic culture, Iceland diaries, journalism about modern Icelandic famine, and a hefty bundle of Iceland-related letters to Icelandophile friends: such is the stuff of a big book rather than a single chapter. One way of making a path through the mass of Morris's northern writings is to examine the *Burnt Njal*-derived poem that Jón Sigurðsson rejected when Morris sent it to him in 1872: 'Gunnars Howe above the House at Lithend'. In it we may find, in conveniently distillate form, many of the characteristic pulses discernible in Morris's lengthier northern writings.

'Gunnar's Howe'

It was Morris, more than any other Victorian, who signalled Hlíðarendi the place, and *Njáls saga* the work, as worthy of serious artistic contemplation. He visited the region in 1871, with his knowledge of the saga enabling him to animate every desolate location he visited, and leading him to demand this same visionary quality in other people. Whilst still on-board ship, peering through the mist, he locates every feature of the land in terms of *Njáls saga*: Svínafell is the mountain 'under which Flosi the Burner lived', whilst the Vestmannaeyjar stand 'just opposite to Njal's house at Bergthorsknoll'.[37] He can hardly wait to arrive in the district. Riding to the actual sites in a high state of excitement, his imagination soon converts a mound near the Bergþórshvoll farmhouse into the site of Njáll's dwelling (43); the next day he finds the (now much eroded) hollow where Flosi and the hundred burners hid before the attack; the pond where the burning Kári slaked his clothes proves to be little more than a patch of marshy ground but there were signs that a brook had once flowed from there; more excitingly, the farmer assures the travellers that he had come across a bed of ashes when digging the foundations for a new parlour. Moving inland, Morris reaches the Lithe as he (like Dasent) calls it. Time and tide have 'sadly wasted and diminished' (47) meadows which had once been 'Gunnar's great wealth'; but Morris is still able to examine the traditional site of Gunnarr's hall, the hollow where his Irish hound howled a last loyal message to its master (48), and 'Gunnar's Howe', in which, one moonlit night, Skarpheðinn and Hǫgni catch sight of the slain Gunnarr singing merrily, surrounded by lights.

Morris was not the first English poet to write about the hero's mound at Hlíðarendi. Richard Hole's 'The Tomb of Gunnar', published in the *Gentleman's Magazine* in 1789,[38] was, however, created from books rather than life; he came across extracts from *Njáls saga* in Bartholin's *Antiqvitatum Danicarum*

---

[36] Amongst them 'The King of Denmark's Sons', 'Hildebrand and Hillelil', 'Agnes and the Hill Man', 'Hafbur and Signy', in Morris 1910–15, IX 140–5, 203–5, 211–12, 213–24.
[37] Morris 1910–15, VIII 21.
[38] Hole 1789, 937.

(1689).[39] The scene that caught Hole's eye tells of Gunnarr's cheerful afterlife in his grave-mound. We may recall the scene as worded in Dasent's *Burnt Njal*, well known to Morris:

> Now these two, Skarphedinn and Hogni, were out of doors one evening by Gunnar's cairn on the south side. The moon and stars were shining clear and bright, but every now and then the clouds drove over them. Then all at once they thought they saw the cairn standing open, and lo! Gunnar had turned himself in the cairn and looked at the moon. They thought they saw four lights burning in the cairn, and none of them threw a shadow. They saw that Gunnar was merry, and he wore a joyful face. He sang a song, and so loud, that it might have been heard though they had been further off.
>
> > '. . . I will die the prop of battle,
> > Sooner die than yield an inch,
> > Yes, sooner die than yield an inch.'
>
> After that the cairn was shut up again.
>
> 'Wouldst thou believe these tokens if Njal or I told them to thee?' says Skarphedinn.
>
> 'I would believe them,' he says, 'if Njal told them, for it is said that he never lies.'
>
> 'Such tokens as these mean much,' says Skarphedinn, 'when he shows himself to us, he who would sooner die than yield to his foes; and see how he has taught us what we ought to do.'
>
> 'I shall be able to bring nothing to pass,' says Hogni, 'unless thou wilt stand by me.'
>
> 'Now,' says Skarphedinn, 'will I bear in mind how Gunnar behaved after the slaying of your kinsman Sigmund; now I will yield you such help as I may. My father gave his word to Gunnar to do that whenever thou or thy mother had need of it.'
>
> After that they go home to Lithend.[40]

Hole decorates the scene with the familiar images and diction of the sanguinary sublime. The sylvan shepherd with his very eighteenth-century 'fleecy train' soon flees the scene: Sarhedine and Hogner (the nearest Hole comes to these unfamiliar names) are made of sterner stuff, however. The poet and his congested noun phrases are in full flow: the two men make for the tomb 'While darkly-rolling vapours hide / In their dun veil night's glittering pride.' The 'fearless' pair are suddenly confronted with the figure of the dead Gunnarr, clad in his battle-gear and in high good humour. Picked out by the moonlight and with a smile playing across his 'awful brows', the hero's sentiments are impeccably Bartholinean:

> 'Unmanly flight the brave despise;
> Conquest of death's the warrior's prize;

---

[39] Bartholin 1689, 279–81.
[40] Dasent 1861, I 250–1; *Njáls saga*, ch. 78.

> The strife of spears disdain to shun,
> Nor blast the fame by Gunnar won!'

No time is wasted on whether Gunnarr is to be believed; there is no hint of Hǫgni's sense of personal inadequacy, nor of Skarpheðinn's feelings of indebtedness. The call to arms is immediate:

> 'Grasp the sword, and gird the mail!
> Scorning alike to yield or fly,
> Resolve to conquer, or to die!
> A banquet for the wolf prepare,
> And glut the ravenous birds of air!'

Morris's 'Gunnar's Howe' reflections on the same scene are very different. He had twice visited the saga-stead, which is no surprise given his belief that 'I don't know anything more consoling or grander in all literature (to use a beastly French word) than Gunnar's singing in his house under the moon and the drifting clouds.'[41] He had also taken the trouble to translate a portion of the scene in his Journal. Of his first visit he writes:

> we come at last on a big mound rising up from the hollow, and that is Gunnar's Howe: it is most dramatically situated to remind one of the beautiful passage in the Njala where Gunnar sings in his tomb: the sweet grassy flowery valley with a few big grey stones about it has a steep bank above, which hides the higher hilltop; but down the hill the slope is shallow, and about midways of it is the howe; from the top of which you can see looking to right and left all along the Lithe, and up into the valley of Thorsmark.[42]

It was to that 'terrible' valley that his party was to journey on the following morning. But for now they lie around Gunnar's howe, climb further up the slope, and then return to the mound site at eleven o'clock that night, with the moon reduced to a 'little thin crescent', not enough to illuminate the saga hero had he obligingly reappeared.

Morris's brief snatch of translation from this 'beautiful passage in the Njala' bears his unmistakable voice-print:

> Skarphedin and Hogni were abroad one evening by Gunnar's howe, on the south side thereof: the moonshine was bright but whiles the clouds drew over: them seemed the howe opened and Gunnar had turned in the howe, and lay meeting the moon; and they thought they saw four lights burning in the howe, and no shadow cast from any: they saw that Gunnar was merry, and exceeding glad of counte-

41 Kelvin 1984–96, I 344.
42 Morris 1910–15, VIII 48–49; second visit 207.

nance: and he sang a song so high that they had heard of it even had they been farther off.[43]

When compared with Dasent's version of the same passage (quoted above) Morris proves to be sometimes more accurate,[44] allowing himself few Dasentian liberties – the Icelandic text has no 'stars'; nothing was shining 'clear'; the repose of 'drew' for *dró fyrir* works better than the more active 'drove', and the drama of Dasent's 'all at once' is the translator's own invention. On the other hand, Morris's insistence on the closely cognate nature of the two languages leads to moments of fussy eccentricity – instead of Dasent's straightforward 'every now and then' for *stundum* we find the archaistic 'whiles'; the impersonal Icelandic *þeim sýndisk* seems better served by Dasent's 'they thought they saw' than by Morris's transliterated 'them seemed'; and what is a reader who knows no Icelandic to make of Morris's '[Gunnar] lay meeting the moon'? Elsewhere the contest between these two old northern titans is more even: 'exceeding glad of countenance' sounds distractingly biblical as a rendering of *með gleðimóti miklu*, yet Morris would have disliked Dasent's 'wore a joyful face', with its 'beastly' French loan word and failure to signal the intensifying *miklu*. Dasent, the pragmatic proselytising Icelandicist, seems always to have a readership in mind; for Morris translation was more a private communion with the past.

In seeking to express in verse what this scene and its saga-stead meant to him, Morris would have needed no reminding that literary times and tastes had changed since the days of Richard Hole. Edward Young's *Night Thoughts* were no longer in fashion, though adjectival Gothicism finds a surprising new lease of life in Morris's Iceland Journal.[45] In the manuscript that Morris sent to Jón Sigurðsson the poem's title is simply 'Gunnar's Howe' – neither poet nor recipient needed its location identifying. For the 1891 first publication, however, the title has been adjusted ('above the House at Lithend') to nod in the direction of Dasent ('Lithend'); 'Howe' (OI *haugr*) was never likely to succumb to Dasent's Gaelic-derived 'cairn'. Morris may have heard, and his great admirer W.G. Collingwood will have known,[46] that amongst the many -*howe* place names in the English Lake District was 'Gunner's How'.[47]

It is soon apparent, also, that the Morris poem's first-person narrator is addressing a very different audience from Hole's third-person figure:

Ye who have come o'er the sea to behold this grey minster of lands,
Whose floor is the tomb of time past, and whose walls by the toil of dead hands
Show pictures amidst of the ruin of deeds that have overpast death,
Stay by this tomb in a tomb to ask of who lieth beneath.

---

[43] Ibid., 49; *Brennu-Njáls saga*, ÍF XII, 192–3.
[44] But not always: for example *ópinn* is an adjective rather than a past participle.
[45] See Morris 1910–15, VIII 28, 41, 113–114, 150, 154, 170.
[46] Collingwood and Jón Stefánsson 1899, 29 includes a sketch of the site.
[47] Ellwood 1894, 58. For the text of the poem, see Morris 1910–15, IX 179.

The language is archaic, 'Ye', 'o'er', 'behold', 'lieth', but the present tense suggests immediacy. We may take it that Morris is addressing modern travellers. The solemnity of tone reflects the awe that such travellers ought to feel as they move from saga-stead to saga-stead. The imagery in the first verse is, we may recall, exactly what Jón Sigurðsson disliked. Iceland is a 'tomb' (three instances), it is linked with 'death' and 'dead hands' and 'ruin', and, recalling the *gráleit* criticism, it is 'grey'. Yet Jón surely misunderstood Morris's use of the adjective, a favourite when describing Iceland. It occurs four times in this poem, twice in 'Iceland first seen', it is all over 'The Lovers of Gudrun' and *Sigurd the Volsung*, and can be found over a hundred times in his Iceland Journals, in describing lava, moss, streams, clouds, cliffs, plains, skies, seas and slopes. They are all 'grey', but 'grey' is far from being a dull colour for Morris. It was as important for describing Iceland, as it was in his fabric designs. In 1875, whilst hard at work on *Sigurd the Volsung*, Morris's correspondence with Thomas Wardle, his Staffordshire-based colour specialist, makes it clear that achieving the 'required shade' in 'the battle about the "Grey"' was causing them trouble, and that Morris was a demanding taskmaster.[48] It is, after all, only against the correctly dyed dark grey background that the vivid foreground colours of curtain or carpet are shown to best advantage. So it is in the Iceland Journal. There is no 'monotony of greyness' there.[49] We find 'grey', 'dark grey', 'not very dark grey', 'dark . . . and dreadful grey', 'lightish grey', 'dark ashen grey', 'light green and grey', 'greyer than grey', 'light grey-blue', 'yellowish grey', 'ragged grey', 'inky grey', 'woeful grey', 'spotted grey', 'dark grey bordered with white', 'heavy grey', 'cold-grey', light grey becoming 'greyer and greyer', and many other shades. When Morris returns home to England in 1871, it is on a 'soft warm grey morning', sailing on a 'calm and grey sea', that he spots the 'long grey line' of Scottish coast.[50] Awaiting him in Oxfordshire was the light grey stone of his old college and of Kelmscott Manor. Writing to Georgiana Burne-Jones from Verona in 1878 we find Morris confessing boredom with the buildings: 'I long . . . for the heap of grey stones with a grey roof that we call a house north-away.'[51] Grey, then, was a solemn, dramatic, ever-changing colour for William Morris; and in the Journals it is the essential background tone against which the stunning primary colours of Iceland flicker across page after page like the northern lights. Small wonder that, when Morris can find so much colour in a grey modern Icelandic landscape, he has no trouble in finding the right shade of grey for his old northern saga-steads, their interior decorations, and even the eyes of the heroes and heroines in his lengthy narrative poems.

Morris's 'Gunnar's Howe' landscape is not just 'grey' it is a 'grey minster of lands'. Morris knew all about grey minsters, Oxford college chapels, London abbeys, European cathedrals, and, not least, the many churches all over England

---

[48] Kelvin 1984–96, I 267–8.
[49] MacCarthy 1994, 283.
[50] Morris 1910–15, VIII 184.
[51] Kelvin 1984–96, I 487.

for which his firm had supplied stained glass and interior furnishings during the 1860s. The experienced Victorian travellers and tourists addressed by Morris in the poem expect to visit minsters. If they fail to find any in Iceland, they are urged to use their imaginations. Sometimes the 1871 Journal views rockscapes with the eye of the ecclesiastical architect: 'ruined-minster-looking rocks';[52] one mountain 'like a huge church with a transept' (37), and another 'just the shape of Castle St. Angelo at Rome' (131). In the poem the travellers are invited to think of the lava-strewn ground of Iceland as a minster floor: its walls and the pictures they support can be imagined, thanks to the toil of dead hands (saga writers) who tell of ruined deeds whose fame lives on for Victorian enthusiasts through saga translations. The Jón Sigurðsson manuscript of the poem shows that Morris is thinking of sagas – for 'deeds' he writes first 'great tales'. Gunnar's 'Howe' is a small tomb within the great minster of Icelandic land and landscape. It is a tomb within a tomb – a place of mystery, history, beauty and solemnity. No saga-age location was less 'scrawny, drab and sad'.

At the heart of his poem is Morris's fascination with the idea of Iceland's great past living on in its present. It is a past with which Morris seeks personal identification. His demands on it are insistent and revealing. He wants to 'have a part / In that great sorrow of thy children dead';[53] he wants Grettir as a 'friend . . . life's void to fill';[54] and, ever the unfulfilled lover, he wants Iceland, as mother, sister and lover 'all in one', to 'wrap me in the grief of long ago'.[55] He is also eager for his fellow English travellers to 'have a part' in the tale of Gunnarr and Njáll. The Viking-age heroes whose deeds gave rise to the sagas are long dead, as are the early hands that created the sagas and the later ones that copied the manuscripts. Through an almost infinite process of working backwards, dead also are the eddic heroes whose deeds begat the banquet tales and tapestries which decorated the walls at Herdholt in 'The Lovers of Gudrun', and the halls of the Lymdalers and Niblungs in *Sigurd the Volsung*.[56] Through the 'toil' of hands, whether of minstrel on harp, weaver on loom, saga-man on vellum, or translator and poet on paper, the past can be partially retrieved for the present. In 'Iceland first seen', the continuity of Iceland is celebrated 'amid waning of realms and of riches and death of things worshipped and sure'.[57] George Stephens would have understood the mood. Iceland itself voices the explanation – 'I abide here the spouse of a God, and I made and I make and I endure.' If 'making', in either the word's medieval poetic sense or its more familiar modern meanings, could help to fill the silences of 'life's void', then Morris, an old northern workaholic, had nothing to fear.

---

[52] Morris 1910–15, VIII 151.
[53] Ibid., IX 116.
[54] Ibid., VII xxxvi.
[55] Morris 1910–15, 116.
[56] Morris 1877, 173, 217: the wall hangings of the Niblung hall have images of Viking vessels, the Valkyrie, Mímir's fountain, and Miðgarðsormr.
[57] Morris 1910–15, IX 126.

As 'Gunnar's Howe' develops, Morris's anxiety – impatience even – that everyone should share his own vivid engagement soon becomes apparent:

> Ah! the world changeth too soon, that ye stand there with unbated breath,
> As I name him that Gunnar of old, who erst in the haymaking tide
> Felt all the land fragrant and fresh, as amidst of the edges he died.
> Too swiftly fame fadeth away, if ye tremble not lest once again
> The grey mound should open and show him glad-eyed without grudging or pain.
> Little labour methinks to behold him but the tale-teller laboured in vain.

For all its Augustan filigree Richard Hole's 1789 poem had followed the saga scene's narrative line doggedly. With his reference to Gunnar falling 'in the hay-making tide', Morris here touches the events of the saga for the only time in his poem. The tone seems feverish. What happens if someone comes to Iceland and fails to fall under the spell of Gunnar when visiting Hlíðarendi? It could happen. As we shall see in Chapter 10, people visited Iceland for many reasons, not all of them literary. The oblivion which could result from an insensate onlooker's heedlessness was to prompt Morris in *Sigurd the Volsung* to a memorable passage in which Regin tells the youthful Sigurd how he had once taught mankind to reap, sow, sail, sing and weave only to find, within a generation, that perverse euhemerism now attributed these gifts to the gods Freyr, Þórr, Bragi and Freyja respectively.[58] In 'Gunnar's Howe' it seems unthinkable to Morris that the 'tale-teller laboured in vain'; yet in 1873 he was himself to dis-cover just how fragile could be the 'thin thread of insight and imagination'[59] that linked saga past to Victorian present. Visiting the 'Howe' again he finds that the bright evening of 1871 had given way to a wet and 'melancholy' morning of 1873. More than a 'little labour' was needed to recapture the fugi-tive essence, the excitement and awe, of two years earlier:

> it was not until I got back from the howe and wandered by myself about the said site of Gunnar's hall and looked out thence over the great grey plain that I could answer to the echoes of the beautiful story – but then at all events I did not fail.[60]

In the 1872 poem, the 'thin thread' is still securely in place, with appropriate philolological underpinning. In the second verse 'tide', 'edges' and 'methinks' all derive from old northern forms.

In the poem's third stanza talk of tombs, and death gives way to a celebration of death's defeat. The memorable song of a 'man unremembered' can bring the world and its heroes back to life. Passed down through the generations, the story serves to bridge 'all the days that have been':

[58] Morris 1877, 111.
[59] Morris 1910–15, VIII 168.
[60] Ibid., 207.

Little labour for ears that may hearken to hear his death-conquering song,
Till the heart swells to think of the gladness undying that overcame wrong.
O young is the world yet, meseemeth, and the hope of it flourishing green,
When the words of a man unremembered so bridge all the days that have been.
As we look round about on the land that these nine hundred years he hath seen.

Here is the life-affirming optimism that Jón Sigurðsson missed, but which Morris always found in ancient and modern Iceland. If fragile words can sound so loud generations later, then the world is still young, hope is still green, and the human heart can rejoice. So it is that the last verse returns from broad humanitarian musings to the dusk of the summer evening of 21 July 1871 which, Morris recalls, never quite grows dark and which finds nature bustling with activity:

Dusk is abroad on the grass of this valley amidst of the hill:
Dusk that shall never be dark till the dawn hard on midnight shall fill
The trench under Eyjafell's snow, and the grey plain the sea meeteth grey.
White, high aloft hangs the moon that no dark night shall brighten ere day,
For here day and night toileth the summer lest deedless his time pass away.

The three stages of an Icelandic summer circle of the sun are linked by alliteration in the verse – dusk, dawn, day. Each dissolves into the other before dark has a chance to take hold and require the intervention of the moon. Just as there are no sharp divisions between day and night, so the demarcation line between land and sea is unclear from a distance. The one runs into the other which runs into the one again. The sense is always of process and continuity, and the final line highlights energy, progress and vitality – the summer season not wishing to leave without having *done* something. The poem began with 'deeds' preserved through the words of a saga; in July 1871 new deeds were being done, many or most or all of which would be rewarded with oblivion. But the deeds were to be done just the same. Gunnarr had sung of doing brave deeds irrespective of death. For Morris those brave deeds live on undyingly through the labours of the long-dead saga writer; his Icelandic saga lives on undyingly through the toil of many Icelandic scribes and a single English translator; Dasent's translation lived vividly in the mind of William Morris the traveller; and Morris's travels will live on in the lines of 'Gunnar's Howe'.

Salute from Iceland

Morris was not to know it, but his own death produced a Gunnarr-related literary deed even beyond the narrative span of his own poem. Gunnarr of Hlíðarendi can be found paying tribute to Morris. Morris's celebrity in Iceland as a champion of their old literature led to several generous tributes being published in Iceland at the time of his death.[61] One which has escaped the attention of

[61] Ellison 1988.

Morris scholars is Matthías Jochumsson's striking commemorative poem 'Vilhjálmur Morris'.[62] Matthías's poem celebrates Morris the champion of the old northern muse and of the modern socialist cause. From amidst the recycled eddic diction we learn that Morris drank in the north with his mother's milk; and that Iceland ('Snælands dóttir') never set eyes on a more gifted poetic genius ('snjallari snilling'). Revered Icelandic historians and saga heroes voice their tributes: Ari Þorgilsson rejoices that Icelandic history now has a voice in England; Egill Skallagrímsson states that no warrior was more valued by King Athelstan than William Morris is valued by Iceland; Snorri Sturluson, the Sturlungs, and Sæmundr fróði salute the English hero; and, last in the parade, we meet a group of the saga heroes whom Morris had helped to make famous in Britain or for whom he had a special affection – characters from 'The Lovers of Gudrun', *Gunnlaugs saga* and *Burnt Njal*:

> Good report they gave
> the glorious guest –
> each and all
> of the action men:
> Gunnarr and Gestr,
> Gizurr and Hjalti,
> Einarr and Kjartan,
> Wormtongue and Njáll.[63]

Matthías then turns to Morris's death, and registers his esteem for *Sigurd the Volsung*. We see Morris attacking the Fáfnir-like monster of injustice, oppression, and grievous inequalities of wealth distribution which held London in thrall:

> Lies the serpent
> round London;
> know we that fearsome creature,
> foulest in the world,
> sprays with destructive fire
> the fettered folk,
> the monster of a billion
> burdens of Grani.[64]

Scorning wealth, safety (and the advice of Reginn), Morris (like his Volsung Sigurd) sets off for Gnítaheiði, where he dies an heroic death:

[62] Matthías Jochumsson 1956–8, I 567–71. Written 1896, published 1923 in *Eimreiðin* 29, 257–61.
[63] 'Mæltu orðheill / ítrum gesti / einn ok sérhverr / afreksmanna: / Gunnar ok Gestr, / Gizur ok Hjalti, / Einar ok Kjartan, / Ormstunga, Njáll': Matthías Jochumsson 1956–8, I 569.
[64] 'Liggr linni / um Lundúnaborg; / þá vitum meinvætt / mesta í heimi, / eys hrælogum / á hremmdar dróttir / gandr þúsundað / granabyrða': Matthías Jochumsson 1956–8, I 570–1.

> he rushed thus into the flames
> flayed the mighty monster:
> resounded wide in the world
> of us all. *There fell Morris*.[65]

But the poet lives on in the mind of Iceland:

> May high in praise
> Bragi's art-rich hero,
> – may man teach this to man –
> Morris in Snorri's land.[66]

Translating the Sagas

Matthías's tribute prompts us to direct our attention towards the saga translations and, more importantly, to the two narrative poems that tower over the rest
of Morris's Icelandic literary and scholarly activity. The Iceland Journals are rich
and compelling works, but were not published until 1911.[67] Similarly 'Gunnar's
Howe' and Morris's other old northern ballads and lyrics were not published
until 1891. Morris's early reputation as an old northernist was based on his
work as a translator and narrative poet. By securing their publication both in
journals and *Three Northern Love Stories* (1875), Morris and Eiríkur Magnússon
introduced *Víglundar saga* to Victorian England,[68] reacquainted people with
Gunnlaugs saga, and reminded old northernists that the story of Frithiof began
life as an old Icelandic saga and not as a modern Swedish poem. The 1875
volume and its reprints assuredly found a readership, and so, a generation later,
did the six volumes of the Saga Library (1891–1905), the last four of which
provided an alternative to Laing's reprinted *Heimskringla* translation, whilst the
first two volumes made available for the first time English translations of
Hávarðar saga Ísfirðings, *Hænsa-Þóris saga*, and *Eyrbyggja saga*. This latter work
was the source of the 'Wonders of Froda' incidents,[69] which an ebullient Morris
translates over dinner for his companions while visiting Stykkishólmur in
1871.[70]

The substance of Frederick York Powell's celebrated attack on the studied

[65] 'Vóð svá Vafurlogann / vann á Jörmungandi: / Dundi vítt í veröld / vorri. *Þar fell Morris*.': ibid., I
571.
[66] 'Hátt í lofi lifi / listfagr ástvin Braga, / – maðr kenni þat manni! – / Morris á foldu Snorra!': ibid.
[67] MacCarthy 1994, 310.
[68] Morris 1910–15, VIII 139, 151.
[69] Chapters 51–5.
[70] Morris 1910–15, VIII 120, 135; see also 161. The story was popular in late Victorian England:
Stevenson 1916 (written *c*.1890); Craigie in Lang 1897, 273–87; Major and Speight 1905, 115–25
include a version of Morris and Eiríkr Magnússon 1891–1905, II 139–52.

archaisms of Morris's translation style[71] is rejected by Eiríkur Magnússon, but it is sometimes difficult to resist the sense that Morris was reaching out to an audience of initiates rather than seeking to win converts. It was (and perhaps still is) hard for readers to appreciate – and even harder still to relish – the philological exuberance which Morris brought to the task of translation. In *Gunnlaugs saga* the young hero has arrived in Norway, eager to assert his strength of mind and body:

> Jarl mælti: 'Hvat er fœti þínum, Íslendingr?'
> 'Sullr er á, herra,' sagði hann.
> 'Ok gekk þú þó ekki haltr?'
> Gunnlaugr svarar: 'Eigi skal haltr ganga, meðan báðir fœtr eru jafnlangir.'[72]

The Morris and Eiríkur Magnússon translation reads as follows:

> The earl asked, 'What ails thy foot, Icelander?'
> 'A boil, lord,' said he.
> 'And yet thou wentest not halt.'
> Gunnlaug answers, 'Why go halt while both legs are long alike?'[73]

The translation stays closely in touch with Icelandic vocabulary ('earl', 'halt'), with pronoun usage, and with the forms and tense shifts of the tag verbs. Omission of a verb from each of Gunnlaugr's responses creates even greater terseness. Yet concern for inversion, morphology, and the retention of compounds can produce 'thou wentest not halt' and 'while both legs are long alike', locutions better suited to the taste of a dedicated connoisseur.

This is even more the case with the verses. With Eiríkur to guide him, Morris relishes the challenge of complex Icelandic prosody and opaque imagery. Indeed, in the six-year gap between the original and revised versions of *Gunnlaugs saga*, Morris grew more ambitious. The 1875 *Three Northern Love Stories* version confirms that Morris had worked hard on his revisions; replacing uncongenial French forms with old northern equivalents, introducing compound nouns and adjectives, and inverting English word order to reflect traditional Icelandic practice. Thus, when Gunnlaugr is accused by a farmer of having offered a coin of too little value as compensation for having slapped his son, the poet replies:

> To this close-fist the right I gave
> A new mark, grey of face to have;
> O slow thy gold from thee to spit,
> I bid thee long to look at it!

---

[71] Morris's name is glaringly absent from the list of successful translators in Gudbrand Vigfusson and Powell 1883, I cxv. Eiríkur responds in Morris and Eiríkr Magnússon 1891–1905, VI vii, note.
[72] Sigurður Nordal and Guðni Jónsson 1938, 69.
[73] Morris and Eiríkr Magnússon 1875, 20.

> For thou shalt think it no good thing
> If thou must tighten thy purse string,
> Missing so much of deep-sea's sheen
> As on this day thine eyes have seen.[74]

The meaning seems to be: take what you have been offered, or you will lose even that money which is currently in your purse. In the revised version a closer eye has been kept on the Icelandic original:

> Bade I the *m*iddling *m*ighty
> To ha<u>ve</u> a *m*ark of w<u>aves</u>' flame;
> Giver of *g*rey seas' *g*litter,
> This *g*ift shalt thou make sh<u>ift</u> with.
> If the *e*lf-sun of the waters
> From <u>*out*</u> of purse thou <u>lett</u>est,
> O *w*aster of the *w*orm's bed,
> A*w*<u>aits</u> thee sorrow <u>later</u>.[75]

We notice the interlinear alliteration and internal rhyme (perfect, half and eye). As Gary Aho remarks, 'In these revised "vísur" we can watch the Victorian skald matching wits with Gunnlaug and Raven'.[76]

It is, however, possible to exaggerate Morris's radicalism, or at least to overstate his uniqueness in this respect. Indeed when his treatment of *Friðþjófs saga* is compared with George Stephens' 1839 version, it is Stephens who can sometimes seems the more mannered and archaistic. During the turbulent sea voyage to the Orkneys the hero climbs to the top of the mast to survey the wild seas, and on his descent reports strange sightings:

'. . . Moreover I saw two women on the back of the whale, and they it is who will have brought this great storm on us with the worst of spells and witchcraft; but now we shall try which may prevail, my fortune or their devilry, so steer ye at your straightest, and I will smite these evil things with beams.'
Therewith he sang a stave:
> See I *t*roll women
> *T*wain on the billows,
> E'en they whom *H*elgi
> *H*ither hath sent.
> *E*llidi now
> Or *e*ver her way stop
> Shall *s*mite the backs
> Of these a*s*under.[77]

[74] Aho 1996, xxv–vi.
[75] Morris and Eiríkr Magnússon 1875, 16: my italics.
[76] Aho 1996, xxvi.
[77] Morris and Eiríkr Magnússon 1875, 62: my italics.

The equivalent passage in Stephens reads as follows:

> Two women see I on the back of that Whale; they it is who, with their *w*orst spells and blackest *w*itchcraft, cause this *h*orrible *h*ead-storm. Now will we try whether our fortune or their incantations avail the most; steer ye right onward as before; myself, with a *d*art-club, will bruise these evil *d*emons.' Then sang he this song:
>
> > *W*eird *w*itches see I,
> > Two, on the *w*ave there; –
> > *H*elge has sent them,
> > *H*ither to meet us:
> > Ellida shall *s*nap a-
> > *S*under i' th' middest
> > Their *b*acks, – ere o'er *b*illows
> > *B*ounds she right onward.[78]

The Icelandic text from which both poets worked reads thus, with the verse alliteration highlighted:

> konur sè ek 2 á baki hvalnum, ok munu þær valda þessum ófriðar-stormi með sínum versta seið ok göldrum; nú skulu vèr til reyna, hvort meira má, hamíngja vor, eða tröllskapr þeirra, ok skulu þið stýra at sem beinast, en ek skal með lurkum berja þessi óvætti, ok kvað vísu:
>
> > Sè ek *t*röllkonur
> > *t*vær á báru,
> > þær *h*efir *H*elgi
> > *h*íngat sendar;
> > þeim skal *s*níða
> > *s*undr í miðju
> > hrygg *E*lliði
> > *á*ðr enn *a*f för skríðr.[79]

Both translators retain the alliteration; Morris is noticeably bolder than Stephens in following the word and phrase order of the original, but it is the Stephens verse which ends with a burst of heroic energy matching the Icelandic. In the prose Stephens' greater accuracy in translating *vor* as 'our fortune' and not 'my fortune' is thematically important: Friðþjófr is a leader of men in their apparently darkest hour, whereas Morris breaks the hero's link with his crew. Stephens is also more scrupulous than Morris in retaining Icelandic present tense forms. Morris shuns Stephens's unauthorised amplification in '*worst* spells and *blackest* witchcraft' [my italics], and his extra alliterative colouring. Morris, too, finds a more telling translation for *tröllskapr* ('devilry') than the Latinate and over-specific 'incantations'; and he preserves the superlative form in 'straightest' as a translation of *beinast*, compared with Stephens's more diffuse

---

[78] Stephens 1839, 18: my italics.
[79] Rafn 1829–30, II 79: my italics.

'right onward'. The balance of evidence from this comparison of passages reminds us that Morris was not the first philologically alert Icelandicist to tackle a saga translation. In this instance, indeed, Morris's strength lies perhaps not so much in greater accuracy (or eccentricity) but in his greater restraint.

The Legacy of Laxdæla

Few Victorians had the linguistic knowledge to engage with such niceties. Philological fine-tuning was a rarified pleasure and could not match the more immediate narrative pleasures offered by the poem Morris derived from *Laxdæla saga*, 'The Lovers of Gudrun', his own favourite tale from the vast narrative corpus of his *Earthly Paradise*.[80] Largely unread today, this vast compendium of ancient stories was once 'the mainstay of mid Victorian picnics',[81] and the work that George Eliot used to take out into the woods to read out loud.[82] 'The Lovers of Gudrun' achieved particular celebrity. It was published as a separate work in the United States, enjoying great success. Morris distributed copies as gifts during his 1871 Iceland visit.[83] Its composition seems to have been a brisk labour of love; Morris claims that on a single Sunday in June 1869 he composed 728 long lines of the poem.[84] Moreover, having created in apparent haste, Morris had little reason to repent at leisure, for the poem was hugely popular. Eiríkur Magnússon points to the 'Gudrun' poem as a major reason why 'interest for [Icelandic literature] has spread into wider circles, in this country, and will continue to do so'.[85] Wider circles included women and children. W.G. Collingwood, the Iceland explorer, saga translator, and artist could read *Laxdæla saga* in Icelandic but his letters from Iceland to his wife assume that she and her children would be following his saga-stead pilgrimage in the pages of Morris's poem.[86]

It is certainly tempting to look for links between Morris's domestic woes and the series of sagas about love and romance that he translated, or put into verse paraphrase, or prepared illuminated manuscripts of. At exactly the time when his friend Rossetti was having an affair with his wife, the unhappy Morris chose to translate a series of (mostly) sad old northern love stories – *Laxdæla saga* (his unfinished translation feeds into 'The Lovers of Gudrun'),[87] *Vǫlsunga saga* (the translation, published 1870, underpins *Sigurd the Volsung*), *Kormáks saga* (completed in the 1870s though unpublished until 1970), *Víglundar saga*, *Friðþjófs*

---

[80] 'the most important thing I have written' (Kelvin 1984–96, I 82); the *Earthly Paradise* 'would have done me more credit if there had been nothing in it but Gudrun' (ibid. 100).

[81] MacCarthy 1994, 264.

[82] Ibid.

[83] Morris 1910–15, V xxxiv.

[84] Ibid., xxxiv; see also Kelvin 1984–96, I 310.

[85] Morris and Eiríkr Magnússon 1891–1905, VI x.

[86] Collingwood transcripts, WGC to his wife, 8 July 1897.

[87] Kelvin 1984–96, I 109–10.

saga, and *Gunnlaugs saga ormstungu*. Some sagas patently do not fit the pattern: the patient Friðþjófr woos and eventually wins Ingibjǫrg, with no challenge from any rival thereafter; the fixated Kormákr pursues but never marries Steingerðr; and Gunnlaugr and Hrafn kill each other. Moreover, if the parallels between Morris and Bolli in *Laxdæla* merit investigation, so do those between Morris and the eponymous hero of *Grettis saga*, not to mention Hallbjǫrn Oddsson in *Landnámabók*, characters never normally mentioned in this context.

Morris's 'Of the Wooing of Hallbiorn the Strong' poem[88] may help us in this domestic *roman à clef* context: it also offers us a striking example of Morris's transforming imagination at work when confronted with an Icelandic text. Morris found the story in the 1829 Copenhagen edition of *Landnámabók*.[89] Hallbjǫrn Oddsson is married to Hallgerðr Tungu-Oddsdóttir. In the spring Hallbjǫrn prepares to leave for home, while Tungu-Oddr, already aware that there is little love in the marriage, absents himself diplomatically. The terse *Landnámabók* entry suddenly grows expansive as it tells of Hallgerðr, seated on the dais combing her magnificent long locks of hair, wrapped in sullen silence as Hallbjǫrn announces three times that they are to leave. Tugging in vain at his disobedient wife's hair he finally draws his sword and cuts off her head. Oddr, learning of his daughter's death, asks another guest Snæbjǫrn Eyvindsson to exact revenge, which he does.

Morris transforms laconic prose into balladic verse paragraphs, each one beginning and ending with the same sad refrain about the clash between summer healing and winter strife. We find end-stopped lines, structural triads, incremental repetition, traditional alliterative doublet phrases and monosyllabic balladic vocabulary. There are no significant old northern archaisms. Whenever Victorian poets, from George Borrow to Beatrice Barmby, adopt balladic measure for saga scenes the results are invariably powerful, and its merits are easily identifiable in 'Hallbiorn the Strong'. In terms of the narrative raw material, Morris expands the early part of the *Landnámabók* entry in order to motivate Snæbiorn's role in the poem. Hallbiorn arrives with his heart set on Hallgerd, whilst her cousin Snæbiorn has a secure role in the hall as musician and craftsman, and a firm place in her affections:

> Hallgerd's hands undid his weed,
> Hallgerd's hands poured out the mead.
> Her fingers at his breast he felt,
> As her hair fell down about his belt.
> Her fingers with the cup he took,
> And o'er its rim at her did look.
> Cold cup, warm hand, and fingers slim,
> Before his eyes were waxen dim.

---

[88] Morris 1910–15, IX 95–102.

[89] Ibid., 95: subtitle, 'A Story from the Land Settling Book of Iceland, Chapter XXX'. See *Landnámabók* (Copenhagen, 1829), 116–20 (ch. 30).

> And if the feast were foul or fair,
> He knew not, save that she was there. (96)

Morris has created a love triangle where none existed in the Icelandic text. The account of the winter stay is expanded to draw attention to what it was that made the season bearable for Hallgerd: 'Dark are the days, and the nights are long, / And sweet and fair was Snæbiorn's song' (97). The narrative stage management anticipates Morris's favourite motifs and methods in his longer poems. We find a dusting of rural specificity in references to the normal life outside the fraught walls of the banqueting halls: lambs bleating and salmon swimming in Iceland, wheat growing and honey-bees flying in England, laden beasts gathered in the trading towns of Norway. There are knowing references to ancient howes which men still 'behold today'; and one senses that Morris's great hall of Tongue came within a whisker of having its walls adorned with tapestries showing the great stories of eddic gods and heroes. Seasonal change lies at the heart of the ballad. The presentation of Hallgerd, still and stubborn, seems like a trial run for the role of Gudrun in the final book of *Sigurd the Volsung*, with the sunlight on her golden hair also anticipating the interwoven patterns of such imagery in his longer poem. The *Landnámabók* beheading scene is rendered less cruelly perfunctory and more sensually suggestive: 'The bitter point was in Hallgerd's breast / That Snæbiorn's lips of love had pressed' (99). Finally, unlike the Icelandic text, Morris's Snæbiorn is not allowed to die the robust death of Hallbiorn, whose sights are set on supper with Odin. He is not even permitted the more squalid finality of dying in a squabble over money with his Viking companions. His fate points rather to a life of lonely exile in Greenland, a land without 'love alive', and a grave where 'there is nought with grief to strive' (102). Hallgerd marries the wrong man and shows him no love; her trusted lover lives on in desolation. It would require some interpretative elasticity to fit Morris's own life into all aspects of this tale of frustrated love, but, at the very least, the story represents one more variation on a painful general theme.

The case for identifying Morris himself in the figure of Bodli in 'The Lovers of Gudrun' has more substance to it, but that was not the reason that the poem enjoyed such popularity in Victorian England. 'The Lovers of Gudrun' won its readership as an arresting tale in its own right, full of narrative colour and diversity of mood. Following the example of Tegnér and Longfellow, Morris trimmed the saga down to a sequence of nineteen juxtaposed narrative episodes, like the stories painted on the panelling and roof boards at Herdholt. The opening chapters of the saga, rich in genealogical detail, in which the family background of the principal protagonists is slowly unveiled, are jettisoned, and the saga's ending is also much pared down. Morris makes no bones about why he did this:

> The saga itself is full of interesting incident, but has no pretensions to artistic unity
> . . . it is disjointed . . . and in some important places very bald, much more so than
> in any of the good translated sagas: [the saga has] coarsenesses both of manners
> and character that seemed alien to other parts of the characters therein, and

wh[ich] I thought I had a right to soften or disregard: All these things, to my mind, joining with the magnificent story made it the better subject for a poem as one could fairly say that the story had never been properly told.[90]

William Morris had no wish to play the saga on original instruments, or in following the printed score to the letter. Like the great concert pianists of his day, he chose to make the work his own.[91]

In seeking to 'tell the story properly' Morris avoids the chiselled intensity of complex lyric verse, developing instead an accessible and (in a sense) democratic style that cries out to be read out loud, just as, within the narrative frame, ancient tales entertain attentive listeners at feasts. Morris can colour a scene like the pre-Raphaelite painter he was. His style certainly exhibits 'rhyme and measure deftly intertwined',[92] elements that provide an unobtrusive controlling framework within which Morris's characteristic long-breathed sentences and paragraphs could wind their sinewy way. With his variations of narrative pace, rapid switches of (as it were) camera angle and microphone position, Morris is able to dissolve stretches of heraldic grandeur into moments of darting unease. In character descriptions Morris, like his beloved Chaucer, deploys a slippery but suggestive vocabulary of moral appraisal. Thus, when Kjartan meets Gudrun for the first time upon his return to Iceland, what is the reader to make of 'He smiled upon her *kindly*' (322; my italics)? The forms 'kind', 'kindness' and 'kindly' appear thereafter a dozen times over ten pages (330–9) and sound ambiguously through the rest of the poem. Morris's diction exploits old northern vocabulary shrewdly, yet distanced solemnity is achieved more by contractions, elliptical word order, unfamiliar past tense formations, and even by using 'a' as the indefinite object form before a vowel.

So it is in the scene when Gudrun stands at the door of Bathstead, longing for Kjartan to return. Her 'wide' and (it need hardly be added) 'grey' eyes gaze southwards:

> Until upon the wind she seemed to hear
> The sound of horse-hoofs, and 'twixt hope and fear
> She trembled, as more clear the far sounds grew;
> And thitherward it seemed from Herdhold drew;
> So now at last to meet that sound she went,
> Until her eyes, on the hill's brow intent,
> Beheld a spear rising against the sky
> O'er the grey road, and therewith presently
> A gilded helm rose up beneath the spear,
> And then her trembling limbs no more might bear
> Her body forward; scarce alive she stood,
> And saw a man in raiment red as blood

[90] Kelvin 1984–96, I 109–10.
[91] For reservations, see Ellison 1972, 159–66.
[92] Morris 1910–15, V 274.

Rise o'er the hill's brow, who when he did gain
The highest part of the grey road, drew rein
To gaze on Bathstead spreading 'neath him there,
Its bright vanes glittering in the morning air.
She stared upon him panting, and belike
He saw her now, for he his spurs did strike
Into his horse, and, while her quivering face
Grew hard and stern, rode swiftly to the place
Whereas she stood, and clattering leapt adown
Unto the earth, and met her troubled frown
And pale face, with the sad imploring eyes
Of Bodli Thorleikson. (305)

In terms of the presentation of the heroine, quivering in anticipation of her lover's return, it is not as the saga has it, nor as some late twentieth-century readers might wish it. In terms of narrative artistry, however, even if not every rift is loaded with ore, a deft practitioner is unquestionably at work here. The vacant gazing, the distant noise of hoofs, the instant bewildered reaction, the growing sense that the horses are heading towards her home, the spear on the brow of the hill, followed by the helmet, and finally the bloody red raiment set against the (as ever) grey[93] road and reminiscent of sunsets in the Icelandic Journals. We then find the rider pausing to gaze on Bathstead's glittering roof; the first moment of mutual recognition; the speed of the rider set against the stillness of Gudrun; troubled frown meets sad imploring eyes, and Gudrun (her hopes cruelly thwarted) meets Bodli.[94]

While the poem follows the main contours of the saga respectfully, some areas of conflict are heightened. We note, for instance, that when Kjartan (already betrothed to Gudrun and anxious to win renown overseas) and Bodli go abroad, Bodli is shown to be already furtively lusting after his friend's beloved. Indeed, throughout the poem, the character of Bodli – passionate, jealous, self-abnegating, the prisoner of a loveless marriage that he had schemed to bring about and lived to regret – is probed with such energy and sympathy that readings of the poem which identify Rossetti and Morris as Kjartan and Bodli do little injury to the poem. Guðrún's vengefulness towards Kjartan in the saga is largely transferred to her brothers in the poem, so that the presentation of the heroine retains its emotional decorum. The poem thus loses the famous and memorable exchange (at least as printed in the 1826 Copenhagen edition from which Morris worked)[95] when Bolli returns to report his killing of

---

[93] Grey is everywhere in the poem: the ewes at Herdholt (Morris 1910–15, V 262) and Freyia's cats on the tapestries (263); the skies when Kjartan first sailed away from Gudrun (287); the eyes of Gudrun (305, 334, 340) and Refna (321); Gudrun's stirring passion is like a 'grey dove' caught in a net (310); Kjartan confronts Gudrun as Bodli's bride at Bathstead on a grey day (323); the stones (356–7) behind which Refna hides on overhearing gossip about Kjartan's cowardliness; and Gudrun's grey face and the grey porch to which Bodli returns having killed Kjartan (382).

[94] See, too, Kjartan's eventual return: Morris 1910–15, V 327–8.

[95] The text remains problematic: Ólafur Halldórsson 1990, 271–4, Louis-Jensen 1993.

Kjartan and hears Guðrún announcing cheerfully that 'Harm spurs on to hard deeds (work); I have spun yarn for twelve ells of homespun and you have killed Kjartan'.[96] It is replaced by one of Morris's 'glooming' dusk scenes, with the 'faint noises of gathering night', the 'faint clink of mail-rings' give way to the 'dead hush of the hall', soon to be shattered by Gudrun's grief-stricken shriek (383–4).

We recall, from the final stanza of 'Gunnar's Howe', Morris's fondness for the gloaming light of Icelandic summer nights. Never is this better exploited than in the hideous confrontation between Bodli and Gudrun, once the truth of Kjartan's return to Iceland has been digested. The hall lights go out one by one until just a single flame casts its eerie glow, making 'the well-known things as strange as death' (329); the last breath of the summer breeze and the final glimmerings of a summer night are felt or seen through the windows; Bodli hears footsteps, and a figure stands beside him in the 'half dusk of the departing night'; Bodli is paralysed in wind and limb, and night cannot protect him from the lash of Gudrun's thrice cursing tongue; he longs for death, and she underlines the intensity of her love for Kjartan; as the wildfowl signal the dawn of another desolate day, their eyes meet and Bodli reaches helplessly towards her – only for Gudrun to flee:

> And left him 'twixt the dark night and the day,
> 'Twixt good and ill, 'twixt love and struggling hate,
> The coming hours of restless pain to wait. (331)

William Morris grew up at a time when narrative poetry could still teach lessons to the aspiring young writer: atmospheric description, the use of omniscient narration, motif deployment, and flexibility in the presentation of speech and conversation. In his case the lessons had been well learnt.

Through all the buzz and flux of incident and emotion in the poem, its overall shape is unmistakably a mighty old northern struggle between fate and human free will, in which virtue resides as much in the capacity of humans to cope with the blows fashioned by fate, as in their capacity to fashion destiny with their own hands. Fatalism shadows the story from the long opening sequence in which Guest the soothsayer foretells the fate of Gudrun's four husbands, and then at Herdholt when, tearfully, he senses the bloody fate of Bodli and Kjartan as the two youths play happily together. Guest explains the significance of Gudrun's dreams, each relating to a future husband who will die before his time. But to foreknow is not to evade; it involves rather bearing a greater burden than those who live in blissful ignorance:

---

[96] Press 1899, 178; compare Howard 1902, 101, 'Believe me, / I shall go home and spin twelve ells of yarn, / Deeming my day well spent, – and yours, my husband'; also Proctor 1903, 161, 'Mickle Prowess hath been done; I have spun yarn for twelve ells, and thou hast slain Kjartan'. Proctor died in an Alpine climbing accident in 1903 – 'like many a Viking wanderer in the days of old, no man knows how he perished, or where his body lies': *Saga-Book* 3 (1901–3), 489.

> Yet little from my foresight shalt thou win,
> Since both the blind, and they who see full well,
> Go the same road, and leave a tale to tell
> Of interwoven miseries, lest they
> Who after them a while on earth must stay,
> Should have no pleasure in the winter night,
> When this man's pain is made that man's delight. (258)

Through Guest's words Morris voices a central concern in his artistic and personal engagement with the old north. The deeds and suffering of fated heroes, through the toiling hands of the saga man, can bring pleasure to (or at least can stiffen the resolve of) later generations whose own winter nights would otherwise stretch joylessly ahead.

Morris knew that this was true in his own life and the poem is ever alert to variations on the theme. We see Guest visiting Herdholt. The 'new-built hall' is a place of peace and plenty and industry; the cloth-room, the buttery, the women's chamber as well as the main hall catch the eye in the cool and dusk of evening; we see Flemish linen and English honey, wine casks and cloth presses, silks and silver and gold. On the high panelling and roof-boards Guest's eyes rest on 'noble stories, painted fair'. But these are tales of eddic myth, of the vulnerability and eventual doom of the gods:

> And Heimdall, with the gold horn slung behind,
> That in the God's-dusk he shall surely wind,
> Sickening all hearts with fear; and last of all
> Was Odin's sorrow wrought upon the wall,
> As slow-paced, weary-faced, he went along,
> Anxious with all the tales of woe and wrong
> His ravens, Thought and Memory, bring to him. (263)

Guest knows that the real Norse gods cannot be contained within a tapestry for the pleasure of uninvolved onlookers. The gods gaze down on Laxdale, just as Morris shows them shadowing the tracks of the Volsungs in *Sigurd the Volsung*. The soothsayer understands Odin's burden of suffering; he shares it as much as any human can. Within a hundred lines he has spotted Kjartan and Bodli dressing in their grey clothes, sitting on a grey rock, with Kjartan clutching a grey blade, and, he tearfully tells his son, long after he (Guest) is under a grey cairn, that these two youths will destroy each other (267). Guest tells his son to 'be blind' but the father must walk on all-knowing, all-seeing, and ever helpless.

In the poem characters recognise and even relish the responsibilities which they bear. Indeed, they behave as if conscious of how their fate will read in some subsequent saga account to be retold at some later feast in some other hall. Thus Kjartan rouses his worried companions as he proposes defiance to King Olaf Tryggvason during their Norwegian captivity: the worst that can happen 'shall be a tale to tell / Ere all is o'er' and 'How shall it be when folk our story tell / If we die grey-haired' (292, 293). Or again, Bodli tells Kjartan that if the worst comes to the worst in Trondheim, they must die together.

> as in Atli's Hall
> The Niblungs fell; nor worser will it sound
> That thus it was, when we are underground,
> And over there our Gudrun hears the tale. (295)

Yet Bodli knew, better than anyone, that he and Kjartan were far from being as inseparable as Gunnarr and Hǫgni, and that the phrase 'our Gudrun' meant different things to each of them. When Bodli returns to Iceland and meets Gudrun, she rejoices that Kjartan is 'Alive and well! / And doing deeds whereof the skalds shall tell!' (306). When urged by his father once more to visit Bathstead, Kjartan's fatalism is again expressed in terms of the emerging story in which he finds himself trapped as a character:

> 'Well,' Kiartan said, 'if so I deemed, that fate
> Might be turned back of men, or foolish hate
> Die out for lack of fuel, no more would I
> Unto the Bathstead hall-door draw anigh;
> But forasmuch as now I know full well,
> That the same story there shall be to tell
> Whether I go, or whether I refrain,
> Let all be as thou wilt . . .' (350)

Later, as Bodli sets off for his final fateful assault on Kjartan, he bids Gudrun farewell – 'Of me, too, shall there be a tale to tell' (363), and indeed in 'The Lovers of Gudrun' the brooding fantasies of Bodli receive far more attention than in the saga. In the scene of Kjartan's death there are past, present and future tales criss-crossing each other everywhere (372–3).

This accumulated evidence from 'The Lovers of Gudrun' anticipates precisely the point that Morris was to make in 'Gunnar's Howe'. There is a noble sequence of narrative transmission and reception in which each element has its 'part in that great sorrow', each has its own validity, each participant is aware of what has gone before and of what comes afterwards. The sequence takes in hero and heroine; heroic deeds; oral transmission of accounts of such deeds; the creation of a more permanent record by saga-men, artists, weavers of tapestries; transmission of sagas through the work of scribes; the eventual emergence of scholarly editions as scribal texts are sifted by eighteenth- and nineteenth-century editors; the use of one such edition to create a narrative poem based on a saga; visits to the saga sites by enthusiastic readers of saga and poem; a poem written to mark a visit to such a site; the celebration by later poets of that and other works; the publication of an Icelandic *Reader* featuring as its largest edited extract a section of the saga in question;[97] two translations of the saga including one by a close disciple of the poet;[98] the dissemination of translated extracts in

---

[97] Gudbrand Vigfusson and Powell 1879, 20–82.
[98] Press 1899, Proctor 1903.

school books;[99] a play staged in London based on one of the two translations.[100] This was the life cycle of *Laxdœla saga* from its misty origins in medieval Iceland to the gas lights of Drury Lane in Edwardian London.

Though the eddic gods are confined to the Herdholt tapestries and to Kjartan's song on his final journey, the fixity of fate which they embody lies at the heart of 'The Lovers of Gudrun'. Each of the principal characters strives to play the role that fate has assigned them. *Sigurd The Volsung*, based on *Vǫlsunga saga*, 'that most glorious of stories',[101] investigates these same struggles on an even grander epic scale.

'It is the greatest book': Sigurd the Volsung

Morris's initial view of *Vǫlsunga saga*, in the summer of 1869, was that it was 'rather of the monstrous order',[102] but he soon found himself 'swallowed up' with its grandeur, tenderness and tragedy.[103] He also admired the eddic poems based on the same tales: 'the 1st lay of Gudrun (her lament over Sigurd dead): it is a wonderful poem, entirely free from any affectation or quaintness, as simple and direct as the finest classical poems'.[104] He found a publisher for his translation of the saga, and remained on the lookout for sympathetic reviewers: 'the public are shy of Icelandic books and can't tell what the book may be by the title'.[105] Though initially reluctant to write a poem based on the saga,[106] by 1876 the 306 pages and 11,000 lines of *Sigurd the Volsung* were ready for the reading public, from whom it received mixed notices. Swinburne loathed the poem as much as he had liked 'The Lovers of Gudrun',[107] but Charles Sayle thought that it was simply wonderful:

> I casually took up Morris's 'Sigurd the Volsung' the other night about 8 o'clock just after dinner, not having read it but always having meant to. It so 'got possession of me' in the reading that I did not stop from my labours until 7 o'clock next morning when I finished the whole epic from beginning to end in one sitting of eleven hours! It is the greatest book – as new books go nowadays – that I have read for many many months. As a work of art it is one of the most perfect that I have ever read.[108]

---

[99] Speight and Major 1905, 53–70 (the tale of Melkorka). See also Eiríkur Magnússon's translation of Torfhildur Hólm's play *Kjartan og Guðrún*, perhaps used as a teaching text in Cambridge: Lbs. 2182 4to.

[100] Howard 1902.

[101] Kelvin 1984–96, I 344.

[102] Ibid., 89.

[103] Ibid., 99.

[104] Ibid., 110.

[105] Ibid., 119; the addressee was the critic Sidney Colvin.

[106] Ibid., 98–9.

[107] Lang 1959–62, IV 307: AS to Theodore Watts, 13 October 1882.

[108] Lbs. 2188a 4to, Charles Sayle to EM, 30 January 1887; see also Kelvin 1984–96, I 552.

By the end of the century it had achieved school textbook status;[109] and, as we noted in Chapter 6, amongst the prescribed homework topics in a school edition of tales from *Njáls saga* we find pupils being invited to rewrite a scene from the saga in 'the metre of Sigurd the Volsung'.[110]

There is nothing childish about the poem itself. At the end of 'Iceland first seen' Morris ponders the day 'when Balder comes back' bringing peace and healing to Iceland. Unlike Tegnér Morris seems strangely reluctant to embrace the possibility:

> Ah! when thy Balder comes back and we gather the gains he hath won,
> Shall we not linger a little to talk of thy sweetness of old,
> Yea, turn back awhile to thy travail whence the Gods stood aloof to behold?[111]

And what was this 'sweetness' and 'travail' of old Iceland which Morris and his fellow Icelandophiles expect to linger over? It stands identified as the poet addresses the land:

> O Queen of the grief without knowledge, of the courage that may not avail
> Of the longing that may not attain, of the love that shall never forget,
> More joy than the gladness of laughter thy voice hath amidst of its wail:
> More hope than of pleasure fulfilled amidst thy blindness is set;
> More glorious than gaining of all thine unfaltering hand that shall fail:
> For what is the mark on thy brow but the brand that thy Brynhild doth bear?
> Lone once, and loved and undone by a love that no ages outwear.

Grief without knowledge, unattainable longings, wailing, blindness, failure of the unfaltering hand, unavailing courage, the sorrow of timeless and unforgettable love: all these are to be found in full measure in *Sigurd the Volsung*, with the 'brand' of Brynhild bearing its full weight of responsibility.

Sigurd leaves the Iceland of 'The Lovers of Gudrun' far behind. Its settings combine tapestried richness with mythic vagueness. The solid splendour of the hall in Lymdale dissolves into the crystalline eeriness of Brynhild's residence; peaceful rural English landscapes change within a few lines into impenetrable forest and then into nightmarish grey moonscapes which recall the lava wastes described in Morris's Iceland Journals. Time of day and season of year, too, swirl giddily past characters as they struggle for a toe-hold on existence; it is as if, in their world, the only constant is mutability. For every moment spent in the secure hierarchies of hall life, there are others to be devoted to travelling in defiant splendour to hostile lands, with their icy invitations, hollow welcomes, and treacherous inversions of civilised life. At every stage and on every page, readers are reminded that 'Heavy and hard are the Norns: but each man his

---

[109] Morris 1905. Lang 1890, 357–67 was a much abbreviated version of the tale, based on Morris's poem.
[110] Dasent 1917, 123.
[111] Morris 1910–15, IX 126.

burden bears'.[112] Within the poem most individuals bear these burdens with dignity and stoicism. The 'gleaming-grey' (6, 68) kirtled Odin hovers over the action throughout the poem, observing the heroes in their spring-time glory, and, like Morris's Gunnar, in their harvest-time fall (69).[113] Morris caters to the Victorian fondness for images of the sea-going Viking. Sigmund and Sinfjotli spend their due share of time on the 'swan-bath' (17) in their 'golden dragons' (66); and visiting sea-kings raise a howe for King Sigmund (73). Yet when the treacherous King Siggeir seeks to buy off the Volsungs' voyage of vengeance, the rebuke to Viking freebooting is unmistakable:

> 'Nay no such men are we,
> No tuggers at the hawser, no wasters of the sea:
> We will have the gold and the purple when we list such things to win;
> But now we think on our fathers, and avenging of our kin.' (50)[114]

Later in the poem, Sigurd, by now renowned for his commitment to justice ('the sheaf shall be for the plougher, and the loaf for him that sowed'; 203), rides with the Niblungs to 'chase the sons of plunder that curse the ocean-side', and a fully-fledged battle ensues (209–10). Yet if the poem presents both sides of the Viking case, the dragon ships in which they sail lie at the heart of the narrator's memorable image of making and enduring with which the poem's first book ends. Sigmund's home, with its high-seat, hangings and harps appears to have been 'fashioned in vain'. The king is dead and his loyal kin have perished. But life often stubbornly reasserts itself – as in the construction of a Viking long-ship:

> Lo, the noble oak of the forest with his feet in the flowers and grass, . . .
> And there it stands in the forest, an exceeding glorious thing:
> Then come the axes of men, and low it lies on the ground,
> And the crane comes out of the southland, and its nest is nowhere found,
> And bare and shorn of its blossoms is the house of the deer of the wood.
> But the tree is a golden dragon; and fair it floats on the flood,
> And beareth the kings and the earl-folk, and is shield-hung all without:
> And it seeth the blaze of the beacons, and heareth the war-God's shout.
> There are tidings wherever it cometh, and the tale of its time shall be told.
> A dear name it hath got like a king, and a fame that groweth not old. (74).

Man culls to create, as the furniture catalogue of Morris's firm confirmed.

Images of tale telling in *Sigurd* perform a related function. Stories created about the fallen king and of Sinfjotli live on in the ears of his widow as she weans the newly-born Sigurd (85). And, in due time, it is in order to provide material for future songs, and to replenish the ranks of heroes in Valhalla, that

---

112 Morris 1877, 14.
113 The death of Sigmund's troop who fall 'like seeded hay / Before the brown scythes' sweeping'.
114 Sigurd rode with the Niblungs to 'chase the sons of plunder that curse the ocean-side' (209).

the youthful Sigurd longs to explore the wide world 'filled with deeds unwrought'. (93) Like Dasent's Beorn the Welshman he is no 'acre-bider' (87); home can no more hold him than a hazel copse can hold the light of the morning sun (87, 89). Even when he knows his fate, not to follow his star, not to face the 'ash-grey' Fafnir, would be to conspire in some destructive process of regression which could consume the civilised world:

> 'Arise, O Sigurd, lest the hour be overlate!
> For the sun in the mid-noon shineth, and swift is the hand of Fate:
> Arise! lest the world run backward and the blind heart have its will,
> And once again be tangled the sundered good and ill;
> Lest love and hatred perish, lest the world forget its tale,
> And the Gods themselves sit deedless, dreaming, in the high-walled heavenly vale.'
>
> (149)

Stasis was not an option for a hero, except the drugged paralysis arising from Grimhild's baleful love potion; and nor was solitude amidst the bleak 'ash-grey' landscape of the Glittering Heath (153). For all the dangers to which it exposes him, Sigurd needs contact with

> The house and the ship and the island, the loom and the mine and the stall,
> The beds of bane and healing, the crafts that slay and save,
> The temple of God and the Doom-ring, the cradle and the grave. (165)

His approach to Lymdale brings the great hero to an idyllic spring-season world of rural contentment described in language sometimes reminiscent of eighteenth-century pastoral verse (180). Sigurd, 'in mighty honour holden' after his triumphant return from his slaying of Regin, seeks out wild forest bulls and lonely wolves for want of greater stimulus in that time of peace:

> For as then no other warfare do the lords of Lymdale know,
> And the axe-age and the sword-age seem dead a while ago,
> And the age of the cleaving of shields, and of brother by brother slain,
> And the bitter days of the whoredom, and the hardened lust of gain. (184)

No Victorian reader familiar with the overall shape of the eddic myths, and with the significance of our Chapter Seven benchmark lines echoed here, would need reminding that *Voluspá* refers not to a past that will never return, as the folk of Lymdale believed, but rather to a future from which none may escape. It thus marks a fateful moment in the poem. It is while out riding in the meadows that Sigurd's falcon flies off over the ramparts of a castle, and lands on the window of Brynhild's gold-roofed residence. It is in pursuit of the bird that Sigurd encounters Brynhild for the first time since their fateful meeting on the hero's way home from the dragon slaying. The pledges of love and loyalty made then are now renewed with great lyricism and sensuality and are thereafter subjected to every test that fate and human malevolence can contrive. As repeated references over the remainder of the poem confirm, the threat of an axe-age and sword-age is ever present, and so is the hideous familial betrayal signified in 'brother by brother slain'. When Gunnar's horse refuses to brave the flame wall, he rails at the forces responsible, whoever they are – his fosterbrother Sigurd, his younger siblings, his mother, 'Or thou, O God of the Goths, wilt thou hide and laugh thy fill, / While the hands of the fosterbrethren the blood of brothers spill?' (240). At the end of her life, Brynhild summons Gunnar, her husband only by guile, her beloved Sigurd's killer by design. She describes a dream she has had and a voice she has heard:

> 'O woe for the broken troth,
> And the heavy Need of the Niblungs, and the Sorrow of Odin the Goth!
> Then I saw the halls of the strangers, and the hills and the dark-blue sea,
> Nor knew of their names and their nations, for earth was afar from me,
> But brother rose up against brother, and blood swam over the board,
> And women smote and spared not, and the fire was master and lord . . .' (306)

Foreshadowed here is treachery towards Sigurd's brothers-in-law Gunnar and Hogni, and the final conflagration that overwhelms her last home and resting-place:

> Like breedeth like in his house, and venom, and guile, and the knife
> Oft lie 'twixt brother and brother, and the son and the father's life. (327)

With the sulphurous elements of sexual jealousy and frustration, sibling rivalry, maternal possessiveness, and family vengefulness brought together and allowed to ferment towards the end of the poem's third book, familiar narrative motifs take on new significance. Tale-telling sequences, whether woven into a tapestry, sung by minstrels at an evening feast, or pondered by individuals in private, are a case in point. When adorning the halls or entertaining the hall-dwellers in times of peace, the tales represent a celebration of the prowess of the tribe, and a kind of mission statement about future conduct. Sigurd's errant hawk leads its master to Brynhild who is weaving a tapestry that records once again the hero's life and triumphs. Sigurd's whole life stands eerily in front of him, stretched out on the loom (187). The still unwoven threads will eventually tell of his visit to Niblung country, home of the snare-spinning, net-weaving Grimhild, Gudrun's mother, from whose 'cunning' there are no eagle voices to save him. When Brynhild and Gudrun meet while swimming, Sigurd's heroic deeds are rehearsed again, but Gudrun's version includes, for the first time in the poem, an additional deadly revelation that Sigurd had undertaken Gunnar's wooing of Brynhild for him (267). It comes as no surprise that Gudrun's curse (303), seeking to fix the future, soon takes the place of tapestries and tale-telling about the past.

But the final images of *Sigurd the Volsung* are not of humans fashioning their own destinies. They show instead, firstly, Grimhild's belated and helpless realisation (reminiscent of that of Norna of the Fitful Head) that long-term control of others is beyond her powers; and, secondly, that heroes are more comfortable when reacting than when creating. The folly, small-mindedness and wilfulness which create the confusions are forgotten. There remains time only for courage, always in abundant supply amongst Volsungs and Niblungs alike. Atli's hall represents a stage on which, with Gudrun's ashen face and deafening silence as the backdrop, Gunnar and Hogni can die the deaths and create the raw material for tales to be told and woven for the generations to come. The brothers are unrepentant, dignified, and content to submit to the ultimate decrees of the gods.

An Old Northern Socialist

Morris found the raw material for his narrative poems in Iceland, but did he also find his socialism there? A remark from Morris's self-portrait written for the benefit of the Austrian refugee socialist Andreas Scheu has assumed canonical importance in recent discussions: 'I learned one lesson there [in Iceland], thoroughly I hope, that the most grinding poverty is a trifling evil compared with the inequality of classes.'[115] Morris told a lecture audience in 1887 that there was no disgrace attached to manual work in Iceland and 'no class of degradation'.[116] If it were indeed the case that visiting Iceland had been the key moment in the political awakening of one of Britain's pioneering practical socialist activists, this would indeed be an important additional colour to the rainbow of political allegiances reflected amongst other Victorian old northernists: Stanley the Whiggish gentleman in rural retreat; Stephens the fiery ex-patriate brother of a Chartist-sympathising methodist; Carlyle the Tory patriarch; Dasent the Darwinian maverick. Yet, though Morris's socialism is not in doubt, its putative Icelandic origin seems less certain on the evidence of his written works. Morris's Iceland Journals have no substantive references to the 'trifling evil' of poverty.[117] Instead we read of Morris's impatience (136) with comically unreliable service from the Co-operative organisation in Reykjavík (25–7), to be set alongside his subsequent claim that the solution to Iceland's economic ills lay in the promotion of 'the simplest form of co-operative commonwealth'.[118] We may also note Morris's bouts of dissatisfaction with the service provided by district guides (64, 87); his obsession with lice whenever forced to enter a farmer's house (44, 81); and the disdain directed at an 'unsavoury idiot' at Barkarstaðir (56, 206), a bellows-blower in Hrutafjörður (103), and a 'vulgar Danish Jew' in Stykkishólmur (123). The nameless peasantry function in the Journals as a deeply recessed background presence, like the *huldufolk* of folklore, who either service the everyday needs of the riders (a saddle-maker; a smith: 58), or who abandon their

[115] Kelvin 1984–96, II 229, 15 September 1883; cited by MacCarthy in Morris 1996, xi.
[116] Le Mire 1969, 181, 184–5: 1887 lecture at Kelmscott House, Hammersmith.
[117] Though see Morris 1910–15, VIII 99, 113.
[118] Le Mire 1969, 198.

scythes momentarily to watch the great English skald pass grandly (and incuriously) by (29, 57, 225, 227).[119] If all men were equal in Iceland, Morris's progress brought him frequently into contact with those who were more equal than others. It was hard to learn much about 'degradation' when the poet was forever the guest of merchants (36, 101, 144), sheriffs (59), well-situated priests (40, 63, 114, 147), doctors (89–93), and friends of Eiríkur Magnússon (96, 99, 107, 120). Even amongst those 'bonders' with whom he meets and talks, we find that one in Víðidalur had spent time in Scotland, was fluent in English, and was discontented with the Iceland to which he returned (94); that another owned no less than 200 ewes and was considered to be 'rich' (209); that a third was 'somewhat of a magnate, a man who could trace his direct descent to a "landnámsman" ' (96) and had a collection of antique pewter, fine silver and tapestries, and seventeenth-century manuscripts including Morris's beloved Vǫlsunga saga. Morris and his party can hardly be blamed for the inevitably limited nature of their exposure to the warp and weft of Icelandic society. But self-authenticating political testimonies built on such brittle memories and undernourished understandings ought perhaps to be taken with a pinch of Icelandic nose tobacco. Happily, when told by Eiríkur Magnússon of the distress triggered by famine in Iceland 1875 and 1882, Morris's reaction was not to see the directly ensuing poverty as 'trifling' but to raise money with characteristic verve and generosity of spirit.[120]

Yet it may be that at least one other set of references from the Iceland Journals does point to the kind of strongly-localised, democratic community life which Morris favoured in his late prose romances. During his Laxárdalur travels, Morris visits 'Auð's Thingstead and doom-ring' (111); in the Rangá district he visits mounds that he believes represent 'Thingbooths' and a further circular mound 'presumably the doom-ring' (195). The Íslendingasögur have few specific references to 'doom-rings' but Morris knew one of them well. In Eyrbyggja saga the narrator (in Morris and Eiríkur Magnússon's translation) states at one point:

> There is yet to be seen the Doom-ring, where men were doomed to the sacrifice. In that ring stands the stone of Thor over which those men were broken who were sacrificed, and the colour of the blood on that stone is yet to be seen.[121]

Here the doom-ring is associated with religious sacrifice. In Sigurd the Volsung a similar location is the hallowed spot where Sigurd and the Niblung brothers swear oaths of allegiance. It is the place of royal law where, particularly when Sigurd is present, the poor man can rely on due justice as 'the tangle straighteneth before him, and the maze of crooked things'.[122] Elsewhere in the poem it

---

[119] Haymakers who ignore the passing Englishmen are commented on: Morris 1910–15, VIII 43.
[120] See Harris 1978–81, Ellison 1987–8.
[121] Morris and Eiríkr Magnússon 1891–1905, II 18.
[122] Morris 1877, 233.

is the place 'for the sifting of troublous things' (275) by the royal participants. It is by no means a people's court and it seems not always to command universal assent; Sigurd is unique in the trust that he enjoys from ordinary folk (278). Morris's late balladic piece 'The Folk-Mote by the River',[123] celebrates such sites and traditions – outdoors, accessible, in touch with land and folk. People can gather, watch, listen, react and feel involved. In the poem, against a background of Chaucerian spring freshness, and guided by a venerable figure speaking from the Elders' Mound, people resolve to fight the oppression of the feudal Earl Hugh, and secure their freedom, albeit that some will perish in the struggle. They will bow the knee to God in heaven but to no-one on earth. Morris celebrates this resolve in ballad metre whose traditional folk roots make it an ideal non-feudal medium of expression.[124] In *The Roots of the Mountains* (1889), though the Doom-ring functions as a place of religious observance, private oaths, and avowals between lovers, its role is also judicial and political, as tribal customary law is promoted and decisions about common action are made. It stands at the heart of the hallowed 'Folk-mote' sites used by the people of Burgstead and Silverdale.[125] In *The Roots of the Mountains* people gather to discuss how best to protect their 'fellowship' from the threat of 'mastery' posed by the predatory Dusky Riders from outside their territory.[126] The decisions are made in common, acted on with courage, and the traditions of freedom are successfully defended. The dead are honoured at the Doom-ring site and the lovers united.

Morris's old northern romance world may have been of indeterminate location, but at every turn its narrative style recalls if not Icelandic sagas then perhaps the kind of common old northern style that existed in the minds of George Stephens and Morris. The tale shows neighbouring tribes united through marriage of their young folk (Face-of-God and Sun-Beam), and it dramatises a form of localised decision making and dispute resolution in which both leaders and led have a part to play. Such distant ideals energised Morris during his decade of service to the emerging socialist cause in Britain. How pure in form and attractive in spirit the folk-mote ideal must have seemed after a decade of mind-numbing tedium and fractiousness at meetings of the Socialist League, the Socialist Union, the Social-Democratic Federation, the Hammersmith Socialist Society, the Committee of Socialist Bodies, the Orthodox Anarchists, the Fabians, the Collectivists, and all the other gatherings which he took

---

[123] Morris 1910–15, IX 169–76. In this politicised vision, set in rural England, the people unite to resist Earl Hugh's oppression, and secure their freedom.

[124] Morris 1910–15, XXIII 52, 'Feudal England' (1888) – a few ballad stanzas are better than 'a cartload of whining introspective lyrics of to-day'.

[125] Longman's Pocket Library edition (1913), I 11, 119, 133; II 187, 229.

[126] Morris 1910–15, XXIII 58 argues that the final socialist workers' revolution will ensure the end of 'mastery' and the triumph of 'fellowship'.

the trouble to attend and address. During this period of draughty committee room service Morris will have needed no reminding that the fissure between the ideals of Viking-age decision making and the Victorian realities was an unbridgeable *ginnungagap*.

SECTION FOUR

LIVING THE OLD NORTH

CHAPTER TEN

Travels, Trips and Trots

The Saga-student . . . had better content himself with reading; . . . the phenomenon of the Thingfield [Þingvellir] . . . has not an interesting feature.
(W.G. Lock 1882, 70)

Why do we long to wend forth through the length and breadth of a land,
Dreadful with grinding of ice, and record of scarce hidden fire,
But that there 'mid the grey grassy dales sore scarred by the ruining streams
Lives the tale of the Northland of old and the undying glory of dreams?
(William Morris 1891)[1]

[Iceland] is to-day a living Pompeii where the northmen races can read their past.
(Jón Stefánsson 1907, 294)

Travel, Tourism and Pilgrimage

In his glowing 1861 review of Dasent's *Burnt Njal* Robert Lowe, Viscount Sherbrooke, notes that Njáll's home at Bergþórshvoll stood very near Portland Head, a staging point site for the proposed Transatlantic electronic telegraph.[2] Charles Forbes's 1860 Iceland travel book also links the saga-age with the new technology. Instantaneous communication between Europe and Canada, via Britain, the Faroe Islands, Iceland, and Norway would be a modern symbol of the ancient unity between northern kith and kin. Such a link could buttress traditional freedoms against assault and infiltration from the priest-ridden despotism of southern Europe, and the 'tyrannising' democracy of the United States.[3] Forbes's sentiments are echoed in speeches at a Southampton banquet honouring the departure for northern waters of a survey expedition. A Danish naval officer reports his monarch's pleasure that Danish dominions were to provide landfall for the cable; and that the line will connect people of the same racial origin – at one end will be the Scandinavians, 'from whom descended the Anglo-Saxons, and at the other end their descendants, the Americans

---

[1] From 'Iceland first seen'; quoted from Morris 1910–15, IX 125.
[2] Lowe 1861, 436.
[3] Forbes 1860, 334.

(applause)'.[4] In Hans Christian Andersen's fairy tale the new cable was just an alien sea-snake irritating the indigenous fish on the sea-bed;[5] but for the Danish king and his young naval officer, for a British traveller to Iceland, and for a senior British political figure reviewing a new saga translation, issues of imperial pride, national prestige, and cultural self-definition were involved all the way along the line.

Forbes and other Victorian travellers to Scandinavia and Iceland knew that Viking-age sailing routes had once followed much the same paths now marked out for the cable, but they also understood the difference between instant telegraphic contact, and days of hazardous sailing before medieval travellers from Nidaros or Kirkwall could shake hands with kith and kin in Tórshavn, or Reykjavík, or Brattahlíð – or L'Anse aux Meadows. Victorian travellers had much swifter and somewhat safer vessels, but for all the talk of Iceland's popularity among the 'Cockney trip' class of tourist,[6] travel to the saga-steads of the north was not to be lightly undertaken. In 1834 the Honourable Arthur Dillon, discovering that there were no direct sailings between Iceland and Great Britain, arrived in Copenhagen just too late to catch one of two vessels departing for the north – he heard later that one ship had foundered and the other was long overdue.[7] The advent of steamships around 1870 did not remove the dangers. H. Rider Haggard, on his way home from Iceland with his head full of images for his Viking-age novel *Eric Brighteyes*, was lucky to escape with his life when the *Copeland* sank off the Orkneys in late July 1888.[8] Yet such dangers were part of the challenge to travellers from the land of Drake, Frobisher and Nelson – or 'Njalson' as one *Burnt Njal* reviewer called him.[9] That Victorian gentlemen sailors, 'modern Vikings' every one,[10] were eager to voyage north and explore the coasts of Norway and Iceland was seen as a favourable reflection on the mettle of the nation's youth. At a time when the traditional European tour could seem merely 'insipid', Iceland represented a worthy challenge which the 'dandy order of tourists'[11] would do well to avoid. In the competitive market of Victorian travelling, as the Alps became a penny share, Iceland assumed blue chip status.

Not everyone travelling to the south of Europe would have regarded themselves as 'dandies', or their Italian or Grecian explorations as insipid. Many would have resisted the label 'tourists', insisting instead on the more prestigious term 'travellers'. For a century and more European travel had been a serious business.[12] It involved exhaustive preparatory reading; travellers needed to be

4 [anon. 2] 1861, 58.
5 Andersen 1974, 1006–14.
6 Burton 1875, I xii.
7 Dillon 1840, 1; see also Hooker 1813, I ii–iii.
8 Ponzi 1995, 41.
9 Nicolson 1861, 303.
10 Scott 1863, 460.
11 Ibid., 459–60.
12 Batten 1978.

well versed on all the famous sites, and (having consulted their pocket editions of Byron)[13] to feel all the right feelings at each location; the urge to travel quickly in order to complete the itinerary had to be balanced against the fear of rushing heedlessly past a significant site. They understood the importance of locating the 'fugitive essence' of a foreign land.[14] Dedicated travellers tended to adopt the role of the disdainful anti-tourist, securing credit for undertaking difficult journeys at a time when the Thomas Cook culture was making foreign travel easier. They sought out ever more remotely located antiquities, and made travelling into a kind of competitive cultural performance before a critical audience of fellow travellers and, later, discerning readers.[15] John Pemble[16] has identified what such individuals hoped to find on their travels, and the categories identified offer a helpful framework with which to view the rather different and little commented upon phenomenon of Victorian travel to the Scandinavian and Icelandic north.[17] Some southern travellers went on pilgrimages to shrines and places of sacred art; or to view the famous historical sites of Greece and Rome; or for health cures; or as exiles from the sexual taboos of Victorian Britain; or to practise and perfect eccentricity; or to 'go native'; or to examine papists, popery and the Pope on their home ground. Some, no doubt, went to observe all that was wrong and rotten abroad, in order to return with a clearer sense of why Britannia ruled the waves and a few, perhaps, confronted with the wreckage of fallen empires and paradises lost in Europe and the Middle East, returned home wondering whether comparable signs of decay were yet discernible in Victoria's realms.

Iceland presented a very different set of problems and possibilities for tourists, travellers and pilgrims. There was no chance of flashing too quickly past a hallowed saga-stead on an Icelandic horse moving at even the fastest of its five gaits. No-one in his or her right mind travelled to Iceland for a health cure – the fresh air tended to be delivered in gale force doses, and at the wrong temperature. There had to be more accessible places for a lifetime's moral exile, and few will have set out to look for a freer and easier sexual culture though Lord Byron's grandson, during his winter stay in north Iceland, and with a family reputation to maintain, fell in love with a young woman who eventually chose not to return to England with the young Lothario.[18] An individual would have to be very eccentric indeed to go to Iceland to practise eccentricity under multiple layers of protective oil skins. The chances of 'going native' were minimal, though the family of James Robb, a commercial agent from Liverpool,

---

[13] Buzard 1993, 120.

[14] Ibid., 10.

[15] Ibid., 97.

[16] Pemble 1987.

[17] Against Cotsell 1990, 28, see Aho 1993, Barton 1996, Sumarliði Ísleifsson 1996, 121–207.

[18] Ralph Milbanke lived in Iceland 1861–2. His Copenhagen contacts included Guðbrandur Vigfússon, Jón Sigurðsson and Jón Árnason: SJL MS 3.33, p. 30; see Sveinn Skorri Höskuldsson 1993, 29–30, 35.

managed it.[19] The possibilities of Reykjavík's social whirl were soon exhausted. It was not until the end of the century that the supportive arm of Thomas Cook or the blessings of Murrayolatry extended to the Arctic fringes,[20] whilst the first English-Icelandic phrase book did not appear until after the turn of the century – prepared and published, inevitably, in Germany.[21] It would have been difficult for Iceland travellers not to fulfil Ruskin's dictum that travel should involve travail, in spite of the reassuring advertisements in Lock's 1882 *Guide* identifying the pleasures of a state room on the steamship *Camoens*, the newly-opened billiard room in Hotel Ísland in Reykjavík, odourless leggings 'specially adapted for Iceland' from Scott's of Leith, and a range of tentings bearing suitably imperial names for those wishing to make a radical chic fashion statement – the 'Kabul' was a particular favourite.[22] There would be lots of opportunities for 'prideful revelling'[23] at the challenges of independent travel after nervous Icelandic guides had fled at the first suspicion that fabled outlaws from the uncharted interior were near at hand.[24] One exasperated traveller claimed that 'an Icelander would lose the way between any two places in the world, save the brandy bottle and his mouth'.[25] There was no possibility of slipping into the hapless ways of the vulgar tourist; in every respect – climate, landscape, weather, and language – Iceland offered 'otherness', 'marginality', and 'resistance to closure' in abundance.[26] As for finding escape, repose, peace and freedom, W.H. Auden and Louis MacNeice could speak of their 1936 Icelandic travels as affording 'time for soul to stretch and spit';[27] most shivering, saddle-sore Victorian travellers would have been baffled by the notion as well as the phraseology.

Matthías Jochumsson, a frequent visitor to Britain on behalf of the Unitarian movement, and a popular lecturer, used to enjoy underlining the extent of ancient and modern Icelandic alterity:

> Well, Iceland has no army, no apples . . . no atheists; no bridges, no banks, no beggars, no Baptists . . . no corn, . . . no clubs, no cathedrals; no dukes, no diplomacy, no dynamite; no electricity, no embassadors, no elephants, no exchequer; no fabrics; no gas, no gamblers, no gibbets, no gallows, no generals; no hospitals (except one), no hydrophobia, no hogs, no heterodoxy; no inns, no infirmary . . .

---

[19] Barrow 1835, 108; Burton 1875, I 227.
[20] Many Iceland books after 1860 include travel appendices; Lock 1879, 4 claims that his book will serve as a Murray or Baedeker for Iceland; see also Coles 1882, 250–58, Lock 1882.
[21] [anon.], 1909.
[22] Ponzi 1995, 154.
[23] Buzard 1993, 33.
[24] Forbes 1860, 164–77.
[25] Lock 1879, 16.
[26] Few features of the nineteenth-century colonialist mindset identified by Spurr 1993 seem applicable to Iceland travellers, though see below, p. 302.
[27] Louis MacNeice, in Auden and MacNeice 1937, 261.

no locomotives . . . no laureate; no magazins, no manufactures, no museum, no monks, no monkeys, no Magna Charta; no nihilists . . . no nobility, no night in May, June and July[28]

and so on. Matthías's Iceland seemed a destination not to be missed, a chilly pre-lapsarian paradise; for others it must have seemed a retreat into the stone- or lava-age. By 1880 three shipping lines competed for passenger traffic to Iceland.[29] Return fares were £5 second class, £8 first class – William Morris, of course, travelled pilgrim class. Outward journeys took up to eleven days, and even the seven-day return trips seemed long enough when the wind, fresh out of the north east, was destabilising the digestion. Why, then, were so many Victorian Icelandophiles eager to do business with the shipping lines?

As it had been since the days of John Thomas Stanley, Geysir remained a major attraction, even surviving being purchased in the 1890s by the young Ulsterman Viscount Craigavon from the local farmer for £100 – his furious father ordered the thrusting young entrepreneur to sell it back at once.[30] For other travellers there were fish to catch, birds eggs to market,[31] Iceland spar to refine for spectacle lenses,[32] pit ponies to send down British coal-mines, wool to barter,[33] and sulphur to mine.[34] Iceland, too, continued to offer limitless wonders for the less commercially oriented geologist. It offered the ultimate voyage into matter, in all stages of its dynamic history. To assemble mineral samples was to collect natural hieroglyphs, comparable (in some impressionable eyes) with those of runic writing. For those with more sporting interests, there were rare birds to watch, salmon to catch, rare plants to catalogue, and enough mountains and glaciers to keep enthusiasts from the British Alpine Club on their toes and crampons.[35]

From the late 1850s travellers began to relish the fact that there were also saga-steads to visit and contemplate. As Iceland's popularity grew, it became possible to distinguish between those Victorian summer travellers for whom a trek to Geysir and a trudge round Þingvellir represented sufficient exposure to Iceland's fugitive essence, and a smaller band of highly motivated literary travellers, fortified by a winter's saga reading, for whom even the *Burnt Njal* sites might represent only the beginning of their explorations. Victorian travellers to southern Europe were unlikely to discover major new Greek and Roman texts and antiquities but after 1860 a steady stream of new saga translations

---

[28] Lbs. 2807 4to, undated lecture.
[29] See Lock 1879.
[30] Ervine 1949, 53–5.
[31] Lbs. 2188a 4to, Albert Newton to Eiríkur Magnússon, 7 February 1877.
[32] Lbs. 2186a 4to, Richard Baker to Eiríkur Magnússon, 18 February 1884.
[33] Sim 1886.
[34] Ponzi 1995, 130–33, 170–2; many shareholders in 'The Krisuvik Sulphur Company' were Reform Club members. Þorvaldur Thoroddsen I 44–5 mentions an 1862 Mýrasýsla project. See also Burton 1875, I 329–404.
[35] Longman 1861.

appeared, each identifying new saga-steads worthy of first-hand investigation. In no time at all there were *Víga-Glúms saga* sites,[36] *Grettis saga* sites,[37] *Kjalnesinga saga* sites,[38] *Sturlunga saga* sites,[39] *Hellismanna saga* sites,[40] and Saint Þorlákr sites awaiting visitation[41]. Determinedly non-literary travellers hoping to earn their anti-tourist badges could head off into the remote north west,[42] or stay over a whole winter,[43] or learn to speak Icelandic and thus to enjoy the ultimate Victorian old northernist's experience of conversing with 'the pure full-blooded bonder and peasant class',[44] the descendants of Gunnarr and Grettir, in a language little changed over a thousand years. The hapless tourist was left to shout louder in English. Moreover, for all the talk about the 'manly' old north, late nineteenth-century Iceland attracted a number of well-informed and hardy women travellers, 'English old maids globe trotting', as W.G. Collingwood ungallantly described them to his wife.[45]

Travel to and within Iceland clearly presented Victorians with a different interplay between ancient and modern than did the well-trodden Mediterranean regions. As we saw in Chapter 2, Enlightenment-age travellers to Iceland went with knapsacks full of theodolites and thermometers, and minds full of sentiment and sublimity. Victorian visitors, better clad and shod against the elements, brought minds increasingly well stocked with old northern lore and legend. It is these travellers who are the subject of this chapter, whose title is taken from a cheery Victorian travelogue.[46]

'Shudd'ring Tenants'

The defining text for Enlightenment-age sentimental journeying in Iceland had been lines from Goldsmith, quoted alongside the title-page of Sir George Mackenzie's *Travels in the Island of Iceland* (1811), and often recycled by later writers:

> The shudd'ring tenant of the frigid zone
> Boldly proclaims that happiest spot his own;
> Extols the treasures of his stormy seas,
> And his long nights of revelry and ease . . .

---

[36] Head 1866.
[37] Baring-Gould 1863, 1890.
[38] Smith 1874.
[39] Gudbrand Vigfusson 1878.
[40] Coles 1882. A nineteenth-century saga by Gísli Konráðsson, set in Borgarfjörður and written in traditional style.
[41] Leith 1895b.
[42] Shepherd 1867.
[43] Dillon 1840.
[44] Lock 1879, 3.
[45] Collingwood transcripts, WGC to Mrs C, 30 July 1897. See Pfeiffer 1852, Oswald 1876, 1882, Leith 1897.
[46] See Haraldur Sigurðsson 1991; for travellers to Norway, see Schiötz 1970–86.

Such is the patriot's boast, where'er we roam,
His first best country ever is – at home.[47]

Mackenzie, for all his ignorance of Vikings and sagas, nevertheless feels able to praise saga-age Icelanders for their contentment of spirit, ascribing to them an Icelandic proverb that became a favourite amongst Victorian writers about Iceland: 'Ísland er hinn besta land sem sólin skinnar uppâ' [Iceland is the best land on which the sun shines].[48]

Ebenezer Henderson was a good deal better informed than Mackenzie about Viking- and saga-age literature, but, as he travelled all over Iceland distributing copies of the British and Foreign Bible Society's new Icelandic bible translation, his eyes were more on God's world than Njáll's. In his published travelogue, it is only when he describes Berserkjahraun on the north shores of the Snæfellsnes peninsula that saga literature is allowed brief exposure, via a truncated version of Sir Walter Scott's digest of *Eyrbyggja saga* (II 59–63). Henderson's one extended discussion of Old Icelandic literature, an appendix on eddic and skaldic verse (II 323–400), praises the native simplicity and clarity of the *Poetic Edda*, and condemns the unnatural complications of skaldic diction. Prophetic wisdom (illustrated by extensive quotation from *Vǫluspá*) wins his approval; not so verses marked by 'the tocsin . . . the horrid uproar of war' (II 353).

John Barrow's 1835 painstaking account of travels in Norway and Iceland shares Henderson's tentativeness about old northern literary perspectives. His few literary references tend to be derived from edda (via Thomas Percy)[49] rather than saga, as when a perfunctory 'bird of Odin' flutters across one page (193). The von Troil-derived account of the four ages of Iceland's literary and historical development is also of low voltage (244). Similar modest levels of literary alertness can be found in the Honourable Arthur Dillon's 1840 account of his year-long stay in Iceland.[50] The old Icelandic sources referred to are annals rather than family sagas,[51] and we find no linkage between saga text and saga-stead. As for philology, Dillon's reflections on the meaning of the Almannagjá pass (literally 'Ravine of all men') at Þingvellir are unimpressive: 'the meaning . . . no one appeared to know, not even the natives, but it seems to relate to something in which all mankind is concerned'.[52] George Atkinson's 1833 Iceland expedition journal proves a little more alert in this respect. Though Atkinson 'did not find one legend that would be likely to amuse my kind of reader',[53] he does identify links between the speech of Reykjavík and that of Tyneside. Successful commu-

---

[47] Quoted in Barrow 1835, 241 and [anon.1] 1875, 47.

[48] Henderson 1818, I xxxv; Dillon 1840, 304; Shepherd 1867, 145; van Gruisen 1879, 75; Wedderburn 1880, 229; Howorth 1894, 82.

[49] Barrow 1835, 233.

[50] The copy presented by Disraeli to the Aylesbury Literary and Mechanical Institute in 1840 is in the Lbs. Mark Watson collection.

[51] *Landnámabók, Skírnismál, Færeyinga saga*: Dillon 1840, 27, 269, 272.

[52] Barrow 1835, 139.

[53] Seaton 1989, 28.

nication was achieved with one native by 'talking "Newcastle" to him rather distinctly', anticipating the views of George Stephens and W.G. Collingwood about links between local English dialects and old northern speech:

> Was there not something curious in finding . . . that a rough untutored native of the interior of Iceland, where ages almost may glide by and bring no change to beings so isolated and cut off from the intercourse with strangers . . . where the language spoken is so old a Danish, that it may even be the same as that with which our English was leavened in olden times – was it not curious, that he and I should find such a whimsical means of communication?[54]

High Latitudes

By some way, the most widely read nineteenth-century northern travel book was Lord Dufferin's *Letters from High Latitudes* (1857). Into its tenth edition by the end of the century, its genial style was much imitated and its title much parodied. The 'High Latitudes' in question embraced Spitzbergen and Norway as well as Iceland; the latter section accounts for just a quarter of the whole volume, and, truth to tell, Dufferin's heart does not seem to have been in it, even though Icelanders praised the book, and even though for years afterwards Dufferin and his family stayed in touch with Icelanders befriended during his brief stay, and was able to help Icelandic immigrants during his time as Governor-General of Canada.[55] In Iceland Dufferin was assisted by Sigurður Jónasson, a well-educated young guide,[56] yet his travels did not extend beyond quick visits to the well-trodden haunts of Þingvellir, Hekla and Geysir. Þorleifur Repp writes of Dufferin's enthusiastic predilection for the Icelandic sagas,[57] but we find little sign of it in his book, save for a brainstorm at Þingvellir when he contemplated emulating Flosi Þórðarson's legendary leap over a wide cleft in the rocks known as Flosahlaup.[58]

Dufferin's old northern vision was formed primarily by Laing's *Heimskringla* and its Preliminary Dissertation. One way of contextualising Dufferin's old northern interests is by examining those of the volume's dedicatee, Francis Egerton, Earl of Ellesmere (1800–57). Egerton was an energetic antiquarian, well connected among Copenhagen scholars, as had previously been the case with his uncle, Francis Henry, Earl of Bridgewater.[59] Egerton wrote a play on King Alfred and the Vikings,[60] and compiled his *Guide to Northern Archæology*

---

54 Ibid., 111.
55 Lbs. 631 fol.; also Hjörtur Pálsson 1975, 158.
56 For his correspondence with Dufferin and others, see Lbs. 1484a 4to.
57 Lbs. 1484 4to; Wawn 1991a, 224.
58 Dufferin 1857, 94.
59 The autographed (by Grímur Thorkelin) copy of the 1787 Copenhagen *Sæmundar Edda* is now in the Melsteð Collection, Brotherton Library, University of Leeds.
60 *DNB* VI 573.

. . . for the Use of English Readers (1848), itself very much a work of the old school. An admirer of John Jamieson's 1808 Scottish dictionary, he seemed thoroughly at home with Pinkerton's 'all Picts were Scandinavians with painted bodies' argument,[61] as well as with Robert Jamieson's 1814 theory about the links between Scottish and Scandinavian ballads. He proposed an *Antiqvitates Britannicæ et Hibernicæ* volume (never completed) along the lines of C.C. Rafn's *Antiqvitates Americanæ* (1837), and *Antiquités Russes et Orientales* (1847).[62] Egerton appears not to have been an Iceland man. He believed that all the eddas and many of the sagas had been composed in mainland Scandinavia, and that the common old northern language survived best in Norway. Judging by the space devoted to each literary category in his discussion, Ellesmere's priorities were very much those of the pre-*Burnt Njal* generation: mythical (4 pages) and heroic (5) eddic poems, Snorri's *Prose Edda* (3), *Heimskringla* and other *Fornmannasögur* (3), and last, and by some way least, *Íslendingasögur* (2).

Dufferin will, thus, have found little encouragement from Egerton to look beyond the Norwegian perspectives of Samuel Laing. In serenading Trondheim, he begins 'conjuring pictures from the past' for his British readers. Haraldr Finehair appears before our eyes:

> hot blood deepens the colour of his sun-bronzed cheek; an iron purpose gleams in his earnest eyes, like the flash of a drawn sword; a circlet of gold binds the massive brow, and from beneath it stream to below his waist thick masses of hair, of that dusky red which glows like the heart of a furnace in the sunlight, but deepens earth-brown in the shadow.[63]

By his side stands the fair Gyða, her 'demure and heavy-lidded eyes' tinged with scorn. Dufferin is evidently not an admirer; a king had been turned into a tyrant by a woman. Gyða as presented here is a prime candidate for election to the Victorian hall of female saga infamy, along with Hallgerðr, Gunnhildr and Freydís, the murderous harridan of *Grænlendinga saga*.[64] In Dufferin's vision, amongst the crowd of onlookers who had sold out their ancient udal rights to King Haraldr stands a sad-faced group with their eyes trained on the horizon:

> A dark speck mars that shadowy line . . . It is a ship. Its sides are long, and black, and low; but high in front rises the prow, fashioned into the semblance of a gigantic golden dragon, against whose gleaming breast the divided waters angrily flash and gurgle . . . And who are they that navigate this strange barbaric vessel? – why leave they the sheltering fiords of their beloved Norway? They are the noblest hearts of that noble land – freemen, who value freedom, – who have abandoned all

[61] Egerton 1848 vi.
[62] Ibid., xi.
[63] Dufferin 1857, 346.
[64] As in Ballantyne 1872, 53.

rather than call Harald master, – and now seek a new home even among the desolate crags of Iceland, rather than submit to the tyranny of a usurper.[65]

We find this same dragon-headed Viking ship stamped on the front cover of the second edition. The author's imaginative empathy clearly lies with Norse sea-kings and colonisers. Dufferin's other two noble 'phantoms from Norway's romantic past' sound the same note (352): 'King Hacon's Last Battle' highlights the monarch's steel-spirited scorn of death (349–52),[66] and elegiac ship burial (a favourite Victorian type-scene);[67] and King Ólafr Tryggvason's final battle (356–60).[68]

Claiming that Clarendon, Macaulay and Pepys never did justice to the influence of the old north on British institutions, Dufferin does his best to redress the balance, helped by some very Westminster-oriented cameos. His account of the adoption of Christianity at the Alþingi in the year 1000 is narrated like a debate in the Victorian House of Commons – pagans (Tories) confront Christians (Whigs) until the 'Treasury whips' call for a division (99–100). His wry modern parallel for the image of Flóki's three ravens accompanying him on his voyage of discovery to Iceland is a Victorian Member of Parliament heading for the grouse moor with three spotters (29). The elements of romance, chronicle and Arctic adventurism that mark different sections of the book, also compete for attention when Dufferin looks for a title for the volume.[69] Dufferin's initial idea had been 'Arctic Islands', abandoned when his publisher announced that the public are 'sick of everything Arctic'; 'The Silent Seas' and 'The Isles of the Frozen Seas' and also the more philologically adventurous 'Holmgangir' are all rejected, before his final choice emerges. The days of 'pilgrimages' to 'saga--steads' were still some way off.

Paradigm Shift

Saga-stead days are brought nearer by Charles Forbes, assuredly an anti-tourist before tourism had even begun: 'you must go a long way for romance in these days of steam'.[70] The title of his 1860 travelogue, *Iceland: Its Volcanoes, Geysers and Glaciers*, does scant justice to the volume's determined exploration of the intersection between Iceland's past and present. A visit to the farm at Staðarhraun finds Forbes categorising the inhabitants in terms of the three estates vision of the eddic *Rígsþula* (184); Reykholt triggers references to Snorri's *Heimskringla* and to Laing's translation (129), whilst Oddi prompts

---

65 Dufferin 1857, 347–48.
66 Dufferin used Laing 1844, I 346–8.
67 Not least in art: see Frank Dicksee's 'A Viking's Funeral' in Wilson 1997, 62.
68 See also Laing 1844, I 477–82.
69 See Lbs. Mark Watson Collection, Lord Dufferin to George Dasent, undated; bound into a copy of Dufferin 1857.
70 Forbes 1860, 8.

thoughts of tales about Sæmundr fróði and his studies in magic (293–307);[71] the Berserkjahraun on Snæfellsnes (213) lead Forbes, like Henderson before him, to invoke Scott's *Eyrbyggja saga* summary; and Þingvellir, the 'natural monument of the indomitable pluck of this branch of the Norse section of our family' (79), is contrasted with the new 'Brummagem building' (68) housing the Alþingi in Reykjavík. All these individual observations illuminate the author's summary account of the Iceland settlement story, in which Forbes highlights those features of legal and constitutional practice in Victorian England which represent the fruitful residue of the old northern spirit.

Forbes's book represents the model followed by many literary travellers in the second half of the century. Viking and Victorian images and perceptions stand side by side, though in those (just) pre-*Burnt Njal* days saga references remain few and seem second-hand. The volume was certainly the model for A.J. Symington's *Pen and Pencil Sketches of Faröe and Iceland* (1862).[72] The author is another paid-up Laingean in his understanding of England's old northern origins: the Angles came from Angeln, which (he was still just able to write) 'forms part of Holstein, a province in Denmark' (294),[73] whilst the Germans are a separate branch of the great Gothic family, 'very unlike us in many respects'. Britain has certainly built heroically on its Viking inheritance: it has an empire on which the sun never sets; its great seamen from Drake to Nelson are chips off the old Viking block (301): it is the home of freedom, the sanctuary of the oppressed (308); and its all-conquering language 'bids fair one day to become universal'. *Íslendingasögur* references are limited. Things might have been very different had a desired visit to the *Njála* district proved logistically possible. He inspects Flosi's leap at Þingvellir (87), where Almannagjá produces exactly the sort of extravagant reaction that Sir Richard Burton was later to deride. Amongst the book's enterprising appendices, we find (for the first time in English) a group of Icelandic folktales, collected by Magnús Grímsson and Jón Árnason, and translated by Symington's friend, séra Ólafur Pálsson, George Dasent's Icelandic teacher in Stockholm.[74] Through such texts the Icelandic landscape becomes animated if not with the saga heroes of Hlíðarendi and Bergþórshvoll, then at least with trolls, dwarfs and elfs. Two volumes of such tales translated by Eiríkur Magnússon and his wealthy Welsh backer, George Powell were soon to place this narrative tradition firmly before the Victorian reading public.[75] The Symington volume also includes a set of three 'Poems on Northern Subjects',[76] one ('Death Song of an Old Norse King') by Symington himself, and two ('Lay of the Vikings' and 'The Viking's Raven') by his wife. The gloomy spirit of two of these poems, each in turn translated into Icelandic

---

[71] On Maurer and Iceland, see Baldur Hafstað 1997.
[72] Summarised in Symington 1869.
[73] Angeln is in fact in Schleswig.
[74] Snæbjörn Jónsson 1956.
[75] See Powell and Eiríkr Magnússon 1864, 1866.
[76] Symington 1862, 278–88.

by séra Ólafur, contrasts strikingly with the triumphalism in the editor's preface. Symington's 'Death Song' treads the familiar eighteenth-century path: laughter in the face of death, wine-drinking from foes' skulls, the splendour of ship burial; a life fully lived. Mrs Symington's two poems are markedly different, however. They tell of northern degeneracy since those golden days. Fallen Viking spirits beg for release from 'a land unworthy even to be your tomb'; the narrator states unblinkingly that 'Meet it were that the springtide rain should weep / O'er the degeneracy of your race – / The scattered glory of your father-land' (279). In the fine ballad 'The Viking's Raven', the faithful bird greets the return of an old warrior; his son must be dead and Thorsteing [sic] is now the last of his race: 'Alas! with us will perish / The Vikings' race and name, / That long made foemen tremble / When Scalds rehearsed our fame' (285). By the end even the bird has croaked its last, and the old grey stone on which he perched is uprooted. The Vikings have become a sad symbol of a glory never to return.

Definitive Visions I: Frederick Metcalfe

It is Frederick Metcalfe who can be credited with first bringing saga-steads alive for British readers. He had travelled extensively in Norway and written a colourful book about his experiences;[77] he had learned to read Icelandic sagas and he was a romantic old northern nationalist. The range of Metcalfe's Icelandic reading is impressive. At appropriate saga-steads in his 1861 Iceland travelogue he reveals a hard-won knowledge of *Brennu-Njáls saga, Eyrbyggja saga, Egils saga Skallagrímssonar,* (perhaps) *Finnboga saga ramma, Fóstbræðra saga, Grettis saga Ásmundarsonar, Laxdæla saga, Vatnsdæla saga,* and *Þórðar saga hreðu.*[78] None of these works had been available in an English translation as Metcalfe prepared his book for publication. We may also note his references to untranslated folk-tales such as 'Djákninn á Myrká' (71),[79] to Eggert Ólafsson and Bjarni Pálsson's *Reise igiennem Island* (1772),[80] and to Icelandic folksongs (254–5). It may have been an accident that Metcalfe went to Iceland when he did (1), but his primary source reading had prepared him well for the possibility. Dufferin-style anec-dotes include expressions of undisguised relief after resisting the assistance of an over-eager local farmer's daughter when the time came for 'pulling off my inex-pressibles' (311) before retiring to bed – rather the reverse of his hero Grettir's experiences in similar circumstances. Only first-hand inspection of *Íslendin-*

---

[77] Metcalfe 1856. Two Norwegian scholars supported his candidature for the Oxford Professorship of Anglo-Saxon and Northern Antiquities in 1876. Metcalfe 1881 was prepared at the instigation of Gustav Storm: the original manuscript may have been written in Fountains Abbey, whose monks helped to found the Lysafjord Benedictine house in Norway in 1146.

[78] Respectively, Metcalfe 1861, 358–74, 296–7, 318–24, 229, 264–7, 179–80 and passim, 280–5, 213–15, 232–3.

[79] Powell and Eiríkr Magnússon 1864, 73–7.

[80] Metcalfe 1861, 98, 122; an abridged translation was published in Edinburgh in 1805.

gasögur sites will satisfy his bookish curiosity. He wants to explore the slopes which Grettir once 'clomb' (119), to stroll through the 'easily identified . . . actual localities' where Ingimundr settled in Vatnsdalur, to measure the remains of Hǫskuldr's great hall at Hjarðarholt (285), and to gaze on the tiny burial mound of Sámr, Gunnarr's faithful hound. There was scarcely a cattle byre or twist in the river in the Fljótshlíð district that Metcalfe did not recognise as the site of stirring deeds of old. His excitement can well be imagined when he meets a decrepit old man who, like Sir Walter Scott's Last Minstrel, becomes animated when asked to narrate a story. Metcalfe, saga manuscript in hand, follows the performance with rapt attention and marvels at the faultless memory of the saga man as incident after incident is retold with not a word out of place (185–6).

It was not just in his enthusiasm for saga men and saga-steads that Metcalfe's mindset differs from that of Samuel Laing's generation. He points to questions of language rather than to judicial and parliamentary procedures when discussing old northern influences in modern Britain. Metcalfe relishes modern Icelandic as much as the language of the sagas:

> [it is] almost identical with that [language] in which those bold Vikings expressed their thoughts a thousand years ago; those Vikings to whom Englishmen owe most their dash, their love of enterprise, their frankness, their liberty; a race, whom their admirers compare with the Spartan in deliberate valour and mother wit; with the Athenian in daring and genius. (393)

He quotes snatches of conversation with guides or farmers which he has been able to follow, and to which he may even have been able to contribute by the end of his visit. He enjoys Icelandic proverbs, and it is his ear for authentic Icelandic pronunciation which allows the 'Oxonian in Iceland' to joke that the name Bolli, Kjartan's killer in *Laxdæla saga*, is pronounced 'Bodley, and [is] no doubt an ancestor of the Founder of the Bodleian Library at Oxford' (285). He had previously discovered an 'Oxfjord' in Norway.[81]

Definitive Visions II: Sabine Baring-Gould

Sabine Baring-Gould travelled to Iceland in 1862 and his *Iceland: Its Scenes and Sagas* (1863) offers an even more saturated sense of a saga-rich landscape than that conveyed by Metcalfe's narrative. Baring-Gould has better pictures (several in colour), sections of translation from several sagas and, if we take all his published works on old northern topics into consideration (and also the old northern references in his books on more general medieval topics),[82] his enthusiastic advocacy of Viking- and saga-age culture must have reached a broader audience

[81] Metcalfe 1856, II 156.
[82] Baring-Gould 1865, 8–52 refers to Icelandic tales of outlaws, berserks, shape-shifters, and werewolves. See also Baring-Gould 1868, 307–8. Sir Arthur Conan Doyle wrote *The Hound of the Baskervilles* in Baring-Gould's Dartmoor house.

over a longer period than any other other Victorian old northernist except William Morris, not least because of his contact with young people. The difference which an Icelandic visit could make to a Victorian old northernist is revealed by comparing Baring-Gould's two Iceland-related novels for schoolboys – *Grettir the Outlaw* (1890) and *The Icelander's Sword; or, The Story of Oraefadal* (1894). Both had their origins in his schoolmastering days in the late 1850s as he reoralised sagas while out with his young charges on Sunday afternoon walks. Both were published in single volume editions in the 1890s, in response to requests from former pupils who were now parents on the lookout for suitable books for their own children.[83] *Oraefadal: An Icelandic Tale* (1859–62)[84] exhibits only an arm's length curiosity about the Icelandic locations in which the narrative is set. Gregorius and his family, Norwegian exiles in Iceland, discover the body of a fellow countryman called Onund who had been killed by wolves. In the mistaken belief that Gregorius had murdered her husband, Onund's widow Gudruna incites her son Eric to vengeance. Eric, a student at the Skálholt Cathedral school, loves Gregorius's daughter Ingebjorg. The implacable Gudruna, believing that Ingebjorg is distracting her son from his filial obligations of revenge, arranges to have her held hostage by her sister, a descendant of the legendary Vǫlundr the smith. In the story's climactic fight at Skálholt Eric learns too late the truth about Gregorius's innocent acquisition of his late father's sword. The young man dies in Ingebjorg's arms, albeit restored to communion with the church. The end of the novel is marked by an eruption of Öræfajökull.

This is one of the first Victorian old northern novels by a British author,[85] and reveals a very early nineteenth-century mindset. Its sense of Icelandic geography is vague. The only Icelandic texts cited are *Heimskringla*[86] and the eddic *Vǫlundarkviða* – the novel's ancestral sword motif may derive from *Hervarar saga*.[87] The most personal (to Baring-Gould) saga reference is to *Laurentius saga*, cited in a description of the priests' vestments at Skálholt.[88] Baring-Gould taught at a Woodard school, devoted to educating middle-class boys within a solidly Christian framework. Of high church inclination, he writes dismissively of low church reformers such as Anthony Trollope's atrocious Obadiah Slope who were driving good Anglicans into the arms of Rome.[89] It is no surprise, therefore, that his 1859 tale is set in the vicinity of the cathedral school at Skál-

---

83 Baring-Gould 1890, vi.
84 Baring-Gould 1859–62 and 1894 are textually almost identical.
85 Other candidates include King 1850, a paraphrastic life of St Anskar (see [Charlton] 1850), and [anon.] 1860, an account of Bishop Ísleifr and his Viking disciple Ásbrandr.
86 Laing 1844 created in him 'an ineradicable craving to know Icelandic and to travel to Scandinavia': Baring-Gould 1923, 127.
87 See Kuhn 1986.
88 Elton 1890.
89 Baring-Gould 1923, 296; see also 261–8.

Fig. 9. Illugi defends the dying Grettir. Artist M. Zeno Diemer.
From S. Baring-Gould, *Grettir the Outlaw*.

holt, that it draws on an (until 1890)[90] untranslated saga about a medieval saint, and that it signals the importance of young Eric's dying in the faith.

Baring-Gould began reading *Grettis saga* in England in 1860, nine years before the first English translation of the saga by William Morris and Eiríkur Magnússon. Accordingly, he read it in Icelandic, having first taught himself to use a Danish grammar of Icelandic and an Icelandic-Danish dictionary.[91] *Grettir the Outlaw, a Story of Iceland* (1890) is one of the narrative fruits of those linguistic labours (Fig. 9). The story is a great deal more Icelandic in texture than *Oraefadal*, not just because it follows the contours of a famous saga set in Iceland, but also because Baring-Gould draws on knowledge acquired during his 1862 Iceland travels, when he visited the *Grettis saga* sites. He went in the belief that the saga was a true record of historical events. His novel identifies those saga elements that would tax the credulity of Victorian schoolboys, and rationalises them in terms of geological science, oral tradition, or theories of myth. Thus the boulders that the mighty Grettir is supposed to have thrown were relocated by glacial movement;[92] that 'bearserks' were ordinary folk who had simply lost all self-control (169); that the wonderful valley of Þórisdalur still exists, but the only means of locating it (an angled stone with a hole through it) has shifted during volcanic eruptions (280–86); that Grettir died not through witchcraft but because of his failure to eat enough green vegetables, which rendered him unable to resist blood poisoning in his wound (373); that Glámr was an outlaw around whom increasingly fantastic legends accumulated (148, 244), though older readers are assured that Grettir's fight with Kárr has a mythic significance – it represents the descent of the sun into the grave of winter, whence it will return after having recovered 'the fruits of the earth';[93] and that the legend of the fight under the mere developed because traditional story tellers, like nature, abhor a vacuum and create extravagant tales to fill it (300–3). These rationalisations are accompanied by a steady trickle of authenticating formulae made possible by saga-stead travel – 'I know exactly the road taken by Grettir on this occasion, for I have ridden over it' (114), or 'I have ridden through these rivers' (298). Any young reader troubled by the bloodthirstiness of old Icelandic society is reminded of the harsh lessons of modern colonial experience (195). With the story's authenticity established, Baring-Gould's moral authority is impregnable as he highlights the lessons for life to be absorbed by his young listeners and readers – the importance of being patient, of listening to the advice of elders, of obeying one's father, of bathing daily, and, not least, of learning the three Rs.[94]

The corner-stone of Baring-Gould's great sequence of old northern publica-

[90] Elton O. 1890.

[91] See Baring-Gould 1863, xvi; the references may be to Rask 1811, Björn Halldórsson 1814. Baring-Gould 1923, 282 claims to have learned Icelandic from a German publication.

[92] Baring-Gould 1890, 41, 115, 121.

[93] Baring-Gould 1863, 275.

[94] Ibid., 24, 100, 221–2, 228–9, 100–1.

tions was *Iceland: Its Scenes and Sagas* (1863). We need only look at the title-page quotation to confirm that the author is one of the new post-Metcalfe generation of Iceland travellers. Goldsmith's oft cited 'frigid tenants' of the Arctic have been replaced by lines from Jónas Hallgrímsson's 'Ísland' (1835). The poetry of Jónas did not fall off the shelf at Baring-Gould's feet in the early 1860s – only contact with Iceland and Icelanders would have brought it to his attention. Its presence in the 1863 volume marks the sea-change in English travel books on Iceland that reviewers had begun to notice.[95] The obligatory discussions on history, geology, climate, and economics are ring-fenced in a small print introductory section. From the moment that the print size increases and Chapter One begins, the author reveals himself to be an Icelandic saga man through and through. We notice at once that four substantial sections ('The Berserk "Red Rovers" '; 'The Burning of the Hostel'; 'The Valley of Shadows'; 'The Outlaw's Isle') later to feature in the *Grettir* novel appear in preliminary form as inset narratives.[96] Baring-Gould also includes substantial translated sections from *Vatnsdæla saga* and *Flóamanna saga*, forty years before complete English translations of either saga appeared.[97] With *Vatnsdæla*, as with *Gretla*, Baring-Gould is keen to establish historicity and plausibility wherever possible. He reports having found traces of the fortress occupied by the wretched Hrolleifr when under attack by Þorsteinn and Jǫkull whose father he had killed – a circular mound is discernible though the wall had collapsed in the eighteenth century.[98] There is often the sense with Baring-Gould that real Viking- and saga-age relics were forever just evading his grasp, as they decay, collapse or are buried under lava shortly before his arrival. Baring-Gould also includes a summary of *Bandamana saga*, with sections translated, twenty years before Eiríkur Magnússon's translation appeared as an appendix to John Cole's Iceland travelogue.[99] We find, too, a translation of the *Egils saga* section that tells of the drowning of Egill Skallagrímsson's sons, and contextualises his famous poem 'Sonatorrek', also paraphrased in balladic form by Baring-Gould; it was not until 1893 that any other English translation of material from the saga was published.[100]

Baring-Gould is equally at ease dealing with residual old northern folklore in the British Isles – eddic verses about the children Hjúki and Bil who fetched water from the well Byrgir in the bucket Sœgr survive, he claims, in tales of Jack

---

[95] Scott 1863 reviews Baring-Gould 1863, Dufferin 1857, Mackenzie 1812, Hooker 1813, and Henderson 1818.

[96] Baring-Gould 1890, 48–70, 154–166, 125–38, 313–74 derive from Baring-Gould 1863, 8–22, 76–85, 116–31, 246–73.

[97] In Gudbrand Vigfusson and Powell 1905. Baring-Gould 1863, 138–47 (translation of *Vatnsdæla saga*, chs 22–26: the story of Hrolleifr), and 368–84 (*Flóamanna saga*, chs 20–24, 28, 29: about Greenland).

[98] Baring-Gould 1863, 136.

[99] Coles 1882 Preface; the two other saga translations in the appendix were *Þórðar saga hreðu* and *Hrafnkels saga*.

[100] G[reen] 1893.

and Jill going up the hill. The attendance of both children on the moon (their names, he explains, mean 'the quickening' and 'the failing') 'means that the moon becomes full and then wanes. By the bucket of water I presume is signified the effect of the orb on the weather' (189). Legends from Baring-Gould's native Dartmoor help to explain his interest in Óðinn the wild huntsman (199–203).[101]

Baring-Gould's volume is also the first Iceland travel book to show any real awareness of manuscripts of sagas and eddic poems (225–6). The importance placed by a high-church Englishman on visiting the old episcopal seat at Hólar (235–41) comes as no surprise. Details of liturgical practice, vestments and music are carefully recorded. However, Baring-Gould's Ecclesiological Society dream (shared by other Victorian old northernists)[102] that the Icelandic and Danish churches 'should be restored to the unity of the Church, by receiving succession through our own bishops' (296) tended to receive an icy reception in Scandinavia.

The Jónas Hallgrímsson quotation with which Baring-Gould's book begins points to the beauty of Iceland, but then asks, 'Where are thy olden fame, and freedom, and deeds of greatest prowess?'[103] Some Victorian travellers, beginning, as we have noted, with the Symingtons, pondered just this question. For all its natural splendours, and its unsurpassed medieval literary tradition, what was wrong with Iceland? The faults identified include indolence,[104] mercenariness,[105] poor standards of domestic hygiene,[106] excessive dependence on the Danes, impractical nostalgia,[107] and agricultural conservatism.[108] The familiar solutions of liberal economics are recommended by some.[109] Others saw the answer in better drains, cleaner dairies, the cooperative movement, abolition of the liquor trade, and 'a genuine turning to Him from whom all blessings flow'.[110] A few could see no solution whatever and despaired;[111] and at least one articulate British-based (in Edinburgh) Icelander, Jón Hjaltalín,[112] chal-

[101] See earlier Metcalfe 1861, 123.
[102] Indrebø and Kolsrud 1924–71, I 269–71, 271–4, 300–1; II 61–2 (correspondence between P.A. Munch and G.J.R. Gordon).
[103] 'Hvar er þín fornaldarfrægð, frelsið og manndáðin best?': 'Ísland' (1835), quoted from Haukur Hannesson et al. 1989, I 63.
[104] Pfeiffer 1852, 154, 179; Bryce 1923, 25, 39–40.
[105] Dasent 1876, 223.
[106] Hack 1819.
[107] Chambers 1856, 82–3, Wedderburn 1880, 223.
[108] [anon.] 1876, 169–70. The Lbs. copy was awarded as a prize at Laurel Bank School, Manchester.
[109] Burton 1875, I 208–9. Jón Ólafsson 1875, 41 proposes a new Icelandic colony in Alaska; 100 million strong within a century, it could sweep south and 'bring about the rebirth of the wretched English language' [endrfœtt ina afskræmdu ensku tungu]; see also Hjörtur Pálsson 1975.
[110] Howell 1893, 108; the book reveals an unusually wide knowledge of modern Icelandic poetry – ibid., 84, 91, 103, 121. See also Þórunn Sigurðardóttir 1994, 201–16, 218–19.
[111] Lbs. 2186 4to, W.G. Collingwood to Eiríkur Magnússon, 5 and 8 September 1897.
[112] Jón Hjaltalín [1870], 255–6.

lenged the formulaic criticisms, noting, for instance, that more 'indolent' Ice-landers drowned from fishing boats in 1864 than there were casualties in the Dano-Prussian war.[113]

While several Victorian travellers worry about the faded glories of Iceland, one or two of them even dare to reflect on the possibility of future decline in Britain. Viking blood courses in Victorian veins, just as it had also coursed in Icelandic veins and look what had happened to them. Britain has a tried and tested system of parliamentary government but so did Iceland in the tenth century.[114] Could fabled Victorian energy and enterprise fade away? Could Ice-landic levels of alleged indolence descend on the Victorians? We have noted Dasent's awareness of this unease, and the same mood prompts Baring-Gould to inject some very adult sounding remarks into his schoolboy tale of Oræfadal:

> Whether these stormy passions have wholly spent themselves, or are brooding still over our horizon, it is not for the author to say; whether the ferocity in our nature has at all showed itself of late among our countrymen – whether . . . our gilded leopards have contented themselves with catching mice, or, again, whether the love of excitement, which nowadays quenches itself in a novel, instead of driving men to deeds of heroism, be more wholesome than its first development – are points which must be left to the readers to determine.[115]

Baring-Gould believes that engagement with the old north, whether in travel book, novel or saga translation, can arrest the onset of such degeneracy. The wintry violence and vernal freshness radiating from that long-forgotten medi-eval society contrast with the autumnal rankness and decay of mid ninteenth-century life:

> The Middle Ages were times presenting violent contrasts. With blood-smirched hands, in the place of blazing homesteads, notable deeds of mercy, self-devotion, or valour were performed. Then brightness was dashed into the darkness. If there were keen winds and chill showers, the buds of many flowers burst open in the May of Civilization; and those leaflets which appeared were full of the life of warm gales and soft dews. Now we have lost the frost and winds, and rejoice in our autumn, with its smell of corruption, and its leaves pulled from the branches and strewed for us to trample on, or to scrape together or anatomize.

The native hue of old northern resolution has allowed itself to be 'sicklied o'er' with the pale cast of modern indifference:

> the men of this generation lie under an evenly-graduated sky of gray, wrapt in themselves alone. There was great freshness and reality in the old days, with their long stalking shadows and bright kindling gleams of sun. (108)

---

[113] Ibid., 256.
[114] Metcalfe 1861, 173.
[115] Baring-Gould 1894, 107.

Exposure to the spirit of Grettir and Gunnarr and Skarpheðinn – and to the land which gave them birth – could be a powerful antidote.

A Sceptical Voice

Such brooding about present and future dangers tended, however, to be the exception rather than the rule with Victorian travellers to Iceland. The Gradgrindian Sir Richard Burton would have none of it. He was interested in facts, and scorned those who headed north in search of giddy sensations rather than sober thoughts. He had a point. Travelling in Norway, William and Mary Howitt report an encounter with 'northern lights flickering and rushing with a *crackling sound* [my italics] over their heads'.[116] A contributor to the journal *Science, Art and History* recalls a night at Geysir:

> I . . . dreamt . . . a queer disjointed jumble of Scandinavian myths new and old, of which I only remembered Odin's Raven flapping its wings and leading me to Rabna Floki; seeing that worthy thrash Thor, after having eaten his hammer; and Loki kindling Midgard with fire from the Serpent's eyes; the winds, all the while, sighing a requiem for Baldur, through Igdrasill the ash tree of existence. The rocks were being hurled about by the Jötuns, who in the midst of their conflict opened a space, and respectfully stood aside to allow Professor Chadbourne [a companion] to approach me.[117]

Had someone in the party been spiking the skyr? Burton's 1875 travelogue sets out to deflate the 'wunderbar', 'Iceland on the brain' age of Iceland travel writers,[118] notwithstanding several decidedly 'wunderbar' illustrations in his own book (II 321). The fashion was for travel a book to follow travel within a year, so Burton makes a virtue of waiting three years. Writers always praised the intricacy of the Viking-age Icelandic legal system; Burton wonders whether in the complexity of its *Burnt Njal* workings the cure was not worse than the disease (I 97–8). Space normally assigned to the beauties of Icelandic nature is devoted to statistics and hard information. Anyone looking for the standard historical sketch of Viking-age society will be disappointed (I 78); but for anyone wanting to know the number of saddle-makers in Iceland, the mean temperatures in Stykkishólmur, or the export value of one-fingered mittens or two-threaded guernseys, Burton is the man (I 63, 127, 207). He views Iceland in ways identified by David Spurr as characteristic of Victorian colonists – he surveys, appropriates, commodifies, and classifies.[119] We might note, though, that the same commodifying gaze had been exhibited by native Icelanders

---

[116] Howitt 1852, 15.
[117] Symington 1869, 599.
[118] Burton 1875, II 175, I x.
[119] Spurr 1993.

describing their own land a hundred years earlier.[120] Burton is unawed by the 'awesome' chasms at Þingvellir; he breathes easily when recalling the 'breathtaking' danger of the track around Búlandshöfði[121] and gazes fearlessly up at 'dreadful' Hekla, 'a commonplace heap . . . a mere pigmy compared with the Andine peaks' (II 162). He feels under no obligation to advertise his knowledge of, or enthusiasm for, Icelandic sagas; they are mentioned periodically with elaborate unconcern (II 155). He uses the new 1874 *Icelandic-English Dictionary* to belabour erring etymologies and etymologists, making it sound for all the world as if he had produced the volume himself. In footnotes and even in the main text he is no respecter of the dead – James Johnstone's credulity about the historicity of Ragnarr loðbrók earns him the soubriquet 'O sancta simplicitas' (II 126); Mackenzie's descriptions of Krísuvík are 'prodigiously exaggerated' (II 136), and Scott's novels are full of 'woeful perversions' (II 19). He is not above abusing the living either; Baring-Gould's sad-eyed account of the Icelandic Reformation is ascribed to 'crass ignorance' (I 102n), whilst Eiríkur Magnússon is 'an ultra-disputatious and sub-learned Icelander' whose appointment to the Cambridge University Library can only be attributed to British eccentricity (I 28, II 27).

Burton's discussion of *Grettis saga* is characteristic of his overall treatment of the old north. The saga is introduced in the context of a description of modern Drangey:

> it is known far and wide as the last refuge of Grettir Ásmundarson, popularly 'Grettir the Strong'. The millennial lithograph simply says of this strong man, 'outlaw for twenty years and died in this capacity.' While telling the tale of his well-merited death, the Icelander's eyes, to my wonder and confusion, filled with tears . . . The 'Oxonian' [Metcalfe] abridges the prodigious long yarn spun by the Gretla, and shows the 'William Wallace of Iceland,' as the outlaw is called by the admirers of muscular un-Christianity, to have been, *pace* Mr Morris, even for Iceland, a superior ruffian. With few exceptions, we may say the same of the Saga heroes generally, and it is ethnologically interesting to contrast their excessive Scandinavian destructiveness with the Ishmaelitic turn of the Bedawin. (II 124)

There are no concessions here to sentiment, lyricism, or innocent enthusiasm for saga texts. The old north is not dismissed as a fiction, but is to be taken strictly on Burton's pragmatic terms. We note the distinction between the saga as 'popularly' known, and as an authority (Burton) knows it; the hero's patronymic is given with the accented 'Á' carefully marked; the English gentleman's distaste at public displays of emotion is signalled, particularly over something as

---

[120] Eggert Ólafsson and Bjarni Pálsson 1772, 1805. Wiens 1996 contrasts Burton's 'patronizing and paternalist' tendency to look down on Iceland with William Morris's fondness for gazing upwards from valley plains: yet see Morris 1910–15, VIII 49, 190, 193, 196 and passim, and Burton 1875, II 161–2. Modern academic political correctness can produce readings as problematic as those of any Victorian patriarchal capitalist.

[121] Morris 1910–15, VIII 133 [14 August 1871].

mundane as a literary text,[122] as is his eagerness to keep both saga and hero at arm's length with references to the 'long yarn', and to the work's enthusiasts amongst muscular atheists; Grettir is a 'superior ruffian', *pace* (a smart new idiom by which Burton probably meant, 'with not much respect to')[123] William Morris.[124] Finally, we may note the effortless ease with which the widely travelled knight of the realm plucks a telling comparison with Bedouin culture in the Middle East from his accumulated store of first-hand knowledge. The paragraph is a definitive anti-tourist performance.

The Search for Originality

As late as the 1880s in the ever-more crowded Iceland travel book market there were still ways of catching the public eye: cultivating a satirical style, engaging in archaeological controversy, being a woman, producing a picture book or, as the sub-title to John Coles' *Summer Travelling in Iceland* (1882) confirms, by including 'a literal translation of three sagas [*Bandamanna saga, Hrafnkels saga Freysgoða, Þórðar saga hreðu*]', none of them previously available.[125] We may note that *Þórðar saga hreðu* had to wait over a hundred years before a second English translation appeared. So much for the constrictions of Victorian canonicity; in terms of saga translations their ambition and achievement leave the twentieth century trailing in their wake. Coles's volume also includes summaries of the saga of Grettir, the folktale of Fjalla-Eyvindr, and *Hellismanna saga*,[126] the latter an early nineteenth-century saga written by Gísli Konráðsson, though not identified as such by Coles – it is just another colourful saga of events 'a very long time ago',[127] included at the appropriate geographical point (Surtshellir) in his travelogue.

Originality deriving from private satire marks out *A Narrative of the Voyage of the Argonauts in 1880* (1881).[128] The two factors that had come to dominate Iceland travelogues in the second half of the nineteenth century were sagasteads and a concern for Iceland's future economic development: a fondness for Iceland's literary past encouraged travellers to take an interest in its commercial future. This is even the case with the *Argonauts* volume which, on the surface, seems little more than a privately printed memento[129] of yet another jolly jaunt by well-heeled adventurers. The (by now) formulaic features of Iceland travel

---

122 Browning 1876, 6 claims that Icelanders tell saga stories on horseback during the summer; at each famous spot of valour or vengeance they weep and embrace even though they have seen it twenty times before.

123 Burton's use of *pace* predates the first *OED* citation.

124 Morris 1910–15, VII xix; Morris and Eiríkr Magnússon 1869, facing title-page.

125 Largely the work of Eiríkur Magnússon: Coles 1882 Preface, [ii].

126 See, respectively, Coles 1882, 131–5, 58–60 ('the Icelandic Robin Hood'), 157–9.

127 Coles 1882, 157.

128 By William Mitchell Banks, a Liverpool University teacher: Haraldur Sigurðsson 1991, 14.

129 See also Dalton 1879.

books invite satire – a Dufferinesque alliterating title ('Flecks from the Foam of an Icelandic Fritterer'); a chapter on the all too well-trodden path from Þingvellir to Geysir, headed by a saga quotation (from *Sniggurer's Saga*), and marked by self-referential chattiness, passages of purple prose, howling ignorance (*Burnt Njal* treated as a place rather than a book), and linguistic imperialism.[130] Outside the demarcated satirical sections, though, there are elements of seriousness. The Argonauts were not, in fact, a party of wealthy dimwits. As well as academics from Liverpool's university college, the party included members of families at the heart of the city's commercial and cultural success – for example, the Rathbones and the Holts (owners of a major shipping line). Liverpool was a city with a spring in its commercial and cultural stride, with Iceland links going back a hundred years and more. Travel to Iceland for some members of the party, at least, was in the blood – Mrs George Holt, sister-in-law of Alfred Holt the shipping magnate, was the niece of Sir George Mackenzie's 1810 Iceland companion Dr Richard Bright (73). The party was familiar with Dasent's *Burnt Njal*. The saga is warmly commended as a guide to Þingvellir, a location which 'if he [the reader] has any soul in him, will make his very toes tingle and his pulse beat higher at every fresh battle and duel' (35). It is only when thoughts turn to Iceland's future that spirits droop: 'the glory has departed never to return' (75); the people are intelligent but impractical; the climate is bad; and their balance of trade heavily in deficit. The locals hide from such realities by wrapping themselves 'fondly in the memories of the grander past' (76).

Robert Angus Smith's *To Iceland in a Yacht* (1873) is another privately printed journal with strong claims to originality in its old and modern northern perspectives. Published by the *Burnt Njal* publisher, and with illustrations by Dasent's illustrator Sigurður Guðmundsson, the volume describes an exploration of the Elliðavatn district near Reykjavík. The author, a friend of A.J. Symington, is led by his Icelandic guides to a location in which archaeology, saga scholarship and romantic imagination intersect. Smith examines what many believed to be an old 'Thingstead', a series of stone circles and ruined booths at Þingnes on the shores of the lake. This was said to mark the site of the Kjalarnes Thing, as described in considerable detail in *Kjalnesinga saga*, an almost completely unknown work in Britain at this time. Smith was a chemist whose expertise lay in sewage rather than sagas, but he speculates freely as to whether the structure was a temple or a court.[131] The name Þingnes and the adjacent booths suggested a major Thing-stead, perhaps the oldest in the south west of Iceland, established (according to some sources) by the son of Ingólfr Arnarson. For anyone in Britain with old northern interests who read Icelandic sagas as faithful reports of Viking-age Icelandic reality, or who (like John Thomas Stanley) had wondered about the significance of the circle of stones at Stenness,[132] or

---

130 [Banks] 1881, 38–49.
131 Smith 1874, 18.
132 See also Henderson 1818, I 72.

(even) who liked the last chapter of Scott's *The Pirate* (referred to by Smith),[133] a matter of this significance could not be confined to the pages of a privately published travelogue. Accordingly, all the available evidence was presented as a paper to the Society of Antiquaries of Scotland in 1873: including diagrams a translation of the relevant saga descriptions of the temple of Þórr, and its sacrificial ceremonies and an account of Jónas Hallgrímsson's pioneering 1841 visit to the site.[134] In this whole process, nineteenth-century romantic nationalism encouraged Icelanders to look for confirmatory evidence of the Viking-age judicial and religious practices described in the family sagas. And the visionary rapture in which many visiting Victorians toured the saga-steads made them, in turn, eager to believe what they were told.[135]

Along with satire and on-site archaeology, a third way in which the late nineteenth-century Iceland traveller could strike an original note in the subsequent travelogue was by being a woman. This is certainly the case with *By Fell and Fjord, or Scenes and Studies in Iceland* (1882) by 'E.J. Oswald' – Elizabeth Jane Oswald. The prefatory claim that 'I am not aware of any other book about Iceland [which] has taken the special line that I have attempted to follow in mine – the connection of the land with the sagas' overstates the case, but Miss Oswald, travelling for more than six months in the company of two female companions, proves to be an independent-minded observer, for all the obligatory references to Laing[136] and *The Pirate*.[137] Her identification with the old north is very personal: she identifies an old Icelandic derivation (Ás-valdr, 'power of the summer gods') for her surname.[138] *By Fell and Fjord* is the first Iceland book to include a map specifically identifying the districts in which individual sagas are set, yet the book's most distinctive emphasis is on the role of women in medieval and modern Icelandic society. Oswald is sensitive to the trials of domestic life in nineteenth-century Iceland (notably questions of cleanliness and hygiene; 15, 70), and recommends that women travellers should take their own saddles and inflatable rubber baths (135–7). Women feature prominently in the book's literary references. *By Fell and Fjord* is a book of heroines rather than heroes: of Auðr the Deep-Minded (96–7), of Gísli Súrsson's faithful wife (88), of Njáll's Bergþóra (172); and even of Hallgerðr, 'of all women the most fascinating' (208). Readers are reminded that she and Gunnarr were married for fifteen years, with the strong implication that there had been happy times before the final treachery. When she writes about *Harðar saga* (and she was the first English traveller to do so), it is the heroic behaviour and 'northern

133 Smith 1874, 18.
134 Haukur Hannesson 1989, II 396–401.
135 The interpretation of this site remains controversial: see Guðmundur Ólafsson 1987, Adolf Friðriksson and Orri Vésteinsson 1992, 26–27, Adolf Friðriksson 1994, 129–35.
136 Oswald 1882, 34.
137 Ibid., 86: a gnarled countrywoman reminds her of Norna.
138 Ibid., 50n.

spirit' of the two women Þuríðr and Helga on which she concentrates (64–6). She draws attention to the Helgi lays in the *Edda*, notably *Helgakviða Hundingsbana II*,[139] in which the heroine finds herself in a familiar heroic dilemma as the daughter of a murdered man, the wife of the murderer, and the sister of the avenger:

> It is worth while learning Icelandic, if merely to read these fine poems, as only they can be read, in the original. The women are there represented as brave and true, and as willing to lay down their lives in a just cause as the men. Vindictive and merciless to their foes, yet intensely affectionate and true to their friends, they were worthy of the high respect in which they were held, and of the love of the heroes.[140]

Oswald identifies images of happy domesticity. She translates a scene from *Sturlunga saga* not in order to highlight some calamitous battle amongst rival Sturlung Age chieftains, but in order to illustrate the everyday chatter of two young girls.[141] The 'Deacon from Myrká' folktale about Guðrún and her ghostly abduction is warmly praised (235–6) as is William Morris's 'Lovers of Gudrun' (98). Like Morris, Oswald is certainly no fan of Wagner's 'queer' and 'immoral' operas (277), rejecting the mystical flummery in which simple eddic nature myths had been enveloped. Giants are no more (and no less) than personified natural forces 'which it is the object of all the useful arts to subdue or circumvent', as in Snorri's story of Þórr's visit to Geirrøðr the giant, where the hostility he encounters represents forces of destruction (Geysir, volcanoes) challenging 'the higher vital and intelligent powers' of humanity (73). Addressing the daily practicalities of Viking- and saga-age Icelandic life, Oswald approves of the relative ease with which couples could obtain a divorce, and also the full property rights afforded to women in such circumstances – similar provision in late Victorian Britain 'might liberate' a good many couples (49–50). She contrasts the respect accorded to old northern women with their subject status in eastern cultures. She has doubts about the more robotic claims made for the benefits of free market forces in nineteenth-century Iceland: it is one thing for travellers to suggest economic 'improvements' and quite another to experience the consequences (110). Scotland knew all about 'improvement'; everyone, she claims, now looks spotlessly clean – and as miserable as sin (113). The author acquires a dog called Kári,[142] assuredly named after Burnt Njal's son-in-law, with whose spirit she most closely identifies. Her first glimpse of Iceland had been of Ingólfshöfði, and the sight reminds her not of the pioneering settler but rather of Kári's shipwreck at the end of the saga. Oswald composed a fine ballad based on Kári's visit to the house of Flosi, leader of the Bergþórshvoll burners:

---

[139] Head 1865.
[140] Oswald 1882, 47.
[141] Ibid., 211–12. The passage is from *Haukdœla þáttr*: Örnólfur Thorsson et al. 1988, I 193–4
[142] Lbs. 367 fol., EJO to Grímur Thomsen, 17 July 1870.

'We fear no foe nor any fate,
Let us then knock at Flosi's gate;'
Hark to the wind on the upland fell –
'We are worn-out men and the night is blind,
We'll prove the mettle of Flosi's mind.'
Hark to the dash of the thunderous swell.

Flosi came to the wind-shook door,
'What voice is that in the tempest's roar?'
Oh fires within are bright and warm –
'Who stands so dark against the snow?'
'Kari it is, thy deadliest foe.'
Hold fast the doors against the storm.

'Thou com'st unarmed, a shipwrecked guest,
Kári, avenger, come thou blest.'
Cruelest storms at last will cease –
'Revenge is past, and love shall live;
Ah, doubt not, but the dead forgive.'
Under the grass mounds all is peace. (175)

The two men are reconciled as the storm rages. The vengeful passions of the saga have run their course and the final note is one of forgiveness reaching out from beyond the grave.

Definitive Visions III: W.G. Collingwood

Illustrations, sparingly used in the Oswald book, dominate W.G. Collingwood's *A Pilgrimage to the Saga-Steads of Iceland* (1899). This was not quite the first Victorian 'picture book to illustrate the sagas of Iceland'[143] but it was assuredly the best. Having first read the sagas translated by William Morris and Eiríkur Magnússon, Collingwood then uses his own fictions (discussed in Chapter 11) to examine and recreate the Viking roots of his own northern England. This, in turn, leads to a 'pilgrimage' (his carefully chosen term) to Iceland's saga-steads in the company of a British-based Icelander Dr Jón Stefánsson, and then to the published travelogue with its unique pictorial record – a hundred and fifty sketches of saga sites, including a dozen plates in colour.[144]

Discussion of place names is a major feature of Collingwood's *Saga-Steads* volume, along with repeated expressions of admiration for William Morris, and an inclination to see in every wayside pile of stones the remains of a pagan temple, judgement ring, or Grettistak. The cognate place names in Iceland, Cumberland and Westmoreland tell of rich cultural continuities: ' "fell" as we

---

[143] Collingwood and Jón Stefánsson 1899, Preface. See Campbell 1866 and Howell 1893 for earlier illustrated volumes.
[144] Collingwood and Jón Stefánsson 1899; Haraldur Hannesson 1988.

say in the North of England'; Hlíðarendi, 'Lyth, in Northern English'; Leik-skálavellir, ' "laik-scales" as they might be called in North England'; and Espihól, 'aspen hill – like Esps in the English Lake District'.[145] As for William Morris's influence, Collingwood's first glimpse of Iceland is marked by a quotation from 'Iceland first seen' (4), and thereafter at each appropriate saga-stead we find references to Morris's 'Of the Wooing of Hallbjörn the Strong' (43), 'The Lovers of Gudrun' (55, 92, 122), the *Eyrbyggja saga* translation (67),[146] and *The House on the Glittering Plain* (148). And as for Collingwood's determination to link stead to saga, the picture captions tell their own story: 'Grettir's Hut on Arnar–vatn', 'Gudrun's Grave', 'Kjartan's Grave', 'Skallagrim's Grave in Borgarnes', and (of course) 'Gunnar's How at Lythend'.[147] Collingwood's unpublished letters to his family reveal that he was not always satisfied with viewing the surface of ruins. His 11-year-old daughter learns that her father has dug up Guðrún Ósvífrsdóttir's grave: 'I wouldn't have done it, but antiquaries have poopoohed the tradition; and I put her all back again, except some of the teeth and a bit of her skull.'[148]

For Victorian philologists like Collingwood sensitivity to the romance of ancient and modern Iceland was never a substitute for scholarship but rather a spur:

> We went out to see the very places where events so familiar in books occurred in reality; and we found that the belief was true. For every touch of human interest in the sagas – pastoral, romantic or sublime – there was, and still remains, a landscape setting no less sweet, or strange, or stern. (v)

Sumptuous scenery was no mere decorative background to the noble sentiments of saga – the one grew essentially out of the other:

> Tenderness and passion of a sort may be found wherever human life can be lived; but the intense tenderness and the intense passion of the saga could only be developed among scenery which, whether the actors felt it or not, reacted upon their sentiment.

Or again: 'The modern reader, "out of Iceland" is left wholly at a loss when he tries to *stage* these dramas, to *visualize* the actions and events' (86). Collingwood's *Saga-Steads* volume was a memorable response to that sense of deprivation.

---

[145] Collingwood and Jón Stefánsson 1899, 4, 25, 71, 173.
[146] The miracles at Fróðá.
[147] Respectively Collingwood and Jón Stefánsson 1899, 53, 92, 59, 58, 29.
[148] Collingwood transcripts: WGC to Dora Collingwood, [June 1897]. See also Jón Stefánsson 1898.

Royal Occasions

It might be said that many of the travel books discussed in this chapter, with their insistent sense of the interconnectedness of Icelandic and British past and present, were written for relatively specialised audiences. Yet one event in 1874 with the strongest possible links to Iceland's great Viking-age past enjoyed widespread coverage in newspapers, popular periodicals[149] and travel books on both sides of the Atlantic.[150] In the summer of that year King Christian IX of Denmark undertook a state visit to Iceland to mark the thousandth anniversary of Ingólfr Arnarson's settlement. In London *The Times* reported the events in detail, and there were accounts and full-page illustrations in the *Illustrated London News*, which did its best to make the occasion look like part of the metropolitan social season.[151] The special artist sent by the *News* to cover the story clearly had no interest in chasms leapt over by Flosi, boulders carried by Grettir, or mounds inhabited by Gunnarr of Hlíðarendi. He was on the lookout for architectural splendour, in short supply in Reykjavík. He offered readers Reykjavík 'Cathedral', sketched during a service with the king present; he conjured up a lavish Reykjavík ball in what passed for a lavish Reykjavík ballroom; and the celebratory firework display was shown lighting up the town. Front-page illustrations showed the king at Þingvellir, and Geysir in full gush, and the accompanying reports quivered with deference.[152]

One British writer was able to combine an account of his own visit to Iceland and Norway, with reflections on two royal progresses: that of the Danish monarch in Iceland in 1874, and that of Prince Arthur in Oslo the previous summer. Lord Garvagh's *Pilgrim in Scandinavia* (1875) includes his claim, already noted, that it was in the ship belonging to a Garvagh ancestor from Bristol that Columbus journeyed to Iceland, there to learn of Vínland, and hence to journey to America. Garvagh hears an Icelander celebrate the high quality of old northern stock – 'we are in this country a royal race; descended from no common lot of colonists or settlers' – no other country in the present century was colonised by people 'of that [high] stamp'.[153] Garvagh himself is reluctant to rhapsodise too warmly about Þingvellir in case, a royalist to the tips of his dress spurs, he should descend into 'the customary transports of Republican enthusiasm' (44–5). His most eloquent moment comes when recalling Prince Arthur's Norwegian visit in 1873. Gazing down on the British fleet leaving Oslo fjord with their royal passenger, he recalls the early history of

---

[149] Bryce 1874b.
[150] For example Taylor 1875. Headley 1875 includes a translation of the Ragnarr loðbrók death song (13–17), praise of *Burnt Njal* (207), and Laingean comments from Rasmus Anderson (319).
[151] *ILN* 29 August 1875, title page and 206; 5 September, 216; 12 September, 254, 256–7, 274; 19 September, 271. The journal had previously featured the great northern waterfall Dettifoss, 24 August 1872.
[152] *ILN* 29 August 1874, 206.
[153] Garvagh 1875, 12.

Norway 'in which we learn that Vikings, Norsemen, Danes and other nations of that race, by victories at sea, gave kings to neighbouring lands' (198). Britain was one such land and, like George Stephens, Garvagh looks to the day when the British government will recognise its old northern inheritance by supporting the idea of a united Scandinavia, a much-needed bulwark against the growing threat from a united Germany. Viking-age history and Victorian foreign policy are, once more, securely linked.

Jón Jónsson of Mývatn and George Dasent

The last word in this chapter on Victorian travellers in Iceland belongs to one of their hosts. In 1877 *Fraser's Magazine*, with Sir (as he now was) George Dasent as its editor, achieved something of a coup by publishing 'Jòn [sic] Jònsson's Saga: the Genuine Autobiography of a Modern Icelander'.[154] Written in uncertain but always comprehensible English, here was the story of a genuine Icelandic *bóndi* from Mývatn:

> The 14 Agust, when I was occupied at grass-cutting, I saw a boat, and looking in my glass I perceaved there were foreigners in it, they had come from Skutustad, and came to Reikjahlid in the afternoon. I heard when I came home that one in the boat had been Mr. Dasent (the translator of our most pleasant Saga, or history Njala).[155]

The self-educated Icelandic farmer writing (in English) in the 'homely narrative' style of *Njáls saga* just misses talking to the man who translated that saga into a form of modern English that often sought to conceal its modernity. And he misses him for the noblest of saga-age reasons – he is working to ensure that his modern 'bleikir akrar' become 'slegin tún' before the rains come. We must hope that Dasent and his fellow travellers felt that the fields looked 'fairer than they had ever seemed before', before passing contentedly on their way.

[154] Jón Jónsson 1877.
[155] Ibid., 23; Jón is mentioned in Shepherd 1867, 159.

CHAPTER 11

Telling Viking Tales

> When I have been in Norway, or Denmark, or among Scandinavi-
> ans, I have felt something like a cry of nature from within, assert-
> ing (credibly or otherwise) my nearness to them. In Norway I
> have never felt as if in a foreign country: and this I have discovered
> is a very common experience with British travellers.
>
> (W.E. Gladstone 1893)[1]

Prussian perspectives

On 27 November 1889, H. Rider Haggard dedicated his old northern novel *Eric Brighteyes* to Her Imperial Majesty, the Empress Frederick of Germany, daughter of Queen Victoria, and widow of Frederick III, King of Prussia and German Emperor who had succumbed to throat cancer the previous year.[2] Victoria had travelled to Germany to comfort her dying son-in-law. Rider Haggard's dedication expresses decorous gratitude that the ailing emperor had been 'interested and fascinated' by his earlier works, and reflects on the pleasure which his new novel might have brought to that noble 'lover of peace' and 'soldier of soldiers'. But it was not to be. Like Eric Brighteyes himself, the German emperor had now 'passed through the Hundred Gates into the Valhalla of Renown'; and so the new tale of 'a warrior of long ago, a hero of our Northern stock' must now serve simply as a token of the author's respect and sympathy for the grieving widow.

In 1918, with the four 'dreadful years' of Great War conflict painfully fresh in mind, Maurice Hewlett published *Gudrid the Fair*, the fourth in a series of 'sagas retold' in which the author took the bare narrative bones of texts published in Guðbrandur Vigfússon and Frederick York Powell's *Corpvs Poeticvm Boreale* (1883) and *Origines Islandicae* (1905), and recast them in novelistic form.[3] Hewlett was an important convert to the old northern cause. Now an almost

---

[1] February 1890 letter to Paul du Chaillu; printed in du Chaillu 1893, xx.
[2] First published in 1891; all quotations in this chapter are from a 1951 reprint.
[3] See also Hewlett 1916 (based on *Ögmundar þáttr dytts*), 1917 (*Flóamanna saga*), 1917 (*Kormáks saga*), 1919 (*Gísla saga*), and 1920 (*Fóstbræðra saga*).

forgotten figure, his many works enjoyed great popularity early in the twentieth century. In the *Gudrid* preface, Hewlett acknowledges the demands that old sagas can make on modern readers: their 'frugality freezes the soul', they are 'laconic to [the point of] baldness', and their 'starkness . . . shocks me'.[4] Raw saga narratives (in this instance case *Eiríks saga rauða* and *Grænlendinga saga*) had rusty locks, he claimed, and needed the kind of oil that his novels provided. Hewlett detected a noble continuity between the terseness of ancient saga speech and the gruff jesting of modern soldiers in the trenches.[5] It was the 'Scandinavian blood' of the noble British soldier that had been spilt at Ypres, Passchendaele and the Somme. The Great War served to challenge claims that 'no such heroes were ever given to the world as the heroes of Iceland'[6]

The Haggard and Hewlett Viking-age novels were, thus, more than sources of imaginative escape for adolescent readers. They were politicised texts, minor counters on the boardgame of European diplomacy, whose players included the Victorian House of Hanover, and the mighty German Empire.[7] Accordingly, questions of heritage, ethnicity, nationality, colonialism, sufferage, spirituality and regional pride within Britain hover over the wide range of novelistic fictions that Victorian and Edwardian writers produced.

A wide range there certainly is. We find paraphrases of saga and chronicle that celebrate the Scandinavian and Norman heritage in the British Isles,[8] or the Norse discovery of America.[9] Some old northern tales promote images of stout-hearted masculinity for the schoolboys of middle England as they trained to become pillars of society and empire.[10] There are novels that give imaginative substance to the distinctively regional old northern heritage which British antiquarians had begun to celebrate.[11] Some tales were intended as spiritual and moral fables,[12] while others, a blend of didacticism and sensationalism, transferred easily to the London stage.[13] Readers are reminded that the old north had left its mark across half the world. We find old northern stories set in ninth-century Norway,[14] tenth-century Iceland,[15] eleventh-century England,[16]

---

4 Hewlett 1918, x.
5 Ibid., xi.
6 Ibid., xii.
7 The tradition continues into the twentieth century, notably with Henry Treece's Viking novels, from *Viking's Dawn* (1955) and *The Burning of Njal* (1964), to *Vinland the Good* (1967). Treece (1911–66), a Lincolnshire schoolmaster, was an RAF Flight Lieutenant during the Second World War.
8 Baring-Gould 1890, Leighton 1895, Young 1895.
9 Ballantyne 1872, Liljencrantz 1902.
10 Baring-Gould 1894, Ballantyne 1869.
11 Collingwood 1895, 1896.
12 Howarth 1895.
13 Caine 1904; saga adaptations for the stage included Howard 1902, Winbolt 1902, Fox [1906] and 1929, Bottomley 1953 ('The Riders to Lithend', 1909).
14 Ballantyne 1869.
15 Baring-Gould 1890.
16 Bulwer-Lytton 1844, Kingsley 1866.

and twelfth-century Byzantium;[17] and others with old northern elements located in and around seventeenth-century Trondheim,[18] eighteenth-century Skálholt,[19] and nineteenth-century Liverpool,[20] Monte Carlo,[21] and Shetland.[22] Others take place in less well-defined 'long ago' periods and 'far away' places.[23]

The formats of these works also vary considerably. Some claim to be 'new sagas'.[24] There are dogged two or three volume novels narrated in the third person,[25] and supple short stories featuring 'I' narrators;[26] unmistakably bookish novels[27] take their place alongside narratives whose origins lay in oral tradition;[28] philologically alert works compete with linguistically comatose ones.[29] The vast majority of the novels were by men about men, with all that this can imply in the presentation of women within the novels – loyal wives and self-sacrificial homemakers, gossiping beggarwomen, trouble-making grand-mothers, haughty young shrews in need of the taming that only a good husband could bring, and cackling gap-toothed soothsayers in touch with ele-ments beyond the pale of civilised male society. Of the handful of women novel-ists on old northern topics from the period under review,[30] the temptation must have been to write like an honorary man. With all the novelists, a limited range of narrative motifs works overtime within vague geographical settings – child-hood slavery, Viking ships, heroic sea-battles, ancestral swords, boisterous feast-ing, Baden-Powellite male bonding, revenge sequences, ship burials, and saws about true Vikings having no home save the whale's road. Those novelists better read in old northern primary texts deploy additional narrative colouring – sea-witches, holmgangs, berserks, battle-banners, doom-rings, dreams, pagan temples, witches and wizards, blood oaths, runic prophecies, outlaw chases and escapes – all set against more carefully delineated Icelandic, Scandinavian, British and Vínlandian backgrounds. The illustrators of such novels are similarly predictable: at every turn wild-eyed faces of cross-gartered Viking heroes peer out across ocean or heath from underneath horned or winged helmets.

Of the novelists themselves, most are long forgotten; others, once popular, are now neglected;[31] others are respected in spite of rather than because of their

17 Oswald 1888.
18 Hugo 1885 (novel first published in French 1825).
19 [Flamank] 1837.
20 Downe 1902.
21 Caine 1904.
22 Saxby 1892.
23 de la Motte Fouquet 1815, 1845.
24 Caine 1890.
25 Flamank 1837, Dasent 1875.
26 Kipling 1964 [1893], Risley 1897.
27 du Chaillu 1893.
28 Baring-Gould 1890.
29 Collingwood 1896, 1899; M.R. [Margaret Cartmell] 1879.
30 M.R., E.J. Oswald, Jesse Saxby.
31 Leighton, Ballantyne, Caine, Kipling.

fictional writing;[32] one or two, now unread, remain well known for being well known.[33] Most novels disappeared from view within a year or two of publication, others were republished fitfully over a generation or so, a few found an overseas readership in translation, at least one caused a modest-sized scandal,[34] and a handful served regularly as school prizes or Christmas gifts, winning a loyal following and enjoying a long shelf-life. The present writer's copies of Bulwer-Lytton's *Harold* (1848) and Kingsley's *Hereward the Wake* (1866) are respectively inscribed (on their inside covers), 'Constance Potts from Mother, August 1906' and 'Constance M. Emmerson, Xmas 1896'.[35]

The present chapter seeks to examine the contribution of a representative range of these tales to Victorian and Edwardian understandings of the old north.

Harold and Hereward

The longest Victorian novel about Iceland, *The Curate of Steinhollt, A Tale of Iceland*,[36] is also the earliest, published in the year of Victoria's accession. It is, however, to Edward Bulwer-Lytton's *Harold, Last of the Saxon Kings* that we must look for the first influential Victorian novelistic recreation of the old north. Bulwer-Lytton's family claimed descent from early Norman settlers – 'Bulver or Bölvar . . . is . . . so purely Scandinavian that it is one of the warlike names given to Odin himself by the Norse-scalds.'[37] The novel notes the fusion that has already taken place in England between sluggish Saxon and vigorous Dane before the reign of King Harold Godwinson and celebrates the Scandinavian element.[38] The war sons of the north were 'a magnificent race of men' (39), with their prodigious energy, passion for liberty, and capacity to blend in with those whom they overrun, thereby enabling their best qualities to reanimate former foes. So complete was that process of assimilation over the following centuries that the destabilising regional distinctions and rival monarchies of Anglo-Saxon England find themselves reduced in Victorian England to genteel rivalry between county cricket teams from former Wessex or Danelaw regions.[39] This genial localism surfaces in Lytton's footnotes. Folk in Yorkshire, Norfolk and Cumberland, for instance, are said to be 'noted for their intolerance of all

---

32 Notably Dasent.

33 Most obviously Scott and Kingsley.

34 Collingwood 1896.

35 The Lbs. copy of Ballantyne 1872 (1879 issue) has a note 'To Harold Sands with his Mother's love, January 20, 1880'.

36 By James Flamank. Set in pre-1783 eruption Iceland, the novel owes much to Scott's *Pirate* (the sisters Thorna and Vola are clearly based on Brenda and Minna); literary references are to edda rather than saga; and alongside adventures involving outlaws, caves, misdirected letters, and relentless moralising, we follow the halting progress of Thorna and Marfreda towards marriage.

37 Bulwer-Lytton 1951, 536.

38 Ibid., 141, 163, 245.

39 See annotation in Bulwer-Lytton 1951, 40, 80, 179, 258.

oppression', and more resolutely independent-minded than their fellows in the south and west, as a result of Viking invasion (80).

This old northern element in the English character and constitution frames the novel. If Sir Walter Scott had used history to buttress romance,[40] Lytton now uses romance to give substance and shape to history, and much of that romance derives from the story's old northern elements. Its opening chapters are dominated by the brooding Hilda, widowed Danish sister-in-law of Earl Godwin's wife Gytha, Harold's mother.[41] Clearly modelled on Scott's Norna,[42] Hilda watches over her aspiring royal charges with manipulative care – a 'Scandinavian vala' whose late husband had died like a true sea-king 'amidst the feast of ravens' (43). We find her surrounded by druidical ruins, runic manuscripts, and valkyrie-like handmaidens. A woven battle banner, encrusted with precious stones from Odinic times, flutters emblematically over the novel's final pages.[43] Gurth, Harold's brother, dies wrapped in the banner, his royal brother having already fallen at his feet. The final moments of his companion Leofwine are also unmistakably Bartholinean – he fell 'laughing in death', as if seeking inclusion in some revised edition of the Danish scholar's famous treatise. The narrator reminds the reader constantly that old northern sea-kings' blood still flows in Teutonic veins, both male and female.[44] Edith, Harold's steadfast love, is likened by Hilda to a saga *fylgja* (133, 322, 438) and accordingly, after she is abandoned by Harold in his pursuit of a loveless diplomatic marriage, his fortunes decline. Cultural distinctions between Saxon and Dane can seem trivial, as with attitudes to bathing and drinking (63, 250), but they can also resonate powerfully, as with attitudes to song and minstrelsy. In England, under the influence of the Norman-loving King Edward, native minstrels are neglected (345), whereas memories of traditional heroic song help Gytha and Hilda to recall old northern childhoods (191, 270); Hilda's prophecies are delivered in rhyme (327–33) and it is through rousing verses that the morale of Harold's Anglo-Danish supporters is sustained on the night before the Battle of Hastings, contrasting with the monkish plain chant audible from the Norman side.

Not all old northern images are unambiguously positive: there is stern Saxon criticism of their piracy, idolatry, and horse-flesh eating (182). Norse raiders are still a danger to the state (243, 411) and the blustering King Harald Hardrada's guileless bravery contrasts with Norman discipline and cunning. Yet, with Bulwer-Lytton paraphrasing Laing's *Heimskringla* translation (478–90), we sense an heroic nobility in the verses with which Hardrada rouses his troops in his final moments (485–6), and a dignified melancholy after his death – 'on that bier lay the last son of Berserker and sea-king'. Poignant, too, is the departure of Hardrada's son, the worthy Olave, watched by Harold from the shore – ' "there

---

40 Preface to 3rd edition, 14.

41 By inventing Gytha's sister, Bulwer-Lytton can create old northern atmospherics without distorting an historical figure.

42 Bulwer-Lytton 1951, 327.

43 See Motherwell 1832, 9–20, 'The Battle Flag of Sigurd'.

44 Bulwer-Lytton 1951, 89, 126, 143, 145, 325, 413, 492, 561–2.

glide the last sails that shall ever bear the devastating raven to the shores of England" ' (492). Sadder still, and more fateful, is the death of Hilda herself, whose night-time visions in stone circles had drawn Harold ever closer to her, as she sought to promote her adopted hero's cause – 'the Genius of the dark and fierce, the warlike and wizard North, had expired for ever' (514).

In Bulwer-Lytton's anatomy of the English nation, then, the Vikings had brought Odinic vigour to an inert Saxon body politic[45] but that same energy, rooted in Normandy and tempered by contact with Roman system and order, had created a Norman people capable of triumphing at Hastings. Neither the novel itself nor its successive prefaces rejoice at this. Sir Walter Scott's instinctive sympathy for unity within and between nations leads him in *Count Robert of Paris* (1831) to dramatise the reconciliation process between the exiled Saxon Hereward, now a Varangian guard, and William the Conqueror's crusading son, Count Robert. Thrown together amidst the intrigues of the Byzantine court, their improbable friendship even survives the test of ceremonial single combat.[46] By the end of Scott's novel, Hereward is restored by William Rufus to his ancestral New Forest lands; and, we may note, Victorian memories of old Saxon Free Forester defiance were later to find expression in the traditions of a famously exclusive cricket club. In *Harold*, through the character of young Mallet de Glanville, Bulwer-Lytton establishes a more sympathetic perspective on the invaders than might be derived from the icy Lanfranc or the haughty William. But Lytton's greater concern is to reflect on how England, defended by Saxon staunchness and Danish bravado, had ever been conquered. The sad and lengthy litany of factors is intoned:[47] 'a decrepit monarchy and a fated race';[48] heedlessness after initial victory against Hardrada; disunity between and rebellion within regions; the disloyalty of slavish ranks with no stake in any victory; sibling rivalry within ruling houses; the ascetic Edward's weak leadership;[49] a 'timorous spirit of calculation, which the over-regard for wealth had fostered' (526); military indiscipline; and the 'deep guile' of the Norman chief. Yet the great Saxon and Danish virtues – love of freedom and justice, practicality, stubborn courage, and sense of duty – would still lie at the heart of the post-Conquest English character, nourished by Norman chivalry, sophistication and system.

Such images of a national community's gradual evolution contrast vividly with the revolutionary turmoil of Europe in the 1840s:

> On every side of us thrones totter, and the deep foundations of society are convulsed. Shot and shell sweep the streets of capitals which have long been pointed out as the chosen abodes of order: cavalry and bayonets cannot control populations whose loyalty has become a proverb here.[50]

45 As asserted in, for example, Wheaton 1831, 319, 351–67. More generally, see Simmons 1990.
46 Scott 1831/1905, 558ff. [ch. 33].
47 Lanfranc's characterisation of the English sets the pattern: Bulwer-Lytton 1951, 84–5 (ch. 2).
48 Ibid., 16; preface to third edition.
49 Dasent 1873, II 207–10 reflects Bulwer-Lytton's views; Repp [1853 (for 1845–49)] is more hostile to Godwin and positive towards Edward.
50 Kemble 1849, I [v].

J.M. Kemble's preface to his *The Saxons in England* (1849) celebrates British stability under 'the exalted Lady', the dedicatee of his work. Victoria remains 'secure in the affections of a people whose institutions have given them all the blessings of an equal law'. Lytton's novel will certainly have been read in this light, with the fall of Harold or Hilda representing part of the process of evolutionary development and repair that any society, or species, undergoes.[51] For Bulwer-Lytton, a Tory by the time he wrote the novel, this creative fusion of pre- and post-Conquest political traditions buttressed Victorian stability. His investigation of personal and political tensions through the lives of 'last of the race' novelistic heroes[52] had run its course with *Harold*.

Another 'last of the race' Victorian tale, an invasion narrative[53] with a strong old northern element, is Charles Kingsley's *Hereward the Wake: Last of the English* (1866), published on the 800th anniversary of the Battle of Hastings, and picking up chronologically where Bulwer-Lytton leaves off.[54] A saga enthusiast from his early days, Kingsley deploys in *Hereward* large-scale narrative motifs and small-scale narrative decoration deriving from, or reminiscent of, medieval saga and romance. Hereward's rite of passage from coalbiter to hero to outlaw resembles that of Grettir, though the role of drink and women in his final fall recalls the cautionary tales of Sunday School moralists. Hereward's Danelaw values take many forms: he longs for the life of the 'Creekers' (Vikings) and 'Kempery men';[55] idolises Harald Hardrada;[56] enjoys the company of old Vikings such as the indomitable housecarle Surturbrand and the gigantic Siward (43–5; ch. 1); sings Viking songs (85–6; ch. 3); wins a famous sword; relishes the outlaw life; survives a shipboard trial-by-storm resembling that of Frithiof (116–18; ch. 6); and woos and wins Torfrida his 'saga-wife', the 'pythoness' (392; ch. 31) who comes closest to the apparently obligatory recreation of Scott's Norna (197; ch. 15). After a prolonged European *útanferð*, Hereward returns to his native Fen country to coordinate resistance against the invaders. By daring disguise and open defiance Hereward becomes a thorn in the side of the Norman authorities, and a hero in the eyes of the Danelaw natives. But for all the Anglo-Danish virtues of bathing, beard growing, and hustings attendance, their endemic disunity ('there were a dozen men in England as good as I, every man wanting his own way'; 353, ch. 27), and ignorance of the arts and discipline of war, proves destructive (295; ch. 23). As retreat and defeat take their toll, some perish, or flee to the safety of Scandinavia or the exoticism of life in the Varangian guard, whilst others succumb to despair at the 'cold heart and bloody hand' now ruling England (483, 526; chs

---

51 Stafford 1994, 268–9, 281–3.
52 Discussed in Stafford 1994; but see also Young 1895 and Ker [?1920].
53 On later Victorian invasion narratives, see Brantlinger 1988, 233–6.
54 Lang 1891, 153–8. The novel's dedicatee was Thomas Wright: see Wright 1845.
55 Kingsley 1866/1895, 11, 31 (ch. 1).
56 Ibid., 31, 50 (ch. 1), 58, 62 (ch. 2), 104 (ch. 4), 142 (ch. 8), 199, 203 (ch. 15), 216 (ch. 17). Other role models include Ragnarr loðbrók and Beowulf: ibid., 62.

28, 41). Not even Hereward and Torfrida his wife are immune (422; ch. 33). As they drift apart, Hereward's eye falls on Alftruda, whilst the distraught Torfrida, conscious of having borne Hereward no son and thus condemned him to be yet another 'last of the line' (422; ch. 33), seeks refuge in a nunnery. Torfrida's mental disintegration produces some of Kingsley's finest writing (453–5; ch. 36), with the progress of her funeral barge through the Fens recalling that of Tennyson's Elaine. By the end Hereward serves his defeated people better in death, as songs about his heroic life and resistance cheer his remaining followers in forest or fen, while they wait for a change in their fortunes. In Kingsley's universe defeat takes its place as part of the divine pattern governing social evolution: 'war and disorder, ruin and death, cannot last for ever . . . the true laws of God's universe, peace and order, usefulness and life, will reassert themselves' (529; ch. 42). The fenlands are reclaimed, Crowland Minster is rebuilt, and the 'lying' monks establish a 'little school of letters in a poor town hard by; which became . . . the University of Cambridge' (532; ch. 42). The inscription over Hereward's grave ('Here lies the last of the old English') is matched by one for the Norman Richard of Roulos ('Here lies the first of the new English; who, by the inspiration of God, began to drain the fens'). Old northernism dissolves into Norman progress. Kingsley remains sympathetic to the old northern rebels and identifies the modern lessons still to be learned from them. To take just three instances. Firstly, Norman efficiency would no doubt restore the old Roman roads pillaged by the Saxons and Anglo-Danes for building work: 'Be it so. The neglect of new roads, the destruction of the old ones, was a natural evil consequence of local self-government. A cheap price perhaps, after all, to pay for that power of local self-government which has kept England free unto this day' (484; ch. 38).[57] Secondly, life among a loyal band of fellows, whether in East Anglia, Jómsborg, or on board Frithiof's Viking ship, has its modern parallels: 'Hard knocks in good humour, strict rules, fair play, and equal justice for high and low; this was the old outlaw spirit, which has descended, to this day, the life and marrow of an English public school' (432; ch. 34). Thirdly, the novel includes a genealogical table (241; ch. 18: Fig. 10) tracing the line of King Harald Bluetooth, King Canute, Gyda and Earl Godwin, and King Harold on through to Alexandra (1844–1925), daughter of King Christian IX of Denmark who, we recall, had become Princess of Wales just three years before the novel was published, and enjoyed untarnished public esteem for half a century afterwards.[58] Viking blood had revivified the Victorian royal court; and Kingsley and his fellow old northernists[59] relished the fact.

---

[57] Anderson 1967 identifies the Victorian readership likely to be sympathetic to local government.
[58] Streatfeild 1884 was dedicated to her.
[59] Leith 1895a, 27–9 includes a poem celebrating Hereward.

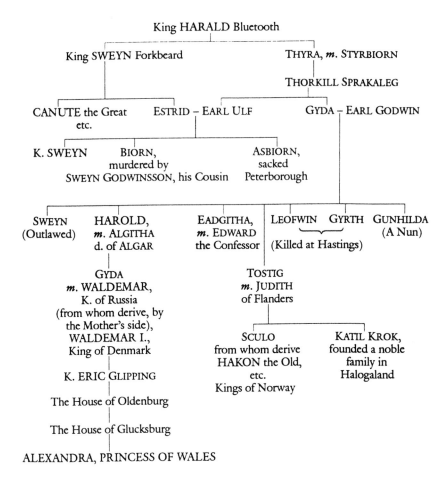

Fig. 10. The genealogy of Alexandra, Princess of Wales.
From Charles Kingsley, *Hereward the Wake*.

Canute as Hero

In the search for pre-Conquest heroes ripe for treatment Victorian old northern novelists might have been expected to make more of King Canute than they did. Apart from his role as Earl Godwin's mentor in *Harold*, the only Victorian-Edwardian novel devoted specifically to his life and reign appears to be *The Ward of King Canute* (1903),[60] by Ottilie Liljencrantz, Scandinavian-American Anglo-Saxophile, born, bred and based in Chicago. The story tells of Randelin, a young woman orphaned after a Saxon attack on a Danish strong-

---

60 Published in Boston and Chicago 1903; London 1904.

hold in northern England. Itching for revenge – 'I am a Norse maiden, the kins-woman of warriors' (29) – she seeks out Canute's support, dressed in her brother Fridtjof's clothes, and having adopted his name. Not only was the Tegnérian spirit still alive but so apparently was that of Ragnarr loðbrók, and Hrothgar in *Beowulf* – for the adviser chosen by Canute to train his new recruit was Rothgar Lodbrok, no less. In further fighting against the Saxons, 'Fridtjof' is captured, but rescued by Lord Silbert of Ivarsdale, an independent-minded Northumbrian who then returns home with his new charge. Randelin helps to foil a Danish siege of Silbert's castle, before being restored to Canute's court. With her true identity revealed, Randelin tells the king of her love for Silbert who, with a priggishness worthy of Hardy's Angel Clare, refuses to forgive her earlier unmaidenly period in disguise. After defeating Edmund Ironside, Canute claims authority over Saxons and Danes alike and is duly crowned; the narrative and political logic of the story also requires the Danish Randelin to marry the Northumbrian Silbert. Overall the novel dramatises the domestication of Viking values in Danelaw England, as raiding gives way to ruling, and as the price for national unity is identified and paid. The heroine, an honorary man for much of the novel, endures privations that match anything endured by the young Olaf Tryggvason in Victorian tales of his Esthonian enslavement. The successful completion of a demanding rite of passage is celebrated through Ran-delin's potentially lively marriage to Silbert.

Horlingdal and Vínland

While Bulwer-Lytton, Kingsley and later Liljencrantz investigate the distinc-tively old northern element as it fused into the English character, novels such as *Erling the Bold* (1869) and *The Norsemen in the West* (1872) by the prolific R.M. Ballantyne, examine its Scandinavian origins. Reissues in 1913 and 1919 con-firmed the British popularity of *Erling*, and it also enjoyed success in the United States, with editions published in Philadelphia and Chicago, and an abridged version in Boston in 1927. In New York it took its place as part of A.L. Burt's Round Table series of children's books, alongside Baring-Gould's *Grettir the Outlaw* and Robert Leighton's *Olaf the Glorious*; these tales had to compete for the attention of young readers with the likes of Fred Wishaw's *Boris the Bear Hunter* (about Peter the Great) and Gordon Stables's *How Jack Mackenzie won his Epaulettes* (about the Crimean War). As we noted briefly in Chapter Four, the Erling tale soon reveals its Laingean credentials with its unsympathetic picture of Harald Fairhair – crafty, predatory and perfunctory in his respect for the hallowed consultative processes of the people's Thing. This had never been the way of the world at Haldorstede in the idyllic north Norwegian district of Horlingdal, where young Erling is brought up to believe in liberty, natural rights and local democracy. Apart from an undernourished sub-plot in which the bright-eyed hero and his morose companion Glum woo and win their brides, the story traces the inexorable pressure exerted by the centralising

monarch on the Horlingdal way of life. The threat from Danish Vikings is recognised, and Harald's impatience with uncoordinated resistance is acknowledged, but the overall sense is that under this monarch the cure was likely to be
worse than the disease. The Horlingdal case is argued boldly in the king's presence. Erling defies the berserks, symbols of King Harald's lust for power, but
ultimately the old rural ways have no place in Harald's new Norway as the
battle at Hafrsfjörðr confirms. Yet, out of this famous defeat and the Horling-
dalers death-defying escape by dragon ship, the community of Iceland was
born, and the book's concluding images are of thriving Icelandic farmsteads
peopled by the prosperous descendants of Erling, Glum and their fellow colonisers. As one of the earliest of the fully-fledged Viking-age Victorian novels
Erling helped to establish the repertoire of narrative moves and motifs that subsequent novels felt obliged to deploy – the arming of the hero at the conclusion
of his rite of passage, Thing debates, berserk fights, ship burials (Guthorm,
Erling's foster-father), and a major naval engagement. Yet the wisps of plot and
slabs of authenticating description serve mainly as anchoring points for forth-
right narratorial statements of old northernism. Thus when Alric, Erling's
younger brother, fights and defeats a wolf,[61] young readers are instructed to
ignore well-meaning but enfeebling adult advice to 'take care' and 'avoid
danger'. Youngsters should practise jumping off high cliffs into deep pools so
that, should the occasion arise, 'you may be able to plunge off the high
bulwarks of a vessel to save a sister, or mother, or child, with as little thought
about yourself as if you were jumping off a sofa'.[62] Was there a copy on-board
the *Titanic*, one wonders? There is also intriguing detail about the old northern
origin of everyday English expressions: 'to take someone down a peg or two' is
said to refer to the studs or pegs set inside Viking drinking vessels – these were
measuring devices, and a bibulous opponent could be tricked by keeping the ale
in one's own cup level with a lower peg.[63] The novel is also one of the first Victorian old northern books to feature a dragon ship as a cover illustration.

Samuel Laing's scholarly spadework underpinned both *Erling* and, notwithstanding the influence of C.C. Rafn's *Antiqvitates Americanæ* (1837),[64] Ballantyne's *The Norsemen in the West; or America before Columbus* (1872). Here was a
work that established the ground rules for the Vínland novel, a genre which has
proved as fertile at the end of the twentieth century as it did at the beginning
(Fig. 11).[65] Alongside his narrative outline of the Vínland voyagers' adventures,
Ballantyne provides a gentle Laingean commentary on his characters' thoughts
and deeds. Readers' attention is drawn to the 'not-sufficiently-appreciated fact
that the blood of the hardy and adventurous vikings of Norway still flows in

---

61 Omitted from the 1927 American adaptation; chapter 17 in Ballantyne 1869. Other omissions
include Guthorm's heroic exploits (ch. 19), and discussion on God's role at Hafrsfjörðr (396–7).
62 Ballantyne 1869, 283.
63 Ibid., 84.
64 Swiftly followed by Beamish 1841.
65 See Barnes G. 1994; the most recent instance, in Icelandic, is Jónas Kristjánsson 1998.

our veins';[66] the decision to abandon the colony is taken at a Thing meeting after full discussion (358–62); and the narrator politicises the differences between oral and lettered cultures, with the inflexibility of written culture originating in authoritarian southern Europe, and with orality harmonising better with democratic practice (58–9, 216–17). Ballantyne is well disposed to the Skraelings ('something almost sublime in the[ir] savage, resolute aspect', 29), and regrets the short-lived nature of early friendships between settler and native. Had such contacts continued American history would have been very different (185).[67] The challenge to traditional gender roles represented by the ferocious Freydis ('one of those women who appear to have been born women by mistake', 53) is soon reduced to the level of music-hall comedy, while the exemplary Gudrun marries Karlsefin. Ballantyne notes both the 'effervescence' (213) of early colonial life, but also the responsibility shouldered by the colonising leader Karlsefin, whose unease as a landlocked sea-king is sympathetically treated (221–2). For younger readers, Ballantyne emphasises the evils of drink (42) and disobedience (287). He develops the figure of Olaf Leifsson to fill the role played by Alric in his *Erling* novel; it is his capture by the Skraelings, while babysitting 'the first Yankee' (200; Gudrun's baby Snorro), that destabilises the community in the period before the final decision is made to abandon the settlement. A specifically British element is developed out of a *Flateyjarbók* detail: two Scottish slaves, Haki and Heika, serve Leif loyally in Vínland, before being freed (a token of the Greenland leader's acceptance of Christianity) to return to Scotland (398–9), where marriage awaits them.

At the turn of the century, it is no surprise to find a trilogy of Vínland tales published in the United States by an American novelist. Pressure had been building up throughout the nineteenth century. Rafn's *Antiqivtates Americanæ*, in either its original or popularised forms, had encouraged scholars to produce translations and undertake studies of the Vínland sagas,[68] to produce speculative identifications of Eastern seaboard sites for Leifr Eiríksson's landfall and settlement,[69] and to indulge in individual displays of old northern conspicuous consumption such as Catherine Wolfe's Vínland stained-glass windows for her new house in Newport, Rhode Island.[70] Moreover, as travel books and newspapers confirmed, Leifr's descendants were still voyaging west in search of a better life. They settled in Wisconsin and the Dakotas, in Manitoba, and a few dreamed of establishing a colony in Alaska.[71] What a novel that community

---

[66] Ballantyne 1872, 52.

[67] The Skraeling fondness for milk rather than ale is reported approvingly (188).

[68] Beamish 1841, Anderson 1874, Sephton 1880, Brown 1887, Reeves 1890, Hebermann 1891, Smith 1892.

[69] See, for example, the passionate advocacy of Horsford E.N. 1888a, 1888b, 1888c, 1893 and Horsford C. 1893 for a Charles River, Boston, site for Leifsbúðir and for Norumbega, allegedly the lost city of the Norsemen. See also Wallace 1991, Fleming 1995.

[70] Kelvin 1984–96, II 182, 423.

[71] Jón Ólafsson 1875, Hjörtur Pálsson 1975. Jón claimed that peoples had always moved from north to south – the Tartars into China, the British into India. The Alaskan Icelanders' manifest destiny was to follow suit.

Fig. 11. The first night in Vinland. Artist Pearson. From R.M. Ballantyne,
The Norsemen in the West.

might have produced. In 1893, at the World Fair in Chicago, the centre of attraction was a replica Viking ship, modelled on the recently discovered Gokstad vessel;[72] centre of attraction would have been *Flateyjarbók*, but strenuous efforts at the highest government levels in Washington and Copenhagen had failed to persuade the Danish library authorities to authorise its transfer.[73]

The time was thus ripe for Ottilie Liljencrantz's *The Thrall of Leif the Lucky* (1902), *The Vinland Champions* (1904), and *Randvar the Songsmith: a Romance of Norumbega* (1906). The novelist's apparent Anglophilia ensures that, in the 1902 work, the 'thrall' is the son of a Northumbrian jarl, seized by Tyrker, Leif's German foster-father. Young Alwin's skill as a rune 'rister', acquired in Britain, earns him a place on an expedition to Greenland, the main purpose of which is to have Leif Eriksson convert his stubbornly pagan father, and later on the voyage to Vínland. However, despite the new colony's democracy and Tyrker's discovery of grapes, the settlement fails and the painful decision is taken to return home. The novel is a mildly celebratory amplification of popular conjectures about the northmen in Vínland. Sympathy for the Skraelings finds fuller expression in *The Viking Champions*. Here, Alrek, obstreperous and disobedient nephew of the law-abiding chieftain Thorfinn Karlsefni, is compelled by his uncle to assemble his own band of Vikings, thereby learning the hard lessons of responsible leadership. It is easy for Brand, one of Alrek's men, to cry, 'Let us live like Fridtjof the Bold, with the ship for our hall, and the sky for our roof';[74] but colonial leadership, whether in the eleventh or nineteenth century, involved dry land dealings with the native peoples. A prominent concern in both novels is Thorfinn's frustrated desire for honest dealings with the Skraelings. Commercial prudence alone suggested that Vínland the Good and (later) 'America the Free' could represent a 'peace-land and a never-emptied treasure house' if only native and settler could have learnt to live together in harmony.[75] The novelist is not clear that the problem is any nearer a solution a thousand years after Thorfinn's voyage.

The Romance of the South

Several nineteenth-century novelists clearly feel more comfortable investigating Viking links with southern Europe than with Vínland. In planning his colourless *Count Robert of Paris* (1831), Sir Walter Scott must have noted the narrative potential of Miklagarðr settings from Baron Friedrich de la Motte-Fouqué's *Thiodolf the Icelander* (1818), perhaps Europe's first old northern novel, and a work that enjoyed considerable early Victorian popularity.[76] Yet, as British

---

[72] Finnbogi Guðmundsson 1991, 34–7.

[73] Petersen 1991.

[74] Liljencrantz 1904, 227. The author claims to draw material from *Frithiofs saga* in her chapter 6 duel scene.

[75] Ibid., 244.

[76] de la Motte-Fouqué died in 1843. New translations were published in London in 1845, 1865, 1877.

knowledge of old northern Norway and Iceland developed through scholarship and travel, the limitations of de la Motte-Fouqué's vision (and narrative method) will have become increasingly apparent. Fouqué depicts Iceland in the formulaic shorthand of enlightenment Europe; characters arrive only as a result of shipwreck; earlier encounters with Normans in southern Europe help them to achieve an almost instantaneous grasp of the Icelandic language; Hekla erupts;[77] the eponymous hero is subject to berserker fits; Mordur, an objectionable Norwegian pirate (the age of the heroic Norse sea-king had yet to arrive), is eliminated by Thiodolf,[78] and the reader follows animated attempts at the Rock of Justice[79] to resolve a conflict between the hero and a local magnate, Gunnar of Hlidarend (no less) – the novelist knew the name, and perhaps the reputed nobility, but assuredly not the whole saga. The improbable figure of Sir Jonas, a priest from England, addresses issues of old northern nationality in ways which would have appalled Laing and Stephens: 'you good Icelanders assuredly belong to that noble German race from which we Englishmen also are proud of having come'.[80] Thiodolf leaves Iceland in search of adventure, along with the bewildered Italian couple rescued from a shipwreck at the novel's opening. The further south in Europe the party travels the more comfortable de la Motte-Fouqué seems to be. Arriving in Constantinople Thiodolf and other Varangians fight bravely against marauding barbarians. The author is also more at home with heroic legend than family saga. In an intriguing scene at the emperor's court, Thiodolf attends a dramatised performance of the Volsung legends. His latent berserker spirit aroused, he rushes on stage and stabs the young actor innocently playing the role of Fáfnir. Rescued by the intercession of Princess Theodore, Thiodolf (along with the novel's other principal characters) marries and, as had long seemed likely, is baptised.

Elizabeth Jane Oswald's *The Dragon of the North: A Tale of the Normans in Italy* (1888) resembles de la Motte-Fouqué's tale in several respects. Heroic legend and Christianity are still well to the fore; sudden shipwreck still stalks the hapless traveller; and fluency in Icelandic continues to be acquired in remarkable ways – Laurentio the narrator learns it by reading the gospels in Gothic. Yet Oswald's scholarly experience and novelistic vision was quite unlike that of de la Motte-Fouqué. As we noted in Chapter 10, she knew both old and modern Icelandic well; she had travelled extensively in Iceland and knew many Icelanders;[81] she was widely read in saga as well as in eddic legend. It is, thus, not long before her specialist knowledge shows through in the novel – Kolbiorn, a retread of Scott's Claude Halcro, and the resident poet on a Viking dragon-ship heading for Italy, ponderously explains the rules of skaldic prosody to his unap-

---

[77] de la Motte Fouqué I vii: all references are to the 1872 New York issue.

[78] Ibid., I 50 (ch. 12).

[79] Ibid., I 44–9 (chs 11–12).

[80] Ibid., I 44 (ch. 11).

[81] The Landsbókasafn Íslands copy of Oswald 1888 is dedicated by the author to Þóra Thoroddsen, wife of Þorvaldur, the distinguished natural scientist and traveller.

preciative fellow passengers. Though the author does not shy away from references to appropriately targeted Viking violence, the novel is no revenge saga. Instead it mimics the twists and turns of a chivalric romance. Its hero, Rainulf the Norman, is worthy of the exemplary Hertha's hand. The heroine's Christian spirituality, integrity, and common sense become important reference points in the novel, along with the gentle pagan stoicism of Thorstein (the captain), which reads like the vows of the Jómsborg Vikings filtered through a Kelvinside sensibility:

> 'I like the northern way, – do not expect more than life gives; meet good and bad fortune with an equal mind; treasure life while you have it; but treasure above it the honour which belongs to a man. And should there be a life beyond, honour will come to meet you; and should there be none, honour will rest on the stones of your cairn, and for a while your name shall live in the thought of men.'[82]

Thorstein's fate involves conversion to Christianity and a fight to the death with a real dragon. The novel's final images are tender and reflective: marriage for Hertha and Rainulf and a memorial statue for the worthy Thorstein.

It would have been surprising if at least one Victorian Viking story had not reminded its readers unambiguously that, viewed through a Laingean lens, southern Europe was the home of slavery, despotism and Catholicism. Hume Nisbet's *Valdmer the Viking. A Romance of the Eleventh Century by Sea and Land* (1893) makes the point through an allegorical fantasy in which Valdmer and his brother Erlend journey overseas from Norway, recording the customs of each country. Reaching the dazzling city of Tulan, they receive a lavish royal welcome, to which Valdmer responds by singing Viking songs. The overall setting is reminiscent of a late William Morris romance. Yet, for all its glister and gold, Tulan proves to be a wretched place, governed by (pagan) priests and served by mindless slaves. Deprived of the civilising energies of free minds and wills, Tulan survives in a state of arrested development, symbolised by the blind and voiceless Vetoria, a thousand-year Sleeping Beauty. No 'fusion' is possible between the vibrant Viking world and the asphyxiating torpor of Tulan. The Vikings escape before a volcano consumes the land. Erlend joins King Canute in Britain; Valdmer heads off on a pilgrimage to Rome and then Palestine.

Family Values

Though most Victorian novelists identified a firm moral basis to life in the old northern lands bordering the Atlantic, they were not slow to investigate the tensions that could grow up between the centrifugal forces of Vikingism and the stabilities and responsibilities of family life. In Mary Howarth's *Stories of Norway* (1895), published by the Society for the Promotion of Christian Knowledge in

---

[82] Oswald 1888, 247–8.

Britain, we meet a boy who wants to be a Viking. He leaves his widowed and impoverished mother and sets off to go to sea. Preoccupied with the excitements ahead, he ignores the dangerous temptation that a washing basket drifting out into the lake represents to the young children of his mother's landlord, but he does heed the testimony of a melancholy Viking who has come to loathe his life on the ocean wave, and is returning home for good. Advised to remember duty to family and friends, the lad also heads for his own home, and arrives in time to rescue the landlord's drowning child, and to assume adult responsibilities towards his mother. Victorian family values are vindicated.[83]

J. Storer Clouston provides a much more complicated narrative about family values in his native isles. *Vandrad the Viking, or the Feud and the Spell* (1898) tells of two Sogn Vikings shipwrecked off Orkney. Eystein and Helgi are saved by Osla, daughter of Andreas the hermit, once known as Thord the Tall, who had been held responsible for the death of Eystein's brother Olaf. Eystein wrestles with conflicting obligations – courtesy to his life-saving hostess, loyalty to his brother's memory. His movements are constantly shadowed by the benevolent Atli, an estranged follower of Eystein's father, and for long an exile amongst the Lapps and Finns from whom he learnt the arts of magic. With Atli's guiding hand the two Vikings escape from a feast at which all their followers are killed. Returning to Sogn, Eystein assumes the throne from his late father. Osla also finds her way to Sogn, having learnt from her own dying father of his responsibility for Olaf's death. Eystein realises that Atli (real name Kolskeg) is Olaf's foster-father, that Olaf's death was the result of a terrible misunderstanding, and that Osla is the woman whom he should marry. Amidst the shipwrecks, rune sticks, magical messages, duplicity, and portentous fatalism, the familiar outline of a medieval romance structure is discernible. As in *Sir Degaré* – or *The Pirate* – children need to identify their parents and siblings before establishing their own family lives as mature adults. A similar structure had earlier been tested to breaking point in Margaret Cartmell's [M.R.] complicated and congested *The Viking, A Novel* (1879). The novelist's addiction to Scott's *The Pirate* is revealed not only by quotations from the novel that head each of the first fourteen chapters, but in her deployment of a Viking-age Minna Troil (Rhunella, daughter of the flamboyant sea-king Oscar), brought to heel (and in this case to marriage) by Eric the not especially strapping hero.

The Truculent Tendency

The novelistic concerns of J.F. Hodgetts and Paul du Chaillu are ethnographic rather than familial, with both writers employing fiction to buttress their mainstream scholarly writings. Hodgetts wrote a set of tales on old English and old northern themes: *The Champion of Odin, or Viking Life in Days of Old* (1885),

---

[83] Similar conclusions are reached by a slightly different route in Saxby [1890], 1892, 1895–6. See also Oertel von Horn 1873.

Edwin the Boy Outlaw; Or, the Dawn of Freedom in England (1887),[84] *Harold the Boy-Earl: A Story of Old England* (1888), and *Kormak the Viking* (1902). He seeks to present 'the myths of their own race' to 'English boys, [who] as a rule, are too open and straightforward to feel any pleasure in the stories of the deities of Olympus'.[85] The *Kormak* novel is entirely representative of the sequence. Borrowing several names but little else from the saga, Hodgetts follows the by this time well-established formulaic pattern: orphaned hero; fosterage; boisterous rite of passage; dragon-ships; Thing meetings; *útanferð* through outlawry; sea-battles; adventures in Orkney, France, and (linking up uneasily with the *Anglo-Saxon Chronicle*) with Hæsten and his great Danish army in England; parental reunion; baptism by a faithful old hermit; and, eventually, loyal service in Alfred's court. The novel represents a shining example of the 'fusion' of Anglo-Scandian elements within society.

An angry spirit lurks beneath the novel's genial surface, however. Hodgetts resents the cultural forces that had denied the old north its proper voice within British culture since the Norman conquest. This is made clear in lectures delivered at the British Museum, subsequently published as *Older England, Illustrated by the Anglo-Saxon Antiquities in the British Museum* (1884). Drawing on the same sources used in his novels (Percy's *Northern Antiquities*, Tegnér's *Frithiof*, the two eddas, and Alfredian chronicles) Hodgetts enterprisingly focuses his lectures not on people or periods, but on the material culture of the Viking age – swords, shields, spears, brooches, rings, jars, runes, books, drinking horns, caskets and coins.[86] The lecturer's tone is belligerent. He mocks the inability of the Roman alphabet to cope adequately with the sonic richness of the old northern language.[87] He excoriates the 'morbid love of Latinity' in the seventeenth and eighteenth centuries; it is he, we may recall, who views the famous mistranslation about Vikings drinking from the skulls of their foes as a deliberate 'slur . . . by the Latinists' on the noble memory of the civilised old north (171). But their days were numbered. 1884 was a time when an Englishman was allowed to talk English and to believe in the culture of England more than that of dead Rome and deader Greece (65).

Paul du Chaillu's *Ivar the Viking* also needs to be read against its author's idiosyncratic scholarly writings. In his vast study *The Viking Age: The Early History, Manners, and Customs of the Ancestors of the English-Speaking Nations* (1889), du Chaillu piles up evidence in support of his views about the nature and date of Viking colonisation in Britain. George Stephens is mentioned as an old friend and it certainly shows. du Chaillu wonders why English-speaking peoples have always been 'far more energetic, daring, adventurous, and prosperous, and understand the art of self-government and of ruling alien peoples far

---

[84] In the *Hereward the Wake* mould; Hodgetts 1884 120–2 echoes Kingsley's politicised interest in the Hereward legends.

[85] Hodgetts 1885, iv.

[86] Compare with the thematic arrangement in Vicary 1887.

[87] Hodgetts 1884, 61.

better than other colonising nations'.[88] And why were the English such a pre-eminently sea-faring people?[89] For du Chaillu, an American by birth, well connected in Copenhagen and widely read in old northern literature, the answer lies in the Viking invasions.[90] There had never been a Saxon invasion of Britain, for the so-called Saxons were in fact Norsemen from the Baltic. 'Anglo-Saxon' influence in Britain is a myth promoted by German scholars – the 'Norse' invasion period of Britain effectively extended from the third to the eleventh century. Potential objections are addressed. Etymologically, the name 'England' derives not from 'Anglo-Saxon', but from Swedish *äng*, or Icelandic *engi*, 'flat grassy land'.[91] Archaeologically, any similarities between findings in Friesland and Britain could be explained in terms of Baltic Norsemen having died in Friesland on their way to Britain, leaving artefacts behind them. As for British naval prowess, this comes not from land-lubberly Saxons, but from Tacitus's sea-going Sueones.

The Viking Age may have cheered the lion of Cheapinghaven, but ran into much scholarly scepticism in Britain,[92] which du Chaillu addresses in the preface to *Ivar the Viking, A Romantic History based upon Authentic Facts of the Third and Fourth Centuries* (1893). He includes a facsimile letter of support from the Prime Minister, no less.[93] The central du Chaillu thesis finds expression in the novel when Ivar visits East Anglia, where his ancestors had lived two hundred years earlier as Roman power waned.[94] His British expedition is one of a cluster of eddic and saga motifs in the novel. The result says much for du Chaillu's wide reading and rather less for his capacity to harmonise the elements into a convincing whole. A request from the youthful Ivar – 'Foster-father, tell me how things were in the beginning, and about the creation' (43) – triggers a sequence in which Gudbrand plays Gylfi to Ivar's Gangleri. Ivar's foster-father offers *Hávamál*-derived counsel before Ivar sets off for England. Ivar and his fellows undergo a *Gísla saga*-style foster-brotherhood ceremony (66–7) and *Vǫlsunga saga* (or at least Morris's *Sigurd the Volsung*) kicks in when Ivar is made to drink a love potion by Ingigerd who believes that he loves another. As we have already noted, the stormy return journey to Scandinavia on-board Ellidi is based on Frithiof's voyage. Hjorvard, Ivar's father, tells him the story of *Skírnismál* before informing him that there is a girl (wholly unsuitable, it turns out) waiting to marry him. *Atlakviða* is the model for Ivar's visit to the house of his father's murderer, in pursuit of the wicked Starkad's daughter, Hervor, whose name derives from *Hervarar saga*, as does her nocturnal visit to Starkad's

88 du Chaillu 1889, I vii.
89 Ibid.
90 du Chaillu's scholarly contacts included Kristian Kålund, Daniel Bruun, and Jón Stefánsson. He had travelled extensively in Norway, Sweden and Lapland.
91 du Chaillu 1893, xii.
92 For example *Edinburgh Review* 173 (1891), 332–59, at 332–3.
93 See note 1, above.
94 du Chaillu 1893, 98–99.

grave mound to persuade him to yield up his ancient sword (195). The novel draws to a close in a flurry of law cases, holmgangs, and sports meetings, at the end of which Ivar the Viking marries his impeccably suitable bride.

All ends happily in the novel, but du Chaillu is not clear that the same will be true for Great Britain, the modern-day colonial powerhouse. Readers of *The Viking Age* are offered a gloomy picture. England, colonised by early Vikings, eventually outpaced Scandinavia in wealth and power – just as America outpaced Britain in the late eighteenth century. The great colonising work of England 'cannot be undone', and further success beckons, but the dark clouds of inevitable historical decline are in sight: 'As ages roll on, England, the mother of nations, cannot escape the fate that awaits all; for on the scroll of time this everlasting truth is written – birth, growth, maturity, decay; – and how difficult for us to realise the fact when in the fulness of power, strength, and pride!'[95] It is as if with every neglected rune-stone and overgrown doom-ring that du Chaillu saw or read about, his awe at Victorian power gave way to a deep unease: 'The ruined and deserted cities, the scanty records of history, which tells us of dead civilisations, the fragmentary traditions of religious beliefs, the wrecks of empires, and the forgotten graves, are the pathetic and silent witnesses of the great past, and a sad suggestion of the inevitable fate in store for all' (ix).

Eric Brighteyes

Arguably the finest Victorian Viking-age novel, H. Rider Haggard's *Eric Brighteyes* (1891) is also set in Iceland. It is now illuminating to read the novel alongside du Chaillu's gloomy historical determinism, but at the time its many devotees, the Prince of Wales and Rudyard Kipling among them, were doubtless too busy enjoying its bristling eventfulness to brood much over angst-ridden subtexts.[96] Recalling first reading the novel under the dormitory bedclothes as an enthralled 9-year-old in 1912, a critic remembers vividly the lump in his throat as he followed the fortunes of the gallant Eric and the predatory Swanhild, and pored over the illustrations.[97] In 1891 Iceland was still an unfamiliar setting for old or modern northern novels. We have noted the tentative Iceland section at the opening of de la Motte-Fouqué's *Thiodolf* novel; Victor Hugo's *Han(s) of Iceland* (1823)[98] situates the wild man from Skálholt in the forests of Trondheim; and in *Journey to the Centre of the Earth*,[99] Jules Verne was more interested in what lay beneath rather than above ground on Snæfellsnes. We have noted, too, that the Icelandic settings are lightly urged in Sabine

[95] du Chaillu 1889, ix.
[96] Haggard 1926, II 4–6; also 1874, iii–iv. 'I don't think much of the boy who can lay it down till it is finished; women of course can't be expected to care for it': Andrew Lang in Tilden 1918, II 4.
[97] Elwin 1939, 253.
[98] Five English translations were published during Victoria's reign.
[99] First published in Paris in 1867; first English translation 1872.

Baring-Gould's 1859–62 *Oraefadal*. Yet by the time of that work's republication in 1894, following Baring-Gould's Iceland-saturated *Grettir the Outlaw* (1890), Victorian Britain's love affair with ancient and modern Iceland was in full bloom, and was certain to find novelistic expression. As well as the two Baring-Gould works, we may mention Hall Caine's *The Bondman; A New Saga* (1890) and *The Prodigal Son* (1904), and Walmer Downe's *The Dane's Daughter; An Icelandic Story* (1902),[100] minor-league family melodramas charged with a kind of salacious morality, and all set in decently detailed modern Icelandic locations.

Rider Haggard's *Eric Brighteyes*, set in medieval Iceland, is an altogether more substantial work by a writer much better versed in Icelandic lore, literature and landscape than Hall Caine, and with greater narrative gifts than Baring-Gould. Haggard had travelled around the island in 1888, with letters of introduction from Eiríkur Magnússon,[101] and had been stirred by the famous saga-steads. With 'saga in hand' he visits both Hlíðarendi and Bergþórshvoll:

> He who digs beneath the surface of the lonely mound that looks across plain and sea to Westman Islands may still find traces of the burning, and see what appears to be the black sand with which the hands of Bergthora and her women strewed the earthen floor some nine hundred yars ago, and even the greasy and clotted remains of the whey that they threw upon the flame to quench it.[102]

Like several before him, he responds to the *ubi sunt* resonances of Þingvellir: 'Every sod, every rock, every square foot of Axe River, is eloquent of the deeds and deaths of great men. Where are they all now? The raven croaks over where they *were*, the whimbrel's wild note echoes against the mountains, and that is the only answer given.'[103] As for the sagas: 'outside of the Bible and Homer there exists . . . no literature more truly interesting', not least because (as Haggard and most Victorians longed to believed) they were 'records of actual facts' (I 288).

On his return home, just three days after almost drowning in a terrible storm in the Pentland Firth, he was at work on the opening pages of *Eric Brighteyes*. Haggard soon found himself drawing on another vivid memory of Iceland, his visit to Gullfoss:

> A most splendid sight. The yellow river, after tumbling down a cliff, bends a little to the right and leaps in two mighty waterfalls, across which a rainbow streams, into a chasm a hundred feet deep, leaving a bare space of cliff between. From the deep of this chasm the spray boils up like steam, a glorious thing to see. (I 286)

---

100 Discussed briefly in Wawn 1994c, 213, 217–18.
101 Lbs. 2187 4to, H. Rider Haggard to Eiríkur Magnússon, 12 June 1888; Lbs. 4373 4to, EM to Geir Zoëga, 11 June 1888; see Lbs. Bréfasafn Stefáns Einarssonar, William Morris to EM, 5 June 1888.
102 Haggard 1891/1974, viii.
103 Haggard 1926, I 285.

The Golden Falls, strangely ignored by the many eighteenth- and nineteenth-century artists attracted to nearby Geysir,[104] certainly make their literary mark in the novel as a vital stage in the hero's heroic progress, as he strives to win the hand of the beautiful Gudruda. Her father, Asmund the chieftain, had devised the ultimate 'impossible task' to test the courage of a suitor as socially inferior as Frithiof had been in the eyes of Ingeborg's brothers: Eric must proceed to the Yuletide feast at Middalhof by descending through the thunderous waters of the falls. Watched in admiring disbelief by Asmund, Eric plunges into the chasm and lives to tell the tale and to admire the rainbow hovering overhead – this, he believed, was the benevolent work of the gods as they sought to unite the star-crossed lovers.

Many more trials await the dauntless hero: a wrestling match with a treacherous rival suitor; the unwelcome attentions of the seductive Swanhild, Gudruda's half sister, who in her jealousy seeks by magic, mischief, and murderous assault to separate the two lovers; the hostility of Gudroda's brother Björn; a three-year exile from Iceland; and treacherous Viking companions. Eric's loyal companion is Skallagrim, a well-meaning but alcoholically challenged berserk. The hero's happiness seems assured when he arrives back from overseas just in time to prevent Gudruda's marriage to an unloved rival, and to marry her himself. The court is overrun by his enemies on that same night, with the sozzled Skallagrim failing to sound the alarm. Gudruda perishes, and the grief-striken Eric takes to the hills, with the insatiable Swanhild in vain but manic pursuit. He defends himself like Gísli Súrsson before confronting death unflinchingly.

Haggard's novel is a remarkable illustration of just how inward a knowledge of Icelandic sagas could be developed in 1890 by a dedicated enthusiast of the old north, even one who was in no real sense a professional philologist. No footnotes draw attention to the weight of reading that lies behind the novel, but few knowledgeable enthusiasts would have needed to be told. Haggard describes the novel as a 'romance founded on the Icelandic Sagas', albeit shorn of the 'endless side plots' and the genealogies that make sagas 'undoubtedly difficult reading';[105] and so it proves. We find interlacings of predictive dreams and curses: the interplay of the natural and supernatural; a strong streak of fatalism; a culture of feud and vengeance; the wondrous sword Whitefire; portentous verses, bloodcurdling oaths, lovers' vows and recognition tokens (notably split coins, as in *Gísla saga*); love potions (from *Vǫlsunga saga*); the hero's fear of the dark (*Grettis saga*); Skallagrim's axe (*Njáls saga*); comic misogyny (perhaps an echo of Dasent's Beorn the Welshman);[106] chattering beggarwomen (*Njáls saga*); the binding on of Hel shoes (*Gísla saga*); the cold hand on the sleeping

---

[104] On artistic representations of Geysir, see Ponzi 1986, 55, 65, 77, 103; Ponzi 1987, 8, 88; Sumarliði Ísleifsson 1996, 95, 114, 136 and passim. On Gullfoss, see Howell 1893, Þórunn Sigurðardóttir 1994, 205–6; see also Lbs. 2877 4to, Björn Jónsson (editor of the *Ísafold* newspaper) to Howell, various dates.

[105] 1974, vii.

[106] In Dasent 1875.

breast (*Gísla saga*); the shapeshifting Swanhild; the demonic Groa (*Eyrbyggja saga* or *Vatnsdæla saga*); Eric's shipboard songs (Tegnér's *Frithiof*); a Viking sea-battle (*Ólafs saga Tryggvasonar*), and defeat and death in a lonely defile (*Gísla saga, Grettis saga*) following a Valkyrie vision (*Njáls saga*). To these elements we may add all the properties with which the stage is dressed – skalds, stockfish, smoked lamb, gods, pagan temples, dwarfs, barrow-dwellers, doom-rings, Viking ships, Gizur the Lawman at the Alþingi, and the drowning pool for women at Þingvellir. The narrative is voiced with the aid of authentic or at least plausible Icelandic proverbs,[107] and attempts to mimic saga style through use of coordinate and paratactic syntax, inverted word order, compounding, archaic pronoun and verb forms, and alliterative doublets.[108] The overall result is a colourful and convincing secondary world. Haggard is no old northern fanatic: he finds the old sagas 'too ample, too prolix, too crowded with detail, they cannot indeed vie in art with the epics of Greece'.[109] But in their depiction of life, simple and heroic, 'they fall beneath no literature in the world, save the Iliad and the Odyssey alone'.

Behind the old northern atmospherics and adventure it is not difficult to read *Eric Brighteyes* as a Dasentian 'melancholy presentiments of dissolution' novel, with its romance elements set within a tragic framework, its hero expiring with no smile on his face and the author offering no consolatory Valhalla afterlife. Eric's foes are relentless, his friends often sadly inadequate, and he dies without issue. At least when Dasent's Jómsborg vikings are destroyed, the young hero Vagn survives, and in his subsequent marriage lies the hope and expectation of future issue and further renown. Frithiof, like Eric, inherits no wealth or high family status to help him through life; his achievements and high repute are his alone. But whereas Frithiof's final role is the exercise of authorised power in Sogn, our final glimpse of Eric Brighteyes is of his funeral barque drifting out to sea, accompanied in death as he had been dogged in life by Swanhild, the malignant hysteric. Far out to sea, they are consumed in a fireball, much as we see in Sir Frank Dicksee's 1893 painting 'Viking's Funeral'.[110] Victorian readers could have been forgiven for thinking that in saga literature, for every admirable Frithiof or Vagn, there seemed always to be two doomed Grettirs, or Gíslis, or Gunnarrs, or Njálls, or Gunnlaugrs, or Kjartans, or Sigurðrs – all destroyed in the prime of life with women prominent amongst the engines of destruction. For every saintly Gudruda or stout-hearted Auðr, there seemed always to be an unfathomable Swanhild, or Hallgerðr, or Brynhildr. That Haggard is content to allow Swanhild's Finnish upbringings to explain her behaviour marks one of the ways in which his well-crafted tale falls short of becoming a searching examina-

---

107 See, for example, Haggard 1891/1951, 33, 54, 104, 138, 177, 179, 192, 228.
108 Haggard 1891/1951, x states that 'archaisms [have been] avoided as much as possible', yet several survive: 'The men busked on their harness' (127); 'smiling as she shore' [past tense of 'shear'] (185); 'she gave me money for my faring' (218).
109 Haggard 1891/1951, x.
110 Wilson 1997, 62.

tion of jealousy in human relations. His finest *Íslendingasögur* models were more daring and more revealing.

The Collingwood Paradigm

Haggard's sense of how quickly noble ideal can degenerate into bleak reality also finds telling expression in W.G. Collingwood's intriguing sequence of old northern fictions. In his short story 'Thurstan at the Thwaite' (1899), set in the Lake District where he lived for much of his life, Collingwood creates the kind of saga story which, he believes, descendants of the early Lake District old northmen would have produced had their oral tales ever been written down. Set in the tenth century, it tells of the last days of Thurstan, an old Cumbrian udaller, whose lands at the Thwaite at Conyngs-tun (Coniston) occupy the site of an ancient Viking-age farmstead. Thurstan's whole way of life ('the old use in these parts was that every man was his own man')[111] is threatened by the church (the Abbot of St Mary's, Furness), and by secular lords (the Baron of Kent-Dale). Even his children are seduced by courtly trappings or monastic ceremony. Only Thurstan remains anxious to assert his origins and instincts. His defiance is signalled as much by the saga-like manner of his speech as the substance. Thurstan's idiolect, as stiff and unyielding as his old northern values, is marked by neologistic compounding, inversion, proverbial saws, unorthodox past tense forms, old northern dialect, and idioms such as 'let do on him his sword', only available to an author familiar with Icelandic auxiliary *láta* in compound verb phrases. The local Thing meeting is interrupted by a message from the Norman king, delivered in the alien language of ancient Rome and European Christendom, and announcing a carve-up of the estate, which was not the king's to divide. Undermined by friends and family, Thurstan makes a last 'withstanding' on his home ground. With a final burst of defiance directed at 'nithings all', the old man dies, ancestral sword in wrinkled but steady hand. Refused 'kirk-burial' by the local priest, Thurstan is laid to rest on a howe similar to those which Victorian old northernists enjoyed visiting – Gunnarr's at Hlíðarendi, King Beli's at Balestrand.

Thurstan is a tale about the cultural footprints left by Viking-age settlers in Cumberland and Westmoreland, a region whose vigorous nineteenth-century cultivation of its old northern roots represented a continuation of a tradition dating back to Bishop William Nicolson of Carlisle in the seventeenth century.[112] Collingwood, like Stanley, Holland and George Stephens a native of Merseyside, became a central figure in the cultivation of Lake District old northernism.[113] After visiting Iceland in 1897, he painted some two hundred

---

[111] Collingwood 1899, [ii].
[112] Harris 1992.
[113] Collingwood 1892–6.

fine water colours of the principal saga-steads,[114] published an account of this 'pilgrimage',[115] and translated a saga about a famous Icelandic poet.[116] He wrote two late Victorian novels about Viking-age Coniston,[117] and became Lake District representative ('Heraths-Umboths-man') in the Viking Society, formed in 1892 to provide a focus for old northern enthusiasms throughout the British Isles.[118] Collingwood lectured to the society in 1898 on 'Gudrun's grave',[119] having excavated the site, and having become a life member of the Hið íslenzka fornleifafélag [The Icelandic Archaeological Society].[120] The developmental sequence of Collingwood's old northern interests – novel writing, place-name study, contact with an Icelander resident in Britain (Jón Stefánsson),[121] Iceland travel, archaeology, sketching and painting, language learning, saga translation, membership of learned society – represents an unusually full version of a familiar late Victorian paradigm.

'Thurstan' draws attention to the long-silent Lake District voices. Around the end of the nineteenth century the Viking-age linguistic residue in northwest England was becoming more widely appreciated in Cumberland and Lancashire,[122] with new publications on local dialect attracting many local subscribers,[123] and with Collingwood's lectures helping to focus local attention. In honour of the thousandth anniversary of the arrival of Vikings in the region, Collingwood read a paper to the Barrow Naturalists' Field Club and Literary and Scientific Association.[124] In it he reflects on the kind of world that Isle of Man Vikings would have encountered when they finally reached the territory long visible to them across the Irish Sea: a no man's land, the least populated part of England, and thus an ideal refuge for invaders, before they had to face the mid tenth-century hostility of the Saxon kings. The region's Norse linguistic residue provided Collingwood with extra rhythmic and linguistic colours when he came to translate the verses of *Kormáks saga* – the saga's stanzas reminded him of the traditional Lakeland poetry 'before the school board and cheap magazines came in'.[125] Lakeland speech, he claims,

> perfectly matches this old Norse, being indeed its direct descendant, and surviving amongt the children of the Vikings in northern England. If the Saga could be

---

114 Haraldur Hannesson 1988.
115 Collingwood and Jón Stefánsson 1899.
116 Collingwood and Jón Stefánsson 1902.
117 Collingwood 1895, 1896
118 Townsend 1992.
119 *Saga-Book* 1897–1900, 212 129.
120 Jón Stefánsson 1898, 39–40.
121 Jón Stefánsson 1949 discusses Jón's links with British old northernists.
122 See Collingwood 1892–6; Sephton 1903, 1904, 1913.
123 Ellwood 1894, 1895, 1898.
124 Collingwood 1895–6.
125 Collingwood and Jón Stefánsson 1902, 7.

turned into the talk of an old-fashioned peasant of Yorkshire or Cumberland it would be precisely represented.[126]

One reason for Collingwood publishing his translation in Ulverston was his eagerness to assert these continuities. And, no doubt, one reason for Collingwood's fondness for identifying links between Cumbrian Viking settlers and eighteenth- and early nineteenth-century sea captains (who fought at sea and farmed at home) was that his own grandfather took over from the fallen Lord Nelson at Trafalgar.[127]

It is, however, in *Thorstein of the Mere; A Saga of the Northmen in Lakeland* (1895),[128] and its controversial sequel *The Bondwoman* (1896) that Collingwood's old northernism achieves its fullest fictional expression.[129] The novels work as a pair: *Thorstein* deals with the inter-tribal hostilities and external threats to the Lake District community in which the young hero grows up, and *The Bondwoman* dramatises domestic tensions in a way that shocked late Victorian readers and reviewers. In *Thorstein* Swein Bjornsson and his followers till uncultivated fields, they trade independently, and Swein's skills as a master smith symbolise old northern self-sufficiency. Politically, the story follows the shifting currents of war and truce, as the Lakeland community finds itself caught up in the attempts of Saxon kings to subdue the sons of Sigtrygg as they attempt to re-establish a power base in York. The conflict was to reach its height at the Battle of Brunanburh, the Anglo-Saxon poetic account of which had been much cited and translated in Britain from Thomas Warton's time onwards, and was now placed in full historical context.[130] Woven in amongst such details of national politics and local history (the northmen established an Althing at Legburthwaite [Logbergfield]), we find yet another rite of passage narrative. Whilst exploring Thurstonwater Thorstein is captured by the fell folk. Aware of the local proverb 'Homely wit has homebred barn',[131] he escapes with his future bride (Rhaineach), and duly follows the familiar *útanferð* trail (Orkney, Iceland, Norway, London). He marries the wrong woman (the scheming Asdis), becomes head of the family after his father's death at Brunanburh, is exiled by jealous siblings, eventually finds the right woman, accepts Christianity and perishes in battle. Unlike the childless Eric Brighteyes, however, Thorstein has fathered three sons who, the implied Victorian reader is invited to believe, founded the ancient dynasties still flourishing in the region.

Collingwood deploys plausible old northern names,[132] Cumbrian saws and dialect with the deftness of a native – 'bealed', 'bield', 'clarty ways', 'a conny bit

---

[126] Ibid., 22.
[127] Jón Stefánsson 1949, 121–3.
[128] Reissued in 1909, 1929 (new format).
[129] Reissued as *The Bondwomen* in 1932, the year of Collingwood's death.
[130] Collingwood would have relished Jón Espólín's unpublished Icelandic translation: Wawn 1994a, 835–7.
[131] In Icelandic, 'heimskt er heimalið barn'.
[132] See Lbs. 2186a, WGC to Eiríkur Magnússon, 25 July 1895.

of flat', 'that great fireflaught in the heavens Gowk-month', 'a gradely good stir-about', 'haybay', 'laiks', 'lait', 'lound', 'slocken', 'snape', 'snod', 'wankle as a wet sark' and many more besides. Readers could check particular forms in Thomas Ellwood's *Lakeland and Iceland, being a Glossary of Words in the Dialect of Cumberland, Westmorland, and North Lancashire which seem allied to or identical with the Icelandic or Norse* (1893), the work of a schoolmaster vicar who had been born, brought up, and had lived all his life in Lakeland.[133] Half-way through the novel, the author digresses from his story in order to clarify the values driving his tale:

> On salt shores, where farming alone could never thrive; on bleak headlands among the seamews' nests; on lone islands veiled in the mist or girdled with the surf, – homes where any but a race of sailors would have hungered slowly to death, or pined into dismal savagery, – there they [the Northmen] bred and multiplied, and sang through the winter, and strove through the summer; their wit and wisdom and valour putting to shame . . . the follies and the vices and the idleness of the South. It were long to reckon up all that we owe them, in thought and speech, in law and custom, in arts and crafts; for without books, they made themselves learned; without schools, they became artists; without examples, they perfected laws; and without bigotry, they found freedom. A wonderful people, and greatly to be gloried in, even yet, by their inheritors; still more by their own children in the day of their strength. For a thousand years ago it might well be said wherever a Northman's keel strake strand there he found his kin to hand; be it west-over-sea from old Norway, in Britain or Ireland or the isles thereabout; or in Greenland or Iceland; or on the Baltic coasts, and thenceaway to the Atlantic, from Finmark and Denmark to Holland and Valland; everywhere the Northman's tongue was heard and the Northman's hand feared.[134]

The soaring style, unmatched anywhere else in the novel, signals the importance that Collingwood attached to this ringing statement of the ideals and emotions powering his many-faceted pursuit of Viking-age culture.

It may well have been Collingwood's determined identification of past with present in *Thorstein of the Mere* that lay behind the turbulent reception of *The Bondwoman* a year later. In his preface to the 1932 reprint Collingwood speaks of 'the little stir it made among a few friends' having been forgotten.[135] A stir there certainly had been. The 1895 *Spectator* reviewer, for example, declared that 'this is a book which ought never to have been written'.[136] Collingwood's irritation at this hostile metropolitan reception led to his using a Cumberland publisher for all his subsequent works. *The Bondwoman* is built around the tensions surrounding Oddi Samsson, a Lakeland settler of old northern origin, after he

---

133 Ellwood's book was published for the English Dialect Society, and attracted over 130 Lake District subscribers, John Ruskin amongst them. Collingwood was Ruskin's secretary.
134 Collingwood 1895, 120–1.
135 Collingwood 1932, [Preface].
136 Edward Thompson in Collingwood 1929, [iii].

introduces Deorwyn, a Saxon bondwoman, into the household. Eyebrows are raised in the Langdale fictional community as Oddi finds himself torn between husbandly loyalty to his long-suffering wife Groa, and the amorous instincts of a free-roving Viking – rationalised in terms of Oddi's anxiety at the failure of his formal marriage to have produced a male heir.[137] Groa has to accommodate the right of Oddi to 'have his heart's desire, and a bit over . . . there were many who had two, and more than two, in those days' (110), even when such freedom leads to his fathering two children – a girl by Deorwyn, and, at last, the longed-for son by Groa. These same tensions trigger another passage of authorial commentary in which Collingwood assesses the qualities of life amongst the Lakeland northmen in the transitional period when Vikings had not yet developed fully into dalesmen:

> The dalesmen, in the time of our story, were Vikings no longer . . . In this mind they were at once better men, and worse, than their fathers before them. Better for the reign of Thor was over, the bearsark [sic] days of rapine and massacre. Better, for there should be none happier nor cleaner souled than he who ploughs his own acres, or feeds his own sheep, in the midst of a peaceful land of hills and dales, among green pastures and besides still waters. But worse they were, because they had lost the old virtues, and had not yet put on the new. They were no longer the riders of the foam, the free-handed ring scatterers, reckless of life and fearless of death. Nor were they yet what their children came to be – the sturdy squires and canny statesmen of the North, dwelling in thrift and industry, and sending out their sons to roam the world, and to rise in it by sheer force of worth and wisdom.
>
> (100–1)

Petty feuding arose within the community, and so did a hunger for personal freedom that was hard for Victorian readers to reconcile with responsible family values:

> Who so free as the woman that left her man at a word, taking the portion that belonged to her, and quitting herself of all ties, – and none blamed her? Who so free as one to whom all his household were as their handmaids to the patriarchs; who needed only silver in his bag to buy what he list of youth and beauty – and none cried shame? (102)

The novel's uneasy reception and Collingwood's prickly reaction are easy to understand. Yet there may be more important issues than Victorian propriety playing round the edges of Collingwood's novel. They offer a minor key coda to this chapter of major key novelistic images. All Collingwood's water colours from Iceland are of unpeopled scenes, bleak and beautiful saga-steads, famous sites which could readily be peopled in the imaginations of the saga-reading public perusing his *Pilgrimage to the Saga-Steads* book. The situation is different with his oil painting 'The Parliament of Ancient Iceland', which he presented to the Viking Club in 1906, and which hung in the Gothic Hall at the King's

---

137 Collingwood 1896, 79.

Weigh House where Club meetings were held. Here is a picture featuring over a hundred figures, with a sense of bustle and animation pulsing everywhere; Þingvellir symbolises the discussion-holding, decision-making culture depicted positively in so many Viking novels. When we examine the artist's letters home as he explored the actual saga-stead we come across moments of exasperation with modern Iceland and Icelanders, as weariness and homesickness eat into his reserves of good humour. He is baffled by the apparent indifference of Iceland-ers to their own history and antiquities.[138] In an interview with an Icelandic journalist before returning home, Collingwood touches gently on some of his negative impressions.[139] A sterner tone can be found in letters to Eiríkur Magnússon written on his return to Britain. He knew well the Cumbrian version of the Icelandic proverb 'glöggt er gests augað',[140] and his own eye had been confronted with many dispiriting Icelandic images: 'If you had lately . . . seen for yourself town and country . . . you would feel that the land is indeed a land of Gotham, and wholly irreclaimable by any teaching or preaching'.[141] Ice-landers have less in common with Vikings 'than we with Red Indians'. He was returning home

> with such a feeling of disheartenment . . . It isn't only vermin and Danes and such like: it's everybody and everything. Of course I know the historical reasons of this degeneracy: but apology for it doesn't cure it. And I don't think any writing will cure it . . . I hope my pictures will not be without use to Iceland in their little way; greater things being left to stronger people.[142]

But how strong were the 'stronger people' of England? Was anyone capable of doing 'greater things' for Iceland? With Collingwood's sense that in modern Britain greatness lay rooted firmly in the old north, the answer ought to have been a positive one. But, as du Chaillu's bleak forecast about the future of Great Britain made clear, empires fall as well as rise. At best the condition of Iceland was cause for real sadness; at worst it could point to the future for any society built on old northern values. If 'writing and preaching' could not cure modern Iceland, they could offer a cautionary word to Collingwood's homeland.

Afterword

With Collingwood's troubled spirit in mind, we may conclude this chapter with a glimpse of a troubled Viking-age narrator struggling to retain his sanity while wrestling with his own sense of of pride and fear, honour and shame. R.V. Ris-

---

138 Collingwood transcripts, WGC to Mrs Collingwood, 30 July 1897.

139 Haraldur Hannesson 1988, 136.

140 'gleg [clear] is a guest's eye': in Lbs. 2186 4to, WGC to Eiríkur Magnússon, [n.d.] October 1897.

141 Ibid., 5 September 1897.

142 Ibid., 8 September 1897.

ley's set of short stories *The Sentimental Vikings* (1897) confirms that Victorian fiction was capable of rejecting all the heartiness of spirit and certainty of purpose that Victorian Vikingism so often represented. In 'The Sweeping of the Hall', an aged narrator, once a Viking, still shudders as he recalls his chief raiding a hall, killing the lord, and seizing the dead man's helpless daughter. In 'The Story of the Oar-Captain', the same narrator's relief at returning at the end of one voyage gives way to despair as the captain announces the start of another. And, in 'The Last Voyage', we find the narrator at the end of his tether. In his final moments, as the snow falls, he hears the call of the pagan gods: 'There is no voice of Christian God, for I have sacked his churches. The snow is in my eyes, and I am mad. I lean my head against the ship. There is no warmth, and I am afraid, alone.'[143] It is a scene of dislocation characteristic of stories in which the characters have no names or specific settings, and where the narrator oscillates between grim memories and glum realities. The brave morning of the Viking sea-king, and the lyric grandeur of the final ship burial, both still celebrated elsewhere,[144] have here given way to the darkest despair.

[143] Risley 1897, 169.
[144] For Vikings as great mariners, see Adams 1883: tales from Laing 1844, and from Vínland sagas, are followed by stories about Cabot, de Soto, Drake and Henry Morgan. On a noble Viking chief's ship burial, see McNab 1906, 2–16.

CHAPTER TWELVE

The Invisible College:
Resources and Networks

> You cannot conceive how interesting it is to an Englishman to find
> that an Icelandic phrase will run almost word for word into his
> own language. (H.G. Liddell 1867).[1]

> Like Casaubon, he cuts through into the jungle of learning, and
> his roads are Roman.
> (Oliver Elton 1890 [viii], on Guðbrandur Vigfússon)

> Give me news of your mistress Lady Lexicon; I hope – if it is not
> indelicate to hope – that she has given birth to a whole litter of
> letters by this time.
> (H.L.D. Ward to Guðbrandur Vigfússon, c.1872)[2]

The Cultivated Boat Builder

In the Introduction to his 1883 *Corpvs Poeticvm Boreale*, Guðbrandur Vigfússon
reflects on the differing intellectual traditions in English-speaking countries and
'abroad', by which he means principally Germany. 'Abroad' a man is 'aut Professor aut nullus'. Not so up and down the shires of Britain: 'often far from big
towns or universities, often little known, humble, and unpresuming, there are
to be found earnest and devoted scholars, who take up and pursue studies of
various kinds, purely from the love of them, without any desire for reward or
fame or publication'.[3] Guðbrandur indicates that it is to these people that the
two volumes of the *Corpvs* are directed with its texts and translations of 'The
Poetry of the Old Northern Tongue from the Earliest Times to the Thirteenth
Century'. He claims that 'all wise men of letters' cultivate some physical activity
as a hobby such as 'carving, turning, boat-building', and recommends in the

---

1 Bodleian MS Eng. Misc. d.131, HGL to GV, 8 January 1867. Liddell was joint compiler of the
Greek-English Lexicon (1843).
2 Bodleian MS Eng. Misc. d.131, undated. Gollancz 1898 is dedicated (in Icelandic) to Ward and
Eiríkur Magnússon.
3 All quotations in the paragraph are taken from Gudbrand Vigfusson and Powell 1883, cxxi.

same way that 'every handicraftsman and trader, great and small' should find some 'literary or artistic occupation or amusement' to fill their moments of leisure. Such folk would find 'no more delightful study than . . . the Old Northern Literature' represented in the *Corpvs*.

We do not know how many horny-handed sons of toil followed Guðbrandur's advice, but there is evidence of the kind of readership that old northern literature achieved in Victorian Britain. The printed word alone offers a lop-sided picture. For every Victorian who published essays or books about Vikings, there were several others who pursued their interest in less public ways. People studied alone at home; they worked in pairs to translate eddic poems; they gathered in groups to read sagas; they supported their local antiquarian societies; they attended lectures from visiting scholars; they prepared old northern tableaux for public performance; they subscribed loyally to old northern publications; and, not least, they corresponded with each other and with acknowledged authorities in the subject area. Sufficient correspondence survives from the last four decades of the century to confirm the existence of (in Philippa Levine's phrase) an 'invisible college'[4] of old northern enthusiasts in Victorian Britain. We learn of the sort of people who were attracted to the idea of the old north; their regional distribution; the particular nature of their interests; the sometimes intricate networks of individuals and institutions involved; and the nature of the scholarly support on which they were able to draw.

Two senior members of the invisible college were Guðbrandur Vigfússon in Oxford and Eiríkur Magnússon in Cambridge.[5] Over three decades Guðbrandur busied himself with a succession of demanding lexicographical and editorial projects; Eiríkur was a full-time librarian, part-time teacher of Icelandic, and spare-time scholar. Yet both men found time to deal patiently with the daily postal enquiries from wearisome (it must sometimes have seemed) enthusiasts from all over Britain. It is on the unpublished correspondence directed to Guðbrandur and Eiríkur, supplemented by letters and papers written to and by other prominent Victorian old northernists, that this chapter draws.

Resources I: Icelandic-English Dictionary (1874)

All the correspondence with Guðbrandur Vigfússon needs to be read in the light of the magisterial sequence of 1870s and 1880s publications with which his name is associated, to which reference is frequently made by his correspondents, and without which the independent study of primary old northern texts in Victorian Britain would have been virtually impossible. These works are *An Icelandic-English Dictionary* (1874), *Sturlunga Saga* (1878), *An Icelandic Prose Reader* (1879), *Corpvs Poeticvm Boreale* (1883), the much delayed edition and

---

4 Levine 1986, 36.
5 On Guðbrandur, see [Jón Þorkelsson] 1894, Benedikz 1989; on Eiríkur, see Stefán Einarsson 1933, 1961.

translation of *Orkneyinga saga* and *Hákonar saga* (1887–94), and *Origines Islandicae* (1905).[6] Individual reviewers with personal axes to grind could and did point out the errors in these volumes,[7] but in the eyes of grateful old northern enthusiasts such pioneering publications were indispensable. There had never been a dictionary of Icelandic in English, nor an English edition of any saga, nor a history of Icelandic literature in English such as that provided by the *Sturlunga* 'Prolegomena'. None of the Icelandic grammar books published earlier in the century could match the 1879 *Reader* in the clarity and authority of its grammatical coverage, or in the range of annotated saga extracts on which students could cut their philological teeth. The two *Corpvs* volumes opened up new horizons to readers ignorant of, intimidated by, or unsympathetic to the complexities of medieval Icelandic prosody and diction, and the volumes' new theories about the British origins of Icelandic eddic poetry represented an additional incentive to engage with these texts. Guðbrandur's edition of *Orkneyinga saga* and *Hákonar saga* also breaks new ground, as do Sir George Dasent's translations, for all the disastrous delays in their publication.[8] The posthumous *Origines* provided readers with a much-needed 'Collection of the More Important Sagas and other Native Writings relating to the Settlement and early History of Iceland'.

Each of these volumes deserves a chapter to itself,[9] but a few paragraphs on two of them must suffice as a prelude to an examination of correspondence that makes such frequent reference to them. Letters to Guðbrandur Vigfússon confirm that the 1874 *Dictionary* was by far the most important work that he produced. It was praised all over the English-speaking world and beyond. Its origins represent a happy combination of accident and design. The intersecting factors were: English gentlemanly leisure (Richard Cleasby), natural disaster (cholera epidemics in southern Europe encouraging Cleasby to visit Scandinavia), availability of learned Icelandic assistance (Konráð Gíslason who taught Cleasby Icelandic in Copenhagen), personal experience of inadequate scholarly provision (Cleasby's studies had been hampered by the lack of a good Icelandic dictionary), and family wealth (which enabled Cleasby to finance Konráð's lexicographical work). To these initial elements we may add a series of subsequent factors: a hammer blow from fate (Cleasby's untimely death in 1847),[10] postmortem confusion (Þorleifur Repp was spoken of as best qualified to take over the project,[11] which was eventually relocated in Britain), individual dynamism (Dasent), decisive Icelandic scholarly input (Guðbrandur Vigfússon), and con-

6 Guðbrandur died in 1889; York Powell in 1904.
7 Notably Eiríkr Magnússon 1905 on Gudbrand Vigfusson and Powell 1905.
8 See Knowles 1963, 118–23; Wawn 1997a, 468–71.
9 On the *Corpvs*, see Benedikt Gröndal 1884, Dronke 1989.
10 'a thunderbolt for us all' [Tordenslag for os alle]: Indrebø and Kolsrud 1924–71, I 245, P.A. Munch to George Stephens, 8 November 1847.
11 Aðalgeir Kristjánsson 1964, 142: Brynjólfur Pétursson to Grímur Thomsen, 9 December 1847.

troversy (over the extent of Guðbrandur's contribution).[12] The early fascicles that appeared in 1869 confirmed that the *Dictionary* would represent for amateur and professional alike the single most important Icelandic-related pedagogical and scholarly resource available in the English language. Its uncompromising preliminary grammar section, stodgy even by Victorian standards, belies the richness and humanity of its individual entries. Whatever the nature of the pre-existing materials inherited from Cleasby and Konráð Gíslason,[13] the guiding hand of Guðbrandur Vigfússon (drawing on the help of informed correspondents from all over Britain) seems discernible in the heavy freight of British literary and cultural reference carried by many of the entries. By leafing through A alone the Victorian reader would have soon noticed this recurrent emphasis:

aflausn Guðbrandur notes a *Fóstbræðra saga* reference to the fisherman's custom of declaring himself free from fishing obligations when he had 'drawn (up) a fish for himself . . . another for his boat, a third for his angle, a fourth for his line'. The reader is assured that 'this way of reckoning their catch is still common with fishermen in many parts of England and Scotland', with a Scottish ballad cited in support.

alin Defined as 'the arm from the elbow to the end of the middle finger'. We learn that the old Icelandic *ell* was doubled in 1200 to match its English equivalent, and prevailed until British trade in Iceland declined at the end of the fifteenth century. Dasent's *Burnt Njal* is cited. A secondary meaning 'a unit of value, viz. an ell . . . of woollen stuff' is linked to English 'woadmal' and equivalent Orkney and Shetland terms.

Amlóði Identified as the 'true name' of Shakespeare's Hamlet. The story's origins are traced to tenth-century Iceland, with its earliest written form (in Saxo) perhaps derived from Icelandic oral tradition; attention is drawn to a manuscript of *Ambales saga* in the British Museum;[14] and, in the word's transfered sense of 'fool, simpleton', Anglo-Saxon parallels are cited.

andsælis The identified meaning 'against the course of the sun' is linked to Scottish dialectal 'widdershins', and to the belief that moving against the direction of the sun is 'universally considered both in England and Scotland to be most unlucky': Jamieson's *Etymological Dictionary* is cited.[15]

áfr The term for an oat-brewed ale. A detailed etymological discussion refers to Scottish *yill*, 'ale', from Robbie Burns' 'Country Lassie'.

---

[12] Re-examined in Aðalgeir Kristjánsson 1996.

[13] See [anon.] 1874, Jakob Benediktsson 1969, 103–4, Knowles 1980, Svavar Sigmundsson 1989, Guðrún Kvaran 1991, 61–7, Aðalgeir Kristjánsson 1996, 30–1.

[14] Gollancz 1898, lii–lv argues for the work's Irish provenance.

[15] J.A. Carlyle discusses the dictionary: Bodleian MS Eng. Misc. d.131, JAC to GV, 18 May 1867, 23 October 1869.

The gentle process of acculturation at work here is nourished by Guðbrandur's network of contacts throughout Britain: the Carlyles in Scotland, the Peacocks in Newcastle, the Sephtons in Liverpool, and scholarly collaborators such as Edmund Head and George Dasent. The eccentric nature of individual etymologies itself results from Guðbrandur's unflagging wish to identify the closest possible cultural links between Iceland and Britain.

Resources II: Sturlunga saga (1878)

Sturlunga saga, Sturla Þórðarson's lengthy chronicle of the last years of the medieval Icelandic commonwealth, is frequently cited in the *Dictionary*, with Guðbrandur drawing on transcripts made in Copenhagen before, at Dasent's instigation, he moved to Britain to begin his lexicographical work. Residence in England, while affording access to important manuscripts, also enabled Guðbrandur to complete his edition of *Sturlunga*.[16] Even with the aid of the *Dictionary* only a few dedicated Victorian souls will have made much headway in Guðbrandur's edited Icelandic text, but any old northernist could read the 'Prolegomena', which was (or were!) intended to serve as an introduction to an integrated text series featuring the commanding heights of medieval Icelandic literature – *Sturlunga saga*, the *Corpvs*, and (eventually) *Origines Islandicae*.[17] Like the *Dictionary* the *Sturlunga* introduction teems with references to British life and letters. The reader learns that Icelandic literature bears the marks of Celtic influence;[18] that early Icelandic land settlement was based on the udal ideals of Norway and Orkney; that Icelandic sagas such as *Laxdœla* resemble Elizabethan drama;[19] that *Beowulf* was the English offshoot of a Scandinavian tradition which in Iceland produced *Grettissaga*;[20] that Sturla is 'the "last minstrel" of the Saga time, . . . left alone, like Ossian, with the dead'.[21] Guðbrandur praises Jón Hjaltalín's 1873 translation of *Orkneyinga saga*;[22] and refers (albeit somewhat dismissively) to *Hákonar saga Hákonarsonar*, the end of which was probably the best known *samtíðarsaga* in Britain.[23] Even when addressing the narrative art of *Sturlunga* itself, British comparisons are invoked: 'you can feel the choking smoke and heat, and hear the roar of the flame in the hall and the clash of the spears in the porches . . . [such] pitiless . . . faithfulness to fact' has

---

[16] He used BM Add. 11127 (*c.*1690), and Advocates' Library MS 21.3.17, both acquired around 1820.

[17] Projected editions of *Njáls saga* and the complete *Konungasögur* never materialised.

[18] Gudbrand Vigfusson 1878, I xxvi.

[19] Ibid., I xxvi.

[20] Ibid., I xlix–l. See discussion in Magnús Fjalldal 1998.

[21] Gudbrand Vigfusson 1878, I lxix.

[22] Ibid., I xcv.

[23] Johnstone 1782a. *Sverris saga* enjoyed late Victorian prominence after Carlyle 1875 and Sephton 1899. Thirteenth-century *samtíðasögur* deal with near contemporary Icelandic history.

been matched by 'Defoe and Carlyle alone of English authors'.[24] Guðbrandur also outlines his new theory of British origin for the eddic lays.[25] With Guðbrandur's 'Prolegomena' directing such an Anglocentric spray over Icelandic culture, the canny Jón Hjaltalín wondered why the essay was not published separately in Britain as 'A History of Old Icelandic Literature',[26] for the benefit of those disinclined to buy *Sturlunga* itself.

The *Dictionary*, the *Sturlunga* 'Prolegomena' and, come to that, the *Prose Reader* and, eventually, the *Orkneyinga saga* edition and translation, are commanding scholarly achievements that answered the long-felt needs of many Victorian old northernists, as many of Guðbrandur's correspondents were happy to acknowledge.

Correspondence with Guðbrandur Vigfússon

Letters to Guðbrandur did not arrive daily in thematically organised bundles from clearly identifiable groups. A random selection hints at the diversity of Guðbrandur's regular postbag. Rev. Pellew Arthur of Gloucester requests guidance with his Old Icelandic reading in the summer of 1888.[27] He has acquired the *Dictionary, Prose Reader,* and *Sturlunga*; he is currently reading *Orkneyinga saga* and finding Icelandic harder to read than Danish; he intends to read *Sturlunga saga* in Guðbrandur's edition and also some of the *Biskupasögur.* Like many another Victorian enthusiast, he also wants to visit Iceland 'where the writers of the sagas lived' and unlike every other correspondent he sends a pair of Christmas pheasants to the Icelander with thanks for any help he can offer. The then terminally ill Guðbrandur is likely to have appreciated the thought more than the gift.[28] Frederick Balfour has noticed the title 'Ancient Icelandic sagas' on the published lecture lists in Oxford; he is not a member of the university but would very much like to attend; would the sessions be too difficult for him as he does not know Icelandic grammar?[29] Marie Brown writes from America; she is completing her fanatically anti-Columbus, anti-Catholic book on the Norse discovery of America and requests advice about an appropriate design for the cover.[30] The Dean of Chichester wants to know the names for the days of the week in Icelandic and any other obscure northern languages.[31] J.W. Cursiter expresses his pleasure at having acquired the *Corpvs Poeticvm*: 'I am

---

[24] Gudbrand Vigfusson 1878, I cvi–cvii.

[25] Ibid., I clxxxiii–vi; rejected by Benedikt Gröndal 1880.

[26] Bodleian MS Icelandic d.1, JH to GV, Easter 1879. Guðbrandur's brother wanted the 'Prolegomena' translating into Icelandic: Bodleian MS Icelandic d.2, Sigurður Vigfússon to GV, 8 May 1881.

[27] Bodleian MS Eng. Misc. d.131, PA to GV, 19 July 1888.

[28] Ibid., [late 1888].

[29] Ibid., FB to GV, [– Jan. 1887].

[30] Ibid., MB to GV, 25 March 1887.

[31] Ibid., John W. Burgeon to GV, 19 January 1887.

beginning to look upon all Scandinavian literature as indispensable altho I can't read it.'[32] Oliver Elton writes from Liverpool University to suggest a new project – a translation of Hallgrímur Pétursson's *Passíusálmar*, the great seventeenth-century work of Icelandic popular piety that was to attract other Victorian translators.[33]

Such letters to Guðbrandur offer some sense of the invisible old northern college in Victorian Britain which emerges: the predominance of male university-educated (or connected) members;[34] the widespread unsatisfied demand for teaching, lectures, and guided reading; the problem of availability of and access to books; the gratitude with which Guðbrandur's own publications were received; the development and politicisation of old northern studies in the United States; and the Anglo-Catholic interest in Icelandic pre- and post-medieval religious literature.

The 1874 *Dictionary* was acknowledged as Guðbrandur's greatest scholarly achievement by his correspondents. Joseph Bosworth, revising his *Dictionary of the Anglo-Saxon Language* (1838), writes in 1871 to check an etymological point, praises the first fascicles of the Icelandic dictionary, and congratulates Guðbrandur on the honorary M.A. that the University of Oxford had newly bestowed upon its tireless lexicographical workhorse.[35] Frederick Metcalfe, the 'Oxonian in Iceland', writes to say that the award of this degree is 'unique in the Annals of Iceland'.[36] We must hope that the untenured and impoverished Guðbrandur realised how lucky he was.[37] Willard Fiske, a wealthy New Englander who spent much of his adult life in Italy and owned an unrivalled collection of old northern books,[38] also writes to praise the *Dictionary*: 'I see many indications that it is already giving an impulse to Icelandic studies on this side of the ocean.'[39] Writing again in 1879, with *Sturlunga* and the *Prose Reader* now also available, Fiske states: 'You deserve the thanks of the whole English-speaking community of scholars for providing them with such an apparatus',[40] and cites Walter Skeat's *Etymological Dictionary of English* (1879–1882) as one of the 'plain results of your painstaking labours'. Skeat himself had been quick to congratulate Guðbrandur:[41] the *Dictionary* is a wonderful achievement, and would have been even better had it included an index of English words derived

---

[32] Ibid., JWC to GV, [n.d.] 1888.

[33] Ibid., OE to GV, [n.d.] September 1886.

[34] Guðbrandur helped Charlotte Sidgewick prepare a children's book on Iceland: Bodleian MS Eng. Misc. d.131, 7 letters *c.*1886.

[35] Ibid., JB to GV, 3 June 1871.

[36] Ibid., FM to GV, 9 June [–].

[37] Guðbrandur's financial plight is highlighted in Bodleian MS Icel. c.112, letters between Max Müller, H.G. Liddell and Henry Smith.

[38] Halldór Hermannsson 1914–27.

[39] Bodleian MS Eng. Misc. d.131, WF to GV, 15 January 1875.

[40] Ibid., WF to GV, 7 June 1879.

[41] Ibid., WWS to GV, 27 December 1869.

from Icelandic as an appendix – Skeat would be willing to prepare such a list.[42] Guðbrandur, ever prickly, chose to take offence at the implied deficiency, and the Cambridge scholar is forced to pour oil on the troubled waters.[43] His suggestion that Guðbrandur should publish a shorter version of the *Dictionary* was eventually acted on by Geir Zoëga in 1910.

Guðbrandur's *Dictionary* becomes the corner-stone for saga-reading groups, such as that run by Arthur Lawrenson in the Shetland Isles.[44] His Lerwick friends have come to depend on the volume, but now the owner has emigrated to New Zealand and taken it with him. They are currently reading *Hávamál* from the *Corpvs Poeticvm*, and Guðbrandur is thanked for making copies available at a discount price. The group members are all proud of their Old Norse ancestry.[45] Captain F.W.L. Thomas of Shetland, nautical surveyor by day and saga enthusiast by night, writes about Old Icelandic terms for sailing and the sea. Thomas expresses gratitude for the *Dictionary* and *Corpvs Poeticvm*, even though he, like many other Victorian old northernists, has little sympathy for the stylistic complexity of skaldic poetry: 'I do not wonder I could never translate the Skaldic verses – it seems as if the words had been shaken up in a bag and then picked out and arranged according not to their sense but to their sound.'[46]

Guðbrandur kept in touch with several of his earliest British contacts. His friendship with Bligh Peacock, 'a merchant and scholar, who knows the Northern languages, Icelandic inclusive',[47] dates from his arrival from Denmark in 1864; thereafter Guðbrandur often stayed with the Peacocks during his northern tours, which normally also took in Liverpool (the Sephtons), the Isle of Man (Ernest Savage), Dumfries (the Carlyles), and Edinburgh (meetings with Capt. Thomas). Twenty years later Bligh's son Septimus writes to announce that his father wishes to dispose of his private library of 1200 books on old northern topics.[48] The existence of such a collection offers a further glimpse of the old northern interests of Victorian antiquarians in the north-east, to set alongside Þorleifur Repp's friendship with Ralph Carr, Carr's own interest in the Maeshowe runes,[49] George Atkinson's Icelandic travels,[50] and the honorary memberships of Finnur Magnússon and George Stephens in the local antiquarian society.

Exasperatingly, one or two of Guðbrandur's more intriguing correspondents disappear without trace. In 1880, a youthful sounding James Platt writes two

42 See Skeat 1876.
43 Bodleian MS Eng. Misc. d.131, WWS to GV, 27 December 1869.
44 See Lawrenson 1882.
45 Bodleian MS Eng. Misc. d.131, AL to GV, 22 December 1879, 5 November 1882. See also Lawrenson 1882.
46 Ibid. See also J.A. Carlyle to GV, 24 April [n.a.].
47 SJL MS 3.32, GV to John Sephton, 29 October 1883.
48 Bodleian MS Eng. Misc. d.131, SP to GV, 8 September 1885.
49 Wawn 1991a, 176–83; also Farrer 1862, Barnes M. 1994.
50 Seaton 1989.

delightful letters to Guðbrandur, his 'fellow Teuton'.[51] Platt is a keen student of Old Icelandic, has made good use of Guðbrandur's *Dictionary* and *Reader*, and is eager to devote himself to the philological life. He has been 'addicted' to northern antiquity for as long as he can remember, but had never found a friend to whom 'I could communicate my ideas on such subjects.' He prepared a vocabulary of Old English when he was just ten years-old; he has a 'remarkable natural inclination' for the northern languages; manifest destiny is calling him – 'I cannot but feel sure that Teutonic philology is the end for which I was born and the only thing which would be a success in my hands.' He requests a testimonial letter, and submits notes on aspects of Icelandic philology for scrutiny, all 'entirely original so far as I know'. The British Library catalogue has no record of any subsequent philological publications: what ever happened to James Platt? Did he succumb to disease or death in battle or did he, like Charlie Mears in Kipling's 'The Finest Story in the World', simply grow out of it?[52] And how many more like him were there in Victorian Britain?

Guðbrandur Vigfússon's links with the Carlyles, forged early, were maintained over a long period. John, younger brother of Thomas, was among Guðbrandur's most loyal correspondents in the decade from 1866. Guðbrandur was instructed always to reply in Icelandic. John well understood the need for the new dictionary,[53] had helped to proof-read the volume,[54] and was a shrewd adviser concerning its contents. He encourages Guðbrandur to highlight the extent of Norse influence in Scotland, and to quote extensively from otherwise inaccessible texts – 'Dictionaries in general . . . have little to enliven them except perhaps the passages which they quote'.[55] Carlyle worries about Guðbrandur's 'alarmingly defective' English, and about the section on Icelandic grammar at the beginning of the *Dictionary* – 'too concentrated'[56] in appearance, and quite unsuitable for nervous beginners. The Clarendon Press should publish a separate Icelandic grammar volume with spacious layout, clear paradigms, and selected graded reading texts – Guðbrandur might care to work on this in the evenings as 'a kind of rest and relaxation' after a day's work on the *Dictionary* entries![57] In its corrected form the *Dictionary* will be a great success, Guðbrandur is assured; the whole enterprise would bring 'great credit and honour to Oxford – the greatest since the time of Hicks [sic] and Wanley'.[58]

John Carlyle's letters range widely over other aspects of the old and modern north.[59] He has read the *Strengleikar* and the *Biskupasögur*,[60] and reflects disap-

51 Bodleian MS Eng., JP to GV, 3 July and 5 July 1880.
52 See 'Coda', below, pp. 370–1.
53 Bodleian MS Eng. Misc. d.131, JAC to GV, 23 March 1866; 30 September 1866.
54 Ibid., 11 October 1866, 25 November 1866
55 Ibid., 26 December 1866.
56 Ibid., 1 October 1869.
57 Ibid., 23 October 1869. Sweet 1886 supplied this need.
58 Ibid., 21 August 1866.
59 Cowan 1979.
60 Bodleian MS Eng. Misc. d.131, 9 April 1867.

provingly on the nature of medieval Catholicism in Iceland.[61] He reports that his brother Thomas still thinks that 'Odin was a man of real flesh and blood', a hero fit to worship,[62] and looks forward to forthcoming articles by Jón Hjaltalín in *Fraser's Magazine*, whose editorship Dasent had taken over.[63] Carlyle clearly has little time for Dasent himself ('rather fat'),[64] or for his much-praised *Burnt Njal* ('I dislike his vulgar translation of the Njals Saga, which in the original is so noble and clear . . . [I] detest the slang which [he] introduces').[65] He nevertheless advises Guðbrandur shrewdly in his stormy relationship with the English scholar.[66]

Guðbrandur Vigfússon's exasperation with Dasent came easily, which makes the patience he extended towards some of his apparently more eccentric correspondents all the more remarkable. He may have rolled his eyes when T.G. Paterson, one of the Kleifarvatn sulphur entrepreneurs, writes to ask where he can obtain a model of the newly-discovered Gokstad ship – a friend wanted to paint some authentic-looking Viking scenes.[67] Sir Garth Wilkinson, whose Swedenborgian study of *Vǫluspá* is discussed in Chapter Seven, pesters Guðbrandur over the best way of organising regular shipments of Icelandic lava for his domestic use – he believed it was good for horses' teeth! Wilkinson's own old northern network extended beyond Oxford. Acquiring Icelandic manuscripts from his fellow Swedenborgian Jón Hjaltalín before the latter's return to Iceland, Wilkinson presents them to Harvard University, with whose librarian he is on good terms. One manuscript contains a copy of Jón Hjaltalín's eddic style 'Victoríukviða'[68] which the Icelander recited for the Queen at Windsor Castle in April 1868, 'there being about 850 years since an Icelander brought a poem to an English sovereign'; this was a reference to the skaldic poems performed before kings of England by Gunnlaugr and Egill as recorded in the sagas which bear their names. The rest of the manuscript contains Jón's 1870 unpublished annotated translation of the *Poetic Edda*. A fair copy[69] was prepared for Anna Maria Helena, Countess de Noailles, a mysterious figure for whom Jón undertook other old northern work. He was paid nine guineas in 1872 for preparing a sample abridgement of the letter A in 'Cleasby's Dictionary' (111 pages), and offers to complete the project for £200.[70] He also lends the Countess an unpublished Icelandic grammar that he had prepared. Corre-

[61] Ibid., 27 April 1867.
[62] Ibid., 1 October 1869.
[63] Ibid., 12 September 1871.
[64] Ibid., 26 December 1866.
[65] Ibid., 25 December 1874.
[66] Ibid., 27 January 1877.
[67] Ibid., TGP to GV, 18 October 1886.
[68] Harvard University Library MS Icel. 55.
[69] Lbs. 2859 4to.
[70] [Hughes] [n.d.], 101–2.

spondence suggests that Jón's client lived in Britain (probably London) during his period of residence in the country.[71]

As has already been noted, Guðbrandur received his fair share of correspondence from America. He was destined never to emulate Leifr Eiríksson and cross the Atlantic, though his friend Jón Stefánsson loyally (and mistakenly) declares that 'they will have to make a professorship for you in Oxford if they want to keep you from the American Universities'.[72] One university-based correspondent in the United States allows us to uncover another chain of contacts involving Guðbrandur. Charles Sprague Smith of Andover, Massachusetts,[73] having spent six months in Oxford studying with Guðbrandur, travelled in Scandinavia with letters of introduction from his mentor. Returning to America in 1880, Sprague Smith was appointed to a post at Columbia College, a school which within a few years would have the accomplished Icelandic scholar William Carpenter as its President.[74] Sprague Smith reports that he has been teaching an Icelandic class, studying the relationship between *Grettis saga* and *Beowulf*,[75] and has presented Longfellow with (appropriately) an early edition of *Ólafs saga Tryggvasonar*, 'of course sowing with the intention of reaping'.[76] Sprague Smith contemplates future visits to Iceland in the company of Guðbrandur; he eventually made the trip alone in 1888, meeting Matthías Jochumsson in Akureyri, who 'exercised' him on passages from *Sturlunga saga*, and pronounced himself well satisfied with the young scholar's progress.[77] In his teaching Sprague Smith used John Sephton's translation of *Eiríks saga Rauða*, as recommended by Guðbrandur,[78] who, writing to Sephton, had once praised 'the freshness (and also the accuracy but that is a matter of course) of your rendering'.[79] These exchanges underline once again the widespread personal and institutional links which Guðbrandur Vigfússon helped to promote, all to the benefit of old northern scholarship, on both sides of the Atlantic.

Only one letter survives from George Stephens, whom Sprague Smith had found 'as long-winded and prosaic in his conversation as in his writings'.[80] Guðbrandur is thanked for his account of recent scholarly skirmishes about Manx runes. Stephens is reminded of 'the heroes of our Northern Walhall, [who] slay each other with gusto day by day and, when "the shades of evening fall", retire to a jolly . . . [wake], like good fellows as they are'.[81] Ernest Savage is

71 Bound in with Lbs. 2859 4to, two letters from Jón to the Countess.
72 Bodleian MS Eng. Misc. d.131, JS to GV, 18 December 1887.
73 His daughter was the medieval scholar Lucy Toulmin Smith.
74 See Carpenter 1881a, 1881b, 1887.
75 See Smith 1881.
76 Bodleian MS Eng. Misc. d.131, CCS to GV, 15 February 1880. See Smith 1889, 1890, 1891a, 1891b, 1892 for Iceland related publications.
77 Bodleian MS Eng. Misc. d.131, CCS to GV, 20 September 1888.
78 SJL MS 3.32, GV to John Sephton, 26 December 1880; also 20 April 1882.
79 Ibid., 25 August 1880.
80 Ibid., GV to John Sephton, 26 December 1880.
81 Bodleian MS Eng. Misc. d.131, GS to GV, 9 March 1887.

much exercised by proposed changes to the Viking-age structure of the Manx parliament, the Tynwald – would Guðbrandur and York Powell intervene?[82] A youthful Henry Sweet[83] requests a testimonial from Guðbrandur to support his application for a position in the British Museum. Sweet writes subsequently to praise Guðbrandur's 'truly noble' dictionary, that has 'revived all my old love for Icelandic'. This is no mere formulaic tribute. Sweet's bitterness at the poverty of his Oxford education is born of its long-lasting after-effects: 'The drudgery of cramming up Greek and Latin . . . made it impossible for me to take any real pleasure in any study whatever.'[84]

Henry Sweet is not the only Victorian scholar to confirm to Guðbrandur that Icelandic studies could reawaken individuals from lethargy or despair. In 1895 John Sephton was appointed Reader in Icelandic Studies at the University College of Liverpool.[85] He owned a fine collection of early Icelandic printed books,[86] published extensively on old northern subjects,[87] and remained in regular contact with Guðbrandur over the last decade of the Icelander's life. In April 1882 Sephton is deeply depressed. His friend and fellow Liverpudlian Icelandophile Sir James Picton is growing old, Icelandic studies in the city are languishing, he himself has not opened a book for months and his only son has just died.[88] A forthcoming book of Guðbrandur's promises to revive his spirits: 'I hope however . . . that the sight of the *Corpvs Poeticvm* . . . will bring me new life.' It was no idle hope. Henry Howorth, a Manchester M.P. and Icelandic enthusiast,[89] had written to York Powell, also in the spring of 1882, with his own tragic tale. One of his children had fallen out of a moving train and been crushed, with Howorth looking on helplessly: 'It would have killed me . . . but for my having Norse studies to resort to.'[90] Both Howorth and Sephton rediscover the will to live and work, and Guðbrandur follows the latter's progress eagerly. Sephton reports that whenever he has 'ten minutes to spare which is not often I fly to the Flatey book'.[91] He decides to translate *Jómsvíkinga þáttr* – 'I am amusing myself with the Wickings of Jomsborg.'[92] A recent lecture on Thor was

---

82 SJL MS 3.33, 101: ES to GV, [n.d.].

83 Bodleian MS Eng. Misc. d.131, HS to GV, 12 March 1869. See Wawn 1990a.

84 Bodleian MS Eng. Misc. d.131, HS to GV, 11 February 1877.

85 Sephton's referees included York Powell and Eiríkur Magnússon: Lbs. 2187b 4to, Edward Jenks to EM, 13 June 1895.

86 Now in the SJL, University of Liverpool. The texts include Skálholt editions of *Landnámabók* (1688) and Einar Eyjólfsson's translation of Arngrímur Jónsson's *Gronlandia* (1688); *Saga . . . Olafs Tryggvasonar Noregs kongs* (1689); devotional works by Hallgrímur Pétursson (1692, 1693), *Guðbrandsbiblía* and *Þorláksbiblía*, Verelius's *Herrauds och Bosa saga* (1666), sermons by Jón Vídalín of Skálholt (1716), and *Elucidarius* (1689).

87 See Sephton 1880, 1887, 1892, 1895, 1896, 1898, 1899, 1912.

88 Bodleian MS Eng. Misc.d.131, JS to GV, 21 April 1882.

89 Howorth 1920; see also [anon.] 1892. Howorth 1894 reviews Howell 1893, Green 1893, Baring-Gould 1894.

90 SJL MS 3.33, HH to GV, 20 April 1882.

91 Bodleian MS Eng. Misc. d.131, JS to GV, 24 December 1887.

92 Ibid., 22 March 1888.

delivered to 'as fine an audience as Liverpool can furnish'; the whole perform-ance was 'nothing but the Corpvs from beginning to end'.[93] This represents an archetypal instance of the trickle-down effect of learned scholarship within Vic-torian society's 'invisible college': an Oxford-based Icelander's scholarship is transmitted both in print and by word of mouth to the worthy burghers of Merseyside by a well-informed and widely respected local disciple.

Sephton's Liverpool circle of old northern enthusiasts is certainly comparable with groups associated with Collingwood in the Lake District group, and Bligh Peacock on Tyneside. Guðbrandur used to dine with local Liverpool members of parliament when staying with the Sephtons, notably Sir James Picton – 'a fine man, and deserving of respect for having literary interests at all in Liver-pool, where all the world rotates around bales of Cotton'.[94] Papers by Picton and others on Grimms' Law, Sanskrit, Saxon settlements, philology, ethnology, and runes were read at the Liverpool Literary and Philosophical Society, and help us to appreciate the high levels of philological curiosity amongst the mid-Victorian provincial intelligentsia.[95] Sephton himself lectured regularly to the society towards the end of the century on runes, Norse religion, and the Norse-men in Greenland and America.[96] He could point to unseemly Viking-age con-tinuities on Merseyside. Discussing Hákon jarl in *Jómsvíkinga saga*, he remarks: 'He certainly upheld the social institution of slavery, and was not averse to the slave-trade any more than his descendants in Wirral and West Derby down to the present century.'[97] But we also find him determined to derive the name 'Litherland', a Merseyside area of no great beauty, from Old Icelandic Hlíðar-endi, as in 'Gunnar's famous home'.[98] This kind of regional enthusiasm eventu-ally achieved national coordination with the formation of the Viking Club in London in 1892.[99]

Resources III: The Victorian Lecture Room

Public lectures were an important focal point for members of the old northern 'invisible college', and were frequently spoken of in their correspondence. We recall that Þorleifur Repp was a colourful lecturer on the Edinburgh circuit in the 1830s; that Thomas Smith lectured on Norse paganism to the Leicester Lit-erary Society in 1838; that Thomas Carlyle's thoughts on Odin and hero worship were first voiced in lectures held in London in 1840; and that by 1876,

---

93 Ibid., 30 March 1887. Guðbrandur learnt of Sephton's successful lectures from a visiting Nor-wegian scholar: SJL MS 3.32, GV to JS, 29 March 1887. Sephton 1887 includes a balladic trans-lation of *Þrymskviða*.
94 SJL MS 3.33, JS to GV, 8 Jan. 1886.
95 Picton 1864, 1865, 1868, 1869; Geldart 1875. See also Wiley 1990.
96 Sephton 1880, 1892, 1896, 1898.
97 Sephton 1892, 125.
98 Sephton 1904, 68.
99 Townsend 1992.

for his set of afternoon lectures on old northern literature, history and ethnography in St George's Hall, Langham Place, George Browning was able to charge 2s 6d for a single lecture, 10s 6d for the set of six, and a guinea for a family ticket. William Morris and James Bryce became star old northern performers in provincial lecture halls, whilst other solid citizens and scholars found eager audiences in their own localities.[100] Native Icelanders inevitably carried a special authority with British audiences. Summaries of lectures were often printed in local, national, and even international newspapers.[101] Like globe-trotting concert pianists, lecturers such as Jón Hjaltalín or Eiríkur Magnússon would prepare a set of lectures for the season and then tour the country with them: during the 1871–2 winter Jón visited Edinburgh, Greenock, Newcastle, Birmingham, and Manchester with lectures 'illustrated by maps and photographic views'.[102] William Lyall, Secretary to the Literary and Philosophical Society of Newcastle,[103] writes to confirm arrangements for Eiríkur's visit in the autumn of 1871; his three lectures are to deal with the sagas, the *Poetic Edda*, and 'Social and Domestic Conditions of the Northmen in Early Times'.[104] Such visits not only spread the old northern word but generated valuable income for impecunious visiting scholars.[105]

Unpublished manuscripts of Eiríkur's lectures indicate what was on offer to the stout citizenry of middle Britain on winter evenings in draughty halls up and down the land. As well as his fund-raising lectures on Anglo-Icelandic relations (discussed in Chapter 1), Eiríkur is well aware that by the 1870s his audiences want to hear about the romance of Iceland and its saga culture – the lonely farmsteads in bleak windswept valleys where during long winter nights miraculous feats of story telling and writing took place. It was the Danish artist August Schiøtt who produced the archetypal portrait of the country *kvöldvaka*: the cosy homestead, the family group at work, father reading from the precious old vellum, his book illuminated by an oil lamp, his face glowing with reflected light from the page[106] – naturalism and symbolism here serve a common cause. Eiríkur was able to draw on his own first-hand childhood experiences. He knew that the lamps were fuelled by codliver oil, or shark oil, or melted seal blubber. He had breathed the dank air of the turf houses, and experienced the interactive nature of the tale telling as all people great and small 'make their laconic remarks

---

100 As with Alex Moffat, whose December 1900 'Palnatoke and Wales' lecture at the Swansea Scientific Society was subsequently published: Moffat 1903.
101 Bodleian MS Icel. d.1, Jón Hjaltalín to GV, 23 May 1871.
102 Ibid., 23 September 1870.
103 Watson R.S. 1897.
104 Lbs. 2188a 4to, WL to EM, 21 September 1871; lectures on the Monday, Wednesday and Friday evenings.
105 'these societies have offered me good fees' [þessi félög hafa boðið mér gott kjör]; Bodleian MS Icel. d.1, Jón Hjaltalín to GV, 23 September 1870.
106 Ponzi 1986, 91.

as the story develops on the character of this or that hero, and on the tragic as well as the comic interest of the whole situation'.[107]

Eiríkur seasons his narrative with seductive atmospherics[108] even when, as in his lecture 'Iceland and England 1875', the cruel actualities of modern Iceland to which Eiríkur draws attention told a different tale. A disastrous volcanic eruption of Öræfajökull in 1874 had caused catastrophic damage to 2,000 square miles of farmland to the south and east of Iceland. Land at Hákonar-staðir that had been offered for sale the previous year at £300 was now worth less than £10 (xlii). Pastures had been devastated and livestock incinerated. The sun became a grotesque 'huge red ball . . . dull, rayless . . . [with an] almost chilling lustre' (xli). People consumed such food as there was along with mouth-fuls of dust – a 'process of repulsive necessity [rather] than of hearty gratifica-tion' (ibid.). Eiríkur is invited to give this lecture in Dorchester in September 1875.[109] Two lectures in Wisbech in July 1876 discussing 'Recent Eruptions in Iceland' and 'The Island's Distress and England's Charity' were almost certainly recycled versions of the same paper.[110] Unlike the southern Icelandic grasslands themselves, lectures of this kind could be dusted off when the spectre of further famine loomed large in the early 1880s.[111]

The Eiríkur Magnússon Circle

When Eiríkur's private correspondence is examined, covering the years from his arrival in Britain in 1862 until his death in 1913, the picture of the invisible college that emerges is somewhat different from that derived from letters to Guðbrandur Vigfússon. This is not wholly surprising, not least because the two men, friends when they arrived in Britain, became deadly enemies in a private philological civil war worthy of the rawest Sturlung Age conflict: the bachelor against the family man; Dalasýsla against Berufjörður; Oxford against Cambridge; the purist against the moderniser in their fierce debate over biblical translation policy;[112] the trouble-making non-contributor against the organiser of the 1875 and 1882 Mansion House Icelandic famine relief campaigns.[113] They squabbled in print over anything and everything.[114] The fires of Hekla could freeze over before Eiríkur and Guðbrandur would be reconciled.

In terms of their correspondents, it is hard to imagine Albany Major, Secre-

[107] Lbs. 406 fol. (1) xli–lxii.
[108] Ibid., (2) xv.
[109] Lbs. 2188b 4to, HCM to EM, 18 September 1875.
[110] Lbs 2186a 4to, J.N. Brightman and N.M. Boulton to EM, 17 and 19 February 1876.
[111] Lbs. 403–4 fol.
[112] Gudbrand Vigfusson 1869; Eiríkr Magnússon 1879.
[113] Eiríkr Magnússon 1882, Harris 1978–81, Ellison 1979, 1987–8, 178.
[114] Morris 1879 objects to Guðbrandur's omission (1878, I 1) of Eiríkur's name when referring to the Morris-Eiríkur *Grettis saga* translation. Eiríkr Magnússon 1875 is dismissed as a reproduction of Unger's 1869 edition: Gudbrand Vigfusson 1878, I cxxxv.

tary of the Viking Club, daring to write to Guðbrandur on headed notepaper identifying the name of his Croydon residence as 'Bifrost' [sic], the eddic rainbow bridge linking heaven and earth.[115] The affliction ran in the family: E.E. Speight, Major's brother-in-law, named his Norwood house 'Nidaros'.[116] Letters to Eiríkur tend to be more informal than those to Guðbrandur, and thus offer a wider-angled shot of old northern enthusiasms up to the end of Edward VII's reign. Albany Major writes tetchily of a Viking pageant on the River Thames as part of the Festival of Empire in the summer of 1910 – his translation of *Bjarkamál* had been used and abused by the participants.[117] Speight and Major had published an enterprising collection of translated saga extracts for school children,[118] with passages selected from material already in print[119] or from their own specially prepared translations. The idea was simple: 'we wish to get the Saga Stories into English Schools, to bring down a little of the Northern atmosphere to the children' for all that 'it is almost sure to be at the expense of our pockets'.[120] Speight admits that 'neither [Albany] Major nor myself have any real training in Icelandic',[121] and wishes that they had known earlier of Eiríkur's offer of help. Other projects are afoot: Speight wants to publish a collection of translated pieces relating to the discovery of Greenland and Vínland; and, having translated the whole of *Flóamanna saga*, he intends to move on to *Eiríks saga rauða*, *Flateyjarbók* and *Konungs skuggsjá*. *Bjarnar saga Hítdælakappa* is another possibility, 'and I have Vatnsdaela in view too'.[122] He wonders whether a publisher could be found for the works in C.C. Rafn's 1829–30 *Fornaldarsögur* edition. Indeed, why not translate the whole medieval saga corpus – 'I wish we could induce some one to lay down sufficient funds for us to produce a cheap uniform edition of popular translations of the Sagas . . . I suppose there are quite 50 volumes which might be counted worthy of inclusion.'[123] Finance need not be a problem, 'if we did fifty copies of each – 160pp. each, I could produce the lot for £160, if there were not many notes in small print'. He feels that it 'might almost be' worth asking for a government grant – 'many men have got Civil List pensions for far less important work'. The format he has in mind is that used for Sigurður Kristjánsson's pocket-sized paperback texts published in Reykjavík with which some British travellers would have been familiar. Speight's missionary zeal is intense:

---

[115] Lbs. 2188b 4to, AM letters to EM.

[116] Lbs. 2189b 4to. EES to EM, 29 August 1899.

[117] Lbs. 2188b 4to, AM to EM, 16 November 1910.

[118] Major and Speight 1899, 1905; see also Major 1894.

[119] For example Sephton 1895 and Morris and Eiríkr Magnússon 1891–1905, I (*Howard the Halt*).

[120] Lbs. 2189b 4to, EES to EM, 14 August 1899.

[121] Ibid., 29 August 1899.

[122] Ibid., 13 November 1903.

[123] Ibid., 29 August 1899.

I shall certainly spend some time in Iceland as soon as possible in order to get the feeling of actuality and nearness to the real life of the people, without which all work of this type is dry bones . . . I am determin'd to do my share in the future of bringing Northern matters before the British public and I am hopeful of spending a good part of my life in the north, where I can learn at first hand Islandsk and Farøsk and study their literature.

Few of Eiríkur's correspondents could match these levels of commitment, but several of them were working hard at learning Icelandic in Eiríkur's presence or through his postal guidance. His earliest pupil was almost certainly Sir Edmund Head, who took three or four lessons a week in 1863 – George Dasent's publisher Williams and Norgate had passed on Eiríkur's address.[124] The young Israel Gollancz enquires about formal Icelandic classes in Cambridge, 'several besides myself would welcome such';[125] we subsequently learn that Gollancz took weekly lessons from Jón Stefánsson, a friend of Eiríkur and W.G. Collingwood.[126] Bertha Skeat, niece of Walter, takes Icelandic classes with Eiríkur in Cambridge in 1885,[127] as does a Miss Reynolds of Newnham College who, with others, reads *Njáls saga* with Eiríkur over a two-year period. Writing later as an established teacher, she reports the belief that she has encountered in Europe that 'of all . . . nations Englishmen appreciate best the literary qualities of the Icelandic language'.[128] Lizzie Marshall once read *Grettissaga* with Eiríkur and writes to send greetings: some of her 'pleasantest memories of Cambridge [are of] you, Grettir and the Library'.[129] Russell Martineau, a British Museum librarian who learnt Icelandic and Danish from Eiríkur, reports that he is off to Norway in 1874, and plans to visit Frithiof's Sognefjord haunts.[130] Charles Barlow, once a pupil, is now a successful lawyer in London. Writing from the Temple, he asks Eiríkur about Scandinavian marriage laws, ancient and modern; he is advising the Foreign Office on a current case.[131] Maria Barlow of Bolton, perhaps a relation of Charles, may never have studied in Cambridge, but she receives postal instruction from Eiríkur during 1885–6 – distance learning ahead of its time. Eiríkur proves to be a demanding task-master; two pages of translation are to be submitted three times a week. While studying Ari Þorgilson's *Íslendingabók* her letters sound like those of any harassed student through the ages – she has not had time to do her translation, the glossary in her text (perhaps Guðbrandur's 1879 *Reader*) seems to 'omit many words', and she feels

---

[124] Lbs. 2187b 4to, Edmund Head to EM, 20 July 1863.

[125] Lbs. 2187a 4to, IG to EM, 30 November 1884.

[126] Lbs. 2185 4to, JS to EM, [n.d.].

[127] Lbs. 2187a 4to, Helen Gladstone to EM, 4 March 1885.

[128] Lbs. 2189a 4to, Miss Reynolds to EM, 23 March 1893.

[129] Lbs. 2188b 4to, LM to EM, 23 December 1891.

[130] Ibid., RM to EM, 10 June 1874. Eiríkur owned four English translations of Tegnér's poem: see Lbs. 405 fol.

[131] Lbs. 2186a 4to, CB to EM, 25 January 1895.

ashamed of her tardy progress. The letters reveal that Eiríkur receives a monthly cheque for his services.[132]

Like Maria Barlow, Gladys Alexander of Birkenhead never studied at the nearby and new Victoria College in Manchester (later Manchester University). She writes to ask whether she could teach herself Icelandic, 'and if so, what Grammar and books to begin with'.[133] Young Fred Harley was more fortunate. He became one of the first English Department graduates at Victoria College to obtain a first class honours degree; after further study in Göttingen and Berlin, he taught at Owens College in Manchester.[134] Applying for a teaching post in Canada, he requests Eiríkur's help. The appointment will be made by the Minister of Education, a man with 'old fashioned notions' who 'is not alive to the improvements of knowledge of Anglo Saxon . . . and the cognate dialects in English studies and is therefore liable to appoint somebody of literary rather than linguistic attainments'. Eiríkur's brief is to argue that 'if they want to give an impetus to English in their University, *language* must be taken as the basis', and to point out 'how indispensable a scientific training in the English language and cognate dialects is in a Professor of English'. Harley's Victoria College syllabus touched all conceivable bases: Anglo-Saxon, Early English, Gothic, Old Icelandic, Old High German, Modern German, Old French, Teutonic philology, Old Saxon, in addition to which 'we were forced to go through a three years' course of Literature under Professor A.W. Ward (though this literature does not find place in the examination which is purely linguistic and philological)'. How times change!

Linguistic discipline and literary sensibility find themselves more harmoniously linked in the brief career of Beatrice Barmby. The precise circumstances that first brought her into postal contact with Eiríkur Magnússon are not clear but a strong scholarly and personal bond was soon established between learned father-figure and young poet and playwright, who died with tragic suddenness in January 1899 at the age of 31. Icelanders who knew Beatrice were struck by her precocious command of their language,[135] with Eiríkur largely responsible for her rapid progress. The 'Dear Sir' of March 1893 has by 1897 become 'Dear Uncle Eiríkur', with Beatrice proving a most attentive student, forever seeking her tutor's advice, borrowing his books, and relishing the opportunity to exchange views about intellectual issues of the day, as well as specifically Icelandic literary topics. Beatrice helps him with his indexing and his English; she deals tactfully with Eiríkur's sometimes stormy relationship with Thomas Ellwood, the keen but incompetent Cumberland-based translator of *Landnámabók*;[136] she speaks feelingly of the impossibility of understanding the sagas without going to Iceland, yet her frail health prevents her from contem-

---

132 Ibid., MB to EM, 9 November 1885.
133 Ibid., GA to EM, May 1 [*c*.1875?].
134 Lbs. 2187a 4to, FH to EM, 25 April 1888.
135 'amazingly gifted in the language' [undravel að sér í tungunni]: Matthías Jóchumsson 1902, iii.
136 Lbs. 2186a 4to, BB to EM, 27 August 1897; see also TE to EM, 21 September 1898.

plating such a visit.[137] Hearing of W.G. Collingwood's disillusion with modern Iceland, she remarks, 'what wouldn't I give to be a strong man and able to do something for Iceland'.[138] It is easy to believe her sister Mabel's remark that Beatrice was 'at her best with clever men'.[139] It was her melancholy duty to inform Eiríkur of Beatrice's sudden death. For W.P. Ker, no man's critical fool, Beatrice 'had a great heart, and a most original mind – more truly heroic I think than any of her contemporaries'.[140] Jón Stefánsson told her mother that Beatrice's poems were more Icelandic in spirit than those of William Morris.[141] In Matthías Jochumsson's view, 'Miss Barmby understood *Sturlunga saga* and its period so well that you could count on the fingers of one hand the men in Scandinavia – including Iceland – who understand the saga better.'[142] She produced a fine ballad on the 1253 burning at Flugumýri scene, a popular episode with Victorian old northernists,[143] whilst her pair of sonnets 'On Sturla's *Íslendinga saga*' reveal the intensity of her personal engagement with the poet and his age. It is hard to believe that Eiríkur Magnússon was not invited to cast his eye over the two poems, of which this is the first:

> Across the waste of barren centuries
>   A voice, a human cry, comes echoing still,
>   Clear-toned, in that monotony of ill
> That ebbed and flowed set in the ice-bound seas.
> A pure, proud, weary heart; not passionate,
>   Though wronged; with wordy transports little stirred,
>   He knew too well the value of his word,
> And, grandly reticent, clasped his hands with fate.
>
> Yet through the years he sets my pulse to his,
> My brother dreamer in an iron race;
>   In field or fight, had we been face to face,
> I could not feel him nearer than he is,
>   Since still to all his silent pride there clings
>   The inborn sense of tears in human things.[144]

Beatrice's melodrama based on *Gísla saga* looms large in letters to Eiríkur.

137 Ibid., BB to EM, 23 March 1893.
138 Ibid., [n.d.; *c*.1898–9].
139 Lbs. 2808 4to, MB to Matthías Jochumsson, 13 January 1903.
140 Ibid., WPK to Matthías Jochumsson, 5 March 1903.
141 Jón Stefánsson 1949, 123.
142 Matthías Jochumsson 1902, v: 'Sturlunga og hennar öld skildi Miss Barmby svo vel, að eg efast um, hvort ekki sé auðvelt at telja á fingrum sér þá menn á Norðurlöndum – meðtöldu Íslandi –, sem skilja hana betur'.
143 Wawn 1997a, 464–6.
144 Barmby 1900, 107. Personal identification remains strong in the second sonnet: 'No longing that he felt, no joy that he knew, / No loss he suffered but I know it too. (Barmby 1900, 108).

Unpublished at the time of her death it was seen into print in both English[145] and Icelandic (in Matthías Jochumsson's translation),[146] read one evening at the Viking Club,[147] publicised amongst the Icelandic community in Manitoba[148] and as far afield as Australia and Buenos Aires,[149] talked of as worth staging in Britain[150] and Iceland,[151] and used (in Matthías's version) by W.P. Ker as an Icelandic teaching text.[152]

If Eiríkur took Beatrice Barmby under his wing, the roles were reversed in his relationship with the Welshman George E.J. Powell (1842–82), a wealthy old Etonian poet,[153] pianist, bon viveur, Wagner devotee,[154] and Icelandophile. Powell and Eiríkur first met on board ship returning from Iceland in 1862.[155] Thereafter they collaborated on translating Icelandic folk-tales from the newly-published Jón Árnason collection.[156] Two volumes were produced, with George Powell, infatuated at the time with all things Icelandic, paying £400 (twice Eiríkur's annual salary as librarian in Cambridge in the 1870s) for the first volume's illustrations, and bankrolling Eiríkur and his artist in their *fjallkona* design for the second volume's frontispiece (Fig. 12).[157] Half a dozen of the translated tales were still doing service for king and country as late as 1940, as reprinted in *The Icelandic Christmas Book*, a volume specially prepared for British soldiers stationed in Reykjavík.

While George Powell bankrolled Eiríkur through his early days in Britain,[158] Eiríkur became Powell's scholarly guide in the Icelandic language, with a trans-

---

145 Barmby 1900. Her short story 'The House of the Hill Folk' (Barmby 1903a, 211–32) tells of a farm boy's escape from robbers in the Icelandic interior and of reunion with a long-lost sister.

146 Matthías Jochumsson 1902. Publication in Winnipeg and a performance in Christiania were mooted: Lbs. 2808 4to, Mabel Barmby to MJ, 17 January 1901, July 2 1902; Steingrímur Matthíasson 1935, 606. Matthías prepared a Danish translation of the play: Lbs. 2806 4to.

147 Lbs. 2808 4to, MB to MJ, 13 January 1903.

148 Ibid., 17 November 1901.

149 Ibid., 12 June 1910.

150 Lbs. 2184 4to, Jón Stefánsson to EM, 1 March 1899. See also Lbs. 2808 4to, Mabel Barmby to Matthías Jochumsson, 3 November 1905: 'I wish any of these great actors would take up our Gísli.'

151 Lbs. 2808 4to, MB to Matthías Jochumsson, 3 December 1911.

152 Ibid., 17 May 1907.

153 See Powell 1860, 1861. Part of the second volume is dedicated to Longfellow; the poet is identified as 'Miölnir', but neither collection contains poems on old northern subjects.

154 According to local legend, Wagner visited Nanteos, saw the so-called Nanteos cup, learnt of its legendary grail vessel status, and returned home to compose *Parzival*. I am grateful to Gerald Morgan and Professor Desmond Slay, both of Aberystwyth, for information about Powell.

155 Thomas 1953–7, 123.

156 Jón Arnason 1862–4.

157 The artist was Gustav Doré: see Lbs. 2189a 4to, GEJP to EM, 16 January 1863; Finnur Sigmundsson 1950, I 25–6. The 1866 artist was J.B. Zwecker.

158 Matthías Jochumsson 1864 is dedicated to Powell. His motives are clarified in a letter to Steingrímur Thorsteinsson, 11 June 1864: 'This Powell to whom I have dedicated [the play] is pretty much my best hope; he is a good sort and wealthy . . . [he] writes to me in extraordinarily complimentary terms – I don't know why, because he hardly understands any Icelandic' [Þessi Powell sem ég dedicera er annars hálfvegis mín vonarstjarna, hann er vænn maður og velauðugur að fé . . .

lation of *Hávarðar saga Ísfirðings* as the focus of their first collaboration. There were regular reading classes: 'a chop at 1 o'clock . . . a cup of tea at 5 or 6 . . . we might then spend the day in going through part of the saga together . . . The time saved by this way of going through the saga will be immense.'[159] Powell's literary enthusiasm is matched by his financial generosity.[160] By 12 April 1870 a note of urgency has crept into Powell's instructions: 'We must, by all means – and that right speedily – get Havard off our hands and consciences.'[161] Yet, for whatever reason, the Powell-Magnússon translation was never published, and thus takes its place on a tantalising list of unpublished Victorian old northern translations, along with Thomas Carlyle's *Færeyinga saga*,[162] Frederick York Powell's *Gull-Þóris saga* and *Hervarar saga*,[163] Robert Proctor's *Vápnfirðinga saga*,[164] and versions of the *Poetic Edda* by Jón Hjaltalín[165] and Eiríkur Magnússon.[166] How many more lay gathering dust in the desk drawers of enthusiasts all over Britain?

To know George Powell was also to be part of yet another Victorian old northern network, involving the politician and diplomat James Bryce, William Morris, the poet A.C. Swinburne, and his cousin Mrs Disney Leith. Swinburne shared Powell's old Etonian fascination with flagellation and saga literature,[167] earning himself the nickname Sveinbjörn. Guy de Maupassant describes meeting the two men on holiday in France in 1867; their rented house was awash with young men and explicit photographs; guests were entertained with recitations of Icelandic folk tales.[168] While at Oxford Swinburne knew Guðbrandur and was a friend of James Bryce, later an influential Icelandophile diplomat. Mrs Disney Leith dedicated a collection of early poems to her cousin. He, in turn, knew William Morris, though he had his doubts about *Sigurd the Volsung* – 'all this dashed and blank Volsungery will end up by eating up all the splendid genius it has already overgrown and incrusted with Icelandic moss'.[169]

Like Guðbrandur, Eiríkur Magnússon numbered influential American old

---

skrífar mér óttaleg kompliment, ekki veit ég fyrir hvað, því hann skilur ekki íslensku nema með kíki] (Steingrímur Matthíasson 1935 14).

[159] Lbs. 2189a 4to [n.d.].

[160] Lbs. 2808 4to, GEJP to EM, 1 January 1869.

[161] Ibid., GEJP to EM, 12 April 1870. The manuscript, NLW MS 19763, ff. 202–85, would repay further study.

[162] Cowan 1979, 174–5.

[163] Elton 1906, I 11. Both the York Powell translations may date from *c*.1868, when, aged 18 and influenced by Dasent 1861, he also translated *Færeyinga saga*, which remained unpublished until 1896.

[164] *DNB*, Second Supplement III 140–1.

[165] See above, note 69.

[166] Lbs. 407 fol.

[167] Lang 1959–62, I 135, 150, 164, 171, 246 and passim. In the *Pall Mall Gazette*, Swinburne lists the *Poetic Edda* and *Burnt Njal* amongst his hundred best books in world literature: Lang 1959–62, V 134.

[168] Henderson 1974, 144–6.

[169] Lang 1959–62, V 134.

Fig. 12. Frontispiece to G.E.J. Powell and Eiríkr Magnússon (trans.)
Icelandic Legends, Collected by Jón Arnason.

northernists amongst his correspondents. Rasmus Anderson assures him that a North American audience of millions awaits his saga translations – by 1875 enthusiasm is 'just awakening'.[170] For the scholar Francis Tupper, the old north is 'the rock whence we are hewn and the mouth of the pit whence we are digged'.[171] Edward Denham of Boston, a saga enthusiast, asks for autographs – Eiríkur's and (if obtainable) William Morris's.[172] Thorstein Veblen offers his translation of *Laxdæla saga* for publication in the Saga Library.[173] Indeed, even the White House was on side. While serving as British Ambassador in Washington, Sir (as he now was) James Bryce used to entertain an enthralled President Teddy Roosevelt with his own versions of saga tales.[174]

To an even greater extent than Guðbrandur, Eiríkur attracted the random British correspondent asking for information or reporting on their work or travels. G.A. Stocks of Barrow in Furness,[175] and Arthur Brooke, the rector of Slingsby,[176] enquire about Old Norse elements in local place names. The Reverend J.T. Brown, an Iceland traveller familiar with Muriel Press's *Laxdæla* translation, asks about pagan baptism by immersion.[177] An agent from *The Times* invites Eiríkur to contribute articles in connection with the 1874 millennial anniversary of the Icelandic commonwealth. G.A. Auden, father of Wystan, and a leading old northern authority in York, follows up an earlier discussion with Eiríkur about the family name's links with 'the Norse name Audun': during a recent visit to Copenhagen he had learnt that in Oehlenschläger's play about Hákon jarl, 'Odin when in disguise assumes the name Auden.'[178] Willard Fiske discusses the 1874 Icelandic constitution, likening the Copenhagen-based Jón Sigurðsson to a transmigrated Njáll, 'with all the increased intelligence and judiciousness which seven or eight additional centuries ought to give'.[179] Walter Besant offers Eiríkur £100 to write a book on Haraldr Finehair for Blackwoods' 'Men of Action' series.[180] Maud Ebbutt, a former pupil, and an enterprising populariser of old northern lore and literature,[181] wonders why ash trees were of such importance to the Teutonic peoples.[182] Gilbert Goudie in Edinburgh, saga translator and friend of Jón Hjaltalín, asks Eiríkur to supply for a friend a list of pony references in the Icelandic sagas?[183] J. Harold Herbert, a Nottingham old

[170] Lbs. 2186b 4to, RA to EM, 20 September 1875.
[171] Lbs. 2189b 4to, FT to EM, 16 June 1910.
[172] Lbs. 2186a 4to, ED to EM, 27 September 1880.
[173] Lbs. 2181a 4to, TV to EM, 25 October 1890; Veblen 1925.
[174] Fisher 1927, I 144.
[175] Lbs. 2188b 4to, GAS to EM, 10 November 1892.
[176] Lbs. 2186a 4to, AB to EM, 14 September 1903.
[177] Ibid., JTB to EM, 14 November 1902.
[178] Lbs. 2186b 4to, GAA to EM, 28 May 1904. On possible answers to Auden's query, see Sveinn Haraldsson 1994.
[179] Lbs. 2187a 4to, WF to EM, 2 June 1874.
[180] Lbs. 2186b 4to, WB to EM, 7 November 1877.
[181] Ebbutt 1910.
[182] Lbs. 2187a 4to, ME to EM, 6 May 1891.
[183] Ibid., GG to EM, 28 November 1910.

northernist who had been twice to Iceland, wants to know how to pronounce 'Viking' correctly; whether there are any pigs in Iceland; and, most important, whether any new saga translations might have escaped his attention – 'the sagas have a great fascination for me, and I am very anxious to study them as far as I am able'.[184] George Rowntree of Sunderland writes tactfully to say that Eiríkur's offer of a lecture on Iceland would 'not be sufficiently appreciated' in his home town.[185] Rowntree was certainly the man to know: a protégé of Bligh Peacock, and a scholar of Clare College in Cambridge, where in 1875 he had been awarded the Chancellor's Medal for a lengthy millennial poem on Iceland in which many familiar Laingean and Carlylean bells are rung.[186] Sir Henry Holland invites Eiríkur to lecture on Icelandic history and geography at the Royal Institute.[187] Henry Sweet welcomes Eiríkur's approval of his 1886 *Icelandic Primer*,[188] noting that he has become ever more aware of deficiencies in Guðbrandur's *Dictionary*, not least the influence of the compiler's 'Westfirth pronunciation'.

The extent of old northern literary penetration into the minds of some of Eiríkur's correspondents is suggested by their fondness for deploying eddic and saga phrases and images in their letters. Alice Zimmerman of Highgate is preparing a version of the old northern myths for children; she apologises for her poor handwriting, caused by rheumatism and advancing years, 'Alas, the secret of Idun's apples is gone for ever.'[189] In the same vein, George Ainslie Hight, Cambridge pupil of Eiríkur, translator of *Grettis saga*, and a faithful correspondent during the Icelander's final years, comments on dismissive remarks made about *Vǫlsunga saga* by a recent translator of *Beowulf*, Wentworth Huyshe: 'Well, tasks differ; I, for one, think that Völsunga S. one of the noblest stories ever told, and incomparably superior to *Beowulf*.'[190] 'Tasks differ' echoes Guðrún Ósvífrsdóttir's famously laconic *Laxdæla saga* response to the news that her husband Bolli has killed Kjartan Ólafsson, the man she loved the most and treated the worst.[191] A memorable saga moment reappears as part of the private language of a saga enthusiast.

Though most Victorian old northernists were drawn to eddic and *Íslendingasögur* narratives, due attention was paid by Eiríkur and his correspondents to less familiar areas of medieval Icelandic literature, notably sacred poetry and the *Biskupasögur*: 'in the midst of the awakening or reviving interest in Norse literature which seems to be going on amongst us, it is surely a great mistake to

184 Lbs. 2187b 4to, JHH to EM, 13 October 1901, 12 January 1902.
185 Lbs. 2189a 4to, GR to EM, 3 April 1875.
186 Rowntree 1875.
187 Lbs. 2187b 4to, HH to EM, 29 January [?1872].
188 Ibid., HS to EM, 6 May 1886.
189 Lbs. 2189b 4to, Alice Zimmerman to EM, June 10 [n.a.].
190 Lbs. 2187b 4to, GAH to EM, 24 September 1907.
191 Discussed above, p. 268.

ignore the religious branch of the Saga'.[192] The Earl of Bute writes to request 'two more copies' of Eiríkur's edition and translation of *Lilja*,[193] 'the first Icelandic text which has ever been published in England itself from manuscript sources'.[194] This Marian poem became a favourite of Anglo- and Roman Catholics. Edward Waterton writes from Boulogne in 1877 to ask where he can obtain a copy of *Lilja*, about which he had read in *The Times*: 'I think, from what I have heard, that the great bulk of the English Catholics – or as it is the fashion to call us – Roman Catholics, are quite unacquainted with *Lilja* . . . but it will not be my fault if it is soon not better known amongst us.'[195] He indicates that he would be taking Eiríkur's edition of *Thómas saga Erkibyskups* to Biarritz over the winter.[196] One of Eiríkur's most revealing young Icelandophile correspondents was Edward Rae of Birkenhead, whom Eiríkur met on the Iceland ship returning from his 1871 visit. Rae, 'a restless creature'[197] with plenty of money and self confidence, knows William Morris, and wants all his books binding in the Morris fashion;[198] is grateful for complimentary copies of *Lilja*[199] and *Three Northern Love Stories*;[200] has acquired a book of Danish folk tales;[201] has visited the Isle of Man, 'I know the Manx Runic crosses by heart';[202] and has written a book about Lapland.[203] As well as collecting runic calendars,[204] Rae announces that 'the restless part of my bosom . . . yearns for old silver',[205] with Iceland clearly a favourite source. Already the proud owner of several Icelandic chalices, he asks Eiríkur to help persuade the Bishop of Skálholt to send another in return for 250 dollars.[206] Unbelievably, Eiríkur does so and, even more unbelievably, the Bishop agrees, as long as a duplicate can be sent from England. He refers to himself jokingly as the 'spoliator'[207] of Icelandic churches, avenging the days when English silver was 'booted by Mrs Magnússon's ancestors in some warlike descent upon the English coast'[208] – Eiríkur's wife Sigríður claimed descent from Egill Skallagrímsson.[209] Rae urges

---

[192] Leith 1895b 5. The volume includes translations from *Hungrvaka* and poems about Skálholt and Saint Þorlákr.

[193] Lbs. 2189b 4to, Earl's Secretary to EM, 23 September 1906.

[194] Eiríkr Magnússon 1870, vi.

[195] Lbs. 2189b 4to, EW to EM, 1 December 1876, 27 January 1877, 7 July 1877.

[196] Ibid., 7 July 1877.

[197] Lbs. 2189a 4to, ER to EM, 31 October 1872.

[198] Ibid., 2 January 1875.

[199] Ibid., 10 August [1872].

[200] Ibid., 26 July 1875. The 'pure vigorous Saxon' of the translations is a model for English writers.

[201] Ibid., 23 November 1871.

[202] Ibid., 17 December 1872, 10 November 1877.

[203] Rae 1875.

[204] Lbs. 2190a 4to, 10 November 1877. See Eiríkr Magnússon 1877, 1888; also Simpson 1891.

[205] Lbs. 2189a 4to, ER to EM, 31 October 1872.

[206] Ibid., 31 October 1872.

[207] Ibid., 15 July 1872.

[208] Ibid., 10 June 1872.

[209] Stefán Einarsson 1933, 277.

Eiríkur to keep in touch on these matters, 'or I'll compose a bitter Rune against you'.[210] Happily, by 1873 we find Rae offering to return a chalice acquired at Mosfell.[211] In his last extant letter to Eiríkur,[212] Rae confirms the high levels of interest that philology enjoyed in Victorian London: Max Müller's lectures were proving so popular that each one has to be delivered twice on the same day.[213]

The Invisible College: Associate Members

Guðbrandur Vigfússon and Eiríkur Magnússon were towering figures in establishing old northern networks in Britain, but other visiting Icelanders played their part as visiting fellows in the invisible college. Jón Stefánsson came to Britain in 1882 to catalogue Icelandic manuscripts, became acquainted with James Bryce and Thomas Ellwood, taught Israel Gollancz, befriended the Tyneside old northernists, and travelled to Iceland with W.G. Collingwood. As a worker in the Unitarian cause the poet Matthías Jochumsson was a frequent visitor to Britain, attracting his own circle of loyal friends. W.P. Ker tells Matthías that, having visited the poet in Akureyri, he now keeps a W.G. Collingwood painting of the house in his study. Ker's letters to Matthías, some of them in Icelandic, delight in utilising phrases from the sagas. Amongst Matthías's other correspondents, we find the familiar names of Edward Rae, Israel Gollancz and Mrs Disney Leith.[214]

To the networks identifiable through extant correspondence, may be added those to be glimpsed through membership lists of learned societies and subscribers to old northern publications. Hið íslenzka fornleifafélag [the Icelandic Archaeological Society] was formed in 1880 by prominent Icelandic scholars who, in the company of Willard Fiske, were returning on horseback to Reykjavík after visiting the historical sites at Þingvellir. The earliest British member was Gilbert Goudie, Jón Hjaltalín's collaborator on their 1873 translation of Orkneyinga saga. Other early British members included the newly appointed British consul in Reykjavík W.G. Spence Paterson, Bligh Peacock, George Stephens, and (by the end of the century) W.G. Collingwood.[215] Early British members of Hið íslenzka bókmenntafélag [the Icelandic Literary Society] included John Adamson (Secretary of the Newcastle Antiquarian Society) Robert Jamieson (Edinburgh), Joseph Bosworth (Oxford), John Bowring (London), John Heath (Cambridge), and Benjamin Thorpe.[216] The Copenhagen-based Det Kongelige Nordiske Oldskrift Selskab [Royal Northern

---

[210] Lbs. 2189a 4to, ER to EM, 17 December 1872.

[211] Ibid., 20 May 1873.

[212] Rae also corresponded with Matthías Jochumsson: Lbs. 2808 4to, 19 May 1874.

[213] Lbs. 2189a 4to, ER to EM, 4 June 1878.

[214] This paragraph draws on correspondence with Matthías in Lbs. 2808 4to.

[215] Membership lists in Árbók Hins íslenska fornleifafélags, notably 1880–1, 116.

[216] Names listed in Skírnir 1 1827. Later members included Ebenezer Henderson and George Stephens; no lists published after 1858.

Old Manuscript Society] has a substantial British membership from the middle of the nineteenth century, with Prince Albert taking his place alongside virtually every crowned head of Europe. Over the years several of Guðbrandur and Eiríkur's correspondents appear in the published lists of members as do Icelandic travellers, provincial antiquarians, and prominent scholars: John Adamson, Paul du Chaillu, the Marquis of Bute, John Bowring, John Earle, Francis Lord Egerton, John Ingram (Oxford), J.M. Kemble, Mountstuart Elphinstone (known to Repp), George Stephens, A.J. Symington, Lord Dufferin, and the Edinburgh professor M.D. Traill. Institutional members in Britain include learned societies in Manchester, Liverpool, Newcastle, Cumberland and Westmoreland, and Edinburgh; also the Society of Antiquaries, the Royal Society of Literature, the Royal Historical Society, the Anthropological Institute of Great Britian and Ireland, the Royal Irish Academy; and, in the furthest reaches of the Empire, societies in Bombay, Calcutta, Ottawa, Sydney and Toronto.

Occasional lists of subscribers supporting old northern publications provide additional evidence of the invisible college's membership in late Victorian Britain. Thomas Ellwood's three old northern publications in the 1890s – *The Landnama Book of Iceland* (1894), *Lakeland and Iceland* (1895), and *The Book of the Settlements of Iceland* (1898) – offer a representative glimpse of the Lake District old northern circle. The three works represent a logical sequence: broad discussion, dialectal glossary, primary text translation. The 1894 volume attracts over 100 subscribers and over 130 sign up for the *Landnámabók* translation. The great majority live locally: colonels, knights of the shires, bishops, archdeacons, deans, justices of the peace, and doctors.[217] It is not difficult to imagine many of them being stirred by the sentiments of Ellwood's 1898 Introduction:

> [the translation] is an attempt to render . . . [*Íslendingabók*] from Icelandic, a language spoken by only about 60,000 or 70,000 people, all told, into English, spoken as it is by a kindred people, a race numbering over one hundred millions, whose maritime enterprize followed by settlement and colonization derived apparently from the Norsemen, have given them the dominion of a great part of the earth.[218]

Eiríkur was worried about the mistakes in the translation; Ellwood's subscribers may not have cared, as they contemplated the glories of imperial conquest.

The Craigie Connection

This survey of invisible college correspondence began with Guðbrandur Vigfússon and has referred frequently to his *Icelandic-English Dictionary*. It seems appropriate, therefore, to conclude by mentioning the early letters to Icelanders

217 Ellwood 1894, 67–69.
218 Ellwood 1898, Preface [unpaginated].

written by W.A. Craigie, who began his long career as an old northern scholar in the 1890s[219] and eventually found himself entrusted, nearly sixty years later, with the task of seeing a revised edition of Guðbrandur's dictionary through the press. Writing to his friend séra Jón Þorvaldsson at Staður on the Reykjanes peninsula, the young Craigie reports the success of his 'well attended' public lectures on Icelandic sagas, on Iceland and Greenland, and on the life and times of the district.[220] There is much talk about new books on Iceland. Craigie has no time for fashionable claims about Celtic influence on saga literature.[221] Like many before him, he believes that the Celts are invariably an influenced rather than an influential people.[222] He announces that he is translating the eddic poems (most of which he believes to have been composed in Iceland), and that the Germans take these pieces 'far too seriously'.[223]

It was not long before all Europe was forced to take the Germans very seriously indeed. During the First World War the work of the invisible college was severely curtailed, and many of its male students called to sterner duties. Craigie's proposed visit to Iceland is abandoned, as are hopes that different modern branches of the Teutonic family of nations could recapture the old northern unity that scholars and laymen in Britain and all over Europe had made their particular focus of study. In 1915 Craigie assures séra Jón that the war has made 'wonderfully little difference';[224] by 1918 we find W.P. Ker striking a much bleaker note – 'we hope for a return of the good days, but nothing can make up for the waste'. Fellow feeling for 'the Gothas' was in very short supply.[225]

---

[219] Craigie 1893a, 1893b, 1896a, 1896b; see Snæbjörn Jónsson 1927.

[220] Lbs. 2692 8vo, WAC to Jón Þorvaldsson, 19 February 1912.

[221] For example, see above, note 14.

[222] Lbs. 2395 4to, WAC to Benedikt Gröndal, 22 July 1906.

[223] Ibid., 14 March 1906.

[224] Lbs. 2692 8vo, WAC to Jón Þorvaldsson, 28 February 1915.

[225] Lbs. 4430 4to, WPK to Guðmundur Magnússon, [29 July] 1918; Lbs. 2808 4to, Miss Spears to Matthías Jochumsson, 5 January 1918.

CODA

'Vikinglife' after Victoria[1]

As a child Rudyard Kipling heard 'Uncle' William Morris retelling stories from *Burnt Njal* and impersonating Norna of the Fitful Head in parlour recreations of scenes from *The Pirate*.[2] As an adult Kipling never lost touch with these old northern voices. In his 'The Finest Story in the World' (1893), we meet young Charlie Mears, by day a London bank clerk and, in his spare time, an aspiring but ungifted poet. The story's anonymous narrator befriends Charlie and discovers that his mind is well stocked with 'notions', staggeringly realistic images of life on board ancient ocean-going vessels – in Greek galleys and Viking longships – Charlie hardly seemed to know the difference. The narrator is astonished at the 'profligate abundance of detail' (113) at Charlie's command and exasperated by his complete inability to verbalise it effectively. The narrator realises that he is dealing not with tin-eared tale-telling but with metempsychosis. Charlie is not imagining the pitching and tossing of an open boat voyaging to Vínland, but had spent part of a previous life experiencing it. By acting as Charlie's amanuensis, the narrator has the chance to produce 'the most marvellous tale in the world' (118).

Charlie is anything but an easy collaborator, however. His eagerness to clothe his adventures in the borrowed feathers of major English poets threatens to allow alien voices and values to contaminate his unique narrative witness. Yet the narrator had every incentive to keep faith when, out of the blue, lines from Longfellow's 'The Saga of King Olaf Tryggvason', or a cow bellowing on a barge passing under London Bridge, could trigger a stream of fire-fresh recollections of voyaging to or rural life in Vínland. Having first consulted a scholar in the British Museum, the narrator later shares his experiences with a young Bengali friend, who is intrigued but pessimistic. Western Christianity cannot tolerate metempsychosis, he claims, because it removes the fear of death. The young man's rare glimpse behind doors that the gods normally keep bolted will not last. There is no chance of regularising the psychic current against the distractions of books, business or, most destructive of all, a girl friend. So it is that the bubble eventually bursts. Charlie arrives one day excited at having com-

[1] Lund 1869, 62.
[2] Kipling 1937, 15–16.

370

posed a love poem. He has lost his heart to a tobacconist's assistant, and the narrator's chance of telling his great tale has disappeared. The mists of a shallow contented forgetfulness descend on the young banking seer; the Vínland visions vanish.

Kipling's subtle story touches on many of the themes that have assumed importance in the present study: the fascination with the old north on both sides of the Atlantic ocean; the uneasy relationship between Graeco-Roman and old northern literary tradition; the relationship between Christianity and old northern paganism; the Indo-European dimension to the Victorian analysis of the old north; the cult of the Viking ship; and the links between specialised scholarship and popular enthusiasm. Kipling's tale also reflects on what might happen to Charlie's Viking narrative after its publication. The narrator notes gloomily that it will be moralised by preachers, colonised by Orientalists, fought over by rival faiths, and feminised by women. How right he was. We have seen Victorian readers, translators, composers, paraphrasers, painters, poets, and play-wrights infusing Viking- and saga-age texts with their own agendas. Eddas and sagas were indeed moralised, allegorised, nationalised, imperialised, colonial-ised, politicised, sectarianised, regionalised, and genderised.

It is, however, precisely because of this capacity to undergo cultural trans-lation and modernisation that the old north has retained its power to attract and intrigue. Unlike Charlie, many post-Victorian Britons never abandoned their old northern 'notions'. It is true that, for a variety of reasons, old northern lit-erature never became a dominant discourse in twentieth-century culture. For all the increased exposure that it enjoyed in schools and universities between the wars, Old Icelandic never replaced Graeco-Roman studies as the dominant fast-track subject area for the prospective Whitehall mandarin. Moreover, no field-commanding work of high art, music or literature drawing on old north-ern themes emerged to command attention during the early decades of the new century. Again, two world wars compromised some old northernists' lingering dreams of celebrating shared values with Saxon kith and kin. The enthusiasm of the fanatical few remained undiminished even in the dark days of 1941: 'Icelandic is a wonderful Culture-speech, with its own words for every-thing and makes one realize how much was lost to English in its bastardization by the Norman Conquest.' But this letter to W.G. Collingwood's Icelandic friend Dr Jón Stefánsson was written in Brixton Prison, where the writer was serving time as a Nazi sympathiser.[3] Another of Jón's wartime correspondents, writing from the British Museum, doubtless voiced the thoughts of many others: 'you must not expect me to share . . . your high opinion of the Vikings. They were brave and skilful men, but were a nuisance in the world they lived in, as other brave and skilful men are today.'[4]

Yet in post-war Britain Vikingism resurfaced more or less intact and has con-

[3] Lbs. 3426 4to: Prisoner 2860 S. Wright, to Dr Jón Stefánsson, 13 June 1941. Wright learnt Ice-landic and Gothic whilst in jail.
[4] Ibid., J. Whitely to JS, 4 July 1942.

tinued to generate more coffee-table books, films, television exposure, tales for children and adults, advertising slogans, cartoons, comic books, and (now) web-sites than its one-time opponents, the Anglo-Saxons. The Vikings, like Robin Hood (and, perhaps, unlike the Anglo-Saxons), have contributed colourfully to the modern Heritage industry. The iconography (long-ships, horned helmets) that the Victorians developed for them remains instantly recognisable and widely deployed, whereas popular Anglo-Saxonism has never found the right logo. The only major twentieth-century writer (Tolkien) to recreate Anglo-Saxon values compellingly denied that he was doing anything of the sort. Professor Shippey has traced this absence of popular Anglo-Saxonism to the political and linguistic domination achieved by England and English during Victoria's reign: 'the developing and potentially powerful image of Anglo-Saxon origins was sacrificed, during the nineteenth century, to the needs of an Imperial and a British, not an English ideology'.[5] No such inhibitions attended the alternative English creation myth represented by Vikingism. In Victorian Britain the Scandinavian devil had the best tunes, many of which are still cheerfully whistled in the new millennium   . Several of the qualities that attracted the Victorians to eddas and sagas remain seductive, their rougher ideological edges smoothed by irony – the robustly poignant myths of the Viking gods, the cartoon-like bravado of eddic heroes, the unflinching assertiveness of saga heroines, and the ultimate vulnerability of communities from Jorvík to Jómsborg, from Bergþórshvoll to Ásgarðr. Nor has it harmed the Viking cause that, in a late twentieth-century devolutionary era, their centres of greatest influence within the British Isles were in Orkney or the Danelaw or the Wirral rather than London. For those repelled by the sanguinary sublime, Viking-age settlers can be made to seem like resourceful small businessmen. Not least, the stiff upper lips of the old north retain the capacity to raise a modern smile. Thomas Bartholin, who solemnly catalogued every old northern heroic joke in 1689, would surely have approved. It was he who set the standard for translating old northern culture into comprehensible post-medieval shapes. Plenty of Victorian writers ran hard with the same baton, and at the beginning of the twenty-first century there seems no shortage of fresh competitors, in both the elite marathon and populist fun-run divisions, eager to make the old north their own.

5   Shippey 2000, 215.

BIBLIOGRAPHY

Entries are generally ordered in accordance with Icelandic alphabetical practice. Entries beginning with or containing accented vowels follow equivalent forms with simple vowels. Thus, Á follows A, Í follows I, Ó follows O and so on; the entry for 'Árngrímur Jónsson' follows the final unaccented A entry; that for 'Fáfnir' follows the final FA entry 'Farrer'. Entries under Þ, Ö follow those for Z. Icelanders are normally listed under their first names, as with Geir Zoëga listed under Geir.

I. MANUSCRIPTS

Bodleian Library
Add.C. 56, Boreales 47, Percy c.7–9, Eng. Lett. d.59, Eng. Misc. c.112, English Misc. d.131, German d.2, Icelandic d.1, d.2, Scandinavian d.1, d.2.

Bristol City Library
B 7473–6, 7480–5.

British Library
Add. 4860, 24972, 31048.

Cheshire County Record Office
DSA 4b, 5/6, 5/8, 5/9a, 7/1–3, 12e, 123/1, 127/1.

Collingwood Transcripts
Letters from W.G. Collingwood to his family: transcripts. Originals in Abbot Hall Art Gallery and Museum, Kendal.

Edinburgh University Library
La. III. 379/757–81.

Harvard University Library
Icel. 55.

Henry E. Huntington Library, San Marino, California
Larpent 1751.

John Rylands Library, Manchester
JRL 716–18, 722.

King's College, University of London
Icelandic 2.

Landsbókasafn Íslands
Lbs. 342c fol., 367 fol., 403–10 fol., 424 fol., 604 fol., 631 fol., 890 fol., 952 fol., 962 fol.
Lbs. 480 4to, 978 4to, 980 4to, 1056 4to, 1484a 4to, 1706 4to, 1760 4to, 1855–60 4to, 2179–90 4to, 2208 4to, 2395 4to, 2399 4to, 2561 4to, 2692 4to, 2807–8 4to, 2859–60 4to, 2877 4to, 3175 4to, 3422 4to, 3426 4to, 3633 4to, 3886–8 4to, 4295 4to, 4373–4 4to, 4430 4to, 4555 4to, 4705 4to, 4840 4to, 4868 4to.
Lbs. 2692 8vo, 3504 8vo.
Lbs. JS 400–2 4to, 141 fol., 143 fol.
Lbs. ÍB 88–90 fol., 93–105 fol., 10 8vo, 124 8vo.
Lbs. Bréfasafn Stefáns Einarssonar.
Lbs. Mark Watson collection: copy of Dufferin 1857: uncatalogued letter from Lord Dufferin to G.W. Dasent [*c*.1857].
Lbs. Repp. Acc. 6/7/1989 fol.

Lunds Universitetsbibliotek
Brevsaml. Stephens G.

National Library of Scotland
NLS Acc. 7515.

National Library of Wales
13533, 19763, Mân Adnau 1407A (Minor Deposit).

Orkney Archive
Memoir by Samuel Laing: transcript.

Scottish Record Office
Heddle GD 263/124.

Shetland Archive
D.I./135, p. 273.

Sidney Jones Library, University of Liverpool
3.32–33.

Þjóðskjalasafn Íslands
E. 10, E. 182.

II. PRINTED SOURCES

Aall, Jacob. 1838–9. Trans. *Snorre Sturlesons Norske Kongers Sagaer*, 2 vols. Christiania.

Aarsleff, Hans. 1983. *The Study of Language in England, 1780–1860.* 2nd edition. Minneapolis.

Acker, Paul. 1993. 'Norse Sagas translated into English: A Supplement', *SS* 65, 66–102.

Adams, W.H.D. 1883. *Mountains and Mountain Climbing.* London.

Adeane, J.H. 1899. *The Early Married Life of Maria Josepha, Lady Stanley.* London.

Adolf Friðriksson. 1994. *Sagas and Popular Antiquarianism in Icelandic Archaeology.* Avebury.

Adolf Friðriksson and Orri Vésteinsson. 1992. 'Dómhringa saga. Grein um fornleifaskýringar', *Saga* 30, 7–79.

Aðalgeir Kristjánsson. 1964. *Brynjólfur Pétursson: Bréf.* Reykjavík.

———. 1996. 'Orðabókastörf Konráðs Gíslasonar', *Íslenskt mál og almenn málfræði* 18, 7–36.

Aho, Gary. 1993. 'Með Ísland á heilanum': Íslandsbækur breskra ferðalanga 1772 til 1897', *Skírnir* 167, 205–58.

———. 1996. Introduction to Morris 1996.

Allchin, A.M. et al. 1994. Eds *Heritage and Prophecy: Grundtvig and the English-Speaking World.* Norwich.

Allen, G.C. [?1912]. Trans. *The Song of Frithiof.* London.

Allen, Ralph Bergen. 1933. *Old Icelandic Sources in the English Novel.* Philadelphia.

Allen, Richard F. 1971. *Fire and Iron: Critical Approaches to* Njáls saga. Pittsburgh.

Allott, Kenneth and Miriam. 1979. Eds *The Poems of Matthew Arnold.* 2nd edition. London and New York.

Andersen, Flemming G. and Lars Ole Sauerberg. 1994. Eds *Traditions and Innovations: Papers Presented to Andreas Haarder.* Odense.

Andersen, Hans Christian. 1974. Trans. Erik Haugaard, *The Complete Fairy Tales and Stories.* London.

Anderson, Sir Charles. 1853. *An Eight Weeks' Journal in Norway . . . in 1852.* London.

———. 1984. Trans. Böðvar Kvaran, *Framandi Land: Dagbókarkorn úr Íslandsferð 1863.* Reykjavík.

Anderson, Olive. 1967. 'The Political Uses of History in mid Nineteenth-Century England', *Past and Present* 36, 87–105.

Anderson, Rasmus B. 1873. *The Scandinavian Languages: their Historical, Linguistic, Literary and Scientific Value.* Madison, Wisconsin.

———. 1874. *America Not Discovered by Columbus: An Historical Sketch of the Discovery of America by the Norseman in the Tenth Century.* Chicago.

———. 1880. *The Younger Edda, also called Snorre's Edda, or The Prose Edda*. Chicago.

Anderson, Rasmus B. 1889. See Laing, Samuel.

Anderson, Rasmus B. 1905–6. Ed. *Norræna. History and Romance of Northern Europe: A Library of Supreme Classics Printed in Complete Form*. 10 vols. London and New York.

Anderson, Rasmus B. and Jón Bjarnason. 1877. Trans. *Viking Tales of the North*. Chicago.

Anderson, Robert. 1990. *Elgar in Manuscript*. London.

———. 1993. *Elgar*. London.

Anderton, H. Orsmond. 1893. *Baldur. A Lyrical Drama*. London.

Andrés Björnsson. 1990. 'Grímur Thomsen og Uppsalamótið 1856', *LÍÁ 1988*, nýr flokkur 14, 5–15.

Anna Agnarsdóttir. 1979. 'Ráðagerðir um innlimun Íslands í Bretaveldi á árunum 1785–1815', *Saga* 17, 5–58.

———. 1989. 'Eftirmál byltingarinnar 1809: Viðbrögð breskra stjórnvalda', *Saga* 27, 67–101.

———. 1993. 'Ráðabrugg á dulmáli: Hugleiðingar um skjal frá 1785', *Ný Saga* 6, 28–41.

———. 1994. 'Sir Joseph Banks and the Exploration of Iceland', in R.E.R. Banks et al. 1994, 31–48.

[anon.1]. 1763. [Review of Percy 1763], *MR* 28, 281–86.

[anon.2]. 1763. [Review of Percy 1763], *QR* 15, 307–10.

[anon.]. 1813. *Memoir of the Causes of the Present Distressed State of the Icelanders, and the Easy and Certain Means of Permanently Bettering their Condition*. London.

[anon.]. 1820. 'On the State of the Cultivation of the Ancient Literature of the North at the Present Period', *LM* 1, 391–401.

[anon.]. 1821. 'On the Songs of the People of Gothic or Teutonic Race', *LM* 3, 143–53; 4, 41–47, 412–17.

[anon.]. 1821–2. [Review of Scott 1822], *QR* 26, 434–74.

[anon.]. 1825. *The Juvenile Rambler: Early Reading Lessons designed for Children*. [London].

[anon.]. 1831. *A Walk in Shetland by Two Eccentrics*. Edinburgh.

[anon.]. 1850. *Domestic Scenes in Greenland and Iceland*. 2nd edition. London.

[anon.1]. 1852. *Stories of the Norseman*. London.

[anon.2]. [1852]. *Jon of Iceland: A Story of the Far North and other Tales*. London.

[anon.]. [1860]. *The Northern Light: A Tale of Iceland and Greenland in the Eleventh Century*. London.

[anon.1]. 1861. *Kormak, An Icelandic Romance of the Tenth Century*. Boston.

[anon.2]. 1861. *The North Atlantic Telegraph, via the Faröe Isles, Iceland and Greenland. Miscellaneous Reports, Speeches and Papers*. London.

[anon.]. 1866. 'Recent Work on Icelandic literature', *GM* (August), 232–8.

[anon.]. 1871. *Portrait of Sir Walter Scott and Fine Engravings in Illustration of*

The Pirate *for the Members of the Royal Association for the Promotion of Fine Arts in Scotland*. Edinburgh.

[anon.]. 1874. [Review of Cleasby and Gudbrand Vigfusson 1874], *The Times* 2 March, 4.

[anon.1]. 1875. *Half Hours in the Far North: Life amid Snow and Ice*. London.

[anon.2]. 1875. [Review of Dasent 1875], *The Times* 17 May, 8.

[anon.]. 1876. *The Arctic World; its Plants, Animals, and Natural Phenomena*. London.

[anon.]. 1878. [Review of Vansittart Conybeare 1877], *SatR* April 20, 498–500.

[anon.]. 1892. 'H. Howorth, Kt., M.P.', *Papers of the Manchester Literary Club* 467–71.

[anon.]. 1895. [Review of Sephton 1895], *Liverpool Daily Post* 13 March.

[anon.]. 1909. *The Englishman on Iceland: How to Make Yourself Understood*. Bonn.

[anon.]. 1916. *Hið íslenzka bókmenntafjelag 1816–1916: Minningarrit*. Reykjavík.

[anon.]. 1940. *The Iceland Christmas Book*. Reykjavík.

[anon.]. 1971. *Summary Catalogue of the Advocates' Manuscripts*. Edinburgh.

Anster, John. 1853. 'Rhymes from the Edda. Thor and Thrym; or, Thor's Hammer brought home', *DUM* 41, 578–82.

Antonsen, Elmer et al. 1990. Eds *The Grimm Brothers and the Germanic Past*. Amsterdam.

Arngrímur Jónsson. 1593. *Brevis commentarius de Islandia*. Copenhagen.

———. 1609. *Crymogæa sive rerum Islandicarum*. Hamburg.

Arnold, Matthew. See Allott K. and M. 1979.

Arwidsson, Adolph Ivar. 1834–42. *Svenska fornsånger*. Stockholm.

[Asbjörnsen P. et al.]. 1876. *Testimonials in Favour of the Rev. F. Metcalfe, Candidate for the Chair of Anglo-Saxon and Northern Antiquities*. [?Oxford].

Aspin, J. [1826]. *Cosmorama: A View of the Costumes and Peculiarities of All Nations*. London.

Atkinson, Brooks. 1950. Ed. *The Select Writings of Ralph Waldo Emerson*. New York.

Auden, W.H. and Louis MacNeice. 1937. *Letters from Iceland*. London and New York.

Axelsen, Jens. 1996. 'Rasmus Rask og Thorleifur Gudmundsson Repp', *Rask* 4, 93–110.

Árni Kristjánsson. 1956–8. Ed. Matthías Jochumsson, *Ljóðmæli*. 2 vols. Reykjavík.

Baker, Oscar. 1841. Trans. *The Saga of Frithiof: A Legend*. London.

Baldur Hafstað. 1997. Trans. *Konrad Maurer: Íslandsferð 1858*. Reykjavík.

Ballantyne, R.M. 1869. *Erling the Bold: A Tale of the Norse Sea-Kings*. London.

———. 1872. *The Norsemen in the West; or, America before Columbus. A Tale*. London.

Banks, R.E.R. et al. 1994. Eds *Sir Joseph Banks: A Global Perspective*. Kew.

[Banks, William Mitchell]. 1881. *A Narrative of the Voyage of the Argonauts in 1880; Compiled by the Bard from the Most Authentic Records.* [Edinburgh].

Baring-Gould, Sabine. 1859–62. 'Öraefa-Dal: An Icelandic Tale', *The Hurst Johnian*, I 6–12, 36–44, 67–82, 111–20, 149–65, 189–99, 227–32, 270–80, 309–21, 350–63; II 8–18, 52–9, 93–7, 138–53, 180–90, 227–37, 269–76. Brighton.

———. 1863. *Iceland: its Scenes and Sagas.* London.

———. 1865. *The Book of Werewolves.* London.

———. 1868. *Curious Myths of the Middle Ages.* London.

———. 1890. *Grettir the Outlaw: a Story of Iceland.* London.

———. 1894. *The Icelander's Sword; or, The Story of Oraefa-dal.* London.

———. 1923. *Early Reminiscences, 1834–64.* London.

———. 1925. *Further Reminiscences, 1864–1894.* London.

Barmby, Beatrice. 1900. *Gísli Súrsson: A Drama; Ballads and Poems of the Old Norse Days and Some Translations.* London.

———. 1902. Trans. Matthías Jochumsson, *Gísli Súrsson.* Akureyri.

———. 1903a. *Rosslyn's Raid and Other Tales.* London.

———. 1903b. *Poems.* London.

Barnes, Geraldine et al. 1994. Eds *Old Norse Studies in the New World.* Sydney.

Barnes, Geraldine. 1994. 'Reinventing Paradise: Vínland 1000–1992', in Barnes et al. 1994, 19–32.

Barnes, Michael P. 1992. 'The Gentlemen v. the Scholars: An early Maeshowe controversy', in Hødnebø et al. 1992, 20–8.

———. 1993. 'The Interpretation of the Runic Inscriptions of Maeshowe', in Batey et al. 1993, 349–69. Edinburgh.

———. 1994. *The Runic Inscriptions of Maeshowe, Orkney.* Odense.

Barnes, William. 1863. *A Grammar and Glossary of Dorset with the History, Out-spreading, and Bearings of South-Western English.* Berlin.

———. 1869. *Early England and the Saxon-English, with Some Notes on the Father-Stock of the Saxon-English, the Frisian.* London.

Barribeau, James Leigh. 1984. *The Vikings and England: The Ninth and the Nineteenth Centuries.* Doctoral Dissertation, Cornell University.

———. 1983. 'William Morris and saga translation: 'The Story of King Magnus, son of Erling', in Farrell 1983, 39–61.

Barrow, John. 1835. *A Visit to Iceland by Way of Tronyem, in the 'Flower of Yarrow' Yacht, in the Summer of 1834.* London.

Bartholin, Thomas. 1689. *Antiqvitatum Danicarum de causis contemptæ a Danis adhuc gentilibus mortis.* Copenhagen.

Barton, H. Arnold. 1996. '*Iter Scandinavicum*: Foreign Travelers' Views of the Late Eighteenth-Century North', *SS* 68, 1–18.

Batey, Colleen, Judith Jesch and Christopher Morris. 1993. Eds *The Viking Age in Caithness, Orkney and the North Atlantic: Select Papers from the Proceedings of the Eleventh Viking Congress, Thurso and Kirkwall, 22 August – 1 September 1989.* Edinburgh.

Batten, C.L. 1978. *Pleasurable Instruction. Form and Convention in Eighteenth-Century Travel Literature*. Berkeley.

Bayerschmidt, Carl F. and Erik J. Friis. 1965. Eds *Scandinavian Studies: Essays Presented to Dr. Henry Goddard Leach on the Occasion of his Eighty-Fifth Birthday*. Seattle.

Bayerschmidt, Carl F. and Lee M. Hollander. 1955. Trans. *Njál's Saga*. New York.

Bayldon, George. 1870. *An Elementary Grammar of the Old Norse or Icelandic Language*. London.

Beamish, North Ludlow. 1841. *The Discovery of America by the Northmen*. London.

Beattie, James. 1776. *The Minstrel; or the Progress of Genius. a Poem in Two Books*. Edinburgh.

Beck, Richard. 1972. *Útverðir íslenzkrar menningar*. Reykjavík.

Beer, Gillian. 1989. 'Darwin and the Growth of Language Theory', in Shuttleworth and Christie 1989, 152–70.

Bell, Alan. 1973. Ed. *Scott Bicentenary Essays*. Edinburgh and London.

Bellot, H. Hale. 1929. *University College, London, 1826–1926*. London.

Benedikt Sveinbjarnarson Gröndal. 1971. *Sagan af Heljarslóðarorrustu*. Reykjavík. [First published 1861].

———. 1880. 'Um Sturlungasaga og Prolegomena eptir Dr Gudbrand Vigfússon', *Tímarit Hins íslenzka bókmentafjelags* 1, 5–32.

———. 1884. 'Um *Corpvs Poeticvm Boreale*', *Tímarit Hins íslenzka bókmentafjelags* 5, 116–42.

Benedikz, B.S. 1961. Ed. *Studia Centenalia in honorem memoriae Benedikt S. Þórarinsson*. Reykjavík.

———. 1970. 'Grímur Thorkelín, the University of Saint Andrews, and the Codex Scardensis', *SS* 42/4, 385–93.

———. 1989. 'Guðbrandur Vigfússon. A Biographical Sketch', in McTurk and Wawn 1989, 11–33.

Bennett. 1882. *Bennett's Hand-Book for Travellers in Norway*. 22nd edition. Christiania.

Bennett, J.A.W. 1937. 'The Beginnings of Norse Studies in England', *SBVS* 12/1, 35–42.

———. 1938. *The History of Old English and Old Norse Studies in England from the Time of Francis Junius to the End of the Eighteenth Century*. Doctoral Dissertation, University of Oxford.

———. 1950–1. 'The Beginnings of Runic Studies in England', *SBVS* 13/4, 269–83.

[Bennett, Joseph]. 1896. [Review of Elgar's *King Olaf*] in Redwood 1982, 15–20.

Bennett, Joseph. [n.d.]. *Scenes from the Saga of King Olaf . . . Book of Words with Analytical Notes*. London.

Benson, Adolphe B. 1926. 'A List of the English Translations of the Frithjofs Saga', *Germanic Review* 1, 142–67.

Bergesen, Robert. 1997. *Vinland Bibliography: Writings Relating to the Norse in Greenland and America*. Tromsø.

[Bevan, F.L.]. 1886. *Near Home; or, The Countries of Europe Described*. 4th edition. London.

Bird, John. 1976. *Percy Grainger*. London.

Bjarni Aðalbjarnarson. 1941–51. Snorri Sturluson, *Heimskringla*, 3 vols. Reykjavík [Íslensk fornrit 26–28].

Björn Halldórsson. 1814. Ed. Rasmus Rask, *Lexicon Islandico-Latinum-Danicum Biörnonis Halldorsonii*. 2 vols. Copenhagen.

Björn Þorsteinsson. 1957–61. 'Henry VIII and Iceland', *SBVS* 15, 67–101.

———. 1970. *Enska öldin í sögu Íslendinga*. Reykjavík.

Björner, E.J. 1737. *Nordiska kämpa dater*. Stockholm.

Black, Joseph. 1794. 'An Analysis of the Waters of Some Hot Springs in Iceland', *TRSE* 3, 95–126.

Blackley, W. L. 1857. Trans. *The Frithiof Saga; or, Lay of Frithiof*. Dublin.

———. 1914. Trans. *Frithiofs Saga*, in Lieder 1914.

Blackwell, I.A. 1847. See Percy, Thomas

Blair, Hugh. 1763. *A Critical Dissertation on the Poems of Ossian*. Edinburgh.

Blake, N.F. 1962. *The Saga of the Jomsvikings*. London.

Blaksley, John. 1903. *Travels, Trips and Trots*. London.

Blind, Karl. 1877. 'The Teutonic Tree of Existence', *FM* n.s. 15, 101–17.

———. 1879. 'Discovery of Odinic Songs of Shetland', *The Nineteenth Century* 5, 1091–1113.

———. 1894. 'The Boar's Head Dinner at Oxford and a Teutonic Sun-God', *SBVS* 1, 90–105.

———. 1896. 'The "Song to Ægir" ', *ScotR* 27, 95–104.

———. 1899. 'Odin and the Royal Family of England', *ScotR* 33, 371–79.

Booth, Susan. 1969. 'The Early Career of Alexander Runciman and his Relations with Sir James Clerk of Penicuik', *JWCI* 32, 332–43.

Borrow, George. 1889. Trans. Johannes Ewald, *The Death of Balder*. London.

———. 1923–24. Ed. Clement K. Shorter, *The Works of George Borrow*. 16 vols. London and New York. [vols 7–9, *The Songs of Scandinavia and Other Poems and Ballads*].

Bossche, Christopher Vanden. 1989. 'Carlyle's *Færeyinga saga* translation', *The Carlyle Annual* 10, 64–79.

Bosworth, Joseph. 1839. *Scandinavian Literature*. London.

Bottomley, Gordon. 1953. Ed. Claude C. Abbott and Anthony Bertram. *Poems and Plays*. London.

Boucher, Odile. 1983. 'The Criticism of Fiction in *Tait's Edinburgh Magazine*, 1832–50', *SSL* 18, 75–84.

Bourdillon, F.W. 1914. *Christmas Roses for 1914*. London.

Bowler, Peter J. 1989. *The Invention of Progress: the Victorians and the Past*. Oxford.

Bowring, Sir John and George Borrow. 1832. 'Literature and Literary Societies in Iceland', *FQR* 9, 41–77.

Boyer, Régis. 1994. 'Vikings, Sagas and Wasa Bread', in Wawn 1994b, 69–81.

Boyesen, Hjalmar. 1895. *Essays on Scandinavian Literature*. New York.

Bradley, S.A.J. 1994. ' "The First New European Literature": N.F.S. Grundtvig's Reception of Anglo-Saxon Literature', in Allchin et al. 1994.

B[radley], H[enry]. 1897–8. 'George Stephens (1813–95)', in *DNB* 18, 1060–1.

Brantlinger, Patrick. 1988. *Rule of Darkness: British Literature and Imperialism, 1830–1914*. Ithaca and London.

Bray, Olive. 1908. *The Elder or Poetic Edda, Commonly Known as Sæmund's Edda*. London.

Bredsdorff, Elias. 1960. Ed. *Sir Edmund Gosse's Correspondence with Scandinavian Writers*. Copenhagen.

———. 1965. 'John Heath, M.A., Fellow of King's College, Cambridge', in Bayerschmidt and Friis 1965, 170–201.

Bremer, Frederika. 1844. *Strife and Peace: or Scenes in Norway*. London.

Brinkley, Richard. 1972. 'George Powell of Nanteos: A Further Appreciation', *AWR* 48, 130–34.

Brooks, C.W.S. 1851. *The Poetic Works*. 6 vols. London.

Brooks, Cleanth et al. 1946–77. Eds *The Percy Letters*. 7 vols. New Haven and London.

Brown, Iain Gordon. 1994. Ed. *The Todholes of Aisle*. Edinburgh.

Brown, Marie A. 1887. *The Icelandic Discoverers of America; or, Honour to whom Honour is Due*. London.

Browne, G.F. 1915. *The Recollections of a Bishop*. London.

Browning, George. 1876. *The Edda Songs and Sagas of Iceland*. London.

Bruce, Michael. 1782. *Poems on Several Occasions*. Stirling.

Bryce, James Viscount. 1874a. 'Notes on mountain climbing in Iceland', *AJ* 7, 50–2.

———. 1874b. 'Impressions of Iceland', *CM* 29, 553–70.

———. 1902. *The Relation of the Advanced and the Backward Races of Mankind*. Oxford.

———. 1915. *Race Sentiment as a Factor in History*. London.

———. 1923. *Memoirs of Travel*. London.

Bryndís Sverrisdóttir et al. 1990. *Frá Englum og Keltum: English and Celtic Artefacts and Influence* [Exhibition, Þjóðminjasafn Íslands]. Reykjavík.

Br[ynjólfur] J[ónsson]. 1900. 'Fjögur kvæði eftir Mrs D. Leith', *Eimreiðin* 6, 170–3.

Brøndsted, Johannes. 1969. *Danmarks historie* [Vol. 1: *De ældste tider indtil år 600*]. Copenhagen.

Buchanan, Robert. 1866. Trans. *Ballad Stories of the Affections, from the Scandinavian*. London.

———. 1877. 'Balder the Beautiful: A Song of Divine Death', in *The Complete Poetic Works*, 2 vols, I 427–92. London.

———. 1901. *The Complete Works of Robert Buchanan*. 2 vols. London.

Bugge, S. 1881–9. *Studier over de nordiske Gude- og Heltesagns Oprindelse*. Christiania.

Bulwer-Lytton, E.R. [*c*.1900]. *Harold: Last of the Saxons*. 3rd edition. London. [1st edition 1848].

Burton, Sir Richard Francis. 1875. *Ultima Thule; or, A Summer in Iceland*. 2 vols. London and Edinburgh.

[Busk, Mary Margaret]. 1828–9. 'Tegner's *Legend of Frithiof*', *FQR* 3, 254–82.

[———]. 1835. 'Scandinavian Mythology and the Nature of its Allegory', *BEM* 38, 25–36.

[———]. 1836. 'Mythology of the North', *FQR* 16, 436–44.

Butt, John. 1963. Ed. *The Poems of Alexander Pope*. London.

Buzard, James. 1993. *The Beaten Track: European Tourism, Literature and the Ways to Culture, 1800–1918*. Oxford.

Caine, Hall. 1890. *The Bondman; A New Saga*. London.

———. 1904. *The Prodigal Son*. London.

———. 1905. *The Prodigal Son*. London [Prompt copy, in Lbs.].

Call, W.M.W. 1875 [First edition 1849]. *Reverberations*. London.

Calverley, W.S. 1881–2. 'The Sculptured Cross at Gosforth, West Cumberland', *Transactions of the Cumberland and Westmorland Antiquarian and Archaeological Society* 6, 373–404.

Camden, William. 1695. *Britannia*. [Facsimile reprint, 1971]. Newton Abbot.

Campbell, A. 1959. *Old English Grammar*. Oxford.

[Campbell, John]. 1741. *The Polite Correspondence: or Rational Amusement*. London.

Campbell, J.F. 1866. *Frost and Fire: Natural Engines, Tool-Marks and Chips, with Sketches Taken at Home and Abroad by a Traveller*. 2 vols. Edinburgh.

Cannadine, David. 1983. 'The Context, Performance and Meaning of Ritual: The British Monarchy and "The Invention of Tradition" ', in Hobsbawm and Ranger 1983, 101–64.

Cappel, Emily S. [1882]. *Old Norse Saga*. Fairy Tales of All Nations, e.s. 1. London.

Carling, John R. 1904. *The Viking's Skull*. London.

Carlyle, Thomas. 1875a. 'The Early Kings of Norway', *FM* n.s. 11, 1–26, 235–55, 273–88.

———. 1875b. *The Early Kings of Norway; also An Essay on the Portraits of John Knox*. London.

———. 1892. Ed. R.P. Karkaria. *Lectures on the History of Literature or the Successive Periods of European Culture delivered in 1838 . . . now first published*. London and Bombay.

———. 1897. *On Heroes, Hero Worship and the Heroic in History*. [Vol. 5 in *The Works of Thomas Carlyle*. Centenary edition. 30 vols]. London.

———. 1899. *Critical and Miscellaneous Essays*. 5 vols. London.

Carpenter, William. 1881a. *Grundriss der neuisländischen Grammatik*. Leipzig.

———. 1881b. Nikolásdrápa Halls Prests. *An Icelandic Poem from Circa A.D. 1400*. Doctoral Dissertation, University of Freiburg. Halle.

————. 1887. 'An Icelandic Novelist', *New Englander and Yale Review*, 469–76.

Carr, Ralph. 1868. 'Observations on Some of the Runic Inscriptions at Mae-showe, Orkney', *PSAS* 6, 70–83.

Carus-Wilson, E.M. 1967. *English Merchant Venturers*. 2nd edition. London.

Chambers, E.K. 1903. *The Medieval Stage*. 2 vols. Oxford.

Chambers, R.W. 1939. 'Philologists at University College, London. The Begin-nings (1828–1889)', in *Man's Unconquerable Mind*, 342–58. London and Toronto.

Chambers, Robert. 1856. *Tracings of Iceland and the Faröe Islands*. Edinburgh.

[Charlton, Edward]. 1850. 'Northern Literature', *DR* 29, 354–70.

————. 1852a. 'Scandinavian Literature', *DR* 32, 97–124.

————. 1852b. 'The Literature and Romance of Northern Europe' [Review of Howitt 1852], *DR* 33, 112–39.

Chitnis, Anand C. 1970. 'The University of Edinburgh's Natural History Museum and the Huttonian-Wernerian debate', *Annals of Science* 27, 85–94.

[Christophers, Samuel W.] 1859. 'The Teutonic Tribes in England' [Reviews of Latham 1840, Kemble 1849, Dasent 1859], *LQR* 12 (July), 355–86.

Clark, J.W. 1861. 'Journal of a Yacht Voyage to the Faroe Islands and Iceland', in Galton 1861, 318–61.

Clay, Beatrice. [?1909]. *Stories from the Saga of Burnt Njal. Part 1: The Story of Gunnar*. London.

————. [n.d.]. Ed. *The Saga of King Olaf*. London.

Cleasby, Richard, and Gudbrand Vigfusson. 1874. *An Icelandic-English Diction-ary Based on the Manuscript Collection of the late R. Cleasby, Enlarged and Com-pleted by Gudbrand Vigfusson*. Oxford.

[Clerke, Agnes Mary]. 1891. 'Scandinavian Antiquities', *ER* 173, 332–59.

[Clifford, Charles]. 1863. *A Tour Twenty Years Ago*. London.

[————]. 1865. *Travels by 'Umbra'*. Edinburgh.

Clouston, J. Storer. 1897. *Vandrad the Viking: Or, The Feud and the Spell*. London.

Clunies Ross, Margaret. 1994. 'Percy and Mallet: The Genesis of *Northern Antiquities*', in Gísli Sigurðsson et al. 1994, 107–117.

————. 1998a. *The Norse Muse in Britain 1750–1820*. Trieste.

————. 1998b. 'Revaluing the Work of Edward Lye, an Eighteenth-Century Septentrional Scholar', *Studies in Medievalism* 9, 1–15.

[Cochrane, John]. 1838. *Catalogue of the Library of Abbotsford*. Edinburgh.

Cole, Owen Blayney. 1880. *Thorstein and Gudrún; An Icelandic Idyll*. Portis-head.

————. 1881. *Eyolf and Astrida; An Icelandic Saga*. Portishead.

————. 1882. *Edmund and Anlaf; A Tragic Interlude in Five Scenes*. Portishead.

Coles, John. 1882. *Summer Travelling in Iceland: Being the Narrative of Two Jour-neys across the Island by Unfrequented Routes*. London.

Collingwood, W.G. 1892–6. 'The Vikings in Lakeland: Their Place-Names, Remains, History', *SBVS* 1/2, 182–96.

————. 1895. *Thorstein of the Mere*. London. [Reissued 1909, Kendal].

———. 1895–6. 'Furness a thousand years ago', *Reports and Proceedings of the Barrow Naturalists Field Club and Literary and Scientific Association*, 1–9.

———. 1896. *The Bondwoman: A Saga of Langdale*. London.

———. 1899. *Thurstan at the Thwaite: A Coniston Tale*. [1990 Llanerch Press reprint from *Coniston Tales*].

———. 1929. *Thorstein of the Mere: A Saga of the Northmen in Lakeland*. 2nd ed. London.

———. 1932. *The Bondwomen: A Saga of Langdale*. 2nd ed. London.

Collingwood, W.G., and Jón Stefánsson. 1899. *A Pilgrimage to the Saga-Steads of Iceland*. Ulverston.

———. 1902. Trans. *The Life and Death of Cormac the Skald*. Ulverston.

Colwell, W.A. 1909. 'On an Eighteenth-Century Translation of Bürger's *Lenore*', *MLN* 24, 254–5.

Conybeare, C.A. Vansittart. 1877. *The Place of Iceland in the History of European Literature*. Oxford.

Cook, Robert. 1998. 'The Dasent shift', in *Guðrúnarhvöt kveðin Guðrúnu Ásu Grímsdóttur, fimmtugri, 23 sept. 1998*, 83–5. Reykjavík.

Coomaraswamy, Ananda. 1905. Trans. *Voluspa Done into English Out of the Icelandic of the the Elder Edda*. Kandy.

Corelli, Marie. 1887. *Thelma*. 2nd edition. Leipzig.

Corson, J.C. 1943. Ed. *A Bibliography of Sir Walter Scott . . . 1797–1940*. Reprinted 1968. New York.

Cotsell, M. 1990. Ed. *Creditable Warriors*. London and Atlantic Highlands.

Cottle, Amos, 1797. *Icelandic Poetry, or The Edda of Saemund*. Bristol.

Cottle, Joseph. 1816. *Alfred*. Third edition. 2 vols. London.

Cowan, Edward J. 1979. 'The Sage and the Sagas: The Brothers Carlyle and "Early Kings" ', *The Bibliothek* 9, 161–83.

Cowan, Edward J. and Hermann Pálsson. 1972. Eds Grímur Thomsen, *On the Character of the Old Northern Poetry*, Studia Islandica 31. Reykjavík.

Cox, George W. 1871. 'Morris's *Earthly Paradise*', *ER* 133, 243–66.

———. 1872. *The Mythology of the Aryan Nations*. Rev. edition. London.

———. Trans. *The Children's Norse Tales*. London.

Cox, George W. and Eustace H. Jones, 1872. *Tales of Teutonic Lands*. London.

Craigie, W.A. 1893a. 'The Oldest Icelandic Folk-lore', *Folk-Lore* 4, 219–32.

———. 1893b. 'Oldnordiske ord i det gæliske sprog', *Arkiv för nordisk filologi* 10, 149–66.

———. 1896a. Trans. *Scandinavian Folklore*. Paisley and London.

———. 1896b. 'The Poetry of the Skalds', *ScotR* 33, 331–46.

———. 1913. *The Icelandic Sagas*. Cambridge.

Cramp, Rosemary, R.N. Bailey, J. Lang et al. 1984–91. *Corpus of Anglo-Saxon Stone Sculpture*. 3 vols. New York.

Crane, R.S. 1922. 'An Early Eighteenth-Century Enthusiast for Primitive Poetry: John Husbands', *MLN* 37, 27–36.

[Crolly, George]. 1852. Review of Worsaae 1852, *DR* 32, 184–220.

Cross, F.L. and E.A. Livingstone. 1974. Eds *The Oxford History of the Christian Church*. 2nd edition. Oxford.

Crusell, B. [1825]. *Tolf sånger ur Frithiofs saga*. Stockholm.

Curtis, L.P. 1968. *Anglo-Saxons and Celts: A Study of Anti-Irish Prejudice in Victorian England*. Bridgeport, CN.

Dalton, Charles. 1879. *Journal of a Tour in Iceland, 1878*. Hull.

Damico, Helen. 1998. Ed. *Medieval Scholarship. Biographical Studies on the Formation of a Discipline: II Literature and Philology*. New York and London.

D'Arcy, Julian. 1996. *Scottish Skalds and Sagamen: Old Norse Influence on Modern Scottish Literature*. East Linton.

D'Arcy, Julian and Kirsten Wolf. 1987. 'Sir Walter Scott and *Eyrbyggja saga*', *SSL* 22, 30–43.

Darwin, Erasmus. 1799. *The Botanic Garden. Part One*. 4th edition. London.

Dasent, George Webbe. 1842. Trans. *The Prose or Younger Edda Commonly Ascribed to Snorri Sturluson*. Stockholm.

———. 1843. Trans. *A Grammar of the Icelandic or Old Norse Tongue translated from the Swedish of Erasmus Rask*. London and Frankfurt.

———. 1845. Trans. *Theophilus in Icelandic, Low German and Other Tongues*. London.

———. 1851. 'The Master Thief: a Norse Popular Tale', *BEM* 70, 595–604.

———. 1858. 'The Norsemen in Iceland', *Oxford Essays*, 165–214. Oxford.

———. 1859. Trans. *Popular Tales from the Norse*. Edinburgh.

———. 1861. Trans. *The Story of Burnt Njal; or, Life in Iceland at the End of the Tenth Century*. 2 vols. Edinburgh.

———. 1866. Trans. *The Story of Gisli the Outlaw*. Edinburgh.

———. 1873. *Jest and Earnest: A Collection of Essays and Reviews*. 2 vols. London.

[———]. 1874a. [Review of Cleasby and Gudbrand Vigfusson 1874], *The Times* 2 March, 4d.

[———.]. 1874b. [Review of Cleasby and Gudbrand Vigfusson 1874], *ER* 140, 228–258.

———. 1875. *The Vikings of the Baltic*. 3 vols. London.

[———]. 1876. 'Iceland and its Explorers' [Review of Burton 1875], *ER* 143, 222–50

[———]. 1882. 'The Land of the Midnight Sun', *ER* 155, 256–79.

———. 1900. Trans. *The Story of Burnt Njal from the Icelandic of the Njals Saga*. London. [Revised E.V. Lucas].

———. [?1900]. Trans. *The Story of Gisli the Outlaw*. London.

———. 1903. Trans. *Popular Tales from the Norse*. Rev. edition with memoir by A.I. Dasent. Edinburgh.

———. 1905. See French, Allan.

———. 1906. Trans. *The Story of Burnt Njal, the Great Icelandic Tribune, Jurist, and Counsellor*. Norrœna Society. London et al.

———. [1909]. *Gisli the Outlaw. From the Icelandic by George Webbe Dasent D.C.L. Retold by Rev. A. E. Sims*. All Time Tales, 12. London and Glasgow.

———. 1917. See Malim, H.

Dasent, George Webbe. See also Gudbrand Vigfusson and Dasent.

Davenport Adams, W.H. 1883. *Stories and Sea; or, Stories of Great Vikings and Sea Captains*. London.

Davis, B.H. 1989. *Thomas Percy. A Scholar-Critic in the Age of Johnson*. Philadelphia.

Davis T. 1842. 'Udalism and Feudalism', *DM* 218–37, 293–315.

de Costa, B.F. 1868. *The Pre-Columbian Discovery of America*. New York.

de la Motte-Fouquet, F. 1815. *Die Fahrten Thiodolfs den Isländer*. Upsala.

———. 1845. Trans. *Thiodolf the Icelander*. London.

de Vere, A.T. 1884. *The Poetic Works*. London.

Dehn-Nielsen, Henning. 1933–44. 'George Stephens', in C.F. Bricka, Povl Engelstoft and Svend Dahl (Eds), *Dansk Biografisk Leksikon* 16 vols, XIV 99–100. 3rd edition. Copenhagen.

Demarest, Anthony. 1975. *Coleridge and the Elder Edda: 1795–1798*. Doctoral Dissertation, Fordham University, New York.

Desmond, Adrian and James Moore. 1992. *Darwin*. London.

Dibdin, T.J. 1822. *The Pirate, a Melodramatic Romance, Taken from the Novel*. London.

Dillmann, François-Xavier. 1996. 'Frankrig og den nordiske fortid—de første etaper af genopdagelsen', in Roesdahl and Sørensen 1996, 13–26.

Dillon, Hon. Arthur. 1840. *A Winter in Iceland and Lapland*. 2 vols. London.

Dobbie, Elliot van Kirk. 1942. Ed. *The Anglo-Saxon Poetic Records*. 6 vols. New York.

Dowling, Linda. 1986. *Language and Decadence in the Victorian Fin de Siècle*. Princeton.

———. 1994. *Hellenism and Homosexuality in Victorian Oxford*. Ithaca and London.

Downe, Walmer. 1902. *The Dane's Daughter, An Icelandic Story*. London.

Dronke, Ursula. 1989. 'The Scope of the *Corpvs Poeticvm Borealis*', in McTurk and Wawn 1989, 93–112.

Drummond, Sir William. 1817. *Odin; a Poem. Part One*. London.

Dryden, John. 1716. *Poetical Miscellanies*. VI. London.

Dubozy, Maria. 1998. 'The Brothers Grimm: Jacob Ludwig Carl (1785–1863), Wilhelm Carl (1786–1859)', in Damico 1998, 93–108.

du Chaillu, Paul. 1889. *The Viking Age: The Early History, Manners, and Customs of the Ancestors of the English-Speaking Nations*. 2 vols. London.

———. 1893. *Ivar the Viking*. London.

Dufferin, Lord. 1857. *Letters from High Latitudes; Being an Account of a Voyage to Iceland, Jan Mayen, and Spitzbergen, in 1856*. 2 vols. London.

Dunn, Hugh. 1894. 'Is our Race degenerating?', *NC* 36, 301–14.

[Dunne, David B.]. 1861. 'Iceland', *DR* 50, 1–59.

[Earle, John]. 1875. 'Icelandic Illustrations of English', *QR* 139, 433–65.

Ebbutt, Maud Isabel, 1910. *Hero Myths and Legends of the British Race*. London and New York.

Edmonston, Arthur. 1809. *A View of the Past and Present State of the Zetland Islands*. Edinburgh.

Egerton, Francis. 1848. *Guide to Northern Archaeology, by the Royal Society of Northern Antiquaries of Copenhagen for the Use of English Readers*. London.

Egerton-Warburton, R.E. 1877. *Poems, Epigrams, and Sonnets*. London.

Eggert Ólafsson and Bjarni Pálsson. 1772. *Reise igiennem Island*. Sorøe.

————. 1805. *Travels in Iceland*. London.

Ehrleman, Lloyd Wendell. 1940. *A Victorian Rebel: The Life of William Morris*. New York.

Einar Ólafur Sveinsson. 1954. *Brennu-Njáls saga*. Íslenzk fornrit 13. Reykjavík.

Eiríkr Magnússon. 1869. 'Iceland for the Americans', *SR* 3 July, 28.

————. 1869. [Review of Cleasby and Gudbrand Vigfusson 1874; first fascicles], *SR* 6 November, 610.

————. 1870. Ed. and Trans. Eysteinn Ásgrímsson, *The Lily: An Icelandic Poem of the Fourteenth Century*. London.

————. 1875–83. Ed. and Trans. *Thómas saga Erkibyskups*. 2 vols. London.

————. 1877. *On an Early Runic Calendar, Found in Lapland 1866*. Cambridge.

————. 1879. *Dr Gudbrand Vigfusson's Ideal of an Icelandic New Testament Translation, or The Gospel of St Matthew by Lawman Odd Gottskalksson*. Cambridge.

————. 1882. *Mr Vigfusson and the Distress in Iceland*. Cambridge.

————. 1888. *On Four Runic Calendars*. Cambridge.

————. 1895. *On Odin's horse Yggdrasill*. London.

————. 1896. *Edda. Its Derivation and Meaning*. London.

————. 1896–7. 'William Morris', *Cambridge Review* 18, 109–10.

————. 1905. [Review of Gudbrand Vigfusson and York Powell 1905], *SBVS* 4/2, 415–67.

Elgar, Sir Edward. 1896. *Scenes from the Saga of King Olaf*. London.

————. See Bennett, Joseph.

Eliot, George. 1960. Ed. Anthea Bell, *The Mill on The Floss*. London.

Ellison, Ruth C. 1972. ' "The Undying Glory of Dreams": William Morris and "The Northland of Old" ', *Victorian Poetry*, Stratford-upon-Avon Studies 15, 139–75. London.

————. 1979. 'Hallæri og hneykslismál', *Andvari*, nýr flokkur 20, 62–79.

————. 1987–8. 'The Alleged Famine in Iceland', *SBVS* 22 3/4, 165–79.

————. 1988. 'Icelandic Obituaries of William Morris', *Journal of the William Morris Society* 8, 35–41.

Ellwood, Thomas. 1894. *The Landnama Book of Iceland as it illustrates the Dialect, Folk Lore and Antiquities of Cumberland, Westmorland and North Lancashire*. Kendal.

————. 1895. *Lakeland and Iceland: Being a Glossary of Words in the Dialect of Cumbria, Westmorland and North Lancashire which seem Allied to or Identical with the Icelandic or Norse*. London.

————. 1898. Trans. *The Book of the Settlement of Iceland*. Kendal.

Elsa E. Guðjónsson. 1985. 'Íslenskur brúðarbúningur í ensku safni', *Árbók hins íslenzka fornleifafélags 1984*, 49–80.

Elstob, Elizabeth. 1715. *The Rudiments of Grammar for the English-Saxon Tongue*. London.

Elton, Charles. 1890. 'The Viking Age' [Review of du Chaillu 1889], *QR* 347–69.

Elton, Oliver. 1890. Trans. *The Life of Laurence Bishop of Hólar in Iceland (Laurentius Saga) by Einar Haflidarson*. London.

———. 1894. Trans. *The Nine Books of the Danish History of Saxo Grammaticus*. London.

———. 1906. *Frederick York Powell, A Life*. 2 vols. Oxford.

Elwin, Malcolm. 1939. *Old Gods Falling*. London.

Emerson, Ralph Waldo. 1950. Ed. Brooks Atkinson, *Selected Writings*. New York.

Engesæter, Aage. [n.d. ?1990]. *Turistaden Balestrand. Om reiselivsnæringi i Balestrand før 1914*. Sogndal.

Erslev, Thomas Hansen. 1858–68. *Almindeligt Forfatter-Lexicon for Kongeriget Danmark med tilhørende Bilande–Supplement*. 3 vols, III 268–78. Copenhagen.

Ervine, St. John. 1949. *Craigavon: Ulsterman*. London.

Ewald, Johannes. 1889. Trans. George Borrow, *The Death of Balder*. London.

Fahlcrantz, Carl Johan. 1829. *Framnäs och Balestrand. Frithiofs och Ingeborgs hem*. Stockholm.

Fallowes, E.H. et al. 1967. Eds *English Madrigal Verse 1588–1632*. Rev. 3rd edition. Oxford.

Faraday, Winifred. 1902. *The Edda: I. Divine Mythology*. London.

Farley, Frank E. 1903. *Scandinavian Influence in the English Romantic Movement*. Cambridge, Mass.

———. 1906. 'Three "Lapland Songs" ', *PMLA* 21, 1–39.

Farrell, R.T. 1983. Ed. *The Vikings*. Ithaca.

Farrer, James. 1862. *Notice of Runic Inscriptions Discovered during Recent Excavations in the Orkneys*. [Edinburgh].

Faulkes, Anthony. 1977. 'Edda', *Gripla* 2, 32–39.

Faulkes, Anthony and Richard Perkins. 1993. Eds *Viking Revaluations*. London.

Felix Ólafsson. 1992. *Ebenezer Henderson og Hið íslenska Biblíufélag*. Reykjavík.

Fell, Christine. 1986. 'Old English *Wicing*: A Question of Semantics', *Publications of the British Academy* 72, 295–316.

———. 1987. 'Modern English Viking', *LSE* 18, 111–22.

———. 1992. 'Norse Studies: Then, Now and Hereafter', in Faulkes and Perkins 1993, 85–99.

———. 1996. 'The First Publication of Old Norse Literature in England and its Relation to its Sources', in Roesdahl and Sørensen 1996, 27–57.

Ferguson, R.M. 1896. *The Viking's Bride and other Poems*. Paisley.

[Ferguson, Sir Samuel]. 1833. 'Death-Song of Regner Lodbrog', *BEM* 33, 910–23.

Fielding, K.J. 1984. 'Carlyle and Esaias Tegnér: An Unpublished Manuscript', *Carlyle Newsletter* 5, 3–10, 35.

Finnbogi Guðmundsson. 1971. 'Um þjóðlegan metnað Jóns Sigurðssonar', *Andvari*, nýr flokkur 13, 118–45.

———. 1991. 'Um Chicagoför sr. Matthíasar Jochumssonar 1893', *LÍA 1989*, nýr flokkur 17, 27–39.

Finnur Jónsson. 1772–8. *Historia ecclesiastica Islandiæ*. 4 vols. Copenhagen.

Finnur Magnússon. 1824–6. *Eddalæren*. 4 vols. Copenhagen.

———. 1836–7. 'Om Obelisken i Ruthwell og om de Angel-Saxiske Runer', *Annaler for Nordisk Oldkyndighed* 243–337.

Finnur Sigmundsson. 1950. Ed. *Úr fórum Jóns Árnasonar.* 2 vols. Reykjavík.

Fisher, H.A.L. 1927. *James Bryce (Viscount Bryce of Dechment, O.M.).* 2 vols. London.

Fjalldal, Magnús. See Magnús Fjalldal.

[Flamank, John]. 1837. *The Curate of Steinhollt. A Tale of Iceland*. 2 vols. London.

Fleming, Robin. 1995. 'Picturesque History and the Medieval in Nineteenth-Century America', *AHR* 100, 1061–94.

Foote, Peter. 1996–8. See Olaus Magnus.

Forbes, Charles. 1860. *Iceland: Its Volcanoes, Geysers and Glaciers*. London.

Forester, Thomas. 1850. *Norway in 1848 and 1849*. London.

———. 1853. *Norway and its Scenery*. London.

[Forman, Henry]. 1871. [Review of Stephens 1839, Laing 1844, Dasent 1861 and 1866, Head 1866, Morris and Eiríkr Magnússon 1869 and 1870], *LQR* 36, 35–65.

Fox, E.M. [1906]. *Graysteel; or the Bearsarks come to Surnadale*. Sheffield.

———. 1929. *The Tale of the Men of Laxdale*. Teaching of English Literature Series. London.

Frantzen, Allen J. and J.D. Niles. 1997. Eds *Anglo-Saxonism and the Construction of Social Identity*. Gainesville, Flor.

Frazer, J.G. 1913. *Balder the Beautiful; the Fire-Festivals and the Doctrines of the External Soul*. London.

French, Allen. 1904. *The Story of Rolf and the Viking's Bow*. Boston.

———. 1905. *Heroes of Iceland, Adapted from Dasent's Translation of* The Story of Burnt Njal, *the Great Icelandic Saga*. London.

Fry, Donald K. 1980. *Norse Sagas Translated into English*. New York.

F[rye], W.E. 1835. *Frithiof's Saga; or The Legend of Frithiof*. London.

Frye, W.E. 1845. See Oehlenschläger 1819.

Furnivall, F.J. 1870. Ed. Andrew Boorde, *The Fyrst Boke of the Introduction of Knowledge (1542)*. EETS e.s. 10. London.

Gades, Charles R. et al. 1970–90. Eds *The Collected Letters of Thomas and Jane Welsh Carlyle*. 18 vols. Durham, N.C. and London.

Galbraith, Georgina. 1965. *The Journal of the Rev. William Bagshaw Stevens*. Oxford.

———. 1971. *Collected Poems of the Rev. William Bagshaw Stevens*. London.

[Galt, John]. 1803. 'An Extract from a Gothic Poem', *The Scots Magazine* 65, 272–4.

Galton, Francis. 1861. *Vacation Tourists and Notes of Travels in 1860*. London.

Garvagh, Lord. 1875. *The Pilgrim of Scandinavia*. London.

Gash, Norman. 1965. *Reaction and Reconstruction in English Politics, 1832–52*. Oxford.

Geijer, Erik Gustaf and Arvid August Afzelius. 1880. Eds *Svenska Folkvisor*. Stockholm.

Geldart, E.M. 1875. 'Illustrations of Grimm's Law', *PLLPS* 29, 351–78.

Gísli Sigurðsson [et al.]. 1994. Eds *Sagnaþing, helgað Jónasi Kristjánssyni sjötugum*. 2 vols. Reykjavík.

Goblirsch, Kurt Gustav et al. 1997. Eds *Germanic Studies in Honor of Anatoly Liberman*. Odense.

Goddard, Julia. 1871. *Wonderful Stories from Northern Lands*. London.

[Goldsmith, Oliver]. 1757. [Review of Mallet 1755, 1756], *MR* 16, 377–81.

Gollancz, Israel. 1898. *Hamlet in Iceland*. London.

Gordon, E.V. 1957. *An Introduction to Old Norse*. 2nd edition, rev. A.R. Taylor. Oxford.

G[osse], E[dmund] W. 1879. 'The "Egils saga" ', *CM* 40, 21–39.

———. 1880. 'The "Eyrbyggja saga" ', *CM* 41, 712–22.

Gould, C.N. 1921–3. 'The Friðþjófssaga, an Oriental Tale', *SS* 7, 219–50.

G[reen], W.C. 1893. Trans. *The Story of Egil Skallagrimsson: An Icelandic Family History of the Ninth and Tenth Centuries*. London.

———. 1905. [Review of Wagner 1904], *SBVS* 4, 253–4.

Green. W.C. 1908. *Translations from the Icelandic: Being Select Passages Introductory to Icelandic Literature*. London.

Greenway, John. 1977. *Mythic Imagination and the Nordic Past*. Athens, Georgia.

Grierson, Sir Herbert. 1932–7. Ed. *The Letters of Sir Walter Scott*. 12 vols. London.

Grimm, Jakob. 1812–15. *Kinder- und Hausmärchen*. 2 vols. Berlin.

———. 1815. *Lieder der alten Edda*. I. Berlin.

———. 1819–37. *Deutsche Grammatik*, 4 vols. Göttingen. [2nd edition 1822].

Grímur Thomsen. 1859. 'The Northmen in Iceland' [Review of Dasent 1858], *Société Royale des Antiquaires du Nord* 4–16. Copenhagen.

Grímur Jónsson Thorkelin. 1788. Trans. *Fragments of English and Irish History in the Ninth and Tenth Century*. London.

——— [?] et al. 1809a. Ed. and Trans. *Egils-saga sive Egilli Skallagrimii vita*. Copenhagen.

——— [?] et al. 1809b. Trans. *Nials-Saga. Historia Niali et filiorum*. Copenhagen.

———. 1815. Ed. and Trans. *De Danorum rebus gestis secul. III & IV. Pöema Danicum dialecto Anglosaxonica*. Copenhagen.

Guðbrandur Vigfússon. 1855. 'Ferðasaga úr Noregi', *NF* 15, 1–83.

———. 1861. 'Álit um ritgjörðir' [Review of Dasent 1861], *NF* 21, 128–36.

Guðbrandr Vigfusson. 1865. 'On the word *Rúnhenda* or *Rímhenda* and the Introduction of Rhyme into Iceland', *TPS* 200–17.

———. 1866. 'Some Remarks upon the Use of the Reflexive Pronoun in Icelandic', *TPS* 80–112.

Gudbrand Vigfusson [Guðbrandur Vigfússon]. 1869. *A Few Parallel Specimens from the First Three Gospels*. Oxford.

———. 1878. Ed. *Sturlunga Saga Including the Islendinga Saga of Lawman Sturla Thordsson*. 2 vols. Oxford.

Gudbrand Vigfusson and Sir G.W. Dasent. 1887–94. Eds and Trans. *Icelandic Sagas and other Historical Documents relating to the Settlements and Descents of the Northmen on the British Isles*. Rolls Series. 4 vols. London.

Gudbrand Vigfusson and F. York Powell. 1879. Eds *An Icelandic Prose Reader*. Oxford.

———. 1883. Eds and Trans. *Corpvs Poeticvm Boreale. The Poetry of the Old Northern Tongue from the Earliest Times to the Thirteenth Century*. 2 vols. Oxford.

———. 1886. *Sigfred-Arminivs and Other Papers*. Oxford and London.

———. 1905. Eds *Origines Islandicae*. 2 vols. Oxford.

Guðbrandur Vigfússon and C.R. Unger. 1860–8. Eds *Flateyjarbók*. Christiania.

Guðmundur Ólafsson. 1987. 'Þingnes by Elliðavatn: The First Local Assembly in Iceland?', *Proceedings of the Tenth Viking Congress, Larkollen, Norway 1985* 343–49. Oslo.

Guðrún Kvaran. 1991. 'Konráð Gíslason, málfræðingur og orðabókahöfundur', *Skagfirðingabók* 20, 47–70.

Guðrún Kvaran and Sigurður Jónsson. 1991. *Nöfn Íslendinga*. Reykjavík.

Guerber, H.A. 1908. *Myths of the Norsemen*. London.

Gunnar Guðmundsson. 1993. 'Frú Disney Leith og Ísland', *LÍÁ 1992*, nýr flokkur 18, 27–40.

Gunnell, Terry. 1995. *The Origins of Drama in Scandinavia*. Cambridge.

Göransson, Johann. [1746]. *De Yfverborna Atlingars: eller Sviogötars ok Nordmänners Edda*. Uppsala.

H.L. 1882. *Odin Sagas and Other Poems*. Manchester.

Haarder, Andreas. 1982. Ed. *The Medieval Legacy*. Odense.

Hack, Maria. 1819. *Winter Evenings; or, Tales of Travellers*. 4 vols. London.

Haggard, H.Rider. 1891/1951. *Eric Brighteyes*. London. [Reissue].

———. 1891/1974. *Eric Brighteyes*. London. [Reprinted Hollywood, Calif.].

———. 1926. *The Days of My Life*. 2 vols. London.

Haigh, Daniel. 1861. *The Anglo-Saxon Sagas*. London.

Hakluyt, R. 1599–1600. Trans. *The Principal Navigations, Voiages, Traffiques and Discoveries of the English Nation*. 3 vols. London. [Translation of Arngrímur Jónsson 1593].

Hall, Mrs A.W. [?1900]. *Icelandic Fairy Tales*. London and New York.

Halldór Hermannsson. 1919. 'Sir George Webbe Dasent', *Skírnir* 93, 117–40.

———. 1914–27. *Catalogue of the Icelandic Collection bequeathed by Willard Fiske*. 3 vols in 2. Ithaca, NY.

———. 1928. *Sir Joseph Banks and Iceland*. Islandica 18. Ithaca, NY.

Hamel, Leopold. 1874. Trans. *Frithiof's Saga*. London.

Handley, Vernon. 1987/1994. Conductor. *Scenes from the Saga of King Olaf.* EMI CMS 5 65104. London.

Haraldur Hannesson. 1988. Trans. *Fegurð Íslands og fornir sögustaðir.* Reykjavík.

Haraldur Sigurðsson. 1971–8. *Kortasaga Íslands.* 2 vols. Reykjavík.

———. 1991. *Ísland í skrifum erlendra manna um þjóðlíf og náttúru landsins. Ritaskrá.* Reykjavík.

Harley, Ethel. 1889. *A Girl's Ride in Iceland.* London and Sydney.

Harris, Richard L. 1970. 'The Lion-Knight Legend in Iceland and the Valþjófsstaðir Door', *Viator* 1, 125–45.

———. 1978–81. 'William Morris, Eiríkur Magnússon and the Icelandic Famine Relief Efforts of 1882', *SBVS* 20 1/2, 31–41.

———. 1992. Ed. *A Chorus of Grammars: The Correspondence of George Hickes and his Collaborators on the* Thesaurus linguarum septentrionalium. Toronto.

Harvey, Charles and Jon Press. 1991. *William Morris. Design and Enterprise in Victorian Britain.* Manchester.

Harvey Wood, E.H. 1972. *Letters to an Antiquary: The Literary Correspondence of G.J. Thorkelin (1752–1829).* Doctoral Dissertation, University of Edinburgh.

Haughton, Walter E. et al. 1966–89. *The Wellesley Index to Victorian Periodicals, 1824–1900.* 5 vols. Toronto and Buffalo.

Haukur Hannesson et al. 1989. Eds *Ritverk Jónasar Hallgrímssonar.* 4 vols. Reykjavík.

Hazlitt, William. 1822. [Review of Scott 1822], *LM* 25, 80–89.

Head, Sir Edmund. 1865. Trans. 'Free Translation from the Icelandic of the Edda: Helgakviða Hundingsbana II', *FM* 72, 370–4.

———. 1866. *The Story of Víga-Glum.* London.

Headley, P.C. 1875. *The Island of Fire; or, A Thousand Years of the Old Northmen's Home, 874–1874.* Boston.

Heanley, R.M. 1901–3. 'The Vikings: Their Folklore in Marshland', *SBVS* 3, 35–62.

Heath, John. 1827. Trans. *The Little Shepherd Boy. An Idyll.* Copenhagen.

Hebermann, Charles G. 1891. Trans. *The History of Ancient Vinland by Thormod Torfason.* New York.

Heckethorne, C.W. 1856. Trans. *The Frithjof Saga; A Scandinavian Romance.* London.

Heimir Pálsson et al. 1990. Eds *Yrkja: Afmælisrit til Vigdísar Finnbogadóttur 15. apríl 1990.* Reykjavík.

Henderson, Ebenezer. 1818. *Iceland; Or the Journal of a Residence in that Island, during the Years 1814 and 1815.* 2 vols. in 1. Edinburgh.

———. 1819. *Iceland; Or the Journal of a Residence in that Island, during the Years 1814 and 1815.* Edinburgh.

———. 1831. *Iceland; Or the Journal of a Residence in that Island, during the Years 1814 and 1815.* Abridged edition. Boston.

———. 1832. [On Jón Þorláksson and Pope], *FQR,* 73–4.

Henderson, J. 1872. Trans. *The Story of Frithiof.* London and Edinburgh.

Henderson, Philip. 1974. *Swinburne: the Portrait of a Poet.* London.

Henderson, Thulia S. [1859]. *Memoir of the Rev. E. Henderson, D.D., Ph.D.* London.

Henty, G.A. [n.d.]. *The Dragon and the Raven.* London.

Herbert, William. 1806. *Select Icelandic Poetry, Translated from the Originals.* 2 parts. London.

———. 1815. *Helga: A Poem.* London.

———. 1820. *Hedin; or, The Spectre of the Tomb. A Tale.* London.

———. 1838. *Attila, or The Triumph of Christianity.* London.

Herford, C.H. 1918–20. 'Northern Myth in English Poetry', *BJRL* 5, 75–101.

Hermann Pálsson. 1970. *Tólfta öldin. Þættir um menn og málefni.* Reykjavík.

Hewlett, Maurice. 1916. *Frey and His Wife.* London.

———. 1917. *A Lover's Tale.* London.

———. 1917. *Thorgils of Treadholt.* London.

———. 1918. *Gudrid the Fair.* London.

———. 1919. *The Outlaw.* London.

———. 1920. *The Light Heart.* London.

Hibbert, Christopher. 1976. *George IV.* London.

Hickes, George. 1703–5. *Linguarum vett. septentrionalium thesaurus grammatico-criticus et archæologicus.* 2 vols. Oxford.

Hilen, Andrew. 1947. *Longfellow and Scandinavia: A Study of the Poet's Relationship with the Northern Languages and Literature.* New Haven.

Hill, G.B. 1934–50. Ed. *Boswell's Life of Johnson.* 6 vols. Oxford.

Hjörtur Pálsson. 1975. *Alaskaför Jóns Ólafssonar.* Reykjavík.

Hobsbawm, Eric and Terence Ranger. 1983. Eds *The Invention of Tradition.* Cambridge.

Hodgetts, J. Frederick. 1884. *Older England, Illustrated by the Anglo-Saxon Antiquities in the British Museum in a Course of Six Lectures.* London.

———. 1885. *The Champion of Odin; Or Viking Life in the Days of Old.* London.

———. 1902. *Kormak the Viking.* London.

Hodgkin, Thomas. 1895. 'Professor George Stephens', *Archæologia Aeliana* 18, 50–53.

Hogg, John. 1859. 'On the History of Iceland and the Icelandic Language and Literature', *Transactions of the Royal Society of Literature* n.s. 6, 1–60.

Holcomb, T.A.F. and Martha A. Lyons. 1892. Trans. *Frithiofs saga.* 3rd edition. Chicago and London.

Hole, Richard. 1789. 'The Tomb of Gunnar', *GM* 59, 937.

Holland, Henry. 1808. *A General View of the Agriculture of Cheshire.* London.

———. 1811. *De morbis Islandiae.* Edinburgh.

[Holland, Henry]. 1861. 'Forbes's *Iceland*', *ER* 113, 532–54.

Hooker, William Jackson. 1813. *Journal of a Tour in Iceland in the Summer of 1809.* 2 vols in 1. 2nd edition. London.

Horrebow, Niels. 1758. *A Natural History of Iceland.* London.

Horsford, Cornelia. 1893. *Graves of the Northmen.* Boston.

Horsford, E.N. 1888a. *The Discovery of America by the Northmen.* Boston.

———. 1888b. *The Problem of the Northmen.* Cambridge, Mass.

———. 1888c. *Discovery of America by Northmen: Address at the Unveiling of the Statue of Leif Erikson . . . Oct. 29, 1887.* Boston and New York.

———. 1892. *The Landfall of Leif Erikson, A.D. 1000, and the Site of his Houses in Vineland.* Boston.

———. 1893. *Leif's Home in Vinland.* Boston.

Horsman, R. 1976. 'The Origins of Racial Anglo-Saxonism in Great Britain before 1850', *JHI* 37, 387–410.

Hougen, Pål. 1996. 'Kaiser Wilhelm II og Norges heroiske fortid', in Roesdahl and Sørensen 1996, 147–55.

Howard, Newman. 1902. *Kiartan the Icelander.* London.

Howarth, Mary. 1895. *Stories of Norway in the Saga Days.* London.

Howell, Frederick W.W. 1893. *Icelandic Pictures drawn with Pen and Pencil.* London.

Howitt, William and Mary. 1852. *The Literature and Romance of Northern Europe, Constituting a Complete History of the Literature of Sweden, Denmark, Norway and Iceland.* 2 vols. London.

Howorth, Henry. 1894. 'Iceland today', *QR* 357, 58–82.

———. 1920. 'Harald Fairhair and his Ancestors', *SBVS* 9/1, 1–252.

Hueffer, Francis Xavier. 1876. 'The Story of Sigurd and its Sources', *GM* 19, 46–56.

[Hughes, Shaun F.D.]. [n.d.]. *Skrá um íslensk handrit í Harvard.* Typescript copy in Stofnun Árna Magnússonar, Reykjavík.

Hughes, Thomas. 1859. *The Scouring of the White Horse.* London. [1989 reprint].

———. 1869. *Alfred the Great.* London.

Hugo, Victor. 1885. Trans. Sir Gilbert Campbell, *The Outlaw of Iceland, A Romance.* London.

Hustvedt, Lloyd. 1966. *Rasmus Bjørn Anderson: Pioneering Scholar.* Northfield, Minnesota.

Hødnebø, Finn et al. 1992. Eds *Eyvindarbók. Festskrift til Eyvind Fjeld Halvorsen.* Oslo.

Ibsen, Henrik. 1962. Trans. J.W. McFarlane, *The Vikings of Helgoland.* Oxford.

Indrebø, Gustav and Olof Kolsrud. 1924–71. *Lærde brev fraa og til P.A. Munch.* 3 vols. Oslo.

Ingi Sigurðsson. 1980. 'Viðhorf Íslendinga til Skotlands og Skota á 19. og 20. öld', *Saga* 18, 115–78.

Íslensk sagnablöð. 1826. *Íslensk sagnablöð útgefin að tilhlutan Hins íslenzka bókmenntafélags.* Copenhagen.

Jakob Ásgeirsson. 1998. 'Hann þýddi Njálu', *Morgunblaðið,* 26 April, 24–5.

Jakob Benediktsson. 1969. 'Íslenzk orðabókarstörf á 19. öld', *Andvari,* nýr flokkur 11, 96–108.

Jamieson, John. 1814. *Hermes Scythicus; or, The Radical Affinities of the Greek and Latin Languages to the Gothic.* Edinburgh.

———. 1885. Ed. John Longmuir, *An Etymological Dictionary of the Scottish*

Language. Rev. abridged version of 2nd edition, 4 vols. 1829–32. Edinburgh.

[Jamieson, Robert et al.]. 1814. Eds and Trans. *Illustrations of Northern Antiquities from the Earlier Teutonic and Scandinavian Romances*. Edinburgh.

[Jamieson, Robert]. [?1840]. Ed. and Trans. Þorleifur Guðmundsson Repp, *Deeds Relating to Orkney and Zetland 1433–1631*. [?Copenhagen].

Jensen, Minna Skafte. 1995. *A History of Nordic Neo-Latin Literature*. Odense.

Johnson, Edgar. 1970. *Sir Walter Scott: The Great Unknown*. 2 vols. London.

[Johnstone, Christian Isobel]. 1844. [Review of Laing 1844], *TEM* 44, 281–93, 369–81.

Johnstone, James. 1780. Ed. and Trans. *Anecdotes of Olave the Black, King of Man, and the Hebridian Princes of the Somerled Family, to which are added XVIII. Eulogies on Haco, King of Norway, by Snorro Sturlson*. [Copenhagen].

———. 1782a. Ed. and Trans. *The Norwegian Account of Haco's Expedition against Scotland, A.D. mcclxiii.* [Copenhagen].

———. 1782b. Ed. and Trans. *Lodbrokar-Quida; or the Death-Song of Lodbroc; now First Correctly Printed from Various Manuscripts, with a Free English Translation*. [Copenhagen].

———. 1784. Ed. and Trans. *Chronicon Manniæ, or a Chronicle of the Kings of Man . . . With the Norwegian Account of Olave the Black King of Man, and of Haco's Expedition Against Scotland*. Perth.

———. 1786. Ed. and Trans. *Antiquitates Celto-Scandicæ; sive series rerum gestarum inter nationes Britannicarum insularum et gentis septentrionales*. Copenhagen.

Jón Árnason. 1862–4. *Íslenzkar þjóðsögur og æfintýri*. 2 vols. Leipzig.

Jón Eiríksson 1775. Ed. *Sagan af Gunnlaugi ormstungu ok Skalld-Rafni*. Copenhagen.

Jón Karl Helgason. 1998. *Hetjan og höfundurinn. Brot úr íslenskri menningarsögu*. Reykjavík.

———. 1999. *The Rewriting of Njáls saga: Translation, Politics and Icelandic Sagas*. Clevedon, Buffalo, Toronto, Sydney.

Jón Hjaltalín. 1868. 'On the Civilisation of the First Icelandic Colonists, with a Short Account of Some of their Manners and Customs', *Transactions of the Ethnological Society of London* n.s. 6, 176–82.

———. [1870]. 'An Icelander's Notes on Iceland', *Illustrated Travels* 252–6, 265–70, 301–6.

———. 1871. 'Traces of Animal Worship among the Old Scandinavians', *FM* n.s. 4, 13–25.

———. 1872. 'Rights of Women among the Old Scandinavians', *Journal of Jurisprudence* 16, 505–26.

———. 1874. *The Thousandth Anniversary of the Norwegian Settlement in Iceland*. Reykjavík.

Jón A. Hjaltalín and Gilbert Goudie. 1873. Trans. (Joseph Anderson, Ed.), *The Orkneyinga Saga*. Edinburgh.

Jón Jónsson. 1877. G.R.F. Cole, Ed., 'Jòn Jònsson's [sic] Saga: the Genuine Autobiography of a Modern Icelander', *FM* 15, 1–33.

Jón Ólafsson. 1875. *Alaska. Lýsing á landi og landskostum, ásamt skýrslu innar íslensku sendinefndar um stofnun íslenzkrár nýlendu.* Washington, D.C.

Jón Samsonarson. 1991. 'Marghala Grýla í görðum vesturnorrænna eyþjóða', in Gísli Sigurðsson and Örnólfur Thorsson, Eds *Lygisögur sagðar Sverri Tómassyni*, 48–54. Reykjavík.

Jón Stefánsson. 1890a. 'An Icelander upon "The Bondman"', *The Academy* 12 July 1890.

———. 1890b. 'Íslenzk áhrif á enskar bókmenntir', *Tímarit Hins íslenzka bókmentafjelags* 11, 278–94.

———. 1898. 'Leiði Guðrúnar Ósvífrsdóttur', *Árbók Hins íslenzka fornleifafjelags 1898*, 39–46.

———. 1949. *Úti í heimi: Endurminningar.* Reykjavík.

[Jón Þorkelsson]. 1894. 'Guðbrandur Vigfússon', *Andvari* 19, 1–43.

Jónas Jónsson. 1780. Ed. and Trans. *Orkneyinga saga, sive Historia Orcadensium.* Copenhagen.

Jónas Kristjánsson. 1994. 'Er Egilssaga "Norse" ', *Skáldskaparmál* 3, 216–31.

———. 1998. *Veröld víð.* Reykjavík.

Jones, Julia Clinton. 1878. *Valhalla, The Myths of Norseland.* San Francisco.

Jorgensen, Peter A. 1997. *The Story of Jonatas in Iceland.* Reykjavík.

Kabell, Inge. 1996. 'Et portræt af George Stephens', *Magasin fra Det kongelige Bibliotek* 11, 21–41.

Kalinke, Marianne. 1990. *Bridal-Quest Romance in Medieval Iceland.* Ithaca.

Kavanagh, Morgan Peter. 1844. *The Discovery of the Science of Languages*, 2 vols. London.

———. 1856. *Myths traced to their Primary Source through Language.* London.

Keary, A. and E. 1857. *The Heroes of Asgard and the Giants of Jötunheim, Or, the Week and Its Story.* London.

———. [?1860]. *Christmas Week and its Stories; Or, the Heroes of Asgard.* London.

———. 1883. *The Heroes of Asgard: Tales from Scandinavian Mythology.* London.

———. 1901. *The Heroes of Asgard: Tales from Scandinavian Mythology.* London.

Keary, C.F. 1890. [Review of Dasent and Gudbrand Vigfusson 1887–94], *EHR* 5, 127–32.

———. 1891. *The Vikings in Western Christendom AD 789 to AD 888.* London.

[Keary, Elizabeth]. 1882. *Memoir of Annie Keary.* London.

[Keightley, T.]. 1828a. *The Fairy Mythology, Illustrative of the Romance and Superstitions of Various Countries.* 2 vols. London.

———. 1828b. [Review of Eddic scholarship], *FQR* 2, 210–43.

———. 1829. 'Scandinavian Mythology', *FQR* 3, 102–39.

———. 1832. 'The Northern Runes' [Review of L. Ettmüller's *Völuspá*], *FQR* 9, 438–46.

———. 1834. *Tales and Popular Fictions: Their Resemblance and Transmission from Country to Country.* London.

———. 1850. *The Fairy Mythology, Illustrative of the Romance and Superstitions of Various Countries*. 2nd edition. London.

Kellett, E.E. 1903. *The Passing of Scyld and Other Poems*. London. [Review in *SBVS* 3/2, 285–6].

Kelvin, Norman. 1984–96. *The Collected Letters of William Morris*. 5 vols in 4. Princeton.

Kemble, J.M. 1840. 'On Anglo-Saxon Runes', *Archæologia* 28, 327–72.

———. 1849. *The Saxons in England: a History of the English Commonwealth till the Period of the Norman Conquest*. 2 vols. London.

[Kennedy, Patrick]. 1864. 'Icelandic Legends' [Rev. of Powell and Eiríkr Magnússon 1864], *DUM* 64, 65–72.

———. 1872. 'The Old Norse Mythology', *DUM* 79, 481–9, 599–612.

Ker, David. [?1920]. *The Last of the Vikings*. London.

Ker, W. P. 1896. *Epic and Romance: Essays on Medieval Literature*. London.

———. 1905. [Review of Gudbrand Vigfusson and York Powell 1905], *EHR* 20, 779–81.

———. 1906. *Sturla the Historian*. Oxford.

———. 1908. *Iceland and the Humanities*. London.

Keyser, Rudolf. 1854. Trans. Barclay Pennock, *The Religion of the Northmen*. New York.

———. 1868. Trans. M.R. Barnard, *The Private Life of the Old Northmen*. London.

Kidd, Colin. 1995. 'Teutonist Ethnology and Scottish Nationalist Inhibition, 1780–1880', *SHR* 74, 45–68.

Kiernan, Kevin S. 1983. 'Thorkelin's Trip to Great Britain, 1786–91', *The Library* 6th series 5/1, 1–21.

———. 1986. *The Thorkelin Transcripts of Beowulf*. Copenhagen.

King, Richard J. 1850. *Anschar: A Tale of the North*. London.

———. 1862. 'Iceland: the Change of Faith', *QR* 111, 115–47.

———. 1876a. 'Runes and Rune-Stones', [Review of Stephens 1866–68] *FM* 94, 747–57.

———. 1876b. 'The Orkneys and Rude Stone Monuments', *QR* 142, 126–60.

Kingsley, Charles. 1866/1895. *Hereward the Wake: Last of the English*. London. [Macmillan Pocket edition].

Kingsley, Fanny. 1891. Ed. *Charles Kingsley: His Letters, and Memoirs of his Life*. 2 vols. London.

Kipling, Rudyard. 1893. *Many Inventions*. London.

———. 1937. *Something of Myself*. New York.

———. 1993. Ed. Donald Mackenzie, *Puck of Pook's Hill and Rewards and Fairies*. Oxford.

Kirby, W.F. 1912. 'William Herbert and his Scandinavian Poetry', *SBVS* 7/2, 206–19.

Kjartan Ólafsson. 1986. 'Áform Frakka um nýlendu við Dýrafjörð', *Saga* 24, 147–203.

———. 1987. 'Dýrafjarðarmálið. Jón forseti og Ísfirðingar á öndverðum meiði', *Saga* 25, 89–166.

Kliger, Samuel. 1952. *The Goths in England: A Study of Seventeenth- and Eighteenth-Century Thought*. Cambridge, Mass.

Knowles, David. 1963. *Great Historical Enterprises*. London.

Knowles, Elizabeth. 1980. 'Notes on the First Edition of "Cleasby-Vigfússon" ', *SBVS* 20/3, 165–78.

Koerner, E.F.K. 1983. Ed. *Linguistics and Evolutionary Theory*. Amsterdam.

Kuhn, Hans. 1962. Ed. *Edda*. Heidelberg.

Kuhn, Hans. 1986. 'Die Geschichte von blutrünstigen Schwert. Bearbeitungen der *Hervarar saga* in der skandinavischen Romantik', in Hans-Peter Naumann Ed. *Festschrift für Oskar Bandle*. Basel and Frankfurt am Main.

L., H. 1882 [1881]. *Odin Sagas and Other Poems*. Manchester.

Laing, R.M. 1841. *Hours in Norway: Poems. To which is added a version of Oehlenschläger's* Axel and Valborg. London.

———. 1842. *A Bard's Last Dream: A Poem in Three Fits*. Christiania.

Laing, Samuel. 1833. *Address to the Electors of Scotland by Samuel Laing, Esq. of Papdale*. Edinburgh.

———. 1839. *A Tour in Sweden in 1838*. London.

———. 1842. *Notes of a Traveller on the Social and Political State of France, Prussia, Switzerland, Italy and Other parts of Europe During the Present Century*. Edinburgh.

———. 1844. Trans. *The Heimskringla; or, Chronicle of the Kings of Norway*. 3 vols. London.

———. 1848. 'Provençal and Scandinavian Poetry', *ER* 88, 1–32.

———. 1852. *Observations on the Social and Political State of Denmark, and the Duchies of Sleswick and Holstein in 1851*. London.

———. 1854. *Journal of a Residence in Norway During the Years 1834, 1835, and 1836 Made With a View to Enquire into the Moral and Political Economy of that Country, and the Condition of its Inhabitants*. 2nd edition [1st edition 1836]. London.

———. 1889. Trans. and Ed. Rasmus B. Anderson, *The Heimskringla or The Sagas of the Norse Kings*. 4 vols. London.

L[ang], A[ndrew]. 1874. ' "The Gripis-Spa" '. From the Elder Edda', *FM* 8 February, 227–34.

Lang, Andrew. 1891. 'The Sagas', in *Essays in Little*, 141–51. London.

———. 1897. *The Book of Dreams and Ghosts*. London.

Lang, Cecil Y. 1959–62. Ed. *The Swinburne Letters*. 6 vols. New Haven and London.

Langebek, J. et al. 1772–1878. Ed. *Scriptores rerum Danicarum medii ævi*. 9 vols. Copenhagen.

Larsson, Ludwig. 1901. Ed. *Friðþjófs saga ins frækna*. Halle.

Latham, R. G. 1838. Trans. *Frithiof, A Norwegian Story*. London.

———. 1840. *Norway and the Norwegians*. 2 vols. London.

———. 1862. *The English Language*. London.

Lawrence, Daniel H. 1965. Ed. Bernard Shaw, *Collected Letters*. London.

[Lawrence, Hannah]. 1861. 'Old Iceland—The Burnt Njal' [Review of Dasent 1861], *BQR* 34, 323–49.

Lawrenson, Arthur. 1882. 'The Colour Sense in the Edda', *Transactions of the Royal Society of Literature* 2nd series 12, 723–48.

Lehman, David. 1992. *Signs of the Times: Deconstruction and the Fall of Paul de Man*. New York.

Leighton, Robert. 1895. *Olaf the Glorious*. London.

[Leighton, William]. 1861. *Kormak: An Icelandic Romance of the Tenth Century*. Boston.

Leith, Mrs Disney. 1895a. *Original Verses and Translations*. London.

[———]. 1895b. Trans. *Stories of the Bishops*. London.

———. 1897. *Three Visits to Iceland*. London.

———. 1908. *Peeps at Many Lands: Iceland*. London.

Le Mire, Eugene D. 1969. *The Unpublished Lectures of William Morris*. Detroit.

Levine, Philippa. 1986. *The Amateur and the Professional: Antiquarians, Historians and Archaeologists in Victorian England, 1838–1886*. Cambridge.

Lewis, C.S. 1955. *Surprised by Joy*. London.

Lewis Jones, David. 1971. 'George Powell–Swinburne's "Friend of Many a Season" ', *AWR* 19, 75–85.

[Lidderdale, T.W.]. 1864. *Numerical List of the Icelandic Manuscripts in the British Museum*. London.

Lieder, P.R. 1914. *Poems by Tegner*. New York.

———. 1920. *Scott and Scandinavian Literature*. Smith College Studies in Modern Languages 2, 8–57.

Liljencrantz, Ottilie A. 1902. *The Thrall of Leif the Lucky: A Story of Viking Days*. Chicago, Boston and London.

———. 1903. *The Ward of King Canute*. Chicago. [London edition 1904].

———. 1904. *The Viking Champions*. Chicago.

———. 1906. *Randver the Songsmith: A Romance of Norumbega*. Chicago.

Litzenberg, Karl. 1935. 'William Morris and Scandinavian Literature: A Bibliographical Essay', *SSN* 13, 93–105.

———. 1936. 'William Morris and *Heimskringla*', *SSN* 14, 33–9.

———. 1936. 'William Morris and *The Burning of Njal*', *SSN* 14, 40–1.

———. 1936. 'William Morris and the Reviews: A Study in the Fame of the Poet', *RES* 12, 413–28.

———. 1947–8. *The Victorians and the Vikings*. Ann Arbor, Mich.

Lock, Charles G. Warnford. 1879. *The Home of the Eddas*. London.

Lock, W.G. 1882. *Guide to Iceland; A Useful Handbook for Travellers and Sportsmen*. London.

———. 1883. *Icelandic Troubles and Mansion House Muddles*. London.

Lockhart, J.G. 1838. *Memoirs of the Life of Sir Walter Scott*. 4 vols. Paris.

Locock, C.D. 1924. Trans. *Fritiof's saga*. New York and London.

Longfellow, H.M. 1904. *Poetical Works*. Oxford.

———. [1907]. Ed. Beatrice Clay, *The Saga of King Olaf*. London.

Longman, William. 1861. *Suggestions for the Exploration of Iceland*. London.

Lonsdale, Roger. 1969. Ed. *The Poems of Gray, Collins, and Goldsmith*. London.

Lottner, Carl. 1861. 'The Edda', *FM* 64, 190–98.

Louis-Jensen, Jonna. 1993. 'A Good Day's Work: *Laxdæla Saga*, Ch. 49', *Nowele* 21/2, 267–82.

Lowe, Robert. 1861. '*The Story of Burnt Njal*' [Review of Dasent 1861], *ER* 114, 425–55.

Lund, H. 1869. *A Short Method of Learning the Old Norse Tongue . . . After the Danish of E. Rask, With an Icelandic Reader by H. Lund*. London.

Lundgreen-Nielsen, Flemming. 1994. 'Grundtvig's Northern Mythology: An Experiment that Failed', in Wawn 1994b, 41–67.

Lutyens, William Enderby. [1929]. *Balder the Beautiful*. London.

Luxdorph B.F. et al. 1787–1828. Eds *Edda Sæmundar hinns fróda*. 3 vols. Copenhagen.

Lúðvík Kristjánsson. 1961. *Á slóðum Jóns Sigurðssonar*. Reykjavík.

Lyall, Edna. 1889. *A Hardy Norseman*. London.

Lönnroth, Lars. 1988. 'The Academy of Odin: Grundtvig's Political Instrumentalization of Old Norse Mythology', in Weber 1988, 339–54.

———. 1994. 'Mallet och det nordiska sublima', in Gísli Sigurðsson et al. 1994, II 527–37.

Lüning, Hermann. 1859. Ed. *Die Edda*. Zürich.

M. R. [Cartmell, Margaret Richmond]. 1879. *The Viking. A Novel*. London.

MacCarthy, Fiona. 1994. *William Morris: A Life for Our Time*. London.

Mackenzie, Sir George S. 1811. *Travels in the Island of Iceland in the Summer of the Year MDCCCX*. Edinburgh.

———. 1812. *Travels in the Island of Iceland in the Summer of the Year MDCCCX*. 2nd edition. Edinburgh.

———. 1842. *Travels in Iceland*. Edinburgh.

Mackenzie, Henry. 1808. *Works*. 8 vols. Edinburgh.

Macleod, Donald. 1879. Ed. *Good Words*. London.

Macpherson, James. 1765. *The Works of Ossian, Son of Fingal. Translated from the Galic Language by James Macpherson*. 2 vols. Edinburgh

McDaniel, S. 1886. *The Life of St Olave, Martyr and King and Patron of Norway*. London.

McDowall, M.W. 1884. Trans. (Anson, W.S.W., Ed.), *Asgard and the Gods: The Tales and Traditions of our Northern Ancestors*. 3rd edition. London.

McKerrow, R.B. 1958. *The Works of Thomas Nashe*. Rev. edition. Oxford.

McKillop, A.D. 1933. 'A Critic of 1741 on Early Poetry', *SP* 30, 504–21.

[McMahon, Patrick]. 1848. [Review of Laing 1836/1854, 1839, 1842], *DR* 14, 278–320.

McNab, Hugh. 1906. *The Viking and Other Poems*. London.

McTurk, Rory and Andrew Wawn. 1989. Eds *Úr Dölum til Dala: Guðbrandur Vigfússon Centenary Essays*. Leeds Texts and Monographs, n.s. 11. Leeds.

Madden, Frederic. 1828. Ed. *The Ancient English Romance of Havelok the Dane*. Roxburghe Club. London.

Magnús Fjalldal. 1998. *The Long Arm of Coincidence: The Frustrated Connection between* Beowulf *and* Grettis saga. Toronto.

Magnus Magnusson and Hermann Pálsson. 1960. Trans. *Njal's saga*. Harmondsworth.

Major, Albany F. 1894. Ed. *Sagas and Songs of the Norsemen*. London.

────── and E.E. Speight. 1899. Ed. *Stories from the Northern Sagas*. London.

────── and E.E. Speight. 1905. Ed. *Stories from the Northern Sagas*. 2nd edition. London.

──────. 1906. [Review of Morris and Eiríkr Magnússon 1891–1905], *SBVS* 4/2, 468–70.

Malim, H. 1917. Ed. *Njal and Gunnar, A Tale of Old Iceland, Retold for Boys from Sir G.W. Dasent's* Story of Burnt Njal. London.

Mallet, Paul-Henri. 1755. *Introduction à l'Histoire de Dannemarc*. Copenhagen.

──────. 1756. *Monumens de la Mythologie et de la Poésie des Celtes*. Copenhagen.

Malling, Ove. 1807. *Great and Good Deeds of Danes, Norwegians and Holsteinians*. London.

Marschall, Birgit. 1991. *Reiser und Regieren: Die Nordlandfahrten Kaiser Wilhelms II*. Bremerhaven.

Marsh, Caroline C. 1888. *Life and Letters of George Perkins Marsh*. New York.

Marsh, George P. 1838. *A Compendious Grammar of the Old-Northern or Icelandic Language*. Burlington, Vermont.

Mason, William. 1811. *The Works of William Mason*. 4 vols. London.

Massey, Gerald. 1861. *Poetical Works*. London.

Masson, D. 1861. 'Gaelic and Norse Popular Tales: An Apology for the Celt', *Macmillan's Magazine* 3, 211–24.

Mathias, T.J. 1781. *Runic Odes imitated from the Norse Tongue in the Manner of Mr Gray*. London.

Matthías Jochumsson. 1864. *Útilegumennirnir*. Reykjavík.

──────. 1866. Trans. *Friðþjófssaga*. Reykjavík.

──────. 1902. See Barmby 1902.

──────. 1922. *Sögukaflar af sjálfum mér*. Reykjavík.

──────. 1923. 'Vilhjálmur Morris', *Eimreiðin* 29, 257–89.

──────. 1956–8. Ed. Árni Kristjánsson, *Matthías Jochumsson, Ljóðmæli*. 2 vols. Reykjavík.

Matthías Johannessen. 1958. *Njála í íslenzkum skáldskap*. Reykjavík.

Melman, B. 1991. 'The Invention of Anglo-Saxon Tradition', *Journal of Contemporary History* 26, 575–95.

Metcalfe, Frederick. 1856. *The Oxonian in Norway; or Notes of Excursions in that Country in 1854–5*. 2 vols. London.

──────. 1861. *The Oxonian in Iceland*. London.

──────. 1867. *The Oxonian in Iceland*. ['Cheap edition']. London.

──────. 1869. 'The Faröese Saga', *BEM* 106, 618–30, 701–19.

──────. 1876. *The Saxon and the Norseman; Or, A Plea for the Study of Icelandic Conjointly with Anglo-Saxon*. Oxford.

──────. 1877. 'Old Norse Mirror of Men and Manners', *QR* 143, 51–82.

————. 1880. *The Englishman and the Scandinavian*. London.

————. 1881. Ed. *Passio et Miracula Beati Olaui*. Oxford.

[————]. 1884. 'The Eddic Poems' [Review of Gudbrand Vigfusson and York Powell 1883], *SR* 3, 299–320.

Metcalfe W. 1890. 'The Vikings' [Review of du Chaillu 1889], *SR* 15, 55–82.

Miles, Pliny. 1854. *Norðurfari; or Rambles in Iceland*. London.

Miller, John B. 1905. Trans. *Frithiofs saga*. Chicago.

Miller, William. 1862. *Our Scandinavian Forefathers: Two Lectures*. Edinburgh.

[Milnes, Richard Monckton]. 1857. 'A Voyage to Iceland', *QR* 102, 438–53.

Mitchell, Jerome. 1987. *Scott, Chaucer and Medieval Romance*. Lexington, Kentucky.

Mitchell, Stephen A. 1991. *Heroic Sagas and Ballads: Myth and Poetics*. Ithaca.

Mjöberg, Jöran. 1967. *Drömmen om sagatiden*. Stockholm.

————. 1980. 'Romanticism and Revival', in Wilson 1980, 207–38. New York.

Moffatt, A.G. 1903. 'Palnatoki in Wales', *SBVS* 3/2, 163–73.

Moore, Jerrold Northrop. 1984. *Edward Elgar, A Life in Music*. Oxford.

————. 1987. *Elgar and his Publishers: Letters of a Creative Life*. 2 vols. Oxford.

Morris, Kevin L. 1984. *The Image of the Middle Ages in Romantic and Victorian Literature*. London et al.

Morris, William. 1876. *The Story of Sigurd the Volsung and the Fall of the Niblungs*. London.

————. 1877. *The Story of Sigurd the Volsung and the Fall of the Niblungs*. 2nd edition. London.

————. 1879. [Letter], *Athenaeum* 17 May, 632–3.

————. 1891. *Poems by the Way*. London.

————. 1905. *The Story of Sigurd the Volsung* [with sections condensed into prose]. London.

————. 1910–15. Ed. May Morris, *The Collected Works of William Morris*. 24 vols. London.

————. 1996. [No editor named], *Icelandic Journals*. London.

Morris, William, and Eiríkr Magnússon. 1869. Trans. *The Story of Grettir the Strong*. London.

————. 1871. Trans. 'The Story of Frithiof the Bold', *The Dark Blue* 1, 42–58, 176–82.

————. 1875. Trans. *Three Northern Love Stories*. London. [Reprinted Bristol, 1996; introduction by Gary Aho].

————. 1891–1905. Trans. *The Saga Library*. 6 vols. London.

————. 1900. Trans. 'The Story of Frithiof the Bold', *Poet-Lore* 12, 353–84.

Morris, William, and Eiríkur Magnússon. 1970. Trans. *The Story of Kormak, the Son of Ogmund* [Introduction by Grace J. Calder]. London.

[Mortimer, Favell Lee]. 1878. *Near Home; or, The Countries of Europe Described*. London.

Motherwell, William. 1832. *Poems Narrative and Lyrical*. Glasgow.

————. 1847. *The Poetic Works of William Motherwell*. Glasgow.

Muckleston, R. 1862. Trans. *The Frithiof Saga: A Poem*. London.

Munch, P.A. 1847. Ed. *Den ældre Edda*. Christiania.

Murray, K.M.E. 1977. *Caught in the Web of Words*. New Haven.

Müller, P.E. 1817–20. *Sagabibliothek*. 3 vols. Copenhagen.

Nanna Ólafsdóttir. 1982. 'Bréf Willards Fiskes til Íslendinga', *LÍÁ 1981*, nýr flokkur 7, 28–68.

[Neaves, Charles]. 1842. 'Dr Jamieson's Scottish Dictionary', *BEM* 52, 61–73.

[———]. 1845. [Review of Laing 1844], *ER* 82, 267–318.

[Neuberg, Joseph]. 1854. 'The Odin-Religion', *WR* n.s. 6, 312–42.

Nicolaysen, N. 1882. Trans. Thomas Krag. *The Viking-Ship Discovered at Gokstad in Norway*. Christiania.

Nicoll, Allardyce. 1946. *A History of Late Nineteenth-Century Drama, 1850–1900*. 2 vols. Cambridge.

———. 1959. *Late Nineteenth-Century Drama, 1850–1900*. Cambridge.

[Nicoll, James]. 1840. *An Historical and Descriptive Account of Iceland, Greenland and the Faroe Islands*. Edinburgh.

Nicolson, Alexander. 1861. [Review of Dasent 1861], *Macmillan's Magazine* 4, 294–305.

Nielsen, Hans Friede. 1990. 'Jacob Grimm and the German Dialects', in Antonsen 1990, 25–32.

Nielsen, Jørgen-Erik. 1986. 'Andreas Andersen Feldborg. In Denmark English and in England Danish', *Angles on the English Speaking World* 2, 51–63.

Nisbet, Hume. 1893. *Valdmer the Viking. A Romance of the Eleventh Century by Sea and Land*. London.

Nordal, Sigurður. See Sigurður Nordal.

Northern Books. Rulon-Miller Books. 1991. *Catalogue 99* [Books owned by George Stephens]. St Paul, Minnesota.

Nugent, Ermengarda Greville. 1884. *The Rueing of Gudrun and Other Poems*. London.

Oehlenschläger, Adam. 1819. *Nordens guder: et episk digt*. Copenhagen.

———. 1845. Trans. W.E. Frye, *The Gods of the North*. London and Paris.

Oertel von Horn, W. 1873. Trans. Rev. Matthías Steenleigh, *Olaf Thorlaksen, An Iceland Narrative*. Philadelphia.

Okun, Henry. 1967. 'Ossian in Painting', *Journal of the Warburg and Courtauld Institutes* 30, 327–56.

Olaus Magnus. 1555. *Historia de gentibus septentrionalibus*. Rome. [facsimile edition, Copenhagen 1972].

———. 1558. [C. Scribonius], *Historia de gentibus septentrionalibus sic in epitomen redacta*. Antwerp.

———. 1658. [anon.]. Trans. *A Compendious History of the Goths, Swedes and Vandals*. London.

———. 1996–8. Trans. P. Fisher and H. Higgens, Ed. Peter Foote, *A Description of the Northern Peoples*. 3 vols. Hakluyt Society, Series II 182. London.

Olaus Olavius. 1772. Ed. *Sagan af Niali Þorgeirssyni ok sonum hans*. Copenhagen.

Olender, Maurice. 1992. Trans. Arthur Goldhammer, *The Languages of Paradise: Race, Religion and Philology in the Nineteenth Century*. Cambridge, Mass.

Omberg, Margaret. 1976. *Scandinavian Themes in English Poetry, 1760–1800*. Uppsala.

Oswald, E.J. 1876. 'In Iceland', *Good Words* July, August, 472–8, 543–9.

———. 1882. *By Fell and Fjord, or Scenes and Studies in Iceland*. Edinburgh and London.

———. 1888. *The Dragon of the North. A Tale of the Normans in Italy*. London.

Outram, Mary Frances. [1909]. *In the Van of the Vikings; or, How Olaf Tryggvason Lost and Won*. London.

Ólafur Halldórsson. 1990. *Grettisfærsla*. Reykjavík.

Page, R.I. 1962–5. ' "Lapland Sorcerers" ', *SBVS* 16/3, 215–32.

———. 1973. *An Introduction to English Runes*. London.

———. 1980. 'Some Thoughts on Manx Runes', *SBVS* 20/3, 179–99.

———. 1987. *'A Most Vile People': Early English Historians on the Vikings*. London.

———. 1995. *Runes and Runic Inscriptions: Collected Essays on Anglo-Saxon and Viking Runes*. Woodbridge.

Paget, Clara Lady. 1891. *Notes on Northern Words*. Cambridge.

———. 1894. *King Bele of the Sogn District, Norway, and Jarl Angantyr of the Orkney Isles*. Cambridge.

Paijkull, C.W. 1868. Trans. M.R. Barnard, *A Summer in Iceland*. Uppsala.

Palmer, A.S. 1883. [Articles on Gudbrand Vigfusson 1874], *Notes and Queries*, 6th series, 7, 259, 346.

Parker, Charles Arundel. 1881–2. 'Notes on Gosforth Church and Churchyard and on Sculptured Fragments there', *Transactions of the Cumberland and Westmorland Antiquarian and Archaeological Society* 6, 405–12.

———. 1896. *The Ancient Crosses at Gosforth, Cumberland*. London.

———. 1909. *Shelagh, Olaf Cuaran's Daughter. A Saga of the North in Cumbria in the Tenth Century*. Kendal.

Páll Eggert Ólafsson. 1918–37. *Skrá um handritasöfn Landsbókasafnsins*. 3 vols. Reykjavík.

———. 1929–33. *Jón Sigurðsson*, 5 vols. Reykjavík.

Pemble, John. 1987. *The Mediterranean Passion: Victorians and Edwardians in the South*. Oxford.

Percy, Thomas. 1761. Trans. 'Fragments of Celtic Poetry, from Olaus Verelius, a German Writer; literally translated', *Annual Register* 4, 236–7.

[———]. 1763. Trans. *Five Pieces of Runic Poetry Translated from the Islandic Language*. London.

[———]. 1770. Trans. *Northern Antiquities: or, A Description of the Manners, Customs, Religion and Laws of the Ancient Danes, and other Northern Nations; Including those of Our Own Saxon Ancestors*. 2 vols. London.

[———]. 1809. Trans. *Northern Antiquities: or, A Description of the Manners, Customs, Religion and Laws of the Ancient Danes, including those of Our Own Saxon Ancestors*. Edinburgh.

————. 1847. Trans. I.A. Blackwell, Ed. *Northern Antiquities; or, An Historical Account of the Manners, Customs, Religion and Laws, Maritime Expeditions and Discoveries, Language and Literature of the Ancient Scandinavians*. London.

————. 1859. Trans. I.A. Blackwell, Ed. *Northern Antiquities; or, An Historical Account of the Manners, Customs, Religion and Laws, Maritime Expeditions and Discoveries, Language and Literature of the Ancient Scandinavians*. New issue. London.

Peringskiöld, Johan. 1697. Ed. *Heims Kringla*. Stockholm.

Perkins, Richard. 1989. 'Objects and Oral Tradition in Medieval Iceland', in McTurk and Wawn 1989, 239–66.

Petersen, Erik. 1991. 'Vínlandsferð Flateyjarbókar', *LÍÁ 1989*, nýr flokkur 17, 5–25.

Petersen, N.M. 1849. *Nordisk mythologi*. Copenhagen.

Petterson, John. 1826. *The Spirit of Odin, or The Father's Curse*. New York.

Pfeiffer, Ida. 1852. *A Visit to Iceland and the Scandinavian North*. London.

Phillpotts, Bertha. 1920. *The Elder Edda and Ancient Scandinavian Drama*. Cambridge.

Picton, Sir James. 1864. 'On Sanskrit Roots and English Derivatives', *PLLPS* 18, 31–64

————. 1865. *Notes on the South Lancashire Dialect*. Liverpool.

————. 1868. 'On Social Life Among the Teutonic Races in Early Times', *PLLPS* 22, 68–98.

————. 1869. 'Our Mother Tongue and its Congeners', *PLLPS* 23, 52–84.

Pigott, Granville. 1839. *A Manual of Scandinavian Mythology Containing a Popular Account of the Two Eddas and of the Religion of the North*. London.

Pinkerton, John. 1787. *A Dissertation on the Origin and Progress of the Scythians or Goths, Being an Introduction to the Ancient and Modern History of Europe*. London.

————. 1789. *An Enquiry into the History of Scotland*, 2 vols. London.

Pitt, Ruth J. 1893. *The Tragedy of the Norse Gods*. London.

Polwhele, Richard. 1792. Ed. *Poems, Chiefly by Gentlemen of Devon and Cornwall*. Bath.

Ponzi, Frank. 1986. *Ísland á nítjándu öld*. Reykjavík.

————. 1987. *Ísland á átjándu öld*. Reykjavík.

————. 1995. *Iceland: The Dire Years*. Mossfellsbaer.

Poole, Russell. 1994. 'Constructions of Fate in Victorian Philology and Literature', in Barnes et al. 1994, 110–19.

Pope, Rev. Alexander. 1866. Trans. *Ancient History of Orkney, Caithness and the North*. Wick.

Pope, Alexander. See Butt, John.

Porter, Bernard. 1998. 'Virtue and vice in the North: the Scandinavian writings of Samuel Laing', *Scandinavian Journal of History* 23, 153–72.

Potter, F. Scarlett. [1876]. *Erling, or the Days of St Olaf*. London.

[Powell, G.E.J.; pseud. Miölnir]. 1860. *Poems*. Aberystwyth.

————. 1861. *Poems*. Aberystwyth.

Powell, G.E.J. and Eiríkr Magnússon. 1864. Trans. *Icelandic Legends, Collected by Jón Arnason*. London.

———. 1866. Trans. *Icelandic Legends, Collected by Jón Arnason*. London.

Pratt, Mary Louise. 1992. *Imperial Eyes: Travel Writing and Acculturation*. New York.

Press, Muriel. 1899. Trans. *The Laxdale Saga*. London.

Prior, R.C. Alexander. 1860. Trans. *Ancient Danish Ballads*. London.

Proctor, Robert. 1903. *The Story of the Laxdalers*. London.

Prowett, J. 1816. *The Voluspa or Speech of the Prophetess, with Other Poems*. London.

Pulsiano, Philip et al. 1993. Eds *Medieval Scandinavia: An Encyclopedia*. New York and London.

———. 1998. 'Benjamin Thorpe (1782–1870)', in Damico 1998, 75–92.

Purchas, Samuel. 1625. *Purchas his Pilgrimes*. London.

Quinn, Judy and Margaret Clunies Ross. 1994. 'The Image of Norse Poetry and Myth in Seventeenth-Century England', in Wawn 1994b, 189–210.

Rae, Edward. 1875. *The Land of the North Wind*. London.

Rafn, C.C. 1821–6. *Nordiske Kæmpe-Historier*. 3 vols. Copenhagen.

———. 1829–30. *Fornaldarsögur Nordrlanda*. 3 vols. Copenhagen.

———. 1837. *Antiqvitates Americanæ*. Copenhagen.

Ragozin, Zenaïde A. 1899. *Frithjof the Viking of Norway and Roland the Paladin of France*. New York and London.

Rask, Rasmus. 1811. *Vejledning til det Islandske eller gamle Nordiske Sprog*. Stockholm.

———. 1818a. *Undersøgelse om det gamle Nordiske eller Islandske Sprogs Oprindelse*. Copenhagen.

———. 1818b. *Anvisning till Isländskan eller Nordiska Fornspråket*. Stockholm.

———. 1818c. Ed. *Edda Sæmundar hinns Fróda*. Stockholm.

———. 1818d. Ed. *Snorra-Edda*. Stockholm.

Rawlins, T.F.S. [?1850]. *The Hall of Odin*. [?Oxford].

Reaney, P.H. et al. 1991. *A Dictionary of English Surnames*. 3rd edition. London.

Redwood, Christopher. 1982. *An Elgar Companion*. Ashbourne.

Reed, Mrs Joseph J. 1865. *The Adventures of Olaf Tryggveson: King of Norway*. London.

Reeves, Arthur Middleton. 1890. *The Finding of Wineland*. London.

Repp, Þorleifur Guðmundsson. 1826. Trans. *Laxdæla saga*. Copenhagen.

———. 1831. 'On the Scottish Formula of Congratulations on the New Year's Eve, "Hogmannay, Trollalay" ', *Archæologia Scotica* 4, 202–12.

———. 1832. *An Historical Treatise on Trial by Jury, Wager of Law, and other Co-ordinate Forensic Institutions formerly in use in Scandinavia and in Iceland*. Edinburgh.

———. 1834. Ed. *Certificates in Favour of Mr Thorleif Gudmundson Repp, A.M.* Edinburgh.

———. [1853 (for 1845–9)]. Trans. 'The Saga of King Edward the Confessor', *Mémoires de la Société Royale des Antiquaires du Nord*, 272–86.

—————— and Jón Sigurðsson. 1854. Eds 'Saga Ósvalds Konungs hins helga', *Annaler for Nordisk Oldkyndighed og Historie* 3–91.

Ricks, Christopher. 1986. Ed. *The Poems of Tennyson*. 3 vols. Harlow.

R[igg], J.M. 1892. 'Samuel Laing', *DNB* 31, 404–6.

Risley, R.V. 1897. *The Sentimental Vikings*. London.

Robertson, F. 1870. *Torquil, or the Days of Olaf Tryggvason*. Edinburgh.

Roesdahl, Else and Preben Meulengracht Sørensen. 1996. Eds *The Waking of Angantyr: The Scandinavian Past in European Culture*. Aarhus.

Roscoe, William Caldwell. 1852–3. 'The Eddas', *Prospective Review* 8–9, 456–527.

—————. 1863. 'Fragments of Scandinavian Legend', *DUM* 62, 552–63.

Rowntree, George. 1875. *Iceland. A Poem Which Obtained the Chancellor's Medal at the Cambridge Commencement, MDCCCLXXV.* Cambridge.

Rudwick, M.J.S. 1962–3. 'Hutton and Werner compared: George Greenough's geological tour of Scotland', *BJHS* 1, 117–35.

[Russell, C.W.]. 1844. [Review of Frederika Bremer's novels], *DR* 17, 351–76.

Samson, Ross. 1991. Ed. *Social Approaches to Viking Studies*. Glasgow.

Saxby, Jessie. [1890]. *Wrecked on the Shetlands; or, the Little Sea-King*. London.

—————. 1892. *Viking-Boys. A Tale*. London.

—————. 1895, 1896. *The Sagabook of Lunda, Wherein is Recorded Some More of the Notable Adventures of Viking-Boys and their Friends*. London.

Schepelern, H.D. 1965. Ed. *Breve fra og til Ole Worm*. Copenhagen.

Schiötz, Eiler H. 1970–86. *Utlendingers reiser i Norge: En bibliografi*. 2 vols. Oslo, Bergen, Tromso.

Schlegel, Friedrich. 1818. Trans. J.G. Lockhart, *Lectures On the History of Literature, Ancient and Modern*. 2 vols. Edinburgh.

Schöning G. et al. 1777–83. Eds *Heimskringla edr Noregs Konunga-Sögor*, 3 vols. Copenhagen.

Scott, James Anderson. 1863. 'Fragments of Scandinavian Legend', *DUM* 62, 459–68.

Scott, Sir Walter. 1806. [Review of Herbert 1806], *ER* 9, 211–23.

—————. 1808. Ed. *The Works of John Dryden*. 18 vols. London.

—————. 1810. See Seward 1810.

[—————]. 1812. [*Helga*: Prologue and Epilogue], *The Scots Magazine*, February 134–5, 153–4.

—————. 1816. *The Antiquary*. Edinburgh.

—————. 1822. *The Pirate*. Edinburgh. [Reprinted Lerwick 1996].

—————. 1830. *Letters on Demonology and Witchcraft*. London.

—————. 1831/1905. *Count Robert of Paris*. Edinburgh.

—————. 1904. Ed. J. Logue Robertson, *Poetical Works*. London.

—————. 1982. Ed. William F. Laughlan, *Northern Lights, or A Voyage in the Lighthouse Yacht to Nova Zembla and the Lord knows where in the Summer of 1814*. Hawick.

Scragg, D. 2000. Ed. *Changing Perceptions of the Anglo-Saxons: Cultural Theory from the Twelfth Century to the Present Day*. Cambridge.

Scudder, Horace. 1885. *The Champion of Odin; or Viking Life in Days of Old*. Boston.

Seaton, A.V. 1989. Ed. George Clayton Atkinson, *Journal of an Expedition to the Feroe and Westman Islands and Iceland 1833*. Newcastle upon Tyne.

Seaton, Ethel. 1935. *Literary Relations of England and Scandinavia in the Seventeenth Century*. Oxford.

Sephton, John. 1880. 'Translation of Eirik the Red's Saga', *PLLPS* 34, 183–212.

———. 1887. *Thor and His Sway*. Liverpool.

———. 1892. 'The Religion of the Eddas and Sagas', *PLLPS* 46, 107–26.

———. 1894. 'A Translation of the Saga of Frithiof the Fearless', *PLLPS* 48, 69–97.

———. 1895. Trans. *The Saga of King Olaf Tryggwason who reigned over Norway A.D. 995 to 1000*. London.

———. 1896. 'On Some Runic Remains', *PLLPS* 50, 183–209.

———. 1898. 'What the Sagas say of Greenland', *PLLPS* 52, 119–54.

———. 1899. Trans. *Sverrissaga. The Saga of King Sverri of Norway*. London.

———. 1903. 'Notes on a Lancashire Dialect', *Otia Merseiana* 3, 4–22.

———. 1904. 'Notes on South Lancashire Place-Names in Doomsday Book', *Otia Merseiana* 4, 65–74.

———. 1912. 'On the Study of Icelandic', *The Library*, 3rd series 12/3, 385–411.

———. 1913. *A Handbook of Lancashire Place Names*. Liverpool.

Seward, Anna. 1810. Ed. Sir Walter Scott, *The Poetical Works*. 3 vols. Edinburgh.

Shand, Alexander. 1882. 'Ladies in Iceland', *BEM* August, 242–51.

Shaw, Clement B. 1908. Trans. *Frithiof's saga, A Legend of Ancient Norway*. Chicago and London.

Sheehan, James J. 1988. *German History, 1770–1866*. Oxford.

[Shelton, Maurice]. 1735. Trans. *Wotton's Short View of G. Hickes's Grammatico-Critical and Archaeological Treasure of the Ancient Northern Languages*. London.

Shepherd, C.W. 1867. *The North-West Peninsula of Iceland; Being the Journal of a Tour in Iceland in the Spring and Summer of 1862*. London.

Sherman, L.A. 1877. Trans. *Frithiofs Saga, A Legend of Ancient Norway*. Boston.

Shippey, T.A. 1979. 'Goths and Huns: the Rediscovery of the Northern Cultures in the Nineteenth Century', in Haarder 1982, 51–69.

———. 1982. *The Road to Middle Earth*. London.

———. 1994a. 'Local Patriotism and the Early Interpretations of Beowulf', in Andersen and Sauerberg 1994, 303–18. Odense.

———. 1994b. [Review of Stanley 1994], *Times Literary Supplement* 22 July 1994, 22.

———. 2000. 'The Underdeveloped Image: Anglo-Saxon in Popular Consciousness from Turner to Tolkien', in Scragg 2000, 215–36.

Shippey, T.A. and Andreas Haarder. 1998. Eds *Beowulf: The Critical Heritage*. London and New York.

Shuttleworth, Sally and John Christie. 1989. Eds *Nature Transformed: Science and Literature 1700–1900*. Manchester.

Sigfús Blöndal. 1905. 'Max Müller um Gudbrand Vigfússon', *Eimreiðin* 11, 27–9.

———. 1929. 'William Morris og Ísland', *Ársrit Hins íslenska frœðafjelags í Kaupmannahöfn* 11, 65–84.

Sigurður Nordal. 1952. *Time and Vellum*. London.

Sigurður Nordal and Guðni Jónsson. 1938. Eds *Borgfirðinga sögur*, ÍF 3. Reykjavík.

Sim, George Charles. 1886. *From England to Iceland; A Summer Trip to the Arctic Circle*. Bradford.

Sims, Albert E. 1909. *Gisli the Outlaw*. London.

Simmons, Clare A. 1990. *Reversing the Conquest. History and Myth in 19th-Century British Literature*. New Brunswick and London.

———. 1992. ' "Iron-Worded Proof" ': Victorian Identity and the Old English Language', *Studies in Medievalism* 4, 202–14.

Simpson, John. 1973. '*Eyrbyggja saga* and Nineteenth-Century Scholarship', in Foote 1973, 360–94.

———. 1973. 'Scott and Old Norse Literature', in Bell 1973, 300–13.

Sinding, Paul Christian. 1862. *History of Scandinavia; from the Earliest Times of the Northmen; The Sea-Kings and Vikings, Their Manners, Maritime Expeditions, Struggles and Wars; The Discovery and Thousand Years' Anniversary of Iceland*. 5th edition. Pittsburgh.

Skeat, Walter W. 1876. *A List of English Words: the Etymology of which is illustrated by a Comparison with Iceland . . . an Appendix to Cleasby and Vigfusson's Icelandic-English Dictionary*. Oxford.

———. 1879–82. *A Concise Etymological Dictionary of the English Language*. Oxford.

Skene, W.F. 1834. 'Extracts from the Northern Sagas', *Transactions of the Iona Club* 1, 67–9.

Sladden, Dilnot. 1834. *The Northmen; A Poem in Four Cantos*. Canterbury.

Smedley, Menella Bute. 1863. *The Story of Queen Isabel and Other Verses*. London.

Smith, Charles Sprague. 1881. 'Beówulf Gretti', *The New Englander* 4, 49–67.

———. 1889. 'A Summer in Iceland', *Scribner's Magazine* 6, 451–72.

———. 1890. 'Modern Iceland', *BAGS* 22, 442–73.

———. 1891a. Trans. *The Sun's Song*. Boston.

———. 1891b. 'Orkney and Shetland', *BAGS* 23, 131–55.

———. 1892. 'The Vinland voyages', *BAGS* 24, 510–35.

Smith, Margaret M. 1988. 'Thomas Percy, William Shenstone, *Five Pieces of Runic Poetry* and *The Relics*', *Bodleian Library Record* 12, 471–7.

Smith, Robert Angus. 1873. *To Iceland in a Yacht*. Edinburgh.

————. 1874. 'On Some Ruins at Ellida Vatn and Kjalarnes in Iceland', *PSAS* 10, 3–29.

Smith, T. 1838. *The* Völuspá: *Read Before the Leicestershire Literary Society.* Leicester.

[Smyth, Mrs A. Gillespie]. 1828. 'Frithioff: A Swedish poem', *BEM* 23, 137–61.

Snæbjörn Jónsson. 1927. 'W.A. Craigie', *Eimreiðin* 33, 150–65.

————. 1956. 'Hver kenndi Dasent íslensku', *Lesbók Morgunblaðsins* 168–9.

Southey, Robert. 1824. *The Book of the Church.* 2 vols. London.

————. 1829. *The Poetical Works.* Paris.

Spalding, H. 1872. Trans. *The Tale of Frithiof.* London.

Sparkes, W.E. 1912. *Sigurd and Gudrun: An Ancient Tale of Constancy in Love.* [London].

Speight, E.E. 1903. *Children of Odin.* London.

Speight, E.E. and Albany Major 1899. Ed. *Stories from the Northern Sagas.* London. [Rev. 2nd edition 1905].

Spender, Edward. 1857. 'Lord Dufferin's Yacht Voyage', [Review of Dufferin 1857] *LQR* 9, 174–90.

Splain, Rev. James F. 1885. 'To Iceland and Back', *The Month* 55, 489–501.

Spurr, David. 1993. *The Rhetoric of Empire.* Durham, North Carolina.

Stafford, Barbara Maria. 1984. *Voyage into Substance. Art, Science and the Illustrated Travel Account, 1760–1840.* Cambridge, Mass.

Stafford, Fiona J. 1988. *The Sublime Savage: A Study of James MacPherson and the Poems of Ossian.* Edinburgh.

————. 1994. *The Last of the Race; the Growth of a Myth from Milton to Darwin.* Oxford.

Stanley, E.G. 1975. *The Search for Anglo-Saxon Paganism.* Cambridge.

————. 1994. *In the Foreground*: Beowulf. Cambridge.

Stanley, John Thomas. 1794. 'An Account of the Hot Springs in Iceland with an Analysis of their Waters', *TRSE* 3, 127–37, 138–53.

Steen-Nøkleberg, Einar. 1995. Introductory notes to *Grieg Piano Music, Vol. 11* (Naxos DDD 8.553397). Munich.

Stefán Einarsson. 1933. *Saga Eiríks Magnússonar.* Reykjavík.

————. 1961. 'Eiríkur Magnússon –The Forgotten Pioneer', in Benedikz 1961, 33–50.

Steindór Steindórsson. 1979. *Íslands leiðangur Stanleys 1789.* Reykjavík.

Steingrímur Matthíasson. 1935. *Bréf Matthíasar Jochumssonar.* Akureyri.

Steingrímur Thorsteinsson. [1879]. *Kvæði flutt Prof. W. Fiske og Herra A.M. Reeves í . . . Reykjavík (Glasgow).* Reykjavík.

Stephens, George. 1835. *The Tempest, An Outline Sketch of the Play by William Shakespear.* Stockholm.

————. 1837. *Conversational Outlines of English Grammar.* Stockholm.

————. 1839. *Frithiof's saga, A Legend of Norway.* Stockholm.

————. 1840a. 'Sweden as it is', *FQR* 27, 143–73, 433–55.

————. 1840b. 'Old Popular Ballads of Sweden', *FQR* 25, 25–48.

———. 1841. *Engelskt och Svenskt Handlexicon*. Stockholm.

———. 1843–5. 'Forslag til Islændernes uudgivne folkesagns og sanges opteg-nelse og bevaring', *Antikvarisk Tidsskrift* 1, 191–2.

———. 1844. 'The King of Birds; or, the Lay of the Phoenix: An Anglo-Saxon Song of the Tenth or Eleventh Century', *Archæologia* 30, 256–322.

———. 1847–58. Ed. *Ett Forn-Svenskt Legendarium*. 2 vols. Stockholm.

———. 1848. Trans. Oscar I, King of Norway and Sweden, *Port-Regulations for the City of Stockholm*. Stockholm.

[———]. 1852a. ' "English" or "Anglo-Saxon" ', *GM* 36, 323–7, 472–6.

———. 1852b. Ed. *Brottstycken av en Dominikaner-Ordens eller Predikare-Brödernas Statut eller Capitel-Bok från XIII. Århundradet, och gällende för Pro-vincia Dacia eller de Nordiska Riken*. Copenhagen.

———. 1853a. Trans. *Tvende Old-Engelske Digte*. Copenhagen.

———. 1853b. *Defence of the Full Hereditary Right according to the Lex Regia of the Kings and Royal House of Denmark*. Copenhagen.

———. 1855. *The Shakespear Story-Teller; Introductory Leaves or Outline Sketches, with Choice Extracts in the Words of the Poet Himself*. Copenhagen.

———. 1857. *Revenge, or Woman's Love*. Copenhagen.

[———]. 1858. *The Scandinavian Question. Practical Reflections by Arnliot Gellina. Translated from the Swedish Original by an English Scandinavian*. Cheapinghaven.

———. [1859a]. *The Rescue of Robert Burns, February 1759. A Centenary Poem*. Cheapinghaven and London.

———. 1859b. *Seventeen Songs and Chants etc. to Prof. G. Stephens's Melodrama Revenge, or Woman's Love. Nearly all Composed by Prof. G. Stephens, and Har-monized for the Piano by B. Vilh. Hallberg, Dir. Mus. Landskrona, Sweden*. Cheapinghaven.

———. 1860a. Ed. *Two Leaves of King Waldere's Lay. A Hitherto Unknown Old-English Epic of the Eighth Century, belonging to the Saga-Cyclus of King Theodric and his Men*. Cheapinghaven.

———. 1860b. Ed. *Ghost-thanks, or the Grateful Unburied, A Mythic Tale in its Oldest European Form, Sir Amadace, a Middle-Northern-English Metrical Romance of the Thirteenth Century*. Cheapinghaven.

———. 1863. *Queen Dagmar's Cross, Facsimile in Gold and Colors of the Enam-eled Jewel in the Old-Northern Museum, Cheapinghaven, Denmark*. London and Cheapinghaven.

———. 1866–1901. *The Old-Northern Runic Monuments of Scandinavia and England*. 4 vols [Vol. 4 Ed. S.O.M. Soderberg]. London and Copenhagen.

———. 1868. *The Runic Hall in the Danish Old-Northern Museum*. Cheaping-haven.

———. 1870. *Scandinavian Runic Stones which speak of Knut the Great*. London. [Originally published in *Archæologia* 43 (1870), 97–117].

———. 1872. 'On a Runic Door in Iceland', *Archæologia Scotica* 5, 249–60.

———. 1878. *Thunor the Thunderer Carved on a Scandinavian Font of about the Year 1000*. London, Edinburgh and Copenhagen.

411

———. 1879. *On the Dialect of the First Book Printed in Swedish*. Upsala.

———. 1879–80. 'Runic Inscription found at Brough, Westmorland. Date about A.D. 550–600', *Transactions of the Cumberland and Westmorland Antiquarian and Archæological Society* 5, 291–310.

———. 1883. *Professor S. Bugge's Studies on Northern Mythology Shortly Examined*. London and Copenhagen.

———. 1884. *Handbook of the Old-Northern Runic Monuments of Scandinavia and England*. London, Edinburgh and Cheapinghaven.

———. 1888. *A Cantata at the Copenhagen-University Festival, November 17, 1888 in Commemoration of the Royal Jubilee, November 15 1888, the 25th Year of H.M. Christian IX, King*. Copenhagen.

———. 1890. *Er Engelsk et Tysk Sprog*. Copenhagen.

———. 1894. *The Runes and Whence They Came*. London and Copenhagen.

Stephens, George and J.V. Liffman. 1845–9. Eds *Herr Ivan lejon-riddaren*, Samlingar utgifna af Svenska Fornskrift-Sällskapet. Stockholm.

Stephens, George and H. Cavallius. 1882. Trans. Albert Alberg, *Old Norse Fairy Tales*. London.

Sterling, Joseph. 1789. *Poems*. Dublin.

Stevens, William Bagshaw. 1775. *Poems, Consisting of Indian Odes and Miscellaneous Poems*. Oxford.

Stevenson, Robert Louis. 1916. *The Waif Woman*. London.

Stock, Brian. 1990. *Listening for the Text. On the Uses of the Past*. Baltimore.

Stockbridge, George Herbert. 1894. *Balder the Poet and Other Verses*. London.

Stockdale, Percival. 1778. *An Enquiry into the Nature and Genuine Laws of Poetry*. London.

Stone, Olivia M. 1882. *Norway in June*. London.

Streatfeild, G.S. 1884. *Lincolnshire and the Danes*. London.

Strong, Roy. 1978. *Recreating the Past: British History and the Victorian Painters*. London and New York.

Strong, William. [1833]. Trans. William Strong. *Frithiof's Saga: A Scandinavian Legend of Royal Love*. London.

Strongi'th'arm. [pseud. Charles Wickstead Armstrong]. 1892. *The Yorl of the Northmen; or, the Fate of the English Race, Being a Romance of a Monarchical Utopia*. London.

Suhm, P.F. et al. 1773. *Kristni-saga, sive Historia Religionis Christianæ in Islandiam introductæ*. Copenhagen.

Sumarliði Ísleifsson. 1996. *Ísland: Framandi land*. Reykjavík.

Sutherland Graeme, P.N. 1953. 'The Parliamentary Representation of Orkney and Shetland, 1754–1900', *Orkney Miscellany* 1, 64–104.

Sutherland, John. 1995. *Sir Walter Scott. A Critical Biography*. London.

Svavar Sigmundsson. 1989. 'Guðbrandur Vigfússon as Lexicographer', in Wawn and McTurk 1989, 287–316.

Sveinn Haraldsson. 1994. ' "The North begins inside": Auden, Ancestry and Iceland' in Wawn 1994b, 255–84.

Sveinn Skorri Höskuldsson. 1993. *Benedikt á Auðnum*. Reykjavík.

Sverrir Jakobsson. 1994. ' "Þá þrengir oss vor áliggjandi nauðsyn annara meðala að leita": Siglingar Englendinga til Íslands á 17. öld', *Sagnir* 15, 36–48.

Sweet, Henry. 1885. *The Oldest English Texts*, EETS o.s. 83. London.

———. 1886. *An Icelandic Primer.* Oxford.

Symington, A.J. 1862. *Pen and Pencil Sketches of Faröe and Iceland.* London.

———. 1869. 'Faröe and Iceland', *Science, Art and History*, 436–42, 493–500, 542–52, 593–604, 652–60.

Syndergaard, Larry E. 1995. *English Translations of the Scandinavian Medieval Ballads. An Analytical Guide and Bibliography.* Turku.

[Talfour, Thomas Noon]. 1822. [Review of Scott 1822], *New Monthly Magazine* 4, 188–92.

Tattersall, J.F. 1890. *The Baptism of the Viking and other Verse.* London.

Taylor, Arnold. 1969. '*Hauksbók* and Ælfric's *De falsis diis*', *LSE* n.s. 3, 101–9.

Taylor, Bayard. 1858. *Northern Travel: Summer and Winter Pictures of Sweden, Denmark and Lapland.* New York.

———. 1875. *Egypt and Iceland in the Year 1874.* London.

———. 1886. *Boys of other Countries.* New York and London.

Tegnér, Esaias. See Strong [1833], F[rye] 1835, Latham 1838, Stephens 1839, Baker 1841, Heckethorne 1856, Blackley 1857, Mucklestone 1862, Matthías Jochumsson 1866, Spalding 1872, Henderson 1872, Hamel 1874, Holcomb and Lyons 1892, Watson 1897, Miller 1905, Upton 1907, Allen [1912], Blackley 1913, Locock 1924.

Temple, William. 1690. 'Of Heroick Virtue', in *Miscellanea. The Second Part. In Four Essays.* London.

Thimm, Franz. 1869. *A Short Practical and Easy Method of Learning the Old Norsk Tongue or Icelandic Language after the Danish of E. Rask. With An Icelandic Reader, An Account of the Norsk Poetry and the Sagas, and a Modern Icelandic Vocabulary for Travellers.* 2nd edition. London.

Thomas, R.G. 1953–7. 'George E.J. Powell, Eiríkr Magnússon and Jón Sigurðsson: A Chapter in Icelandic Literary History', *SBVS* 14/1–2, 113–30.

Thomson, William P.L. 1985. 'The Udal League', *Orkney View* 2, 15–17.

Thompson, Francis. 1990. 'John Francis Campbell (1821–85)', *Folklore* 101, 88–96.

Thorpe, Benjamin. 1851–2. *Northern Mythology, Comprising the Principal Popular Traditions and Superstitions of Scandinavia, North Germany and the Netherlands.* 3 vols. London.

———. 1853. *Yule-Tide Stories. A Collection of Scandinavian and North German Popular Tales and Traditions.* London.

———. 1866. Trans. *The Edda of Sæmund the Learned from the Old Norse or Icelandic, with a Mythological Index.* 2 vols. in 1. London.

Thorsteinn Erlingsson. 1899. *Ruins of the Saga Time: Being an Account of Travels and Explorations in Iceland in the Summer of 1895.* London.

Thwaite, Ann. 1984. *Edmund Gosse: A Literary Landscape, 1849–1928.* London.

Tilden, Sir William A. 1918. *Sir William Tilden, K.C.B., F.R.S.: Memorials of his Life and Work.* London.

Todd, James Henthorn. 1867. Ed. *The War of the Gaedhil with the Gaill, or the Invasions of Ireland by the Danes and Other Norsemen*. London.

Toland, J. 1966. *The Last Hundred Days*. New York.

Tomlinson, Henry. 1930. *Great Sea Stories of All Nations*. London.

Tompkins, Peter. 1960. Ed. *To a Young Actress: The Letters of Bernard Shaw to Molly Tompkins*. London.

Townsend, J.A.B. 1992. 'The Viking Society: A Centenary History', *SBVS* 23/4, 180–212.

Toynbee, Paget and L. Whibley. 1935. Eds *Correspondence of Thomas Gray*. 3 vols. Oxford.

Tremenheere, Sir Hugh Seymour]. 1837. 'Laing's *Residence in Norway*', *ER* 65, 39–61.

[———]. 1839. [Review of Laing 1839], *ER* 69, 349–65.

Trevor-Roper, Hugh. 1983. 'The Invention of Tradition: the Highland Tradition of Scotland', in Cannadine 1983, 15–42.

Troil, Uno von. 1780. *Letters on Iceland*. 2nd edition. London.

Trollope, Anthony. 1878a. 'Iceland', *FR* n.s. 30, 175–90.

———. 1878b. *How the 'Mastiffs' went to Iceland*. London.

Troup, George. 1849. 'Our Anglo-Saxon Empire', *TEM* n.s. 16, 687–95.

Tucker, Susie I. 1963–4. 'Scandinavica for the Eighteenth-Century Common Reader', *SBVS* 16, 233–47.

Tudsbury, Francis W.T. 1907. *Brunanburh A.D. 937*. London and Chester.

[Turnbull, George V.]. 1900. *Handbook to Iceland*. 2nd edition. Leith.

Turner, Sharon. 1823. *The History of the Anglo-Saxons: Comprising the History of England from the Earliest Period to the Norman Conquest*, 3 vols. London.

Uhland, Ludwig. 1836. *Der Mythus von Thór nach nordischen Quellen*. Stuttgart.

Upton, George. 1907. Trans. *The Frithiof Saga*. Chicago.

Valentine, William Christopher. [?1850]. *The Hall of Odin*. [?Oxford].

Valtýr Guðmundsson. 1893. 'Ritsjá nokkurra útlendra bóka, er snerta Ísland og íslenzkar bókmenntir (1891)', *Tímarit Hins íslenzka bókmenntafjelags* 40, 205–73.

van Gruisen, N.L. 1879. *A Holiday in Iceland*. London.

Veblen, Thorstein. 1925. Trans. *The Laxdæla Saga*. New York.

Venn, J. and J.A. 1922–54. *Alumni Cantabrigienses*. 6 vols. Cambridge.

Verelius, Olaus. 1672. Ed. *Hervarar saga*. Uppsala.

Verne, Jules. 1992. Trans. William Butcher, *Journey to the Centre of the Earth*. Oxford.

Vicary, J. Fulford. 1886. *Olav the King, and Olav, King and Martyr*. London.

———. 1887. *Saga Time*. London.

Viðar Hreinsson et al. 1997. Eds *The Complete Sagas of Icelanders*. 5 vols. Reykjavík.

Waddell, P. Hately. 1875. *Oscar and the Clyde, Fingal in Ireland, Oscar in Iceland; or, Ossian Historical and Authentic*. Glasgow.

Wagner, Felix. 1904. Ed. *La saga de Fridthjof le fort*. Louvain.

Wainwright, H.T. 1975. Ed. H.P.R. Finberg, *Scandinavian England*. Chichester.

Wallace, Birgitta Linderoth. 1991. 'The Vikings in North America: Myth and Reality', in Samson 1991, 207–19.

Wallace, Horatio. 1917. *The Song of the Madness of the Children of Odin and Other Poems*. Winnipeg.

Waller, S.E. 1874. *Six Weeks in the Saddle: A Painter's Journal*. London.

[Ward, H.L.D.]. 1864. *Numerical List of the Icelandic Manuscripts in the British Museum. November 1864*. Copy of manuscript in Stofnun Árna Magnússonar, Reykjavík.

Warner, G. 1926. Ed. *Libelle of Englyshe Polycye. A Poem on the Use of Sea Power 1436*. Oxford.

Warton, Thomas. 1748. *Poems on Several Occasions*. London.

———. 1774–81. *The History of English Poetry*. 3 vols. London.

Waterhouse, G. 1931. 'G.J. Thorkelin and the Rev. James Johnstone', *MLR* 26, 436–44.

Watson, Margaret. 1897. Trans. 'Frithjof's Saga', *DR* 121, 30–40.

Watson, Robert Spence. 1897. *History of the Literary and Philosophical Society of Newcastle-upon-Tyne 1793–1896*. Newcastle-upon-Tyne.

Watts, W.L. 1874. 'On the Vatna Jökull', *FM* 10, 175–90.

———. 1876. 'Ascent of Myrdals Jökull', *AJ* 7, 179–91.

Wawn, Andrew. 1981. 'John Thomas Stanley and Iceland: The Sense and Sensibility of an Eighteenth-Century Explorer', *SS* 53, 52–76.

———. 1982. '*Gunnlaugs saga ormstungu* and the Theatre Royal, Edinburgh: Melodrama, Mineralogy and Sir George Mackenzie', *Scandinavica* 21, 139–51.

———. 1983. 'James Six and the Court of Brunswick 1781–2', *ASSL* 220/135, 241–67.

———. 1985. 'Hundadagadrottningin. Bréf frá Íslandi: Guðrún Johnsen og Stanleyfjölskyldan frá Cheshire, 1814–16', *Saga* 23, 99–133.

———. 1987. *The Iceland Journal of Henry Holland 1810*. Hakluyt Society, 2nd series, 168. London.

———. 1990a. 'Henry Sweet, Guðbrandur Vigfússon and "Runic Lore" ', *Henry Sweet Society for the History of Linguistic Ideas: Newsletter* 15, 4–9.

———. 1990b. 'The Silk-Clad Varangian: Þorleifur Repp and *Færeyinga saga*', *SBVS* 23/1, 46–72.

———. 1991a. *The Anglo Man. Þorleifur Repp, Britain and Enlightenment Philology*. Studia Islandica 49. Reykjavík.

———. 1991b. 'The Assistance of Icelanders to George Webbe Dasent', *LÍÁ 1989*, nýr flokkur 15, 73–92.

———. 1993. 'Shrieks at the Stones: The Vikings, the Orkneys and the Scottish Enlightenment', in Batey et al. 1993, 408–22.

———. 1994a. 'Óðinn, Ossian and Iceland' in Gísli Sigurðsson et al. 1994, II 829–40.

———. 1994b. Ed. *Northern Antiquity: The Post-Medieval Reception of Edda and Saga*. Enfield Lock.

———. 1994c. 'The Cult of "Stalwart Frith-thjof" in Victorian Britain', in Wawn 1994b, 213–58.

———. 1995. 'George Stephens, Cheapinghaven and Old Northern Antiquity', *Studies in Medievalism* 7, 1–42.

———. 1997a. ' "Brass-brained rivalries": *Sturlunga saga* in Victorian Britain', in Goblirsch et al. 1997, 463–82.

———. 1997b. 'W.G. Collingwood and *Njála*. An unpublished poem', in Rósa Þorsteinsdóttir et al. Eds *Bókahnútur brygðinn Olöfu Benediktsdóttur*. Reykjavík.

———. 1998. 'King Ólafr Tryggvason, Sir Edward Elgar, and *The Musician's Tale*', *LSE* n.s. 29, 381–400.

Weber, Gerd Wolfgang. 1988. Ed. *Idee, Gestalt, Geschichte. Festschrift Klaus von See*. Odense.

Wedderburn, David. 1880. 'Iceland', *NC* 8, 218–36.

Wenz, Gustav. 1914. Ed. *Die Friðþjófssaga*. Halle.

West, John F. 1970–6. Ed. *The Journals of the Stanley Expedition to the Faroe Islands and Iceland*. Tórshavn.

West, William. 1837. 'Laing's Residence in Norway', *DUM* 9, 443–52.

Wheaton, Henry and Andrew Crichton. 1831. *History of the Northmen; Or, Danes and Normans: From the Earliest Times to the Conquest of England by William of Normandy*. London.

Whistler, Charles W. 1896. *A Thane of Wessex: Being a Story of the Great Viking Raids into Somerset*. London.

———. 1897. *Wulfric the Weapon-Thane. A Study of the Danish Invasion of East Anglia in the Days of Edmund the Martyr*. London.

———. 1899. *King Alfred's Viking: a Story of the First English Fleet*. London.

White, H.A. 1927. *Sir Walter Scott's Novels on the Stage*. New Haven and London.

White, John. 1861. *The Vikings; a Poem Recited in the Theatre, Oxford, June XII, MDCCCLXI*. Oxford.

Whittier, John G. 1843. *Lays of My Home and Other Poems*. Boston.

Wiener, M.J. 1981. *English Culture and the Decline of the Industrial Spirit*. Cambridge.

Wiens, Pamela Bracken. 1996. 'Fire and Ice: Clashing Visions of Iceland in the Travel Narratives of Morris and Burton', *JWMS* 11, 12–18.

Wiley, Raymond A. 1981. Ed. *John Mitchell Kemble and Jakob Grimm. A Correspondence 1832–52*. Leiden.

———. 1990. 'Grimm's Grammar gains ground in England, 1832–52', in Antonsen 1990, 33–42.

Wilkinson, James John Garth. 1897. *The Book of Edda called Völuspá, A Study in its Scriptural and Spiritual Correspondences*. London.

Williams, David. 1982. *A World of his Own: The Double Life of George Borrow*. Oxford.

Williams, W. 1790. 'The Hervarer Saga, a Gothic Ode, From the Septentrionalium Thesaurus of Dr Hickes', *GM* 60, 844.

Wilson, David. 1980. Ed. *The Northern World: The History and Heritage of Northern Europe, AD 400–1100*. London.

———. 1996. 'The Viking Age in British Literature and History in the Eighteenth and Nineteenth Centuries', in Roesdahl and Sørensen 1996, 58–71.

———. 1997. *Vikings and Gods in European Art*. Højbjerg.

[Wilson, Lucy S.]. 1825. *The Juvenile Rambler: Early Reading Lessons designed for Children*. [London].

Winbolt, Frederick I. 1902. *Frithiof the Bold: A Drama Based upon the Ancient Scandinavian Legend*. London.

Wolf, Kirsten. 1998. 'Rasmus Rask', in Damico 1998, 109–24.

Worm, Christian. 1716. *Arae multiscii schedae de Islandia*. Oxford.

Worm, Ole. 1636. *Runer seu Danica literatura antiqvissima*. Copenhagen.

Worsaae, J.J.A. 1843. *Danmarks Oldtid oplyst ved Oldsager og Gravhøie*. Copenhagen.

———. 1846. *The Antiquities of Ireland and Denmark, Being the Substance of Two Communications Made to the Royal Irish Academy, at its Meetings, November 30th and December 7th, 1846*. Dublin.

———. 1849. Trans. William J. Thoms, *The Primeval Antiquities of Denmark*. London.

———. 1852. *An Account of the Danes and Norwegians in England, Scotland and Ireland*. London.

Wotton, William. 1735. Trans. Maurice Shelton, *Wotton's Short View of George Hickes's Grammatico-Critical and Archaeological Treasure of the Ancient Northern-Languages*. London.

Wright, Joseph. 1898–1905. *The English Dialect Dictionary*. 6 vols. London.

Wright, Thomas. 1845. 'Hereward the Saxon', *Ainsworth's Magazine* 7, 437–41, 512–18.

York Powell, F. 1894. 'Saga Growth', *Folk-Lore* 5, 97–106.

———. 1896. Trans. *The Tale of Thrond of Gate, commonly called* Færeyinga saga. London.

Young, Captain Charles. 1895. *The Last of the Vikings. A Book for Boys*. London.

———. 1911. *Harald, First of the Vikings*. London.

Zavarr [pseud.]. 1849. *The Viking; An Epic*. London.

Zernack, Julia. 1997. *Bibliographie der deutschsprachigen Sagaübersetzungen 1791–1995*. Berlin.

Örnólfur Thorsson et al. 1988. Eds *Sturlunga saga*. Reykjavík.

Þormóður Torfason. 1697. *Orcades, seu rerum Orcadensium historiæ*. Copenhagen.

Þorvaldur Thoroddsen. 1922. *Minningabók*. 2 vols. Copenhagen.

Þórunn Sigurðardóttir. 1994. *Manuscript Material, Correspondence, and Graphic Material in the Fiske Icelandic Collection*. Islandica 48. Ithaca and London.

Þórunn Valdimarsdóttir. 1990. 'Um gagnkvæma ást manna og meyjar (fjallkonunnar)', in Heimir Pálsson et al. 1990, 288–94.

417

INDEX

The entries in this index are generally ordered in accordance with Icelandic alphabetical practice. Entries beginning with or containing accented vowels follow equivalent forms with simple vowels. Thus, Á follows A (the entry for 'Árngrímur Jónsson' follows the final unaccented A entry; 'Fáfnir' follows the final FA entry 'Farrer'), Í follows I and so on. Entries under letters Ö, Þ follow those for Z. Icelanders are listed under their first names, as with Jón Sigurðsson listed under Jón.

358–60; and Rider Haggard 332;
Bandamanna saga translation 299;
Lilja 366–7; *Poetic Edda* translation
362; *Thómas saga Erkibyskups* 366;
Three Northern Love Stories 366
electronic telegraph, Transatlantic 283
Elgar, Sir Edward 8, 111–15
Eliot, George: *Middlemarch* 153; *Mill on the Floss* 81; *Silas Marner* 151
Elizabeth I, Queen 14, 17
Elliðavatn 305
Ellwood, Thomas 5, 128, 338, 359, 367; Lake District subscribers to publications 368
Elstob, Elizabeth 3
Elton, Oliver 161, 342, 348
Elucidarius 353
Elvey, George 60
Emerson, Ralph Waldo 111, 208
entrepreneurialism 176
Eric Brighteyes: *see* Haggard, H. Rider
Erling the Bold: *see* Ballantyne, R.M.
Espólín, Jón: *see* Jón Espólín
Estlin, J.P. 57
ethnicity: characteristics of Danes, Saxons, Normans 317–19; fusion of English, Scandinavian or Norman elements 329; Icelanders as Teutons 326; and philology 146, 238; Transatlantic telegraph joining northern kith and kin 283
Etymological Dictionary of English: *see* Skeat, Walter
Evans, Evan 26, 30–1
Ewald, Johannes 205
Eyrbyggja saga 38, 45, 55–6, 84, 86, 259, 294, 333; 'Wonders of Froda [Fróðá]' 259, 309

Faroe Islands 40, 283
Farrer, James 235
Fáfnir 258; in *Sigurd the Volsung* 274
Feldborg, Andreas 120
feudalism 98–9, 107, 278
Festival of Empire 1910 357
Finnboga saga ramma 294
Finnur Jónsson 55
Finnur Magnússon 13, 85, 185, 349; comparative mythology 190; nature myth interpretations of eddas 189, 192, 202, of sagas 298
Fiske, Willard 210, 348, 364, 367
Fjalarr 209
Fjalla-Eyvindr 304

Flamank, James 315
Flateyjarbók 323, 325, 353, 357
Flosahlaup 290
Flóamanna saga 299, 312, 357
Flóki Vilgerðarson 48
folklore and folktales 7–8, 150, 186–7, 194, 197, 217, 366; Boar's Head traditions 197; Dasent's theory of origin 150; 'Djákninn á Myrká' 294, 307; eddas and ritual drama 193–4; Fjalla-Eyvindr 304; Freyr and chariot drawing in Yorkshire 199; Jack the Giant Killer 191; 'Jack and Jill go up the hill' 299–300; Óðinn's ravens and 'a little bird told me' 197; Óðinn as wild huntsman 186, 194, 300; Ólafur Pálsson and Symington translations of 293; Powell and Eiríkur Magnússon translations of 293, 351, 363; Viking drinking tradition and 'taken down a peg or two' 322; William Tell and Pálna-Toki 180; Yuletide 197, 199
Forbes, Charles 247, 283, 292
Forester, Thomas 139
Forseti 192
Fountains Abbey 294
Fox, E.M. 313
Fóstbræðra saga 294, 312, 345
France 362
Frazer, Sir James 193
Frederick III, King of Prussia 312
Frederik VII, King of Denmark 218
Free Foresters 317
French, Allen 165
Freyja 200, 204, 256
Freyr 199, 256
Friðþjófs saga 117, 129, 183, 264
Frithiofs saga: *see* Tegnér, E.
Frobisher, Sir Martin 284
Froelich, Lorenz 162
Froissart, Jean 95
Frye, W.E. 201
Furnivall, F.J. 14
Færeyinga saga 40, 84, 289, 362

Garvagh, Lord 13, 310–11
Gaukr Trandilsson 235
Geijer, Erik Gustaf 122, 229
Geir Zoëga 210, 349
Geirrøðr 307
gender: attitudes to saga women 153, 291, 306; masculinity 154, 313; Tegnér and femininity 134–5; Tegnér